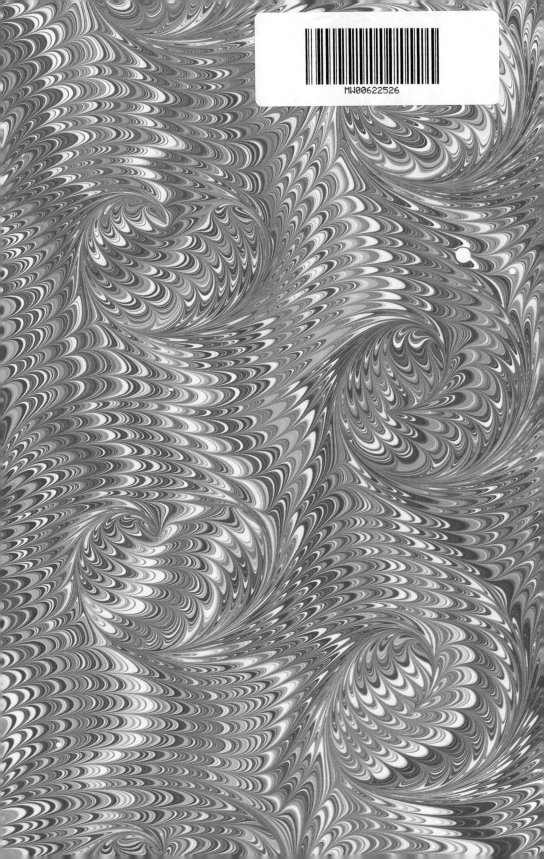

THE SKY MEN

16 June 2001

to John Costello:

hoping you enjoy my
view of the "Greatest
generation" —

All the Best,

Kirk Ross

THE SKY MEN

A Parachute Rifle Company's Story of the Battle of the Bulge and the Jump Across the Rhine

Kirk B. Ross

Schiffer Military History
Atglen, PA

Book design by Robert Biondi.

Printed in China.
ISBN: 0-7643-1172-7

We are always looking for people to write books on new and related subjects. If you have an idea for
a book, please contact us at the address below.

Published by Schiffer Publishing Ltd.
4880 Lower Valley Road
Atglen, PA 19310
Phone: (610) 593-1777
FAX: (610) 593-2002
E-mail: Schifferbk@aol.com.
Visit our web site at: www.schifferbooks.com
Please write for a free catalog.
This book may be purchased from the publisher.
Please include $3.95 postage.
Try your bookstore first.

In Europe, Schiffer books are distributed by:
Bushwood Books
6 Marksbury Ave.
Kew Gardens
Surrey TW9 4JF
England
Phone: 44 (0)208 392-8585
FAX: 44 (0)208 392-9876
E-mail: Bushwd@aol.com.
Free postage in the UK. Europe: air mail at cost.
Try your bookstore first.

Preface

An essential immediacy accompanies war. No place is it felt more intensely than among the young men whose job it is to do the actual killing.

At the time this story takes place most of the men in it were only nineteen years old. Like all young men, they were a complex mix of fear, love, desire, and dreams. They carried with them a youthful sense of adventure, a general disregard for authority, and the capacity to slide into base and even cruel behavior. The United States had been at war for almost two years when enlistment or the draft inducted them into the brotherhood of war and began to instill in them a new morality, one which made killing a virtue and proclaimed Duty its god. The army didn't want any choir boys. What they needed was "a bunch of damn killers in uniforms," and that's what they got. One historian who reviewed this manuscript actually labeled these men "hoodlums." Maybe they were, but it was a war. *The Sky Men* is their story.

Dedication
For F Company, 513th Parachute Infantry Regiment
of the Seventeenth Airborne Division
When Duty called, they came,
When Country called, they died.

Contents

Prologue

In 1787 Benjamin Franklin, inspired by his contemporary Montgolfier's success with the hot air balloon, first proposed the use of an airborne assault in warfare when he stated: "Where is the Prince who can afford so to cover his country with troops for its defense, as that ten thousand men descending from the clouds, might not, in many places, do an infinite amount of mischief before a force could be brought together to repel them?"[1] By the time the Wright Brothers first flew at Kitty Hawk in 1903, the parachute was already six centuries old, but it was not until the First World War that the first serious suggestions for the military application of the parachute for airborne forces arose.[2]

Brigadier General Billy Mitchell, commander of the American Air Service in France during World War I, suggested the first airborne assault in October 1918. Envisioned to support the anticipated Spring 1919 offensive, General Mitchell proposed to deploy the better part of the 1st U.S. Infantry Division by parachute behind the German lines around Metz. The 'Airdoughs,' armed with a large number of automatic weapons, would be dropped from heavy bombers, protected by an umbrella of fighter aircraft, and resupplied by air. Though the operation was seriously considered, the armistice arrived before it became a reality. It is an interesting footnote, however, that working out the details of Mitchell's "wild" proposal was "a young Air Service staff officer," Lewis H. Brereton, "the future commander of the First Allied Airborne Army in 1944-1945."[3]

After the First World War, several European nations, including France, Italy, and Great Britain, began experimenting with the concept of airborne operations. However, it was Nazi Germany and the Soviet Union that undertook the most serious study of this new kind of warfare. The Soviets were the first to apply airborne concepts when, during the Red Army maneuvers near Moscow in 1930, they landed a lieutenant and eight men by parachute. By 1935 the Soviets had organized an Airlanding Corps capable of transporting an entire division. The following year the Russians jumped two battalions of infantry – one thousand men – supported by sixteen artillery pieces and one hundred fifty machine-guns in less than eight minutes during tactical exercises near Kiev. The force assembled and rapidly occupied a town that was their objective. An additional four thousand reinforcements were then air-landed and joined the paratroopers.

The exercises made a mixed impression on most of the foreign observers. In Germany, however, the Airborne concept was enthusiastically embraced.[4] Germany may have also been impressed by the remark made by Red Air Force Marshal Michal Schtscherbakov to "French Marshal Petain during a tour of the Maginot Line: 'Fortresses like this may well be superfluous in the future if your potential adversary . . . parachutes over them'."[5] The Germans began the rapid development of an airborne arm within the Luftwaffe with the activation of the *1st Jäger Battalion, Regiment 'Herman Göring'* in January 1936. A second battalion was formed by the army that same month. By the time of the invasion of Poland, the Germans had organized most of the *7.Flieger-Division*. Though these men did not participate in the Polish campaign, Hitler promised their commander, General der Flieger Kurt Student that they would see action in the west.[6]

And so they did. The arrival of parachute troops in Norway, Holland, and Belgium, in advance of the Germans' main forces, paved "the way for the capture of airfields and reduction of fortifications in 1940 [and] startled anew a world not yet recovered from the accounts of air-ground blitzkrieg in Poland and Scandinavia." Spearheading the German drive through the low countries in May, a small force of five hundred parachutists captured the crossings of the Albert Canal intact. Further, two officers and seventy-eight men arrived by glider atop the broad roof of the great Belgian fort Eben Emael and held the garrison at bay until mechanized infantry arrived the next day. Then, in April 1941 Germans used gliderborne troops in the seizure of Corinth. Less than a month later they offered their final demonstration that airborne troops were "here to stay" – the parachute, glider, and airlanding assault on Crete. The capture of that strategic island in the Mediterranean left a lasting impression on the Allied armies" and the dramatic display of German airborne power served to spur on the United States Army's fledgling Airborne Effort.[7]

Despite the fact that the United States had developed emergency parachutes for its aviators as early as 1918, the Army did not begin experimenting with parachutes for the deployment of airborne forces until 1928. That year, on 29 April, General Billy Mitchell watched as three volunteers from the 2nd Infantry Division jumped at Kelly Field near San Antonio, Texas. The three men assembled and fired a machine-gun as part of the exercise. Unfortunately, no further experiments were conducted until May 1939, when the Chief of Infantry again raised the question of "air infantry." By 2 January 1940, it had been ordered that a test platoon be formed under the Infantry Board. The cooperation of the Air Corps was ordered as well and what was to become known as the Airborne Effort had begun.[8]

The pioneer days of American airborne began on 25 June 1940 under the red clay bluffs of Fort Benning, Georgia, the home of the Infantry School, with the activation of the Parachute Test Platoon.[9] "Thus," wrote General James M. Gavin, the famed commander of the 82nd Airborne Division, "it is a historical fact that airborne warfare, at least in a modern sense, was originated by the Russians and developed to a state of combat effectiveness by the Germans. But it is also a historical fact that the American Army took this new instrument of warfare and, with the British, refined and improved it and unleashed upon our enemies airborne forces of such power and perfection as even they had not dreamed of."[10] Of the two hundred men from the 29th Infantry Regiment who volunteered, forty-eight men were selected. Training began right away with the first jumps being made on 16 August and a mass jump being made on the twenty-ninth. Even as these men worked, a new battle was beginning as the services vied over the control of the new arm.[11]

For more than a year there had been a debate within the Army over who would control the airborne troops. After the Air Corps was approached regarding air transportation for "air infantry" they suggested that airborne forces be brought under their control and be named "Air Grenadiers." Even the Corps of Engineers suggested that, in light of Airborne's role as saboteurs operating behind enemy lines, they be placed under their command. It was not until mid-1940 that the Army's Deputy Chief of Staff finally directed that airborne forces, whose primary mission was ground combat, remain under the Chief of Infantry and train at Fort Benning. Things then began to heat up.

On 16 September 1940, the 501st Parachute Infantry Battalion was activated, absorbing the members of the original test platoon. The following summer saw the creation of the 502nd Parachute Battalion which drew on the 501st for cadre. New training areas and additional drop zones were eventually created to cope with the growing needs of the Airborne Effort. By the end of 1941, two more parachute infantry battalions would be formed, the 503rd and the 504th.[12] Parachute field artillery and other formations were soon to follow.[13] The growth of the Airborne program had occurred not a moment too soon as war was declared on 8 December 1941, the day after the surprise Japanese attack of the American Naval Base at Pearl Harbor, Hawaii.

Throughout 1942, the Airborne Effort intensified. On 21 March, the Provisional Parachute Group was redesignated Airborne Command and all existing airborne units were placed under its authority. Airborne Command served to coordinate all aspects of the Airborne Effort including the activation of the various formations, training of personnel, and coordination of air transportation with the Army Air Forces. At the same time, the role these men were to play was also being discussed.

In May 1942, the mission of airborne forces was put forth in Field Manual 31-30, *Tactics and Techniques of Air-borne Troops*: parachute troops were considered "the spearhead of a vertical envelopment or the advance and guard element of airlanding troops or other forces." The concept of airborne warfare generally was one which envisioned the seizure of suitable landing areas by parachute troops, and then their reinforcement by troops arriving by glider or airplane. Accompanying this was listed a whole series of possible objectives for airborne troops: "river and canal crossings, defiles, establishing bridgeheads; attack of defended positions by landing on flank or in rear, or within the perimeter; destruction of enemy supply and communication installations; consolidation and holding of ground taken by armored forces until the arrival of other ground units; and assistance to ground offensives by vertical envelopment."[14]

War Department Training Circular No. 113, *The Employment of Airborne and Troop Carrier Forces*, of 9 October 1943, further detailed the use of the new arm. It stated that these forces would be deployed in mass, but went on to say that:

"Airborne troops should not be employed unless they can be supported by other ground or naval forces within approximately 3 days, or unless they can be withdrawn after their mission has been accomplished."[15] This was later proven by operations to be sound doctrine. The circular also stated: "[airborne forces presented] a constant threat by their mere presence in the theater of operations thereby causing the enemy to disperse his forces over a wide area in order to protect his vital installations."[16] The new airborne arm, therefore, provided the Army with the means to apply the naval concept of "Fleet in Being" and, as a footnote, espoused Benjamin Franklin's vision of mighty armies descending from the clouds.[17] As Airborne Command worked out the details that would put these ideas into practice, new volunteers were being trained to fill the ranks of the ever increasing airborne arm.

1

What I Call Southern Charm

Basic Training & The Parachute School
11 January - 13 November 1943

"Oh, is this bitch hot!" lamented seventeen-year-old Private Frank Munafo, from New York. Shifting in the ranks around him, other men gabbed nervously amongst themselves while the midsummer heat, still intense though the day was slipping away to dusk, raised beads of sweat which ran down their backs and stained their uniforms. It was early August 1943. Munafo, like most of the new men, had been in service little more than a month.[1]

That morning, approximately two thousand enlisted personnel assembled at Fort Benning had collected their gear and marched from their barracks in Benning's 'Frying Pan' area all the way to the muddy Chattahoochee River, "their River Styx," in the words of one man. There, a civilian ferry conveyed them to the Alabama side to the river, and the march continued on "for [another] four miles through a dismal countryside of ['goober'] patches and anemic pine woods."[2] The column stopped at a run of one story, tar-paper and plywood hutments situated on a recently cleared patch of Alabama jungle.[3] A sign there read '513th Parachute Infantry Regiment.' The camp was officially known as Fort Mitchell, Alabama, but was better known to the men at The Parachute School as the 'Alabama Area'.

The men were formed-up in companies – fourteen all together – each one a part of Colonel Albert H. Dickerson's new 513th Parachute Infantry Regiment (PIR). Munafo's company, F Company, was one of three rifle companies in Major Nicholas Willis' 2nd Battalion. Each of the regiment's three battalions had a Headquarters and Headquarters Company (HHC) as well, and Regiment had a Headquarters Company and an attached Service Company. 1st Lieutenant Walter Rydesky, 2nd Battalion's 81mm mortar platoon leader, took one look at the throng of awkward, untrained recruits that had arrived and lamented to Lieutenant McGee, one of the other 2nd Battalion officers, "Mack, this is the worse bunch of people I've ever seen. Ain't none of us ever coming back alive."[4]

A tall – about six feet, three or four – blue-eyed sergeant walked with measured cadence before the body of restless trainees that made up F Company. The sergeant wore only a white tee-shirt, well-pressed khaki jump trousers, and brown Corcoran boots – the type issued to paratroopers. On his khaki overseas cap was a round, infantry blue patch on which a white parachute was embroidered. He was obviously a man of some experience and in excellent physical condition. All talk silenced immediately when the tough-expressioned soldier before them called the formation to attention. "All right," he said in a solid, authoritative voice that, coming from his young, somewhat of a "baby-face," seemed somehow out of place. "I'm gonna tell you how things are gonna be. When I tell you to do something, you do it right now. You do it quick. And if you don't do it quick enough, you're gonna give me twenty-five push-ups. If I don't like the way you're doing the twenty-five push-ups, you'll give me fifty push-ups." Some of the men in ranks groaned. The sergeant paused, but for a moment. "And if you don't like that," said the stern instructor, "you'll give me a hundred push-ups."

"Now, I imagine there's some of you guys in there that think you'd like to whip my ass," another pause, "and I'm gonna give you a chance." The sergeant then bellowed, "Open ranks, March!" When the formation had executed the order, the sergeant continued. "All you guys that think you can whip my ass come out over here on the right end and line up. I'll give you a chance right now." Not one of F Company's scores of volunteers even dared to move. After waiting a few minutes in silence, the sergeant continued. He let the men know what they were going to do, that they were going to do it, and that if they didn't measure up they were out. The sons of democracy wouldn't be strong enough to beat the Germans. The instructors knew it would take men trained and hardened for the task, cold-blooded killers in uniforms, and it was the instructors' job to make them so. Munafo listened intently, hanging on every word, but it was the end of the sergeant's speech that most galvanized him – he told the men that they were the best and the bravest. Munafo, for one, was glad he'd volunteered.[5]

The formation broke up when F Company's First Sergeant, Arthur A. Clark, started down the list of about 130 names, assigning the men to platoons. Clark went down the list alphabetically. Privates James Arrowood, Philip Cavaleri, Edward R. Dahlberg, Wayne DeHaven, Willis B. Grice, and Sidney Laufer, along with about thirty more, were assigned to the First Platoon.

For a year after high school, Philip Cavaleri of South Boston, Massachusetts had worked as a negative engraver for a paper company, preparing negatives in the production of large printing plates. The following year, 1942, Cavaleri worked as a stevedore at a busy Boston Army base, loading and unloading freight cars and ships, all kinds of war materiel and munitions. He and his pals spent their lunch breaks seated atop five hundred pound bombs, occasionally scrawling a "This is for Hitler" or "This is for Mussolini" on them. During his first month on the docks, one of Cavaleri's work mates was drafted. A couple of months later, however, his friend was back working on the docks, only this time as a soldier assigned to a quartermaster company. His friend was upset because civilian stevedores like Cavaleri were making $45-$50 a week, while he was making only $50 a month as a private. A couple of weeks were all Cavaleri had to enjoy his friend's frustration because he too received his notice to report for service.

Cavaleri's first choice was the Army Air Forces, but he was rejected when a test revealed he was color deficient. His next choice was the infantry. Cavaleri had had four years of military-type drill in high school; thus, he was used to handling rifles and marching. "Would you like to join the paratroopers?" asked the recruiting sergeant. "They're looking for infantrymen."

"Sure. Okay," Cavaleri replied. That was it. He didn't even know paratroopers received an extra $50 a month until he arrived at Fort Benning. "We were just kids from the city," said Cavaleri. "What did we know?"

Private Willis B. Grice was a farmer's son from Nashville, Tennessee. Lured by higher wages, both he and his father had left the farm to work at the nearby Vultee aircraft factory when Grice received his notice to report for service. He volunteered for Airborne immediately and went directly to Benning. "Sixteen of us come down from Camp Oglethorpe, Tennessee," remembered Grice. It was about midnight when they stopped along a row of barracks and were immediately introduced to the Airborne's demanding training methods. In the dark, a sergeant assembled the men and told them to drop their bags. The sergeant then started the men running down the road, four miles, up to the Alabama Area and back. When the men, breathing heavily, got back to their piled up duffel bags, the sergeant asked the group of panting trainees, "How many want to quit?" Four men fell out, but Grice, who had "stayed close to the sergeant" the whole way, spoke right up. "If that's all it is," he stated, "then I'm gonna stay."[6]

Private Sidney Laufer was a Jewish kid of Rumanian descent from Hartford, Connecticut. He hadn't spent much time thinking about the war before he'd enlisted, mostly because he didn't know much about it. "Here I was a kid," Laufer explained. His attitude was, "Who gives a shit about what happened in Europe as long as it's not in my back yard."[7]

In 1937, two of Laufer's cousins traveled from Europe on, they said, a visit. The girls ended up staying for years. The cousins' mother arrived a couple of years later, and then finally their brother as well. Their father, however, never came; he would eventually die in a concentration camp. The girls didn't speak English at first, so Sid's parents translated their stories about what was happening in Hitler's Europe for him. Still, Laufer thought, "It's over there. Who cares?"[8]

After Pearl Harbor, Laufer's feelings changed. Other young men around him were rushing to register or enlist. Meanwhile, rumors spread in Connecticut that Japanese and German submarines were just off the coast, near the Navy's submarine base in New London. Being too young to enlist – Laufer was only sixteen in late 1941 – he volunteered as a fire watcher for the Connecticut Defense Council. At the same time he attended high school and worked part-time at Colt Patent Firearms in the cold storage division. Laufer's job was to pack the unfinished frames for the M1911A1 pistol in long boxes for transport by mules to the first machining operation. "All I did was put those things into little slots" at 70 cents an hour. Laufer turned eighteen on 18 March 1943 and by May had volunteered. "The flags were waving and all the kids were signing up. And – Oh shit – I just signed up with them," he recalled. Laufer felt an additional obligation, too. His older brother, Abraham, was already in the Army.[9]

The Navy turned Laufer down because he was color blind. "It was a big disappointment," he admitted. So, he turned to the Army. Laufer left his job at Colt on 20 July and reported to Fort Devins, Massachusetts. There, with all the other enlistees, he was given his shots, was administered the Army General Classification Test, and received uniforms. "Nothing fit right," Laufer remarked. "They just threw them at you. They didn't give a shit because they were recruits, too." At Devins, Laufer suffered the same brand of 'chicken' treatment that was the burden of all new soldiers. "Who can drive a truck?" asked a sergeant. A man raised his hand thinking he was going to get out of some regular duty by so volunteering. What he didn't know was that the Army already knew all the tricks of the trade. Instead of a truck, the sergeant gave the man a wheelbarrow to drive.[10]

At Devins, all the arms and services of the Army were there recruiting. An Army Air Forces recruiter informed Laufer that color blind people could distinguish camouflage better than those with normal vision, and suggested that he should train as a bombardier. "Forget it," he said, "that's not for me." Then a soldier got up on stage with "this fancy outfit on, fancy boots, and give me all this bull that I'm gonna learn how to ride motorcycles, and run trains, and we're going behind the enemy lines, and do all this stuff and demolitions. All kinds of crap! And of course, being a young kid, my eyes were that big and I said, 'That's for me!' Especially one of those fancy uniforms." With a friend, Joe DiSaro who wound up in the same battalion, Laufer signed up for the paratroopers.[11]

"All of a sudden," recalls Bob Greenstrand, "I heard the name Elwyn H. Greenstrand called." Greenstrand could tell the First Sergeant was having some trouble with his first name. "I believe he called out Evelyn!" When Greenstrand answered "Here!" loud and clear, and sergeant saw that he was a man, Greenstrand thought Clark looked relieved. "I am sure that he thought a WAC had been shipped by mistake." Greenstrand was assigned to the Second Platoon's first squad. With him went Private Paul Imre who was assigned to the platoon's 60mm mortar squad, Private Clarence F. Knigge, Jr., and another thirty or so men.

Before he turned eighteen, in April 1943, Imre joined the Army's Enlisted Reserve Corps at the University of Illinois where he was studying bio-chemistry and German – the only thing that he had learned in college that would prove to be valuable in service. When the spring semester ended in May, he went home to the Bronx. In June, Imre received notice to report to Fort Dix, New Jersey for active duty on 23 July 1943.

At Dix, Imre was inducted and issued his basic uniforms and equipment – from identification tags to foot powder to GI socks. Then he mailed his civilian stuff back home. A couple of days later, he was given the Army General Classification Test (AGCT). The AGCT was designed to assay an inductee's ability to learn, measuring "a compound of native endowments" and "the effects of schooling and social experience." The score determined an inductee's "intelligence" in terms of its usefulness to the Army. Scores were ranked, high to low, as Class I, II, III, IV, and V. More often than not, Class I, II, and III men were assigned to fill technical positions in the Army Air Forces or the service branches of the Army Ground Forces (AGF). So great were the demands of the service branches for top-scoring men that the combat branches of the AGF – especially the Infantry – were forced to operate with fewer than their specified number of upper score men, while at the same time being crowded with Class IV and V enlistees to well in excess. The only exception to this rule was found in airborne units of the AGF which were allowed to cull out their excess Class IV and V men and, therefore, had a higher total proportion of upper scores than other combat branches.[12]

The day before the AGCT was administered, Imre suffered the standard battery of inoculations for typhus, typhoid, small pox, tetanus, and other diseases. These made him and the other recruits very ill. "Everyone was kinda sick and throwing up," remembered Imre. "No one ate much, but they were terribly thirsty all the time and had diarrhea." Imre developed a 103-degree fever from the shots, but this didn't prevent him for scoring well. In three days he was over his fever and Imre joined a rookie company at Fort Dix. This was the start of his orientation to the U.S. Army.

Imre's rookie company practiced close-order drill, military courtesy, and learned the Articles of War – all the real chicken stuff. Their drill instructor was a tough little Polish sergeant named Lideck who soon proved himself to be an expert in all things chicken.

Sergeant Lideck knew some of the men in the company had gone to college, so one day he decided to have some fun at their expense. "Okay," said Lideck, "dis is a class in education. Okay, all you guys that went to college, stand up." The college guys stood up. "The rest of you dumb bastards sit down, and watch. Now," directing his remarks to the standing college men, "would you guys show us how to pick up anything that's not living from here to the mess hall and back – on you hands and knees. And you dumb bastards," he said, redirecting his remarks to those men still seated, "sit down there and watch and learn." Imre got the message right away that his previous educational efforts were really not esteemed by the Army.

Imre soon had enough of Lideck's chickenshit and volunteered for parachute infantry. Besides, he knew that's what he wanted to do from the beginning. So, sometime in August, Imre traveled by train to Fort Benning, Georgia.[13]

"It looked like a hell hole, really!" said Imre, remembering his first impression of Fort Mitchell. "Sand. It looked like the Sahara." The quarters, just shacks, were furnished only with bunks and were surrounded by red clay hills and goober patches. To Imre, the whole place looked as if it were devoid of anything living. Imre couldn't believe that this was a place you'd go to learn how to be a soldier. He soon found out it wasn't: Fort Mitchell was a place where you learned how to be a paratrooper.

The First Sergeant continued to call out names until he'd expended all those on the list. The balance of the company's men, including Privates John I. Hall, Frank Munafo, and Richard H. Murray went to the Third Platoon.

Frank Munafo had wanted to be a paratrooper since he was sixteen years old. He was riding on a bus one day, coming home from roller skating with his friends, when he saw a soldier, "a big, tall, strapping, nice lookin' guy," hop on the bus. "Oh, what a nice uniform," Munafo thought, "dressed to kill." The soldier had on high-laced brown boots, the emblem of the parachute on his overseas cap, and sterling wings and ribbons on his chest. Munafo sat just looking at the guy, couldn't take his eyes off him. "Oh jeez, what does he do? What kind of a service is he in?" he thought to himself. Finally, he worked up the nerve to ask him. Munafo sat down in the seat across the aisle and asked, "Hey mister, what to you do?"

"I'm a United States paratrooper," the young soldier replied.

"It stood in my mind – that's what I want to be," recalled Munafo. "I never forgot it."

After the war started, Munafo couldn't wait to get in the service. His mother had passed away, his father was living in Pennsylvania working for the government, and his brother had already been drafted and was serving with the engineers. Munafo hated living by himself, so, as soon as he could, he went to the local induction center. To his disappointment, however, the sergeant there told him "You have to wait till you're called." Not to be put off, Munafo quit high school, went back, and finally wore the sergeant down. The sergeant knew he was too young, but he "screwed around" with Munafo's birth certificate. Munafo was inducted in Jersey City and, as soon as he got to Dix, he volunteered for Airborne.[14]

A few of the other men in the company, Privates Neil Haggard, Edward D. Sorenson, and George Vondrasek among them, had previous training. Private Haggard was serving with the 144th Infantry Regiment of the 44th Division, New Jersey National Guard, when he volunteered for Airborne. The 44th was a chickenshit outfit, as far as Haggard was concerned, filled with smart-ass NCOs and lazy officers, and he wanted out. When told to choose between a thirty-day furlough and a transfer to The Parachute School, Haggard told his old commanding officer to "stick the furlough." When he arrived at Benning, the NCO greeted him with, "Cut that non-combatant patch off your uniform right now. Where you're going, you're going to see combat!" Haggard loved it.[15]

Haggard, from St. Louis, asked to go into communications and was assigned to company HQ. Together with Sorenson, Vondrasek, and another radio man, they were put in a tent, separated from the barracks which housed the rest of F Company. Because they had already gone through basic training with other outfits, they wouldn't have to repeat it. They were required, however, to make the twenty-five mile road marchs.[16]

F Company's Commanding Officer (CO) was Captain Gates Ivy, Jr. Captain Ivy, very tall, dark complexioned, and handsome, was a native Mississippian. He stood rigidly erect, like he was at attention at all times – the men would come to see this was his normal posture. "He talked slow and he moved slow," commented Staff Sergeant John O. Paul, platoon sergeant of Third Platoon, "but he moved fast when he had to." Likewise, though he was usually quiet and polite, Ivy would bark orders when he had to. Ivy's Executive Officer was 1st Lieutenant Sam Dean. A contrast to Ivy, Dean was short, had bow-legs, and being affable by nature was popular with the men. The fact that he spoke with a distinct Southern drawl was about the only thing Dean and the CO had in common.[17]

The platoon leaders were 2nd Lieutenant Lawrence P. O'Donnell and 2nd Lieutenant Leonard P. Sims with the First Platoon, 1st Lieutenant Frank Chappell and 2nd Lieutenant Samuel Calhoun with the Second Platoon, and 1st Lieutenant Ivan Stositch with Third Platoon. "Our officers," said Laufer, "were the handsomest sonsabitches!" "Stositch was so good looking – he should have been a movie star," said Munafo, "not a platoon leader." Something like freshmen athletes, F Company men looked to their officers as team captains and the officers' bearing, ability, and patent good looks inspired confidence and loyalty from the recruits. According to Major Irwin A. Edwards, 2nd Battalion's Executive Officer, "F Company probably had the youngest, and the finest. . . officers" in the regiment.[18]

On 6 March 1943, shortly after being formed, the 513th's headquarters was moved from the Frying Pan to the Fort Mitchell, a location completely isolated from the rest of the post. Unfortunately, the 513th Parachute Infantry had been earmarked to serve as The Parachute School Replacement Pool. The mission of the Replacement Pool was to supply trained parachute replacements to the Army's several airborne divisions, independent regiments and battalions, as well as to the Organization for Strategic Services (OSS). Colonel Dickerson, however, constantly looked forward to the day when his regiment would be activated as a combat unit, and conducted business accordingly.

Major Irwin A. 'Boppy' Edwards, like Dickerson, recognized immediately the advantage the 513th's administration of the Replacement Pool would have on the regiment's future. Tall, lean, and handsome, Edwards was an Oklahoma native, a graduate of the Oklahoma Military Academy and ROTC, and like many airborne officers, a former cavalryman. 'Boppy' was the name his daughter had given him when she'd learned to talk, and Edwards preferred it to Irwin. The only Irwins he'd ever known, said Edwards, "were fancy butchers or hair dressers." As commander of I Company – all the Replacement Pool's officers were assigned to I Company – Major Edwards screened all the commissioned personnel as they came through the system. "We had selected the good ones [officers] as they come out of The Parachute School," said Edwards. The best of the officer replacements were kept for the 513th, and the same held true of the enlisted men. "We ended up with. . . from the standpoint of motivation, honesty, and integrity. . . a superior group of soldiers," said Edwards, ". . . absolutely superb youngsters. And that was a big advantage."[19]

The order Colonel Dickerson was waiting for arrived 31 May 1943. The 513th Parachute Infantry was relieved of its duties administering the Parachute Replacement Pool, and authorized to fill its ranks to full strength "as per the appropriate T/O, & E by orders." Men had begun arriving almost immediately.[21]

When all of F Company's men had been organized, the company was assembled. Captain Ivy then got up in front of the men and gave a short speech. Ivy reiterated what they had already been told, but added one more thing. "Do not get too close to your buddies," he said, "because when you get into combat and he's killed, you might do something to get yourself killed. So don't get too close to your buddy."[21]

Training was begun immediately. For F Company, their careers as paratroopers began with thirteen weeks of Basic Training which was devoted to the skills all soldiers needed. The first two weeks were called the 'recruit period' during which the soldiers would be instructed in military discipline and courtesy, the Articles of War, Army regulations, military sanitation and first aid, individual defense against chemical attacks, individual defense against air and mechanized attacks, marches and bivouacs, close-order and extended-order drill, care of clothing and equipment, packs and tent pitching, and interior guard duty. The basic training schedule for the paratroops was identical to that of any other new recruits in the Army except that the drill instructors in the Alabama Area were intent on pushing their Airborne trainees harder both physically and mentally than regular troops.

The first morning of Basic, the men were taken on a three or four-mile run before breakfast. The next day, it was six miles. Captain Ivy, the men found, never accompanied the men on the morning runs. Ivy chose instead to run alone, and if he happened into the company in the course, he'd just give everyone a smile and keep going.[22]

Most of the recruits were already athletic. Tec 5 Ray R. Rafalovich was fanatical about his body. Munafo remembers "he once did several hundred sit ups while the men took turns holding down his feet. Every time you saw him he was doing push-ups or sit-ups." Many of the others, like Munafo, Imre, and Private Howard R. McClain had lettered in track. "That's all we did when we were kids," comments Munafo, "we didn't have anything else to do."[23]

Privates Imre and McClain, who had run on the track teams at the Universities of Illinois and Florida respectively, found the runs easy, so easy that they decided they could embarrass their platoon leader, Lieutenant Chappell, by beating him in a race. In reply, Chappell smiled, and said, "We'll go out for a little jog, boys." He turned to his assistant. "These poor bastards can go back," he said, instructing Calhoun to take the rest of the men to the barracks. Then his eyes returned to Imre and McClain. "Just follow me, boys," he said, "and when you get tired – let me know."

Imre and McClain started running but the lieutenant quickly passed both of them, charging ahead at a fast pace. Imre thought to himself, "This guy can't keep this pace up for a half mile – it would be a world's record." But Chappell kept on going, widening the gap. At the half way point, the lieutenant taunted the two freshmen, "Time to turn around and go back. Come on, girls!"

When Imre and McClain finally dragged themselves back to the barracks, they found the lieutenant waiting, laughing and grinning. "Good try, kids. Let's try it again tomorrow. Better again, how 'bout before lunch!" Imre and McClain felt sick. They didn't even want to eat their breakfasts. Chappell smiled some more and got up. "Any time, boys," he said, waving his hand as he walked off. It was a small lesson in humility.

The road marches were made as strenuous as possible. The men were marched "through half the state of Alabama. The officers," believed Greenstrand, "would intentionally pray for rain or terribly hot weather simply to punish us." At first, Greenstrand thought he was going to collapse or even fail, but found inspiration from an unlikely source. "I probably would have [quit] if it hadn't been for [Private] Dolph Greene," said Greenstrand. "He was an actor from New York, overweight and more out of shape than I was. This guy would run until he dropped but would never quit. I followed him alphabetically through all the training at jump school and when it was his turn to do something he was on his feet and never hesitated. Dolph gave me the will I needed to keep going until I got in shape myself."[24]

Two weeks after basic training began, Lieutenant Chappell was reassigned as an instructor at The Parachute School and 2nd Lieutenant Calhoun took over the Second Platoon. Lieutenant Calhoun had grown up on his father's farm in Fresno, California. There, he'd spent his summers swimming in the canals and riding horses, and playing Cowboys and Indians with his best friend.

Calhoun had been in the Army since 1938 when he'd enlisted in the 185th Infantry Regiment, a National Guard outfit, at Camp San Luis Obispo. The following summer and winter, Calhoun spent training in California with the 159th Infantry. By 1941, Calhoun had enlisted in the regular Army and was eventually assigned to H Company, 15th Infantry where he performed various duties from machine-gunner to company runner for Captain George P. Howell, H Company's CO. There, Calhoun was promoted to private first class.

In 1942, two more promotions followed and soon Calhoun was ordered to Fort Benning, Georgia, to attend Officers Candidate School Class 172. Calhoun established an exemplary record at OCS, graduated, and was commissioned a Second Lieutenant in the Infantry. Shortly after graduation, Calhoun ran into his former company commander from the 15th Infantry, George Howell who had risen to the rank of brigadier general and was in command of The Parachute School. General Howell talked Calhoun into volunteering for airborne training and he was assigned to Class 128. Calhoun graduated The Parachute School and the Demolitions School in early 1943 and was assigned to the 513th Parachute Infantry Regiment's officer pool.

While awaiting their assignments, officers and men in the pool continued to train, undertaking field problems that took them all over the local countryside. On many occasions, lieutenants were loaded into the back of two-and-a-half-ton trucks, which had their tarpaulins drawn down, and were driven into the Alabama countryside. A 'bird dog' – one of the NCO instructors – sat at the back of the truck to make sure the lieutenants couldn't see out. After about an hour, the trucks pulled off the road and the tarpaulins were thrown back. Each instructor informed his charges that they were now "behind enemy lines" and that their own lines were in this or that direction, so many miles away. When the trucks drove away, the men had to get back on their own.

On his first time out, Calhoun's group was dropped off on a logging road at about 0800. The men started walking, but within minutes, along came a big semi-truck. Since the men had been instructed to commandeer transportation when behind enemy lines, Calhoun, exercising his native resourcefulness, flagged down the truck and asked the driver if he could take them all to Fort Mitchell, Alabama. As the driver was already headed for Phenix City, Alabama and would pass the road to Fort Mitchell on the way, he was more than happy to oblige. The men climbed on board and rode the logs all the way. At the road leading to the Alabama Area, they hitched a ride to within about a mile of camp and walked the rest of the way, arriving at about 1000 hours. The instructors were furious. It was early, about 0800, when Calhoun's group was dropped off, and the brass hats were all hollering that they'd gotten back too soon. They were about to take them out to do it all over again when Calhoun explained that they were only following their instructions to appropriate local transportation. Calhoun's reasoning seemed to appease them. Meanwhile, the rest of the lieutenants walked all the way and didn't get back to camp until late that night. Not surprisingly, Calhoun was one of the first officers in the Replacement Pool to be selected by Edwards for the 513th.[25]

Calhoun struck the men as being very young, and some saw in him a "boyish innocence." Calhoun "always tried to sound tougher or more military than he really was I believe," said Greenstrand. Private Donald O. Newhouse agreed. "Calhoun was always business-like. . . always acting stern and in charge." However young he looked, Calhoun threw himself wholeheartedly into the platoon's training. Calhoun had grown up with the idyllic belief that the good guys were always supposed to win, and he pushed his men because of it. "This was the way to win a war" was the way Calhoun looked at paratrooping. Yet, and perhaps because he had been an enlisted man himself, he treated his men with dignity.[26]

Before the first week of training had passed, the men came to despise the camp, and the instructors did everything in their power to make it miserable for the trainees. There was a juke box in Fort Mitchell's mess hall and starting the first morning at 0530, and every morning thereafter remembered Laufer, "some sonofabitch would get up and start playing *Pistol Packin' Momma.*" Roaches scurried across the floors. Maggots covered the garbage. "Some men went AWOL," recalled Laufer. "Oh, it was terrible!"[27]

The shacks, long things with screening all round and covers that came down when it rained, were hotter than hell. "In the barracks, at night time, it was so hot and humid," complained Munafo, "very damp, very uncomfortable." For Private Murray, from Boothbay, Maine, the heat was sheer torture. While his men smothered in the shacks, however, Captain Ivy lived in an air-conditioned trailer.[28]

"The food was plentiful, but bad," said Imre, "but the guys were so hungry they soon overcame their reluctance." PFC Imre figured that this was the Army's way of saying that "theirs was not going to be a life of ease." They would have to make do with what they got and still perform to the satisfaction of the instructors. There was a lot of SOS – of the ground beef and white sauce variety. The biscuits were browned on the outside, but, on one occasion, on the inside they were raw. It made some of the guys mad, remembered Neal Haggard, so they got up and started throwing them. "Throw them damn biscuits, you bastards," hollered one of the cooks, "but whenever you're on KP, you're gonna clean em up just like the KPs this morning are gonna clean em up. So just throw em. I don't care." The cook's speech just made the men that much madder so they got up and really started throwing them. After a while, though, some of the men grew to love the chow. Grice, in fact, volunteered for KP every chance he got. He'd gone into the service at 160 pounds and quickly gained twenty more.[29]

The second phase of basic was the 'company period'. During these eight weeks, all training focused on the weapons and tactics of the rifle company, and nearly a fifth of the schedule was devoted to the M1 rifle alone. "Sighting, cleaning, nomenclature," states Laufer. "There was no reason men didn't know what they were carrying. They gave you all the training in the world. Everything was explained and they explained it thoroughly." Laufer, who had only fired .22s in civilian life, couldn't wait to get his hands on one.[30]

Imre, who had never fired a rifle before entering service, thought the M1 "was a very light rifle, [though on marches] it got heavier with each mile. At the end of twenty-five miles, it felt like ninety-six pounds." The weapon's weight notwithstanding, Imre was excited by the fact that he could hit what he was aiming at: it was a "damn miracle to pull the trigger and put a hole in something two hundred, three hundred, four hundred yards away." Lieutenant Calhoun required every one of his men to put at least eight of ten in the bulls-eye, and, by the end of basic, his men had become terrific marksmen.

Day or night, rain or shine, even with live fire crackling thirty inches over their heads, the men could take their weapons apart and put them back together. In the way of practice, First Sergeant Clark would throw the pieces of a weapon into a dark room, push a man in, and shut the door. There, in the dark, it was to be reassembled. This training was intended not only to bolster the men's self confidence, but was also a way of developing a vital skill. In a combat jump, the M1, dismantled in its Griswold Bag, had to be reassembled quickly upon landing. Most of the heavy weapons used by paratroopers had to be assembled after landing as well.

The men were also instructed in the care, maintenance, and use of the infantry's other basic weapons, including the .30 caliber M1918A2 Browning Automatic Rifle, the M1919A4 light machine-gun, the .45 caliber M1911A1 automatic pistol, hand grenades, and the bayonet. The NCOs performed most of the instruction.

Most of F Company's NCOs – Sergeant Arthur A. 'Snuffy' Bowers, Staff Sergeant Henry Kaczmarek who was covered with tattoos, and Sergeant Milton C. Smith – had come up from Panama and the 501st Parachute Infantry Regiment or the 507th. They were a tough bunch. Sergeant Smith, Second Platoon's guide, had picked up a few tricks from The Parachute School's NCOs.[31] "He trained us," said Imre. "He trained us with what I call a kind of Southern charm." Every order Smith gave started with, "All right, you dumb bastards. . ." Stositch's platoon sergeant was John O. Paul, from Pineville, Louisiana. "Paul was a rough sonofabitch," says Laufer, "but he was a good sergeant, he knew his work, and the men respected him." Paul had only been in service since June of 1942, but had already completed The Parachute School and Demolitions School. Intelligent, conscientious, and efficient, he had risen quickly to the rank of staff sergeant.

Calhoun's platoon sergeant was Staff Sergeant Raymond O. Nix. At six feet and two hundred pounds, every inch of Sergeant Nix was an enormous example of the hard-living, hard-drinking, prewar Regular Army. The men didn't know much about all that, however; to them, he was just a "mean son of a bitch." Even Lieutenant Calhoun considered Nix be one of the roughest men in the paratroops. Nix was a skilled soldier, and once held the Army championship in bayonet combat. To no one's surprise, Nix relished leading F Company's bayonet instruction; he taunting the men, daring them to try and stick him. The few men who really did try ended up on their asses. To his detriment, though, Sergeant Nix had another passion: drinking schnapps, which often led to fights in one of Columbus, Georgia's bars. Nix was known to disappear on benders after these fights. "He'd show up a couple of days later and they'd bust him down only to raise him back up," observed Private Marvin Harris. And Nix's drinking binges wouldn't endear him to any of the men either. "Nix was usually broke a day or two after pay day," remembered Greenstrand, so "when he went to town, he normally requested to borrow a few dollars. The word was: 'You had best invest it with him.' Of course interest rates were not very good and it was rare that you ever seen that green again."[32]

During the company period, individual tactical training covered hasty entrenchments, camouflage, map and aerial photograph reading, observer training, messenger training, and tactical training of the individual soldier. Unit tactics covered the offensive and defensive formations of rifle squads, platoons, and the company as well as night operations. Weeks eleven and twelve of Basic Training were the 'battalion period', and the last week was the 'regimental period', all which covered similar training subjects but which focused on tactical exercises involving those larger formations.

Shortly before F Company finished basic, they were treated to an exhibition jump over the Alabama Area. The men were sat while the instructors explained what was about to happen when the planes came over. The planes started their pass over the drop zone "and sure as shit," remembered Munafo, "you see the one stick come out and you'd see the one coming right down. The chute didn't open. You could see him trying to open the pack but he just couldn't. That day, about three or four guys chickened out. . . that was it."[33]

The Parachute School, located at Ft. Benning's Lawson Field in the infamous Frying Pan area, was established on 30 April 1941. Throughout training, parachute troops were subject to the most "intense and continuous physical training course" provided by the Army. This was instituted in order to "minimize the number of landing injuries" and to prepare troopers for the immense physical challenges routine to airborne operations. The course, composed of four training stages – A, B, C, and D – was conducted over four weeks, one week for each phase. The curriculum was intended to instill in every trainee the ability to pack, inspect, and maintain his T-5 or T-7 parachute, familiarize him with tactical jumping, and instruct him how to properly load and drop aerial delivery units containing heavy equipment.[34]

The men of Major Willis' 2nd Battalion began A Stage of parachute training on 20 October 1943. A Stage was physical conditioning, pure and simple, and arguably the most important part of paratrooper training. It set the tone.

The instructors told the men that in order to be paratroopers, they would have to perform physically "beyond their wildest dreams," that they must be instantaneously obedient, and yet still be able to act independently, and that they would be doing things that they'd never done before in their lives and would probably never do again. Airborne operations required that paratroopers carry almost all of their weapons and equipment, everything they needed, with them into battle. Therefore, they had to be in top physical condition. In battle, they would regularly be required to perform acts of valor that other soldiers would call crazy. They would be extraordinary soldiers, elite, the best. For them, there would be no alternative to victory. To "sluff off – to be second best – meant losing their lives and their country."

In The Parachute School, the men, even officers, came under the control of the school's NCO instructors – 'white tee-shirt commandos' as they were known. At Fort Benning, the sergeant was king. The men were up and out in the pitch darkness – 0400 to 0430 hours – to make formation and start 'calihoopies' – calisthenics. "The whole regiment would have to fall out, including the officers, even the colonels," said Laufer. "When it came to calihoopies, it was the sergeants from Ft. Benning that were in charge. And believe me, when they gave an order, the men carried it out at a dead run." The instructors, many combat veterans, instilled obedience through punishment and intimidation, methods that got the men's attention. "Parachute School instructors," Imre said, "treated the new recruits like animals that needed to be beaten. They trained the men like people who believed in training dogs by beating them." Even the officers had to obey them, and, remembered Laufer, "some of the sergeants gave the officers a real hard time."[35]

The first exercise was always push-ups, followed by a run. The very first day, the instructors informed the men they were going to run three miles down to the Alabama border and back, and if anybody dropped out, he was out of the paratroops. After the run there were more push-ups. Finally an instructor ordered the formation to quick-march in place. "Anybody that doesn't want to continue," hollered the instructor, "stand fast." Then he double-timed the company to the mess hall for breakfast. Any man that stood fast was removed, along with his belongings, before breakfast had ended. This weeding-out took place every morning for a week.[36]

The food at Benning was a big improvement over the Alabama Area. F Company men, according to Private John La Riccia, "couldn't eat better" than they did in The Parachute School. The men got all the milk, cereal, hotcakes, and French toast they could handle.

After chow, the men formed up again for more exercises. To develop muscles needed in parachute manipulation, the men climbed ropes to the top of the hangers using only their arms. Then the trainees performed platform jumps and tumbling exercises over and over again to learn how to land without injury. Then arm-circles with the Indian clubs – a torture second only to the push-ups in the instructors' favor. After three minutes of exercising, the instructor would jest, "Now I'm gonna give you guys a rest. We're gonna go the other way." Some men passed out. Imre recalled once letting his arms down, but when an instructor fixed his withering gaze on him, and mouthed the words, "chickenshit," Imre's arms shot back up.[37]

Next came squat-thrusts, sit-ups, the bend-and-reach, the turn-and-bounce, duck walking, arm-circles, more push-ups, more arm-circles, and 'jabs' – an exercise unique to The Parachute School. Jabs were meant to foster instant, unthinking reactions and quick reflexes – and to keep the men alert. When an instructor yelled "Jab!" no matter what the trainee was doing, he was to stop and immediately strike his chest with his right fist. Sometimes an instructor yelled jab in the middle of a lecture to catch the guys who had gone to sleep or who just weren't interested. "If you didn't jab fast enough," recalled Laufer, "it was your ass." Trainees who didn't perform the jab fast enough to please the instructor, or loud enough for the instructor to hear, had to do twenty-five push-ups. "A lot of men fell out, embarrassed, to do a lot of push-ups while their friends grinned at them from ranks," recalled Imre. There was a purpose to this, however. "Alertness, precision, neatness, and discipline" were qualities "indispensable" for paratroopers and all training, including jabs, was designed to "demand and develop these characteristics." By the end of parachute training, most troopers realized that jabs had developed a reflex reaction that might save their life if their main canopy failed to deploy properly on a jump: the handle of their reserve parachute was located on their chest.[38]

The instructors pushed every man to do more push-ups, to run farther and faster by telling him that no matter how well he thought he was doing, it was not good enough. "We did a million push-ups and jabs," remembered Greenstrand, and "ran round the training field swinging our risers. . . singing 'I screwed up,' or 'I'm a B-29,' or something to that effect." "Some sergeants would give you fifty push-ups for blinking your eyes," recalled Corporal Marvin Harris. When the trainee recovered, the sergeants sometimes asked, "Did you cheat?" "No, Sergeant!" came the reply. "A good paratrooper always cheats," the sergeant would bellow back and the trainee had to do twenty-five more. Again the sergeant asked, "Did you cheat?" "Yes, Sergeant!" came the reply. "A good paratrooper never cheats," and it was twenty-five more.[39]

"When a sergeant told you to do push-ups, trainees could demand of the instructor, 'Do 'em with me', noted Laufer, but when you got up, "he'd really ream your ass out for twenty-five more whether you cheated or not." It was a practice unique to the Airborne. The Parachute School instructors, as well as the officers of the regiment, did everything they asked the men to do. Officers and instructors alike demonstrated to recruits that they were tough and, through this behavior, gained the respect of the men. "Do you want me to show you how to do push-ups?" Lieutenant Calhoun would ask. Then he'd get down and lead the men saying, "I'll show you how to do push-ups and you're gonna do 'em with me. This is how to do 'em," he'd say. "Now, keep up with me." Lieutenant Calhoun strictly adhered to this credo. "If he told you to run [for punishment], he'd run with you," remembered Munafo. "He was a bitch, but he was all heart."[40]

Rounding out A Stage was hand-to-hand combat training. The instructor, Tech Sergeant Gasdon, was a big blond fellow who made the slight Lieutenant Calhoun his guinea pig. On one occasion, Gasdon threw the lieutenant completely out of the sawdust ring and into the hard-packed earth. "Come back," Gasdon instructed Lieutenant Calhoun. "Let's do that again." Sergeant Gasdon was a perfectionist.

By the end of A Stage, every man could run five miles in fifty minutes, do at least fifty push-ups, sixteen chin ups, and climb a forty foot rope using only his arms. The constant exercise had not only toughened the men, but had taught them that they were able to go beyond the limits of ordinary physical exertion. It also instilled in the men the confidence that they were serving with men they could trust in combat, men who wouldn't quit when things got rough. More importantly, each man knew that if he dug down deep inside himself he could find the will to keep going, no matter what. This set the paratroopers apart from other soldiers. At the same time, a camaraderie had developed among F Company men – all for one and one for all – with the instructors becoming their common enemy. That's where the hard, ruthless character of the unit was formed. "What do you do when they're down?" the instructors asked. The correct response was, "Kill 'em, kill 'em!!" In time, this aggressive attitude would be unleashed upon the Germans.

The second week of parachute training introduced the men to parachute packing and apparatus training. The men were issued their jump suits for the first time – two outfits, jump boots, and new M1C helmets and jump liners. The trainees weren't allowed to blouse their trousers over their boots, though, until they earned their wings. If one of the paratroopers on the installation caught a trainee doing it, he'd cut his boots down to GI shoes. The men were trucked to the packing sheds at Lawson Field where two enormous hangers with concrete floors had been converted into rigger sheds, these occupied by long tables for parachute packing, heavy-duty sewing machines for rigger's work, and opposite them, a row of offices and supply rooms. At the end of each hanger were towers – parachute shake-out and drying rooms – where chutes were hung after jumps to dry and be cleared of debris.

Technical parachute training, or B Stage, began with the packing course which occupied fifty-two hours on the training schedule. One officer was assigned to each group of 250 trainees. Large classes were divided and NCO instructors were assigned to supervise smaller groups of eighteen students working at six tables in the packing shed. Each trainee was provided with a text outlining the nomenclature and operation of a complete parachute assembly and students were graded on both their "recitation of the text assignments" and their "practical work" every day. Instructors worked to eliminate the trainees' natural fears of jumping by replacing "ignorance and resultant fear" with a "thorough knowledge and familiarity with the parachute and confidence in its capabilities."[41]

The basic packing course consisted of a lecture on the purpose and method of conducting the course, and instruction in the care of equipment; the nomenclature and functioning of the parachute; the laying out of the parachute; the removal of twists and tangles in suspension lines; the inspection of the parachute, panel folding for both the right-hand and left-hand groups of panels; the complete folding of the canopy, the stowing of the suspension lines in the pack, the closing and sewing of the pack including necessary tacking; the complete packing of the back pack; the lay-out of the reserve parachute; the complete packing of the reserve parachute; harness adjustment; the maintaining of associated records and forms; the hanging and checking of the parachute for drying; collecting parachutes and bin storage; and field folding.[44]

Following the packing course was a two-hour written examination, and a six-hour practical examination in which the student had to successfully complete the packing of a troop type parachute, both main and reserve. Students who scored seventy-five percent on the written exam of fifty questions, who completely packed a parachute "so as to insure its proper functioning in a live jump or drop test" under the supervision of instructor, and who had achieved passing grades on the daily exercises were considered "qualified" to advance to the next stage of training.[43]

It took the troopers about two hours to properly pack their chutes, getting every crease out of the canopy, leaving an air hole up through the chute to ensure it would open fast enough. The men used shot bags to hold the slippery silk in place while they worked and sometimes these got packed in the chute by mistake. "When [the parachute] opens [the shot bag] hits you in the damn head," said Staff Sergeant Paul. But, added Imre, at least "then you knew it was open."

Initially, the canopy of the T-5 parachute was fitted with a little 'pilot' chute to help pull the main chute from the container, but the enlisted men cut these off for souvenirs. The Parachute School instructors finally eliminated them all together. "The enlisted men swiped so many of them they just cut out buying them," remembered Calhoun.

Taking place in conjunction with the packing course, and an integral part of B Stage, was the jump training course. Jump training was intended to produce trainees who could endure the "physical shocks" confronted in parachute landings, jump from a plane in flight "without hesitation and without endangering fellow jumpers," and adequately control their parachute during decent "so as to land in a suitable area" and without injury. Men trained in groups of fifty or less supervised by two NCO instructors. One officer was present for every 150 trainees.[44]

The jump training course required fifty-two hours of instruction to complete. The first six hours of training were in the suspended harness – known by the men as the 'ball breaker' – learning parachute manipulation, the basic control of the parachute in descent, checking oscillation, the proper landing position, and the correct posture for water, tree, and wire landings. To slip backwards, trainees pulled down on the two back risers, spilling the air from the front of the chute. To go forward, trainees pulled down on the front risers. Slipping left and right were accomplished in similar fashion. To make the chute turn, the trainees reached behind their heads for one riser while pulling on its diagonal opposite in the front. Left unchecked, the resultant motion would "screw you right into the ground," joked Clarence Knigge. The ball breaker was followed by six hours of door practice, learning techniques for individual and mass jumping – every step from loading-up to the jump until they could do it in their sleep.

Six hours were spent in the landing trainer practicing the parachute landing fall, in jumps from the 'Incline Rail and Trolly' and the forty-foot high 'Mock-up Tower' which gave "a good approximation to the force and direction of an actual parachute landing."[45] A large number of men washed out at the forty-foot tower, perhaps more than did in D Stage. To Private Grice, however, "it wasn't nothin'." Raised on a farm, he'd grown up jumping off the roof of the barn into stacks of hay.

The mock-up tower was followed by six more hours of tumbling and "platform jumps with accompanying rolls," six hours of trampoline and stall bar exercises to build coordination and strength, and ten hours on the trainasium, a kind of jungle gym on a grand scale devised to develop and limber up those muscles most needed by the jumper, and build mental toughness in the trainee. Finally, the men sat through four hours of lectures and films on jumping and technique.[46]

At the end of the training schedule, trainees were given eight hours of written and practical qualification tests. Students were required to achieve a grade of seventy-five percent or better on both the written examination and the practical tests on the various apparatus to qualify. This completed, trainees were half way through jump school and if they made it this far, the rest would be downhill.[47]

The third week of jump school was C Stage, the Tower Training Course. F Company "went to the towers to look them over" and take their first ride in the buddy seat. Though the trainees would continue to practice packing parachutes, the course's focus was now directed on having the trainees demonstrate their ability to make live parachute jumps and land safely. There also was an increased effort on the part of the instructors to eliminate men who showed signs of fear or were unable to master the techniques.[48]

The thirty-six hour Tower Training Course consisted of seat descents, rigging drills, harness descents, shock absorber harness drills, collapsing and collecting parachutes, recovery from drag, ten hours of review, and ten hours of free descents (forward descents, checking oscillation, slipping, and body turns) from the tower. To advance, the trainee had to make two correct landings from the free tower, and demonstrate his ability to collect a parachute, to collapse a parachute in the wind, and to recover from a drag position.

The first part of tower training took place on the controlled tower. Four 250-foot training towers, which had been originally erected as parachute rides for 1939 New York World's Fair, had been purchased by Airborne Command and, reconfiguring them for their own purpose, moved to Lawson Field. For Private Laufer it was his second time on the towers: he had ridden a parachute down from one of them with his cousin at the World's Fair. It had been a big thrill.

In controlled tower training, two trainees, strapped into a swing seat called the 'buddy seat', which was hung under a fully deployed parachute canopy, were hoisted to the top of the tower by a cable. The parachute was secured to the hoisting cable by a spring release. When the parachute reached the top of the tower, the spring release was compressed and the parachute – and the trainees – were set free to descend safely regulated by guide cables. Following buddy seat rides, individual trainees performed the same maneuver while strapped into a harness.

To the men's surprise, 1st Lieutenant Frank Chappell, who had transferred out of F Company's Second Platoon, was now in charge of C Stage. To the recruits, Chappell was known alternately as 'Flash Gordon' or 'Atlas Maidenswoon', two comic book heroes of the day. Chappell apparently deserved such nicknames having earned quite a reputation as the 'reserve parachute tester' at The Parachute School. He had jumped on his reserve chute thirty-four times from aircraft, sometimes opening both the main and the reserve together just to see what would happen. On one occasion, Chappell drove a motorcycle out of a C-47 and then opened his parachute. The opening shock caused him to let go of the motorcycle though, and it crashed to the ground. Even more daringly, Chappell had on several occasions jumped on his reserve from the top of the 250-foot practice towers. After climbing to the top, he would walk the end of one of the tower's cross arms, spill the chute, and jump into the breeze.

Amazingly, it was Chappell's physique, not his reckless courage, that inspired the most admiration. Flash Gordon was "built like a 'V' from top to bottom, barrel chested, tan, blond, flashing his teeth, anything you wanted to be, he was it. . . He was a god of Adonis," recalled Imre. Flash Gordon could do one hundred push-ups, and then do twenty-five on his right hand and twenty-five on his left, according to Laufer. "The guy was just fantastic."[49]

To build up the men's confidence in the equipment, Flash Gordon walked out and took hold of the harness of a parachute with both hands. The men's jaws hit the ground when the chute was hoisted up the tower with Flash Gordon dangling underneath gripping on to the harness. Set free at the top, Chappell came safely floating down. "He was either brave or nuts," commented Laufer.

As the week passed, the men progressed into free descents from the towers. In free tower training, the third phase of C Stage, individual trainees were strapped into parachute harnesses and lifted to the top of the towers. When released, the trainee would descend under his own control. When Private Imre stepped up for his first solo flight, the instructor handed him a little piece of toilet paper. At first, Private Imre thought "it was because you just about needed it," but the instructor informed him that he was to release it at the top of the tower in order to determine the wind's direction and, therefore, the direction in which to slip to clear the tower.

The final phase of C Stage was practice in collapsing parachutes in high winds. For this purpose, an airplane engine had been converted into a wind machine. Men, dragged across the ground behind a canopy inflated by the wind machine, learned how to collapse their chutes, and 'figure 8' suspension lines.

With the exception of a few men, including Private Grice, F Company by-passed shock absorber harness training. The shock absorber harness was devised to simulate the effects of a parachute's opening shock. Trainees suspended at some height in the contraption, pulled a rip cord and began to fall. After the trooper had fallen fifteen feet from the shock harness frame, one-inch-thick elastics attached to the risers began to stretch, giving some approximation of a canopy's opening jerk. There was a mat below to break the fall, but it didn't really soften the landing. "As they pulled you up," said Staff Sergeant Paul who went through The Parachute School in October 1942, "that damn mat down there kept getting smaller and smaller. It looked like a matchbox."

Though it was generally conceded among those who'd already trained on it that the shock harness had no practical value, it took a fatal accident to have it removed from the curriculum. In June 1943, a lieutenant from Calhoun's class had been killed on the apparatus when the metal frame's connections broke free of the cable. The lieutenant hit the ground and was decapitated when the falling metal frame fell on him.

The final part of Technical Parachute Training was Qualification Jumping, or D Stage. To earn his wings, a trainee had to complete five jumps from various altitudes, two of which were 'mass jumps' of twelve men. The men also received additional training in packing, loading, ejecting, and recovering aerial delivery units, and lectures on the history of parachute troops and the principles of vertical envelopment tactics. Before each jump, the students packed their own parachutes.

The men were excited. Their ordeal was almost over and they knew they were going to make it. They were going to earn their wings and the right to be called "a United States paratrooper."

Each student was assigned a parachute, kit bag, and a helmet which were kept in marked bins in the packing sheds. Groups of twelve men – a 'stick' – were assigned to one jumpmaster who was responsible for them. On the day of a jump, sticks were marched as a unit to the bin rooms to draw their parachutes. The men paired up and helped each other put on their parachutes, at which time the whole stick was inspected by a rigger or an officer. After all twelve men were inspected, the officer in charge of the packing shed assigned the stick to a plane and sent them to the 'sweat shed' where they waited until the NCO dispatcher conducted them to their plane.

While waiting in the sweat shed, each man rechecked his equipment. "That's when you really was thinking," remembered Munafo, especially before the last jump on Saturday – the men had packed their chutes on Friday night in one big hurry so they could get to town and then they all wondered if they had done a good job or not. When their plane was ready, the dispatcher directed the stick onto the loading apron where the jumpmaster inspected each man's equipment for the final time and told the men to "Load up!"[50]

Once airborne, it was the jumpmaster's job to ensure the plane reached the correct altitude and was on course. From his position in the door, the jumpmaster looked for the 'jump-off point,' indicated by two red marker panels on the ground. On the first pass over the field, the jumpmaster threw out 'Oscar,' – a wind dummy – to test the accuracy of the jump-off point. If Oscar landed okay, two parallel white marker panels, placed in the center of the drop zone (DZ), indicated that it was safe for the students to jump. As the ship approached the DZ, the jumpmaster instructed the first jumper to "Stand Up!. . . Hook Up!" and the jumpmaster insured the student took the correct position in the door. Over the jump-off point, the jumpmaster gave the signal to jump – "Go!" and a good-luck slap on the butt.[51]

The day before the first jump, Privates Russell A. Hataway, Robert C. Hultman, Paul Imre, and Clifford T. Harding helped each other pack their chutes. That evening, Hultman jibed, "Goddammit, Imre. I can't remember whether we put rubber bands around those suspension lines or not. Hataway, did we do that?" Hataway shrugged.

Imre glared at his buddy, "Hultman, I'm gonna tell you something. If that thing doesn't work, my reserve *is* gonna work, and I'll come back, and I'll cut you to pieces – slowly – and with the back of the knife!" Hultman started laughing. He just couldn't take Imre's threats seriously.

The first jump took place on a beautiful, sunny afternoon. The men donned their chutes and pulled the straps tight – so much so they couldn't really stand up straight. The sticks climbed aboard the C-47s and sat in the cold metal seats that ran along both sides of the cabin. The seats, to Laufer, always felt cold no matter how hot it was outside. Then the engines roared to life, exhaust streaming in the prop blast. The noise was terrific and the whole plane started shaking. Laufer took it all in with great excitement; he had never flown before.[52]

Gaining speed, the plane hit a few bumps. Then it was peaceful. As they climbed higher and higher, the men's attention fixed on the planes' little windows and the world beyond them. "Oh wow, is this gorgeous!" Laufer remembered thinking. "Noisy – but gorgeous." On the way up to jump altitude, the men exchanged grave-yard humor. "Who do want us to notify if your chute doesn't open," and so on. Then the planes had leveled off at 1,500 feet. All of a sudden, the jumpmaster "hollered at the top of his voice, 'Stand up and hook up!' Check you equipment. Sound off for equipment check'."[53]

"What the hell am I doin' here?" a voice suddenly shouted inside Laufer's head. The men stood up and each hooked the snap-fastener of his static line to the anchor line running along the top of the cabin. When a man jumped, the static line would deploy. At its full length, it pulled the blow-out panel off the back of the chute pack and pulled out the container holding the canopy. The man would continue to fall, and the risers and suspension lines deployed until at the end, the break cord – which fixed the canopy to the static line – would snap and the canopy would open.

Each man checked the chute of the man ahead of him. "Number twelve okay!" yelled the last man in the stick as he slapped the man ahead of him. "Number eleven, okay!" yelled the next man in line. This continued until the last man in the stick yelled "All okay!"

"Stand in the door!" yelled the jumpmaster to the first man. "Go!" and the man disappeared.

The jumpmaster took his time, letting each man feel comfortable before he jumped. The next jumper was told to stand in the door. "Go!" If a man froze in the door – he went out anyway, assisted out by a well-placed boot. And there was a lot of hesitation as each man looked at the unfamiliar green blur of the fields speeding past below.

The men shuffled forward. "Stand in the door!" came the command again. As Laufer stood in the door he saw the ground below. Moving fast, different colors – dark green, light green, plowed fields, goober fields – Laufer could see every-thing. He concentrated on the ground below while the engines and the wind roared in his ears. "Go!" Out the door and right underneath the tail he went. It was a beautiful feeling.

The static line deployed. Then there was the pop of the opening shock. "Oh, thank God!" was the first thing out of Laufer's mouth.

Haggard jumped and started counting – the men were supposed to count – but the prop blast took his breath away. By the time he'd recovered and started count-ing, the chute was already open.

On the way down, Private Cavaleri was determined to keep his eyes open. Around him men were shouting, "Hey, look at me. I'm flyin'!" or "Bump my chute." Then up came the ground.

Laufer hit the ground like a "sack of shit." "Thank God it's over," he said to himself as he rolled up his chute and stuffed it in his kit bag. Trucks took the men to the packing shed where the chutes would be hung up, shaken out, and repacked.

When all the guys were back in the barracks that evening "the bullshit started." "Oh, it was nothing!" "I LOVE IT! I'm gonna do it tomorrow!" Tomorrow came and they were nervous wrecks – every one of them "scarred shitless," remarked Laufer. The next evening in the barracks, it was the "same shit."

On the first jump, one man on Imre's plane refused to jump. Private Donald A. Bacon went back down in the plane. "It was an embarrassing situation," remem-bered Laufer, "cuz he was in the First Platoon." The regiment "played it up real big that he was a quitter." While he stood in front, the First Platoon fell into formation, followed by the Second and the Third Platoons of F Company, then the rest of the regiment. His boots were cut off in front of the entire regiment, and "they packed his stuff and took him out," said Imre. The men felt a little sorry for him, remembered Laufer.

"The first jump was easy," said Laufer. The next jumps would be rougher. Men knew now that they would land hard. A few men had already been injured. Some men didn't take time to pack their chutes correctly, or screwed up and had to make do. There was only a short amount of time for each man to get the job done right, and the men waiting in line didn't want any one cutting into their time. In the packing shed after his second jump, Greenstrand carefully laid out the chute, straightened the canopy and suspension lines, and started to fold it up. Just as he was preparing to tie the break cord from the back pack to the static line, the whole pile of silk fell off the table and onto the floor. "I about wet my pants," said Greenstrand. One of the instructors walked over, picked up the canopy, and dumped the whole mess back on the table. "Finish packing," he said. "That damn chute will open." That was the instructor's way of telling him to do it right the first time. Greenstrand followed orders and stuffed the whole tangled mess into the container. Greenstrand sweat it out all night but the next day the chute "blossomed perfectly."[54]

By the third jump, F Company troopers had become more outwardly concerned for their own safety. Mass jumping was a hazardous undertaking. Grice, who had hurt his leg on the second jump, was told he could wait it out. But "Lieutenant said I could – I'm gonna jump," was his attitude. Inwardly, he was afraid if he didn't jump then, he wouldn't be willing to jump later.[55]

During this jump, several men were blown off the DZ. "It [the wind] changed while we were up there, I gather," said Cavaleri. "The damn guys was coming down there on top of the PX and on the road in front of it," remembered Paul. PFC Grice jumped way out over the woods. He kept slipping and slipping until he finally said to himself, "I am not gonna make it." Grice then wished he'd taken the officers up on their offer to sit it out until his injury healed. He crossed his legs and came crashing down into the trees. When he came to rest, he was hanging twelve or fourteen feet in the air. PFC Walter Day came down in a pig pen situated adjacent to a goober patch and emerged covered with pig manure from head to toe.

The men had all been told what to do in the event of a malfunction or accident. "If your main chute doesn't open," the men were instructed, "pull the rip cord for the reserve, and take it and throw it out [and in a manner] hand it up to the next

39

guy." If a jumper, during a descent, came down on the canopy of another parachute descending below him, he was instructed walk across the top. If he didn't, the parachute below would steal the air from the one above and collapse its canopy. Some men got so scared they opened their reserve chutes anyway, malfunction or not.[56]

Lieutenant Calhoun had experienced more than his fare share of problems in D Stage. On one of his own qualifying jumps, his parachute didn't deploy. Calhoun counted, "one thousand, two thousand, three thousand" and looked up to see that the chute had still not opened. Thinking that he had counted too fast, he started over again. Finally, there came the opening shock. He had one big swing and landed on the ground so hard he injured his knee.[57]

Calhoun's luck on his fourth jump was no better. It had begun raining and, due to the weather, the instructors canceled the jump, but not before Calhoun's ship went aloft. The pilot flew north to Macon, Georgia and then turned and headed south, back to Benning. When the ship came over the field the jumpmasters gave the men the go ahead to jump. As Calhoun went out the door, however, the plane hit turbulent air and lost altitude dramatically.

Calhoun heard a bang and looked up to see a large white star surrounded by a blue background right beside him. "The plane [had] come down with me," said Calhoun. The lieutenant pushed away from the star, but his feet were forced back into the side of the aircraft by the wind pressure. He pushed away with his feet and his shoulders came back. It just sucked him in. Finally he slid down under the fuselage, down near the tail wheel. Calhoun was reaching out for the wheel when, suddenly, his chute popped open and, and he was violently wrenched backward and away from the plane by the rapidly filling canopy. Calhoun landed safely but was met by one of the NCO instructors who angrily told him, "Lieutenant, you didn't jump far enough when you left that plane." Calhoun didn't argue long. Instead, from then on, he jumped as far away as he could.

The fifth and last qualifying jump for F Company was made at night with equipment, onto F Field, a small drop zone in the Alabama Area across which ran a high power line. Everyone was at once excited and just plain scared at the prospect, including the officers that had to pack their own chutes and jump with the men. Many of the officers hadn't jumped for three or four months and had not packed a parachute in six.[58] But Major Nicholas Willis, 2nd Battalion's CO, had ordered it. It rained during the day but on towards evening the skies cleared and the moon shown brightly over the Southern countryside. When the ships roared into the air over Lawson Field, everything looked good. A week earlier, a plane had come down in flames on a night jump. Privately, some of the men prayed this wouldn't happen to them.

As the C-47s navigated toward the drop zone, the men looked around the cabins at each other, their pale faces a variety of expressions bathed in the warm, crimson glow of the red light. Outside the ships, the moon hung cheerily, save for the transports a solitary ornament in an otherwise empty night sky. Men with faces pressed against the windows could make out scores of little lights dotting the countryside. Troopers standing in the doors could see sparks leaping from the port engine's exhausts running past the open door and into the darkness. "Will they set my chute on fire?" some wondered. Beside them, jumpmasters scanned the shadowy landscape below for the first signs of the drop zone, oblivious both to the dancing exhaust flames and the fear tightening in the guts of the young men next to them.

"Wonder where the trees are?" Munafo thought while he rested his hand on the .30 caliber machine-gun he would jump with for the first time. The warning light came on and the men went through the normal pre-jump equipment checks. Green light. "GO!!!"

Like a flood, men and equipment spilled from the planes. Under their canopies, troopers strained to see the horizon, each anticipating the inevitable collision with the invisible earth rising quickly toward them. Below, moonlight reflected on the Chattahoochee River. "We went out so happy," remembered Imre. "Now we were gonna get those damn wings."

Haggard heard a whooshing sound from above and looked up expecting to see that he'd blown a panel. Instead he saw another F Company man, Private Walter 'Red' Hart, coming down on top of him, his feet tangled up in the suspension lines. "Red Hart, steer your damn chute away from me," Haggard hollered up. "You get your damn chute out of the way," Hart yelled back, swearing. "I'm having enough trouble." Haggard steered clear and both landed okay.

Private Cavaleri landed with a thud, but safely. Nearby, Cavaleri saw Lieutenant Colonel Allan C. Miller, the regimental Executive Officer, walking upright through the middle of the field, observing the jumpers. Cavaleri got out of his harness and began immediately to look for the equipment bundle containing his .30 caliber machine-gun, its tripod, and ammunition.

Miller saw Cavaleri and turned to approach him. "Soldier, what are you doing?" he asked.

"I'm looking for my machine-gun, sir," answered Cavaleri.

"Don't you know you're under fire," declared Miller, in an attempt to uphold the spirit of the exercise. "Get out of here. Go find your group."

During a combat jump, the men would likely be under enemy fire but Miller made a mistake in ordering Cavaleri search for his company before locating his weapon. Miller's order was "ass-backwards," commented Major Edwards. "I didn't hear that conversation. If I had I would have refuted it," added Edwards. A parachute infantry company had only nine light machine-guns and three 60mm mortars to provide supporting fires. The loss of just one gun could prove catastrophic in combat. Miller's 'putting the cart before the horse' logic was bound to endanger the lives of his men when they got into real combat. Colonel Miller and Major Edwards had a working agreement, and fortunately, Miller usually listened to Edwards. But Miller was known to do things like that.

Running parallel to the river's course was a hard-surfaced road. The road, still wet from the rain that had fallen during the afternoon, reflected the moonlight deceivingly. Disoriented by the darkness and excitement, many troopers mistook that road for the Chattahoochee River. To avoid being dragged under by the weight of the wet canopy and drowned, the men had been instructed to escape from their chute before landing in water. Canadians jumping with Staff Sergeant John O. Paul above Lawson Field the year before – the airstrip being situated along side and parallel to the Chattahoochee – had made the same mistake, a dozen or so breaking their legs. "They thought they were above the river so they all made water landings," remarked Paul.

On this night, a few men ended up with broken bones when they mistakenly released above the road. One man released at one hundred feet in the air and was killed instantly. Although he was from another company, the news of the man's death came hard to Captain Ivy's men. The only problem experienced in F Company was by Private Richard Murray. His reserve deployed while he was still on board his transport. He unfastened it and cleared away the pile of silk, but the jumpmaster wouldn't let him jump without it. Murray had to wait to jump the next evening. For the rest of the company, the darkness and the rain weren't big problems. The men all landed safely, rolled up their chutes, and threw them on the trucks just smiling.[59]

The graduation ceremony was held on Saturday morning, 13 November 1943. The company's officers were proud. Captain Ivy went down the ranks and pinned the wings on the men, and each man was given a diploma. Every man in F Company knew he deserved them. The wings and the bloused boots – they were just confirmation that someone else knew it. "Of course by that time, you couldn't talk to none of us," remembered Laufer. "We were fucking big men. We were the best. We were killers. I was nine feet tall and 280 pounds – all muscle – when they put those wings on me."[60]

2

Out of the Frying Pan

*Fort Bragg, Camp Mackall, The Tennessee Maneuvers, Camp Forrest,
and Camp Miles Standish
13 November 1943 - 13 August 1944*

As soon as the graduation ceremony was over, the men headed out to celebrate. Although soldiers in what was called the "New Army," F Company men imitated the ways of the regulars in "blowing off steam" manifested in evenings of liquor, sex, and often fights. Soldiers stationed at Fort Benning "had at hand the most celebrated 'good-time town' in the country," Phenix City, Alabama. Situated just across the Chattahoochee River, Phenix City's principal industry was sex and Fort Benning's GIs were its principal customers.[1]

Phenix City was a rough and tumble place. Bartenders shorted the men on drinks and then shorted them on their change. Serviceman were rolled by the locals, or even other GIs, frequently. The place was so violent, in fact, that the MPs, while present, didn't like to get mixed up in the fights if they could avoid them.

On the night of graduation, a man in the Second Platoon 'lost' his wallet in one of the bars, and Lieutenant Calhoun organized a search party to go back into town and look for it. Private Imre couldn't believe it when Calhoun instructed the dozen or so men to take their weapons with them. When they got to town, one of the men pointed out the establishment and Calhoun led them inside the dim and musty room. With his men spreading out behind him, the lieutenant approached the bartender. "Okay," Calhoun said in a low, even voice, "one of my men came in here and lost his wallet, and I'm sure the wallet's still around. It sure would be nice if someone returned it." Calhoun paused for a moment to let that sink in and then added, "Or else we'll turn this place into match sticks." The room fell into a dead silence, everyone was motionless, staring at Calhoun and the group of tough and armed young men he was leading. After a moment, the wallet appeared on the bar. "Thank you," said Calhoun cordially, and he and his men backed out of the place.

Despite the scrapes GIs experienced in Phenix City, they all had one good reason to keep going back. "The town was off limits," remembered Munafo. "We were not allowed to go there, but we used to go there [anyway] looking for women. There were a lot of women." One of Phenix City's biggest attractions, according to PFC Laufer, was a live show featuring a prostitute having sex with a mule or a dog. "The guys went crazy for that shit," Laufer testified.

That night, Private Laufer took off for town on foot. He was walking across the bridge over the Chattahoochee when a friend pulled past in a cab. Laufer could see his pal asking the driver to stop, but the cabby would not. Apparently, cabbies didn't want to let two soldiers ride on the same fare if they could avoid it. When the cabby refused, Laufer's friend tried to grab the wheel. The cabby, in turn, smacked the trooper's hand with a billy club. When the trooper hit the cabby in the face, the driver stopped the car and got out, and he and the trooper really got into it. Pretty soon, more cabbies and more paratroopers arrived and joined the fray. Meanwhile, Laufer had drifted off to the side and took a seat on the bridge railing. He was laughing his head off when somebody threw a bottle at him, hit him square in the face, and knocked him backwards off the bridge and into the Chattahoochee. When Laufer climbed out, he decided that was enough entertainment for one night and he made his way back to camp.

While some of the men went to Phenix City, others ventured off into Columbus, Georgia. The Beachy Howard's, a combination bar and bordello, was the favorite of Lieutenants Dean and Calhoun, who sat in one of the back rooms and drank while the madam served drinks and women to the enlisted men in the front rooms. Calhoun always kept an eye on the back door in case the police raided the house.

More popular among enlisted men, however, was Town Pump. "Everybody hung out there," said Munafo. There were mirrors behind the bar, a lot of cheap tables, and a nickelodeon. "It was a dumpy place," but big, and it was always full of women.[2]

During the week, paratroopers usually had no problems there, "but on the weekends, that's when the fights broke out." And there were a lot of fights, mostly with the tankers stationed at Benning's Sand Hill area. The Airborne officers had told their men that any one paratrooper could lick any ten tankers. The problem was that the tankers had been told the reverse by their officers. "If you wanted trouble you'd go in there," explained Munafo, "and paratroopers were always in trouble. They were always going to Town Pump, getting drunk, and ripping the place up."[3]

Despite his unpredictable temper when he was drinking, everybody wanted to go to town with Private Robert Lopes, a Mexican trooper from Los Angeles. Lopes was a prize fighter, "a golden glover. . . and fast with his hands," said Munafo. But "if he got a few drinks in him, he went crazy." In fact, Lopes badly beat a woman in Town Pump and only stopped when his buddies pulled him off. "You knew these guys," stated Munafo, "but when they got drunk, a complete different person."[4]

On post, the enlisted man's bar served up something called '2.1% beer.' "You could drink all you wanted," remembered Munafo. "You didn't feel nothin', you know. It was like drinking a coke. When we'd get into town, where the bars served the regular strength product, a couple of beers is all it took us and we were stoned."

It was raining cats and dogs that Sunday night, and Munafo stepped drunkenly off a curb and fell face down in the rain swollen gutter. "Moon," exclaimed Private John Hall, "what happened, what happened?" Munafo, though, had passed out. Hall, Munafo's ammunition bearer and best buddy, loved to "dump 'em" himself, but he had a high tolerance for alcohol and, fortunately for Munafo, seldom got drunk. Hall picked Munafo up, sobered him up, and managed to get him back to camp in time to stand roll call – and thus avoid Sergeant Paul's wrath – Monday morning.[5]

On Monday, 15 November 1943, the 513th Parachute Infantry moved to Fort Bragg, North Carolina to join the 13th Airborne Division and begin thirteen weeks of advanced individual training, which was to conclude on 8 January 1944. In advanced training, soldiers received additional instruction in their Military Occupation Specialty (MOS).

The next morning, Lieutenant Calhoun paced deliberately in front of his platoon which had formed up in the company street which ran between the rows of barracks. "What's the big deal?" asked Calhoun, letting some of the air out of their recently inflated egos. "Now you've got to learn how to work," he told the men.

Calhoun then shouted out, "Anybody know how to do column left, column right from a stand-still?"

"I do," shot Private Knigge from the back of the ranks.

"Get up in the front!" ordered Calhoun. Knigge, promoted to sergeant that fast, was "going to stay up there forever," he remembered. Sometimes he questioned whether or not he should have been a squad leader, "but," Knigge later rationalized, "I made more money!" Lieutenant Calhoun made a few other adjustments and then got things moving. Lieutenants O'Donnell and Stositch had likewise started working with their platoons.

Monday through Friday, the men were up at 0400 to march out to the field, and stayed in the field until about 2000. The officers spent their Saturdays and Sundays riding out to survey their assigned training areas on small-wheeled motor scooters. They then returned to their quarters to write up the problems for the next week.

During field problems, Lieutenant Colonel Nicholas Willis, 2nd Battalion's commander, would ride out to F Company's area in his jeep. The men would call out, "Tally ho, the Fox!" when Willis' jeep approached, a practice which Calhoun and the other officers were at a loss to explain. Willis drove up to Second Platoon's area and Calhoun reported, explaining what his platoon was working on. A football star at Texas A&M University, Willis was of Russian descent and spoke with a distinctive accent that some officers found unpleasant. After observing the men for a short time, Willis motioned to his driver and they were off to the next platoon. Again the cry, "Tally ho, the Fox!" rose across the countryside. Loosely translated, it meant "There goes the sonofabitch."[6]

Because every parachute infantry regiment required trained jumpmasters and experts in demolitions and communications, specialists courses were opened to volunteers following jump school. The sixteen-hour jumpmaster course familiarized officers and noncoms with the techniques required to organize mass drops. Troopers learned how to construct sand tables, read aerial photographs, brief pilots and jumpmasters, and drop aerial delivery units.

The 176-hour Communications School trained newly qualified jumpers in all communications methods suitable to parachute operations. The men learned how to use and maintain radios, telephones, signaling flags, and blinkers, as well as several forms of code, "and the care and feeding of qualified, five jump, Parapigeons." Sergeant Wayne H. DeHaven, from St. Paul, Minnesota was assigned as

F Company's communications sergeant, and Private Neal Haggard was assigned as his assistant. Several other men were assigned as radio-telephone operators for the platoons.[7]

The Demolitions and Sabotage School, an eighty-eight hour course of instruction, was given over a two week period. The men were trained how to use flame-throwers, bazookas, and a variety of explosives – including dynamite and black powder – against such potential targets as trains, concrete fortifications, and even underwater obstacles. Earlier airborne demolitions training had included learning to drive trains and ride motorcycles, but this was discontinued by the time F Company passed through.

Several of F Company's officers and noncoms had already gone through the course and were teaching it to the new troopers. Lieutenant Calhoun and Lieutenant Walter Rydesky led F Company's demolitions training. On the afternoon Calhoun was instructing the men in the use of prima cord[8] – teaching them how to rig it with a trip wire – another company began to cross the field through their display area. Calhoun was out in a foxhole dug in front of the class, meticulously checking the different loops of the trip-wire and did not notice the approach of the other company. Lieutenant Rydesky, who was standing on a platform, had a better view and sent a man over to tell the other company not to enter the area. In the process, the man tripped over the wire leading to a charge Calhoun was rigging. A powerful blast erupted in the hole under Calhoun, throwing him head over heels out of the hole and onto the ground. Rydesky started yelling, "We wanted that to happen. Lieutenant Calhoun is just putting on a demonstration. He's not hurt." However, Calhoun – laid sprawled on the dry grass under a showering of dusty little clods – although uninjured, was shaking like a leaf. His head was throbbing and he could hardly hear anything above the roaring in his ears. The men recognized immediately that it was no joke, but "most of us laughed, anyway," remembered Cavaleri.

In the early days of jump school, before safety was an issue, demolitions trainees made practice jumps early on Saturday mornings. "And hell," remembered Staff Sergeant Paul, "we jumped at three hundred damn feet. Sometimes we didn't even have a reserve on because we jumped so low." Officers were routinely 'volunteered' to test new equipment and exotic devices, and they could not refuse. Lieutenant Calhoun had jumped over the stump field with a thermite grenade, which burned hot enough to weld steel when ignited, in his leg pocket. He hadn't even been told how dangerous the exercise was until after it was all over.

Most of the men, however, enjoyed the demolitions school immensely. "It was fun," remarked Private Don Newhouse, who would join F Company as a replacement in England.[9] The men learned how to place demolition charges and shaped charges. C2 was the usual type of explosive used and, as Private Laufer soon learned, unlike dynamite, C2 was very stable but extremely destructive.

Private Laufer had volunteered for the demolitions school right away as a way of avoiding regular duty. On the first day, the instructor asked him if he knew anything about explosives. "Oh yeah, sure," said Laufer in a comfortable voice. Laufer was, as he later admitted, "bullshitting the instructor."

The instructor ordered Laufer, "You see that tree over there, private? Blow it up."

"Yes, Sir," Laufer replied, savoring the moment. Laufer picked up several blocks of explosives and wrapped them one right against the other around the trunk of the designated tree. Carefully, Laufer pushed a blasting cap into the hole in one of the blocks, and, stringing the wire behind him, he returned to cover.

The resulting blast was shattering. When Laufer looked up, the tree had disappeared. Private Laufer was dismissed immediately from demolitions school.

The majority of men in any parachute infantry regiment were designated MOS 745, Rifleman, the men who in any army did most of the fighting and dying. Private Imre, who assumed he would be assigned as such, was surprised when he was assigned to be the assistant gunner in Second Platoon's 60mm mortar squad.

Along with its nine .30 caliber Browning machine-guns, the units three 60mm mortars – one being assigned to each of the three rifle platoons – comprised the basic, organic support weapons of a parachute rifle company. As assistant gunner, Imre was responsible for carrying the mortar's baseplate and sight in addition to his regular burden of an M1 rifle, ammunition, and other equipment. It took time for the squad – Hultman, Hataway, Harding, and Imre – to learn how to set up the mortar quickly. They had to focus on their job to do it properly, to zero-in on one task and forget about everything else. "If you don't get [the weapon] zeroed-in," Imre was told, "you might as well throw the damn thing away." Hultman became most adept in leveling the mortar and Imre was close behind. Lieutenant Calhoun didn't want ammunition wasted bracketing-in, so he insisted Second Platoon's mortar squad be accurate with the first shot. They learned how to be. Yet despite this, Imre didn't have a great deal of regard for what he called an "awkward weapon." "You could see the effects of a machine-gun right away," commented one trooper, "but you had to wait for the mortar shell to land." When the shell detonated, Imre found its effect less than impressive. "It wouldn't knock shingles off a house."[10] The mortar also took time to erect – too much for Imre. "Charge 2, charge 1, you look up a chart," complained Imre, "and then you have to angle it, place an aiming stake, level the weapon. By the time you get that thing set up," thought Imre, "you're dead."

During the week following his demolitions accident, Lieutenant Calhoun was leading another class in the use of explosives. The men, seated in bleachers, were following along enthusiastically until they became distracted by jumping over the nearby airfield. "Here comes a streamer!" one of the men shouted. The men were on their feet immediately and Lieutenant Calhoun turned around to look as well. The jumper, his chute fluttering uselessly behind, fell until he met the ground about five hundred yards away. His body struck with such force that it bounced into the air and left a nine-inch-deep depression in the earth. That night Lieutenant Calhoun learned that Lieutenant Colonel John R. Weikel, commanding the 513th's 1st Battalion, had set out to prove that a wet parachute would always open and had soaked his backpack in a tub of water the night before. Weikel, apparently, had been mistaken.[11]

Despite the intensive training, the men still had the time and energy to play tricks on each other. Some men were tied to trees and left out all night. One man was tied to his bunk when there was an important roll call and lost a whole month's worth of weekend passes.

Private Imre received his own share of this hazing. During one inspection, while the men stood in formation, their weapons shouldered, a trooper in the back rank dropped a pine sprig down the barrel of Imre's rifle. When the inspecting officer, Lieutenant Calhoun, came, he gasped, "There's a damn tree down there, isn't there?"

"Sir?" Imre replied, confused.

"Take a look, soldier," Calhoun directed.

Imre took the rifle off his shoulder and saw a foot-long pine branch sticking out of the muzzle. Lieutenant Calhoun knew somebody had played a trick on Imre, but made an example of him anyway, in order to teach him to be alert.

On another inspection, someone managed to paint mud on the heels of Imre's boots. Imre knew somebody had done something, but he couldn't do anything about it because the formation was at attention. The inspecting officer came up behind him and said, "Oh, soldier, looks like you didn't polish your boots."

Again, Imre was sure the officers already knew what had happened, but didn't say anything other than "Yes, Sir!"

"You know what that will cost you? A weekend pass."

"Yes, Sir!"

"Do you think you can take care of your boots next time?"

"Yes, Sir!"

"Do we have to lock them in a vault for you so they remain clean while you walk around barefoot?"

"No, Sir!"

The fun taken at Imre's expense stemmed from two causes. First, he was from New York City and had a pronounced Bronx accent. The Southerners in the outfit found it hilarious. The second reason was Imre's small size: among the Second Platoon, Imre was known as 'The Runt.' Bunches of Southern boys, Private Grice among them, often would gather around Imre's bunk and ask him to pronounce words; his responses provoked laughter, giggles, and slapped thighs. Imre knew they were only teasing him out some sort of odd affection, and he didn't mind the attention either. It was fun.

To most of F Company's Northerners, the Southern boys were "just a bunch of 'ridgerunners'," and Northern boys, like Imre, and Third Platoon's Frank Munafo, couldn't understand the Southerners any better than the Southerners understood them. According to Munafo, "all the Northerners used to make digs at them like, 'Take that shit out of your mouth there, Rebel.' It wasn't all good-natured either." According to Munafo, "there was a lot of fights I'll tell you – a regular war right in Company F. . . There was one little short Southerner from Columbus, Georgia, [Private Henry D. Nobles, and] he used to sing all them hillbilly songs that we hated like *The Wabash Cannonball* – all them Rebel songs. . . and we used to tell him, 'Shut up, you little Rebel!!' There were always fights in the barracks. That's why Sergeant Paul used to get involved. The Rebels didn't like the Yanks and the Yanks didn't like the Rebels. That's all there is to it."[12]

The worst prank perpetrated on Imre came one evening when his barracks mates got some Sloan's Lineament and painted it on his testicles while he was sleeping. After about fifteen or twenty minutes, Imre woke up. He was just sweating and his "balls were really hot, burning." He leapt from his bunk with a scream and charged for the showers on the far side of the barracks.

"Hey, what's wrong?" his friends inquired feigning innocence.

Imre had the cold water on full blast scrubbing the affected area.

"Hey, man, the hot water's here," one of his friends pointed out. "Do you want us to turn it on for you?"

The advice and questions were so solicitous Imre didn't suspect anything at first. Then he felt the greasy lineament and he knew. The pain was awful, but he didn't say anything right away. When he'd finished his shower, he walked back into the barracks, picked up his rifle, and fixed the bayonet. "Okay, who's it?"

"Boys, don't give him any ammunition," howled Private William C. Kuntz as the men cleared the barracks and fled outside. Imre chased them and the men ran around the barracks and went up the trees in mock fear.

Imre figured that Kuntz and a couple of the other guys were behind the act, but after a while he got tired of waiting, and gave up with a sigh and an "Oh, shit!" He disarmed and went back into the barracks.

"Is it safe to come in now?" his friends called from the dark outside. "You're not going to pull a grenade on us are you?"

"No," replied Imre. "But somebody's bunk's on fire!"

When looking back on it fifty years later, Imre saw it as just their way of making friends. All the hazing and kids' pranks were part of how the platoon came together. "Boys will be boys," explained Imre.

Fortunately for Private Imre, on most the evenings, the men were so tired they just took a shower and laid down. Privates Walter H. Balben and Russell Hataway had guitars and would often play songs like *In the Church by the Dell*. Others played cards, chess, or checkers. By 2100 most of the platoon had turned in. The next morning at 0500 hours, *Pistol Packin' Mama* blared out again, and that, according to Laufer, "was a sonofabitch."[13]

At Fort Bragg, F Company received passes to go into town almost every weekend, but sometimes the officers held boxing matches for the coveted passes. Fights went three rounds and often the officers bet on the outcome. On one occasion, Munafo and Laufer squared off. "He [Laufer] never looked at you," remembered Munafo. "He always used to look at your feet [to] distract your attention. For Christ sake!" Munafo thought. "What is he looking at my feet for?!. . . and then he'd throw one." The fight was close, but Munafo won the pass and headed off to town to find a big time.[14]

Drunk and disorderly paratroopers from Fort Bragg usually found their way into a Fayetteville drunktank for the night, and Private Frank Munafo "wound up in jail a few times." Jailed troopers were let out early on Sunday mornings, but that didn't leave them much time to get back to camp to answer reveille. Although he tried to hitch rides, Munafo was often late. Back at camp, the company had formed-up for roll call and Staff Sergeant Paul was standing on his toes and stretching his neck, bellowing, "Munafo! Where's Munafo?!"

Private Munafo had gotten off on the wrong foot with his platoon sergeant, Staff Sergeant Paul, from the very start, a combative relationship that persisted throughout training. "I didn't like him and he didn't like me," commented Munafo when asked for the reasons. His friends, however, had another explanation. "Munafo," said Laufer, "was a fuckup with a cloud over his head like Joe in Little Abner." Sergeant Paul might have known that Munafo didn't mean to screw up so much, but he didn't let up on him for a minute. On field problems, Paul "would be with one of the lieutenants scheming something up," but during calisthenics, Paul always came down on Munafo. "Munafo, what did I say?" Paul hollered at the straining private. "Pick your legs up higher, Munafo. Pick your legs up higher." And he always had some kind of chore waiting for Munafo when he screwed up, such as mopping the barracks, digging a six-square (often threatened but never imposed), or push-ups. "That's all I ever did was push-ups," Munafo recalled.[15]

Finally, Munafo recounted, "Oh Christ, I got broke." Munafo found himself standing before the Captain who told him, "PFC Munafo, we have to reduce you to a grade of private." "I was a PFC," said Munafo, "and they took my stripe away. As if I gave a damn! I didn't give a shit about that stripe." It was by no means an uncommon opinion. When Anthony J. Rybka, who joined F Company at Chalons-sur-Marne, France in 1945, had his PFC stripe taken away, he told his commanding officer, "I'll pay you the $3.75 and you can wear it yourself."[16]

There was one silver lining in Munafo's dark cloud. When he was 'gig made' for the weekend, Munafo, who had his own iron, would press the clothes of his buddies who were going to town, charging a quarter for pants and the same for shirts. It added up – that and what he got for the half a carton of cigarettes he was issued every week which he sold for a nickel a pack. "I'd make like ten dollars on a weekend."[17]

A new top-kick, First Sergeant Royal W. Donovan, was assigned to F Company in November. Donovan, from La Farge, Wisconsin, stood five-feet-seven and was 180 pounds – all muscle. He was also about as Irish as they come.

Donovan had come early to the Airborne. He had enlisted in September 1940 and volunteered for the paratroops while serving with the 9th Infantry Division at Fort Benning. After graduating from The Parachute School Class Number Six in 1941, he joined the new 502nd Parachute Infantry Battalion, which soon was expanded to a regiment. In the Fall of 1942, Donovan was promoted to first sergeant and reassigned to Headquarters Company, 1st Battalion of the new 508th Parachute Infantry Regiment at Camp Blanding, Florida. The 508th was the first parachute infantry regiment to go through basic training and The Parachute School as a unit. Just as it had been in the 513th, the 508th had known precisely what kind of men it wanted. More than half of the original eight thousand volunteers were washed out in training.

In 1943, after appeals to "every general in Airborne Command," First Sergeant Donovan was selected to attend OCS at Fort Benning. After the fifteenth week, Donovan was ready to graduate and had even ordered his officer's uniforms. Unfortunately, four warrant officers and every first sergeant in his class were tossed out in the last week when their bus arrived late to camp and they missed bed check. During his time in OCS, Donovan had missed the 508th, and in any case, the OCS officials told him that, as an old first sergeant, he "talked too tough" to be an officer anyway. To his disappointment, however, Donovan was told there were no billets for his grade in the 508th, but there was a billet for a first sergeant in F Company, 513th Parachute Infantry. That would have to do, thought Donovan. Any port in a storm.[18]

After reporting to company headquarters, First Sergeant Donovan walked down behind the latrines to the row of tents housing F Company. He looked in one of the tents and, although it was well past reveille, all six residents were still inside, asleep. He found the same thing in more than half of the tents. Private Munafo often slept in while Hall went to the company mess. "He would bring me food and I'd sleep late," explained Munafo, "and then I would bring him food and he would sleep late." That way he could steal an extra half hour's sleep "which meant a lot."[19]

Donovan discovered that the company, although nearly at full strength, was "disorganized as hell." Arthur Clark, F Company's First Sergeant since September

1943, and whom Donovan was replacing, had transferred to the regimental medical detachment. Clark had let the company's records go, and Captain Ivy, Donovan found, "was looking for something better." The next morning at 0530, Donovan ordered one of the platoon sergeants to fall the company out. Only about half the men responded. Donovan put an end to that right away. He wasn't very popular for a while, but Donovan was determined to get F Company in shape. "Everybody bitched and griped about it," recalled Donovan, "but it paid off."[20]

Captain Ivy did eventually find something better – he was bumped up to regiment as the new S-2. 1st Lieutenant Sam Dean took over as company CO, but that was only a temporary arrangement. Captain Fred McGoldrick, from Tennessee, was assigned as the new company commander and Dean reverted to company Executive Officer.[21]

On 15 January 1944, the 513th completed the Individual and Physical Tests, ABC, and moved to Camp Mackall, North Carolina. Mackall was home to Airborne Command and was a superb example of the Army's wartime building program. The post contained 1,750 buildings including a 1,200 bed hospital and heated barracks, sixty-five miles of hard stand road, five theaters, six beer gardens, and an all-weather airfield with three five thousand foot runways.[22] At Mackall, the men began "Unit Training." This, the fourth phase of training for all parachute troops, "approximate[d] that of rifle regiment units of comparable size, particularly in the mechanical training with weapons" – parachute troops were required to be "proficient in the use of all weapons organic to the platoon." – "range practice, combat principles, and the basic training subjects."

Practice jumping continued. Once a month, F Company jumped in order to earn their jump pay – the extra $50 a month paratroopers were entitled to. Lieutenant Calhoun acted as jumpmaster on squad problems. After each stick had exited, Calhoun wrote up a report describing how the men had cleared the plane and turned it in at the field. On one jump, a D Company trooper hesitated in the door. Then, all of a sudden, he was turned sideways in the door and the next guy in line ran into him, bumping the hesitating man back into the plane. The impact of the collision caused the trailing man to fall out the door backwards. Calhoun had been sitting on his knees and had not been in a position to prevent him from falling. "When they're going out," explained Calhoun, "it's pretty hard to stop them. They're all pushing to get out." When all the jumpers cleared the plane, Calhoun looked out to count chutes. There were only eleven and there should have been twelve. Worriedly, Calhoun filled out his report.

When the plane landed, Captain Ivy was waiting for him. "Calhoun, get a parachute," commanded Ivy. "We're gonna jump." Ivy and Calhoun went out with the next plane load of troopers over the same DZ. When they landed, Calhoun found a parachute harness laying on the ground beside a depression approximating the size of a body and about six inches deep. The ground was stained with blood. Ivy questioned Calhoun about his conduct in the exercise, but Calhoun was cleared of any personal blame. Interestingly, it was discovered that the dead jumper was wearing another man's dog tags. No one was really sure why, but it was presumed he was covering for a friend who was AWOL.[23]

Three days before the regiment moved to Mackall, Colonel Dickerson, the CO of the 513th, had been relieved of command and transferred to a staff position with the 13th Airborne Division. The Army apparently thought he was too old to command a combat regiment. Dickerson's replacement was Lieutenant Colonel James Winfield Coutts, a West Pointer, who assumed command of the 513th on 21 January. In the interim, Lieutenant Colonel Allen C. Miller had been placed in temporary command of the regiment. With Coutts' arrival, Miller returned to his position as the regimental Executive Officer, the position he had held since 17 April 1943.

About three weeks later, Lieutenant Colonel Nicholas Willis, appreciative of the solid effort his men had shown in the field after arriving at Mackall, gave every man in the 2nd Battalion a three day pass. The camp cleared out immediately. It was on that day, however, that Lieutenant Colonel Coutts called down to 2nd Battalion for men to clean out the headquarters building. Since his whole command was on pass, Willis couldn't send any. Coutts tersely said to Willis, "If you can't send any men, then *you* come up here." Willis was relieved. On 19 February, Coutts brought in Lieutenant Colonel Ward S. Ryan as regimental Executive Officer and Miller was reassigned to command the 2nd Battalion.

Five-foot, four-inch and 118 pound Allen C. Miller grew up in Northern California's Plumas County. He was taught to believe he could accomplish anything he set his sights on and, "since he was old enough to shoot a BB gun, [he had] set his sights on West Point." Miller entered the "class of 1936, with a two-year stopover at VMI." After graduation from West Point, the 'shave tail' 2nd Lieutenant Miller was assigned to Headquarters Company, 25th Infantry at Fort

Huachuca, Arizona. There, Miller became "the last American officer to command the Army's famed Apache Indian Scouts and the only American officer authorized to wear" their insignia. The scouts, formed in 1866, were disbanded a month after Miller's tour at Huachuca ended. "I was never happier," remembered Miller, "than when I could escape from the post into the wilderness with my scouts." After two years in Arizona, Miller was posted in 1938 to the Philippines where he trained the Philippine Scouts to handle pack mules through the trackless countryside of the Bataan Peninsula.[24]

In 1939, after a "whirlwind courtship," Miller married Jean Holderness, the sister of a West Point classmate and "daughter of Colonel A. W. Holderness, Chief of Staff, General Douglas MacArthur's headquarters, Manila." Among those attending the wedding were then-Major and Mrs. Dwight Eisenhower. Miller and Eisenhower occasionally played golf together, and afterwards shook dice for drinks. Eisenhower beat Miller at golf but, as Miller once boasted, Ike always ended up buying the drinks.[25]

In 1940, Miller was ordered to Fort Ord, California as supply officer for the 53rd Infantry Regiment, 7th U.S. Infantry Division. Miller's roommate and West Point classmate, Phil Gage (who later, while serving with the 101st Airborne Division, lost an arm in the Normandy Invasion and survived the war as a PW) described him as a "maverick – an iconoclast with a passionate dislike for the mediocre."[26]

Colonel Coutts remarked that "Miller was the best battalion commander [he] had. [He was] fearless, just a terrific combatant. One of the greatest soldiers I ever met," said Coutts. Miller was, in fact, one of only a handful of Americans to participate in the disastrous Dieppe Raid of 1942. At the time, Miller was a lieutenant serving with the Rangers.

Despite the praise earned from his superiors during and after the war, Miller was absolutely loathed by the men. Known as 'Ace' to his friends, the men nicknamed him 'Acey-Deucy' or 'Boots and Helmet Liner,' the latter diminutive a derogatory expression of Miller's slight stature; his jump boots laced nearly all the way to his knees and his helmet practically covered his eyes. "He was a misfit, physically," commented Lieutenant Walter Rydesky. Rydesky just couldn't believe Miller was suited to command an Airborne outfit. "It was hard to take orders from [Miller]," commented First Sergeant Donovan, who sat in on meetings with the battalion's officers. "Half of what Miller said was erroneous." Staff Sergeant

Paul remembered Acey-Deucy from the replacement pool's compass course. "Oh yeah, yeah, I know how to use a compass," Miller and another officer had assured Paul. "Hell," recalled Paul, "neither one of them [the two officers] knew how to [use a compass] and they ended up getting lost." Neal haggard remembered, "I never saw any fear out of him, and he always urged his men along, but", he added, "Miller had maverick ideas."[27]

His wife's connections didn't have much to do with Miller's command. Rather, according to Major Edwards, it was his association with Colonel Dickerson and his West Point connections that got Miller his job. "Dickerson had always been the captain of the baseball team, basketball team. . . Ace Miller was very popular in his class at the academy. He was a wrestler and he won a lot of his matches." However, Edwards continued, Miller just "didn't know a fucking thing about how to fight a unit in combat." This, to Edwards, was not only accurate of Miller, but true of Colonel Coutts and General Miley as well. "They didn't know how to organize to fight. They never determined what. . . was available to support an attack before committing to it. That sort of [planning] never existed."

Major Edwards saw Miller, like he saw most West Point graduates, as nothing more than a professional military politician. Moreover, "Miller's idea of discipline – and this is so true of many academy graduates who don't seem to be able to make the transition from plebe year bullshit (when everybody stood at attention and [asked,] 'Sir, may I have the potatoes?'), to Army discipline" – was immature and vindictive. Miller's retaliatory behavior was to have particular impact on F Company, and especially Lieutenant Calhoun.[28]

For some unfathomable reason, Regiment commenced serving the men "a hell of a lot of stew," recalled Private Haggard. In fact, it was stew for breakfast, lunch, and dinner. Haggard, who was Charge of Quarters on one particular morning, remembered the effect it had on morale. As CQ, Haggard's job was to run through the barracks in the morning to wake the men and then meet them as they fell out in the company street. That morning, Haggard went through the barracks rousing the men, but when he came on the street he found that hardly any of the guys had fallen out. Haggard went back into one of the barracks and asked one of the men, "What the hell's goin' on?"

"We're tired of the food we're getting," the trooper replied, "and we're not gonna go to work today." Then, 1st Lieutenant Dean, who was Officer of the Day, walked into the barracks and ordered Haggard to "Get the men out of here!"

"Hell, Sir," professed Haggard desperately, "I've been through the barracks twice. They're mad about something and they're not gonna turn out." Dean accepted Haggard's explanation and decided to attempt to reason with the men. Dean was well thought of in the company. Instead of barking orders, he always tried to persuade the men to follow his lead. After he found out what the men's gripe was, he gave them a choice. "If you guys will straighten up and fall out, [and] go about your normal duties, I'll see what I can do about correcting the situation. But if you don't, the whole company will go to the guard house." That must have been a reasonable request because within a few minutes, the company was assembled in the street.[29] The men, however, were beginning to test their boundaries.

One day in the battalion mess, Private Charles Fuller, who was on KP, took it upon himself to aid Lieutenant Dean. Fuller, apparently, was aware that many of the officers in the rifle companies had been issued motor scooters, but that Dean was not among them. So, in the middle of a meal, Fuller walked out from behind the serving line, past the enlisted men dining from their mess kits, and straight up to one of the tables where the 2nd Battalion's officers sat eating from white china. Seemingly at random, Fuller chose one of the field grade officers and put his arm around him as if they were old friends. "Say," said Fuller as the officer sat bolt upright, "we got a little, short-legged sonofabitch down at F Company. His name is Lieutenant Sam Dean and he's a good officer. We want a motor scooter down there tomorrow morning for him." A couple of the officers seated across the table from the man in Fuller's friendly grasp winked to let the officer know that Fuller wasn't right in the head. This, however, was not the first time Fuller had tried to buck the system.

Fuller was not crazy, and all of his goldbricking didn't bother the men. In fact, they thought it entertaining and even rooted him on. To Fuller, the Army was an inconvenience. He stuck his tongue out at F Company's officers, and constantly worked the system to his advantage to get three day passes from battalion or regiment whenever the company turned him down, and it seemed he was always disappearing for three days at a time. Fuller, however, just wanted out of the Army and was doing his best to forward his plans. He eventually got out, too, but only after he had stolen drugs from the medics and threatened to poison the whole company.[30]

The men chafed against discipline in smaller ways, too. One day on the machine-gun range, the range officer, a young lieutenant, while walking out to start the class ordered the men, "Nobody fires unless I give the command." At that moment a large rabbit ran across the middle of the range. Every one of the men opened up and the rabbit was blown to bits. The lieutenant went ballistic, recalled Private Marvin Harris, "pissed off puts it mildly."

Fuller's one-man uprising had been an isolated incident and the rabbit, well, it was still only a minor event. Bigger insurgencies were brewing, however.[31]

While Rydesky went on leave, Lieutenant Calhoun was put in temporary command of Lieutenant Rydesky's 81mm mortar platoon in Headquarters Company. Battalion assigned 1st Lieutenant Randall Purcell to take over Second Platoon. One of the first things Purcell did was replace Staff Sergeant Nix with Staff Sergeant Milton Smith. This was, at least, welcome. According to his platoon, though tough, Smith, from Bessemer, Alabama, was soft spoken and competent, and the men all liked him. But Purcell was strict, and the switch in command style had a profound effect on Second Platoon. "Wow, what a change," lamented Bob Greenstrand. "None of us liked Purcell and he was changing our whole way of life." Since Purcell was a 1st lieutenant, the grade specified to command a parachute rifle platoon, and Calhoun was only a 2nd lieutenant, to the men the situation looked as if it would be permanent. "After a few weeks," recalled Greenstrand, "morale was in the basement so a few of us got to talking and a small committee of us from the platoon went to discuss the problem with Capt[ain] McGoldrick. Someone in the group mentioned a petition (which was unheard of in the Army) and we kind of decided to try it."[32]

Captain McGoldrick said that he would forward the petition to Battalion HQ, but from there it would be out of his hands, suggesting only that the men sign their names in a circle so it could not be determined who had signed first. McGoldrick was well-liked by the men but, according to Royal Donovan, "you could tell him anything" and he'd go along with it. The whole platoon signed the petition and it was presented to the battalion commander, Colonel Miller. In a couple of weeks, Lieutenant Purcell was transferred to E Company and Lieutenant Calhoun returned. The men couldn't have been happier.[33]

What Second Platoon didn't know, however, was just how angry Colonel Miller was over the petition. Lieutenant Calhoun got grilled, but the subsequent investigation by Captain Ivy found no evidence that the lieutenant had any knowledge of the plot. Yet to Colonel Miller, the matter was far from closed. Miller apparently held a grudge against Lieutenant Calhoun, and the men began to wonder if all the "shit details" they began to receive were because of it. Calhoun didn't let the matter rest either. He pinned up Captain Ivy's inquiry findings on the wall over his bunk to antagonize Miller. This had the desired effect, too. When Miller discovered the shrine on an inspection of the officers' quarters, he became angry and brusquely ordered Calhoun to remove the documents from the wall immediately.[34]

On 10 March, the 513th Parachute Infantry was reassigned from the 13th Airborne Division to the 17th Airborne and moved to Lebanon, Tennessee on 20 March 1944 for the Tennessee Maneuvers. The maneuvers consisted of a variety of field exercises over varying terrain. There was even one massed parachute jump. Day or night, all assigned objectives were to be accomplished within specific time perimeters. "It was all bullshit – sleeping outside in the woods," remembered Munafo. The weather was cold – there was even snow on the ground – and the food was lousy. "Some of our cooks could fuck up corn flakes," commented Laufer.

The 517th Parachute Infantry, not the 513th, originally had been assigned to the 17th Airborne Division, but half way through the maneuvers they were relieved from their assignment to the division for shooting pigs – at least that's how the story being circulated went. A few troopers from the 517th, perhaps more than a few, had carved wooden bullets and tipped the ends of their blank cartridges with them. The troopers shot several pigs with the wooden bullets which, as the story went, upset the hell out of their owner who reported them to the general presiding over the maneuvers. The next thing anyone knew, the 517th was on its way overseas and the 513th was taking their place in Major General William M. Miley's division. Due to the strange circumstances, the 513th's maneuver period was cut to only four days.[35]

On 22 March, General Leslie McNair, Commanding General, Army Ground Forces, visited the new 17th Airborne Division. Though to the men it was little more than camping, the Tennessee Maneuvers were in fact, as General George C. Marshall earlier said of the Louisiana Maneuvers in 1941, "a combat college for troop leading." It was a test of the division's ability to conduct large-scale operations and of the leadership ability of its officers. If mistakes in tactics were going to be made, it was better that they occurred in Tennessee where they could be fixed, rather than in Europe or the Pacific.[36]

The exercises took place in the Roan Mountains, hills familiar to Private Bill Kuntz who was, in fact, from a town called Roan Mountain, Tennessee. Kuntz "was a tough guy raised in tough circumstances and a different kind of culture," Imre recalled. He was also the oldest man in the Second Platoon, about thirty-three years old. Colonel Coutts, the Regimental CO, was only thirty-six.[37]

It was rumored within the company that Kuntz's father had been a moon-shiner until somebody killed him to put him out of business. After that, the rumor went, Kuntz and his mother ran the still. When a local sheriff came to close down young Bill, Kuntz killed him. At the trial, the judge told him to either volunteer for the paratroopers or face the gallows. In spite of all that, or perhaps because of it, Second Platoon men respected and admired him. "He was a hell of a soldier," said Greenstrand. "If you're in combat and you're lost, he can find your way home," added Imre, "day or night, with or without a compass." Kuntz had a knack for fighting which became apparent during basic training and which remained when the unit went into combat. "He was wily about German defenses and knew how to take advantage of them. He understood small unit tactics instinctively. He didn't know much about Hannibal, but he knew a lot about laying down a field of fire."

In spite of the skill of Private Kuntz, and the other officers and men, the 513th did not do well at first. The men couldn't believe they were beaten in the maneuvers by, as Lieutenant Calhoun dubbed them, the 'Hungry and Sick Division' (the 106th Infantry Division). "And when we lost, we were bad losers," said Paul Imre. "You weren't supposed to beat us – we were elite." The men's spirits improved, however, when they quickly recovered their edge and started beating their opponents.

The Tennessee hills were full of little farms and homesteads, and the people there had grown accustomed to the trampling of GI feet. Walking in the back woods, some First Platoon men came upon a little cabin. The house was propped up on stilts, and, in the yard, some fifty or so chickens flitted about. Laufer went up to the door and he could smell the aroma of hot biscuits cooking inside. "My God, they smell good," Laufer exclaimed when the door opened and a colored woman, eld-erly and frail, came out.

"Man, come on in and have breakfast," invited the woman.

The woman went out the back of the house and cut quarter inch slices off a slab of bacon. When she returned, she prepared bacon, eggs, hot biscuits, and coffee for Laufer and his buddies. Laufer watched as she dropped the grounds in the boiling water and then put in an egg shell to settle them. Then she poured the coffee from the enamel pot. It was the best breakfast Laufer had ever had. The woman even offered to cook a chicken, but everyone told her she'd already been too kind. When he was finished, Laufer gave her five dollars, then another man gave her ten and, soon, all the men followed suit.

"Would you all like something to drink?" she asked. She again went out back and returned this time with a couple of Ball jars full of 'white lightning,' about 180 proof. The guys took it back to camp and mixed it with grapefruit and orange juice. Some of the Rebels, however, drank it straight.

Private Haggard had a similar experience when he knocked on the door of another country shack. A young woman of about twenty-four answered. Two small kids were clinging to her legs. Haggard got straight to the point and asked for a dozen eggs. "Do you want me to put them in a poke?" asked the woman. "A what?" asked Haggard, confused. "A poke-sack," answered the woman, holding up a small burlap bag. Haggard then understood. "Do you want anything else?" she asked. Haggard asked for a can of tomatoes. After he had paid and thanked the young woman, Haggard returned to the company to prepare a "slum gully" in his mess kit.

After leading his platoon against the 106th, Lieutenant Calhoun acted as an umpire during for the 11th Airborne Division's maneuvers. At the end of the week's exercises, the umpires met on Saturday at the University of Tennessee at Lebanon, from about 0800 to 1000 hours, to critique the participants. After that, the men were excused until 1500 Sunday. Calhoun and his assistants, Corporal Thomas D. Harvey and the newly promoted Sergeant Clarence Knigge, went down to Chattanooga. They found a basement bar downtown and the three decided to give it a try. Inside were a bunch of other soldiers – men from the Ordnance Corps – accompanied by their dates. Being 'good paratroopers,' they waited until some of the ordnance men had to visit the rest room, and then they moved in to take over their girls.

When the ordnance men emerged from the rest room and saw the troopers with their dates, they were ready to start a fight. The girls announcement that they liked the company of the paratroopers better didn't help matters.

After a few angry words were exchanged, Tom Harvey approached the ordnance men.

"Soldier. . .," they said, bringing Harvey up short.

"Soldier, hell!" cried Harvey. "I'm a trooper!" With that, every ordnance man in the place stood up. At that moment, Lieutenant Calhoun realized he and his men were grossly outnumbered and decided it was time to go.

The bartender yelled to Calhoun, "Lieutenant, get your men out of here!" Not needing and further coaxing, Calhoun, Knigge, and Harvey, and with their new companions leading, backed up the stairway and grabbed a taxi to the Patton Hotel. The next morning they were back in the field.

After the maneuvers were over, on 24 March the 513th was assigned to Camp Forrest, Tennessee, near Tullahoma, a typical small 'GI town' with jewelry shops, stores selling knickknacks, places to drink, and a busy train station. As was usual in such towns, there were plenty of fights. Occasionally, a few men amused themselves at the expense of the local police and MPs. Some 513th troopers set off nitrostarch or TNT charges on one side of the town, and then, when the police had gathered around the site of the explosion, they set charges off on the other side of town. The men just set back and laughed cruelly at the commotion.

F Company, the whole regiment in fact, had been promised one furlough between each phase of training, but until they reached Camp Forrest, they had received none. Coutts, however, finally came through with one at the end of March. Let out on a Friday, the men were given seven days plus travel time. The troopers, however, were ready to blow off some steam and they took advantage of the situation. When many failed to return on time, Acey-Deucy, furious over the insubordinate behavior, complained bitterly to Colonel Coutts, "Half my battalion's AWOL." Coutts' response was pragmatic: "What the hell can you do? Forget about it."[38]

When Haggard asked for a twenty-four hour pass to visit his folks in St. Louis, McGoldrick, staring at Haggard with a "jaundiced eye," allowed it but warned him, "I'm gonna sign this pass for you, but if you're not back by reveille Monday morning, I'll have you thrown so far into the stockade it'll take a .50 caliber machine-gun to shoot beans to you." Haggard made it back by 0400 on Monday. It is unlikely, however, that McGoldrick would have punished Haggard if he was not. McGoldrick was known to run things on a somewhat longer reign than Miller. When another man was AWOL for 101 days, McGoldrick had the morning reports altered to show he was in the hospital so the trooper would escape prosecution.[39]

Before they left camp, every man spent hours ironing his uniforms and polishing his boots, smoking as many as fifteen coats of polish over a candle until the brown boots had turned almost black. It was their boots that paratroopers were most proud of, they were their mark of distinction. Moreover, paratroopers were always sharp dressers, a manifestation of the pride they felt in themselves as elite troops.[40]

While he was home, Haggard was constantly asked what kind of a soldier he was. The folks at home had heard about paratroopers, but many had never seen one in the flesh. Private Greenstrand, like most of the men, was excited about going home and showing off a little. He spent a lot of time back in Blue Earth, Minnesota walking up and down Main Street in his uniform just to make sure everybody saw him – especially the girls.[41]

After a day-long train ride to the Bronx, Private Imre was met at the station by his Uncle Sol, his Aunt, and his Grandmother. Everywhere he went, people wanted to buy him a drink. One evening, while having dinner at Jack Dempsey's restaurant with his younger cousin, someone again offered to by the young soldier a libation. "Thanks a lot," Imre said with a smile, "I'll have a Coke." Imre returned to Camp Forrest two days late, but was more or less forgiven.

When Private Laufer walked around Hartford in a tee-shirt, jump pants, and boots, some people gawked at his exotic uniform and asked, "What the hell kind of Army guy is that?" His father, however, who had initially had some reservations about his son's desire to be a paratrooper, was proud. "That's my boy!" he shouted to everyone he met.

Laufer's sister was planning to be married on the next Sunday, so Laufer sent a telegram back to Captain McGoldrick requesting an extension of his leave. McGoldrick, probably feeling the heat from Miller, wouldn't give it to him. "The hell with it," said Laufer, "I'm gonna stay anyway." By Monday, Laufer was AWOL. That day, he followed his sister and her new husband to New York, and then went on by train to Washington, D.C.

"Washington during the war was a tremendous place if you were a serviceman," commented Laufer. "There were a lot of available women," and Laufer soon made friends with a WAC. All the hotels were filled, so she took him to Arlington Cemetery. There, they found a secluded corner and, as Laufer puts it, "screwed all night." They were not alone. The cemetery was filled with other young couples, doing the same thing on the benches, on the ground, and on the graves. Laufer stayed in Washington for two days before he finally made his way back to Camp Forrest.

Laufer's reception committee was Staff Sergeant Henry Kaczmarek, and though he expected to get drilled for being late, Kaczmarek never said a word. Instead,

Kaczmarek told Laufer that F Company had just picked up a new man, one Tech Sergeant Louis P. Walker, and he almost immediately had gone AWOL. Walker had been caught in Fort Sheridan, Illinois and Kaczmarek was going to go get him. Since the rest of the outfit was on a problem, he invited Laufer to tag along.

Kaczmarek – being an old-time soldier from Panama – knew that if a prisoner escaped while in his custody, that he would have to serve the time, so his speech was prepared when they arrived to pick up Walker. Kaczmarek told Walker right off the bat, "Look, if you're gonna make a break, do it now and I'll shoot you now because I'm not gonna worry about shootin' you later and I'm not gonna do your time – I'm gonna shoot ya." The thought of actually shooting Walker had Laufer "scared shitless."

They had to wait a day before returning to camp, so Kaczmarek got them a room at a hotel. Kaczmarek handcuffed Walker to the wrought iron bed in the room and told Laufer, "I'm going down and get a drink." About three hours later, he came back with a girl and a bottle of booze. "Kaczmarek and the girl climbed into the bed to which Walker was handcuffed and screwed all night long," remembered Laufer, who spent the night in the other bed listening, hysterical with laughter.

The next morning at the train station there was a peddler making up fake newspaper headlines. Laufer purchased several and sent them home to his father and to everyone he knew. Kaczmarek even sent one to Captain McGoldrick. The headline read: PARATROOPERS TAKE OVER CHICAGO. LAUFER AND KACZMAREK ARE TOPS.

Staff Sergeant Kaczmarek's bravado didn't sit well with everyone, however. One day, while on exercises, Kaczmarek loaded part of his platoon onto a two-and-a-half ton truck. There was only one small space left when Kaczmarek jumped up on the rear end of the truck, roughly tapped Private Francis 'Chips' Giard, and ordered, "Move over." Chips, a tall, handsome kid from Blackstone, Massachusetts, instead growled and knocked Kaczmarek off the truck.

Angrily dusting himself off, Kaczmarek told Giard, "When we get back, we're gonna look into this." Back at camp, Chips tried his best to beg out of the fight, but Kaczmarek wasn't going to let it go and pulled Giard behind the mess hall. Kaczmarek hit Giard hard in the face and his knees buckled, but as he was going down, Chips came straight up with an upper cut. The lucky punch nearly broke Kaczmarek's jaw. Kaczmarek had to get his teeth wired together, and was on soup-only for some time. After he recovered, however, Kaczmarek and Giard became good friends.[42]

Captain McGoldrick allowed PFC Grice to go home almost every weekend. Grice, apparently, had convinced McGoldrick that his brother, Major Charles Grice – a P-38 Lightning pilot fighting in the Pacific – was himself home on a long furlough. Since PFC Grice lived in Nashville, only a short distance away, Captain McGoldrick didn't see any reason to deny his frequent requests. Whenever he went home, Grice took along Laufer – his best friend – and another buddy for company. Laufer was treated like one of the family, and he loved the home cooking.

One weekend, Grice's sixteen-year-old brother, John, came to visit early. "Daddy let him drive the car down on Wednesday," recalled Grice, and Captain McGoldrick said that it would be all right for him to stay until the weekend. McGoldrick, however, cautioned Grice. "You tell him to be very careful," he said, adding that if his brother were injured or killed, it would be McGoldrick's ass. Grice and Laufer dressed John up in one of Private Evangelos J. Kondiditsiotes' uniforms, which fit perfectly, and then Grice introduced him to the rest of his platoon. "This is my brother," said Grice, thrusting John before them. "He's just staying till the weekend." Grice's platoon mates couldn't believe that McGoldrick let him get away with it, but John followed his big brother everywhere, even to the rifle range. "He shot just like we did," recalled Grice.[43]

When Saturday rolled around, Laufer, Haggard, and the brothers Grice, took off for Nashville with John at the wheel. They were headed down the Mercersburg Road at a good clip when, "[they] heard a sireen." John was too young to have a driver's license (the legal age was eighteen in Tennessee). Without stopping, Willie slid under his brother and John moved to the middle of the front seat between his brother and Laufer. Then, with the police cruiser pulling up behind, Grice pulled to the shoulder.

The deputy stepped from his car and slapped the door closed. Grice watched him in the mirror as he stepped up to his side of the car and announced in a thick drawl, "I know you wasn't driving this car. I know that guy in the middle was driving. But, I also know that your gonna deny. . ."

"That's right," Grice shot back. "I *was* driving."

"I know you wasn't driving," the officer repeated, "but it won't do me any good to write you a ticket 'cause you got two guys that are gonna lie for you. So I ain't gonna write you a ticket, but I want you to know that I know you wasn't driving this damn car. I'm gonna let you go."

Grice, Laufer, Haggard and John all had a good laugh over that as they took off down the road.[44]

When the unit returned from leave, training recommenced. On 19 and 20 May, the division staged a two-day field exercise. Then, on the morning of 30 May, an air-ground demonstration was held for the regiment. The purpose of the exercise was to illustrate the combined destructive power of all a battalion's weapons when they were concentrated on a designated target. And the men were suitably impressed.

One daytime jump was made by each battalion at Manchester, Tennessee and, on 29 and 30 May, the regiment made night practice jumps. F Company's jump was on the 30th. That night, however, black clouds spawning lightning and strong winds boiled up over the airfield. The men of 2nd Battalion waited under the wings of the C-47s for the wind to let up, but it didn't. The commander of the transports told Colonel Coutts, "If you give me an order, I'll make 'em fly. But if you're not going to give me an order, then these men are not going to fly these planes with that storm like it is."

Colonel Coutts told the airmen that nobody was going to slide and ordered three planes to go up and test the weather. F Company drew the duty. "My God, the wind. . . tore you up," remembered Staff Sergeant Paul. Hail battered and high winds buffeted the ships. Almost everyone got sick. Private Harris and the men on his plane were able to stand up and get ready to jump, but they had to hold on to the anchor line in order to keep upright. Fortunately, the jump was called off and the planes landed.[45]

Haggard watched the radioman from his plane get out, kneel, and kiss the ground. "What the hell's the matter with you?" asked the amused troopers.

"Didn't you feel the plane loose speed and altitude, and hear the engine shut down?" the radioman asked. The troopers agreed that they had. "Well," said the airman, "we damn near cut the tail off of another C-47 when we got out of order."

On 5 June, every man in the division packed his kit and nightmarched ten miles through a "malarious" section of the reservation to settle into an overnight tactical bivouac for another phase of training aimed at familiarizing the troopers with basic medical subjects. Troopers were graded on their performance during the march, their selection of a bivouac site, water discipline, and the sanitary measures undertaken including precautions against malaria. During the march realistic scenarios were presented for the troopers. For example, the troops were subjected to a mock mustard gas attack. Casualties were assessed and their symptoms designated by the umpires. Similar exercises continued over the next fortnight.[46]

One morning after F Company got back in the barracks, Munafo was lying in his bunk reading an old newspaper. "Jeez, look at this, John – D-Day," he said to his buddy in the bunk below. The long-awaited opening of the second front had finally come.

"You know," Munafo told Hall, "I would have been there had they not lost my records at Fort Dix." The news of the invasion was updated on the company bulletin board and everyone followed it closely. Munafo and the others all wanted to see combat. The men had chosen the paratroops because the Airborne was supposed to be a fighting unit. In Normandy the Allies had begun the liberation of Europe, but in Tennessee the 17th Airborne Division was still training. F Company men were thrilled by the battle news, but somehow disappointed that they weren't yet in on the fighting themselves.[47]

On 17 June, the regiment completed its unit training and tests, and that night F Company blew off some steam at a company party. All of F Company's officers and men attended, as well as a few officers from the other companies. During the revelry, Private Greenstrand got up on stage and rolled up his pants legs to show all of his boots, put on a helmet liner, and started into a boisterous impersonation of Colonel Miller. Just as Greenstrand really got rolling, Colonel Miller himself paid them a visit. "Captain McGoldrick about had a stroke trying to get word to me to knock it off and get the hell out of there," remembered Greenstrand.[48]

Greenstrand was always getting into something, and when another man from Second Platoon, Private Howard Goddard, who was quite blond already, peroxided his hair and set in the sun until it turned very light. Greenstrand thought he'd try it too, a few days before the regiment moved to Boston, Greenstrand talked two of his buddies, Privates George Gohn and George Graupensperger, into doing it as well. Something went terribly wrong though and they all ended up red heads. "We were in trouble again," recollected Greenstrand. There were regulations against changing your appearance, so they got sent to the barber and it was all clipped off. "We went overseas looking like three skinheads."[49]

On 29 June 1944, 'Jump For Joy,' a two-act musical comedy written by two 513th troopers and starring twenty-five 513th men, including F Company's Privates Greene, Imre, Munafo, and Laufer, was presented at the Grand Theatre in Huntsville, Alabama for the benefit of the Fifth War Loan Campaign. A receipt for a $500 war bond got patrons a seat on the main floor. $100 receipts got seats further back while $25 receipts purchased balcony seating. The show was a complete sell-out – 852 theater seats worth $153,400 in war bonds – and for the patrons it was a ruckus, knee-slapping good time as the company soared through the parodied arrangements, poking fun at the Army and their officers. It was also F Company's last hurrah in the States. The next day, the men were ordered to begin packing for movement overseas.[50]

On the company's last day at Camp Forrest, Private James W. Row and Private Louis P. Walker – who had been busted from Tech Sergeant – were transferred out of the company. They left on the heels of another trouble maker, Private Joseph R. Pilger, Jr. Around the barracks, little things had started to disappear. Cavaleri lost his wings and other men lost collar brass or minor personal possessions. It was not until Private William C. Podkulski's new A-2 leather flight jacket turned up missing, however, that the culprit was revealed. It was only by chance that Podkulski was passing a store in Tullahoma when he spotted a woman wrapping a flight jacket for the mail. When he inquired about it, Podkulski discovered that it was indeed his jacket. He also found out the name of the trooper who'd asked to have it wrapped, Joe Pilger. Podkulski returned to camp and went directly after Pilger, putting him in the hospital. Pilger had always been a little out of step with the rest of the company; a "screw-up," who always was on extra duty for something. However, no one could understand Pilger's motivation for the thefts. He didn't need the money, his parents owned a candy business and by all accounts were rich. Once trouble like this started in a unit, however, the commander had little recourse. Captain McGoldrick did not bother to discern the reason either; he transferred Pilger out immediately.

F Company's officers and enlisted men said goodbye to Camp Forrest at 1000 hours 10 August, and soon were in on a troop train en route for Camp Miles Standish, Massachusetts, in preparation for deployment overseas. Everything about the move was kept hush-hush. Not even the officers – with the exception of Captain McGoldrick – had any idea which theater they were bound for. The men, however, soon recognized landmarks. Outside of New York City, the train went into a tunnel and then emerged near the Meadows at Tonnelle Avenue. There was a junk yard there – Adam's Auto Parts. "Look at that, look at the junk yard," Munafo shouted, pressing himself to the window, gazing at all the junked cars. "I used to hang out there," he told his friends.

"When I seen that place," remembered Munafo, "oh, did I feel bad – 'cause I was alone." It was like a bucket of cold water had been thrown on him, Munafo was stunned by his sudden realization that he might not make it back, that he might even be killed. As the train rolled on through New York and into Connecticut, Munafo thought to himself, "I'll never see this again."

3

McGoldrick and his Forty Thieves

Boston POE, Tidworth Barracks & Camp Barton Stacey
13 August - 15 December 1944

The train carrying the 513th arrived at Camp Miles Standish in Boston on 13 August. On 20 August, the 513th moved to the Boston Port of Embarkation for passage overseas. For security reasons, division patches were removed from uniforms and jump boots were covered with GI leggings. F Company men weren't sure where exactly they were headed, but the rumors were rampant. One whisper declared that the woolen GIs they were wearing had been issued to camouflage the fact they were bound for the Pacific; some, like PFC Imre, believed it. Another report alleged the sun-tans were issued because they were bound for the jungle. Whatever the direction, they were surely headed for the fighting.

Before leaving, Captain McGoldrick, on 17 August, mailed a letter of reassurance to the parents of every men in the company. They probably knew it was a form letter, but it made them feel important nevertheless.

> I would like to take this opportunity to drop you an informal note, stating to you the high regard I have for your son. Never in my military experience have I felt more satisfied with a group of men as I do with the members of the Company which I am privileged to command.
>
> Your son has had many long hours of work, hard work, and there has been quite a number along the way who did not possess the qualities necessary for a good paratrooper - Qualities such as: courage, discipline, courtesy,

physical stamina and the ability to keep going when the going is toughest, but not so with your son. Through it all he has proven that he has what it takes. This hard work had brought results, because today your son has been through a period of training that is the most thorough possible and each of his buddies is just as well prepared.

Above all, I would like you to be assured that there is nothing within my power that I won't do to see that your son is well cared for, for I know that whatever mission I should have to send him on, no matter how difficult or hazardous, without a moments hesitation, he will say "Yes Sir, I'll do it." - And he would.

Sincerely yours,
FRED (NMI) MC GOLDRICK
Captain, Infantry
Commanding.

At 1900 hours, 20 August, with the music of a five-piece band to accompany them, F Company men picked up their duffel bags and slung their rifles, and marched aboard the tall, sea-gray-painted troopship USS *Wakefield*. Gazing out over South Boston from the ship's deck, Private Cavaleri could see the striped roof of his house at 576 E. 2nd Street, not too far away. Cavaleri tried his best to talk Captain McGoldrick into letting him go home for one last goodbye. McGoldrick, though sympathetic, could not. Regulations were regulations and no one could be allowed to leave the ship. Despondently, Cavaleri wondered what his folks were doing and if he'd ever see them again.[1]

The *Wakefield* was not built to be a troopship. She originally was the luxury passenger liner *Manhattan* of the United States Lines. In August 1932, on her maiden voyage, *Manhattan* steamed from Hamburg, Germany to New York in five days, fourteen hours, and twenty-eight minutes, then a record for passenger liners and a feat which earned *Manhattan* the title of "the fastest cabin ship in the world." With the outbreak of war apparently eminent, the Navy chartered the *Manhattan* on 6 June 1941 and, ten days later, she was commissioned the USS *Wakefield*. Because of her high speed, *Wakefield* often operated as a 'lone wolf', sailing without escort across the Atlantic. Her primary port of call was Liverpool, England, prompting her crew to nickname her 'The Boston and Liverpool Ferry,' and eventually she would carry some 110,563 troops to Europe. On this, her latest sortie, she would be carrying more than eight thousand men from the 17th Airborne Division, packed three tiers high into collapsible canvas shelves, each one with just enough room for a GI, his rifle, and his duffel bag.[2]

At nightfall, the hawsers were cast off and *Wakefield* slipped quietly out of the harbor. The voyage from Boston to Liverpool would take nine days of "ZIG for 15 minutes and ZAG for 15 minutes" in order to discourage and U-boats she encountered. At dawn, men on deck spotted the air escort which had closed during the night and which was now shadowing the ship. Soon, however, the planes turned back and the *Wakefield* was pacing solitary over the cold, green Atlantic waves headed east toward Europe.[3]

Travel aboard the troopship *Wakefield* was not the luxury cruise the passengers of the *Manhattan* had enjoyed. Unless one counted the daily battle against seasickness as fun, there wasn't much available in the line of recreation. Relief came when the men were called out on deck for calisthenics, or when they were allowed on the fantail to look for whales – or whatever else it was they thought was out there.[4] The ship's mess served meals continuously starting at 0530 until 1730 hours, but only two meals were served to each man per day because of the large numbers of men aboard. Having grown accustomed to airborne rations, most F Company troopers considered the food to be terrible, however; Private Munafo professed a liking for the Navy's SOS. The *Wakefield's* heads were distinctly unluxurious – they consisted of slabs of wood, wide enough for fifteen men to sit next to each other in a row, situated over a trough through which sea water constantly flowed. At 1700 hours every day, the *Wakefield's* water system was converted from fresh to sea water so the men could shower. For this purpose, a special lye soap which lathered in salt water was issued.[5]

Worse than trying to fight the boredom was trying to sleep confined in the *Wakefield's* hot and airless hold. Berthed below the waterline, the men could hear the screws turning and the water rushing by the hull. If a man had claustrophobia he'd know it then. "The hell with this shit!" Munafo declared vehemently the first hour. He had already had enough and he, John Hall, and Private Raymond W. Slocomb snuck out on deck with their sleeping bags. To their surprise, nobody bothered them. They slept with their faces exposed to the freezing ocean winds, but at least the air was fresh. They repeated their routine every night. Afterward, Munafo vowed he'd "never be a Navy man."[6]

Two days out of Boston, Private Laufer squatted disconsolately on the *Wakefield*'s forward deck, a soft ocean breeze tugging at his coat. Though lulled somewhat by the big ship's constant rolling, Laufer was too seasick and too hungry to be comfortable. The sound of feet landing heavily on the deck ahead distracted him and he turned to see one of the sailors had jumped out of the forward gun tub. Laufer detected something familiar in the sailor's face and soon realized he knew this sailor from back in New Haven. He was Dominic Curilly, whose brother was 'Big Boy' Curilly, a heavyweight fighter who had sparred with Joe Lewis and whose father owned a grinder shop in New Haven where they had all congregated before the war. Laufer shouted, "Dominic!" He sprang to his feet and was hugging his friend almost before the sailor had time to recognize him. The two men recounted their lives since joining the service, then Curilly went to the sailors' PX, which was off limits to the soldiers, and got Laufer a box of Hershey Bars. From there on out, Laufer never had to worry about food.

On the crossing, the officers were substantially better quartered than the men. So, remembered 2nd Lieutenant Charles D. Puckett, the "lieutenants of the 2nd Battalion took turns down in the hold with the men to keep up their morale. Lieutenant Calhoun was scheduled to run the rosters and [shrewdly] scheduled himself on the tours that covered midnight when all the clocks were set ahead one hour for the time change heading east, thus shortening his tour one hour." Several of the other lieutenants of the battalion confronted Calhoun on this point, but Calhoun "laughed it off as a joke." To Puckett, who was at that time in E Company, it was no laughing matter. Rather, it became a source of hard feelings.[7]

On 28 August, *Wakefield* came within range of British fighters which provided an escort for the ship into the harbor at Liverpool, England's busiest wartime port. Easing through the harbor traffic, the massive gray troopship came to rest along the quayside. In short order, F Company got their duffel bags and other equipment squared away, and marched down the gang plank to the waiting six-by-six trucks and moved to an assembly area. The following day, the 513th traveled by train to tent accommodations at Tidworth Barracks on Windmill Hill, located a quarter mile northeast of North Tidworth. "They were nice tents," commented Munafo, "set in a big, open field."[8]

About a week after arriving at Liverpool, Lieutenant Calhoun read in the division's general orders that a general, who had accompanied the regiment overseas on the *Wakefield*, was awarded the Distinguished Service Cross for making the "hazardous, unescorted crossing of the Atlantic." Calhoun laughed – the other eight thousand men who'd been on board had taken the same risk, but hadn't gotten a thing. Calhoun decided that was the reason generals got so many medals.

Tidworth Barracks, only a short distance from Andover on the Salisbury Plain, had formerly served as a British cavalry garrison but had been more recently a home for many of the American GIs training in England. Tidworth House, the manor home of the Duke of Glouchester, had been converted by the Duke and served as a Red Cross club. There, the 507th Parachute Infantry Regiment, that had recently returned from Normandy and which was now assigned to the 17th Airborne Division, camped on the opposite side of Windmill Hill. The glidermen and the division headquarters were established in and around Swindon.

F Company had arrived at Tidworth Barracks with nine officers and 120 enlisted men present for duty, but new men would soon be arriving to bring the company up to T/O & E strength – 176 men. On 4 September 1944, twenty new men joined F Company from the 54th Replacement Battalion. Among them were Staff Sergeant August C. Seacott, Private John D. La Riccia, Private Edward R. Sarrell, and Private Charles W. Simpson. Replacements were graduates of The Parachute School, but had undergone training as individuals rather than as part of a unit. After reporting for duty, the new men were quickly integrated into the company.

"Gus" Seacott was from Superior, Wisconsin and joined F Company's First Platoon as a squad leader. Seacott had followed his older brother Norman into the paratroops. Norman Seacott was a squad leader in E Company of the same battalion. The Seacotts had been closer once – they had both been in the same rifle company of the 3rd Infantry Regiment at Fort Benning.

John La Riccia, from Cleveland, Ohio, was only five-feet, three-inches tall, but he was stocky – "built like a little bull," said Munafo – and a natural athlete. He didn't mind living in tents – he'd been doing so since Basic at Camp Wheeler in Macon, Georgia. And Bing Crosby wouldn't be there to sing the men to sleep as he had during the crossing on the *Ile de France*, but La Riccia "didn't expect to be in no hotel, [they] weren't going 'over there' to visit." La Riccia was promoted to sergeant on 21 November and assigned to Third Platoon's first squad as the assistant squad leader under Staff Sergeant Francis V. McDevitt.[9]

Ed Sarrell, from Embarrass, Minnesota, was a blond-haired Midwesterner with deep-set eyes and a strong chin. He was assigned to Third Platoon. Charlie Simpson was a Southerner from Bremmen, Georgia and was nineteen years old. Simpson was assigned to Second Platoon as an ammunition bearer for PFC Paul M. Evans, a machine-gunner from Monroe, Louisiana.[10]

On 6 September, ten more men joined the company from the 54th Replacement Battalion. One of them was Private Donald O. Newhouse. Twenty-two and married, Newhouse wanted to fly Corsairs against the Japanese but had washed out of the Navy's aviation program. In September 1943, having been denied flight training by the Army Air Forces, he decided the extra pay paratroopers received was attractive. After enduring the tough naval aviator training, Newhouse breezed through The Parachute School. He'd never get to land the plane, but at least he'd still get to fly.[11]

Five more men, including Private Roderick MacKenzie, Jr., joined F Company from the 4th Replacement Depot on 11 September. MacKenzie, from Flanders, New Jersey, had come over from the 66th Infantry Division in which he had served as a divisional Ranger. MacKenzie, who'd found pleasure in the tough training he'd received in the Rangers and at Benning, was assigned as a rifleman and later as a machine-gunner in Lieutenant Calhoun's platoon.[12]

On 13 September, seven officers and 119 enlisted men were awarded the European-African-Middle Eastern Theater Ribbon in recognition of their service in the ETO. The new men – who brought the company to nearly full strength – received their ribbons on 15 September. The next day, another ceremony was held at which the 513th, having more than ninety percent of their men passing the test which followed unit training, was officially designated an Expert Infantry Regiment. In addition, three officers and 104 enlisted men from F Company qualified for the Expert Infantry Badge and F Company was presented with a streamer for their guidon. First Sergeant Donovan was proud because, as he attested, the company was "well trained – really." Before the ceremony concluded, Colonel Coutts, who had just received his promotion from lieutenant colonel, said a few words. He was proud of the regiment, he told them, and gave them all the credit for his recent promotion. "See these chickens," he said, polishing one of his new silver eagles with his coat cuff. "You men put them there." "Twenty-five hundred men came to their feet" cheering, remembered Haggard.[13]

Britain's cold, wet, and foggy climate made living in a tent an absolutely miserable experience. The showers were cold as was the shaving water. "Not a damn stove," remembered the also recently promoted Tech Sergeant Paul, had been provided for any of the tents. Not willing to sacrifice their comfort though roughing it on the English moors, F Company men set out immediately to appropriate for themselves – from neighboring installations – what the Army had apparently overlooked. Heading up the effort was Corporal Edward A. Keeling, Jr., the company armorer-artifacer who joined F Company on 27 September from Service Company. The men nicknamed him 'Stealing Keeling' because he could steal anything the company commander needed and was never caught. Keeling himself referred to his mission as "appropriating." Within a week's time, almost every tent in the F Company area had a stove burning luxuriously inside. The larcenous activities of Keeling and his accomplices soon earned F Company the sobriquet of 'McGoldrick and His Forty Thieves'.[14]

Not every tent had a stove, however, so Newhouse lined his cot with newspapers and a GI blanket, and covered himself with another. The cold, wet weather "wrung the urine right out of you," commented Newhouse. Men getting up in the middle of the night to use the slit-trench latrines behind the tents inevitably drew some grief from their tentmates for leaving the tent flap open. So, the men started keeping jars or cans under their bunks so they wouldn't have to go outside to urinate.[15]

The rain didn't stop the venereal disease inspections – known as 'short-arm inspections' under Army regulations – which had occurred every two weeks since Benning. Since weekend passes to London had been issued to the men almost immediately after they arrived in Britain, the short arms were a necessary measure to prevent the spread of VD. "At 0400, they'd yell, 'Fall out for short arm inspection'," remembered Grice. The men had to be inspected before they had had a chance to go to the latrine. In the dark, the men stumbled out into formation, naked except for their overcoats and boots. What inspectors didn't know was that, several of the division's doctors participated in covering-up VD cases in their regiments by doling out sulfadiazine tablets to their men before they went on pass. When the men later stood for a short arm inspections, stated Dr. Loran Morgan, Battalion Surgeon of the 466th Parachute Field Artillery Battalion, the sulfa drugs masked many of the symptoms.

Early every Saturday morning, a locomotive pulling ten passenger cars rolled up on the tracks skirting camp. The train was leased by the 513th's Athletic and Recreation Department for the purpose of conveying men on pass to London; the A&R Department also provided hotels where both the officers and men of the regiment could stay. At 0800 hours every Saturday morning, the men formed up on the south side of the camp near the railroad tracks to stand inspection. By 0900, the inspection was completed and those who had passed were on their way to Charing Cross Station, about an hour away. The men could hardly wait to get to London and start blowing off steam. This was not an uncommon thought among American servicemen. After all, it was, says historian Norman Longmate, "every GI's ambition to visit, or better still be stationed in, London."[16]

Initially, the enlisted men gravitated to the enlisted man's club at Rainbow Corner which was run by the Red Cross and largely staffed by British Red Cross girls who Private Laufer thought were beautiful. One night, Laufer asked one of the pretty girls serving coffee for a deck of playing cards and was charged a dollar for them. When he opened them up, they were stamped "Compliments of the VFW." After that, Laufer, whose affection for the girls never diminished, never cared very much for the Red Cross. Private La Riccia also was let down by the Red Cross. The club charged GIs twenty-five cents for a coffee and a doughnut while the Salvation Army, La Riccia discovered, served them at no charge. Not even the attractive British Red Cross girls were enough to get him to go back.[17]

Upon his arrival, Tec 5 Haggard took a room in the Strand Palace, a hotel across the street from the London Savoy. One of the first things he did was to purchase a membership in the Royal Opera House. Haggard was not an opera lover, but the opera house had a big dance floor and the music never stopped. When one band got tired, the next would get up on the revolving stage and pick up the tune. The girls were lined up three rows deep – the aggressive girls up front, the ones not-so-aggressive behind them, and the wall flowers behind them all. Haggard loved that he never had to ask a girl to dance. New girls just came right up and cut in.[18] The English girls loved it too. "No one could dance like the American boys," one recalled.

Private Jean Paul Morin was determined to uphold his self-proclaimed reputation as a ladies man. Morin had married his first wife the day before he was to ship out to the paratroops. The next morning, while waiting for his train to Benning, Morin realized he'd forgotten something and returned home to find his new bride in bed with another man. Following the divorce, Morin met and married another girl from Macon, Georgia. This marriage didn't even last the wedding night. Police broke down the door to their hotel room and arrested her for jewel theft. It was, in fact, Morin's frequent bouts with VD that earned him the nickname 'Snake' and a transfer from Regimental Headquarters Company down to Company F.

Morin spent his Sunday nights spinning tales about the girls – one such encounter featured a "Princess Tonya" – he'd romanced on the subway while on pass. Morin's stories probably didn't interest men like La Riccia who described himself as a "square" who never went in for the drinking and running around with girls. Although there were many men like him, there were just as many if not more who were determined to drink and defile themselves as much as possible.[19]

It was in London that many of the young soldiers had their first sexual encounter. When, on his first trip to London Private Imre and his three buddies hailed a cab, a prostitute riding in the back opened the door and invited them inside. Instead of being scared off by the unblushing solicitation, "the four of us took part, you know," said Imre. "We were sort of bonded that way." That was Imre's first sexual experience and his first encounter with London's infamous prostitutes.

Whenever Private Newhouse was asked if he wanted a pass to London, his answer was emphatic: "Oh hell yeah!" On Saturdays, he and PFC Frank J. Kinkus, Jr. rushed to catch the train to Charing Cross Station, only a short walk from Piccadilly Circus. Piccadilly Circus was the city's 'Times Square' and held for every GI its own peculiar promises and pitfalls. London's streets were always crowded with thousands of soldiers, sailors, and airmen from all over the world. Everybody was on the muscle and the mix was volatile. Bobbies, the Shore Patrol, and MPs were ever present, as were the prostitutes. "You couldn't walk ten feet without being propositioned," remarked Dahlberg. And the crowd was kept moving by the Bobbies who "wouldn't let people stand still." Street corner vendors were hawking their wares, calling out, "Newspapers – Newspapers, Batteries – Batteries, Rubbers – Rubbers." The entire mob was on the move, trolling – "everybody was out for a roll in the sack."[20]

F Company's officers warned the men to stay out of the red light district and the men all swore they would, but they must have had their fingers crossed. The girls stood in doorways and the words "Hey, mate," drifted on the blackout night air. Torches flashed on and off – almost every prostitute carried a flashlight and so did almost every serviceman. The only other lights in London were the little blue lights, hanging under reflectors, that marked the pro-stations and they were almost everywhere. Despite the official blackout, London fairly glowed.[21]

Some girls took an even more direct approach, grabbing a man by his testicles, and saying, "Cough!" An argument over the price often followed. "I don't want to buy the thing," one trooper remarked repeatedly. "I just want to pay to use it a little while." Then it was down into one of the air raid shelters.[22]

"Do you wanna' fuck?" a voice invited PFC Laufer from the darkness. Her torch revealed a "gorgeous blond."

"Well, yeah," said Laufer. "Let's go some place."

"Oh no. Right here, standing up."

At the train stations, GIs paid girls a pound note for a "kiss good-bye," and backed them against a convenient wall. The word was that, according to British law, if you were lying down it was prostitution, but if you did it standing up it was not. "Some of the guys tried to break their backs doing that," commented Laufer. "Me, I like comfort. I wouldn't do that."[23]

Signs dressed the empty store windows advertising "Greek culture" or "French culture," anything imaginable underscored with two words: "call me." "There was a photograph and next to it, 'My name is Mary Lou and I'm into. . .' Some guys went crazy for that shit," said Laufer, "and some didn't. For the American serviceman in London, it was there if you wanted it and many did."[24]

After PFC Imre lost almost $200 to a friend at cards, his friend declared that, "so there wouldn't be any bad feelings," they should go out and spend the money. Imre agreed and with his friend and two more buddies out they went. They had a "terrific meal" and "great booze," and then went to an off-limits area – which was really a "posh cat house" – where each of the four picked a girl. Not really knowing why, probably because they were buddies, they asked the girls to leave the doors to their rooms open. As each of the men finished, he got up and walked around, kidding the other guys. Eventually, Imre's three pals came into his room and sat down on his bed. "Imre," said one, "you're not doing it right!" The others started laughing, and shooting spit balls and rubber bands. Imre was too embarrassed do anything after that.

The Army's attitude toward sexual behavior was considerably more liberal than the average young man had previously been accustomed to in civilian life. The Army was concerned a great deal more with the manpower losses to venereal disease than it was with guiding the men morally so, rather than trying to eliminate prostitution, took steps to limit the spread of the disease. Before engaging in intercourse, most prostitutes required servicemen to wash themselves with a potassium-permanganate solution *and* use a condom. Sometimes these could be obtained at a prophylactic station like the one at the Rainbow Corner club in London. Every month, Army regulations required an officer to give a sexual hygiene inspection and lecture to the company. Yet the Army's instruction in sexual hygiene was more often than not an "occasion for ribaldry" rather than serious instruction. To demonstrate the proper use of the prophylactic kit, Lieutenant Puckett employed a broomstick. It always made the men snicker. PFC Laufer was particularly amused by one cartoon in which Sad Sack had just seen a VD film warning him about the dangers of contact with the opposite sex. So, before he shook the hand of his sergeant's girl, he donned a condom like a glove.[25]

When Lieutenant General Matthew B. Ridgeway, commander of the American XVIII Airborne Corps, visited the 513th's area on 6 September, he found training well underway. Road marches and company maneuvers filled the schedule. "We had to keep the guys busy doing something," explained Donovan, "or they'd go whacko." Donovan was only joking; field exercises were, in fact, taken very seriously by the men. The constantly foul weather, however, had most of them down and the "persistent, light rain. . . didn't stop the training." Colonel Miller had the men in the field in spite of it. "Drill, drill, drill, something new and wet every day," Greenstrand recalled. Some field problems lasted as long as ten days, the men sleeping on the cold ground in their pup tents. Eventually, half the company had colds. Most of the men thought Acey-Deucy was just out to make them miserable. Before two weeks had elapsed Captain McGoldrick himself was fed up with Colonel Miller and told him so.[26]

On 14 September, matters came to a head. During an inspection that morning, Miller instructed Captain McGoldrick to "put Calhoun in for promotion to 1st Lieutenant." McGoldrick had First Sergeant Donovan type up the papers. McGoldrick then signed them and sent them up to battalion. Within an hour, McGoldrick had the paperwork back – disapproved by Colonel Miller. The same thing had happened with Calhoun's promotion on at least a half dozen earlier occasions, but this was the last straw. McGoldrick walked to Miller's office to find out what was going on and, during the exchange, McGoldrick lost his temper. So did Miller, and he put McGoldrick up on charges.[27]

When the paperwork reached Colonel Coutts, he called McGoldrick to his office and asked for his side of the story. Captain McGoldrick told Coutts, "You bring Colonel Miller and stand him beside me and I'll tell you everything that man has done wrong, but as long as he's not here I'm not even gonna talk about it." Coutts laughed and told him that he understood. McGoldrick was promoted to major and got shipped up to division. Captain William E. Jakes, from Service

Company, was assigned as the new F Company CO, but since he was in the hospital at the time, 1st Lieutenant Sam Dean assumed command instead.

First Sergeant Donovan, whose responsibilities put him in contact with Miller on a daily basis, always had sympathized with McGoldrick. Ace Miller "was a flighty bastard," commented Donovan, "just a pain in the ass." Miller had offered Donovan the S-1 job (the battalion adjutant) at 2nd Battalion Headquarters. Although it meant a promotion to the grade of warrant officer, Donovan turned it down, declaring to his friends that he'd go AWOL and swim home before he'd work for Colonel Miller. Donovan's sympathy for McGoldrick, however, had no bearing on the showdown's inevitable outcome. At the end of the incident, Calhoun still hadn't gotten his promotion, however; for F Company, McGoldrick's transfer would turn out to be a blessing in disguise.[28]

The American Army was renowned for the quantity and quality of its equipment and supplies, but after being in service for nearly two years, many men could no longer palate Spam. Although plentiful, Army chow was monotonous and the men always looked to supplement their diet. When it was discovered that rabbits, pheasants, ducks, and other small game abounded on local farms, the men set out to do to these what they'd done to the stoves. During field problems on local farms, the men flushed out rabbits and fowl and bagged them. The farmers, upset by the loss of their game and sure of the reason for its loss, complained to the regimental commander who instructed the Officer of the Day to search the barracks nightly for poached game. Such searches were rarely productive.[29]

The men also collected local produce. Before being consumed, vegetables were treated with microlene to prevent cholera; English farmers were spreading night soil on their fields for fertilizer. Every day, an Englishman – the men teased the Brits about being honeydippers, but they just shrugged it off – arrived in a tank truck to collect the human waist from Windmill Hill's outdoor latrines which consisted of metal honey buckets under a row of wooden seats. To get the stuff into the tank, somebody had to hand the buckets up to another trooper on the truck who would pour it in. This task was usually assigned as punishment. Once, when he returned late on a pass, PFC Laufer was detailed as a honeydipper for two days. "The trooper on the truck, if he didn't like you, and he'd shake it, the piss and shit would come all over you. You'd stink. . . like hell." Laufer smelled so bad he had to bathe in the creek – clothes and all – before his friends would let him back in the tent. But even honeydipping was there to teach a simple lesson, said Laufer: DON'T FUCK UP.[30]

The officers came up with all kinds of creative ways to punish infractions. On one road march in the middle of October, Staff Sergeant Seacott and Staff Sergeant Kaczmarek screwed up and as atonement for their mistake were ordered to paint a big 'X' on the telephone poles on the right side of the road, and big 'O' on those on the left – all the way back to camp. The officers must have brought the paint with them waiting for a chance to use it. With all the painting and climbing over fences, it was dark before Seacott and Kaczmarek returned. Kaczmarek was subsequently reduced to private.[31]

Several F Company men had gone to the tattoo parlor in Ludgershall, a small village southeast of camp. PFC Greenstrand got branded with one that read "Death Before Dishonour." That was okay with the officers, but some of the guys got tattoos of jump wings or other unit identifications. These were against regulations and in some instances they were nearly skinned off.[32]

Many infractions, however, went unpunished. On one field exercise, Tech Sergeant Smith put Private Newhouse on guard duty. Newhouse shrugged off the assignment and burrowed into a haystack, lining it with his shelter half to shield himself from the cold, wet ground. A few hours later, Newhouse was shaken awake by Smith. Newhouse knew he'd screwed up, but Smith didn't get mad. The company had been out living in holes for five or six days and were worn out. Newhouse's offense was extremely serious, but for some reason Smith was understanding that night.[33]

Usually, when a man climbed into a haystack near Windmill Hill, he wasn't looking to get any sleep. At the foot of Windmill Hill, there was a row of about a dozen haystacks. English farmers constructed them by placing bundles of straw together and fixing more bundles on top to form a thatched roof. This kept the straw in the center dry. Troopers pulled the bundles out of the center of the stacks and made little rooms in them for the local prostitutes who the men dubbed 'Haystack Annies.' Troopers returning from London arrived at the train station in Ludgershall and walked back along the tracks, past the stacks, to camp. On any given night, if a man was of a mind to take a look down there, he might see flashlights switching on and off around them.[34]

One night, an F Company trooper brought one of the Annies back to camp and put her in his tent. Since there were no lights inside the tents at Windmill Hill, the men lined up in the dark outside to wait their turn. While he was waiting, one of the men got the idea to cut up an old LIFE magazine into pieces the size of British pound notes. He then handed a 'note' to every man in line. Inside the tent, the poor Annie didn't bother to look at the notes as they were handed to her, she just tossed them onto the growing pile under her cot. The next morning, all she had was a handful of useless paper. The woman went to the regimental headquarters to complain, but, since prostitution was illegal, her complaint was ignored. After that, the girls started using a flashlight.[35]

2nd Lieutenant Charles D. Puckett, a tall Californian, came over from E Company on 18 September. Puckett was a West Point officer, but he had been appointed to the Academy from the enlisted ranks. He joined the 513th at Camp Forrest, Tennessee and served with the 2nd Battalion until being assigned to F Company. According to Sam Calhoun, most West Pointers automatically received a promotion to 1st lieutenant upon the completion of Jump school, but Puckett was still a 2nd lieutenant. "He must of got on somebody's shit list," thought Calhoun. Lieutenant Puckett was aloof with the men, and seldomly socialized with them – unlike Lieutenant Calhoun who had also been an enlisted man. 1st Lieutenant Robert J. Gilles, a West Pointer who replaced Lieutenant O'Donnell at Camp Forrest, even remarked that Puckett was a "dunderhead." Private Sarrell, for one, didn't agree with their estimate of Puckett. He and Puckett had once sat together at a movie at Barton Stacey during which Puckett displayed a jovial demeanor.[36] Even Lieutenant Calhoun, however, had his detractors. Usually easy with the men he liked, Calhoun was a martinet with those he did not. If Calhoun saw that one of these men failed to recognize him as an officer, whether on post or in London, he would stop him instantly. "Where's your salute, soldier?" he'd ask, pointing to his lieutenant's bars.

Lieutenant Puckett was assigned as Lieutenant Stositch's assistant platoon leader. Stositch greeted him into the platoon with the remark, "F Company is called the fuckup company because they send here all those who have fucked up." More than fifty years later, Puckett would write, "This remark later proved to be prophetic."[37]

On 25 September, the regiment made a mass exhibition jump over Windmill Hill. For the first time, the men used the 'British parachutes' – T-7s – equipped with the British-designed quick-release device. Troopers had to make one jump a month to earn their jump pay, but jumping for the brass, risking life and limb in an exhibition jump, wasn't something the men favored.[38]

The day before the jump was to take place, loading lists were prepared. When Lieutenant Puckett discovered that he and Lieutenant Stositch were slated to go on the same plane he asked, "I thought the reason for two [lieutenants] per platoon was for a backup. Why are we both in the same plane?" Lieutenant Stositch changed the roster and "put Lieutenant Puckett in jumpmaster position on another plane. Later that day, orders came down from Regimental Headquarters limiting one platoon lieutenant per plane." For Puckett, the event had given him an opportunity to demonstrate his competence to the other officers.[39]

"It was [usually] awful windy at Windmill Hill," remembered Grice, "but it wasn't windy that day." But though the weather was cooperative, the jump went off in far from routine fashion. Lieutenant Puckett's plane passed less than fifty feet above the top of Windmill Hill. The ground started falling away as the red and green jump signals went on. Lieutenant Puckett was the last to jump, and only had time to check his chute opening and then prepare to land. Those who had preceded Puckett out undoubtedly had suffered harder landings.[40]

Private Munafo went out wrong getting one of his legs caught upside down. He had jumped in a pair of regular field boots instead of paratrooper boots and their integral gaiters became tangled in the risers or suspension lines. Munafo came down, one leg in the air, right on top of his canteen. The impact was so hard it knocked the breath out of him, he thought he'd broken his ribs. Munafo was picked up in a jeep and taken to the hospital for treatment.[41]

In almost every stick there were problems. When the green light was flashed over the drop zone, Private Arrowood, the second man in his stick, was pushed to the floor. Arrowood's ship had to make a second pass. By that time, there were parachutes everywhere, dotting the fields.

After he landed, Private Sarrell looked up just in time to see a man hit the earth right beside him. Sarrell was stunned; the trooper's leg bone was sticking out of his stomach. The man's parachute hadn't opened at all. Indeed, many men were injured on the jump and around a dozen men were killed. The parachutes had been packed in the States and never repacked after they got to England. This, apparently, accounted for the high number of streamers and reserve chutes open that day.[42]

On 4 October, F Company marched with the regiment to Barton-Stacey Camp A, about 2 miles north of the village of Barton Stacey near Andover. The camp's permanent wooden barracks – though dirty, worn out, and old looking – were a welcome change from the outdoor living. The men had beds – the mattresses were filled with hay – and the barracks did have stoves. There was no coal to fuel them, however, but that had not been a problem before and would not be a problem now. F Company men appropriated what coal they needed from the mess hall supply or from the British coal dump located about a mile from camp.[43]

The camp was "right close to town [Andover]," remembered Munafo. He discovered a small shop in the village that served fish & chips wrapped up in newspaper. He instantly was hooked on this staple of English cuisine. Munafo and Hall took turns sneaking into town at night to get whole packs of fish & chips. Tech Sergeant Paul, however, was wise to them. Both of them were caught several times while sneaking back into camp and Paul gave them hell for it.[44]

Though most of the men still preferred to go to London – it was only a forty-five minute train ride away from the new camp – a few troopers found the slower pace of villages like Andover and Winchester much more to their liking. Andover boasted only a single cinema and a NAAFI canteen – the NAAFI was a close British cousin of the American Red Cross – but the Bank of England, which had evacuated the capital sometime after the beginning of the war, had relocated near Andover. On Saturday nights, therefore, the regiment sent trucks to the collect the female employees of the Bank of England and convey them to Barton Stacey for a dance. The officers' dance was held in the officer's club, and the enlisted men's in the gymnasium. Although many GIs indulged in sexual excess in London, just as many – if not more – were looking for, at dances, service clubs, church socials, and USO clubs, "nice girls" with whom they might find true companionship and, perhaps, love.[45] The problem was that there just weren't enough "so-called non-professional sexual partners available" for all the American soldiers in Britain; thus many men spent their passes searching for these relatively few women.[46] Privates Munafo and Hall went all the way to Oxford University to look for girls. "Did you know," Calhoun stated, "that we'd tell girls at college that they had to give up ten thousand brassieres so that we men could have one silk parachute. That's what the Army told paratroopers during the war, that it took ten thousand brassieres to make one parachute."

"When I found that out," joked Private Imre, "I ruined ten parachutes!"

Private Laufer took up riding and was lucky enough to be befriended by the family from whom he rented the horse. When he wasn't spending weekends in London, he tried to content himself by riding around their property, but Laufer longed for a girl he'd met while on pass in London. She came from Toddingham, and was, said Laufer, a "lovely young lady." On the weekends they spent together in London, she showed him all the city's famous attractions – Trafalgar Square, the changing of the Guard, and Petticoat Lane were peddlers hawked their wares from push-carts. "It was a real pleasure," he recalled fondly. After the war, Laufer was sorry he'd lost her address.

Private Edward Sarrell fell for a girl from Highbonnet, north of London. Sarrell had returned late from pass at least three times after spending a weekend with her, and First Sergeant Donovan had slapped him with a twenty-five dollar fine each time. The money was supposed to go into a soldier's deposit but didn't make it, Sarrell suspects, any further than Donovan's pocket.[47]

First Sergeant Donovan, the men had discovered, "knew how to connive real well." The men nicknamed him 'Hard Cash Donovan' and 'Diamond Dick.' Donovan routinely cleaned up at pay day poker games. "Did he win? Always," recalled Newhouse. A big time operator, Donovan palled around with Dean Swem, the First Sergeant from I Company, an established friend who had been booted from the same OCS class Donovan had been. On the pretext of getting fuel for the stoves, Swem and Donovan would take a gallon container down to the NCO club where Donovan was on the Board of Governors. One of his men would admit them before the club opened at 1700 hours and Donovan and Swem would then return with a gallon of beer that they quickly drained.[48]

Private Newhouse continued to spend his weekend passes in London with his best friend, PFC Frank Kinkus. Kinkus, like Newhouse, had been married just before leaving the States. Kinkus, however, was "convinced he was going to be killed," and, therefore, decided he would "live dangerously." He "always tried to bring a broad back with him from London," said Newhouse. In the barracks at Barton Stacey were shower rooms, and behind the shower rooms were boiler rooms where the men hung their towels to dry. Kinkus would throw a few blankets on the boiler room floor and stash the girl or often girls. Then he'd go pimp her around camp. It didn't take too long for the officers to catch on, though. They would come to "roust out the gals and [then convey them to the officers' quarters to] use them for themselves."[49]

In September, on their only pass to London, Munafo and Hall arrived in the evening. The city was already blacked-out. Buzz bombs – V1 rockets – were hitting the area, and, therefore, the two joined the Londoners taking shelter in the subways. Cold and cramped, some sleeping, all were there to avoid the bombs. To their delight, what at first was an inconvenience presented them with chance to meet a couple of girls. "They were good girls," remembered Munafo, and they invited the two paratroopers home to meet their parents. Munafo and Hall even had Sunday dinner with them. Munafo found the people gracious – they genuinely wanted to do something nice for the American soldiers.[50]

However, not all Britons felt fondly toward the paratroopers. The British soldiers competed, though unevenly, against the swaggering troopers for women. It was difficult for the 'Tommies' because the paratroopers earned a lot more money than the average British soldier. As a private, a trooper earned $110 a month while his British counterpart earned the equivalent of $12. The Americans' relative wealth attracted many women and the Tommies resented it.[51]

Their relative wealth wasn't all that many Britons found unattractive about the Yanks. Americans, or at least many of them, had a swash about them, an almost belligerent attitude, that did not square with many British ideas of propriety. On one pass to London, Private Connolly suggested to his chum, PFC Arthur Bricmont: "Let's call up Churchill and let him know we're here." His friend agreed so there, in Trafalgar Square, the two squeezed into a phone booth and placed a call to 10 Downing Street, informing the operator that he would "like to speak to Mr. Churchill." A voice came on – it was an aide to the Prime Minister. Connolly told him this: "Tell Churchill he can sleep easier tonight because the 513th Parachute Infantry Regiment of the 17th Airborne Division has arrived and is on its way to France to put an end to the war!" Without pause the aid answered, "I'd be delighted to pass along that heartwarming message to the Prime Minister." Connolly sincerely hoped he would.[52]

Alas, a great proportion of the Americans' bravado was far from innocent in its style and intent. The attitude of many Americans was summed up by Private Laufer: "You have to remember," he pointed out, "that we went over there as conquering heroes and our attitude was real bad. We were there to save England. Fuck the Queen and fuck the King. . . Get a girlfriend – fuck her and forget her. Don't give a shit about anybody else except you. You're an American. When the British queued-up to get on a bus, the American soldier would jump right to the front of the line. Common courtesy? Forget it. He didn't give a shit."[53]

All the drinking by GIs didn't help matters. One of the biggest problems facing the U.S. Army in Europe was the startlingly high level of alcohol use. Historian William O'Neill suggested that not only did American servicemen overseas seldom turn down an opportunity to get drunk, but that during World War II, "America floated to victory on a tidal wave of booze."[54] Across England, the GIs' love of drink, and his capacity to drink in quantity, became famous. Though most Americans preferred hard liquor, many finally submitted to consuming the warm, flat British beer that was much more plentiful, especially after they discovered just how intoxicating it really was. Nevertheless, one soldier's announcement to an English brewer that he had "come for the piss," suggests some Americans' true regard for the stuff. Public drunkenness by many American servicemen contributed greatly to tensions between themselves and their British allies. Aside from the many instances of short-term AWOL and the numerous traffic offenses, drunkenness was the greatest cause of discipline problems and crime in England. One Army report asserted that "intoxication was the largest contributing factor to crime in the European Theater of Operations."[55]

Furthermore, servicemen of all nationalities had been whipped into a fighting spirit which manifested itself outwardly in a brand of brash cockiness. As Laufer put it, "everybody was on the muscle." After a few drinks, it sometimes took only one crooked look or an imagined slight to spark a fight. "It didn't have to be Rebels neither," recalled Munafo. "It could be Northerners too, but from a different outfit." In London, there was a standing feud between the paratroops and the Air Corps. The reason, said Laufer, was that the airmen had been stationed in England since 1943 and, therefore, "they had all the broads." At a club one evening, Laufer sat watching a gorgeous blond dance with one of the flyboys. "Abee," his friends coaxed him, "go ask her to dance." "I don't give a shit" said Laufer, accepting his friend's dare. Laufer had a reputation as a man who didn't give a damn about anything and he often lived up to it. "He'd do anything to get everyone's attention," recalled Imre.

"Do you mind if I cut in?" Laufer asked, tapping the airman on the shoulder.

"Screw! Don't mess with me and my girlfriend!" the airman shot back. A few more words were exchanged but before Laufer could take any action a buddy's fist come right over his shoulder and hit the airman square in the mouth.

The fact is, a lot of the other outfits just didn't like paratroopers either. "That's why," said Munafo, "you never went in town alone. . ." Munafo, Hall, and Slocomb always buddied up when going into town. Of course, paratroopers never seemed to shy away from confrontations, perhaps, as a trooper from the 101st Airborne said, because "paratroopers were always on edge." Their training had seen to that – a kind of survival reflex. Moreover, paratrooper training had every trooper thinking he was better than everyone else. It went to their heads and made many sadistic. It was this attitude, this arrogance, that made many British and Americans despise the paratroopers. Troopers were "continually fighting" British civilians and other American GIs. PFC Joseph B. Gutt, from Chicago, a small, lean, hunched trooper with big feet, would start bumming for a drink the moment he walked into a pub, and more often than not, he'd get involved in a fight. Worse yet was the fact that Gutt almost always lost. He just never learned.[56]

With all the drinking, brawling, and sex, it was inevitable that some troopers found themselves in serious trouble. According to Sam Calhoun, charges pressed against GIs were made to the local government who informed SHAEF. Through channels, word reached individual units from SHAEF and a soldier was brought up on charges. Soldiers of the 513th guilty of minor crimes against a Briton, or of some military offenses, sometimes found themselves serving time in the regimental stockade, a thirty-foot square, eighteen-foot deep pit covered with barbed wire. The hole had been dug by order of Lieutenant Poe, the 513th's Police and Prisons Officer. When it rained, the stockade turned into a mud-hole earning it its name 'Poe's Pig Pen'.

Carrying only their sleeping bags and shelter halves with them, prisoners descended into the pit on a ladder which was then removed. They were allowed out three times a day for meals, and, though F Company's chow was served on a first come-first serve basis, the prisoners always ate last. Their meals were served through the window of the mess hall and the prisoners ate sitting outside on a log – rain or shine – and prisoners got no second helpings. The only other time a prisoner was allowed out of the hole was when he was required for duties such as coal details, yet, the prisoners remained enterprising. Across the street from the Poe's Pig Pen was the camp theater. One night, Private Newhouse, who had pulled guard duty at the theater, heard a pecking on the back door. When he opened it, he found all the prisoners from the stockade standing outside. They had dug a hole under the wire and escaped, all just to watch the movie. Newhouse let them in and, after the film, the prisoners, probably not wishing to add desertion to their list of offenses, snuck back.[57]

On 5 October 1944, Captain William E. Jakes, still in the hospital, was officially relieved from command of F Company and transferred back to the Service Company. That same day, Captain Marshall M. Reynolds joined F Company from the 16th Replacement Depot and assumed command. Born 16 June 1919, Reynolds was a native of Berryville, Virginia and had graduated from the Virginia Military Institute, Class of 1940. Reynolds was a short man – about five feet, six inches tall – bow legged, and, depending on who describes him, a rather mean looking or homely man. Some thought he looked just like Edward G. Robinson. Part of one ear had been burned off and he had burn scars on his face, but Reynolds' neck was all muscle and he had big shoulders and eyes that, when you looked into them, looked like you were staring into a freight train coming down on you; a characteristic which prompted his VMI classmates to nickname him 'The Cannonball'.[58]

In a letter from Reynolds to General Charles Kilbourne, the superintendent of VMI, he detailed his career before joining F Company:

A brief summary of my service is as follows: I was called to active duty in February of 1942 and reported at Camp Robinson, Arkansas as a second lieutenant. From there I sailed to Oahu and was assigned to the 19th Infantry of the 24 Division in May of the same year. I received my promotion to first lieutenant in October and transferred to the 35th Infantry of the 25th Division on the 1st November 1942, as a volunteer, prior to the Division's move to the Solomons. Landed at Guadalcanal in December as Battalion antitank officer. Was injured in a gasoline explosion and returned to the United States for hospitalization, arriving in March 1943. Returned to duty in May at Camp Roberts, California as a stopover prior to attending the Officers Basic Course at Fort Benning. Completed the Course in November 1943 and was assigned as a tactical officer at the Officer Candidate School. Remained there until February 1944, at which time I transferred to The Parachute School for a course in Parachute Training. Completed the Course in March and was assigned as company commander to the Second Parachute Training Regiment. Received my promotion to Captain in July and departed for service in the European Theatre in September. Was assigned to the 513th Parachute Infantry of the 17th Airborne Division on 25 September as a Rifle Company Commander and have continued in that capacity until the present.[59]

Upon his arrival, Captain Reynolds gathered the men and delivered brief talk to let the men know just exactly what he expected of them. He told the men he would go to Hell for them, but if they crossed him he would send them to Hell himself. "I want F Company," Reynolds said, "to be the fightenest fuckingest company in the 17th Airborne Division." F Company had finally gotten a leader that matched its collective self image.

Reynolds "was an animal," said Laufer, "a bulldog," and he set out immediately to prove his mettle to the men. On training marches, Reynolds took turns carrying the .30 caliber machine-guns, the tripods, the 60mm mortar tubes, and the baseplates, setting a good example for the officers and winning the respect of the men right away. There was nothing he would ask his men to do that he wasn't willing to do himself. Shortly after assuming command, Reynolds observed Sergeant Wayne DeHaven, the communications sergeant, and a couple other men working out tactical problems, sketching them in the dirt. "That's the way I like to see you acting," he told them approvingly. DeHaven could tell by his tone that Reynolds genuinely liked his men. The men liked him, too.[60]

On matters of discipline, Reynolds was what many officers claimed to be but weren't: firm but fair. Private Munafo, who had to go before Reynolds a couple of times, said of the Captain, "he was easy." Reynolds punished AWOLs and other infractions with a 'soldier's deposit' – pay was withheld until discharge. There was one thing, however, that Reynolds would not tolerate, a soldier who stole from the men of his own company. "He said if anyone was caught stealing from someone," remembered Greenstrand, "unless he had the hell beaten out of him before he was taken to Captain Reynolds, he [Reynolds] would turn him loose. But, if he had the hell beat out of him, he would throw the book at him."[61]

One man 'Bud' Reynolds didn't hit it off with was Colonel Miller. "Marshall Reynolds," commented Laufer, "would not take any shit from Acey-Deucy." Soon, a rumor was circulating through the company that Reynolds was going to "knock Acey-Deucy on his ass." Though the origins of their inimical relationship are not clear, it nevertheless only served to increase Miller's animosity toward F Company and, specifically, the Second Platoon. "I don't believe," commented Greenstrand, Miller "ever forgave the men of the Second Platoon for. . . signing that petition to get Lieutenant Calhoun back to the platoon."

On 20 November, Private Thomas E. Connolly, from West Newton, Massachusetts, joined F Company. Connolly had falsified his birth certificate and enlisted at seventeen. After induction, he was placed in the ASTP program and started classes at the University of Cincinnati. When the program was scrapped, he was sent to the 19th Armored Infantry Battalion of the 14th Armored Division at Fort Campbell, Kentucky. Connolly, however, volunteered for parachute training immediately. Before he left, his company was formed up and those men who were going to Benning were put on display. "Take a good look at these men," his first sergeant told the assembled company, "they won't be coming back. They're volunteering to go into the paratroops." Connolly graduated parachute training in September 1944, class number 138.

Private Connolly crossed the Atlantic on the *Queen Mary*. Troopers aboard, he happily discovered, were treated almost as well as the Hollywood stars, like Mickey Rooney, with whom they shared passage. Paratroopers were assigned to state rooms, four men per cabin, and each cabin had a private bath. To top it off, no extra duty was assigned to the paratroopers. Connolly finally asked one of the British sailors why they were getting the special treatment. "You lads deserve the best," the sailor told him, "you may not make it home." In 1998, Connolly explained that "the Brits knew more than we knew;" they had witnessed the Airborne casualties from Normandy and Holland returning to English hospitals. But like many other young men, Connolly figured he'd live forever; getting killed was something that happened to the other guy. Because he was an ASTP 'whiz kid', his new friends in the Third Platoon nicknamed him 'Professor'.[62]

"The 17th Division – probably – was the best prepared unit that ever went into combat," stated Major Edwards. "I can't think of any outfit that I ever served in that was better." Training continued extensively – a lot of walking followed by a lot of griping – but the men endured it, not only because of the NCOs' and officers' insistence upon it, but because they all knew combat was not far away. By this time, most of the men had adopted a "take-it-as-it-comes" attitude and didn't let the work or the weather bother them too much. Around Halloween, the 2nd Battalion was trucked to Southampton, which had been heavily bombed by the Germans, for a one day course in street fighting. "The whole town's pregnant," PFC Dahlberg joked the men next to him soon after they arrived. Nearly every woman their truck column passed as they rode into the town was pushing a baby buggy or soon would be, he observed. The men arrived early and, while they waited, somebody found a place to buy fresh-baked brown bread.[63]

The street fighting course was designed to teach the men the basic tactics of house clearing and close quarters combat. It was run by a British officer who would throw a brick at any man who stuck his head out or gave away his position. The most interesting part of the exercise was the grenade demonstration. Cardboard silhouettes were placed inside a room into which a grenade was thrown. The perforated silhouettes left little doubt as to the effectiveness of the weapon. Pole charges, demolition charges, and bazookas were all discussed, and "no bazooka gunners were better trained than those of the 513th," said one paratrooper. Gunners went to the firing ranges frequently, spending five and six hours at a time firing on moving targets; expending whole truck loads of bazooka ammunition a day. This training would prove invaluable in the hard days of fighting to follow.[64]

While the 17th Airborne Division had been getting used to their new quarters and their English cousins, one British and two American Airborne divisions were engaged in bitter struggle in Holland. On 17 September 1944, and over the next several days, the three Allied Airborne divisions were landed in Holland between the Belgian border and Arnhem in Operation MARKET-GARDEN. The goal was the capture bridges over the Rhine at Arnhem, thereby providing the Allies with an avenue to sweep onto the Northern German Plain – good tank country – but the plan had failed to achieve its objectives. After the initial momentum of MARKET-GARDEN stalled, Allied troops moved into static positions on the 'Island' and so began a campaign that soon developed into essentially an artillery duel.

The Island Campaign, fought on the five kilometer wide stretch of land that lay between the Neder Rijn to the north, and the Waal River to the south, took place from early October until the end of November 1944. German forces of the *II SS Panzer Korp* held the high ground north of the Lower Rhine and west of Opheusden on the Island. British and American troops settled in for two months of static, trench warfare more characteristic of WWI than of WWII.

The Island was composed mostly of agricultural land which, like much of Holland, was below sea level. Holding back the sea were levees, some more than twenty feet high and two hundred feet across at their bases with roads along their tops. Below the levees lay drainage ditches and boggy grazing land. Allied infantry served as forward observers or, in the event of a breakthrough, defenders of the dikes they occupied. High ground on the northern bank of the Neder Rijn allowed German gunners to place accurate fire on virtually any point, and even snipe at individual men in the open with their dreaded 88mm guns, thus, movement during the day was limited. Patrols were sent out every night to maintain contact with the enemy, but for the most part Allied troops just had to sit there and take it.

To gain combat experience, on 6 November, one officer from each company of the 17th Airborne was selected to serve in Holland as an observer attached to either the 101st or the 82nd Airborne. Since Lieutenant Calhoun was the officer who stood roll call on the morning of selection, the duty fell to him. Calhoun, along with Lieutenant Harry Kenyon from E Company and the other officers of the 17th, was issued a parachute, ammunition, and rations, and waited around half a day to board a C-47 in Fairfield in preparation for a jump into Eindhoven, Holland.

During the flight, reports of enemy action over the drop zone forced a change in plans; the jump was canceled and the men were told they would land in Brussels, Belgium. However, upon nearing Brussels, the plans changed again. The Luftwaffe was bombing the runway and it was too dangerous to chance a landing. The officers were informed that the British had captured an airfield near Eindhoven and Calhoun's C-47 turned to land there. En route, several fighters were spotted, but they were too far away to determine if they were friend or foe. As the fighters rapidly closed on the transport, everyone on board braced themselves for the worst, but then they were recognized as friendlies, P-51 Mustangs. The fighters overtook the C-47 quickly, passing so close that the ship rocked.

Lieutenant Calhoun's plane finally touched down on the Eindhoven airstrip. The plane rolled onto one of the flanking taxiways and kept rolling. Calhoun was told to throw out his bag first and jump out after it. As soon as the officers were off the plane, the C-47 taxied back around to the top of the runway and took off. All during this time, British fighters were landing, refueling and rearming, and were taking off again to go back into action. It was a "hot area," Calhoun thought.

The 17th Airborne's officers first were taken to the 101st Airborne Division's headquarters, which had been established in a local monastery. They then were taken by truck by the 101st to the 82nd Airborne's headquarters in Nijmagen to meet with Brigadier General James M. Gavin, the commander of the 82nd. Gavin's headquarters was set up near the 'Baby Hatchery,' as the men called the four-story hospital being used by the SS for the procreation of the Master Race. There, Dutch women who had become pregnant by SS men bore their 'Aryan' children. Gavin had kicked out the women and moved in his own wounded. Lieutenant Calhoun slept overnight in the hospital and, the next morning, he and the others met with Gavin.

Gavin split the officers up, some went to the 82nd and some to the 101st. Back at the 101st's headquarters, General Maxwell Taylor told the officers coming to his division, "I'm gonna put you in the front lines and I don't want to see you back here except Friday nights to take a shower. Then you'll get right back up to the front lines. I'm gonna send you on every patrol they'll go on up there. You're gonna get some experience." Calhoun and E Company's Kenyon were sent to the 501st Parachute Infantry on the Island near Heteren, about two miles from Arnhem. Colonel 'Jumpy' Johnson, in command of the 501st, told Calhoun to stick with A and F Companies, both of which were on the line. Calhoun spent a total of nine days in Holland, dodging 88mms and starlight flares, and patrolling the line.

On 15 November, Lieutenant Calhoun returned from Holland. That same day, the regiment marched to Chilbolten Airfield, located about one half mile south-west of Chilbolten proper, for its first overseas review. The review was organized exclusively by the enlisted men of the regiment and First Sergeant Donovan, being the most senior first sergeant, was in charge of the whole thing. Accompanying Major General William M. Miley, the 17th Airborne's CO, were Lieutenant General Louis Brereton, commander of the First Allied Airborne Army, Major General Matthew B. Ridgeway, commander of XVIII Airborne Corps, and Major General Paul L. Williams, commanding the IXth Troop Carrier Command. During the ceremony, troopers of the 507th Parachute Infantry were decorated for their role in the Normandy invasion, while overhead the division's artillery liaison planes flew past the reviewing stand.[65] All the brass agreed that it was the best review they had ever observed, and Donovan was rightly proud of the remarks. On the twenty-third, General Miley announced that 1st Battalion, 513th was judged best in review by General Ridgeway.

On 20 November, eighteen replacements joined the company from the 12th Replacement Depot. F Company was now carrying eight officers and 170 enlisted men on its roster. Among the new men was twenty-one year old Private Raymond L. 'Sam' Lightcap from Hazel Green, Wisconsin. In 1941, Lightcap was working in Washington, D.C., pushing paper for the Department of Agriculture. Even then, he could see the United States was heading towards war. "We were shipping war materials to England by the thousands of tons," he said, and German U-boats were sinking American ships. "I remember stoning the Japanese embassy on that Sunday in the afternoon after we heard the news [of Pearl Harbor]. There must have been five thousand people there doing the same thing I was till the police come along and run us out of there." After Pearl Harbor, Lightcap returned home, hoping to be "pulled into service" with some of his friends. Two weeks after giving up his government job deferment, Lightcap was called into service and reported to Fort Meade, Maryland. Eventually he was assigned to the 87th Infantry Division at Camp McCain, Mississippi.[66]

Lightcap and his company commander, Captain Hicks, didn't get along. Lightcap and another private were put on guard duty one afternoon and never relieved. When the battalion commander caught wind of it, Captain Hicks caught hell. Hicks struck at Lightcap and the other soldier by having them dig ten-squares that night and then assigning him to every shitty detail for the next two months. Lightcap figured the only way he could get away from Hicks was to join the paratroopers. In late November, with parachute training completed, Lightcap boarded the *Queen Mary* at Camp Shanks, New York and sailed to Glasgow, Scotland.[67]

Lightcap found Barton Stacey spare with regard to comforts, and discovered it difficult to penetrate the circle of F Company's old timers. He had plenty of opportunity to talk with the other men, he went to chow with them, he even became a barber and tailor to some of them, but he never got to know any of them well. Many of the other new men were in the same situation he was.[68]

On 25 November, the 513th held a "regimental parade" at which 140 enlisted men of the 513th, including ten from F Company, received the Army Good Conduct Medal from Colonel Coutts and Major Moir, the regimental adjutant. Some men said it was the hardest medal to earn in the Army. "I never got it," remembered Munafo. "I never gave a damn anyway. It was a Boy Scout medal." Private Imre saw the awards as contradictory. "Here we were training to kill people with piano wire and their giving us good conduct medals," said Imre. "I thought it was laughable."

On Thanksgiving Day, the division celebrated this peculiarly American holiday with a peculiarly American institution: the Thanksgiving Day football game. The 513th Parachute Infantry Regiment's football team played the 507th's. "It was just like a pro game," commented Grice, who made first-string guard and tackle. At the final gun, however, the 513th had lost 20 to 0. "They just had a better quarterback than us," Grice insisted. After the game, General Miley, Colonel Edson

Raff of the 507th, General Whitelaw, the division Chief of Staff, and Colonel Coutts visited the regimental area for dinner.[69]

Even though they were away from home, the men spent Thanksgiving with their pals and had a great time. For dinner, the division consumed some "7 tons of turkey, 1,407 pounds of candy, 93 pounds of cranberry makin's, 703 pounds of dehydrated sweet potatoes and 1128 number 2 1/2 cans of pumpkin."[70] Unfortunately, the glider infantrymen of the 194th received something they didn't want. They were served a batch of poorly stored turkeys and the whole regiment ended up with the 'GIs'.

On the morning of 11 December, F Company and the rest of regiment left Barton-Stacey Camp A and moved sixty miles by truck to a marshaling area. The only good thing about the waiting was all the food, especially the steaks. When the men lined up for chow one day, Sergeant John La Riccia, eyeing the spread, commented to one of the Air Corps KPs, "Boy, what a great job you got." "What?" the airman replied. "I don't get none of that." La Riccia took the good food as affirmation of Airborne's elite status. For four days, the men sat at the airport ready to go, waiting for the orders that would take them to battle. Though rumors of the division's target abounded, according to Major I. A. Edwards, the 17th was preparing to drop into Holland north of the Rhine. "The aircraft were parked and loaded," said Edwards. "Everybody chuted-up three times," but the operation was called off.[71]

At 1445 hours on 15 December, F Company left the marshaling area and returned to Barton-Stacey Camp A. Private Frank Munafo was happy to be back. He and his friend, PFC John Hall, immediately resumed their nocturnal jaunts into Andover for the fish & chips they so dearly loved. Likewise, PFC Greenstrand and Private William I. 'Tommy' Thomson, Second Platoon's medic whom Greenstrand had grown close to, returned to their weekend trips to the little basement pub they frequented in Winchester, one of the quaint villages near Salisbury. After he returned from Holland, Lieutenant Calhoun, never really willing to draw firmly the line that separated officers from enlisted men, would occasionally join them. Greenstrand had captured the favor of the pub's small crowd of locals and GIs when he started singing *I've Got A Lovely Bunch of Coconuts* in the improvised British accent he had adopted. Calhoun envied Greenstrand his gift. Not only was Greenstrand a good soldier, but all his joking and carrying on gave Second Platoon's morale a constant shot in the arm and endeared him to the English. The lieutenant was equally fond of Thomson.

Just before Christmas, Lieutenant Calhoun sent the following letter to Private Bob Greenstrand's mother:

I wish to take this opportunity to write to you in regards to your fine son Elwin (Bob), whom I have had the pleasure to work with as his Platoon Leader for the Past 18 Months.

He is An Outstanding Soldier & One of the hardest workers in the Platoon. He has helped Out excellently in Keeping the Boys Morale up with his jokes & Actions. Since we have been in England He has mastered the way English people talk & no matter where he goes he makes friends quickly with both Soldiers & Civilians by Joking with them in their English brogue.

I Know that I Can depend upon him in any Mission I & My Platoon are sent on in Actual Combat.

When Greenstrand had finished his song, he returned to his friends. Lieutenant Calhoun, who was sitting at one of the tables, started to tell them about how he was trying to get them promoted. Greenstrand and Tommy just leaned against a post listening to the lieutenant. Both of them were getting drunk, which, according to Calhoun, was their custom. Suddenly, Greenstrand raised his hand and interrupted the lieutenant mid stream. "Not me," he said, objecting to even the thought of a promotion. "I don't want any responsibility in this army. I just want to get this over with and go home."

4

And into the Fire

Defense of the Meuse River
16 December 1944 - 3 January 1945

During the fall of 1944, the battle on the central western front was being fought by the American First, Third and Ninth Armies, which together comprised the Twelfth Army Group. On the northern flank along the Roer River near Aachen and only thirty miles from Germany was the Ninth Army. In the south, in Luxembourg, was the Third Army under Lieutenant General George S. Patton, Jr. In the center of the front was the First Army. The southernmost and largest part of the First Army sector was held by the VIII Corps under Major General Troy H. Middleton whose headquarters were at Bastogne, Belgium. There, in the Ardennes Forrest, the front stretched from Losheim, Germany in the north, south to the Our River's intersection with the Franco-German border – eighty-eight miles of "rugged hills, high plateaus, deep cut valleys, and restricted road nets." "The Ardennes," a popular travel guide states, "are an ancient mountain range worn down to wooded hills, largely bypassed by modern development, where villages and isolated farmhouses all have slate walls and slate roofs, and where you can walk alone for hours."[1]

Rotated through Middleton's VIII Corps were green divisions received for combat indoctrination and battle-weary divisions released from the front for "re-equipment and rest." On 16 December, VIII Corps was composed of the 4th, 28th, and 106th Infantry Divisions, Combat Command B of the 9th Armored Division, and the 14th Cavalry Group. The 4th Division had been badly mauled in the Huertgen Forest. Likewise, the 28th Division had recently experienced heavy action with the First Army in its drive to the Roer. Combat Command B was green, as was the 106th Division which had arrived at the front only four days earlier. VIII Corps' reserves consisted of one armored combat command and four battalions of combat engineers.[2]

Information gathered from prisoners captured by 28th Infantry Division patrols early in the month indicated that there were only four German divisions, the *18th Infantry*, *26th Volksgrenadier*, *352d Infantry*, and *212th Infantry*, between Middleton's command and the Rhine River. The Allied command was firmly convinced that these formations did not have the men or material to undertake offensive operations. Furthermore, in spite of the fact that there were approximately one million Wehrmacht troops defending Hitler's West Wall, there was still an air of confidence among the Allies that the Germans would stay on the defensive. Therefore, from 12 December on, when forward elements of the 28th Division reported hearing the sounds of vehicle formations moving inside the German lines, the reports were ignored. Rumors of panzer divisions massing behind the enemy front reached American headquarters, but they remained unconfirmed. The credibility of any such rumors, especially from civilian sources, would have to be established before the Allies would concede an army they believed to be all-but-defeated would go on the offensive in the heart of the worst European winter in forty years. Confirmation of the rumors came abruptly on 16 December at 0500 hours, when, amid a clinging predawn fog, German guns spoke along the entire length of the Ardennes front. By 0800 hours, twenty-five German divisions had launched on what would be one of Hitler's greatest gambles of the war.[3]

Three hours after the attack began, German spearheads, driving north toward St. Vith, had penetrated three miles into the positions of the 14th Cavalry Group. The German advance was only temporarily slowed when the 106th Infantry Division was committed in support of the 14th Cavalry. At that same moment, in the south, Combat Command B and the 4th Infantry Division received German feints which effectively prevented them from deploying northward. Meanwhile, the 28th Infantry Division found itself fighting alone against the *2nd SS Panzer Division*, *Panzer Lehr*, three infantry divisions, and the *5th Fallschirmjäger Division*. German thrusts penetrated four and a half miles through the Keystone Division's sector cutting the North-South Highway.[4]

If successful, the operation – *Wacht am Rhein* (Watch on the Rhine) as it was dubbed by the Germans – would split the Allied front in two. 250,000 German soldiers would drive northwest for the Belgian port city of Antwerp, seizing stock-piles of Allied supplies at Liège on their way. In the north, the British 21st Army Group would be cut-off from its bases of supply and forced to withdraw as they had done at Dunkirk four years earlier. Thus left, the American armies, it was hoped, might abandon their campaign in Europe as well. At the very least, Hitler hoped to hold off the Allies long enough for Germany to develop its super weap-ons with which to force them into submission or into a negotiated peace.[5] With his western border thus secured, Hitler then would shift divisions to the Eastern Front where it was hoped they could stem the advancing tide of the Red Army.

On the seventeenth, German pressure increased all along the front. In the north the, situation at St. Vith became critical. To defend the town, General Middleton assigned Combat Command B and the 168th Engineer Combat Battalion which had been committed from VIII Corps reserves the day before. They were sup-ported by elements of the 7th Armored Division that had been released from Major General Leonard T. Gerow's V Corps further north. More critical than St. Vith, however, was the situation of the 106th Infantry Division, which was receiving the heaviest enemy concentrations in its sector. By 0900 hours, two of the division's infantry regiments were cut-off and surrounded and most of its infantrymen were out of ammunition. Meanwhile, under intense German pressure, the 28th Infantry Division was forced to withdraw to the west bank of the Our River. On the south-ern shoulder of the German penetration, only the 4th Infantry Division still held its ground.[6]

After some initial sluggishness, the Supreme Commander, General Dwight D. Eisenhower, began to respond to the German attack on the evening of the sev-enteenth. Reports indicated that the main axis of the German advance was turning perceptibly to the north and northwest. SHEAF correctly ascertained from this information that the initial German objective was the capture of the great supply depot at Liège and that the ultimate objective was the capture of the port of Antwerp. Eisenhower took immediate steps, therefore, to reinforce the Ardennes front and establish a strong defense of the Meuse River, the last natural barrier resting be-tween the Germans and Liège and Antwerp. At 1930 hours, XVIII Airborne Corps, headquartered at Epernay, France, received orders from SHAEF by telephone. Lieu-tenant General Matthew B. Ridgeway, its commander, was at that time in England overseeing readiness tests at the 17th Airborne Division's 'rear' headquarters with its commander, General William Miley. General Eisenhower left word for Ridgeway that the only two divisions in the SHAEF reserve – the 101st and 82nd Airborne – were to be committed to the battle.[7]

In Ridgeway's absence, Major General James M. Gavin, commander of the 82nd Airborne Division headquartered at Sissonne, France, assumed command of the XVIII Airborne Corps early on the evening of the seventeenth. The next morning, Gavin met with General Courtney Hodges, commander of the First U.S. Army, in Spa, Belgium to discuss the deployment of the two airborne divisions. Rather than being sent to reinforce the Meuse River line, the 101st and 82nd were assigned to General Bradley's 12th Army Group who needed them in First Army's zone to fill the widening gap between the V Corps and VIII Corps. The 101st Airborne Division was committed to the defense of Bastogne; the 82nd Airborne Division to the high ground in the vicinity of Werbomont, twelve miles southeast of Spa, on the Bulge's northern shoulder.[8]

Later that day, First Allied Airborne Army (FAAA) was ordered by Eisenhower to transport the 17th Airborne Division to the Continent by air. The defense of the Meuse would fall to this green division. Joining Miley's 17th in this emergency reinforcement was the British 6th Airborne Division – to be transported from England by ship – and the 11th Armored Division, just arrived to the Continent.[9] The remaining divisions that were yet to be transported from England to the Continent – the 66th, 69th, and 76th Infantry, and the 8th Armored – were committed to the battle as well. By the end of January, no American divisions would remain in England.[10]

The hasty deployments were warranted. Throughout the eighteenth, the American situation in the Ardennes continued to deteriorate. With its lines overstretched, its communications shattered, and its headquarters at Wiltz overrun, the 28th Division, which had been fighting virtually unsupported against overwhelming odds, finally collapsed.[11]

That same day, accompanied by Air Chief Marshall Tedder, General Eisenhower met in Verdun with Generals Omar Bradley, George S. Patton, and Jacob L. Devers to discuss the developments in the Ardennes. Eisenhower started the meeting off confidently: "The present situation is to be regarded as one of opportunity for us and not of disaster. There will be only cheerful faces at this conference table." General Patton jumped in enthusiastically, "Hell, let's have the guts to let the [sonsabitches] go all the way to Paris. Then we'll really cut 'em off and chew 'em up." Everyone smiled at Patton's remark, however; Eisenhower informed the assembly that the German attack would not be permitted to cross the Meuse River. Ike wanted to begin counterattacking as soon as possible but decided it was not imperative that a counterattack begin from both flanks at once. He wanted Field Marshal Sir Bernard Law Montgomery's 21st Army Group to "plug the holes in the north" while Patton launched a "co-ordinated attack from the south." Eisenhower informed Field Marshal Montgomery of his intentions that day.[12]

Movement orders reached General Miley at 17th Airborne Division headquarters on 19 December. Though urgent, the division's move was delayed as the C-47s of the 53rd Wing, IX Troop Carrier Command, originally slated to transport the division to France, were diverted for emergency resupply drops to "encircled ground forces in the Ardennes and to the Third and First Armies." The job of moving the 17th fell, therefore, to the 50th and 52nd Troop Carrier Wings and the IX Pathfinder Group. By the time things were sorted out, however, the weather closed in grounding the IX Troop Carrier Command for three days. In the meantime, movement orders were issued to the several organizations of the division which began preparations.[13]

At Barton Stacey, the 513th Parachute Infantry Regiment began preparing for its move south to the airfield at Chilbolton from where they would fly to France. Captain Reynolds went to his company and said simply, "This is it; we're going. You've got six hours to pack your two duffel bags." PFC Greenstrand stuffed his belongings into the bags, not knowing he wouldn't see them again for nearly two months. Staff Sergeant Seacott never saw his again at all. Italian prisoners being housed near Barton Stacey broke into the storage room and stole his and several others.[14]

Officers knew something of the nature of the mission, but the enlisted men, according to Laufer, "didn't know shit." The only thing they did know was that it was something big. "It was pretty traumatic in a way," commented Don Newhouse. However, the division had been sitting in England since August and the men were ready to go. "Send us," said Imre confidently.[15]

Private Munafo stripped his .30 caliber machine-gun, cleaned it up and oiled it, and put it back together. Then he cleaned up his M1, checked his sleeping bag, shovel, trench knife, and other equipment, and filled his canteen. He also drew a bandoleer of ammunition for his M1, and two boxes of .30 caliber machine-gun ammunition. Outside, the temperature was dropping and a soft snow had begun to fall. The officers started the men on assembly problems – jumping out of the back of trucks to gage how fast they could organize. The men's boots left prints in the new white blanket covering the ground.[16]

Private Charles Simpson had been in the hospital for two weeks recuperating from a bout with pneumonia he had contracted after three days of exercises in the rain and a tiring trip to London when word of the move arrived. Simpson knew he should have reported himself sick before going on pass, but he hadn't wanted to give up his only opportunity to see London. Not wanting to be left behind either, Simpson asked his buddy, Private Bill Maxwell, to do him a favor. Through the back window of the hospital ward, Simpson told Maxwell to get him out. "He was just a private like myself," commented Simpson, "but he had a line." Maxwell convinced the doctors that Captain Reynolds needed Simpson back desperately, so they let him go.[17]

Early on the morning of the twentieth, British Field Marshal Montgomery, acting independently, ordered his XXX Corps to positions near Namur and Liège where it could reinforce a retreat to the Meuse River if one became necessary. XXX Corps also prepared the bridges over the Meuse for demolitions in the event they had to be destroyed. That day, Montgomery wrote to Sir Alan Brooke, the British Chief of Staff, that the American leaders had lost control of the situation in the Ardennes. "The American forces," he said, "have been cut clean in half and the Germans can reach the Meuse at Namur without any opposition."[18]

Later that same morning, General Patton arrived in Luxembourg at Twelfth Army Group Headquarters to confer with General Bradley. Just after 0900 hours, the telephone rang. It was Eisenhower informing Bradley that Montgomery was being given operational control of American forces in the northern sector of the Bulge. Patton was upset by the news but maintained his composure. He then ordered General Troy Middleton's VIII Corps to give ground. If the Bulge was getting bigger, then Patton would let it. The further the Germans advanced, the closer they would come to overextended themselves. When they did, Patton planned to strike from the south, into their left flank.[19]

On the morning of the twenty-first, the 695 men of the 2nd Battalion, 513th Parachute Infantry formed up at the motor pool area. With the addition of the service company and the demolitions platoon, all together, Lieutenant Colonel Miller had 792 men under his command. By 0900 hours, the 2nd Battalion, mounted in vans, trucks, and buses, was speeding past the east exit of Camp Barton Stacey bound for the Chilbolton airfield. Preceding Miller's command, the 1st Battalion, with 853 men, and the 3rd Battalion, with 735 men, had departed for Chilbolton earlier that morning. All tolled, a total of 2,380 men were in the 513th when it left for Europe.

F Company arrived at Chilbolton, one of seven airfields designated for marshaling and embarkation for the 17th Airborne Division's move to the Continent, at 1015 hours. Very near the division's barracks at Barton Stacey, Chilbolton had previously served a variety of formations. The field had been occupied until 23 August by the Ninth Air Force's 368th Fighter Group until they were redeployed to France. Following their departure, the field became home to the IX Troop Carrier Command's 442nd Troop Carrier Group of the 53rd Troop Carrier Wing for Operation MARKET. Following to the Holland drop, the 442nd was transferred to the Continent and the field became the United Kingdom support airfield for the 53rd Wing.[20]

Four airfields near Rheims were designated to receive the 17th Airborne. The 513th had been scheduled to depart for one of them, A-70, starting at 1000 hours – the 2nd Battalion and F Company being scheduled to fly with the 3rd Serial at 1200 hours – but poor flying conditions prevented the airborne echelons from leaving. The division's seaborne echelon, however, sailed for France as planned.[21]

Inadvertently, the 513th was forced into a 'hurry up and wait' situation. 2nd Battalion was billeted in buildings in the airfield's warehouse area. Companies drew two blankets for each man for their stay; the Air Corps ordered that they were to be "neatly folded" and left on the cots in the barracks when the battalion departed. A dispensary was opened and sick call was held after breakfast. Guards were mounted by the 1st Battalion and all personnel were prevented from entering or leaving the field. Blackout regulations were enforced.[22]

Meanwhile, preparations for movement were forwarded. Colonel Coutts ordered all men to sew American flags on their right shoulder for the purpose of identification. K and D rations were issued and during the afternoon the men were checked to ensure that they had the authorized loads of ammunition (most men drew as much as they could carry). In addition, Fifty-eight tons of ammunition were being brought with the regiment to France by air. PFC Imre's burden included his personal load, the baseplate and additional ammunition for Second Platoon's 60mm mortar, and thirty pounds of C2. To prevent accidents with loaded weapons and explosives, the officers instructed the men not to load their weapons or even insert loaded clips into them, and, furthermore, no Gamon grenades were issued.[23]

Although the men were supplied with an abundance of ammunition, there was one glaring deficiency – winter clothing, especially footwear. The winter of 1944-1945 was the coldest Europe had experienced in four decades and the American Army was ill prepared for it. Although there were many reasons for this shortage, the average infantryman was simply disgusted by what seemed to be the Army's ineptitude. In 1997, Ed Sarrell still had harsh words for the American Service of Supply. "They knew where we were going and they had the time," he said, "but we never received satisfactory winter clothing."[24]

Privates Newhouse and Laufer were among those lucky enough to have over-shoes, but most men didn't. Among those issued overshoes, many threw them away as soon as they got to the front because they were cumbersome and prevented a man from running fast. Many men didn't go into the fighting with a change of socks either. The move to the marshaling area was so hurried that there had been no time to issue them. Newhouse scrounged up a couple pairs of thick, homespun English wool socks which he put on right away. Laufer tucked his one extra pair safely into a leg pocket. There weren't enough overcoats or gloves, and some of the men were already cutting up the issued gray blankets, those that were to have been left on the cots "neatly folded," to make scarves or hoods. Winter sleeping bags with blanket linings were issued, but after F Company left Rheims they never saw them again.[25]

The shortages bred a 'me-first' attitude among the men. This is not to say that they would not risk their lives for each other in combat, but when it came to staying warm, everyone had to look out for himself, to make sure he got socks, that he got new boots, that he got the overshoes. "Hurrah for me and to hell with everybody else," was Laufer's attitude, and he wasn't alone.

On 21 December, F Company men were exercised in the morning. In the afternoon, they cleaned their weapons for an inspection by the officers, and for more than two hours were lectured on the prevention of trench foot and about the seriousness of looting. The men were then further occupied with the policing of the area. Later in the afternoon there were more calisthenics.[26]

That same morning, with the weather showing signs of clearing, General Williams, commanding the IX Troop Carrier Command, contacted Brigadier General Julian M. Chappell of the 50th Troop Carrier Wing at Chartres. Williams ordered Chappell, "get an airline operation in action to transport passengers and cargo of the 17th Airborne Division from England to France." Consequently, Chappell ordered 224 C-47s to fly to three airfields in England on the twenty-third to begin the airlift.[27]

On Friday, 22 December, the routine of inspections and calisthenics, and lectures and policing continued, but, at 2024 hours, Colonel Coutts issued instructions to Ace Miller for the upcoming move:

> Info received some destination fields already strafed by Germans. On arrival at destination fields, all individual weapons loaded and deployment made with utmost speed. All troops not actually engaged in unloading quickly move to assembly areas off field and dispersed foxholes and slit trenches dug. Airguards posted at destination fields in assembly areas and during movement to concentration areas. Extended interval maintained between vehicles during movement. Airguards posted on each truck, tops off trucks. Radio silence except for 610's, 300's and 536's.[28]

The 17th Airborne Division was about to begin its movement to France.

At dawn on 23 December, 112 C-47s flew to Chilbolton and the first echelon – including the 513th Regimental Headquarters, and 1st Battalion and advance details from all units – departed for Airfield A-70 at Crepy, six miles northwest of Laon/Couvran, France.[29]

On Christmas Eve, the second echelon of the 513th, including F Company, loaded into C-47s and, at 1005 hours, took off for Airfield A-70. Private Lightcap's plane had gone about a third of the way down the runway when it stopped. The barracks bags had been loaded into the tail making it so heavy the pilot couldn't get the ship up. The bags were redistributed, the plane returned to the runway, and Lightcap's ship was soon airborne. First Sergeant Donovan, the company clerk Corporal John M. Eibert, and three men from company headquarters took the next to the last C-47, "loaded to the gills with C-2."[30]

By the time the planes arrived at A-70 and the men had unloaded their equipment it was 1330 hours. The field was about twenty-five miles northwest of Rheims and from there it was another forty miles by motor convoy in six-by-six trucks to Camp Mourmelon Le Grande (headquarters of the 101st Airborne Division). Airguards were posted – two motor columns had been strafed by the Germans southeast of Rheims that morning – and the trucks pulled out. The 1st echelon, already en route when F Company landed in France, arrived in Mourmelon in the afternoon. The 2nd echelon, and the seaborne echelon, arrived later the same day. Donovan and Eibert waited at A-70 for Captain Reynolds, who had taken the last plane and, together, they moved on to Mourmelon, arriving at 1435. Going into the Bulge, the 17th Airborne numbered 832 officers and 12,711 enlisted men. F Company listed eight officers and 161 enlisted men. According to Royal Donovan, morale was high among the men and they seemed eager to get into the fight.[31]

At Mourmelon, the officers had the company fall out and so they could check the roster for AWOLs. Then, each platoon was assigned to one of the numerous small barracks. The accommodations were anything but comfortable. There was no hot food and, because the barracks were small, the men had to sleep two-to-a-bunk or take turns. For most it was a miserable night, but many of the men were too excited to sleep anyway. The idea that action was immanent was reinforced when the order came for every two men to double-up on duffel bags to save space in the trucks when the regiment moved. Privates Kinkus and Newhouse were among those who packed their belongings into a single bag, leaving behind all but the most essential of their possessions.[32]

Meanwhile, General Miley went ahead to VIII Corps headquarters at Florenville. There, Miley was told that the commander of the 11th Armored Division, General Charles S. Kilburn, was "greatly disturbed about the condition of the defenses of the Meuse River line." Upon a visit to the 11th Armored, Miley was informed by the 11th Armored's Chief of Staff that Kilburn wanted General Miley to move the 17th Airborne Division up to the Meuse River as quickly as possible. "Feed them up one battalion at a time if you can't get them there any other way," were the instructions Kilburn left. At that time, however, the 17th Airborne Division had not yet been assigned to VIII Corps. Therefore, Miley informed Kilburn's Chief of Staff that he [Miley] was still attached to the 12th Army Group with the general mission of defending the Meuse from Givet north and "had no authority to proceed in this manner."[33]

No special services were held to mark Christmas Day, nor was there any hot Christmas dinner. Instead, the men were raised for calihoopies and a run. Officers tried to keep the men occupied by reviewing the nomenclature of the M1 rifle, but some of the troopers snuck off to town. "They didn't know where the hell they were going, but a lot of them went anyway", remembered Laufer. Showers were made available, but only the first got hot water. The others boiled water in their helmets over their GI stoves so they could "douche themselves off," as they put it.

During the day, General Miley called 12th Army Group headquarters. From the tone of the conversation, Miley recognized that General Bradley was intensely concerned about the safety of the Meuse defensive line. At that time, the enemy penetration had reached to within only miles of Dinant. Therefore, 12th Army Group informed Miley then that the 17th Airborne had been placed under the operational control of VIII Corps. When Miley contacted General Troy Middleton, he was told to get his division up to the Meuse and build a defense around the towns of Montmayon, Stenay, Sedan, and Verdun. The 11th Armored, which had held these positions, was ordered to take up a supporting position to back up the paratroopers. Forthwith, Miley immediately returned to Mourmelon to prepare the division to move.[34]

Each regiment of the 17th Airborne Division had been assigned bridges over the Meuse River to defend "at all cost" – a task requiring the division to be spread thinly along an eighty-mile-long front extending from Verdun north to Givet in northern France. General Miley divided the division front in two. General Whitelaw was placed in command of the northern sector, from Sedan to Givet. The southern sector, from Sedan to Verdun, was the charge of General Phelps, the division artillery officer. Each of these sectors was in turn divided into two sub-sectors. The 513th was given the southern-most section of the line.[35]

The 2nd Battalion, 513th was instructed to hold all the bridges across the Meuse River in the Stenay area. All bridges and approaching road surfaces were to be prepared for demolitions and each charge was set with a minimum of three means of detonation. Each bridge was under the command of an officer who was instructed that they could blow a bridge, but only to prevent it from falling to the enemy, and then only on the orders of the commander of the 11th Armored Division or VIII Corps. Defended roadblocks were established on the east side of the Meuse to prevent the penetration of enemy armor, and all outposts were to be provided with adequate signals equipment. 3rd Battalion of the 513th had a similar mission in the Verdun area and 1st Battalion, with the attached 411th Quartermaster Truck Company, established a mobile reserve in the vicinity of Cornay.[36]

It was about 1700 hours and, through the falling snow, a long line of open semi-trailers closed up on Mourmelon. 2nd Battalion was ordered to fall out, and as "each unit assembled," wrote Calhoun, "we marched into the large open trailers." As Private Newhouse walked by the mess hall on his way to the trucks, he yelled to the cooks, "Have you cooked up the turkey yet?"[37]

"Yeah," one of them replied, "but we're saving it for the 101st as soon as we can get it up to them." Newhouse was not as disappointed as one might expect, however. Everybody was a little homesick, but F Company men were their own family. The men were all gung-ho, and most were happy to be spending Christmas together in spite of the circumstances.[38]

"As soon as they had it full the tail gate went up," reported Calhoun. "[Then, they] gave us, 'At Ease'." At about 1900 hours, with the battalion loaded, the trucks moved out, "destination secret." Captain Reynolds may have known where they were headed, but, according to Lieutenant Calhoun, no one else had been briefed on their objective.[39]

Before leaving Mourmelon, Private Dwight Caton, a rifleman in the First Platoon, composed a letter to his mother from 'Somewhere in France'. "Dear Mom," Caton wrote, "I know it has been an awfully long time since I wrote you and I am really sorry. Here it is Christmas and it don't seem like Christmas at all here in France. For dinner we will have "C" rations. Maybe next Christmas I'll be home to enjoy a real dinner with you. I wish you would write & tell me whether or not you received that $160.00 I sent you. Well, Mom, that is just about all I can say except that it may be a long time before you hear from me again. Your loving son, Dwight."[40]

F Company's ride through the frozen French countryside was a long and cold one, and the trucks didn't stop. "There was no way to sit down," wrote Calhoun; the men were packed tight and "the open sides of the trailer came up to our arm pits." "Pee calls," remembered Greenstrand, "were very difficult. You had to work your way to the side and have some of the guys hoist you up high enough to get it over the side. I think we peed icicles anyway." The metal trailer beds radiated intense cold and some of the men were already developing the first stages of frostbite on their feet.[41]

The trucks came to a halt at about 0700 on the twenty-sixth, and the men unloaded, glad to be able to move their numb bodies again. Lieutenant Calhoun was informed that they "were in Stenay, France, on the Meuse River." E and F Companies were instructed to set up in and around an abandoned papermill and connected warehouse. The structure was situated on the west bank of the Meuse, about three hundred yards from the river. The mill and warehouse building was very large, and made entirely of local field stone. A waterwheel, set in the Meuse but now idle, had once powered the mill's machinery. "It wasn't much warmer than outside," recalled Greenstrand of his new home, "but at least we were out of the elements." The men were not allowed to have any fires so to get warm they buried themselves in the stacks of paper stored inside the mill. Eventually their own body heat warmed them up. Amid the debris scattered in the paper warehouse, Greenstrand found a German magazine. In it, he discovered a cartoon, blatantly anti-American and anti-Semitic. The artist had rendered a withered milk cow in the crude likeness of President Roosevelt. Hanging around Mr. Roosevelt's neck, in place of the cow bell, was the Star of David swinging prominently. The cow's business end, and a pile of dung, stared at Greenstrand from the page. The caption read, "*Europeesche Kultuur ? . . . prrrt.*"[42]

There were two bridges at Stenay. The first spanned a small tributary about three hundred yards south of the warehouse. The main military bridge crossed the river about one thousand yards southeast of the mill. A twenty-foot-wide, hard-surfaced road passed over both bridges and continued into Stenay, on the eastern side of the river. Two 60mm mortars and three .50 caliber machine-guns were set up around the main bridge, and four .50 caliber machine-guns were positioned around the smaller bridge. Some 37mm and 57mm antitank guns and additional mortars and machine-guns were situated to cover the approaches to both bridges and the roads leading to the bridges on the enemy side of the town. The battalion's four 81mm mortars were set up behind the paper mill. As this was done, the bridges were wired for demolition.

Railroad tracks running parallel to the river's course passed behind the warehouse. From PW Camp 2019, located in the southern corner of the town, hundreds of German prisoners were being led across the bridges to this rail line where they were shoved into a long line of 'forty & eights', boxcars designed to hold forty men or eight horses. The American guards, what some of the fighting men called "limited service bastards," were beating the Germans prisoners and cursing them as they prodded them into box cars. "There's no sense in it," thought Lightcap as he watched, horrified. "The German prisoners were going as fast as they could into these damn cars." The guards, Lightcap thought, were just trying to show "what big men they were."[43]

F Company's mission was to guard the western bridge approaches to Stenay. The platoon leaders placed the men in some old foxholes along the river and ordered improvements to the positions. Digging was tough work, though. Most of the foxholes were shallow scrapes with the hard earth cut from the holes stacked around them forming makeshift parapets. One trooper decided to try and crack through the layer of frost with a grenade. He carefully placed the grenade on the ground and took off, but as he ran away, he "stumbled and fell, breaking his thumb." The grenade went off with a loud *chunk*, but it had no effect on the frozen ground.[44]

Lieutenant Gilles reviewed his platoon's positions, shifting fields of fire and ordering some holes dug deeper. He wanted to know where every man was and make sure they were all protected. "He was good that way," stated Laufer. Many other men, however, like Staff Sergeant Gus Seacott, a squad leader in First Platoon, saw Gilles differently. Seacott thought Gilles was always "too 'by the book'." Seacott often joked that, before Gilles did anything, he had to consult the appropriate Army pamphlet on the subject. Yet, according to Private Tom Connolly, and despite his exertions to distance himself from the enlisted men, "Gilles had a side that. . . some of the men didn't see – a warmth, consideration, and an interest in the men." After Gilles was done touring the platoon's positions, he, Private Arrowood, and four other men setup the platoon's headquarters in an abandoned boxcar that overlooked the mill and the bridge.[45]

Private Tom Connolly was following in his father's footsteps – almost literally. "Merry Christmas," he wrote to his family. "I love you people at home. I think I'm standing where dad stood in WWI." Connolly's father, who still suffered from exposure to mustard gas, had fought over the same ground with the 26th 'Yankee' Division in the Great War.[46]

Lieutenant Calhoun was ordered to defend the roadblock at the main bridge and placed his men on the south side of the road. He set up Second Platoon's CP in the switching house about a quarter mile south of the papermill. It wasn't close but it was good shelter. The wreckage of a German Me-109 protruded from the snow between the two buildings. "The Third Platoon did traffic control and identified and questioned all passengers of vehicles approaching the roadblock." The men defending the roadblocks kept carefully concealed while a few men waved flashlights and shouted "Halt!" to stop approaching vehicles. After a vehicle came to a halt, a guard approached from the rear while the occupants were covered. The men on check-point duty paid special attention to prevent the "enemy from infiltrating through their lines employing ruses and disguise." All of the men were constantly apprised of the signs and countersigns. Often the passwords were words that, the soldiers thought, the average German couldn't pronounce.[47]

Most of the men's time manning the roadblocks was spent trying to keep warm. Private Newhouse and five other troopers constructed a dug-out a few yards from the bridge, and just forward of one of the battalion's .50 caliber machine-gun positions. It was only about four feet deep, but they scrounged up some pierced steel planking to make a roof and covered that over with cardboard and then with dirt. Then they filled the floor with straw. They then filled bottles with diesel and cut pieces of their jump ropes to fashion wicks. These provided light, but they "smoked like hell" and covered them with soot.[48]

When Private Frank DeSanto, one of the November replacements, was ordered to work a shift on the road block, he asked Newhouse if he could borrow his wristwatch. The watch, a gift from his wife, was valuable – his wife had paid $125 for it – but, reluctantly, Newhouse loaned it to him. Four hours later DeSanto returned, claiming he'd lost the watch. It was a dilemma for Newhouse; he couldn't just accuse the guy of being a thief. Newhouse decided to keep silent, hoping the situation would work itself out. Still, deep down, he figured he'd been robbed.[49]

When the company was bedded down that night and it was quiet, Staff Sergeant Seacott decided to have a talk with his brother. E Company was dug in only about fifty yards away, so Seacott figured it would be okay to leave his squad for a few minutes. The brothers discussed what to tell their parents if one or the other of them didn't make it, then Seacott told his brother "Good Luck" and returned to his squad. He found Lieutenant Gilles waiting, furious. Gilles reduced him to private on the spot and took his squad away. Seacott was flabbergasted.[50]

At 2145 hours, a plane was heard approaching the company's positions. Graup, Greenstrand, and Sergeant Gohn, were manning their machine-gun as the plane passed overhead (prior to the move, Staff Sergeant Dean H. Utt, a squad leader in F Company's Second Platoon, went AWOL temporarily, so Lieutenant Calhoun took away Utt's squad and appointed Private Gohn as the new squad leader and promoted him to sergeant). Suddenly, two small bombs detonated with bright flashes about five hundred yards south of the papermill. All of the .50 calibers opened up, filling the sky with arching lines of tracers. Haggard, roused from slumber in the papermill, wasn't sure what was going on until bullets smacked into the concrete floor, then he ran for cover. First Platoon's boxcar was "strafed full of holes," sending Lieutenant Gilles, Arrowood, and the other men running for their lives. Although they were not supposed to, when the .50s started up, Graup, Gohn, and Greenstrand started firing too – Gohn firing the machine-gun from the hip, and Graup and Greenstrand their M1s.[51]

"PFC Slocomb. . . took his light machine-gun in his arms and sprayed the sky with bullets just as [the plane] arrived at the bridge. No hits [were scored] on the German, but several members [of Third Platoon] were mad because it gave our position away," recalled Puckett.[52]

All the extra firing didn't escape Colonel Miller who came down to find out who had been doing the shooting. "I don't know if he ever found out," said Greenstrand, "Calhoun probably saved us again."[53]

After all the commotion was over, Gilles and Arrowood, feeling lucky to be alive, hopped back in their boxcar and went to sleep. "The next night," wrote Arrowood, "we found a house to stay in."

An hour later, the German plane again appeared, this time over Stenay. The only hits the plane scored, however, were on the PW camp wounding fifteen fellow Germans with incendiary bombs.

Every evening thereafter, "a German plane came flying down the river," recalled Puckett. "The men dubbed him 'Bedcheck Charlie' for the hour of his arrival." The only casualty Charlie scored among F Company, however, was a man who, in a rush to take a shot at the plane, shot himself in the foot by mistake.[54]

On 26 December, after having held out for more than ten days, the defenders of Bastogne were relieved by elements of the 4th U.S. Armored Division. Patton was elated, "The German has shot his wad. Prisoners have had no food for from three to five days. We should attack." Patton was convinced that the Germans were finished, and was even more certain that he should begin his attack to close the Bulge immediately, rather than hesitate and run the chance of leaving the Germans a way out as the Allies had done at Falaise in August. But still Montgomery stalled.[55]

Despite the relief of Bastogne, there did not seem to be any drift in German intentions to continue driving northwest for Antwerp. At the same time, numerous "vague and unconfirmed" reports of enemy parachute drops west of the Meuse persisted, requiring further patrols to investigate. No drops were ever confirmed – one excited American report turned out to be equipment bundles dropped from their own planes. Still, Allied planners maintained, the possibility of an enemy parachute drop of division strength existed, and 17th Airborne intelligence reported more than 180,000 German soldiers, and as many as nine hundred tanks, were now fighting in the salient. Not a trivial force at all.[56]

The following day, the responsibility for the destruction of primary bridges in the 17th Airborne's sector passed from the 11th Armored Division to the 17th

Airborne Division. The enemy advance had been stopped and the Germans were engaged in reorganizing their forces. Meanwhile, the 17th Airborne would continue defending the Meuse River line, thus, Miley ordered mine fields to be laid in order to strengthen the division's position. At the same time, the 513th continued to patrol in an attempt to pick up the reported enemy parachutists while elements of the 9th Armored Division, the 41st Cavalry Reconnaissance Squadron (Mechanized), and the 7th Tank Destroyer Group maintained a reconnaissance screen on the east side of the Meuse.[57]

At the roadblock, Lieutenant Puckett and Sergeant Johnnie A. Rutherford were in command of the day shift from 0600 to 1800 hours. Lieutenant Stositch and Tech Sergeant Paul had the night shift. Lieutenants Calhoun and Sims had been given the duty of blowing up the bridge if the Germans tried to cross. When men were not working the road block, they slept in the reams of paper in the mill. Calhoun and Sims, however, had selected a house close to the bridge to bunk in. According to Puckett, the house was owned by an Italian family, man and wife and their blond, twenty-one year old daughter. Around noon on 27 December, Lieutenant Colonel Miller appeared to inspect the bridge defenses. Miller asked Sergeant Rutherford where the lieutenant in charge of the bridge's demolition was, and Rutherford pointed toward the Italian family's house. "Colonel Miller disappeared through the doorway," remembered Puckett. "Minutes later the two lieutenants came running out of the house with Colonel Miller close behind. It turned out that it was Lieutenant Sims' turn on duty." Sims told Miller that he had the plunger to the detonator in his pocket, and, therefore, no one but he could set off the explosives. Miller, apparently, wasn't satisfied with Sims' explanation and Sims "was relieved on the spot and sent to division for action."[58]

Since there was little danger of being fired on, during the days Private Newhouse ventured into town to get a shave from a barber who still had hot water. At night, Newhouse sometimes walked along the railroad tracks to stretch his legs and think. One evening, a train pulling a long line of boxcars stopped along the siding near the papermill. Grice, Haggard, and some of the other men slipped up to it to investigate. They found it loaded with "hoe cake bread and orange marmalade," so they helped themselves. It was a welcome addition to K rations. An MP arrived, however, and stopped them, telling them that the food in the boxcars was for the German prisoners. Grice remembered feeling a little like a prisoner himself. Haggard was burned up; the German prisoners, he thought, were eating better than they were.[59]

On 28 December, General Bradley, reasoning that the German offensive had finally stalled out, convinced SHAEF that his armies should go over to the offensive and cut the German salient at its "waist." The critical area was Houffalize-Vielsalm, said Bradley, and his plan envisioned General Patton's Third Army driving north into the German left flank from Bastogne combined with the simultaneous attack of General Courtney Hodges First Army into the German right. Hodges' army had been placed under the control of British Field Marshal Montgomery's 21st Army Group since the beginning of the Bulge and difficulties in securing the cooperation of the British emerged almost immediately.

Though officially dismissed, German propaganda attempted to spread dissension among the Allies by asserting that the British were taking credit for the successes of American soldiers fighting in the Bulge. There was, however, some truth to the German broadcasts. Field Marshal Montgomery was indeed claiming to have pulled the Americans' chestnuts out of the fire. Yet, when SHAEF asked him to move, Montgomery maintained that Hodges' army was "too weak" to conduct offensive operations, suggesting that First Army would not be able to move for three months. Montgomery then went further, suggesting that Patton's operations should be canceled as well, recommending that Third Army fall back on the Saar. Bradley became irate at these insulting suggestions and demanded vehemently to Lieutenant General Walter Bedell Smith, General Eisenhower's Chief of Staff, that Eisenhower should intervene. It was not until Eisenhower threatened to relieve the mercurial British field marshal that Montgomery opted to launch a counteroffensive in the north in cooperation with Bradley's in the south.[60]

The 12th Army Group's offensive dictated that Patton's Third Army, having relieved the defenders of Bastogne, would continue its attack to the northeast, to Houffalize, St. Vith, and Bitburg. Patton would attack with three corps advancing abreast. John Millikin's III Corps would be in the center; Manton Eddy's XII Corps would be on the right, east of Bastogne; and Troy Middleton's reconstituted VIII Corps would be on the left, west of Bastogne. Among the divisions in Middleton's corps was the 101st Airborne Division and the other units that had participated in Bastogne's defense. The 101st Airborne, however, had suffered numerous casualties and was exhausted from its effort to defend Bastogne. Middleton was also given the 87th Infantry Division, the 11th Armored Division, and the 17th Airborne Division, all fresh from SHAEF reserve. Frank L. Culin's 87th Division had seen limited action in Patton's Saar Campaign, but the other divisions, the 11th

Armored and the 17th Airborne, were – with the exception of the 507th Parachute Infantry Regiment that had seen action in Normandy – composed of green troops.

Unaware of the currents about to sweep them to battle, F Company continued to send patrols out looking for the illusionary enemy parachutists. Although they broke the monotony of manning the defensive positions, patrols were not easy work. On one last patrol, Tech Sergeant Milton Smith led Privates Hataway, Hultman, Harding, Imre, and Joseph R. Kitson south, along the river, and then crossed to the eastern bank by a small boat. Trudging along across the windswept, snow-clad landscape, Private Imre thought he could hear the sounds of small arms fire off in the distance, and once saw what he thought was a German uniform, but, as he admits now, this was only wishful thinking. The patrol moved at a fast gait, but the wind and snow made the going arduous. After four or five hours, the patrol returned, exhausted, cold, hungry.

Late on 27 December, patrols from the 513th finally found what they were looking for. Captain Ivy, the Regimental S-2, sent a message to division intelligence: "Report of captured materiel: 1. Two Parachute harnesses found by patrol 4 3/4 miles SW Verdun at (2258) at 1530 27 Dec. Found in woods and partially buried packing record included. 2. Articles forwarded herewith." It is likely that the chutes were from downed Luftwaffe crews rather than saboteurs, though.

To serve as translators and guides, Colonel Susini, commanding French forces headquartered at nearby Laneuville, attached twelve French enlisted men to each company of the 513th Regiment on 27 December. Two days later, Colonel Miller sent a platoon from the 2nd Battalion to Jametz, another nearby village, to assist local French troops in capturing a band of suspected German parachutists. Apparently, F Company's French guides learned of the parachutists and, as Lt. Calhoun believed, several went off "looking for Germans to kill." They didn't even bother telling Captain Reynolds they were leaving.[61]

Calhoun's platoon had spent the better part of the twenty-ninth making improvements on the roadblock when orders came down to board trucks. The battalion was moving. Laufer, Grice, and Cook finished devouring a couple loaves of French bread they'd begged from another trooper, and packed up their gear. Laufer's anxiety started up again as his mind churned the possibilities over and over. "What's gonna happen?" he thought. "Where are we going? What are we gonna do? Am I gonna get shot? Am I gonna get killed?" Laufer also worried about staying close to his buddy Grice when the fighting started. F Company men did not know it, but they were being pulled off the line in preparation for Patton's attack into the southern shoulder of the Bulge.

2nd Battalion – less D Company which was to stay behind to man the bridges – was ordered to revert to mobile reserve in the vicinity of Romagne. Major Edwards assumed command of D Company and with it responsibility for the bridges in the Stenay area. Supporting D Company were D Company of the 1308th Engineer Regiment; Second Platoon of C Battery, 155th Antitank Battalion; Second Platoon of C Company, 139th Airborne Engineers; B Battery, 466th PFAB; and 2nd Battalion's demolition section.[62]

That day, regiment had learned that the German offensive toward the Meuse had been checked and that some ground had even been regained from the enemy. Still, the threat of a German airborne assault continued to trouble regimental commanders. The men were jumpy, too. At noon, troopers from the 1st Battalion fired at the division's liaison plane as it passed low overhead.[63]

With the exception of the arrival of six cooks for F Company, 30 December passed uneventfully. The next day, the 2nd Battalion, less F Company, moved to a new station at Bantheville, France, west of Stenay. There, Major Edwards and D Company rejoined the battalion. That same day, Colonel Coutts made a request to division for additional jeeps to be distributed to the 513th in preparation for their impending move.

Rather than proceeding to Bantheville with the rest of the battalion, F Company departed Stenay at 1030 hours by truck for the town of Aincreville, some fifteen miles distant. After a half hour ride, F Company arrived at their bivouac area, and the company's French enlisted personnel, most of whom had already run off, were relieved from attachment. Once settled in their new billets, the officers and men alike looked forward to a little relaxation.

At the end of December, Generalfeldmarschall Walther Model, commander of the German forces fighting in the Bulge, suggested that his Army Group B begin a withdrawal from the Bulge salient in an effort to reach the defenses of the Siegfried Line. Hitler, however, dismissed the proposal and ordered that the German forces in the Bulge be reorganized to fight a war of attrition, delaying the Allied drive into the Fatherland as long as possible. Thus, German forces surrendered any further hopes of breaking through in the north and, instead, turned to concentrate on Patton's army in the south. The *Fifth* and *Sixth Panzer Armies* attacked toward Bastogne. The Germans hoped to capture the city, and, by holding it as long as possible, slow the Allied advance east.

On the last day of the year, spearheading Middleton's VIII Corps, the 87th Infantry and 11th Armored Divisions attacked north into the German left. They walked blindly into a scythe. The weather had turned colder than ever. Deep snows, icy roads, and freezing temperatures made it a battle merely to stay alive. Advancing into the flanks of several German divisions marching on Bastogne, the 11th Armored was battered so badly, in fact, that Middleton ordered the 17th Airborne Division rushed from Corps Reserve and into the line.[64]

It was the first day of the new year, and F Company men, since arriving on the Continent, had eaten only cold C, D, and K rations. But, on this day at the French village of Aincreville, "we got our Christmas dinner," remembered Newhouse. "It was turkey with all the trimmings. We ate it in the church yard surrounded by an iron picket fence – I think it was the graveyard." The villagers stood around the fence and watched the men eating. The people appeared to the men to be starving. The children, always with their toboggans in tow, were dressed in rags. Many, Newhouse suspected, suffered from scabies or impetigo. The sight made many troopers feel guilty about the comparative feast they'd been given. "We gave most of it away," said Newhouse. The villagers gave the men presents and the men returned the gesture, giving gifts of gum and chocolate. Some of the men took pictures. To Captain Reynolds, Aincreville's Mayor pointed out the monument in front of his house that bore the names of the nine American soldiers that had been killed in his town during World War I. It was too bad, he said to Captain Reynolds, that a monument could not be built for some of the men of F Company. Captain Reynolds replied that he wouldn't mind a monument to his men, but he didn't think any of his men cared to die in Aincreville in order to be so honored. After dinner, a few men went on patrol and the rest of the troopers set up in some of the farm houses.[65]

At 1710 hours, General Miley sent a field message to Colonel Coutts: "Make plans immediately to assemble your C[ombat] team and be prepared to move on two hours notice." Accompanying the message was a reprimand from General Miley to the entire division. The General, apparently, had observed a "decided laxity in military courtesy and dress" since the division arrived in France. Miley ordered the salute continued and further demanded the men maintain a "high standard of cleanliness and dress," adding, "It is believed that there will be not more than two days left in which to get your men bathed."[66]

Miley probably was concerned by his own G-2 section's estimate of the German situation. The enemy, G-2 said, was placing obvious weight on their defense of southern flank of the Bulge. Already defended by the *1st SS Panzer Division*, *3rd Panzer Grenadier Division*, and the *167th Volksgrenadier Division*, the sector was being reinforced. G-2 also reported the presence of the *12th SS Panzer Division*. This division was believed responsible for the murder of Canadian prisoners in Normandy, and for the Malmédy Massacre of 16 December 1944, the news of which already had swept the American forces. None of this could have been welcome news to the commander of a green division on the eve of an attack into the southern flank of the Bulge.[67]

On 2 January, the 17th Airborne Division was assigned to VIII Corps. General Miley met with General Middleton who instructed Miley to move his division to an assembly area north of Neufchâteau in preparation for "further offensive actions" to the north. Before leaving, Miley requested addition trucks from Oise Base Section and Third Army for the division. Arriving in Neufchâteau, Miley was informed that the location of the assembly area had been changed and was instructed to move the division nine miles further north in preparation for relieving the 11th Armored Division, then fighting west of Bastogne. The new assembly area was located one mile northwest of Bercheux, Luxembourg. At noon, the lead elements of the 513th arrived, and General Miley ordered Colonel Coutts and the other regimental commanders to attend a meeting with the commander of the 11th Armored Division for the purpose of organizing the relief. There, Colonel Coutts made arrangements for his regiment to relieve those elements of the 11th Armored at Mande-St.-Etienne, just a little more than three miles northwest of Bastogne.[68]

Colonel Coutts established the 513th's command post in Flohamont, a small village – heavily damaged by the fighting – nestled amid the rugged hills of the Duchy of Luxembourg. From there, Coutts ordered Lieutenant Colonel Miller to move the 2nd Battalion to the small village of Monty, about four hundred yards south of Mande-St.-Etienne, and to relieve the elements of the 11th Armored Division holding the village. The 1st Battalion, under the command of Lieutenant Colonel Alten R. Taylor, was ordered into the Bois de Fragotte – a dense wood south of Monty. Lieutenant Colonel Edward F. Kent's 3rd Battalion was to remain in reserve in Jodenville. The marches were to be made at night, after all the companies of the regiment had arrived and were assembled.[69]

Meanwhile, at Aincreville, F Company men were making hurried preparations to depart when the village Mayor approached Captain Reynolds to tell him that one of his men had cut the arms of the town's catafalque. Looking for something to sleep on the night before, Sergeant Gohn discovered a strange looking object with several arms protruding from it. He cut the arms off it and made himself a good bed. The next morning, the mayor discovered it where Gohn had tossed it out into the street. Without the catafalque the townspeople had nothing on which to transport the bodies of their deceased to the graveyard for burial. Reynolds took up a collection from the officers and men and gave it to the Mayor to purchase another catafalque. "So much money was donated," said Lieutenant Calhoun, "that the Mayor could have purchased some sort of wheeled vehicle for future use."[70]

Just before the men moved out, a priest arrived. The company was assembled, and the priest granted them absolution for their sins. From then on, everyone knew where they were heading.[71]

Private Lightcap had decided earlier that morning to go hunting for rabbits with his M1 and so struck out toward one of the small neighboring towns. In it, there was a huge monument built in honor of an American captain, a hero of the Great War. The town, in fact, was in the middle of the old World War I battlefield. Outside the village, Lightcap walked alone through the silent trenches, stooping occasionally to shake loose old artillery shells or a spiked German helmet. Lightcap had spent a lot of time back in Hazel Green listening to the older men tell their stories about the Great War. The local veterans told him about Verdun. Now he was here. Nevertheless, it didn't really sink in that he was going into combat and what the consequences might be. Lightcap arrived back at Aincreville to find the rest of the company loading into semi-trailers intended originally not for men, but for cattle. Thankful he'd not missed his ride, Lightcap picked up his extra equipment and bazooka ammunition, milled into the crowd of men, and got onto a truck. At 1230 hours, F Company departed Aincreville for the division assembly area near Bercheux.[72]

F Company moved east with 2nd Battalion all day. As on the ride from Mourmelon, the men were packed so tightly in the trailers they had to stand up. The side rails came up to the men's waists, but since there were no canvas tops on the trucks, the men were exposed to the freezing wind. Sometime in the afternoon, the column stopped to give the men a pee break and the chance to stretch. On numb limbs, the men struggled out of the trucks and stood along the side of the road urinating.[73]

"We were all standing next to the trucks," recalled Newhouse, "it was cold as hell. One of the Second Platoon men went over to the barn [standing along the road], ripped the doors off, and started a fire. Acey-Deucy came up and saw it and raised all kinds of hell." "Second Platoon is a bunch of fuckups!" Miller roared at Lieutenant Calhoun. According to Newhouse, "Acey-Deucy was raving about the smoke, and that the enemy could possibly see it and it would draw artillery fire." Then Miller pulled Calhoun off to the side and continued to rip him up. After Miller left, the men climbed back on the trucks. As the motor convoy started to move, Tech Sergeant Smith told the men what he had overheard Miller saying to Calhoun: "Second Platoon and F Company will be point on the attack."[74]

At more than one incline, the men got out to bull the trucks up the hill. "There was a captain from some other outfit sitting in the cab of our truck" while outside, the men pushed, recalled Ed Costello. Then, from out of nowhere, General Patton appeared. He observed the officer sitting in the cab as the men pushed and "he told the captain: 'Get your ass out and help the boys push.' I guess you know that captain damn near tore the door off getting out of that truck. After some of us had a good laugh we got the trucks up the hill and all loaded up again. There were three or four of us in the rear end, and the General walked up and asked us how things were going. We said, 'O.K.' (what else?) One of the guys said, 'General, we'll get some of those bastards for you.' Well, the General looked at us and said, 'You boys be careful or some sonofabitch will be burying *you* up there.' And, with his pearl-handled guns and all, he walked off."[75]

As night fell, the motor convoy passed through several towns and villages, headlights occasionally illuminated the bodies of dead German and American soldiers, or civilians caught in the fighting. Lieutenant Puckett observed the body of one civilian, clad in black as most were, crushed flat in the middle of the road. In many of the villages, buildings still smoldered from recent fighting. "It was a spooky ride that night," remembered Donovan. "The Germans were on either side of a narrow, half mile wide corridor that we went into." Around 2200 hours, the column arrived at the Bercheux assembly area. The men unloaded from the trucks and moved into the woods and dug holes in which to await further orders while Captain Reynolds scouted the road about a half mile ahead of the column. The men "could see artillery flashes everywhere." The concussion from artillery bombardments shook dirt loose from the sides and on to the men sitting in their hastily dug holes. Occasionally, a round of artillery would pass overhead. "That's our artillery,' they told each other confidently, hoping it really was. In fact, more than twelve battalions of American artillery were firing in the Chenogne area to the east. When Captain Reynolds returned, he told Calhoun that he had run into a German road block. Reynolds ordered the men to load up, and the column was turned around and headed further east.[76]

On Wednesday, 3 January 1945, Field Marshal Montgomery finally consented to begin his attack south, into the right flank of the German army. At 0830 hours that day, Major General Joseph 'Lightning Joe' Collins' VII Corps began its drive south toward Houffalize, the unfortunate town designated as the meeting point of the two Allied armies fighting on the separate shoulders of the Bulge salient. In the south, General Patton, in spite of the costly setbacks suffered by VIII Corps on 30 December, continued to drive his Third U.S. Army north without rest. Patton still believed the attacks would meet little resistance.[77]

Hours before VII Corps' attack began, F Company's trucks pulled to the side of the road and the drivers told the men to dismount. Exhausted and nearly frozen from the all day and all night ride in the open semi-trailers, the men began half hopping and half falling down out of the open trucks. Everyone was stiff with cold and wet through from falling snow. As they milled about in the dark, stamping their boots on the frozen earth trying get the blood in their feet and legs moving again, some men stumbled over the corpses of Germans half buried in snow and ice. There were, in fact, many German bodies. Because of the severe cold, the Germans had stripped bodies of their dead comrades for boots, socks, hats, and any other clothing that they needed. Once discovered, some of the men set to kicking at the corpses, trying to dislodge them, but they had frozen to the earth and did not budge.

Captain Reynolds walked to the head of the column of trucks and immediately began to argue with one of the colored truck drivers. "Hey, you're supposed to take us up here," insisted Reynolds, pointing to a spot on the map he had thrust in the drivers face. The drivers were supposed to have dropped the company at Monty, but had stopped short.

The driver was adamant, however. "No, Sir," he stated flatly, "We ain't goin' no further." For better or for worse, that settled it. Reynolds' runner, PFC Ed Dahlberg, who had been watching his company commander negotiating with the drivers from nearby, could see the flashes of artillery off to the north in the direc-

tion F Company was headed. Dahlberg figured that the artillery was the real reason for their reluctance to continue. He hated the drivers for their cowardice, but
envied them too; they didn't have to go up there where he was going, up to the
fighting and up to the dying. With the truck drivers departing, and thoroughly
disgusted with the situation, Reynolds gave up and went to assemble his men. It
was 0500 hours. F Company had arrived at the end of the line: Chenogne, Belgium.[78]

Only a few miles southwest of Bastogne, the scene of some of the toughest
fighting during the first eight days of the German offensive, the dwellings in the
once-quaint village of Chenogne had been reduced to mere shells by the ebb and
flow of the battle. Officers sent a few men to check out the houses, many smoldering and some still burning. The smoke which the fires illuminated clung low to the
earth as if held down by invisible hands. Tech Sergeant John O. Paul carefully
surveyed the surrounding hills and fields. It gave him a "damn eerie feeling." Here
and there, mute trees broke the monotony of the otherwise still and rolling farmland. Only the smoke moved, a creeping gray-white shroud spreading itself over a
dirty white and silent landscape. To Paul, it looked as if it had been a beautiful
country before the war. Now this place was to him the very portrait of death itself
and, as he looked at the faces around him, he thought every one of his men could
feel it.[79]

Laufer glanced around at the burned-out American tanks and jeeps that littered the landscape. His attention then turned to the carcasses of domestic animals
which were also scattered about. One in particular, a big draught horse which lay
on the side of the road, drew his attention because several possums were eating the
bowels out of it. When one fat possum emerged from its end and darted into the
woods, the sight turned Laufer's stomach. At that moment, Tech Sergeant 'Snuffy'
Bowers, Laufer's platoon sergeant, told the men to check their weapons and equipment, and get ready to move.

The German shelling, which had been falling ahead of them, was slowly working its way south. Captain Reynolds instructed the men to get off the road, get in
among the pine trees, and dig in. The men took out their shovels and started picking away at the frozen earth. After getting down a bit, Dahlberg wrapped himself
in his shelter half and tried to close his eyes, but he was cold and miserable. With
the cold and all the noise from both enemy and friendly artillery firing to the south,
few men could get any real sleep.

At first light, Captain Reynolds, got up and roused Private Lightcap, who was resting a few yards from him. "Go round everybody up," Reynolds instructed Lightcap as he pushed a flashlight into his hand. "We're moving out."[80]

Before long, the company was on its feet and marching northward toward the Bastogne-Marche Highway and Monty; the men were spread out fifty to one hundred feet apart on both sides of the road in an approach-march formation. In the freezing cold, something akin to the marching song *Blood on the Risers* was raised and everyone joined in, accompanied by the crump of artillery which rose in pitch with each step forward. The men were acting like they "didn't think they were in combat yet," commented Gus Seacott. Second Platoon took the lead with First Platoon following and Third Platoon bringing up the rear. Leading the Third Platoon, Lieutenant Gilles set his squads marching on opposite sides of the road. Lieutenant Puckett and a private brought up the rear of the column.[81]

While F Company was organizing at Chenogne, troopers of the 1st Battalion, having moved up to positions the night before, were hit by extremely heavy artillery and mortar fire as they dug slit trenches among the trees in the Bois de Fragotte. They already had endured an attack by a strong mechanized force that had broken through the battalion's lines and severed its communications with corps and division artillery. Though unsupported, the 1st Battalion had held, and eventually forced the enemy to withdraw to the west, up the Bastogne-Marche Highway toward Flamierge, and north to Flamizoulle. Now, as they improved their positions, 1st Battalion troopers could hear the sound of not so distant artillery falling on the 2nd Battalion as it marched toward Monty.[82]

The men had been issued grenades, extra ammunition, and extra rockets for the bazookas before leaving Aincreville. After the company column had progressed some distance, Lieutenant Puckett came upon .30 caliber ammunition boxes and gas masks, discarded by the men ahead of him. Dropping extra ammunition and equipment while on the march was not an uncommon practice throughout the infantry, even among paratroopers, but it was a practice almost always regretted when a fight started. Puckett picked up two boxes of machine-gun ammunition. Each weighed fourteen pounds, but he carried one in each hand in addition to all his other equipment. Meanwhile, the private that accompanied him filled his arms with the discarded gas masks.[83]

The troopers advanced as if they "were on some sort of field problem," said Dahlberg. Unlike the white camouflage snow suits many of the German soldiers were issued, the troopers' uniforms, especially the brown GI overcoats, stood out against the snowy landscape. "On level ground," recalled Lightcap, "the enemy could watch us advance for five miles." Lightcap pondered his vulnerability against the growing chorus of artillery.[84]

As the company marched on, breathing increased from exertion and the air around the men's faces was filled with little frosty clouds. Their boots crunched on the wet snow. Soon they began to pass dead bodies of American soldiers laying here and there. The singing stopped, and after some time a brief halt was ordered. The men pulled off to the side and sat down.

Sprawled in the road nearby was the body of an American lieutenant. One of his knees was bent up and the other leg stuck straight out. He had been a tall man, maybe six feet. From where he sat, Cavaleri and his buddy, PFC Dale J. Auer, could see that the left half of the lieutenant's head was gone, but that the skull was empty, as if it were an empty egg shell. Cavaleri supposed that the shell that killed him must have pulled it all out. The right side was perfect. There was no smell – like everything else, the body was frozen.

Where Third Platoon stopped, there was a cow nearby. The last cow they'd seen had had its side blown out, but it was still walking around. This one looked all right, so one of the Rebels went out, took his helmet off, removed the liner, and started milking the cow, warm milk until his helmet was full.[85]

After about five minutes, Captain Reynolds told Dahlberg, "Bring the company up." The sergeants yelled, "Okay, everybody up! Let's go!" and the men were moving again.[86]

The column was advancing along a cart path to a road junction on the Bastogne-Marche Highway a few hundred yards northwest of Monty. Lieutenant Calhoun was leading with one squad. "Calhoun was always up front," pointed out Don Newhouse, "[he] never held back anything." Lieutenant Isham Fann, Calhoun's assistant platoon leader, followed with the rest of Second Platoon about two hundred yards behind. The Germans began shelling the company as they reached the vicinity of Nivier du Pape, a little more than a half mile southwest of Monty. Light, sporadic mortar fire fell here and there, but its character led Calhoun to believe that the Germans were just test firing concentrations. F Company men dispersed, but kept moving except when a shell struck really close.[87]

Private Lightcap was too dumbfounded by the force of the explosions to take cover when the few first rounds landed nearby. He'd seen artillery fire in training, but he'd never been on the receiving end before. When he heard "those whining bastards coming in" the next time, he buried himself deep in the snow.[88]

2nd Battalion was stretched out for a mile behind Reynolds' men. Behind F Company trailed E Company, followed by Headquarters Company with Colonel Miller, and D Company brought up the rear. At the front of the column, Lieutenant Calhoun's Second Platoon men came upon the body of another German, bare footed, and partially snow covered, near a fence that ran along the road. The claret-colored body was twisted into a grotesque position – "one arm reaching out as if he wanted help getting up." "The sight of him," recalled Greenstrand, "gave us one hell of an awakening and we knew we were getting damn close to combat. I'm not sure but I think a lot of the heroics left most of us at that moment and we all wished we were home or at least in England." They all stood their staring at him until an officer walked up to the group of them and said, "You can stop looking at that German soldier. Where you're going you're gonna see a lot of dead soldiers." The men fell back in ranks and walked on. Meanwhile, mortar and flat trajectory fire, and small arms fire began falling along the road and on the elements at the end of the 2nd Battalion column.

Another halt was ordered by Reynolds and again the men pulled to the side of the road. Sergeant Donald S. Erb, the mortar sergeant from First Platoon, soon came walking down the path swearing his head off. He'd gone off to the side to relieve himself and had been hit by shrapnel and was bleeding from a wound in the back of his head. Erb, F Company's first battle casualty, went to the aid station.[89]

A calvary, standing on the opposite side of the road, marked the spot where Lieutenant Calhoun's men arrived at the Bastogne Highway. It was one of many that dotted the roads and small villages. The lieutenant turned his men southeast and, walking along the highway, marched the last quarter mile into Monty. The tiny village, consisting of a small store, a town hall, and a few dwellings, had been reduced to shells. The Germans had the intersection zeroed in with 88mm guns they'd positioned on high ground just off to the north and they usually fired anytime they spotted movement. Calhoun's men were plainly visible in the growing daylight, however; the artillery was quiet for the moment. A half-track and four or five Sherman tanks of the 11th Armored Division were standing on the side of the crossroads, all warming up their motors, ready to leave. There were also a few German PWs huddled there whom the tankers were guarding closely.[90]

"Hey, look at this guy," said one of the Calhoun's men, pointing to a body. An American soldier, clad in a leather flying jacket, was laying half buried in the snow. A few men gathered around it, gawking with curiosity. Another American was sprawled out near the calvary on the northeast side of the crossroads. "He was really dead," commented Newhouse, "he had parts blown off of him."[91]

Lieutenant Puckett, arriving with the Third Platoon at the end of the company column, spotted a weathered sign that stood forlornly at the crossroads. It read "Bastogne 5 km." 'Bastogne' meant something to Puckett because he had heard about what the 101st had been through. About then, recalled Tech Sergeant Paul, a couple of the armored force men walked up and started explaining that they were getting ready to withdraw some of their damaged vehicles through the road junction and they expected to draw heavy enemy artillery fire. One of them remarked, "Everybody better get 'em a big hole."[92]

The tankers at Monty, elements of the 11th Armored Division's Combat Command B, had good reason to warn the 513th troopers as they had. The area was the ongoing scene of heavy fighting. On 29 December, CCB had been ordered to capture the woods east of Ho mont, and then seize the woods southwest of Mande-St.-Etienne. Their attack was to be led by Task Force Poker – comprised of the 41st Tank Battalion (less one company), and A Company of the 21st Armored Infantry Battalion. Considering the battalion had just completed a 120-mile road march that day, and that they were not afforded the opportunity to make a reconnaissance of the area ahead of them, none of Task Force Poker's officers were "very much pleased at the news."[93]

TF Poker's attack jumped off at 0615 hours on 30 December. Meeting very light resistance initially, Poker advanced cross country guiding on the Morhet road to reach Lavaselle at 1030 hours. Lieutenant Colonel Wray Sagaser, commander of the 41st, recognized that Lavaselle, surrounded by high ground, would be difficult to defend so he elected to push on to Ho mont and Brul, the two towns controlling Lavaselle. TF Poker pushed out ahead, but in doing so put themselves in danger of being isolated if the enemy counterattacked. So, on 31 December, Lieutenant Colonel Sagaser was ordered to wait for "Task Force Pat," (composed of the remainder of the 21st Armored Infantry and one company of the 41st Tank Battalion), to move up abreast and capture Chenogne before it continued.[94]

On the morning of 1 January, the fires of twelve battalions of artillery were brought to bear on the woods north of Chenogne to proceed the attack of TF Pat – more than 550 German bodies were later discovered in these woods. TF Pat jumped off at 1100 hours. By noon, the tanks of the 41st had advanced to the open ground northeast of Ho mont. CCB commander Colonel Wesley Yale "was pressing for the force to drive on to secure a thin line of trees just southwest of Monty." After a delay of over an hour – in which time the battalion suffered several casualties to enemy artillery – the attack resumed. The advance was broken up, however, when Third Platoon of A Company of the 41st became bogged down and mousetrapped in marshy ground near the woods gap through which the attack was supposed to proceed. The entire tank platoon was picked off, one by one, by German 75mm and 88mm antitank guns emplaced along the Bastogne road and on the high ground above Mande-St.-Etienne. The attack was "scotched" and the balance of CCB withdrew into the woods to the southwest.[95]

Throughout that night, small skirmishes erupted between patrols from TF Pat, on CCB's right, and enemy patrols attempting to infiltrate the Americans' lines. German observed direct-fire artillery commanded the countryside south of Monty making vehicular movement venturesome and tree burst artillery caused further casualties among the armored infantrymen.[96]

Lieutenant Colonel Sagaser and Major Patrick Tansey, the commander of the 21st Armored Infantry, agreed that an immediate advance to capture the high ground north of Monty and Mande-St.-Etienne was vital and planned to attack the next day. Proceeding the assault on the morning of 2 January, a platoon of the 41st Cavalry Reconnaissance Squadron (Mecz), brought up the night before to outpost TF Pat's CP and guard the right flank, reconnoitered the towns and made a route reconnaissance of the approaches to Monty to determine a proper axis of attack for the armor. The patrol observed considerable enemy movement in and around the towns but could not determine the significance. At 1500, CCB granted permission for an attack and an air strike and artillery were placed on the towns.[97]

Task Force Poker, attacking on the left, jumped-off at 1600 in a coordinated movement with Task Force Pat on the right. Supported by B Company Shermans, A Company of the 41st made a frontal assault upon the towns. The tanks' guns "set the towns ablaze," but it was not until 2000 hours and darkness "that the combined forces entered Mande-St.-Etienne." Fighting in the town raged throughout the night as the tankers and armored infantrymen clashed with the resolute enemy. When an expected enemy counterattack failed to materialize, Lieutenant Colonel Sagaser decided that, under the circumstances, he could wait for morning to sort out the situation. German soldiers were still holed-up in the cellars and sniping at the Americans at dawn. At 0800 hours, elements of the 17th Airborne division arrived to relieve them. Lieutenant Colonel Sagaser noted the relieving troops' shortages in ammunition and transportation and ordered that some .30 caliber ammunition be left with Miller's battalion when the tankers departed.[98]

Major Edwards took all the company commanders and their first sergeants and went up to take over from the 21st Armored Infantry. The armored infantrymen wanted to trade weapons – mortars, machine-guns, and the like – for the 2nd Battalion's weapons. Edwards refused. "I only had to take one look at two of their weapons and I said, 'There'll be no goddamned exchange of weapons. You people get your weapons and get 'em out of here,' and they left and we kept our clean weapons."[99]

When Colonel Miller arrived at Monty, the commander of the 21st told him tersely, "Couldn't see anything, don't know anything, its your baby." He then ordered his tanks to pull out for Chenogne. As they were leaving, PFC Grice yelled to the tankers, "Gimme some of that canned stuff." One of the tankmen threw off a case of 10-in-1s. Another case was thrown to the Second Platoon. Most F Company men had K-rations, but some men were down to their last or without entirely. Besides, the K-rations were bland. The 10-in-1 rations were better tasting, especially the 'meat and beans.' Private Newhouse opened one of the cans of corned beef hash. It was frozen. He put a frozen chunk in his mouth and held it until it had thawed enough to swallow. Within a half hour, Newhouse had 'the GIs.'[100]

As the armored units started to leave, the enemy began shelling Monty. The ground north of the town was slightly elevated and provided German gunners with a perfect view of Monty and Mande-St.-Etienne itself. Colonel Miller decided that 2nd Battalion would be in a better position in Mande-St.-Etienne and on the surrounding high ground, and immediately ordered an advance. With Lieutenant Calhoun's platoon still leading, F Company crossed over the highway and marched up the cut road to Mande-St.-Etienne, a fairly large town with dozens of buildings. It had been badly damaged in Allied air attacks, however, and few of the buildings remained intact. From their positions on the high ground, Germans gunners worked on those buildings still standing with flat trajectory 88s.[101]

As Calhoun was leading his platoon into the edge of Mande at 0830 hours, Private Newhouse heard a German voice shouting in the distance and the next thing he knew an 88 came in. He and Lieutenant Calhoun took cover under one of the 11th Armored's tanks – not a smart idea if the tanker had decided to get out of there. The German must have been a forward observer, Newhouse thought. The artillery continued, but only sporadically. The platoon regained its feet and continued into the village with the rest of the company close behind.[102]

The Second Platoon walked toward the last house on the north side of the village where they were greeted by two soldiers from the 41st Tank Battalion. According to Lieutenant Calhoun, the 41st's damaged vehicles were spread all across the surrounding countryside. The men of the 41st stopped Calhoun's troopers from going any further, pointing out a group of German soldiers milling around in the trees a few hundred yards to the platoon's front. One of the 41st men told Calhoun, "As long as you don't fire at them, they won't fire at you." This was, apparently, the southern most line of the "Belgian Bulge." Calhoun asked PFC Joseph R. Grubb, his radio-telephone operator, to place a radio call to Captain Reynolds.[103]

Finding the woods ahead were held, Reynolds ordered Lieutenant Calhoun to set up his platoon near a stand of trees on the northwestern edge of the village and there to establish a perimeter defense. So as not to alert the Germans, Lieutenant Calhoun quietly brought up his men and ordered Tech Sergeant Milton Smith to supervise the digging-in. Second Platoon's position covered more than two hundred yards from a stone barn on the northern end of the village, left to a hedgerow that extended northward quite near the trees to F Company's front. Sergeant Gohn's squad set up behind the stone barn and a few of the houses. The ground was as hard as rock and the holes the men dug in it were no more than shallow slit trenches eight to twelve inches deep with the dirt from them stacked around the top.[104]

Imre, Harding, Hataway, and Hultman dug in slightly forward of the rest of the platoon's holes because there they found old shell holes they could improve. This allowed them to dig to about three feet. As they were being used as riflemen, however, they didn't set up their mortar. Imre, worried that the brass buttons on his GI overcoat might draw enemy fire, stopped digging for a moment and pulled them off. Then, he and some of the others put the platoon's ammunition in a small stone well house with shattered windows on the edge of the village. Meanwhile, D Company was setting up on the eastern side of the road which led north, out of the village.[105]

As the balance of F Company filed up Mande's main street, Captain Reynolds instructed the men to dump their gas masks and packs in a stone barn on the left side of the road. The barn's walls were quite intact, though artillery fire had blown several holes in the roof. A little while later, Reynolds told PFC Lightcap to take all of F Company's packs and pull them out of the barn, and to start a fire inside. Many of the company's M1s had frozen up and Reynolds wanted Lightcap to thaw them out and dry them by the fire. The freezing weather created problems with the M1 rifles. If the action of M1 got dirty or oily, and the weather was cold, a trooper "had to kick the shit out of it or look for a new rifle," explained Laufer. With him in the barn Lightcap had a few cases of 10-in-1 rations, and, as long as he was there, he served hot food to any trooper who drifted in.

Reynolds set up his CP in another barn. First Sergeant Donovan straightened out one of the stalls so he could do his paperwork – filling out the daily 'morning reports.' PFC Dahlberg took over another stall and lay down for a few minutes rest. His GI overcoat was wet. His boots were sopping. When he stopped moving, it all began to freeze. Even with that, he "didn't dare take 'em off."[106]

Some of F Company's First Platoon men went into the buildings too, trying to get warm. There was little effort made by them to dig foxholes – the men didn't know how long they were going to stay there. The familiar order to check equipment and take care of their weapons rose from the NCOs, but many men just muddled about. "There was a lot of chaos," Laufer remembered.[107]

There were plenty of German foxholes spread throughout the village. They were well-made affairs with roofs of boards and earth, and the Krauts had lined them with straw from the barns. When they took over these homes, however, some of the troopers discovered that the Germans had relieved themselves in the straw. Private Edward Pierce was aghast. "There was shit everywhere," he recalled. "In all the holes, all the buildings, just everywhere." There was never enough toilet paper, or safe places to use it. Before the battle was over he ended up having to wipe himself off with his hands, and then wipe them off in the snow. The Germans, he guessed, were in just as bad a shape.[108]

Third Platoon set up on F Company's left, just on the eastern side of the Rau de Mande, a small branch running roughly north toward Flamizoulle, which lay less than a mile away. Though covered by ice in places, the little stream mostly ran free. Looking for cover, Third Platoon men found a lot of foxholes there, as well as a lot of dead Germans. While some of the men began digging new holes, Munafo wandered through some of the previously prepared accommodations. With a little effort, he found a beautiful German dugout – cut back into the earth like a cave, but lying in it was the body of a German soldier. "I don't think the guy was dead yet to be honest with you," recalled Munafo. "There was vapor coming out of his mouth." Munafo fired three of four rounds into him, and then jumped in to see if the hole was safe. Munafo scratched around until he found a loaf of black bread, but soon decided he didn't like the way the hole felt and climbed back out. As he later admitted, he was just a kid and he was scared to death. Taking the bread with him, Munafo and Hall searched a while longer until they found a slit trench to lay down in. Slocomb, Munafo's assistant machine-gunner, and another trooper buddied-up in another hole nearby. Sergeant La Riccia buddied-up with Private Spivy and dug a new hole. At thirty-four, the burly but pleasant Louis B. Spivy, from Cincinnati, was the oldest man in F Company.[109]

First Platoon set up in the town in reserve, but a few of the men took it upon themselves to get the lay of the land. There were hedgerows everywhere, observed Cavaleri. Most were at least six feet tall, some were as tall as ten feet. Private Laufer inspected some of the German bodies. Many of the dead were carrying wood-tipped bullets. When one of these hit a man, it splintered and wood went all through his body. The men weren't sure what they were for at first and, fortunately, no one was ever hit by one.[110]

A few German troops were still hiding in the town, sniping at the Americans, and once the 2nd Battalion had assembled in the town, the men set about ruthlessly clearing them out. One German, coaxed from a hole in front of an F Company NCO, was crying, and repeating the words, "Me Polski, me Polski" The sergeant coolly shot him. A small group of prisoners were herded to the rear and shot – one still moving afterwards was finished off with a bayonet. 2nd Lieutenant Isham Fann, who was pushing a German prisoner ahead of him, walked up to Lieutenant Puckett and his men and asked if any of them had a machine-gun. Puckett and the men accompanying him just turned their backs on Fann. Fann took the German to a ditch and shot him with his own carbine. The sight of this made Puckett angry. He knew that when you start killing prisoners you're likely to share the same fate.[111]

By 0930, with what Colonel Miller described as "steady pressure," 2nd Battalion had cleared most of the village. Thirty PWs, all from the *29th Panzergrenadier Regiment*, were taken alive and sent to the rear. The 2nd Battalion, in the process of clearing the town, lost several officers and twenty-five to thirty enlisted men. F Company's casualties included Private Jack Bohn and PFC Lawrence J. Duprey who were slightly wounded by shell fragments; PFC Arthur Bricmont, Jr. who was lightly wounded by rifle fire; and Private Dwight Caton who was seriously wounded by mortar fire.[112]

Caton had been hit by enemy mortar fire and, when medics came to his aid, he was hit again. In all, he received twenty-three shrapnel wounds. After they bandaged him, the medics propped Caton up against a tree to await evacuation. While he was sitting there, his buddies brought up a German prisoner and asked if Caton wanted to shoot him. Caton declined; he couldn't hold a rifle, and even if he could, he didn't want to shoot the man. His buddies, however, had no such qualms and shot him immediately. Caton was put on an ambulance and taken to the rear. On the way, the ambulance passed an old church that had been converted into a field hospital so the driver stopped. Caton was in agony, and the driver thought he could get him a shot of morphine to help ease the pain because they still had a long drive ahead of them. The driver went in and after some discussion, the medics and driver brought Caton inside. Suddenly, a loud explosion rocked the building. The ambulance had taken a direct hit from an artillery shell.

Also wounded while clearing the village was Private Laufer who received a serious gunshot wound in the leg. "Oh thank God it's not worse," he thought – God always showed up right away, said Private Laufer, to help him out with the little things. His friends carried him to a foxhole near the chow truck where he sat until nearly dark before the medics could find room for him on a 'meat wagon'. On the trip to the rear, four wounded men rode in the back on stretchers. Laufer sat in the front seat with the driver. The sense of relief Laufer felt at leaving the battle so early was nothing short of tremendous. Other men were wounded far worse, but he'd escaped he thought. Laufer was soon transported to the 100th General Hospital where he was placed in a ward next to Sergeant Erb.

In ordering the advance into Mande-St.-Etienne, Colonel Miller had marched the 2nd Battalion into a cul-de-sac. The land north of Mande-St.-Etienne, occupied by the Germans, was high ground, but the town, like most Belgian villages in the Ardennes, was situated in a basin. Although Colonel Miller's troops had cleared and occupied the town, 2nd Battalion was under fire from every side except from the east and southeast. A great deal of sniper and automatic fire was coming from the southern edge of the pine forest northwest of town, from the crest of the hill about three hundred yards north, and from a few die-hard snipers that had eluded detection during the men's search of the town. One of F Company's headquarters men, who had taken up residence in a low concrete structure with Tec 5 Haggard, was fired on by a sniper in the church steeple when he went outside to relieve himself. The trooper ran back inside holding his rifle by the sling in one hand and the top of his trousers in the other.[113]

Worse still, during the advance into town, Miller had lost mechanical communications with regiment and snipers were shooting the wire men as they tried to repair the broken phone lines. The battalion CP, located in a building three hundred yards from the front lines on the road from Mande-St.-Etienne to Monty, and the aid station, which had been set up in two of the few intact buildings in town, were being constantly placed under direct fire by German gunners. When an 88 firing from the south put two rounds into one room of the battalion CP, several of the troopers who were there resting were wounded. Fortunately, they were wrapped in their blankets and none were injured seriously. Nevertheless, the CP was taking artillery fire once every five minutes and a sniper was keeping the door constantly covered with a Schmeisser.[114]

To relieve some of this pressure on his command, Miller decided to make an immediate attempt to capture the hills to the north of the town. Holding E Company in reserve, Miller ordered D and F Companies to seize the high ground from which the enemy was directing his fire. D and F Companies moved out, Miller recalled, and "advanced up the road to a point where the trail forks left, but could get no farther." D Company, on the right of the road, tried but could not take the hill crest immediately north of the village. The hill's defenders were dug-in, had several machine-guns, and had no intention of giving up their positions. F Company, on the left of the road, had been ordered to take the forested high ground northwest of the village. Like the hill, the woods were believed to be strongly held. Miller, however, had failed to secure artillery support for his attack. Captain Reynolds probably thought it would be unwise to try it and, therefore, no attempt was made.[115]

By late morning, the enemy artillery had slackened somewhat. Tech Sergeant Paul, who had discovered an abandoned German burrow dug under a large haystack, had set up himself, Staff Sergeant James F. Bassett, the platoon guide, and Lieutenant Stositch inside, and then opened a K-ration and sat in the mouth of the bunker to eat. Nearby was a stock enclosure on the left side of a dirt road that skirted the west side of the village. Cows grazed mildly within the paddock, apparently apathetic about the activity of the town's new occupants, and a few big Belgian draught horses browsed in the fields to the north. A weathered stone barn stood to the right side of the path and appeared to be somewhat intact. At Monty, the 41st men had brought in a retriever vehicle and had begun recovering their damaged armored vehicles. As the first wreck was being hauled through the crossroads, the Germans resumed shelling. Paul ducked back under the haystack while 88s rained down outside.[116]

When Paul emerged from his hole, he saw that the German's shells had hit every one of the cows; their insides dangled from the trees like Christmas decorations. And all but one of the draught horses had been killed by the barrage. The loan surviving horse, its gut torn open, walked about aimlessly while a pig scrambled beneath it, eating the horse's intestines. Paul was a little uncomfortable and even a little embarrassed at the gory spectacle that surrounded him, but he was hungry so he finished his K-rations.[117]

"When the tanks left, it was like a panic," remembered PFC Sarrell. "I really felt that panicky feeling." Apprehension increased that afternoon as periodically enemy tanks were spotted to the east of the town. Three 57mm antitank guns from the 155th Airborne Antitank Battalion had been set up in Mande after the town was secured – two on the east side of the town in the D Company area, and one at a road block on the west side of the town on the Bastogne road. Their gunners had fired several rounds at enemy tanks, but poor visibility limited their accuracy. The gunners were also plagued by a shortage of ammunition – there were only twelve rounds per gun.[118]

The battalion's precarious position was made even more so when its supply train – two two-and-a-half ton-trucks and trailers comprising the entire organic transportation of the battalion – led by the battalion S-4, Lieutenant Stem, was ambushed and destroyed between the Bois de Fragotte and Mande-St.-Etienne. Lieutenant Stem managed to escape and report the loss to Colonel Miller. Miller realized the gravity of his predicament and sent his adjutant, Lieutenant Michael Garafino, to the rear to report the situation to Colonel Coutts at Regimental Headquarters.[119]

Late in the afternoon, 2nd Battalion received some much needed relief. Though Mande-St.-Etienne was shelled throughout the afternoon, the morning fog cleared forcing the enemy's tanks to withdraw "for some distance." Additionally, eleven

Shermans from C Company, 22nd Tank Battalion, which had been attached to the regiment at 0900 hours, were sent to support Miller's battalion. The tanks brought up .30 and .50 caliber machine-gun ammunition, and the tank company commander's radio was used to call back for additional supplies – "1st priority was ammunition for the 6 pounders," recalled Miller. When darkness fell, supplies of all categories arrived, as did two jeep ambulances to evacuate the wounded. The battalion aid station had been amply supplied with plasma and "worked well," said Miller, but nevertheless, not all casualties could be relieved that night.[120]

During the afternoon, Captain Reynolds and his platoon leaders received orders to attend a battalion officers' meeting at the 2nd Battalion CP. "The Battalion Staff briefed us on an attack to be made on January 4th," Calhoun recalled. The attack was to jump off at 0815 hours by divisional order. As Lieutenant Colonel Miller began to outline 2nd Battalion's planned attack to his officers, Captain Reynolds interrupted the meeting to inform Lieutenant Puckett that only platoon leaders were to be present, assistants were to stay with their platoons. Puckett departed and the meeting continued.

According to Lieutenant Colonel Miller, the attack order, which originated at VIII Corps, called for the 87th Infantry Division and the 17th Airborne Division to attack abreast. In General Miley's opinion, to attack so soon after moving into unfamiliar positions "was a large order for a new division." General Patton, however, was adamant: the enemy was withdrawing in front of the 17th Airborne and he ordered attacks to be pressed home. General Middleton had a somewhat more realistic view of the state of the enemy force facing VIII Corps than did Patton, but, like Third Army's commander, he had also badly underestimated their strength.[121]

The 513th Parachute Infantry was ordered to strike north from the vicinity of Monty toward Flamizoulle and the Ourthe River at 0815 hours the next morning. The 194th Glider Infantry Regiment would be assaulting on the 513th's left. Supporting the 513th would be elements of the 155th Airborne Antitank Battalion; the 139th Airborne Engineer Battalion; C Company, 22nd Tank Battalion; and A Company, 630th Tank Destroyer Battalion. Additionally, the 466th Parachute Field Artillery Battalion – armed with 75mm Howitzers – was to fire in direct support of the regiment. D Battery of the 153 Field Artillery Battalion – with 105mms – was assigned to support 2nd Battalion exclusively.[122]

As the briefing continued, some peculiarities in the planned attack, which Colonel Coutts had given to Lieutenant Colonel Miller at the 2nd Battalion CP that afternoon, surfaced. Colonel Coutts had given the attack order to Lieutenant Colonel Miller at the 2nd Battalion CP during the afternoon. Rather than bring the battalions on line "perpendicular to the direction of the attack," 1st and 2nd Battalions, Coutts' ordered, were to jump off from the positions they occupied – 2nd Battalion from positions north of Mande-St.-Etienne, and 1st Battalion, echeloned to the left, from the southern edge of the Bois de Fragotte – yet the attack was to begin simultaneously. Compounding the obvious difficulties of coordinating the attack from the unusual echeloned lines of departure, was the fact that the 513th "had little information of enemy dispositions or terrain over which they were to operate." As the attack developed, the assaulting elements were to sweep north and northeast toward the Ourthe River, driving the Germans north of the regimental zone. Upon reaching the river line, the battalions would destroy the bridges across the Ourthe and establish defensive positions. When he got the word of the goals of the attack, Major Edwards was incredulous: "We attacked with a twelve-mile objective – *Twelve-fucking-mile objective!*"[123]

Miller had already determined that the enemy's center of gravity was the hill rising only two hundred yards north of D Company's position at the edge of town. The capture of this hill would compromise the enemy's position in the woods northwest of the town. Miller, therefore, planned to send E Company through D Company's lines to capture the hill; F Company would take the woods. Miller established his first phase line "across the crest of the immediate hill top and just north of the woods line." Once this line was reached, the companies were to hold until battalion gave them the green light to advance to the next phase line. At the same time, 1st Battalion would attack on 2nd Battalion's left to capture Flamizoulle. Lieutenant Colonel Taylor, commanding 1st Battalion, planned to send B and C Companies and hold A Company in reserve. The dividing line between the assault battalions was the "ravine W of MANDE, N Thru the ravine and trail into FLAMIZOULLE, [and] NNE in the low country to GIVRY, GIVES, and BETHOMONT." Regimental Headquarters was positioned in the Bois des Valets, and 3rd Battalion would be held in reserve.[124]

F Company's officers were completely familiarized with the plan and with their platoons' roles within it. "The Second Platoon of F Company was to be the base platoon in leading [F Company's] attack," recalled Calhoun. The line of departure was to be Second Platoon's defense line. "The phase lines were drawn on the maps where we would coordinate each new move forward as we would try to cut off German Army units west of a line from Bastogne to Houffalize where we would meet units cutting south from the northern edge of the Ardennes Salient."

During the meeting the Germans launched a nebelwerfer attack.[125] From the bottom of a foxhole, Private Laufer, who was still awaiting evacuation, thought the rockets sounded like "a woman getting raped." The huge 185 pound, 280mm high explosive projectiles, coming in six at a time, rolled through the air with sound of thunder and impacted in irregular patterns about thirty or forty yards apart. Rising above the crash of the rocket explosions, was the clatter of rifle fire coming from F Company's area. Colonel Miller broke up the meeting and told the officers to get back to their units and find out what was taking place.

It was snowing and visibility was poor. Graupensperger and Greenstrand had been digging in their machine-gun behind the stone barn. Since Gohn had been promoted to sergeant, Graup had taken over as the gunner. Greenstrand then became the assistant, and Private Alver S. Driggers, from Eustis, Florida, took over as the ammunition bearer. They were all hacking away at the frozen ground, when, suddenly, a German soldier dressed in a white snow suit, jumped up near them and began to run back into the woods. Down the line to the left, Kuntz spotted him first and opened fire with his M1. "All hell broke loose from the woods," said Greenstrand. "If anyone doubted that we were in a combat zone that should have convinced them pronto. The woods, about 250 to 300 yards in front of us was full of Krauts. They had a machine-gun set up on the left flank as well as the right with a deadly crossfire. Then there were German riflemen all over the woods that were firing. We were lucky that we had at least a little depression cut out of the frozen ground, enough to give a little protection."[126]

Staff Sergeant Smith led several of the platoon's NCOs in working their way forward along a cart path, on the platoon's left flank, which ran north toward the trees. Smith moved forward, until he was crouching behind a squat hedgerow near the woodline. As he peered over the top he was tumbled backward, hit squarely in the chest by a bullet.

Imre spotted two enemy soldiers in the field trying to pick up a wounded comrade. He raised his rifle to fire on them but he was stopped by Hataway and Hultman who pushed Imre's rifle down. "You're gonna give us away again," they told Imre. That was probably the only time Hataway refrained from firing on a

German, but, Imre later reasoned, there was already enough incoming fire and they didn't want him drawing any more.

As Lieutenant Calhoun hurried back toward the Second Platoon, more rockets exploded around him. Still more nebelwerfers were passing overhead and exploding in the town. As he passed the First Platoon's area, he could see many of the troopers hunkering low in their holes, raincoats drawn down over their heads. He figured it made them feel a little safer in the barrage.

One of the First Platoon men, Private Cavaleri, had closed his eyes and pulled himself down deep in his hole. There he sat, shaking. The exploding shells sent dirt flying into the holes on top of the men. "What the hell are you doing that for?" he said to himself out loud. "If your gonna get hit you're gonna get hit. That's it!" After that he didn't shake anymore.[127]

As he neared Second Platoon's area, Lieutenant Calhoun could see some of his men running near a wooded area about three hundred yards to the front of his platoon area. They were under fire from the woods. "When I arrived at the left flank of my platoon area I was told that Platoon Sergeant Smith had been shot in the chest by a German sniper as he raised up from behind a hedgerow," recalled Calhoun. The lieutenant got his men, some of whom didn't even know what all the shooting was about because they were so spread out, back into their defensive positions on the line. He then sent the medics out to get Smith.

As the medic brought him in, Smith said jokingly to the men, "I'm getting out of here. If you need any help with them Krauts, let me know and my old man will send over a mule that will kick the hell out of them." Later, the men got the word that Smith had died before reaching the battalion aid station. News of Smith's death spread quickly throughout the company. F Company had lost its first man. The event served to drive home the point that this was it, the real thing, combat. It was quiet for fifteen or twenty minutes. Some of the men went back to look at the body. Many tears were shed. For First Sergeant Donovan, Smith's death also proved that "you didn't dare get real close" to your buddy.[128]

Calhoun, meanwhile, found no one who could explain exactly what Sergeant Smith was doing that far in front of the lines, or why he had taken the NCOs with him leaving the platoon without leaders. Calhoun appointed Staff Sergeant Howard R. McClain of Leesville, Florida as his new platoon sergeant. McClain saw that the men finished preparing their positions and then organized the guard duty rotation for the coming night.[129]

When the shelling had ceased Cavaleri stood up and took a look around. "Look at that!" he exclaimed. Shell holes – a yard across and about six inches deep – dotted the area – some only a few feet away from his own hole. "Look how close that came," said Cavaleri to his foxhole buddy. "Four more feet and they'd got us."[130]

Later that evening, the officers returned to battalion headquarters to receive the rest of the briefing on the next morning's attack. On the way, a D Company man stopped Lieutenant Calhoun to warn him – a German sniper was still occupying the church steeple. Calhoun thanked the trooper and moved ahead a little more cautiously until they reached the CP. Privates Imre and Hataway, who had accompanied Calhoun, waited outside while their platoon leader received the rest of the details concerning the next day's attack.

After only a brief, ten-minute preparatory artillery barrage, the 194th Glider Infantry Regiment (with the 550th Airborne Infantry Battalion attached) and the 513th Parachute Infantry Regiment would lead the attack. The 193rd Glider Infantry Regiment and the 507th Parachute Infantry Regiment were to be held in tactical reserve to repel the expected German counter thrust with the 507th protecting the left flank.[131]

Near the end of the briefing, Colonel Miller hit the officers with what Calhoun thought was a bombshell: "Prisoners will be taken to the S-2 for interrogation and then shot." After Malmédy, commented Don Newhouse, the word was out – 'Don't take any prisoners'." According to Calhoun, Colonel Miller had arranged for First Sergeant Charlie Bell of the Headquarters Company, under the direction of Major Edwards, to have the prisoners shot in one of the village's stone barns. Major Edwards was never aware of the order himself, he said; he was with one of the companies at the time and did not attend the officers meeting. Edwards admitted, however, that, though such an order sounds a little bloodthirsty, it was the Colonel's style: "Miller was an eccentric. . . he was a little bit nutty." Nevertheless, in light of the battalion's predicament, the order was practical. As Don Newhouse explained 54 years later, "Number one, a prisoner is a liability."[132]

After the meeting broke up, F Company's officers returned to their platoons to prepare for the attack. Lieutenant Stositch told Lieutenant Puckett only that they were "going that way [north] as far as we can go." Stositch confided in Tech Sergeant Paul that Battalion didn't expect F Company to encounter any automatics within a thousand yards for the line of departure. Nevertheless, no one could be really sure what to expect.[133]

2nd Battalion, though its lines were spread thin, was well established in the village by nightfall. Two platoons from E Company were set up on the right side of the town and F Company, with Second Platoon on the northwest and Third Platoon on the southwest sides, held the left. D Company manned observation posts surrounding the village and the platoons posted guards in their areas. Battalion headquarters was established in the center.[134]

Despite the fact they were occupying a village, all the men were suffering from the cold. Haggard was down to only his ODs and the temperature was falling. The night before leaving Aincreville, he'd washed his jumpsuit out and hung it out to dry. When the company left sooner than he'd expected, he had had to start scrounging. The first thing he did was find extra socks, nine pairs, and he put them all on. Then he threw away the field boots he had been wearing and put on a pair of goulashes over the socks. He ended up wearing summer underwear, long johns, an OD shirt, a wool sweater, a field jacket, two pairs of OD pants, an overcoat, and a blanket. Even with that he was still cold.

Private Dahlberg had to move out of the barn and sleep in a hole that night. It was very cold, wet and miserable, but at least he had his bed roll. Many of the men had bunched up to use each other's body heat. "We're so close together," remarked Dahlberg to his friends. "What if a shell comes in? We're gonna get it good." The men, however, were too cold to care. Meanwhile, the German sniper in the church fired periodically at the body of a paratrooper that lay in the street nearby, only a few yards from Dahlberg.[135]

Through Slocomb, Sergeant Paul ordered Munafo to "mount the machine-gun at the edge of the woods" west of the town. Sergeant Paul, in fact, usually told Slocomb what he wanted Munafo to do and let Slocomb relay the instructions. Munafo had just finished the final touches on his position when he saw the glow of a fire coming from one of the bombed out buildings. It was just a couple of walls, no roof, but quite a few troopers were using it for shelter and, though he knew it was unwise, Munafo joined them. Before very long, the Germans started bracketing in on the light. One round landed on one side, and then a second landed on the other. "Jesus, that's mortar fire out there," Munafo exclaimed. He recognized the distinctive crunch of the shells and knew instantly what the enemy were doing. "We better get out of here," he told the other men. "If they see a fire, they're gonna figure somebody's by this fire." Everyone got up and hustled out. "Sure as shit, the next one landed right in the middle," Munafo recalled. "Sonofabitch," said Munafo, applauding his good luck, "look at that."[136]

Privates Newhouse and Kinkus were assigned a four hour guard duty in some woods near the village from 2000 to midnight. Newhouse pulled his poncho over his head and smoked a cigarette. They stared so long at the frozen mounds of vegetables in the field that they began to move. Their shift was uneventful, but still they felt awfully alone.[137]

By early morning, German patrols were probing into 2nd Battalion's positions, testing their lines. Some troopers had to fight off enemy attacks where, in many places, the enemy came forward in a dash only to be stopped within yards of the Americans' positions. When an enemy patrol started getting close to Imre and Harding's outpost position, they threw grenades as far away as they could, at least a hundred feet, to draw the Germans' attention and fire. The diversion gave the Germans a noise to shoot at and the two troopers enough time to get to a better position.[138]

The Germans "ran their tanks all night to keep the men scared," said Sarrell, and German artillery and 'screaming meemies' kept up a constant barrage. The artillery of the 17th Airborne answered and knocked out several enemy tanks. The brightly burning remains of German armor, lighting up night, cast ugly shadows on the frozen landscape.[139]

At 2323 hours, Colonel Coutts sent his final field message to Colonel Miller before the attack. It read, "Give 'em hell, Ace."

5

Perfect Targets

Baptism of Fire at Mande-St.-Etienne
Thursday, 4 January 1945

Lieutenant Calhoun woke his Second Platoon men well before dawn to give them time to eat and prepare for the attack. The morning ritual began, each man massaging his numb limbs through several layers of clothing and stamping feet his until he had restored some measure of circulation and dexterity. It was cold, and a light snow was falling. PFC Imre felt sick to his stomach. Around him, the other Second Platoon men crouching in their holes were already nervously picking at cold rations, some trying to make jokes. Others stared up ahead into the trees. Too troubled over the situation to eat much of anything himself, Imre instead packed a snow ball and over it sprinkled the lemonade powder from his K-ration – usually saved to scour his mess kit – and licked it.[1]

Captain Reynolds had discussed F Company's attack the night before with his platoon leaders. Lieutenant Stositch's Third Platoon would be attacking on the left flank with Second Platoon as the base platoon for their attack. E Company would be on the right. Both Reynolds and Lieutenant Calhoun knew that even with artillery to keep the Germans' heads down, an attack across the open ground between Mande-St.-Etienne and the woods would be difficult, almost suicidal – and every man was sure that there were "a hell of a lot of Germans in those woods" as well as enemy tanks lurking in the swirling fog beyond.[2] Lieutenant Calhoun's platoon, Captain Reynolds had decided, would lay down a base of fire on the enemy positions in the edge of the woods while the Third Platoon worked its way from a wooded area on the left and forward, along the cart path with its adjacent embankment which would provide them cover, until they had closed to within thirty-five yards of the left edge of the woods. Then, Second Platoon's base of fire would shift to the right, keeping just ahead of the advancing Third Platoon troopers as they swept through the woods and captured the first objective. It sounded simple enough. Reynolds was sure this would get his men into the woods without too many casualties. At company headquarters, everyone was confident. The word was passed around to PFC Dahlberg: "If we go two miles today, we can get a rest."[3]

At about 0745, the 17th Airborne's artillery began firing the scheduled preparatory barrage along the division's front.[4] High explosive and white phosphorous rounds burst among the pines in the big woods three hundred yards forward of Lieutenant Calhoun's position. Although it was close to the jump off time, Third Platoon had not appeared on the left and E Company had not appeared on the right. Captain Reynolds, who was waiting with Calhoun, told him not to move across the line of departure until he ordered him to do so and left to find out what had happened to Lieutenant Stositch's men and E Company.

At 0800 hours, Lieutenant Colonel Miller, who had been waiting in his observation post (OP) – a tile brick shed or barn that had been hit by artillery allowing Miller to watch the attack through a hole in the front, and the "furthest house on the northern edge of the village" – emerged and marched the seventy-five yards west to the spot where Lieutenant Calhoun was waiting. Miller asked Lieutenant Calhoun why his platoon wasn't attacking. Calhoun explained to Miller that he and Captain Reynolds had discussed the situation the night before, and that they had decided that Second Platoon would "build up a base of fire" to support Third Platoon's attack. Lieutenant Calhoun pointed out the cart path and embankment on the left that Third Platoon, upon crossing the line of departure, would work its way up before dashing into the woods. Calhoun explained that this envelopment would flank the German defenders, and that Stositch would be protected the whole way by Second Platoon's base of fire. Miller, however, was impatient to get the show on the road, and did not approve of Captain Reynolds' plan if it meant waiting for Reynolds to find his lost platoon.

Lieutenant Colonel Miller did not fully appreciate the strength of the German defenses facing F Company in the woods. Rather, based on erroneous information he had received from a patrol, he believed that the Germans had pulled out ahead of 2nd Battalion, and told this to Calhoun. Miller, therefore, ordered Lieutenant

Calhoun to take his men straight across the field, "to attack at once." Calhoun protested; he knew the Germans still held the woods and that his men would have no protection on either flank if they ran into trouble, but he couldn't convince Miller of that fact.

At that moment, Captain Reynolds called on the radio for Lieutenant Calhoun. PFC Joe Grubb, who was squatted in a nearby hole, got up and handed over the Handy-Talky. Reynolds told Calhoun that he had found Lieutenant Stositch and Third Platoon. They had been ambushed and were pinned down. Reynolds had sorted things out, he said, but it would take Third Platoon some time to reach their position on the left flank. Then Captain Reynolds again told Lieutenant Calhoun to put off the attack.

Colonel Miller, who was standing beside Lieutenant Calhoun, asked for the radio. Grabbing it, Miller told Captain Reynolds that he was ordering the Second Platoon to attack now, before the artillery lifted. He then returned the radio to Calhoun.

To Calhoun, Reynolds said only, "Good luck, Sam."

"Without any further resistance to orders," Calhoun formed his men into a skirmish line. When in Service, you do as you're told. Still stiff with cold, the men arose from their holes and crouched in a loose formation. Their brown uniforms stood out starkly against the snowy landscape. Perfect targets.

Sergeant Gohn told Newhouse to assist Private Mabron E. Henderson, the bazooka man. Newhouse said he would do it, but told Gohn he couldn't carry his rifle, the bazooka rockets, *and* a thirty pound satchel of C2. He asked Gohn to take the C2 and Gohn did. The bazooka team then took its place at the rear of the platoon, closest to the village. Gibbs got up on point. Everyone's gut tightened. "I felt like it was World War I and they just said, 'Go over the top!'," remembered Don Newhouse.[5]

Rising gently to the woods ahead, the field before them was flat and white covered with a fresh snow that continued to fall. A barbed wire fence followed the course of the tree line. The artillery barrage was booming now and its roar shattered the cold morning air. Most of the rounds, however, were falling short or off target all together.[6] The men gazed out over the open ground. It was flat – no cover at all. PFC Imre thought it resembled a prairie, and in his brown overcoat, he felt like he was a buffalo about to venture out onto it. The scent of the pines reached his nostrils in spite of the permeating cold – tall, beautiful pines. Then Lieutenant Calhoun gave the word to move out.

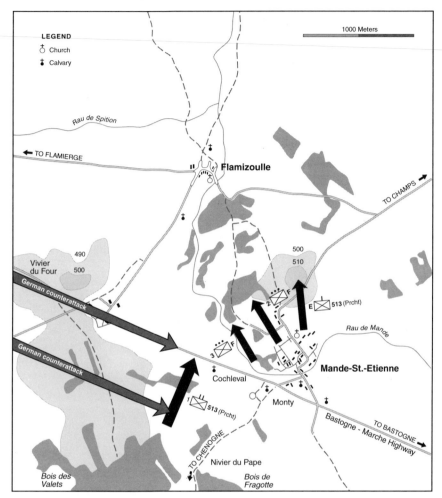

Initial attacks of the 513th Parachute Infantry Regiment at Mande-St.-Etienne, Belgium, 4 January 1945. (Rick Brownlee/R&B Graphic Designs)

Calhoun's men stood up and started across the field slowly. "I think every man held [his] breath waiting for them to open fire," remembered Bob Greenstrand. It wasn't too long before the scout, Private Gibbs, and PFC Kinkus, were approaching the fence some fifteen yards from the edge of the woods line. Lieutenant Calhoun and his runner, PFC Patrick Keller, were following, but were still one hundred fifty yards behind, only about half way across the field. Henderson and Newhouse had just started into the field. Suddenly, the terrible rip of MG-42s broke from the trees. "The Germans must have laughed like hell."[7]

It was a slaughter. Several troopers were knocked down outright. One man who tried to run was shot through his back. Lieutenant Calhoun waved the men to move forward but it was already too late; the Germans unleashed their mortars and artillery. Calhoun's men now were in a trap, boxed in by fire from three sides. One, perhaps two German machine-gunners were firing from positions ahead of the troopers – in the south edge of the forest – and another was on their right flank, firing from the arm of trees extending south more than one hundred yards from the main part of the woods. More machine-gun fire was coming from the Rau de Mande ravine, about two hundred yards away on the platoon's left flank.[8]

Gibbs and Kinkus ran to the fence. They had just scrambled over the wire when they were hit and both dropped. Kinkus was hit by a shell fragment in the thigh. He died, apparently of shock, before anyone could get to him. PFC Gibbs was hit by machine-gun fire. Though wounded, he got to his hands and knees and crawled forward toward a machine-gun on the left front. Sparks flew from his body as he was hit again by another fusillade from the MG-42. Gibbs fell, but again he recovered and crawled forward through the snow toward the machine-gun. Then PFC Greenstrand, watching from just forward of Miller's OP, saw Gibbs fall for the last time. When the medics removed Gibbs' body that evening, they reported that he was clutching a white phosphorous grenade – pinned pulled – in his right hand. Though he made an heroic effort at the cost of his own life, Private Gibbs was never awarded a medal.[9]

Lieutenant Calhoun and PFC Keller were running for the fence when they got pinned down by German fire. The fence, just ahead of them, was itself not a formidable obstacle – men could dive over it – but the withering fire was. To his left, Calhoun could see his men being cut down by the murderous fire. Those who still could had already started to fall back while, around them, tracers ricocheted off the bodies of the dead.

So many men had been hit that it seemed like everyone was calling for the medic, but Private William 'Tommy' Thomson, Second Platoon's medic, had already been killed while assisting PFC Chuck Hester, one of the machine-gunners on the platoon's left. Thomson was clearly identified as a medic, and had been in the field and exposed, helping the wounded from the first shot, when he was killed.[10]

Newhouse and Henderson were in the open, but were the men farthest from the woods. The two pressed themselves down behind a little hump in the ground where they debated whether or not to fire the bazooka or even if they could hit the enemy bunkers – set twenty yards back among the trees – at that range, over three hundred yards. If they did fire, the backblast from the weapon would draw the machine-gunners' attention, they concluded, and that would mean almost certain death. Besides, only the luckiest shot would hit the enemy positions. They decided not to shoot.[11]

More artillery fell in among Calhoun's men only this time it was from 2nd Battalion's own 81mm mortars. The gunners were apparently trying to get the range of the German bunkers and walked several rounds through the pinned men of the Second Platoon. Still more were wounded, and others were hit again.[12]

Greenstrand's squad leader, Sergeant Raymond O. Eide, the blond Norwegian boy from Minnesota the men called 'Hot Damn Eide' because he used the expression so much, was somewhere out ahead of him, but without having to be told, Graupensperger and Greenstrand had gotten their .30 caliber machine-gun set up ahead of Miller's OP and were firing as fast as they could load. They soon ran out of ammunition, however, and Greenstrand yelled for Driggers to bring more. As Greenstrand loaded a fresh belt into the Browning, a bullet struck the ammunition box and it exploded. Greenstrand was blinded for a few seconds but was otherwise all right. Graup, meanwhile, continued firing.[13]

When the firing started, Staff Sergeant Knigge, with second squad, shouted to Lieutenant Calhoun, "What are we gonna do now?" but Calhoun never heard him. Knigge didn't even know if it was Calhoun he was shouting to: "I don't know who the hell I was talking to [but] it was suicide to just keep going forward," remembered Knigge. "The field was completely covered by fire, so I was going back and I got my guys the hell out of there." Knigge's squad had gotten little more than half way across the field when they began to withdraw back to the line of departure. Other men were falling back, too. Taking the bazooka, Newhouse and Henderson fell back to the town as well. Everyone was withdrawing a few yards at a time, stopping only momentarily to return fire and cover their buddies' retreat.[14]

PFC Donald Black, PFC Rod MacKenzie's assistant gunner, got down into a foxhole and began to cry. Black had been married before going overseas and had told Mackenzie, whom he had palled around with in London, that he knew he'd never see his wife again.

First Sergeant Donovan, in a building on the edge of the town, observed the floundering attack in disbelief. Ahead, in the wood line, Donovan spotted a muzzle flash high in a tree. Then a round struck right next to his head, ripping a chunk of wood out of the window sash. Donovan took a pot shot with his M1 at the next muzzle flash and, miraculously, knocked a sniper from his treetop perch. Donovan later discovered that the sniper was a member of the Waffen SS – not one of the old men or boys intelligence had told him to expect.[15] "They weren't Volkssturm or anything like that," Major Edwards, then the battalion exec, agreed in 1997. "They were pros."[16]

Tec 5 Haggard also was watching the attack from behind Miller's observation post with a couple of runners and some of the other company headquarters men when Lieutenant Dean appeared. Dean told Haggard that he didn't know where Reynolds was, and asked Haggard what was going on. Haggard reported that the Second and Third Platoons were pinned down by machine-gun fire, and that he did not know where Reynolds was either. Dean asked Haggard to call the radio men with each of the pinned platoons and instruct them to "crawl up to the officer, and give the radio to the officer," so that he could find out "what the hell was going on." Haggard placed the calls immediately, while volunteering that he didn't know where First Platoon was either. Haggard tried to raise PFC Grubb, Lieutenant Calhoun's RTO, first. All he could hear was garbled screaming. It sounded like the granules in the mic were frozen – Grubb was shouting, but it was nearly inaudible. Haggard just couldn't understand what he was trying to say. Haggard then tried PFC Chuck Craddock with Third Platoon. To Haggard's relief, Craddock answered and Haggard relayed Dean's order.

Craddock was trying to get to Lieutenant Stositch, "He's about thirty feet away," he said, "but I'll try."

"Be careful," said Haggard. That was the last he heard from Craddock. Haggard realized that both radio men had been killed. With that, Lieutenant Dean decided he'd better take off and look for Reynolds himself. When Haggard got the two radios back the next day, the batteries in both were dead and the antenna of one was broken. Both were damaged. Neither was salvageable.[17]

Bullets plowed into the snowy ground all around Greenstrand's position and one round struck him in the right forearm. Greenstrand clutched the limb in fear, but when he inspected the hole in his coat sleeve he realized he wasn't hit. Graup, however, who had suddenly stopped firing, was bleeding badly and grasping his left shoulder in pain. The bullet that cut through Greenstrand's sleeve had hit Graup.

Greenstrand took hold of Graupensperger and helped him back to the foxhole by the barn they had dug the day before. Then Greenstrand ran around the barn and called for a medic. After a few long minutes, the medics came up and started working on Graup. Greenstrand watched them for a moment, helpless. It would be the last time Greenstrand saw him.[18]

Greenstrand then crawled back out to the machine-gun and started firing at the Germans, hoping to keep their heads down. When he was out of ammunition, he again called Driggers to bring more. Driggers came forward, but had trouble loading the first belt, so Greenstrand loaded it and continued firing, sweeping the woods. [19]

It didn't take Greenstrand long to go through the belt and when it was spent, Driggers opened another ammunition box and reached up to reload the gun. At that moment, Driggers was hit. He rolled over onto his back, writhing in pain. Greenstrand grabbed Driggers by the arms, intending to pull him to safety. When he did, Driggers screamed loudly. Greenstrand then saw that Driggers had been hit through both elbows and in the back of one hand. "The German machine-guns," explained Greenstrand, "fired very rapidly. . . and if you caught one slug you usually caught two or three." Greenstrand grabbed Driggers by the shoulder straps of his field jacket and pulled him back to the same foxhole to which he had dragged Graupensperger. Graup was already gone. Greenstrand again ran to the barn and hollered for the medics.[20] The medics from battalion were moving the wounded into Colonel Miller's OP. It was there that they administered first aid to the casualties before moving them to the battalion aid station that was located inside the village proper. Greenstrand again crawled back to the gun and continued firing, calling Private Bernard E. Glanowski, a kid from Buffalo, New York, to carry up more ammunition.[21]

Those Second Platoon men who had managed to get out of the field awaited orders, but none were forthcoming. The assistant platoon leader, 2nd Lieutenant Isham Fann, who had been on patrol the previous evening, had not yet returned to the platoon and no one knew where he was. It later turned out that Fann was in a barn in Mande-St.-Etienne, sleeping.

Meanwhile, as Lieutenant Calhoun lay in the field, bullets ripped past him through the snow, clawing black lines through it and cutting into Keller's body. Calhoun tried to get a response from Keller, but he was dead. Gibbs and Kinkus were dead as well. The only thing Calhoun could do was lie still there among the bodies and hope the German machine-gunners, firing from positions only yards to his front and left, believed he had been killed too.

After about fifteen or twenty minutes the firing quieted down. To Lieutenant Calhoun it felt like he had been laying in the snow for two hours. In the woods, the Germans had relaxed a little and some began smoking. Calhoun had spotted a dirt-covered pile of beets about seventy-five yards to his left rear. Not exactly bullet-proof, but it was the only potential shelter in sight. Calhoun decided to make a run for it.

As soon as he started his dash, it seemed as if every German with a weapon opened fire at him. Calhoun could hear the bullets pop past him and saw the tracers in front of him as some of the German gunners led him, hoping he would run into their fire. Miraculously, Calhoun made it. He leaped over the beet pile and hunkered down behind it. The firing stopped.

From behind Calhoun, a voice called out, "Lieutenant, can I help you?" If there was ever a time he needed help, it was now, Calhoun thought. Calhoun looked around to see a man by a fence post about thirty-five yards south of him. "Who are you?" asked Calhoun. The man identified himself as the forward observer for the battalion's 81mm mortar battery. During the briefing the night before, the officers had been ordered not to call for smoke because the battalion had only sixteen rounds of smoke available. Sam looked around him. His company aidman, Private Thomson, lay dead about thirty-five yards to his left. Some of the wounded men in the field were in agony and begging for help. Without a smoke screen they would never get out. Calhoun considered the situation momentarily and decided to call for the smoke anyway.

This time, the aim of the mortarmen was excellent. They placed six rounds perfectly in front of the enemy positions, blinding the German gunners. Lieutenant Calhoun then directed his remaining men to remove the wounded from the field. Crouching low to avoid being spotted by the German gunners through the drifting smoke, the men went out. Two men grabbed Private Walter Day by his jacket collar – Day had been shot in both legs – and dragged him out while some of the other men fired to cover them.[22] Although already wounded in the leg, Private Bill Kuntz dragged several of the wounded to safety, an act for which he later was awarded the Silver Star.

As soon as the smoke started, Greenstrand jumped up and "ran like hell to the barn." Lieutenant Calhoun arrived soon thereafter and asked him where his machine-gun was, Greenstrand pointed out into the field. "Damn it, Greenstrand," said Calhoun, "we need that gun. Go get it." Greenstrand ran back into the field, and picked up the gun and tripod. He had just started running back for the barn when it dawned on him that the field was still under fire and that a smoke screen couldn't stop a bullet. Greenstrand threw the gun out ahead of him and hit the ground. He then grabbed it by the barrel and dragged it through the snow to the safe side of the barn.[23]

Lieutenant Calhoun took one look at the gun and "wasn't a happy man." The tripod had fallen off while Greenstrand was dragging it and it would not be safe to go back for it. "Field strip that goddamned thing, and get it cleaned up and ready to fire," barked Calhoun. "I did so in darn short order," recalled Greenstrand, "and it wasn't easy because my fingers were about frozen."[24]

It was about 1030 hours. At that moment, Colonel Miller called for Lieutenant Calhoun to report to his observation post. Lieutenant Walter Rydesky, the commander of 2nd Battalion's 81mm mortar platoon, had just been there and left.

Just after 0800, E Company, under Lieutenant John Deam, had made its attack upon the hill north of Mande-St.-Etienne. Artillery placed on the hill kept the heads of the German defenders down as the E Company troopers moved determinedly across the barren, snow-covered ground. Within fifteen minutes, Lieutenant Deam radioed back "that he was on the phase line and the men in enemy fox holes."[25]

While Lieutenant Calhoun's platoon lay pinned down in the field, Rydesky had talked with 2nd Lieutenant Richard E. Manning, who commanded E Company's Third Platoon, and they had devised a plan to get Lieutenant Manning's platoon into the eastern side of the woods where they could relieve the pressure on F Company. Lieutenant Rydesky presented the rather simple plan to Colonel Miller and Captain Jack Lawler, the battalion S-3: Rydesky's 81mm mortars would fire smoke into the tree line, providing cover for Manning's platoon to attack from a nearby road into the woods, behind the German's left flank. Miller at that moment was preoccupied with the battalion's communications situation; the telephone lines to regiment had been cut by enemy artillery and the radios were out. "Colonel Miller looked like he was in shock," remembered Rydesky. The shock lasted only momentarily, however. Miller became hysterical at the proposal – a reaction Rydesky had not expected.

"Are you trying to tell me how to run my outfit?" bellowed Miller. "Get out of here!" Rydesky left uneasy and thought that Miller had fallen apart under the pressure. [26]

Miller, who had been watching the progress of Lieutenant Calhoun's attack from his OP, had already come to the conclusion that Second Platoon would not be able to clear the woods on their own. When Calhoun got pinned down, he called on Lieutenant Deam and told him to continue to hold the crest of the hill with E Company, but to commit his reserve platoon to an attack of the forest. Miller was specific in his orders to Deam, "Go in, but don't swing from the left; Come in from the right [behind them]." This, in fact, was the same plan Rydesky had suggested.

"Don't worry," replied Deam, "I'll start them off myself." Lieutenant Deam called his Third Platoon commander, Lieutenant Manning, and told him to "get his men, fix bayonets, and go on in." As promised, Deam led the attack, but was killed almost immediately by enemy rifle fire. Lieutenant Hall, Manning's assistant was shot in the chest, and another officer, Lieutenant Fagan who had assumed command of E Company, was wounded as well. [27]

At about that moment, Lieutenant Calhoun entered the Colonel's OP. Calhoun was chewed out by an irate Miller for using the smoke. "Manning's crawling up a drainage ditch beside the road on the right with his platoon from E Company," said Miller, "and he'll be over the hill there in about a half hour." From there, Miller said, Lieutenant Manning's platoon would be able to flank the German positions from the right. Then he told Calhoun to round up his platoon and get ready to attack across that field again. "You go out in that field and draw the fire."

Calhoun was well aware that another such attempt would spell certain death for most of his platoon's shaken survivors. "Not my men or me!" Calhoun protested adamantly.

"Just get your men together and await my orders," insisted Miller.

Lieutenant Calhoun wasn't going to take his men out in that field again to get killed regardless of Miller's orders. "It's pretty hard for a guy at the doing level to overcome what senior officers tell him to do," Major Edwards later commented. "It takes a lot of guts." [28] But that is exactly what Calhoun did.

Counting himself, Calhoun had only sixteen men who could still fight. Worsening the situation, the Third Platoon still had not arrived on the line of departure and he still didn't know where Captain Reynolds was. Nevertheless, Lieutenant

Calhoun ordered, "Follow me!" and led his men to the embankment along the cart path running up the left side of the field, the path he and Reynolds had discussed using earlier that morning. The men crawled up the shallow swale and knelt down.

"Fix your bayonets!" ordered Lieutenant Calhoun. Clack came the sound of metal upon metal as the men locked the heavy blades on their M1s. Greenstrand, with the .30 caliber machine-gun, slung the barrel in a bandoleer which he hung around his neck.[29] PFC MacKenzie cut an ammunition belt up into twenty round sections and got ready to load for him.[30]

"Lieutenant Calhoun had a good hold of himself," recalled Don Newhouse.[31] Calhoun knew a surprise dash from the embankment would get his men into the woods too quickly for the Germans to react and probably save lives. He told the men his intentions and then spread them out along the embankment in a skirmish line. Staff Sergeant Knigge took a position on the left. Then, from behind them, a man yelled, "Lieutenant, what outfit's that?" Three men were approaching from the field behind them in the direction of the 1st Battalion.

"Second Platoon, F Company," replied Calhoun.

"I'm the liaison for 1st Battalion. I'm supposed to meet with Colonel Miller. Where's he at?" asked the trooper. Lieutenant Calhoun gave the men the directions to Miller's observation post and off they went.

The woods ahead lay quiet. Lieutenant Calhoun turned to his men and ordered: "Get going you sonsabitches. Do you wanna live forever?"

With one movement, the men rose up and over the side of the embankment. Lieutenant Calhoun led, charging across the open ground, spraying the tree line with his Thompson. Greenstrand was right behind him, firing his .30 caliber machine-gun from his waist. "For Christ sake," yelled Imre, giving him a wide berth, "take it easy!"[32] An enemy machine-gun opened up, but the fire was inaccurate.[33] The attack apparently had caught the Germans off guard. Calhoun's men swept into the trees and pushed nearly 250 yards, reducing German bunkers as they advanced.

Short rounds from American guns started to fall around them and Calhoun hit the ground. A white phosphorus shell landed near his feet, but it was a dud and it fizzled out in the snow. Calhoun, shaken but in one piece, got up and continued.

When the attack broke through from the thick woods, Lieutenant Calhoun could see Lieutenant Manning's platoon on the eastern edge of the woods. Seeing that they were trapped between the two forces, some enemy soldiers started to surrender. Some continued to resist, however. PFC Russell Hataway gored one such German with his bayonet. The man fell dead but the bayonet was stuck between the dead man's ribs. Hataway tried shooting it off but when that didn't work, he unlatched the bayonet and left it sticking in the corpse.[34] Staff Sergeant Knigge was getting ready to throw a grenade into one of the bunkers when one of the men shouted "Hold up!" The trooper called down into the hole and the Germans came out and surrendered. Lieutenant Calhoun yelled, "*Hande hoch. Auf-geben!*" and the rest of the Germans threw down their weapons. It was over. About a dozen enemy soldiers lay dead; another seventeen had surrendered.[35]

While Lieutenant Calhoun was moving his men up the left toward the woods, Lieutenant Manning led his platoon about seventy-five yards north of the farm buildings at the edge of town. Here, the men were about 180 yards from the main part of the forest. E Company's First and Second Platoons were both pinned down in the open ground between the hill crest and the woods. There was intense artillery and machine-gun fire. Manning realized that most of the artillery – save for a single German 88 firing at them – was from American 75mm Howitzers and went to the rear to have the fire shifted into the woods where the German machine-gun fire was coming from. When Lieutenant Manning returned, the next salvo landed right on top of his own position – Manning had given them the wrong corrections. He went back again and this time the artillery "blew the hell out of the woods," silencing the machine-gun that covered the ditch. Manning's men shook their bayonets loose in their scabbards where they had frozen and fixed them. Many of the men then slipped off their overcoats to free themselves up.[36]

Manning's men crawled into the field until they reached the barbed wire fence – about twenty-five yards – and crawled through. PFC Sanchez, the platoon runner, jumped up and yelled, "Let's go!" and charged toward the tree line with the rest of the men following. They could see that artillery had indeed silenced the German machine-gun, the bodies still smoldered from the direct hit. The men tried to form a skirmish line to clear the finger of woods but the artillery had choked the woods with so many felled trees that this was impossible. Manning decided to bypass this section of the woods and reform the platoon on the right edge of the main part of the forest. From here, Lieutenant Manning's men cleared the eastern edge of the woods and then rejoined E Company on the right.[37] Casualties were light in Manning's platoon – only four or five men were wounded in the attack.

Unfortunately, one of them was Manning, severely wounded in the leg by a German grenade. He would loose his leg, but was awarded the Distinguished Service Cross for his efforts.[38]

Back at Lieutenant Calhoun's position, PFC Russell Hataway took a look around at the forest of tall pines and the captured German positions. The trees stood in more or less perfect rows – evidently it was a reforested area. The bunkers were well-constructed affairs, with heavy log and earth roofs and earth was packed up the sides. Some of them had multiple tiers with rifle positions, and were thatched with straw and had straw floors.[39] With the trees growing up around them, to Hataway it looked as if they'd been there for years.[40] The Germans were like groundhogs, thought Imre as he stood over the bunker positions and looked back toward the ground Second Platoon had attacked over earlier that morning. The Germans had had a clear field of fire. "They could see everything." Strangely, however, the Germans had made no attempt to defend their flanks or rear. A lucky break for Lieutenant Calhoun and the Second Platoon.

Not only were the skillfully constructed German fortifications cause for some discomfort, but so too were the German troops who had defended them. Calhoun's men found their prisoners were not young boys and old men but seasoned troops – "a lot of hard-nosed bastards," recalled Neal Haggard.[41] Private Imre got the impression that the enemy force was made up of men from two units. The younger men had fought when the platoon attacked, but the older men – forward observers, Imre thought – gave up right away. The troopers relieved the prisoners of their personal effects, including photographs of their families, and kept them for souvenirs. As this was taking place, one of the Germans pointed to a wound in his shoulder and then at Lieutenant Calhoun's M1A1 Thompson, indicating that it was Calhoun who had wounded him.

Calhoun's own wounded, Sergeant Raymond Eide, and Sergeant Howard McClain whose gloves were covered with blood from a thumb wound, were loaded onto a jeep and taken back to Mande-St.-Etienne for evacuation. Colonel Miller met their jeep as it was heading back, and directed the driver to the battalion aid station where Eide and McClain were given morphine.

Concerned about a possible counterattack, Lieutenant Calhoun ordered his men to set up in the shell holes out in the field forward of the trees, a line which constituted the first phase line. What looked to be about a battalion of Germans were digging in about three hundred yards to his left front, southeast of Flamizoulle and, over to the west, was Flamierge where a German armored division headquarters had been reported to be located. Calhoun had no idea how many Germans might be waiting for them in the bushy hillside in front. All he could do was wait for support to arrive on his right and left flanks.[42] It was the whole situation that troubled Staff Sergeant Knigge. He couldn't understand what they were doing out there all alone in that "idiotic horseshoe" of a position.

While they dug, the Second Platoon troopers saw the outline of a column, about four hundred yards distant, marching to the enemy's rear. Although they couldn't have known it at the time, a large number of troopers from the 1st Battalion had been captured that morning. The Germans were marching them to the rear and to prison camps in Germany.[43]

Despite the falling snow and the consequent poor visibility, the 1st Battalion's attack had begun well enough. B and C Companies had attacked to the northeast, through the Bois des Valets, toward the Bastogne-Marche Highway and Cochleval – a hamlet of one farmhouse and a calvary. With A Company in reserve, the two assault companies advanced through the northern portion of the Bois that morning, encountering light resistance – mainly small arms fire – from a small German force that had infiltrated into the woods during the night. The battalion quickly over-ran the enemy positions, taking twenty-five prisoners.[44]

B and C Companies continued their advance across the open snow fields to the south bank of the Bastogne-Marche Highway at Cochleval. It was there, however, that they were met by "heavy fire from high velocity weapons" and their attack ground to a halt. A few men were able to cross the road, but direct fire from German self-propelled guns to the northwest pinned down the rest and the battalion's casualties mounted quickly. Probably due to poor visibility, elements of the 194th Glider Infantry attacking on their left fired on B and C Companies, too, inflicting several friendly-fire casualties. Lieutenant Colonel Taylor, the 1st Battalion commander, soon decided that the road could not be used as an axis of attack and that it would be impossible to cross the open ground to the north of the Bastogne-Marche Highway in the face of such fire.[45]

A Company, led by Captain John Spears, was ordered to try and flank the enemy by attacking up the Rau de Mande draw, the ditch dividing the zones of the 1st and 2nd Battalions. This attack was blunted, however, by enemy armor that was spread across the entire front of the battalion.[46]

PREVIOUS:
Camp Forrest, Tennessee – June 1944. F Company.

Third Platoon:
Top: Haggard, Elliot, Guidry, Schneck, Sperling, Roebke, Eibert, Bowers; *Middle*: Sorenson, Pilger, Dahlberg, Flynn, Podkulski, Munafo, Holine, Spivey; *Seated*: Rafalovich, DeHaven, Paul, McGoldrick, Dean, Stositch, Donovan, Susol, Rohmann.

Second Platoon:
Top: Harding, Harris, Keller, Imre, Fuller, Hultman, Kinkus, Greene; *Middle*: Gohn, Kitson, Goddard, Hinkley, Hriesik, Greenstrand, Hester, Kuntz; *Seated*: Knigge, Nix, McLain, Graupensperger, Calhoun, Smith, Lage, Halley, Mahoney.

First Platoon:
Top: DePiero, Faulk, Arrowood, Dauer, Bacon, Costello, Laufer; *Middle-Top*: Kaczmarek, Cavaleri, Duprey, Davis, Barbera, Giard, Andrews; *Middle-Bottom*: Duncan, H. Cook, Berg, Anderson, Auer, Balben, Barth, J. Cook, Blackney; *Seated*: Sloan, Moon, Cogan, McGoldrick, O'Donnell, Sims, Vondrasek, Butcher, Cappell.

2nd Lieutenant Samuel Calhoun at home in Fresno, California, in 1943 after completing The Parachute School. (Author's collection via Sam Calhoun)

"Johnny & Rocky" – Tech Sergeant John O. Paul, the platoon sergeant of the Third Platoon, was seriously wounded in action on 4 January 1945. (Courtesy, John O. Paul)

PFC Paul Imre, the assistant 60mm mortar gunner in the Second Platoon, accompanied Lieutenant Calhoun on the bayonet charge, 4 January 1945. (Courtesy, Paul Imre)

Staff Sergeant (then Corporal) Clarence F. Knigge, Jr., a squad leader in the Second Platoon, survived the bayonet charge on 4 January 1945, but was wounded in action three days later. (Author's collection via Clarence Knigge)

Private Frank Munafo, a machine-gunner in the Third Platoon, saved Tech Sergeant Paul's life on 4 January 1945. (Author's collection via Frank Munafo)

RIGHT: PFC James Arrowood of the First Platoon served as runner to 1st Lieutenant Gilles. (Author's collection via James Arrowood)

The trainasium. (Signal Corps photo)

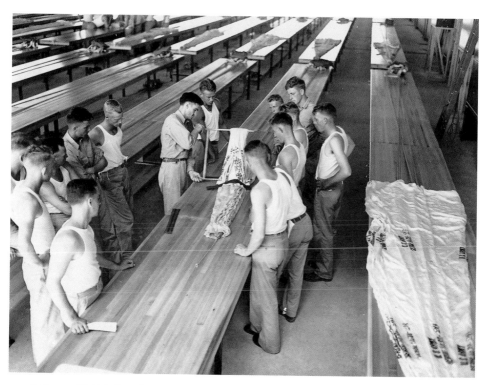

At Lawson Field, trainees learn to properly fold a parachute canopy for packing. (Signal Corps photo)

Trainees learned to steer their parachutes during free descents from the 250' training towers. (Signal Corps photo)

With the aid of a wind machine, a parachute trainee learns to collapse his canopy in high winds. (Signal Corps photo)

Colonel (then Captain) James Winfield Coutts took command of the 513th Parachute Infantry Regiment on 21 January 1944. (Signal Corps photo)

Men of the Second Platoon wait for their turn during practice jumps at Camp Mackall. (Author's collection via Sam Calhoun)

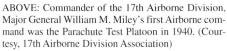

ABOVE: Commander of the 17th Airborne Division, Major General William M. Miley's first Airborne command was the Parachute Test Platoon in 1940. (Courtesy, 17th Airborne Division Association)

ABOVE RIGHT: 2nd Battalion's Commanding Officer, Lieutenant Colonel Allen C. Miller. (Author's collection via Allen Miller, Jr.)

RIGHT: Sam Calhoun at Mackall in 1944. (Author's collection via Sam Calhoun)

At Camp Mackall, PFC Willie Grice was a machine-gunner in the First Platoon. (Author's collection via Sam Calhoun)

PFC Edward R. Dahlberg was the company Commander's runner. (Author's collection via Sam Calhoun)

During the practice jump at Mackall, Private Frank Munafo taped a 'V for Victory' on his helmet. (Author's collection via Frank Munafo)

PFC Willie Grice, PFC Larry Duprey, Sergeant Cliff Butcher, PFC Sid Laufer, and Tec 4 George Vondrasek chuted up for the practice jump at Mackall. (Author's collection via Sam Calhoun)

On guard duty at Camp Forrest, Tennessee, PFC Phil Cavaleri was a machine-gunner in the First Platoon. (Author's collection via Sam Calhoun)

At Camp Forrest, Tennessee, 1944, Private Jack Cook displays F Company's guideon. Cook was only sixteen when, a year later, he was killed in action in Germany. (Author's collection via Bob Greenstrand)

At Camp Forrest, Privates Larry DuPrey and Jack Cook stand guard. (Courtesy, Bob Greenstrand)

PFC Edward R. Dahlberg. (Courtesy, Bob Greenstrand)

Men from the First Platoon. Top: Dahlberg, Cogan, Grice, Kaczmarek, Laufer, Balben, Vondrasek, Cook, and Duprey. Bottom: unidentified, Accomando, Kondiditsiotes, Anderson, Bowers, Faulk, and unidentified. (Author's collection via Sam Calhoun)

At Camp Forrest, a contrasting image of the First Platoon. (Author's collection via Willis Grice)

ABOVE: A graduate of West Point, First Platoon's Commander, 1st Lieutenant Robert J. Gilles was killed in action on 8 January 1945 while covering the company's withdrawal from Mon Nicolay. (Author's collection via Charles Puckett)

ABOVE RIGHT: PFC George Graupensperger and Private Bob Greenstrand on KP duty while at Camp Forrest. (Author's collection via Bob Greenstrand)

RIGHT: Best friends – Privates Sid Laufer and Willie Grice. (Courtesy, Bob Greenstrand)

Harding, Hultman, Accomando, Dauer, Vondrasek, Barbera and Laufer, Cogan, Brewer, unidentified, and Anderson wait in Camp Forrest's mess line. (Author's collection via Bob Greenstrand)

Company Headquarters men Neal Haggard, Wayne DeHaven, and John Flynn. Camp Forrest. (Author's collection via Neal Haggard)

Peeling spuds, Tec 5 Neal Haggard on KP duty at Camp Forrest. (Author's collection via Neal Haggard)

First Platoon men during a road march exercise at Camp Forrest. (Courtesy, Bob Greenstrand)

Camp Forrest's combat city. (Courtesy, Bob Greenstrand)

On a field problem – Paul, Gohn, Knigge, Hataway, Smith, Calhoun, Kaczmarek, and Imre. (Author's collection via Sam Calhoun)

PFC Evangelos J. Kondiditsiotes, PFC Jack Cook, and PFC Russell A. Hataway man a .30 caliber M1919A4 light machine-gun. (Courtesy, Bob Greenstrand)

PFC Francis J. 'Chips' Giard, PFC Willie Grice, and PFC Edward Dahlberg. (Courtesy, Bob Greenstrand)

Private Frank Munafo packing in preparation for movement to the Boston Port of Embarkation. (Author's collection via Frank Munafo)

Amid preparations for movement to the Boston POE, Sergeant Knigge, PFC Duprey, Private Laufer, and PFC Kondiditsiotes pack up Private Munafo for shipping. (Author's collection via Sam Calhoun)

Sergeant (then PFC) George H. Gohn, Jr. and PFC Jacob Hriesik during preparations for movement to the Boston POE, August 1944. Gohn would be killed in action on 4 January 1945. (Author's collection via Sam Calhoun)

On 20 August 1944, F Company, along with more than eight thousand men of the 17th Airborne Division, boarded the USS *Wakefield* for transportation to Europe. *Wakefield's* primary port of call was Liverpool, England, prompting her crew to nickname her "The Boston and Liverpool Ferry." (Author's collection via the U.S. Naval Institute)

PFC Edward R. Sarrell joined F Company on 4 September 1944 and was assigned to the Third Platoon. (Courtesy, Edward Sarrell)

Private Charles W. Simpson, from Bremmen, Georgia, joined F Company on 4 September 1944. He was assigned as an ammunition bearer in the Second Platoon. (Courtesy, Jackie Lauminick)

Before he joined F Company on 11 September 1944, PFC Roderick MacKenzie had served as a divisional Ranger in the 66th Infantry Division. (Author's collection via Rod MacKenzie)

Private Raymond L. Lightcap, from Hazel Green, Wisconsin, joined F Company on 20 November 1944. Lightcap survived the Battle of the Bulge and later served as driver for the Regimental S-2. (Author's collection via Lightcap)

2nd Battalion's Executive Officer, Major Irwin A. 'Boppy' Edwards was the most decorated man in the 513th Parachute Infantry Regiment. (Author's collection via Boppy Edwards)

"Gods Gift To The Women" – PFC Arthur Bricmont and Private Tom Connolly looking for birds in Trafalgar Square. Both men joined F Company on 20 November 1944. (Author's collection via Tom Connolly)

Men of the First Platoon – Barton Stacey Camp A, near Andover, England, 6 October 1944. Private Eddie Barbera, PFC Ed Dahlberg, Tec 5 Bob Anderson, unidentified, PFC Dale Auer, PFC Larry Duprey, PFC Clifford Butcher, PFC Jack Cook, unidentified, Private Maynard Benson, S/Sgt. Harry Cook, PFC Phil Cavaleri, Private Dwight Caton, PFC Ed Costello, and Private Walter Balben. (Author's collection via Phil Cavaleri)

Aincreville, France – the morning of 2 January 1945. F Company officers during preparations for movement to the front near Bastogne, Belgium. 1st Lieutenant Ivan Stositch, 2nd Lieutenant Charles Puckett, Captain Marshall Reynolds, 2nd Lieutenant Samuel Calhoun, and 1st Lieutenant Sam Dean. (Author's collection via Charles Puckett)

2nd Lieutenant Puckett, 1st Lieutenant Stositch, and 1st Lieutenant Dean. (Author's collection via Charles Puckett)

2nd Lieutenant Puckett, Captain Reynolds, and 1st Lieutenant Dean. (Author's collection via Charles Puckett)

After suffering heavy casualties during attacks on 4 and 7 January, troopers of A Company of the 513th move to a reserve position near Senonchamps, Belgium on 10 January 1945. (Signal Corps photo)

During the Battle of the Bulge, German soldiers who attempted to surrender, like these captured by 17th Airborne Division troops on 15 January 1945, were as likely to be shot as deserters by their own officers and NCOs as they were by American soldiers, many of whom chose to take no prisoners. (Signal Corps photo)

While in Division Reserve, men of the 513th Parachute Infantry move to a new assembly area in the vicinity of Liheraine, Belgium on 21 January 1945. (Signal Corps photo)

513th Parachute Infantry moving forward – Liheraine, Belgium on 21 January 1945. (Signal Corps photo)

Towing a 57mm antitank gun, men of the 513th move to Liheraine. (Signal Corps photo)

Bivouac Area, Chalons-sur-Marne, France. When F Company arrived on 11 February 1945, it was down to only about a dozen men. (Courtesy, Margaret Ellis)

2nd Lieutenant Sam Calhoun photographed at Torbay, England on 25 January while recovering from wounds he received in the Bulge. Calhoun was discharged from the hospital, but remained on limited duty until just days before the Rhine operation when he was allowed to return to F Company. (Author's collection via Sam Calhoun)

PFC Charles Chutas and PFC Donald Shay joined F Company in February 1945 and were assigned to the Third Platoon. (Courtesy, Donald Shay)

PFC Kenneth Olson (left), who joined F Company's Third Platoon on 14 February 1945, met his brother in Germany after the war ended. (Author's collection via Ken Olson)

A bazookaman in the First Platoon, Private (later Sergeant) John E. Cobb joined F Company at Chalons. (Author's collection via Sam Calhoun)

Private Hank Contreras (left), one of F Company's cooks, joined just three weeks before Operation VARSITY. (Author's collection via Bob Greenstrand)

At Chalons-sur-Marne, the 513th Parachute Infantry Regiment made practice jumps from the new C-46 Commando transports on 5-10 March 1945. In combat, the C-46 proved to be a "flaming coffin." (Courtesy, 17th Airborne Division Association)

Marshaling area, Achiet Aerodrome, France – 23 March 1945. One of five C-46 Commando transports designated to carry F Company over the Rhine. (Courtesy, Margaret Ellis)

Parapack bundles containing heavy equipment and extra ammunition are secured in their sponsons under a C-46 Commando on the morning of Operation VARSITY. (Robert Capa/Magnum Photos, Inc.)

Lieutenant Calhoun's lead scout, PFC Robert E. Guiles, seated atop a parapack bundle of 81mm mortar shells, contemplates what is to come. (Robert Capa/Magnum Photos, Inc.)

On the morning of D-Day, a 513th trooper puts the final touches on his Mohawk. (Robert Capa/Magnum Photos, Inc.)

Colonel Coutts gives his last briefing to officers of the 513th before battle. F Company's CO, Captain Marshall Reynolds is seated fifteenth from the left. (Robert Capa/Magnum Photos, Inc.)

As H-Hour approaches, F Company men don equipment and parachutes. (Robert Capa/Magnum Photos, Inc.)

At that moment, the Germans launched a tank attack on 1st Battalion's left flank. About ten enemy tanks and self-propelled guns came down the Bastogne Highway and drove into the woods and into the rear of B and C Companies. Still more German tanks set up on the hill crest about 1,400 yards to the northwest and brought a devastating enfilade fire to bear on Taylor's battalion. The German tanks that had moved into the woods behind B and C Companies soon advanced to within a hundred yards of their positions along the highway. It was at this point that Lieutenant Colonel Taylor apparently broke down. He "froze in the foxhole, wouldn't get out," recalled Major Irwin Edwards.

Major Harry F. Kies, Taylor's executive, went out and talked briefly with the company commanders, and then, to avoid becoming cut off by the advancing German tanks himself, quickly returned to the battalion CP. The men, Kies found, had become demoralized – many had lost their weapons and ammunition – and casualties among the battalion, especially among the officers, were heavy. In fact, all the officers of B and C Companies, save one, were killed or wounded. Within a half an hour of Kies departure, more than a hundred men of the battalion were surrounded and taken prisoner. Many more were killed or wounded. Only the Third Platoon of B Company, which had not advanced as far as the rest of the battalion, was able to get some of their men back. [47]

General Miley and Colonel Coutts later relieved Colonel Taylor and put Major Kies in command of 1st Battalion. However, they reassigned Taylor, who, according to Irwin Edwards, "was a personal close buddy of Miley and Lou Coutts," to Division Headquarters. Edwards was further disgusted that Taylor later was appointed to be Chairman of the division's Awards and Decorations Committee, "The sonofabitch who had been relieved for cowardice. That's the sort of thing that [happened] in the 513th particularly," explained Edwards. "[It] didn't happen in the 194th or the 507th because of [Colonel Edson] Raff [CO of the 507th] and [Colonel James R.] Pierce [CO of the 194th] who were real soldiers." [48]

Just before Lieutenant Calhoun's platoon launched their attack into the forest at 0800, F Company's Third Platoon began making their way to the line of departure. Just as he had Lieutenant Puckett the night before, Lieutenant Stositch informed Tech Sergeant Paul that they were going to attack north "as far as they could go." Intelligence reports indicated that they would be able to advance more than a thousand yards before they ran into the first automatic weapons. At a little before 0800, Staff Sergeant Frank McDevitt's first squad, following closely behind Lieutenant Stositch and Tech Sergeant Paul, led the platoon north along a cart path, more of a depression in the snow, out of the woods. Lieutenant Puckett took up the rear to make sure the other rifle squads and the 60mm mortar squad did not fall behind. A low hedgerow and a wire fence followed the track of the cart path a few yards to the right. Stositch did not send scouts out but instead walked out into the open along the path.[49]

First squad passed through a gap in the hedgerow which ran roughly north to south, then scrambled across the wire fence. About fifty yards ahead was another hedgerow, running parallel to the first. McDevitt turned left, making his way northward, out into an open, rolling pasture between the two hedgerows. Sergeant La Riccia, the assistant squad leader, was a couple hundred yards back, bringing up first squad's rear; the body of the squad was dispersed in between.

Suddenly, the distinct the pop, pop, pop of Mauser rifles erupted from the woods to the front left. Simultaneously, a deluge of grazing machine-gun fire, pouring out of the woods, ripped up the earth and cracked through the air around the advancing men. Staff Sergeant McDevitt was hit in the hand. He yelled back to Sergeant La Riccia, "Get these guys moving! Get to the hedgerow – get to the hedgerow!!" and then started back to help La Riccia bring up the rest of the squad. Before he had gone very far, he was hit in the back and killed. Lieutenant Stositch and Sergeant Paul had crossed the first hedgerow and were near the second. They dashed forward and hit the ground behind it. At this spot, the hedgerow curved to the left, across the platoon's front, before winding back north towards the woods.[50]

Sergeant La Riccia moved forward in bounds and reached the second hedgerow. Stositch, Paul, and Slocomb were the only other men there. Looking back he could see Private Arthur Wisner lying motionless in the pasture. Wisner was such a nice guy the men had nicknamed him 'Wiz – The Best Kid There Is.' Now he was killed. Several other men were spread out in the field as well, perfect targets for the German marksmen. In fact, most of the first squad had been killed or wounded in the first few seconds. Up ahead, La Riccia could see vapor from the muzzle blast of a German machine-gun about three hundred yards away. It was coming from a low, snow covered mound just at the edge of the forest. The snipers – La Riccia figured that there had to be at least two of them considering the volume and accuracy of the fire – were concealed. He stuck the muzzle of his M1 through the thick, prickly hedge to fire at the machine-gun, but he quickly pulled it back a bit. He didn't want the muzzle blast from his own weapon to give away his position. He fired about twelve rounds, but he couldn't tell if he'd hit anything.[51] At least he hadn't drawn any return fire.

PFC Patrick Phillips and PFC Leroy Halley were lying in the pasture between the two hedgerows. The machine-gun had opened up just as Phillips, the machine-gunner in La Riccia's squad, was crossing the break in the first hedgerow. Phillips was hit in both legs – his left leg was only grazed but a slug had lodged in the right. Halley, his assistant, then turned to run and was shot through the buttocks by a sniper. Halley fell – he was conscious but couldn't move under his own power. Phillips couldn't walk either, but he could crawl. When the firing died down a little, he crawled back behind the hedgerow, dragging Halley. Amazingly, the movement did not draw sniper fire, and they managed to get out of the pasture and eventually reached the rear where a jeep took them to the aid station.[52]

After about twenty minutes, the German fire let up. Keeping as low as possible, Sergeant La Riccia went out into the pasture to look for the rest of his squad. He found Private John Waters who was mortally wounded and PFC Ed Schneck who had been wounded in the buttocks. PFC Jack Tomasch was lying face down in the snow with a big hole in his back. Braving the threat of snipers, Private Earl 'Pete' Petersen, the medic, was on his knees, working on him.[53]

Lieutenant Stositch shouted to PFC Charles Craddock, his RTO who was lying several yards behind him in the pasture, to call for smoke. Craddock placed the call and the mission was fired. Munafo, laying on his stomach in the snow some several yards behind the first hedge, watched as the shells landed east of the second hedgerow, rather than near the woods where the fire was coming from. "Jesus Christ," he exclaimed in frustration, "They're shooting in the wrong place." At that moment, Lieutenant Stositch got up and shouted to the men behind him: "Let's go forward!" The few remaining men of the first squad and part of the second squad moved up and took shelter against the second low hedgerow.[54]

Munafo slouched as he ran forward through the gap in the hedgerow with Hall, his ammunition bearer. Together with Sergeant Sorenson, his assistant squad leader, they made it all the way to the spot where Lieutenant Stositch lay. The three started crawling a couple of yards through a narrow gap in this hedgerow. On the way, Hall was hit. Munafo, desperately wanting to get his .30 caliber machine-gun into action, called to Slocomb, his assistant gunner, to bring up the tripod. Slocomb sprang toward him, dropping down on Munafo's left to set up the tripod. However, Slocomb was up on his knees, completely exposed to enemy fire.[55]

"Get down," cried Munafo, who was lying as flat as he could to mask himself from the hail of small arms fire. "Get do. . ."

Slocomb lurched and fell, shot by a sniper – there was a little red circle in the front of his head marking the spot. For a moment, Munafo just lay there, stunned by Slocomb's death. He soon gathered himself. He didn't have any ammunition – Hall was nowhere to be seen – so the .30 caliber was useless. But Munafo still had his M1. He shouldered it and started firing at the puffs of smoke he saw springing up among the trees. Immediately, bullets cracked past his head – "bullets made the sound of firecrackers when they passed" – the snipers were firing on him. Sergeant Edward D. Sorenson, nearby, was hit by a rifle slug, but it was stopped by his military shaving kit.[56]

Munafo continued to fire into the trees ahead of him and to the left. "The barrel got so hot" steam rose from it. Meanwhile, the enemy's volume of fire increased. A ricochet hit Munafo's boot. He was okay, but some of the men pinned in the pasture were being dismembered as German machine-gun fire hit them again and again.[57]

Private Richard Murray, behind the first hedgerow with PFC Studinarz, had gotten their .30 caliber machine-gun going. He'd been told back in Basic Training that the life expectancy of a machine-gunner in combat was about three minutes, and he "had three bullet holes in the ammunition can sitting next to [him] before three minutes was up." That fire, he determined, was coming from behind the platoon's position. Murray took cover for a minute and then, using the entry angle as a guide, sighted back through the bullet holes in the ammunition box and saw that the shots had been fired from the church steeple in town. Murray swung the .30 caliber around and raked the steeple. Later that day, he found the body of a German sniper in the tower.[58]

Mortar shells began to fall among the pinned-down men, ripping up the field and throwing frozen chunks of earth and hot bits of shrapnel over them. Sergeant La Riccia ran back for the cover of the hedge but before he made it was hit in the left hand, elbow, and left leg. Pete the medic, however, continued to work on Tomasch. It suddenly got quiet again, and La Riccia went back out to look for his squad. Then, just as suddenly, the rifle fire and mortars started back up – only now joined by 88s. One of the snipers killed the heretofore lucky Petersen and La Riccia was hit again, this time in the back of both legs by shell fragments.[59]

The men had been in the field for about a half hour. They couldn't move forward and were being slaughtered while they sat there. A German sniper, well concealed in the trees to the left, killed the man lying directly in front of Sergeant Paul with a head shot. Snipers shot several more of the men in the head.[60]

Paul turned his head to tell the men behind him to run and was himself hit by a sniper's bullet. He could feel the round pass his ear before it tore down into his upper right arm. Paul managed to yell, "Get the hell out of here!" Then Paul was struck again. Shell fragments laid his legs open like "beef steak," and machine-gun bullets blew the heel off one of his boots. Another burst shot the seat out of Paul's trousers, cutting through the several layers of clothing and skinning his buttocks. Paul looked around for Lieutenant Stositch but could not see him. Another man in the field moved and he too drew deadly fire. Paul decided the only thing he could do was lay still and watch his blood freeze in the snow.[61]

Lieutenant Stositch, fifteen feet to Munafo's left, was shot through the base of his neck, the bullet nicking his spine. Stositch looked up and saw Munafo. "Frank, I'm hit. I'm hit," cried the lieutenant. "What are we gonna do?"

"We're pinned down," Munafo shouted back. "I don't see nobody, but I know we're being shot at. We got to get outa' here."

"Give the order to retreat," Stositch told him. "You take over and give the commands."

"No, I don't want to do it," Munafo replied. "I'll get somebody else – you take it Sorenson." Sorenson was just ahead on the ground.

"All right," said Sorenson.

"Let's get out of here!" said Munafo. As he began to move back, his only thought was, "Somebody screwed up." [62]

Everybody ran like hell for the first hedgerow. Lieutenant Stositch was yelling for the men to fall back to Mande-St.-Etienne. Leaving his machine-gun, Munafo grabbed Stositch and pulled him across the pasture, over the fence, and to shelter behind the first hedgerow.[63] Lieutenant Puckett, who had assembled the rest of the Third Platoon there before himself moving out to attempt to flank the German positions, left word for the men to stay put. "Don't go any further forward," he had told them. "Everyone up there is dead."[64]

It was then that Munafo saw Sergeant Paul still laying in the field. Paul lifted his head up – he was still alive. Without regard for his own safety – and without taking time to think about what he was getting into – Munafo dropped his helmet in the snow and bolted forward through the gap. Munafo crossed the wire fence and ran to Sergeant Paul. When he reached him, Munafo dragged Paul to his feet and together they walked back, fifty yards across the open ground while around them all hell was breaking loose. By the time they reached the fence the bullets were flying so thick they were zinging off the wire. Munafo brought Paul to the medic from the First Platoon, 'Doc' Sloan, who was working on the wounded behind the first hedge.

"Take care of Sergeant Paul," Munafo commanded Sloan. Munafo took out his trench knife to cut off Paul's web gear, but stopped – he wanted to help Paul but didn't know if he should cut off Paul's equipment because, in training, Paul "was a fuss-pot with his freakin' uniform."

"Sarge, you want me to cut it?" he asked.

"Yeah," said Paul. "Cut it, cut it off, cut it off."

"Are you sure?" asked Munafo again, scared to death because he could see Paul was bleeding all over the place.

"Yeah, cut it off," Paul groaned.

Munafo sawed through the thick webbing of the field suspenders and unfastened Paul's cartridge belt. Then he cut open Paul's uniform to get to the wounds. Paul's right arm was mangled. Munafo ripped open the parapack bandage tied to Paul's helmet, poured the sulfanilamide powder in the wound, and wrapped the bandage around it. "Get him out of here," Munafo yelled at Sloan.

While Lieutenant Stositch and the others were trapped in the pasture, the third squad and the 60mm mortar squad, which had been "following behind the lead elements [of the Third Platoon] came to a halt in the woods. Lieutenant Puckett moved forward to the front edge of the woods, but could not see the rest of the platoon."

Puckett advanced into the open and then dropped to the ground. As soon as he did, a bullet struck the ground only inches from his head. Puckett rolled over and slid into the sunken cart path as another bullet struck the spot he had just left. Puckett got up and quickly moved back into the woods.

As Puckett was approaching, Private Ervin D. Schmidt asked, "Lieutenant, did you see that tracer bullet that just missed your head?" Puckett, however, "just shrugged his shoulders and moved on to where the mortar squad was resting and told Sergeant Johnnie Rutherford to bring his squad and follow him."

Puckett then moved to the northeast side of the woods and from there entered the end of the open pasture. He had begun heading northwest, cutting down hill, across the pasture, when another bullet cracked past his head. Puckett hit the ground immediately. It was then that he saw PFC Slocomb's body "lying face down on the ground off to the right. Sloc[omb] had a bullet hole in his forehead."[65]

Lieutenant Puckett had also noticed that Sergeant Rutherford's 60mm mortar squad wasn't following and so returned to the woods once more to find out why. Instead of Rutherford, Puckett found Captain Reynolds, who had been looking for the Third Platoon, accompanied by Lieutenant Dean and Tec 5 Wayne DeHaven with the SCR-300 radio.

The mortar squad had not even left the woods yet. Lieutenant Dean told Puckett that he had taken the squad and that he was placing them under Company Headquarters' control.[66]

"Something's happened to Stosh," Reynolds told Lieutenant Puckett. "I can't raise him on the radio. Go see what's going on."

Puckett was sweating so he took off his trench coat. He took the grenades out of the pocket of his trench coat and stuffed them in the pockets of his field jacket. Then he gave his trench coat to DeHaven, asking him to hold on to it as he would need it later. Grasping his M1, he moved out.

Lieutenant Puckett began to re-cross the pasture, this time moving to the left, along the cart path to the edge of the pasture where he flopped down among the men of the third squad. Third Platoon's second squad, he saw, was dispersed all round. Peering over the top of the squat hedgerow into the pasture ahead of him, he saw the dead of the first squad. Lieutenant Puckett could see PFC Craddock, Lieutenant Stositch's radio operator, lying in the field among the bodies.[67]

Captain Reynolds appeared directly and flopped down in the sunken path next to Puckett. "Go out and get the radio," he ordered Puckett.

Lieutenant Puckett ran out into the pasture and hit the ground, grabbing at the radio still in Craddock's cold hand. He could see the wound in the right side of Craddock's head.[68]

"Is anyone still kicking?" Puckett called out. One man raised up. From his position, Puckett couldn't make out the man's face. Then the German machine-gunner fired a long burst and the man fell prone quickly. Lieutenant Puckett started to scramble back over the ground, bullets snapping past him. A German soldier fired a rifle-grenade which landed in the snow some twenty-five feet away and exploded, but Puckett was not hurt.[69]

After Puckett made it back to the cover of the sunken cart path Captain Reynolds grabbed the radio from his hands and tried it. It didn't work.

"Try and go around the [left] flank," Captain Reynolds next ordered Lieutenant Puckett. "I'm going to find the Second Platoon."

"Okay," replied Puckett. "We'll give it a try."[70] Reynolds got up and left. According to Donovan, Reynolds already knew where the Second Platoon was. What Reynolds really wanted was to get to Colonel Miller to ask for support or a tank so he could get F Company into the woods.[71]

PFC Studinarz from the third squad was firing a .30 caliber machine-gun into the trees to his front. Lieutenant Puckett told him, "Give me five minutes. I'm going into those woods."[72]

Lieutenant Puckett, with Sergeant Larry J. Sperling and Private Vincent J. Sherlock, Jr. of the third squad, moved to the left flank of the Germans. Angered by seeing the German machine-gunner fire on the wounded men of the first squad lying helplessly in the field, Lieutenant Puckett instructed the men, "Don't give 'em a chance." Then Puckett ordered, "Fix bayonets."

"Lieutenant," said Private Sherlock, "I'm not gonna get that close to 'em."

On Puckett's word, Sergeant Sperling stepped out into the field and, running across the open ground, disappeared into the left side of the woods, edging his way in among the snow-laden boughs. A few moments later, a single shot rang out from behind the curtain of trees.

Lieutenant Puckett ordered Private Sherlock out next. Before he had gone only a few steps, a German soldier darted from the left edge of the trees. Sherlock leveled his M1 and fired, striking the German squarely with a bullet in the back. The man dropped immediately.

Following Sherlock into the field, Lieutenant Puckett approached the body of Sherlock's German. He was lying face down in the snow so he rolled him over. The wound came out through the German's chest. Puckett poked the body with his bayonet but the German lay still, so Puckett continued into the edge of the trees following Sperling and Sherlock.

The men were gathered around a log and earth-covered dugout that was situated in a part of the woods that protruded into the field. In the mouth of the bunker was an MG-42 and the body of German soldier. Sergeant Sperling explained that he had killed the German while he was pushing the machine-gun out of the bunker ahead of him in an attempt to escape.

"Do you have a grenade, Lieutenant?" Sperling asked. Lieutenant Puckett reached into the waist pocket of his field jacket, took out a white phosphorous grenade, and handed it to Sperling. Sperling pulled the pin and tossed the grenade down into the hole. There was an explosion, muffled by the bunker, and a lot of acrid chemical smoke poured from the hole.

Lieutenant Puckett turned to Private Sherlock and asked, "Do you want a pistol?"

Sherlock frowned, a little puzzled.

"The German you shot in the field has one. I saw it while I was over there."

With a broad grin, Sherlock thanked the lieutenant and went after his trophy.

Only a short time had elapsed since the beginning of the attack that morning and reaching the woods. "Things were happening fast," remembered Lieutenant Puckett, "but time was moving in slow motion."

The men moved to the edge of the woods to discuss their next move. Private Schmidt and Private David A. Sigal came up. No sooner than they did, Schmidt fired his rifle in the direction of the German bunker.

"What the hell are you shooting at?" asked Lieutenant Puckett.

"There was another German in the hole and he was getting ready to fire at us with the machine-gun!" answered Schmidt.

Sure enough, there was another German in the mouth of the dugout. But Schmidt had put an end to whatever his plans were with a bullet in the head. Not willing to stand any more difficulty from the bunker, the men proceeded to tear it apart.

Acrid smoke, still thickly filling bowels of the dugout, slowly escaped into the air as the men tore away at the layers of earth and logs covering the bunker. When the last had been cast off, the men were astonished to see that yet one more German soldier, miraculously surviving the burst of the white phosphorous grenade, was still inside. The men pulled him up and out into the light.

The young German wore a bandage covering a head wound. As the men started through his pockets, Lieutenant Puckett looked the man over. The frightened face he saw was so youthful it hadn't even any fuzz. Puckett ordered Private Sigal to take the prisoner to the rear.

The men started through the pockets of the two corpses at the mouth of the bunker. Someone uncovered several cigars and the men lit up. Lieutenant Puckett didn't smoke so someone tossed him a can of sardines as a consolation. Puckett read the label: "NORWAY." The lieutenant had lost his can opener so he saved them for later, tucking them safely into a pocket.

After the men had finished searching the bodies, Sergeant Sperling and Privates Sherlock and Schmidt drifted to the edge of the trees, looking back in the direction they had come. Sperling raised his M1. Sherlock's German was not dead after all. He was alive and was waving his arm, trying to attract the attention of other Germans. Sperling shot the man in the head. He stopped waving. Angered, Sperling turned on Sherlock, "You dumb son-of-a-bitch. I told you to shoot him in the head!"

"Don't talk to me like that!" Sherlock shouted back. "Tensions were running high," remembered Lieutenant Puckett.

A group of Germans had worked their way into some woods behind Puckett's men and they too must have watched Sperling shoot the German in the field. "It must have made them mad," recalled Puckett, because the air came instantly alive with the crack of bullets and the tree line was lit with muzzle flashes.

Lieutenant Puckett went for cover behind a fallen log, about ten feet from the bunker, and between the bunker and the edge of the trees. A German grenade exploded just on the other side of the log, the concussion knocking his helmet off. Everyone began to return fire while the lieutenant put his helmet back on.

Third Platoon apparently had become fragmented even before their attack began. Several men from Third Platoon had taken shelter in a hay loft sitting atop a ridge on the west edge of town near a stone barn. The loft was about twenty feet square and made of wood with a tile roof. Inside, the men sat quietly talking. Though it provided some protection from the elements, it did not provide much protection against enemy fire. Private Edward Sarrell's .30 caliber machine-gun, which was set up outside, had apparently been spotted by the Germans giving away their position and was drawing enemy machine-gun fire. Occasionally, one of the men would try to spot the enemy gunner through a place in the wall where a few boards were missing. This inevitably drew a burst of enemy machine-gun fire which ripped through the building.[73]

When Third Platoon's attack began, these men were ordered to move forward to the sunken cart path a few hundred yards to the north. Setting out warily from the hay loft, the men moved down the northern side of the slope toward the sunken road. When they had advanced about half the way they began to receive enemy machine-gun fire. The men instinctively rushed forward toward the road, where they flopped down. Most of the group made it, however, as Private Sarrell discovered, Private Roger Soucy was shot in the foot on the way. This made Sarrell "damn mad" because Soucy had been wearing his good boots at the time. Nevertheless, in the cart path, the group "was hidden well and they knew the Germans couldn't get at them." Meanwhile, unbeknownst to them, the rest of the Third Platoon, further ahead, had become pinned down in the pasture.

Sarrell determined that over two hundred yards of open ground lay between his position and the trees ahead concealing the German gunners. Although he could not see any Germans, the sound of the firing was growing louder. He took out the hunting knife his father had given him and cut a .30 caliber ammunition belt into twenty round sections. He loaded his machine-gun with one of these and put the others in his pockets. Accompanied by PFC Joe Gutt and PFC George L. Shaughnessy, Sarrell, staying as low as possible, started crawling up the ditch toward the trees. With considerable effort they made it to the southwest corner of the trees and crawled into them about thirty yards.[74]

Three or four German soldiers were walking around ahead of them. They made easy targets for the paratroopers, but they let them pass. The men were more interested in two German bunkers situated back on the edge of the tree line to their right. After assuring themselves that their weapons were ready, the group got up and rushed the German positions from behind, firing their weapons to keep the Germans' heads down. When they had advanced to within a few yards, Sarrell and the others threw white phosphorous and fragmentation grenades into the bunkers. Three Germans – just sixteen-year-old kids, Sarrell thought – were taken prisoner. After the position was secured, Sarrell noticed the bodies of the several American paratroopers sprawled in the field in front of the bunkers.[75]

Firing around the widely dispersed Third Platoon area eventually quieted down and some of the men back in the pasture started dragging the dead and wounded back. However, because there just weren't that many men left, the platoon's cohesion had dissolved. Munafo looked for Sorenson but he had disappeared, so Munafo ended up with a group of about half a dozen troopers in a farm house until he rejoined the company in the woods that evening.[76]

Lieutenant Puckett had taken with him a number of men, however, the men who had been in the pasture started off in small groups or began digging in on their own. Meanwhile, the wounded were helped to the aid station as quickly as possible.

Men from the First Platoon pitched in. Staff Sergeant Seacott carried one trooper whose foot was practically shot off. The shelling by German 88s continued, however, and on the way Seacott had to hit the ground nearly twenty times to avoid being hit.[77]

Though his friends told him to go get patched up, Sergeant La Riccia didn't know exactly where the aid station was, and, since he could walk, he decided to stay on the line.[78] PFC Studinarz had been hit in the stomach by shrapnel, so Private Murray helped him to the aid station, narrowly avoiding being hit himself when he made his way back to the platoon.[79]

Tech Sergeant Paul was placed in a jeep for transportation to the battalion aid station. When he was carried inside the aid station, the battalion surgeon exclaimed, "It's Sergeant Paul!" Paul had gotten to know the doctors and they were obviously concerned with his condition. He could see there were a lot of other wounded men already inside the aid station. While the medics started him on a series of penicillin, he watched the surgeons working on another boy. "Every time they fixed one hole, another started bleeding," he recalled.[80]

Medics tagged Paul for immediate evacuation. At the clearing station, Paul was informed by the doctors: "We're going to operate on you here." Rather than perform a skin graft on Paul, surgeons simply stretched skin closed over his wounds, which eventually left terrible scars. All the time, the hospital was under constant shelling – very window had been blown out. Sergeant Paul was in such severe pain he finally passed out. At the next hospital back, while he lay unconscious, somebody stole his jump boots.

It was about 1130 hours when Captain Reynolds and Private Dahlberg arrived in the woods. Second Platoon's prisoners were being detained near the south edge of the trees. While the Captain went up ahead to find Lieutenant Calhoun, Dahlberg stayed behind to look over the captives. The German prisoners had fought skillfully, but their cunning had meant that many of his friends had been killed. In fact, by this time the men were so dispersed, it was believed that as many as one hundred F Company men had been killed or wounded. Dahlberg pointed to his M1 and then to the head of one of the prisoners. "You're gonna die pretty soon," he told the German coldly. He didn't know if the prisoner understood or not, but he really didn't care.

Lieutenant Calhoun was sending the prisoners to the rear under the guard of Hataway and Hultman. Later, Calhoun was told that the two of them shot the prisoners in accordance with Miller's directive.[81]

Paul Imre, however, offered an eye-witness account of the prisoners' executions. Kuntz, Hataway, Imre, Kitson, Harding, and Hultman escorted the Germans back to a barnyard located on the edge of Mande-St.-Etienne where they waited for the regimental S-2, Captain Gates Ivy, Jr., to interrogate them. Soon afterward, Captain Ivy arrived, and he quickly determined that they were SS. When the troopers discovered just who they had captured, they became infuriated, almost "trembling with a white rage," remembered Imre. They had just recently been told of the atrocity committed against American prisoners at Malmédy at the hands of SS troops. Ivy ordered that their hands be bound behind them as he thought they might try to escape. The men, however, wanted to exact a little revenge.

It took Kuntz about fifteen minutes to gather enough rope. He and the other men herded the prisoners into the barn, put nooses around their necks, and stood them up on benches. Then they booted the benches from under them. "We left them there kicking," said Imre. Kuntz cut the finger off of one SS man, swinging but still alive, just to get his ring. Except for Ivy, who apparently just stood aside, no officers were present and the event was never mentioned again.

It wasn't uncommon for men in line companies, in combat, to give no quarter to prisoners, especially SS troops. One trooper with the 101st Airborne Division in Normandy and Holland, reported that "if they [German prisoners] were scared, we'd take them prisoner, but if they were arrogant, one of our guys would just shoot 'em right in the head. And if they had trooper boots – forget it, they were dead."[82]

An official VIII Corps combat interview suggested that executions of prisoners by 513th troopers had taken place on higher authority: Only twenty-three Germans were taken prisoner in the woods – these included "a captain and a number of English speaking men," the report stated, concluding that the troopers were not inclined to take more prisoners than those that might be beneficial to the S-2.[83] The interview stated further that when the woods north of Mande-St.-Etienne were finally cleared, more than two hundred enemy were reported dead. Lieutenant Calhoun and every other man interviewed by this author stated that there were hardly more than fifty Germans in the woods all tolled. It is possible that the 513th officers interviewed by VIII Corps on 14-16 January 1945 accounted for the large number of German dead in this way rather than admitting to their executions. Most troopers remembered how hard it had been to control prisoners. "There was no place to put the prisoners," explained First Sergeant Royal Donovan, "so consequently a lot of them got shot."[84]

"It really cost," said Imre of the event in 1997. "We were all eighteen years old and true blue – and we did terrible things."

By late morning, the whole 513th attack was losing momentum. 2nd Battalion was in the woods and on the first phase line, but the badly depleted 1st Battalion had made little progress. Though a further advance would surely expose his battalion to flank attacks by the enemy, Miller wanted to continue forward. E Company was thinly spread across the hill far to F Company's right, so Colonel Miller made them reserve and ordered D Company, which had been brought up behind E Company, to pass through their lines and continue to attack north on F Company's right.[85]

In attempting to clear the southern edge of another forested area northeast of F Company's positions, D Company met considerable resistance. After artillery fired a concentration on the woods, D Company charged, firing bazookas as they advanced. The combined effort compelled the Germans to withdraw. However, to the north, German armor, veiled by swirling fog, continued to rove unrestrained across the entire 2nd Battalion front and poor visibility made further artillery support for D Company nearly impossible.[86]

On the first phase line, Lieutenant Calhoun pointed out to Captain Reynolds the Germans digging in forward of his own position. Reynolds told Calhoun that Gilles' First Platoon would be on the line shortly. Calhoun also was waiting for the main body of E Company to show up on the right. Apparently unaware of Miller's plans, Captain Reynolds told Calhoun that because E Company had lost three officers – including Captain Deam and Lieutenant Fagen – already while advancing to the line of departure, it would take E Company some time to get itself pulled together and on line with F Company.

Lieutenant Sam Dean had arrived by then and wanted someone to get the men spread out. He turned to PFC Dahlberg, "You're the oldest guy here, I think you better take over this squad," he said, motioning to a group of men.

Dahlberg took one look and said, "Forget it." The men were all "bitching, complaining, and moaning." Everybody was wondering where they were going, what they were going to do, and when they were going to get something to eat. He was only nineteen and didn't feel like being the sergeant. PFC James J. Gresher from Chicago was given the job instead.

Dahlberg did not get to rest, however. Captain Reynolds ordered him back to find the rest of the company and bring them up. At Mande-St.-Etienne, Dahlberg caught up with First Sergeant Donovan and relayed Reynolds' order to take whatever was left of F Company, and move it up to the new position on the first phase line. "God," replied Donovan, "I guess we're not gonna get a break." Then Dahlberg went out to find Lieutenant Puckett and relay the same order.

Back on the first phase line, Reynolds lay his map on the ground between he and Lieutenant Calhoun and began discussing the company's next move – into Flamizoulle. Almost immediately, a sniper began to fire at them from the bushy hillside to the left.

"What the hell is that?" said Reynolds as the first bullet cracked past. Calhoun's response was to ask Reynolds if they should move. "No," replied Reynolds. "He's not got close to us yet." "Sam," he continued, "send one of your people over to take care of that." Not waiting for Calhoun, Reynolds turned to the first man he saw, "Sergeant Knigge, go over there and see what the hell's goin' on."[87]

Knigge moved down on the left, picked up Sergeant Gohn, and the two men started toward the hill. Advancing along a hedgerow, they went a short way, and then Knigge saw what looked like an armored vehicle ahead of them in the open field between them and the bushy hill. Stopping, Knigge told Gohn, "Go back and see if you can get some artillery." Gohn took off.

Knigge sat there for a while, but Gohn was "gone so damn long," he decided to investigate the armored vehicle alone. Knigge crept up close enough to see it had been knocked-out. Since there were no Germans in sight, he advanced farther, into the copse of trees.

Sergeant Gohn returned to Second Platoon's position just as enemy artillery fire started falling heavily. "The shelling got so bad it was almost suicide to stay," remembered Sarrell.[88] Gohn jumped into a foxhole only a few yards from Greenstrand's. An explosion shook Greenstrand, so hard that it lifted him off the ground. Greenstrand looked up and saw that a shell had landed right on top of Gohn.[89] Gohn had been carrying the thirty-pound satchel of C2 that Newhouse had given him that morning. It all went up when the shell hit, leaving only Gohn's legs which had been thrown out of the hole – the top of his body was completely missing.[90]

Knigge edged through the trees until he came through to the far eastern side. There was a break there and another stand of trees stood beyond about two hundred yards to the east. In the space between, there were a few German foxholes spread every fifty feet or so but there were no Germans in sight. Knigge decided to investigate them. The holes were well dug. There was bread and a few pieces of personal equipment inside the first and the same in the second. Since he'd not been able to find the sniper, Knigge decided to make his way back to the trees. As he reached the edge of the woods, he glanced over his left shoulder and, to his surprise, he saw three Germans standing in front of the trees to the east. "Holy shit!" Knigge exclaimed. "What am I gonna do now?"

Knigge dove behind a tree. One of the Germans signaled to his men and they hit the ground. Then the German, armed with a machine-pistol, started walking toward Knigge, apparently undaunted by the fact that he presented an easy target to the American paratrooper. When Sergeant Knigge peered out from behind the tree, the German was just a few feet away. "Okay, *Deutscher*," Knigge shouted, "*Hande hoch!*"

"*Nien! Nien!*" howled the advancing German in alarm. Knigge saw the German's finger move toward the trigger. Knigge squeezed off one round from his M1 and the German answered with an abbreviated burst from his Schmeisser. The German's aim was unsteady and the bullets flew past Knigge without effect. Knigge wasn't sure if he had hit the German, but the frightened man dropped his weapon in the snow and ran. Knigge raised his M1 to kill the fleeing German, but when he pulled the trigger nothing happened; his weapon was empty. Knigge had gone on patrol with only one round left in his rifle. Knigge got up and started to run like hell himself, back to the company.[91]

As he made his way back across the open field to the platoon, he looked behind him toward the foxholes he had investigated. To the right of them, there were a large number of German infantry supported by an assault gun advancing out of the woods. There was a foxhole nearby so he jumped in and began preparations for a "last stand," putting his grenades and extra ammunition up on the side of the hole. "Here I am with just this rifle," he thought, but, despite his solitary position he began firing anyway – "What the hell!" After only a few seconds, he decided to get out of the holes and back to the platoon. The first man he saw was Sergeant Harold E. Hinkley who was heating a can of some C-rations over sterno. "Goddamn, I'm hungry," he said to Hinkley, and despite the shelling, they had something to eat.[92]

While Staff Sergeant Knigge was in the woods, two more rounds popped past Calhoun and Reynolds. The sniper's fourth shot put a hole in the middle of the map spread out between them. "Now he's getting close," said Reynolds. "It's time to move."

Calhoun heard the sniper's rifle fire again but did not hear the bullet pass. Something cold began to run down his right sleeve. "Captain, I've been hit!" cried Calhoun.

"No shit!" Reynolds said in a matter-of-fact tone. Reynolds, who apparently wanted to take care of the sniper himself, got up and announced, "We're gonna go into the next woods." From the Second Platoon men scattered in holes nearby arose Privates Fredrick Altmiller, Bernard Glanowski, Clifford Harding, John Mahoney, Wilmer Brewer, Don Newhouse, Mabron Henderson, and Bob Greenstrand. Advancing with Reynolds, they made it across the field and then rushed into the woods. Brewer ran almost directly into a German soldier; both men were so frightened they ran in opposite directions, neither firing a shot.

As the men pushed in among the pines they were met only by scattered small arms fire. In seconds, they closed on three Germans who surrendered immediately. Greenstrand wasn't sure why these three had stuck around – perhaps they wanted to surrender – as the rest had apparently left. The troopers started shaking them down; Newhouse took one of the soldier's paybooks as a souvenir. As they did so, all the men could hear the voice of a German officer yelling at his men from deeper in the forest. More troublesome yet, the sound of German tanks could be heard plainly beyond the tree line. Captain Reynolds told the men he was going to reconnoiter the area beyond the trees. He then told them how to deal with the prisoners. "Shoot the sonsabitches and get the hell out of here. I'll be back in a couple of minutes."[93] As Don Newhouse admitted, "I hadn't expected that one."[94]

Private Dahlberg found Lieutenant Puckett in a small stand of trees west of the main woods above the town where he and his men had been exchanging fire intermittently for about a half hour with a small group of German soldiers. "Captain says don't lose any more men."[95]

"Why?" Puckett thought to himself. "It's only the Germans who are losing any men!"[96]

The enemy firing had petered out so Lieutenant Puckett, with as many men as he could gather, got moving forward to the new company position in the big woods. As Puckett passed the field where Craddock had been killed earlier that morning, he went over and picked up something from it.

"What's that, Lieutenant?" asked a private carrying the SCR-300.

"My glove!" answered the lieutenant.

When Lieutenant Puckett arrived at the company position, he got a message to report to Captain Reynolds who was standing in the clump of trees about fifty yards forward and to the right of the company position across an open field. Puckett ran a few yards out into the field and the Germans started firing. Puckett dove for the ground. He could see where the bullets were falling, but the Germans probably couldn't, he figured, and that gave him the confidence to press forward. After waiting for the German to stop firing he got up and ran again and in two more such dashes he reached the Captain.

Reynolds – who moments earlier had left Greenstrand and company to deal with their prisoners – had, by this time, been joined by his radioman, Tec 5 DeHaven, another officer – a captain, a forward observer for artillery – and a sergeant who was the FO's radio man.

"Where's your platoon?" Reynolds asked Puckett.

"The message said that you wanted to see me, not the whole platoon." Puckett responded.

Reynolds frowned and pointed at the woods about seventy-five yards away to the left where Greenstrand and company were waiting. "Second Platoon's in that woods. I want you to take the Third Platoon and join them there."

"Sir," Puckett replied, "the Second Platoon isn't in those woods, the Germans are in those woods. They fired on me as I came over here."

"Shut up!" barked Reynolds. "Take your men over there." Bud Reynolds had a short temper and did not take time to explain that he had taken the remnants of the Second Platoon into the woods.

Puckett said, "Yes, Sir," and re-crossed the field, dodging the machine-gun fire again and rejoined the twenty-eight remaining men of the Third Platoon.

Meanwhile, Greenstrand and the other men had been waiting for Reynolds to return. The prisoners were laying on the ground in front of the men, but so far, no one had gotten up the nerve to carry out the Captain's order. Soon after he had finished with Puckett, Reynolds reappeared and, according to Greenstrand, seeing the prisoners hadn't been shot, he shot them himself. He then turned to the men and said, "Next time I give an order, follow it." It was obvious to Greenstrand that Reynolds was angry, but then, in a fatherly tone, he told the men, "Listen boys, I didn't like doing that either but if the shoe'd been on the other foot – and they'd taken you prisoner – they'd done the same thing. Now get the hell out of here!" "He must have been awfully disgusted with us at the time," recalled Greenstrand, "and I guess we were somewhat lucky he didn't shoot us."[97]

Greenstrand and the others didn't have long to think about what Reynolds had just done because suddenly the Germans began to attack through the woods forward of Reynolds and the group of Second Platoon men. Two enemy tanks approached, the first, loaded with panzergrenadiers, in the gap between the two woods – Newhouse was sure it was a Tiger – and the other was heard coming around on the west side of the woods. Most of the men dropped their extra equipment and made a run for it. Henderson and Altmiller, however, waited because each had a bazooka. Altmiller told Henderson, "Take a shot then get the hell out of here." Even though he knew a direct hit probably would do no damage, Henderson obliged, but missed altogether. He then took off. Altmiller waited until the tank closed to within twenty-five yards to fire. The round struck the tank at the point where the turret joins the upper hull. The explosion didn't seem to damage the tank but, from the way they started hollering, the shrapnel must have ripped into the Germans who were riding on it. Then Altmiller retreated, too.[98]

The men who had left ahead of him yelled to Altmiller, "Come on! Come on! Come on!" Altmiller did so, and as he did German machine-gun bullets splashed in the snow all around him. When he reached the big woods, Altmiller found three bullet holes in the barrel of his bazooka.

Meanwhile, approaching through the gap, the turret of the Tiger traversed right and then left a couple of times and then it withdrew back into the space between trees, covered by the fog. It is possible that the German tank crew was not willing to venture further without more support.[99]

As Greenstrand took a look around, he discovered Captain Reynolds was missing.[100] Someone told him that as they ran from the woods, the tank in the gap had fired its machine-gun. Reynolds had fallen forward in the snow and lay still.[101]

At about this time, Lieutenant Gilles' First Platoon had arrived on the first phase line and was taking up positions in the field to Second Platoon's left. They, too, had spent the better part of the morning under artillery fire. "A lot of guys were calling 'Medic'," commented Grice. Gilles ordered two squads to spread out and dig foxholes along a hedgerow on the left of Second Platoon's positions.[102]

At a pause in the shelling, PFC Raymond Jacobs ran out in the field with his shovel and got on his knees and started hitting the frozen earth. It was like cement. "You're crazy," yelled PFC Phil Cavaleri. Within thirty seconds, the German shelling resumed. One round seemed to land right between Jacobs' feet. The blast threw dirt, snow, and ice into the air in the shape of an upside-down funnel and blew Jacobs backwards. To Cavaleri, who was watching his friend, it all appeared to happen in slow motion. [103]

Cavaleri yelled, "Lieutenant, look up ahead!"

Lying belly down in the snow, Lieutenant Gilles replied, "Well, go out and take a look at him."

Jacobs was bleeding from a hole in back of his head – Cavaleri had found a shallow pool of blood in his helmet. Jacobs also had a piece of shrapnel in each wrist – these wounds were not bleeding – and one of his legs was twisted under him. Slowly, Cavaleri straightened the leg out, slit the pants leg, and checked the bones; the leg seemed to be all right. Cavaleri then bandaged the wound in Jacobs' head to stop the bleeding and administered a shot of morphine. He wanted to wrap Jacobs' wrists as well in order to alert the medics to the wounds, but he was out of bandages and so yelled back for help.[104]

As he worked, the field was shelled twice more. Each time, Cavaleri threw his own body over Jacobs. Another trooper came half way out and threw Cavaleri another bandage. Cavaleri ripped it in two and tied the pieces around the wrist wounds. He then wrapped Jacobs' handkerchief around his injured leg in case he had a fracture. Another shelling began, much more intense than before, and Cavaleri began to fear he would surely be wounded himself.

Private Thomas Connolly, lying six feet from Gilles leaned over and said, "Could we go forward?" Gilles and Connolly dug their elbows into the snow prepared to move when another trooper, nicknamed 'Moose,' went down ahead of them. Connolly dressed the wound, making sure to use the wounded trooper's parapack instead of his own in case he would be hit. Then he started dragging Moose back to the battalion aid station.[105] Finally Lieutenant Gilles shouted, "Let's get out of here."

"Well how 'bout Jacobs?" asked Cavaleri.

"We'll come back and get him," answered Gilles. The men withdrew into the woods; some men went back down to the barn Colonel Miller was using as an observation post.[106] When the shelling stopped, Lieutenant Gilles and another trooper grabbed a stretcher, fetched Jacobs, and carried him back to the barn.[107] Moments later, Connolly, who had withdrawn back to the barn with Gilles, was hit by mortar shell fragments. He sustained a concussion and minor shrapnel wounds in his legs and feet. In addition, Connolly had developed frozen feet. He and Jacobs were soon evacuated.[108]

After being wounded, Lieutenant Calhoun moved forward to a snow-covered embankment behind a barbed wire fence to take cover from the sniper's fire. Hitting the ground, he had rolled over on his wounded arm and could not get off it. The sniper continued 'searching by fire' for Calhoun, but his bullets struck only the snow bank, kicking snow in Calhoun's face. Eventually, the sniper gave up.

Tec 4 George Vondrasek, arriving with First Platoon, saw that Calhoun was wounded and asked, "Lieutenant, my rifle is frozen and won't shoot. Can I have your Tommy gun?"

"Get me off my arm," replied Calhoun, "and you can have anything I've got."

Vondrasek lifted Calhoun off his arm, and then took Calhoun's Thompson, ammunition, and rations. Vondrasek asked Calhoun if he wanted a morphine shot.

Calhoun was worried the stuff was addictive. "No," he declined, "I'll go with the pain."

First Sergeant Donovan then came up to Calhoun, "Lieutenant Calhoun, you're supposed to go back to the aid station. I'm supposed to take over your platoon. Where are they?"

"That's them down there in those holes, dug in," replied Calhoun, motioning to the handful of men still out there in the field, crouching in the shellholes. With that, he got up off the ground and, clutching his arm to his side to relieve the pain, began to make his way back into Mande-St.-Etienne.

Calhoun passed the 2nd Battalion observation post on his way to the company CP where Doc Sloan was taking care of the wounded. Colonel Miller called Calhoun inside and asked him where F Company was. Calhoun pointed to the first phase line on the map.

"You can't be there," said Miller. "We're shelling that area by artillery."

"Colonel," said Calhoun in disgust, "you've been shelling on top of F Company or behind it all day. Stop the shelling and just go up on top of the ridge and look down and you'll see F Company at the phase line waiting for E Company to take up its position to the left of the road."

Colonel Miller did not reply to Calhoun's observation. Instead, he pointed to a crease on Calhoun's helmet where a bullet had ricocheted off. Apparently, the bullet that had hit him in the shoulder had been a ricochet. It hit his arm sideways, not straight by its nose, turning when it hit the bone and taking out a large piece of flesh when it exited out the back. Miller could see that Calhoun, still holding his arm tight against his side, was in a lot of pain and told him to go get it taken care of. Then, acting on Calhoun's suggestion, Miller started out to the ridge to look over the situation for himself, covering himself in a white sheet before departing.[109]

Calhoun went into the house behind Miller's OP that served as F Company's command post. Inside were Lieutenant Dean and Doc Sloan, who were collecting F Company's wounded. After the other medics, Thomson and Peterson, were killed earlier that morning, Captain Reynolds ordered Sloan: "Stay inside that building. We'll send the wounded people to you." Private Simpson from Third Platoon was in there with a bullet wound from the first attack; he'd made it to the aid station on his own. Calhoun also noticed PFC Donald Black among the wounded, suffering a severe shrapnel wound. All tolled, there were about thirty men waiting to be evacuated.

Calhoun's wound was too painful for him to remove his coat, so Sloan took a big pair of scissors and started cutting it off so he could get to work on Calhoun's shoulder. Going into combat, the officers of the 17th Airborne Division had been ordered to wear their neckties, officer's coats, insignia shining on the epaulettes, the works. Calhoun truly loved that coat – a beautiful, camel hair officer's overcoat. After cutting the coat off, Sloan gave Calhoun sulfanilamide tablets to swallow and then fastened his arm tightly to his side so it would not move.

While Lieutenant Puckett and his men headed for the position Captain Reynolds had specified, they began receiving mortar fire and briefly halted. Then Puckett saw the main body of the company, and called to First Sergeant Donovan.

"Lieutenant, you're the only officer left in the company," said Donovan flatly.

"I just spoke with the Captain," said Puckett, correcting.

DeHaven presented himself and told Puckett that after he met with the Captain, Reynolds had gone out across the field to the position the Second Platoon men were occupying but had been cut off by a tank.

"Why didn't you go with him?" the lieutenant asked DeHaven.

According to Puckett, "I'm not gonna follow that fool," was DeHaven's answer.[110] Apparently, DeHaven had not accompanied Reynolds but instead had returned to where the main body of the company was located.

Donovan informed Puckett that Lieutenant Calhoun was wounded and had been evacuated. The radio man for the artillery forward observer also was present and approached Lieutenant Puckett, crying. "Sir, I want to go look for my captain." Puckett gave the sergeant permission, upon which the sergeant dropped the SCR-300 radio he was carrying and moved off.

Puckett took a couple of moments to assess the chaotic situation. He thought to himself, "I haven't been briefed on the plan. There's no one on our left except the Germans. We've got no artillery support." Puckett decided the best course of action was to withdraw from the field and move back into woods overlooking Mande-St.-Etienne and there to reform the company. He gave Donovan his orders and the sergeant retrieved the few men left in the foxhole line. Puckett then gave instructions to destroy the SCR-300 radio that the FO's radio man had dropped. Rather than see it shot, however, a private volunteered to carry it.

Moving further through the woods, Lieutenant Puckett found Lieutenant Gilles from First Platoon. "We're the only officers left," said Puckett. "You're gonna have to take over the company."

"No," said Gilles, "the exec is still alive. Lieutenant Dean will take over the company." Lieutenant Dean was at the company CP.

Lieutenant Dean was sent for and when he arrived Puckett told him that the Captain had been cut off and that it was left to him to take over the company. When he realized he was responsible for organizing the defense of the company position, Dean's legs started to tremble under him. "I can't do it. I can't do it," he said.[111] Colonel Miller, who had appeared just as the news was broken to Dean, pointed to

Puckett. "Well, he can do it for you," he said. Lieutenant Puckett placed the men in position and checked the fields of fire for the company's heavy weapons. He then returned to Lieutenant Dean and said, "I'm finished. You can have 'em back," and left to join his platoon on the forward edge of the tree line. Reorganizing the line could not hide the fact that F Company had suffered heavily in its first battle; in its rifle platoons there were only sixty-five men – and about thirty in the First, ten in the Second, and twenty-five in the Third.[112] Despite the heavy losses, Miller wanted to keep the battalion moving, and so ordered First Sergeant Donovan to get a patrol into Flamizoulle. Donovan began making preparations.

Not only F Company, but the entire regiment, the entire 17th Airborne Division in fact, was in trouble. The division's other assault regiment, the 194th Glider Infantry, attacking on the 513th Parachute Infantry's left that morning, had started well, rapidly taking the villages of Rechriva, Hubermont, Millomont, and Renuamont, but it then met determined resistance and was unable to go farther. What truly imperiled the division, however, was that the 87th U.S. Infantry Division, which was supposed to have advanced on the left flank of the 17th Airborne Division, did not. The 17th Airborne's left flank, General Miley commented, was "left dangling in the breeze." Making a proper defense even more difficult was the inclement weather which made observed artillery fire all but impossible: "We couldn't get the stuff up close enough to our troops," stated Miley. "They [the 194th] were out on a limb," he continued, "past supporting distance."[113] When the 194th received a strong enemy counterattack, therefore, it was forced back almost to its starting point. As the 194th withdrew, German armored units plunged eastward against the exposed left flank of the 513th Parachute Infantry at Mande-St.-Etienne.

At regimental headquarters, Colonel Coutts was stunned by the speed and ferocity of the German attack. He could not determine if German intentions were a localized counterattack against his regiment or a major push towards Bastogne. Whatever the case, however, 1st Battalion received a savage beating. At 1430 hours, Coutts decided to order the 1st Battalion to withdraw what men it could back to their positions in the Bois des Valets where the battalion could reorganize. He then ordered Lieutenant Colonel Edward Kent's 3rd Battalion to take over the 1st Battalion's line. Kent was told to anchor his right at the roadblock at Monty and extend his line through the Bois des Valets to the woods west of Vivier du Four.

Regimental Headquarters Company was sent to the left of the 3rd Battalion as a rifle company. Coutts then sent word to Lieutenant Colonel Miller to stop the 2nd Battalion and dig in.[114] The 513th had gone from the attack, to the defense of a 4,500 yard line.[115]

Next, in an attempt to counter the German armor, Colonel Coutts brought up what armor and antitank weapons he had available. Five 75mm guns were placed at interval along the line and a section of 57mm antitank guns was deployed in depth behind them. Coutts then ordered C Company of the 22nd Tank Battalion – with its Shermans – to go to Monty to deal with the German armor pressuring his left flank.[116]

C Company of the 22nd Tank Battalion was given the mission of "following the infantry [of the 3rd Battalion] in a supporting role, available as TDs in the eventof [*sic*] an enemy armored counterattack." The infantry, however, rapidly fell behind the tanks and soon C Company was in the lead alone – First Platoon "going to the west toward Flamierge and 2d platoon supplying a base of fire." The tanks soon began receiving fire from every direction. Quickly, six Shermans were hit, three of which were "completely destroyed." Captain Lawrence Minnick, commanding C Company, called for artillery support but none came. Next he tried to raise the 1st Battalion to request that the infantry move up and support the tanks, but since what was left of 1st Battalion had been ordered to return to the Bois des Valets to reorganize, they could not. Captain Minnick had no other choice but to withdraw his surviving tanks.[117]

Though most of the 11th Armored Division had few complaints about their relationship with the 17th Airborne, the officers of the 22nd Tank Battalion were angry about the way in which the 17th Airborne Division split up their battalion into small units, denying it the ability to be employed en masse. They complained bitterly that, under "airborne supervision they were misused as a point force against the strongest enemy defenses, while the infantry was always far behind and never close enough to protect them against bazookas and antitank guns." The tank officers further remarked about the "greenness" of the division, and went on to say that the 17th was, on whole, "an outfit which might be good for guerrilla tactics, but which is undisciplined and uncoordinated; the officers have no control over their men and do not exert leadership in battle. Time after time the glider para infantry broke and ran in the face of enemy armor, leaving the tanks unprotected."[118]

Of course, with German armor advancing unchecked eastward, there was a danger developing. Lieutenant Colonel Miller had not received Colonel Coutts order to stop the 2nd Battalion. Communications were a shambles – telephone lines were cut by artillery and the freezing weather played havoc with the radios – however, according to Major Edwards, not all of the regiment's radios were out. The problem, he asserts, was that "nobody at regiment was trying to communicate with us."[119] Therefore, 2nd Battalion, badly dispersed and short of ammunition, its numbers "dwindling from engaging enemy armor under unequal circumstances," was still advancing when the Germans struck its left flank. The first to be hit was F Company.

Miraculously, First Sergeant Donovan's patrol had gotten into Flamizoulle – a village consisting of a few farm houses and a grain elevator about eight hundred yards northwest of Mande-St.-Etienne – without great difficulty. There, the men set about checking the buildings and the surrounding area. A heavy fog was setting in and the snow was falling faster than ever.

Suddenly, the men heard the sound of engines revving. At first, Private Imre thought it was the sound of heavy bombers coming in low. But then three German tanks, covered by snow and fog until they were almost on top of the village, rolled out of the trees about 150 yards to the north, supported by infantry. They held their fire but began to close rapidly. Two more tanks appeared, one to the east of the village and one to the west. Donovan figured it was time to leave.

"Get the hell outa here," Donovan yelled as enemy artillery erupted in the village. The men took off across the snow-blanketed fields. A few threw away their rifles and helmets. Men scrambled over barbed wire fences, some ran right through them. "I don't know how we could run so fast," remembered Bob Greenstrand. Imre agreed, "They should have clocked us for the Olympics."

From F Company's position above Mande-St.-Etienne, nine enemy tanks were spotted moving into the valley south of Flamizoulle from out of the woods D Company quickly had abandoned, and German infantry reoccupied the two small copses of trees north of the main forest. The blinding snow fall, however, aided most of the D Company troopers in making their escape back to the phase line. Some of Donovan's men ran toward D Company's positions. There, the combined group withdrew toward E Company.[120]

Some men didn't make it, though. Imre, Hataway, and Hriesik had just gotten into a patch of woods when they heard the crackling of small arms fire behind them. Hriesik, following his two buddies, shouted out. Imre and Hataway circled around and went back to find Hriesik lying in the snow severely wounded. He had a hole straight through his right shoulder. Imre thought he could "almost see daylight on the other side."

"You all right?" asked Imre and Hataway.

"Fine," replied Hriesik almost nonchalantly. "It's a clean wound. No problem. I'm going to the aid station."

"We gotta' walk you," said Imre. "This place is crawling with Germans."

But Hriesik declined their offer. "No, no."

So they left Hriesik and that was the last they saw of him. Hriesik made it back to Flamizoulle where he tried to hide in a barn, but was captured. Hriesik spoke enough German to keep his captors from shooting him, but was nevertheless sent to a prisoner of war camp. Because he was a paratrooper, he was treated brutally. In captivity, the Germans made an example of him. He received the most punishment but the least food, he had the most cooler time in the camp, and when there was punishment to be meted out, he was the first.

Just as Doc Sloan was finishing up on Lieutenant Calhoun, a frightened trooper burst into the aid station, "Leave one medic with the wounded and all you walking people get out of here and go back. We're withdrawing now!"

"Who gave that order?" demanded Calhoun.

"Colonel Miller," replied the trooper. Rather than make a stand, Miller had apparently ordered the withdrawal of D and E Companies, leaving F Company to cover the battalion as it retired.

Lieutenant Calhoun, stripped to the waist except for his bandages, went outside into the road a few yards from Miller's observation post. There he met Lieutenant Dean. They were astonished to see D and E Company troopers withdrawing through the town.

"Where the hell are you going?" demanded Lieutenant Calhoun of the men.

"We're pulling out," replied the frightened troopers.

"The hell you're pulling out!" shouted Calhoun, angered by the response. "F Company's out there a half a mile with no support. They've got to pull out first. Then you people can run. So turn around."

"Tanks are coming," insisted the frightened men.

"The hell with tanks!" said Calhoun.

Calhoun cussed them out for being a "bunch of cowards" and, countermanding Colonel Miller's order to withdraw, told them to turn around and go back to the top of the ridge and dig in. The D and E Company men did as they were told and went back up on the ridge where they dug in next to F Company.

Calhoun told Lieutenant Dean to move F Company's wounded to the battalion aid station in Mande-St.-Etienne where they could be evacuated. Supply trucks dumped loads of ammunition behind the building used for as the aid station and then picked up wounded to go to the rear. Walking wounded could hold onto the sides of the trucks if they were strong enough. "[I'll] lead anyone back who [can] walk on his own," said Calhoun.

Miller never came out of his OP.

Covered by a thin fog and the gathering darkness, the enemy tanks continued to approach. F Company's officers and NCOs had a hard time keeping the men calmed down.

Enemy automatic fire laced the trees and snapped all round. Almost immediately, PFC MacKenzie was hit by a round that went through his left shoulder and into his left side. "I was surprised it didn't hurt more – it kinda numbed me." MacKenzie thought he'd never be hit and being wounded came as a shock. Another trooper helped him to the medics. The aid station was under fire too, but MacKenzie was nevertheless "glad to be out of the cold."[121]

As the noise of the tanks came closer, the young trooper next to Cavaleri declared, "I'm gonna get out!"

"Forget about it," Cavaleri told him as sternly as possible. "We're at war now. This is combat!"

"No. I'm gonna do something to get out," the man asserted. Cavaleri just turned away from him.

Cavaleri was given orders to lay down a line of fire with his .30 caliber machine-gun between the two small woods forward of the company position. There was no lack of targets, and soon, all the machine-gunners were crying out for extra ammunition and men were sent to bring up more. Imre and Newhouse ran back to the barn at the edge of town where F Company's extra ammunition was stored. Imre had started to gather his first load when the Germans shells began to drop inside the town. Imre flopped on the floor of the stone shed for protection from the shrapnel, so scared he never considered he was surrounded by stacks of mortar shells and boxes of .30 caliber ammunition. The good news, he later figured, was that one direct hit and he wouldn't have had to worry about it.

Newhouse started back to the company's position, but half way across the field he was pinned down by machine-gun fire from the left [west]. Newhouse flopped down behind a lone sapling; its roots made a hump in the snow and offered some concealment. He laid there until after dark, about 1700, and then scrambled back to the company.[122]

The shelling let up momentarily and Imre dashed back to the line carrying a full load of ammunition, then returned to get extra ammunition for Second Platoon's 60mm mortar. He found out when he returned, however, that the baseplate was missing. He had left it out in the field and wasn't about to go get it. In training, however, he had practiced using a helmet in lieu of the baseplate, so Hataway, Hultman, and Imre set up the mortar that way. Wearing two pairs of gloves, Imre held the tube as steady as he could while the others dropped the rounds down the barrel. "They [the rounds] made noise someplace, scaring somebody," remembered Imre. "Second Platoon's mortar barrage."[123]

Colonel Miller joined E Company on the right. From there, Miller ordered 2nd Battalion's bazooka teams out to face the enemy tanks and SPs. In the face of the American bazooka teams, the German tanks – which did not have much infantry support – were, apparently, reluctant to press their attack and turned back. When the tanks withdrew, however, the artillery started back up.

Throughout the night, the German artillery battered the 513th, most of it falling on the 2nd Battalion in the woods overlooking Mande-St.-Etienne. The concussions of the exploding shells were tremendous. Screaming meemies bounced the men up and down in their shallow scrapes. After every explosion the men yelled out to each other, checking to see if buddies were still all right.

Tec 5 Neal Haggard had dug in under a fallen tree that provided him with protection against the tree bursts. His friend, Private Jean Paul Morin, however, had chosen a spot with little protection. Every time a shell came in close, Haggard would yell to him to get down. After one such close shell, Morin was hit. He had a hole so large in his head Haggard could see his brain. Haggard and another trooper carried him off the hill. In the field, they were relieved by two other troopers who took Morin the rest of the way. The medics at the aid station told them to lay Morin with the bodies of the dead and those who could not be saved. Haggard was left helpless and frustrated.[124]

At about 2000 hours, a jeep towing a 57mm antitank gun pulled up into the woods near the F Company's Second Platoon's foxholes. Almost immediately, a shell struck the jeep setting off the white phosphorous ammunition it was carrying. Burning phosphorous pellets went everywhere, falling on some of the dozen or so men in the surrounding holes. One trooper's hand was burned severely and he screamed in pain. It was clear he had to be evacuated so Newhouse propped his M1 up in his hole and helped the man back to the aid station.

The medics told Newhouse that since he'd forgotten his rifle: "Don't go back up there tonight." That was okay by Newhouse. His overcoat had gotten wet around the skirt and when night came it had frozen up like a board. A night in the aid station would do him good.[125]

Throughout the evening, small groups of troopers continued to make their ways back to E and F Company's positions in the woods. At about 2200 hours, Captain Reynolds turned up. Reynolds, cut off by the tank earlier that afternoon, had buried himself in the snow to avoid being spotted, and then waited for dark to slip back to friendly lines. Reynolds woke up Lieutenant Puckett, looked him in the eyes, and then just walked away. No words were exchanged. Puckett was sure the Captain was angry at him for not trying to rescue him. In any case, every man in the company was glad that Reynolds was back.[126]

The 513th's kitchens had been established since about 1730 hours and First Sergeant Donovan asked for one man from each platoon to come down to the battalion CP and pick up the food. As Private Billy English bent over to pick up one of the containers, a white phosphorous grenade he was carrying in his pocket went off. English ran out of the barn on fire and screaming.

Colonel Miller, standing just outside when the grenade exploded, hollered, "Wrap him in straw," – outside there was a frozen pile of straw and dung which had been cleaned from the barn. "Get the hell out of the way," ordered Donovan who grabbed English and dragged him toward a nearby snow bank. Acey-Deucy was "too damn dumb to do anything [right]," thought Donovan. Donovan packed the wounds with snow. This cut off the air to the phosphorous and prevented it from continuing to burn. English was then put on a jeep and evacuated. Donovan learned later that English had lost his leg.[127]

The cooks brought up insulated containers of hot food close to the company position, but so intense was the shelling that not one of the men braved getting out of their holes to get it. German artillery steadily pounded the woods and F Company was "getting a lot of tree bursts," recalled Greenstrand – shells that hit the trees and detonated, showering the men in shrapnel and splinters.[128] Besides, none of the men could eat it anyway. Some of Second Platoon's survivors had a five pound can of bacon from a 10-in-1, but only stared at it.[129] They just weren't hungry. "The odor of the pine trees, gun powder and death smelled just like cream-styled corn to me," remembered Greenstrand. Men were hollering for the medics all night. Some cried openly.[130]

Although the enemy artillery fire was heavy, at 2330 hours, a patrol was ordered out to reconnoiter the area forward of F Company, and Sergeant La Riccia and two other men were detailed for it. The men had gotten about three hundred yards when the ground gave way beneath their feet. Snow had covered over the ice on the Rau de Mande stream and La Riccia and one of the other men crashed through, getting soaked up to their knees. The Germans heard the noise and sent up two flares immediately – each a burst of daylight before they shimmered down. "Oh my God, they're gonna get us for sure," said La Riccia hoarsely. The three men laid in the snow for about an hour, but finally when nothing happened, they made their way back to the company.[131]

By midnight, Private Imre couldn't feel his feet any more and received permission to go back to the aid station. Imre's feet were swollen – his boots were so tight he couldn't slip a knife between the laces and the tongue to cut them off, so the medics soaked Imre's boots in water, cut the laces with scissors and then cut off the boots. Medics placed his feet in melting snow water until the feeling returned and then dried them off. Imre spent the night at the aid station, allowing his feet to dry out completely and assisting the medics where he could.

Most of the time, however, Imre sat in a place in the corner of the room from which he could observe. Lanterns provided the light inside the aid station. The wounded were placed across cots and on doors, whatever the medics could find. Imre watched the chaplain who stood with one F Company man draped across him while the surgeon worked, steadily picking shrapnel from his lacerated back. The trooper feebly clung to the priest. Then, Imre heard the boy groan and, in the dim light, saw his face turn gray. He was dead. The sound of his last gasp was the worst sound Imre had ever heard.

"Shit!" Imre had never heard the chaplain swear before. The surgeon threw his instrument into the pan angrily and struck a post with his fist. After a moment they moved on, continuing to work on the living.

PFC Dahlberg helped one man into the aid station who had shot himself in the foot. The doctor told the man, "You get over there, away from the men who are really wounded." Private Dahlberg then was asked if he'd volunteer to pick up the dead, but he refused. He just couldn't; he was too tired. He left and, in the dark, found his way back to the old company CP in town and caught a few moments of sleep in the straw.[132] Meanwhile, at F Company's new CP, First Sergeant Donovan tried to get some accurate accounting of those killed, wounded, and missing but he soon gave up. Things were too confused.[133]

Still stripped to the waist, Lieutenant Calhoun was growing very cold. The medics at the aid station gave him a blanket, but it only helped a little. Since he could walk, and was therefore not "seriously wounded," Calhoun waited as those in worse shape were evacuated on the ammunition trucks. As each ammunition truck unloaded, wounded would be put on board and moved further to the rear to the regimental clearing station. At about 0300 on the morning of 5 January, a truck came for Lieutenant Calhoun.

More wounded continued to arrive at the aid station in a steady stream throughout the night. Regimental medical personnel did their best but were unable to cope with the enormous number of casualties. Ambulances and ambulance jeeps from the 513th's medical section transported wounded troopers without pause, as did those of the 224th Medical Company. Eventually, ammunition trucks, and supply trucks bringing up socks, gloves, overshoes, and rations, were pressed into evacuating the wounded.[134] Of the 835 men of the 2nd Battalion who went into Monty and Mande-St.-Etienne the day before, more than half had become casualties by the end of 4 January, and the battle was only just beginning.

6

Swatting at Tigers

The Battle for Dead Man's Ridge
5-13 January 1945

The next morning, Ace Miller had 2nd Battalion's observation posts set up in the woods north of Mande-St.-Etienne, on the regimental right. Two 81mm mortars and three 60mm mortars were set up just to the rear of the woods in support. Backing up these weapons were the 75mm Howitzers of the 466th Parachute Field Artillery Battalion and the 105mm Howitzers of the 274th Field Artillery. Concentrations for artillery had been established at crossroads and on likely approaches to the town. In Mande-St.-Etienne, Major Edwards spoke to a liaison officer from VIII Corps artillery. The liaison officer gave him bad news – it would be another forty-eight hours before any additional artillery would be available to support the 513th.[1]

Enemy patrols had been active all through the night of the fourth, probing the lines, testing for weak spots. Daybreak on the fifth brought relief from the German patrols, but the weather was relentless – cold and with poor visibility. The 513th, on the division right, still held the small amount of ground they had taken the day before, but could claim only 1,680 "fighting mad" combat-effective personnel. On the 513th's front Colonel Coutts had positioned C Company of the 139th Engineers on his left, the 1st and 3rd Battalion's in the middle, and Miller's 2nd Battalion on the far right, contacting elements of the 101st Airborne Division.[2]

The German front line ran from high ground south and west of Flamierge, east, running just north of the woods above Mande-St.-Etienne, to the secondary road tracking northeast to Champs where the 101st had recently beaten back an enemy armored attack. 17th Airborne's G-2 had identified the *1st* and *2nd Battalions* of the *29th Panzergrenadier Regiment*, and the *8th* and *115th Panzergrenadier Regiments*. Interrogation of prisoners revealed that both the *8th* and *29th Panzergrenadiers* had suffered heavily, and now numbered scarcely two hundred men apiece. This was both good and bad news for Miley. On one hand, there weren't many enemy troops ahead; on the other hand, to take such a beating at the hands of such a small force was cause for concern. The Germans' effective use of armor had indeed tipped the scales in their favor.

During the night, the 194th Glider Infantry, on the division left at Renuamont about four thousand yards west of Monty, had been attacked by a force of some fifteen to twenty enemy tanks. The 194th was forced to withdraw, but fighting continued around Renuamont into the afternoon. Some of the glidermen who had been taken prisoner during the early fighting at Renuamont later escaped. They reported observing fifty Germans outfitted in American uniforms in the town and similar sightings were indicated in many intelligence reports.[3]

On the 17th's left, The 87th Infantry Division made an attempt to come up on line with Miley's troopers, but a well-timed German spoiling attack scotched the 87th's move. Miley's left flank would be open for yet another day. In light of the 87th's setback, and of the losses suffered by the 17th Airborne the day before, VIII Corps did not ask General Miley to continue his attack on the fifth.[4]

For one man, the morning brought good news. Private Imre was given dry socks and a pair of jump boots by the medics. Imre wore a size eight-and-a-half boot normally, but the medics had given him a pair of elevens or twelves to accommodate his still-swollen feet. At least they were dry, and, for Imre, that was marvelous! The medics also gave him a dry field jacket, an M1 Rifle, a few bandoleers of ammunition, and a couple grenades. The medics had tagged Imre – who had frozen feet – for evacuation that evening, but he would have to wait until then for a place on an ambulance.

It was still about an hour before first light. There was some sporadic enemy shelling and, since 0510 hours, enemy armored vehicles had been heard two miles west of Monty. Imre left the aid station and walked up through Mande toward F Company's position on the hill. In the fields around the town, troopers were picking up the bodies of the dead. Many already had started to change color. Private Richard Murray was among the volunteers for this gruesome task. At the edge of town, Imre stopped at the spring house and picked up a couple of boxes of .30 caliber machine-gun ammunition to give to PFC Joe Kitson. Imre greatly admired the twenty-six year old Kitson because he seemed to have the answers to all of life's most important questions. In a few minutes, Imre reached the Second Platoon's position and jumped into a hole with Harding. A few yards away, Hataway and Hultman shared another foxhole.[5]

On the south side of the village, First Sergeant Donovan was trying to finish his morning report but the previous day's chaos made it all but impossible to determine just whom from F Company had been killed or wounded. Donovan asked Staff Sergeant Knigge to help him, but Knigge wasn't sure about anything beyond that Second Platoon had gotten the hell kicked out of it. Knigge wondered out loud when they were going to get some relief. "We're not gonna get any relief," bluntly replied Donovan.[6]

Donovan, Staff Sergeant Knigge, and a handful of troopers set out through town, past Miller's observation post to find Captain Reynolds. Donovan, as best he could, apprised Reynolds of the situation. Reynolds decided to combine First and Second Platoons under Gilles' command. Third Platoon would remain under Lieutenant Puckett.

At 0945 hours, a strong artillery preparation on the positions of 2nd and 3rd Battalions signaled the beginning of another German counterattack. As they had done the day before, the Germans attacked with tanks, self-propelled guns, and infantry astride the Bastogne Highway advancing toward Ace Miller's positions west of Monty and north of the highway.

Enemy small arms fire and shell shrapnel ripped through the pines and all around the 2nd Battalion men. Pointing to a foxhole, Lieutenant Puckett told Colonel Miller, who was standing near him when the attack began, "Colonel, it's pretty rough here. You better get in this hole." Miller took Puckett's advice and jumped in. When the shelling became a little hotter, Puckett decided he better get in, too. Then a private jumped in on top of the both of them.[7]

The men had not been able to dig new foxholes in the frozen earth so, during the night, many had improved shellholes that pockmarked the ground. They "were lazy," admitted Private Imre, and they paid for it because the German gunners had the area zeroed in. A near miss sent dirt, rocks, and snow raining down on Imre and Harding. Another shell struck like a bolt of lightning, knocking Imre unconscious. When he came to, stunned, he saw that the shell had blown both he and Harding out of their hole. Kitson hauled Imre up and carried him off the line while another trooper took Harding.

"Jesus, are you dead?" Kitson asked when he saw Imre's eyes open. The question scared the hell out of Imre because blood was running down his face and stinging his eyes. "Put me down," Imre yelled. "Just put me down." Kitson laid Imre on the field. The cold snow was like a salve. Imre glanced over to Harding who had been laid down, too. Harding was still unconscious, and, like Imre, covered with blood running from his nose and ears. Kitson and another trooper applied bandages and stopped what bleeding they could.

"Are you okay?" Kitson again asked Imre.

Imre shook his head. He could see Kitson's lips moving but could hardly hear him.

"Can't you hear me?" asked Kitson.

Imre shook his head again. Now he couldn't talk either. Kitson ran for the medics. When the aidmen removed Imre's overcoat, field jacket, wool shirt, longjohns, and cotton underwear, they found a crescent-shaped hole about as big as a half dollar in his right armpit.

Meanwhile, from the northeast, six enemy tanks came through the valley to attack 2nd Battalion's positions but, under the direction of Major Edwards, the battalion's supporting weapons held off the enemy armor and their supporting infantry. About two hours after the barrage had begun, 2nd Battalion had repulsed the enemy thrust against it as had the 1st Battalion.[8]

When the artillery lifted, the men all climbed out of their scrapes. Miller, at the bottom of the pile in Puckett's hole had been nearly squashed. Miller took one look at the private and demanded of Puckett, "Who's he?"

"He's helping me dig the slit trench," Puckett replied.

"Well," said Miller, in a conciliatory tone, "that's okay."[9]

The attack had been beaten off, but intermittent mortar and artillery fire soon started back up and continued to fall on the regiment throughout the day causing about fifteen casualties per battalion. Among these was the 1st Battalion commander, Lieutenant Colonel Kent. Officially, it was reported by Colonel Coutts that Kent refused medical treatment "until late in the evening" at which time "he was found to have a fractured bone in the lower part of his right leg" and was evacuated on Coutts' order. Major Edwards remembered things differently. "Kent received a shrapnel wound in his leg. He shouldn't have gone back any further than the battalion aid station – just a small piece of shrapnel about the size of a half dollar – went through and went out, a clean wound. But he demanded to be evacuated and he was."[10]

Some Germans were taken prisoner during the attack and some men in F Company decided to exact a little retribution. Four F Company troopers walked up to the barn where Private Lightcap was drying out M1s as he had been instructed. Ahead of them, they were pushing four German prisoners. Lightcap observed that two of the Germans were older men, but the other two were just kids, barely sixteen years old.

"What the hell are you going to do with them?" Lightcap asked the troopers, although he felt he already knew. The four were a group of extremely tough men long known among F Company as 'Murder, Incorporated'. Lightcap considered them regular hoods.

"We're gonna shoot the sonsabitches," they answered.

"Why?"

"Cause they were in a machine-gun nest and they wouldn't give up."

Lightcap started to protest. He even offered to take charge of the prisoners himself, but backed down when the men threatened to shoot him if he tried to stop them. "They took the four Germans out back and backed them up against an old brush pile," remembered Lightcap. "The Germans didn't do a thing, they remained quiet, never speaking a word. Each of the troopers picked out a target. They shot them with their own weapons," said Lightcap. The four troopers walked off, but Lightcap remained, transfixed. The snow that was falling melted on the slain Germans' uniforms. Soon, however, the snow didn't melt any more and began covering the bodies. Later, Lightcap reported the murders to an officer, but the report fell on deaf ears. He was almost glad when, by the end of the Battle of the Bulge, all four of the men were themselves killed.[11]

Private Kaczmarek brought in four prisoners – all young and wearing long overcoats – and he and Seacott had them lean spread-eagle against the side of a shed while they searched them. Seacott took a wristwatch from one of them. Then Kaczmarek pushed them to the rear. Seacott heard some shots and, about two minutes later, Kaczmarek returned. Seacott believed that Kaczmarek had shot them.[12]

The 17th Airborne's official policy stated that prisoners were to be rushed to the regimental collecting points for interrogation. They were not to be permitted to smoke, eat, drink, urinate, or warm themselves until the interrogation was completed. They also would be searched for documents before being sent to the Division PW cage at Sibret. However, apparently many Germans who surrendered or who were taken prisoner never even made it much beyond the front.[13]

The rest of the day passed uneventfully up in the woods north of Mande. Captain Reynolds' CP was set up in one of the old German bunkers. Near the bunker was a big trench. A man could stand in it waist high. Up ahead there was a path leading through the woods. A line of foxholes followed it. Cavaleri was in the last hole manning his .30 caliber machine-gun. As darkness gathered, Corps and Division artillery were harassing the enemy in and around Flamierge, the explosions lighting the night sky. This, however, was no deterrent to the enemy foot patrols who were probing the 17th's lines as they had been the night before.[14]

Cavaleri struggled to mark the changes from the light of the sky and the dark of everything else. Because he was night-blind, this was a particularly difficult task. Tech Sergeant Bowers called to Cavaleri to come down into the bunker. Inside it was lit well enough for Cavaleri to see Captain Reynolds, First Sergeant Donovan, Bowers, Tec 5 Haggard, and another trooper. Reynolds knew Cavaleri's boots were all ripped up and so had an extra pair of boots for him. "The boots are too small for me," said Cavaleri, trying to squeeze into them. "I can't get into them." Cavaleri then moved to leave.

"Where are you going, Cavaleri?" asked Reynolds.

"I'm going back to my hole."

"Stay here a while," said Reynolds.

Cavaleri stayed, shooting the bull together with the other men for another hour.[15]

Meanwhile, Privates Newhouse and Henderson were detailed to set up a bazooka roadblock at the Monty crossroads for a four-hour shift. A soft snow, carried on a light wind from the west, was falling, carried on a light wind from the west, on the quiet landscape and empty roads. The temperature was falling, too, into the low twenties.[16] Under the darkening skies the two men sat, each contemplating silently.

PFC Imre, meanwhile, had been moved to the battalion aid station and was tagged for immediate evacuation. Medics put him in the back of a two-and-a-half ton truck with about a dozen other wounded men. The drivers were scared because no one was sure where the American lines ended or where the German's lines began. In the last truck at the end of the column, Imre, although wounded, was given a .30 caliber machine-gun. The driver told him, "If I turn the engine off and blow the horn twice, start firing and keep firing, don't stop. If the Germans catch you in a Red Cross truck they're gonna torture everyone in there." The driver told Imre the challenge and countersign: "*St. George*" and "*The Dragon*." The MPs [holding little blue lights] were stopping all vehicles at crossroads and asking questions to which only 'real Americans' would know the correct answer.[17]

Nothing had prepared Imre for the sight of all the dead and wounded around the aid station. Imre had been raised in a family where you were taught to be kind and loving to one another, not kill them. That day, on the battlefield, he had seen arms, legs, guts, heads flying through the air. The day before he had rolled a buddy over and there wasn't any top to him, his body was just laid wide open. Imre couldn't get rid of the images.

The trucks pressed on into the darkness, the drivers skillfully reading the roads with only the trucks' little blue headlights to illuminate the way. The uneven roads shook the trucks and bounced the wounded making them even more uncomfortable. Over and over again in his mind Imre repeated "We've got to make it out of here. We've got to make it out of here," this while he tried to remember the password.

F Company's losses on the fifth also included Private Clifford M. Sheffield and Private Lawrence E. Lincoln who were killed in action, Private Howard J. Heaton who was seriously wounded, and Staff Sergeant Utt, Sergeant William E. Ward, PFC Rubin E. McLean, PFC Rex A. Roebke, Private Kaczmarek, and Private Simpson who were evacuated with frostbite. PFC Jacob Hriesik, taken prisoner on the fourth, was officially listed as missing in action.

Morning broke on the sixth with the familiar elements, fog, snow, and German shelling. The 513th remained in defensive positions throughout the day, the men dodging artillery and mortar fire, and the occasional Nebelwerfer. The weather was cold, and the visibility, often limited to less than a mile, prevented air support yet again. Little did the men know but, at Third Army headquarters, General Patton was planning to continue his attack north – again toward Houffalize.[18]

Patton, however, was uneasy over the slow progress of his attacks and was especially concerned by what he considered a lackluster performance by the 17th Airborne Division and its commander Major General Miley. Major Edwards was present, as were fifteen or twenty other officers of the division, when Patton arrived that day at Miley's headquarters to light a fire under the division and its commander. "If I get the chance," Patton bellowed at one point at Miley, "I'll come down here for a couple of days and show you how to fight a division!"[19]

That evening, Colonel Coutts received another attack order from Division for the next day. The 17th Airborne was going to advance northwest the following morning with the town of Flamierge its final objective. The 193rd Glider Infantry, now on the division's right, was ordered to capture Flamizoulle. The 194th Glider Infantry, on the left, was given as its initial objectives the towns of Millomont, Rechriva, and Hubermont. The 513th Parachute Infantry, attacking in the center, was ordered to take Flamierge and the high ground to the southwest that commanded the town which Miley considered "the key ground of the whole terrain." Instead of sending the 513th Parachute Infantry north in its attack, General Miley chose to send it northwest, roughly parallel to the highway. Therefore, if they were met by a counterattack from Flamierge, Miley thought it better that they receive it head on. The 193rd and 194th Regiments were to jump off at 0800 hours with the 513th following at 0900 "so that any attempt at flanking movements by the enemy could be dealt with." The 507th Parachute Infantry took up a position in reserve on the left flank so that, in the event the 87th Infantry Division did not attack as planned, the division's left would be covered.[20]

The 513th was to jump off from its present lines. Major Morris Anderson, now in command of the 3rd Battalion after having taken over for Lieutenant Colonel Kent, was ordered to advance along the right of the highway and take the hill just northwest of the point where the Flamizoulle road intersected with the Bastogne Highway at Vivier du Four. From there, 3rd Battalion would be only twelve hundred yards from the final objective – Flamierge.[21]

Kies' 1st Battalion, attacking on the left of the Bastogne Highway, was ordered initially to take the ridge at Vivier du Four. Once there, the battalion would continue its attack – which would be headed roughly northwest – to seize "the high ridge" with its two small stands of trees which ran southeast to northwest, one thousand yards southwest of Flamierge. From this position, 1st Battalion would be able to support the 3rd Battalion's attack on the town. 2nd Battalion, in reserve, would follow behind the 3rd Battalion.[22]

Supporting the 513th were C Company of the 22nd Tank Battalion, A Company of the 630th Tank Destroyer Battalion, and A Company of the 602nd Tank Destroyer Battalion which had been attached to Coutts' regiment on 5 January. The tank destroyers were ordered to follow the advancing battalions and defend against possible enemy armored counterattacks. The Shermans of the 22nd were to attack targets of opportunity. As was customary, the 466th PFAB would fire in direct support and a field artillery liaison party and forward observer were attached to each battalion of the 513th.[23]

At Mande-St.-Etienne, 2nd Battalion was relieved by the 193rd Glider Infantry who occupied the vicinity of Monty and Mande-St.-Etienne on the division right. The 139th Airborne Engineer Battalion was detached from the 513th at 0900 hours, and the 194th Glider Infantry then closed in positions on the left flank. The 2nd Battalion, now the regimental reserve, was ordered to withdraw to the southeast portion of the Bois des Valets and dig in there. The men packed up their equipment quickly. PFC Sarrell slung eight boxes of ammunition on two ropes and lugged the load some four hundred yards back into Mande. "I thought I was going to die," he remarked.[24]

As F Company passed back through the village, some of the troopers noticed bodies laying behind the farmhouses. "In the back there, it was backed up with German soldiers that were brought behind there," remembered Munafo. "I don't know who did it but, I know it was airborne troops. . . lined 'em up and riddled 'em down. Couldn't take prisoners," said Munafo, "Couldn't take prisoners." This was not some rationale used by privates to excuse brutality. There attitude was based on orders some received. Indeed, Private Munafo had been given a direct order from Lieutenant Stositch not to take prisoners. "To begin with, I don't think we had enough men to take care of prisoners," explained Munafo. "You had to do what you had to do." They had.[25]

In the Bois, among the pines that reminded Private Lightcap of "glorified Christmas trees," F Company took shelter in a barn. No one was allowed a fire, but Sarrell remembered that at least one trooper had a hay fire going anyway. At least they were out of the wind. "I didn't have any fresh water," remembered Don Newhouse. "There was a well at the low end of the pasture. The water in it was damn near brown from a thousand years of cow shit. I shook a couple of halizone tablets in it." Some men chewed on raw turnips which they'd pulled from the stacks in a nearby field.

Grice, as a Southerner, hated cold weather as a rule, but was now glad it had become colder; he had thrown off his goulashes days before – the colder weather meant the snow wouldn't melt on his boots as fast. "A lot of us had been issued goulashes including me," said Newhouse, "but when we got into combat, we figured we couldn't run in them so we threw them away." Those who could changed their socks, but it didn't make much difference for the men whose boots were already soaked.[26]

Newhouse was given the chance to get warmed up at a nearby farmhouse. The woodstove in the kitchen was burning intensely, but even after an hour he was still cold. Newhouse decided to unlace his boots and put his feet up near the fire. Water blisters grew immediately on his swollen feet, an indication of severe frostbite. He didn't even wait to tell Captain Reynolds – he went straight to the aid station at Monty where the medics tagged him for evacuation.[27]

Meanwhile, the chow truck came up and F Company was able to eat its first hot meal in almost a week – pancakes and hot coffee – and "big pills," some sort of dietary supplement. It was a welcome change; the C rations the men had been eating had ice in them.

In the afternoon, Captain Reynolds sent out a small patrol under Lieutenant Fann. Fann led the men around for hours until finally they were lost in enemy territory. The patrol eventually returned through another outfit's lines before dark, but had stayed out longer than was planned. The entire patrol was cold through and several men passed out from exhaustion. Private Greenstrand's feet were so numb he could hardly walk on them. Exhausted himself, he too was soon overcome by sleep.[28]

When Greenstrand came to, his feet were up against a hearth in which a fire roared. He looked at his boots; they were tight on his feet and laces were stretched. "Being born and raised in Minnesota with their terrible winters, I knew I was in trouble," remembered Greenstrand. "Get me the hell away from here," he hollered. After the medics moved him, Greenstrand cut the laces and removed the jump boots. He had no feeling in his feet and lower legs. When they got him to the aid station, a surgeon poked him in the calves with a scalpel. There was little blood and no feeling in them at all. Greenstrand was evacuated. First Sergeant Donovan listed him as missing in action.[29]

Six more F Company men were evacuated as well. Staff Sergeant Harry E. Cook, PFC Dennis Jordan, and Private Daniel Green all received light shrapnel wounds. Sergeant Harold E. Hinkley, Sergeant Johnnie Rutherford, PFC Harry E. Dauer, and PFC James Arrowood were evacuated with trench foot. Dauer, according to Haggard, was evacuated with combat fatigue. Hinkley, another man reported, deliberately took his boots off so that his feet would freeze.[30]

With the coming of darkness, the small arms fire along the front gradually ceased. The artillery, however, continued to boom through the night. At 0800 hours the next morning, 7 January, the 17th Airborne Division's attack toward the Ourthe River resumed. Again, the weather was cold and gray, with more of the seemingly perpetual fog and snow. "There was almost no visibility and no chance for air support," stated General Miley. "But [Third] Army was still insisting that there was nothing in front of us. Our patrols indicated that they were still out there. We couldn't tell how many. But Army said they were all pulling away from our front. So we pushed."[31]

The enemy, specifically the *3rd Battalion of Kampfgruppe Remmer* and the *29th, 115th,* and *104th Panzergrenadier Regiments*, was indeed in front of the 17th, but had no intention of leaving just yet. The Germans had been hurt badly, however; though the *104th Panzergrenadier Regiment*, for example, had received one hundred replacements during the prior evening, the average strength of its companies was only twenty-five to thirty men. Squads of six to eight men were being ordered to cover frontages of up to two hundred yards. Yet even with their numbers diminishing the Germans fought on tenaciously. At dawn, they sent Miley's men a calling card, shelling the positions of the 513th Regiment with 210mm nebelwerfers and artillery, and from Renuamont, firing on the 194th Glider Infantry with machine-guns.[32]

3rd Battalion's advance got underway on schedule nevertheless. Guiding on the road, Major Anderson deployed I Company to the right of the highway and G Company to its left; H Company was held in reserve. 3rd Battalion's assault companies were directed to advance until they came to the Flamizoulle road, at which time G Company would turn to the right and take the initial objective – a low hill just north of Vivier du Four. A liaison officer and two forward observers from the 466th Parachute Field Artillery Battalion accompanied the battalion. One platoon of I Company was tasked to maintain contact with the 193rd Glider Infantry attacking on the right.[33]

As Anderson's troopers advanced through the knee-deep snow, flat trajectory artillery began crashing into their ranks, and snipers, positioned in buildings near Vivier du Four, fired on G Company as it closed on the road junction. Despite this harassment, Anderson's men cleared the small village, killing some of the snipers and compelling the rest to retire. On the right, I Company drew heavy fire from German panzergrenadiers, half-tracks and tanks positioned along the road south of Flamizoulle and from machine-guns in woods south of the town. Nevertheless, the Germans withdrew as the battalion advanced, apparently never desiring the fighting to become too close.

From the outset, Major Anderson exercised skillful control of the attack, and 3rd Battalion reached its initial objective by 1100 hours where the men were ordered to dig in. Anderson sent this message to Colonel Coutts: "Now at 48.5-59.6. Enemy tanks directly to front of leading elements 300-yds. 3d Bn., Anderson, on line." On the left meanwhile, 1st Battalion had come on line with relative ease. Anderson, for one, was pleased.[34]

H Company and the mortars were ordered up. Though casualties among the men had only been moderate so far, in the advance all of the artillery radios had been destroyed by enemy action. The lack of communications meant that the mortars were the only artillery support immediately available to Major Anderson and getting the 81mm mortars into action was critically important – enemy armor could be seen concentrating on the high ground south of Flamierge. Hard-won experience had taught Division to expect the enemy to throw in their armor so, a half hour before the 513th's attack, General Miley had contacted Colonel Coutts to prepare for such an attack. "If not already in depth, be sure to get in depth against likely tank attack. Defense should consist of local strong points." For Anderson, the low hill would have to serve as his strong point and he called for tank support to help him defend it. In response, the five remaining Shermans of C Company of the 22nd Tank Battalion moved out on the Bastogne-Marche Highway. Captain Minnick, C Company's CO, received a call shortly thereafter saying that C Company could have three tank destroyers from the 630th Tank Destroyer Battalion. These, however, never materialized.[35]

At 1130 hours, as Major Anderson was placing the battalion's mortars and light machine-guns, six German tanks, Mark IV and Mark VI, attacked his positions from the road junction at Mon Nicolay, about one thousand yards up the highway. The panzers advanced down the highway and through the fields "in an extended front of three hundred yards." The troopers on G Company's left, on high ground, took cover in the highway cut. The rest of the battalion "were not completely dug in" and, as the tanks closed, abandoned the hill and withdrew back to the road cut and buildings at the junction of the Flamizoulle and Bastogne roads. The panzers crested the hill and fired down the reverse slope while German half-tracks approached from Anderson's right along the Flamizoulle road firing machine-guns.[36]

Though his battalion was in a tough spot, Major Anderson retained firm control over his unit. He assembled his company commanders and issued new orders. H Company would come up to help attack the hill. When H Company made the crest, I Company would halt and hold the battalion's right until the advance was again taken up. I Company then would follow at six hundred to eight hundred yards. When the tank platoon arrived, two of the Shermans would be sent with H Company, two with I Company, and the last with headquarters. As many men as possible would mount the tanks and storm the hill. Major Anderson would lead from the front – he planned to mount Lieutenant John Dixon's command tank and lead the assault.[37]

Anderson's attack got off to a rough start. Maneuvering to a position at which the troopers could mount them, the Shermans ran into a mine field and three tanks were disabled. The crews, however, were uninjured and elected to stay with their tanks. Therefore, for the rest of the day, the three disabled tanks would be fought as pillboxes. The fourth tank maneuvered to the right to avoid the mines but was soon destroyed by an 88. Three of its crew were injured. The last tank was ordered to withdraw. When Major Anderson discovered that he would have no tank support, he was undaunted and informed his company commanders that the attack would proceed without them "in ten minutes." It was then 1200 hours.[38]

In short order, 3rd Battalion's rifle companies moved out with the disabled tanks firing their guns and machine-guns in support. Bazooka fire compelled the German half-tracks to withdraw toward Flamizoulle. Bazooka and tank fire then was placed on the enemy tanks on the crest of the hill, resulting in the destruction of one of the Tigers. The rest of the enemy tanks then withdrew. Anderson and his radio operator kept to the front and were the first to reach the crest of the hill. The German tanks retreated into Flamierge, some fifteen hundred yards beyond Major Anderson's position joining more tanks already in the town. Together, they numbered thirteen or fourteen.[39]

Prior to the capture of the 513th's initial objectives by Anderson's and Kent's battalions, General Miley had visited Colonel Coutts' command post. While the 513th was advancing, Miley informed Coutts, the regiments on either flank had met considerable resistance. Because of this, General Miley ordered Coutts to halt his attack on the initial objectives and to "hold the line." Now that Anderson had reached the hill crest with the 3rd Battalion, however, Coutts called Miley to ask permission to continue as "the battalion commanders felt they could make their final objectives and the men wanted to try." General Miley gave Coutts the go-ahead.[40]

By yelling, and using runners and hand signals, Anderson got his men to move forward. The advance progressed slowly over the rolling, open fields blanketed in knee-deep snow before Flamierge. The ground, gently downsloping before rising near the town, was completely covered by fire from German tanks, mortars, and machine-guns and, in the open from the start, the troopers were under intense fire. Enemy riflemen concentrated on the officers, machine-gunners, radiomen, and bazookamen. In response, the troopers returned rifle fire as they advanced as did the battalion's 81mm mortars.[41]

Despite the German fire, the 3rd Battalion had advanced forward to within 150 yards of the town when Colonel Coutts, surmising "by guess and by God" that Major Anderson was nearing his objective, called the 466th Parachute Field Artillery for support. The barrage lasted only ten minutes, but the shells, smashing into the streets and buildings of Flamierge, forced the Germans to seek cover "at the critical moment." Anderson took advantage of the situation and in the ten minutes, divided the town along the line of a road through the town and ordered G Company to clear the left half and H Company to clear the right half. When the barrage lifted, the troopers made a "wild charge" into Flamierge.[42]

Some German machine-gunners and snipers stayed behind to harass the troopers, but most of the enemy infantry withdrew to the north. The tanks, however, remained to be dealt with. Bazookamen knocked out two and a third was disabled by a .30 caliber machine-gun. When its crew bailed out, they were cut down in a fusillade of small arms fire. Flamierge was secured by 1515 hours. With the town, Anderson captured enough hot food for three hundred men.[43]

Although successful, the capture of Flamierge was costly. Of the 525 men of the 3rd Battalion who had begun the attack, 150 had become casualties – most when the battalion was driven off its initial objective. Only two of the battalion's medics were left to assist casualties. Fortunately, the town's inhabitants, who had been hiding in their cellars during the attack, now came out to help the wounded.[44]

During the morning, 2nd Battalion was ordered forward in order "to keep it close behind the action." From its reserve position in the Bois des Valets, the battalion moved north at about 0900 hours, in the direction of Vivier du Four and then west behind the 1st Battalion. The march column, about 350 men all together, proceeded with E Company in the lead, followed in order by F Company, Headquarters Company, D Company, and elements of the 155th Airborne Antitank Battalion. E Company reached their initial objective at the same time Major Anderson's 3rd Battalion was fending off the German counter attack on the Vivier du Four hill crest.[45]

Lieutenant Puckett's Third Platoon led F Company from its bivouac area, at the southern side of the Bois des Valets, out to the northern edge of the woods. Third Platoon now numbered only about eighteen men – the second squad was down to two men, Sergeant Wesley E. Fredenburg and his assistant squad leader. As Puckett moved his men into a stretch of open ground ahead, they came under some mortar fire, but the lieutenant kept his men moving roughly north, into and through the next woods. The point man, Private Sherlock stopped when he came to the far edge of the tall, snow-laden pines, unsure whether or not to proceed. Between Sherlock and the Bastogne-Marche Highway was several hundred yards of open ground. Puckett, unable to see what was holding Sherlock up, went forward.

At that moment, Dahlberg came up from behind. "Captain wants to know if you see anything," he told Puckett.

"You tell him I'll let him know if I see anything," replied Puckett brusquely. Ever since the morning of the fourth, when Reynolds had so abruptly dismissed him, Lieutenant Puckett had the feeling that Reynolds either was crazy or trying to get him killed.

"I don't think you should have said that to the Captain," remarked Sherlock after Dahlberg departed. Puckett overlooked Sherlock's admonishment. He didn't care how the Captain took it.

The lieutenant's attention returned to the snowy field in front of him. Near the highway, Puckett spotted Colonel Miller and some troopers from E Company. Moderate enemy small arms fire from the high ground south of the highway at

Vivier du Four was holding up E Company's advance. More enemy fire was coming from the hill crest that 3rd Battalion had been assigned to capture as their initial objective. Puckett concluded that E Company needed help. "Let's go," Puckett told Sherlock, directing him towards the spot where Miller was pacing.

A platoon from A Company of the 630th Tank Destroyer Battalion was positioned about five hundred yards to the east, and Miller had sent word to them to come up in support. The tankers, however, had refused to budge, their commander stating that another platoon of tank destroyers positioned near Cochleval was responsible for the sector in which 2nd Battalion was operating. Miller, therefore, decided to send forward his bazookamen. In the time between sending and receiving these messages, the 3rd Battalion had renewed its attack and secured its initial objective. At the same time, D Company had moved up and was clearing the high ground south of the highway at Vivier du Four. These actions relieved the pressure on E Company.[46]

German shelling continued sporadically as F Company started out onto the field. Private Logan, trudging along beside Grice asked, "Is this time to go?" Logan had been despondent about his chances for days. Grice told him, "Son, you're not going to die till it's your time." Then, trying to change the subject, Grice asked Logan, "Do you want some rations?"

Walking in the footprints of the men ahead of him, PFC Sarrell saw a large pile of US pattern web gear and packs strewn up along the highway to his right, likely the equipment of the B and C Company men captured on the fourth. Suddenly, Captain Reynolds ran past Sarrell, Puckett and Sherlock, and on out to Colonel Miller. Lieutenant Puckett could see that Reynolds was hot about something. The lieutenant suspected that the Captain was upset with the message he had given Reynolds' runner and was trying to get Miller's permission to discipline him. At that moment, a commotion erupted to the platoon' rear which refocused the lieutenant's attention.

As his men had emerged from the trees, a young German soldier – perhaps just sixteen years old – appeared from a foxhole near the Bastogne road gesturing that he wanted to surrender. Third Platoon men took the boy's weapon away and brought him with them, but the German "started going berserk," recalled Ed Sarrell. "He ran from guy to guy to guy, pleading. He thought we were going to shoot him. Then he just took off. He didn't get fifty feet. I think almost everybody shot at him."[47]

Third Platoon's firing instantly provoked more hostile fire. "We saw a couple of puffs come off a big, tall pine tree," recalled Puckett, who watched the sniper's bullets slug into the snow covered earth right between the Captain and Miller. Both men bucked in alarm. "Get that sonofabitch!" yelled Miller. F Company unleashed a terrific volley, firing at least a couple hundred rounds into the suspect tree. No one fell from the branches, but no more sniper fire came from it either.[48]

As Lieutenant Puckett approached the Colonel's position near the road, Miller told him, "Lieutenant, keep moving your platoon." Puckett was glad that Reynolds hadn't been able to get him in trouble – if that was what he'd been trying to do – and was satisfied about it.

Leading the left thrust of the 513th's advance, 1st Battalion troopers had managed to destroy three tanks – two Mk IVs and a Panther – as they moved toward the high ground south of Flamierge. The battalion's forward progress, however, was rapidly petering out; the virtual destruction of B and C Companies on the morning of the fourth left 1st Battalion with insufficient manpower to accomplish their mission. Colonel Coutts, therefore, ordered Lieutenant Colonel Miller to take over for Major Kies' battalion and to capture the 1st Battalion objective. Coutts then asked Miller if he had any suggestions. Ace proposed that 2nd Battalion swing in behind and follow 3rd Battalion until it had advanced to a point from which the battalion could attack south and take the high ground. Coutts endorsed the plan. Miller got his men moving quickly, however; in the course of executing the movement he abruptly modified his plan. Instead of the whole battalion crossing to the north side of the road, Miller ordered only E Company into the 3rd Battalion zone while D Company moved along the left of the road with the rest of the battalion following.[49]

F Company, spread out in the fields south of the highway, tracked northwest towards Flamierge. Near the highway, F Company's medic, Doc Sloan found a seriously wounded trooper that had been left behind by the preceding company. Sloan, however, could see that his wounds were mortal and so he pushed a rifle into the snow and went on.

The further Puckett's platoon advanced out into the open, the more intense the shelling grew. As he advanced, Sergeant DeHaven was relaying a message for the Captain while Tec 5 Haggard, his assistant, kept guard. When the Germans started laying in some really heavy stuff, 15cm shells or nebelwerfers, Haggard concluded that they had attracted the attention of an enemy artillery observer. Then, one of the shells struck close. DeHaven slipped the radio off his shoulders, and let it fall to the ground, then staggered and went down. Dahlberg and Grice rushed forward to render first aid. Shell splinters had pierced DeHaven's helmet in several places, one big hole in the back, and a lot more little ones, but he was still alive. Haggard picked the radio up and took over. It took him a few moments to realize the shell had torn up the top and riddled it with small holes. The radio was useless, but it had absorbed most of the shrapnel and probably saved DeHaven's life.[50]

Staff Sergeant Knigge had been hit too. Knigge was walking near some old foxholes when the shelling started. A sick feeling swept over him. "I better get down in that goddamned hole," he thought, when suddenly a hot blast cracked through the air. The shellburst threw Knigge heavily into the hole where he lay twisted on top of his now bloody right arm. "Where the hell's my arm?" he screamed in fear and pain. "You're laying on it," replied another trooper. Some men pulled Knigge out of the foxhole and a lieutenant, who had rushed up, pulled open his jacket to inspect his wound. "Boy, are you lucky," said the officer, "You got your ZI, buddy!"

"What's that mean?" asked Knigge.

"Zone of Interior!" According to the officer, Knigge's wound was a ticket back to the States.

Also wounded were Corporal Keeling, PFC Al Barth, and Private Henderson who were all listed as lightly wounded in action. Private William W. G. Maxwell was seriously wounded and died later that day. PFC Donald Black was seriously wounded as well. He hung on until 14 January when he too died of his wounds.

When the heavy stuff started coming in, everyone headed for cover. Lieutenant Puckett first had thrown himself on the ground, but quickly got to his feet to push the men forward. "Come on!" he yelled. "Move up!" He knew it would be worse if they stayed. Reluctantly, the men started to move forward. After some effort, the lead platoon reached the point where the road ran north to Flamierge. Left was a sunken cart path and the wooded hillside that was 2nd Battalion's objective.

After Major Anderson's troopers entered Flamierge, 2nd Battalion attacked south. The 2nd Battalion men south of the road had had a less difficult advance, but an easy time by no means. As they approached Flamierge, E Company, in the lead, had fallen victim to the same fire that had been directed at the 3rd Battalion. Now, before them was the woody hill crest south of Flamierge packed with dug in German infantry that had to be blasted out of their holes one by one.[51]

To his left – in the direction of Mon Nicolay – Puckett spotted the muzzle flashes of a German machine-gun. "Lieutenant," asked Private Sherlock. "Don't you have anybody else to be point man?"

"Okay," said Puckett. He turned to Sergeant Fredenburg. "Fredenburg, you're the point man."[52]

"But I'm a squad leader." Fredenburg protested. Fredenburg had a red, round chubby face that turned even redder when he laughed, only Fredenburg wasn't laughing now.

"Where's your squad?" Puckett asked. The lieutenant was being nasty.

At that moment, Captain Reynolds' runner arrived. "Captain says don't go any farther," he told Puckett. The company was going to hold a position astride the highway. That was good news for Fredenburg – he was off the hook.

There were plenty of old foxholes around and the men jumped into them. Private Logan crawled over to Lieutenant Puckett. He had been shot in the arm and wanted to go to the aid station. Puckett gave him permission and told PFC Harry Goldfarb to go with him. Soon after they departed, Captain Reynolds arrived. "Get out of the sunken road," he told Puckett. Reynolds, according to Puckett, launched into some wild explanation about some Confederate soldiers who'd been ambushed and wiped out during the Civil War when they took cover in a sunken road. Puckett couldn't understand what Reynolds was talking about. He was the only man in the sunken road and he knew where the Germans were. Reluctantly, Puckett crawled forward, across the ground, and swung himself down into the hole the wounded private had occupied. It was about 1600 hours. PFC Goldfarb returned a short while later and reported that a sniper had killed Logan on the way to the rear.

D and E Companies continued to push up the hill in the face of tenacious resistance. "Valuable fire," delivered by the field artillery forward observer, assisted 2nd Battalion's attack greatly, but it wasn't until 1700 hours that the positions on the high ground were secured. As soon as he received word the regiment's objectives were taken, Colonel Coutts called to inform General Miley. Miley called back shortly thereafter with General Troy Middleton's personal congratulations on the 513th's accomplishment.[53]

To consolidate his gains, General Miley sent up a battalion of the 507th Parachute Infantry to the capture the high ground left of Lieutenant Colonel Miller's position. The 507th men routed an enemy force of approximately company strength and occupied the position but afterward were subjected to an intense shelling which killed the battalion commander and the regimental chaplain. The battalion, however, held their ground and it appeared that night to General Miley that the division had "a reasonably good line." But Miley was mistaken.[54]

Though the 513th had secured their objectives, the 193rd or 194th Regiments – the two regiments attacking on either side of Coutts – failed to obtain their objectives, critically exposing the 513th's flanks. The attack of the 193rd Infantry had been preceded by a strong artillery bombardment, but the fog and snow were so heavy that observed fire was impossible. The 193rd jumped off on time, but the glidermen almost at once were stopped by heavy German fire. The regiment "bounced off" the enemy and proceeded to swing to the southwest where it renewed its attack on the woods at Flamizoulle's southern edge, this time gaining a toe hold. Heavy enemy shelling, however, caused many casualties among the glidermen and, after an advance of only five hundred yards, the 193rd was forced to withdraw back to their line of departure to reorganize. Commodore 3 [Colonel Messinger, the Division G-3] sent a field message to Colonel Coutts at 1210 hours: "Chalk [the 193rd GIR] is held up in front of Peter [Flamizoulle]. Can you help them?" At that time, however, Coutts had his own problems.[55]

The 194th Glider Infantry, jumping off from the vicinity of Rechriva, was stopped after advancing one mile, 1,200 yards short of its main objective, Renuamont. The regiment's left flank was anchored at Rechriva and the line extended east to the finger of woods that was the westernmost part of the Bois des Valets. To make matters worse, from their positions in Flamierge and on the high ground to the south, 513th troopers observed German soldiers "infiltrating into the areas over which they had" just advanced.[56]

In Flamierge, 3rd Battalion expected to be counterattacked right away and the men were digging in as fast as they could. The platoon from I Company that had been instructed to keep in contact with the 193rd Glider Infantry during 3rd Battalion's advance on the town had not been able to fill the gap between the two regiments as 3rd Battalion advanced. This platoon became pinned down by German machine-gun fire southeast of the battalion's initial objective. 2nd Battalion had by nightfall secured the high ground, but, like 3rd Battalion, had suffered further casualties. E Company, down to only forty men – less than platoon strength – "occupied the forward edge of the forest on the northwest portion of the objective." D Company had reorganized its remaining men into two platoons. One dug in on E Company's left facing west, and the other astride the main highway on E Company's right.[57]

F Company took up a reserve position at the road junction about five hundred yards due south of Flamierge. At the junction, there was a little, shot-up farm building on the south side of the road and two or three knocked out Shermans from some earlier fighting. Sarrell was shocked when he saw how the German antitank guns had ripped holes right through the Shermans. Sarrell, Joe Gutt, and another trooper went across the road and set up their machine-gun in a crater about fifty feet north of the highway. The rest of the company remained on the south side of the road where they took shelter in liberated foxholes or in old shell holes. Lieutenant Dean and Tec 5 Haggard set up an SCR-300 radio in a dugout that had been picked for the company CP. The CP was located along the highway, about a hundred yards behind F Company's position, and about half way between the battalion CP and F Company's front.[58]

Including himself, Captain Reynolds couldn't have counted more than four officers and sixty-four men left in F Company – hardly enough men to hold off a German tank platoon, let alone any sizable attack. To reinforce the position, A Company moved up and tied in with F Company's left flank, and two 57mm antitank guns were emplaced alongside Reynolds; one at the road junction near First Platoon and the other covering the southwest approach and the ground that was to have been captured by the 194th. A field artillery forward observer came forward as well, setting up shop in the shot-up barn near the road. Supplies were brought up to the 2nd Battalion's dump behind its initial objective, but no ammunition – only a few K rations – made it up to the troopers on the line.[59]

Lieutenant Gilles appointed PFC Grice as squad leader, and gave him seven men to watch over. Grice was ordered to go up on the ridge to the company's left and dig in his gun. He stopped when he got to the edge of a little patch of woods – foxholes were already dug there – and the men were spread out along the tree line. Meanwhile, the rest of the company, not too far away, were improving their holes as best they could.[60]

That evening, heavy skies dumped several more inches of fresh snow onto the already thickly blanketed landscape and temperatures sank to below fifteen degrees. The snow and bitter cold increased the suffering of the all the troopers who, for the most part, were without overcoats or blanket rolls. PFC Dahlberg dug on his foxhole all night just to keep from freezing to death. It was extremely cold with driving wind and snow. In such weather, it was almost impossible for the men to sleep comfortably – the combination of perspiration and expelling breath caused hoarfrost, about an inch and a half long, to grow from the roofs of the small tents. To prevent the tents icing up, the men had to sleep taking turns. "It was the most miserable living I ever witnessed in my life," said Private Marvin Harris.[61]

Once the positions had been prepared, two at a time, Reynolds sent the men back to a little farmhouse along the highway where they could warm themselves. Cavaleri and another trooper, who were occupying a hole in a patch of trees along the highway, were the first to go. In the house, they discovered a wood stove burning brightly and two chairs in front of it. Sitting themselves down in front of the open stove, they took of their boots, and stuck their feet as close as they dared to the flames, holding their boots and socks up to allow them to dry out. After about twenty minutes, they put their boots and walked back to their holes so another pair could warm up.[62]

It was relatively quiet until about 2200 hours, when Germans started shelling Flamierge heavily. Fires caused by the shelling were burning brightly in the town. Lieutenant Puckett was watching the lights flickering when Dahlberg appeared behind his hole with a message from Reynolds; he called, "Hey Lieutenant, Captain wants you to send out a patrol." Puckett acknowledged the runner and, pointing northwest, told PFC Goldfarb, "Take another guy and go up the road as far as you can." Goldfarb called out for Sarrell, but since he didn't want to be the dummy on this patrol, he didn't answer. After a short discussion, Goldfarb managed to gather a small group of men and they struck out up the road until they reached a point south and west of Flamierge. A short while later, Goldfarb returned to report, "Ain't nothing out there but a couple of [German] tanks." The officers noted the report, but it didn't seem to raise any alarms.

Across the road, Lieutenant Puckett observed Sergeant Sperling warming himself up at a burning farmhouse in the field about a hundred yards in front of his position. A few of the men had already ventured out to it to warm up, but every time someone got near it the Germans threw in a shell. So far, however, no one had been hit. Puckett took off his boots and socks. Then he put on his extra pair of socks and replaced his boots. Then he got up to talk to Sperling. As he approached the burning building, Puckett could see it was more of a barn. There was smoldering hay on the floor next to a trap door. Puckett and Sperling must have been silhouetted in the firelight, for suddenly, a German mortar shell came in almost on top of them. Sperling was hit in several places and fell to the ground. Lieutenant Puckett was hit in the back and in the right heel. Puckett hobbled to the trap door and jumped into the cellar. When he was sure the Germans weren't going to send over another shell, Puckett climbed out of the cellar and limped back to his platoon's position. "Go get Larry, he's hurt," Puckett told his men. "Take him to the aid station." A couple of men went out and picked up Sperling, and started for the rear.

Meanwhile, Puckett wanted to examine his own wounds. "Do you have a knife?" he asked one of his men. He cut the laces and pulled off the boot to inspect his foot. A shell fragment had torn out all the flesh between the Achilles tendon and the heal bone. He couldn't walk very far on it so, with one man under each arm supporting him, Puckett started back for the aid station himself. As he passed the company CP, no one said a word. This struck the lieutenant as a little odd. Then a voice came out of the dark, "Go away." Puckett felt sure it was Reynolds, but didn't stop to find out. He was just happy to be going to the rear.

The battalion aid station was set up in a house down the road toward Monty. When Puckett arrived, he asked the doctor how Sergeant Sperling was doing. Sperling, who had numerous fragment wounds, was awake and talking, he said. A little while later, however, one of the medics reported to the surgeon, "Doc, he's gone." The doctor attributed Sperling's death to shock, as none of his ten wounds would have been fatal by themselves. At 0500 on the morning of the eighth, a jeep ambulance arrived. Puckett got in the back seat and was driven to the regimental clearing station. From there, he was taken by ambulance to the 109th Evacuation Hospital in Medy, France where he was operated on. Puckett spent several months recovering from his wounds and never rejoined F Company. Also evacuated was First Sergeant Donovan who was hit just at the hairline with a shell fragment from a treeburst. Donovan lost consciousness and had to be carried to the rear.[63]

Around midnight, the Germans began shelling the regiment's positions relentlessly. Between shellbursts, troopers could make out the rattling of enemy tanks off to the northwest – a sound that continued all night long. Most of the men were hungry – some were melting snow for water. Dahlberg heated up some snow in his helmet and mixed in the lemonade powder from a dinner ration. Others talked quietly or smoked, too nervous to go to sleep. From PFC Cavaleri's .30 caliber machine-gun position, set up on the hill near Grice's, the field before him sloped down. Cavaleri and another trooper shared the hole. In the fields, stobs stuck up out of the snow everywhere. In the hours of darkness, after searching the landscape all evening, eyes began to play tricks on the men and they thought things – shadows – were moving in the dim light. Cavaleri called out, "Lieutenant Gilles."

"Don't call out my name," ordered Gilles. The lieutenant "was a young fellow," said Cavaleri, "only maybe twenty-one or twenty-two years old." He supposed that Gilles didn't want the Germans to know there was an officer there.[64]

"I see movement out there," Cavaleri came back. "Can I fire my carbine?" Gilles consented. Borrowing the M1 Carbine from the fellow next to him, Cavaleri fired four shots.

"Cease fire! Cease fire!" yelled Gilles.[65]

Cavaleri sat quietly for a while and then got up to go see his lieutenant. The fronts of his boots were ripped open and his feet were soaking wet. Lieutenant Gilles took a look at Cavaleri's feet and determined they were frostbitten. Reluctantly, Gilles gave Cavaleri permission to go to the aid station. Private Bernard Glanowski went, too.

In Flamierge, 3rd Battalion's troopers were critically short of ammunition; so short that even a small counterattack would have jeopardized their position. By early evening, Major Anderson still had not regained communications with regiment. Lieutenant McClain, a forward observer from the 466th PFAB, and PFC Rolland Bragg, a lightly wounded medic from Headquarters, 3rd Battalion, drove a captured German ambulance to the rear to report the situation. With them, they took along a seriously wounded trooper in the back. Along the way the men captured two German soldiers. McClain placed one of his prisoners between Bragg and himself in the front seat and made the other German stand outside on the running board as a shield against enemy fire. When the German on the running board tried to escape, McClain "cut him down with his tommy gun." The lieutenant's shooting drew enemy machine-gun fire, however. Despite the hail of bullets, both Bragg and McClain arrived uninjured, but the wounded trooper in the back and the second prisoner were killed. PFC Bragg returned to Flamierge at 2330 hours with Lieutenant Paul McGuire, 3rd Battalion S-4, and a supply party.[66]

The 513th's executive officer, Lieutenant Colonel Ward Ryan made a tour of the 513th's battalions at dusk. Upon reaching the 2nd Battalion CP, Lieutenant Colonel Miller provided Ryan with some men for a patrol to Flamierge. Setting out for the town, Ryan saw fire lights in the distance and guided on them. At the edge of town, Ryan was challenged by a sentry. "*Halt*," came the command in a "very German" voice. Lieutenant Colonel Ryan took the German accent for a bad joke and answered sternly, "This is Colonel Ryan." Captain Joseph W. Rawn, 3rd Battalion S-3 (and acting battalion Executive), who was accompanying Ryan, immediately uttered, *"Was wollen zie?"* in his best German. The patrol had apparently become lost amid the snow drifts and had arrived at Flamizoulle by mistake. Rawn's response confused the sentry long enough for the patrol to withdraw without being challenged again. Lieutenant Colonel Ryan returned to the 2nd Battalion, corrected his bearings, and moved on to Flamierge.[67]

At Flamierge, Ryan did what he could to see that 3rd Battalion received support. Ryan requested antitank guns, but the snow made it impossible to move the guns forward. However, ammunition, including four hundred bazooka rockets, was brought up. Ryan also ordered up a platoon of tank destroyers from the 602nd Tank Destroyer Battalion, personally placing them in burned out buildings around the road junction defended by F Company. Then, 3rd Battalion's surgeon made an inspection of the casualty situation in Flamierge and returned at 0100 hours to evacuate the wounded. Finally, telephone wires were laid from the regimental CP to all of the battalions. When this was finished, Ryan started back to the regimental CP.[68]

In Flamierge that night, many Germans were captured trying to infiltrate through the lines – several were dressed in American uniforms. One German so dressed was "vigorously interrogated" by Anderson's troopers. The prisoner was silent at first, but after some "rough treatment" and the promise he would be shot as a spy if he didn't talk, he began to speak. In fluent English, he told his captors that he had gotten the American uniform from his own organization who had bales of them. The prisoner said he wore the uniform "to make possible his desertion." The man then identified the positions of several enemy infantry and armored units concentrating in the vicinity of Tronle, only about eight hundred yards northwest of Flamierge, and warned his captors that the Germans were preparing to hit the 513th, especially the 3rd Battalion in Flamierge, in the morning. During the night, the *8th Panzergrenadier Regiment* had also arrived, reinforcing the German line.[69]

At first, Major Anderson wanted to execute all of the prisoners who were in American uniforms as spies, but then recanted. If the Germans discovered their bodies, he reasoned, his men would get the same treatment should they be captured. He instead sent the prisoners to the rear with an "explanation of the circumstances" and the recommendation that they be shot there. Major Anderson then called for artillery on the enemy positions the prisoner had divulged, but no artillery was granted. Colonel Coutts told Anderson that the line to the artillery had been cut, but Anderson suspected that Coutts simply did not believe the reports were true. Undeterred, Anderson intelligently sent a patrol south to contact the 2nd Battalion to warn them of the attack he believed was impending.[70]

Private Lightcap, whose hole was on the crest of the hill, was awakened at about 0800 hours by one of the other men who was bringing up K-rations. He quickly tossed a few cartons into the hole with Lightcap and his buddy, and told them, "The old man said to get the hell out of here real quick!" The trooper then turned and ran off in the direction of the company CP. Then, almost at once, the first artillery shells came in with a thunderous roar. When the barrage had passed, Lightcap pressed himself up to take a look. Blood was running through holes in the trooper's uniform, but, still standing, the man managed to hobble off.[71]

Lightcap's attention returned to the rolling white fields to the north. The snow and fog was such that he could make out only ghostlike "forms in the haze," but what Lightcap saw terrified him. "Holy shit!" A "whole herd" of enemy tanks, fifteen to twenty at least, could be seen moving upon Flamierge from the north. Still more German armor – five tanks followed by six self-propelled guns – advanced across the snow drifted fields along the highway between the positions of the 2nd and 3rd Battalions. 2nd Battalion troopers in positions along the bald ridge placed small arms fire on these tanks but to no effect. The tanks were still out of range. The men were only wasting what little ammunition they had so Lieutenant Colonel Miller ordered them to stop. The fog was rapidly clearing, though, and Miller's men had a commanding view of the rapidly approaching enemy. Unknown to Lightcap, the artillery FOs had been firing on the enemy in the forward areas since well before daylight, about 0600 hours, and had started calling in white phosphorous shells. So far, however, artillery had set only one of the tanks aflame.[72]

The antitank guns and tank destroyers positioned near F Company might have been sufficient to deal with the panzers, but they did not go into action. The 57mm antitank gun positioned to the south-southwest of F Company had been hit during the early morning shelling and disabled. The firing mechanism of the other gun, positioned at the road junction, had frozen and its crew had abandoned it. Lieutenant Colonel Miller found them cowering in a nearby house. The Colonel ordered them to return to their position, and even threatened them with his sidearm, but Miller's efforts were to no avail. The crew – this was the same crew that had performed so capably at Mande-St.-Etienne only days earlier – were "incapaci-tated by fear." The tank destroyers, too, had deserted their post several hours ear-lier. When he returned to the regimental CP after his tour of the battalions the night before, Lieutenant Colonel Ryan was staggered to discover that the tank destroy-ers had already abandoned their positions at the road junction and had beaten him back to the CP. It was, by that time, too late to return the tank destroyers to the front. Ryan had the officer in command brought up on charges for desertion in the face of the enemy.[73]

PFC Sarrell was shaken awake by the roaring engines of three Germans tanks, "cutting down the road" between his position and the company. He opened his eyes, but at first did not move. During the night, three or four inches of sticky snow had fallen. Snow clung to the men's coats and helmets, the hole, and the machine-gun. "We just blended in perfectly," he remembered.[74]

On the south side of the road, however, F Company's bazooka men opened up on the tanks. Sarrell counted six rounds all together. "Some went over, some glanced off," then one of the bazookas exploded, "one guy's helmet flew fifty feet in the air." Perhaps that bazooka had frozen up, Sarrell didn't know. Then a second ba-zooka appeared to misfire. The three German tanks just rolled through F Company and down the road, seemingly ignoring the hail of small arms fire, and not even bothering to return fire. "We all just sunk," Sarrell recalled. Sarrell left his ma-chine-gun and picked up his M1. He, Gutt, and the other trooper jumped up out of their hole and ran back to the other side of the road. Sarrell was stiff from cold and had no feeling in his feet at first, but moving around started to make it come back.[75]

As soon as he had spotted the three Panthers coming towards his position, Captain Reynolds sent PFC Dahlberg to the battalion CP to report the situation. Dahlberg started back the several hundred yards to the CP at a run, passing a ba-zooka team that was setting up near the highway. There was much confusion at the battalion CP, but they were already aware of the attack, so Dahlberg returned to the company. As he approached the front, he came across five wounded troopers lying along the road. One man, with a gut wound, was being helped by a sergeant from one of the other companies. A little closer to the front, he came across a black mark in the snow caused by an explosion, all that was left of the bazooka team. To Dahlberg, it looked as though they had taken a direct hit and just disappeared.

One of the biggest fears of American infantrymen was an enemy tank attack. Donovan and Captain Reynolds had discussed the company's defense against enemy armor several times, but they couldn't come up with any reasonable ideas. "We had a lot of contingency plans" though, remembered Donovan, "chief among them was to run like hell." The company had been issued four bazookas for use against tanks and fortified positions. These bazookas were accurate up to one hundred yards, but at that range the sight had to be pulled all the way back. They were most effective at point blank ranges where the gunner might disable a tank by breaking its track. But the M1A1 Rocket Launcher, the model of bazooka used by the 17th Airborne during the Bulge, had many drawbacks. Its 2.36" projectile was severely underpowered for use against most German tanks. "Them bazookas were like swatting against those tanks – you had to hit 'em just right," commented Grice. Also, in cold and wet weather, the batteries that provided the electrical charge to ignite the rocket motors sometimes died; ice forming in the tubes was another danger. The night before the attack, First Sergeant Donovan had seen that every bazooka in F Company had been taken apart and dried out, but in spite of this, some bazookas still didn't work when they were needed.[76]

Panicked, some men on the hillside below Lightcap started running northeast, down the hill, and toward the road. Nearby, however, Lieutenant Fann was conducting a one-man stand. He had turned around one of the abandoned 57mm anti-tank guns, loaded one round, and fired. Lightcap didn't wait to see if the shell had any effect. Instead, leaving his rifle behind, Lightcap picked up his shovel and took off to his rear, southwest, across the fields toward the trees several hundred yards away.[77]

As Lightcap zig-zagged his way across the frozen fields, German machine-gun bullets slapped into the snow around him. He dove for the ground, the firing stopped. Then he got up and started running again. There was a terrific explosion and Lightcap felt a terrible pain shoot through his right leg. "Oh, they got me!" he hollered as he fell. Sprawled in the snow, he felt around his agonized limb for almost five minutes looking for a wound but did not find any. "Shit, I'm not hit!" he said, and he got back up and started running again. More 88mm shells hissed past exploding ahead of him, their shrapnel ricocheting off the frozen ground. He knew that if he could hear the shell, it had already missed him so, with his heart pounding through his chest, he kept going. After almost an hour, he reached the woods, his shovel still in his hand. He came upon an antitank unit set up in the trees. The gunners, noting the sounds of intense firing coming from the direction of the highway, told Lightcap that they were content to wait and let the Germans come to them.[78]

By 0830 hours, the main attack was developing along the 2nd Battalion's front, trying to push directly down the Bastogne Highway. "You could hear the tanks," remembered Grice. "I mean, it was scary." Three more tanks supported by infantry came around the left and attacked D and E Companies on the ridgeline. The enemy infantry suffered severely as they trudged through the snow up the barren slope, yet still they came on. D and E Company troopers were equally tenacious and clung to their positions. Soon, they became intermingled with the enemy infantry, and German tanks drove through their positions and into the small woods to the rear of the battalion's positions. It was at this point that Lieutenant Colonel Miller ordered F Company up.[79]

Captain Reynolds gathered as many men as he could and went forward. The fog was heavy, and offered some protection as they advanced northwest, along the south side of the highway. At Mon Nicolay, they were met by enemy tanks advancing south down the Tronle trail. Reynolds was determined not to let them cross the main highway.

Reynolds spread out his troopers, placing Lieutenant Gilles' platoon in an old slit trench well forward. Lieutenant Dean and the rest of the men deployed in depth behind them. Lieutenant Gilles knew Private Seacott was trained in demolitions, and ordered him to go out into the fog and place a charge on one of the advancing tanks. Seacott thought Gilles was crazy and ignored the order.[80]

Lieutenant Fann, meanwhile, now accompanied by Private Altmiller, had gone back for the other 57mm and had dragged it up to the new position. When they tried to fire the gun, they discovered it wouldn't fire. Fann had lost his weapon, so he asked PFC Altmiller for his carbine. Altmiller gave it over to him. Fann then ordered Altmiller to follow him with his bazooka, and they hustled to a position from which they could get a clear shot at a tank trying to get around the company's position, to flank them and cut them off. Altmiller fired his first round at a range of about fifty yards. The rocket struck the tank squarely but clanked off, a dud. Fann loaded their second rocket and Altmiller fired again. This time the round detonated on the tracks, but it failed to inflict any apparent damage. Fortunately for Fann and Altmiller, the German tank commander didn't know the bazooka team had had only two rockets, and backed off. Altmiller dropped the bazooka – without ammunition it was worthless – and picked up an M1 that had been abandoned. The rifle's barrel was bent, but it was better than nothing.[81]

For the time being, Lieutenant Fann had eliminated the threat to the company's flank. However, enemy tanks were pushing head on into Gilles' entrenched men. Behind these men, in another shallow slit trench, were quite a few other troopers huddled down low to keep under the heavy automatic and cannon fire pouring in. Lieutenant Dean, who was squatted next to Private Munafo ordered, "Munafo, go up there and reconnoiter – see what's happening." "Lieutenant Dean," answered Munafo, "I'm not getting out of this trench now. Can't you here the firing that's going on out there?" Munafo suddenly got angry at Dean's cowardly behavior and stood up anyway – just to prove he had guts enough to do it. As he did so, he saw a trooper who he took for Private Clarence Rohmann staggering towards him. The man's face was shattered – his jaw was completely gone – and he was holding the wound with both hands. "Rohmann!" Munafo shouted. "Where' you going?" Munafo was so stunned by the sight he didn't know what else to say – he didn't want to let Rohmann know how bad he looked. The man moaned and staggered on towards the rear. Munafo dropped back into the trench. Around him, however, many men began to flee. A rout was beginning.[82]

Just north of the highway, five enemy tanks had lined up and were placing heavy enfilade fire on the battalion's positions. And at the same time, six more enemy tanks, supported by infantry with flamethrowers, were closing in from the west to support their assault on D and E Companies' positions. Lieutenant Kenyon, commanding D Company on the hill, was with his platoon on the right of the ridge and was unaware of this new threat on his left. Both D and E Companies were low on small arms ammunition and had expended all their bazooka rockets and grenades. Miller, however, realized holding on to his position was hopeless and ordered a withdrawal.[83]

Colonel Miller ordered D Company to hold the hill while E Company fell back on F Company's line. Once E Company had withdrawn successfully, D Company would be allowed to withdraw and reorganize. E Company, however, was quickly overrun and by the time D Company men realized what was happening, most could not escape. The remnants of D Company, joined by a few survivor's from E Company, fell back on F Company's line, but did not make an attempt to reorganize. They simply had no ammunition left with which to defend themselves, therefore, in small groups, D and E Company men withdrew upon the battalion's ammunition dump at the junction of the Flamizoulle and Bastogne roads.[84]

The ammunition dump had been under attack all morning from the direction of Flamizoulle, but Major Edwards, in command, had been able to hold his position with a small band of infantrymen and the three Shermans from C Company, 22nd Tank Battalion that had been disabled the day before. Now, however, the ammunition dump was under the attack of thirteen enemy tanks closing on his position from northeast of Flamierge, and the Germans were systematically picking off Edwards' pillboxes one by one. Two of the Shermans were knocked out by 88s – one of these had been struck eight times in a two-foot diameter circle.[85]

2nd Battalion's riflemen and machine-gunner's had inflicted a terrific number of casualties upon the German infantry before withdrawing, but small arms fire had no effect on the enemy armor. Firing his machine-gun from his position on the hill, Grice did his best to cover the men with Reynolds. "We fired and fired, but they just kept coming up the hill." Five tanks fired on Grice's position at point blank range, but the shells struck above him. "This ain't no place for us!" he hollered wildly, then Grice sprang out of his hole and ran to find Lieutenant Gilles. Grice found his lieutenant among the farm buildings at Mon Nicolay. "What're we gonna do?" shouted Grice at the officer. He didn't want to stay around there to die. "I think we're gonna hold," said Gilles, glancing to the rear. There, about thirty yards away, Grice saw Acey-Deucy, with some other men around him. Gilles sent Grice to get the official word. "I imagine he [Colonel Miller] was just about as scared as I was," recalled Grice, "but he seemed to know what he was doing and he had plenty of protection around him." Miller told Grice that he was ordering a withdrawal back to the woods [the Bois des Valets]. Grice gave the word to Gilles that Battalion was withdrawing and went to get his men. "Listen," shouted Grice to his squad, "they're coming. Let's get off this ridge." With that he grabbed up his gun and took off. "Everybody was so scared – scared of getting killed – they didn't know what was happening."[86]

"Do you know who this is?" came the voice over Tec 5 Haggard's SCR-300. "Yes, Sir," Haggard had immediately recognized the voice of Colonel Miller. "Call on the radio or send a runner up to F Company," ordered Miller, "and tell them to fall back." Haggard sent out one of the runners, but the man came back almost right away with a piece shot out of his ear. It didn't matter if the runner had gotten through, however; the Germans already had sent Reynolds the same message.

While Grice had conferred with Miller, 2nd Battalion had knocked out four more enemy tanks. One was destroyed by mortar, one by artillery, and two more were credited to F Company bazookamen. But despite their losses, the tanks came on. Altmiller saw the artillery FO call fire down on his own position, the barn, and then watched him drive off in a jeep. According to Altmiller, no friendly artillery ever fell, but there was plenty of enemy fire. Altmiller took off across a field, but turned back when one of the officers yelled at him, "You'll get blowed up out there," explaining he was running through a field sown with antitank mines. "What do you think's happening back there," Altmiller replied and kept on running – away from the tree bursts, away from the tanks. Soon other men from the battalion were following.[87]

Seacott had been sitting on top of several empty American K ration boxes in the bottom of the German slit trenches. All the Germans had left were the little tins of cheese, Seacott recalled thinking – "the Germans didn't like the cheese." As the Germans closed in, Seacott figured it was time to get out, but when he tried to get up to run his cold-numbed feet gave out beneath his weight. Next to him, Lieutenant Gilles got up and started walking north, toward the highway, with four or five men following him. Seacott thought that was the last direction Gilles should have chosen – right towards the enemy. Though the German infantry were still at a considerable range, Seacott shouldered his M1 and started firing at them. He was determined not to go down without a fight. He was spared a heroic death by two buddies who grabbed him out of the trench and started to drag him to the rear.[88]

Sarrell began crawling back along the south side of the highway bank because he thought he probably would be under the machine-gun fire. But it was the tanks that posed more of a danger; they roared over the highway embankment and began rolling up the south side of the road, firing their main guns at the fleeing men "point blank, blowing them up," remembered Sarrell. "A jeep was trying to get out of there. Its wheels were spinning and more and more guys kept piling on." One severely wounded trooper hollered, "Shoot me – Shoot me," to Sarrell. The man yelled the same thing to each trooper who passed, and the tanks were closing, less than one hundred yards away. A tank shell struck a man right next to Sarrell. "I saw body parts flying all over," he remembered. Taking off his overcoat and dropping it, discarding anything that would impede his escape, Sarrell got up and began running for the woods.[89]

It was absolute chaos. "We had people running everywhere, jumping and running, that way, and holding their hands up and giving up," remembered Grice. "And they were heading back with not even anybody guarding them."[90]

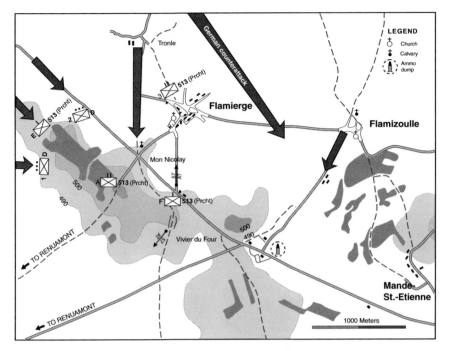

German counterattacks on the positions of the 513th Parachute Infantry Regiment, at Flamierge, Belgium, 8 January 1945. (Rick Brownlee/R&B Graphic Designs)

Captain Reynolds had remained behind to cover the withdrawal of his men. Around him, bullets sizzled past like angry hornets. Nearby, PFC Paul J. Accomando called to Dahlberg, "I can't get out of the hole. My feet are frozen." "Ace," begged Dahlberg, "you better get out of the hole. Tanks are coming." Accomando got up, and on his numb feet, started for the woods. "Get down, Sir," Dahlberg then advised the Captain. Reynolds did not heed his runner, however, and almost immediately he was hit in the right arm. That seemed to be enough for Reynolds; he, Dahlberg, and a surgeon from regimental headquarters who had gotten caught at the front, took off running through the snow fields for the protection of the woods.[91]

Colonel Miller called on the radio again, "Do you know who this is?" Again Haggard answered, "Yes." "Have F Company fall back again," said Miller. The order was superfluous; F Company was already withdrawing. Haggard also recognized that it was time for him to get out. Haggard turned to the six other headquarters men with him and told them to go, one at a time, that "the tanks are beating us out and we're retreating." Outside, a German tank was approaching, firing its big

225

gun as the men broke from the hole. Haggard was amazed that they all made it okay. As he cleared the bunker, Haggard could see that the tank was ignoring him and the other men. Rather, it was firing at a 57mm antitank gun and a jeep that had been abandoned near the bunker. Haggard flopped to the ground just as the tank fired another round. The shell exploded nearby and, although he did not realize it at the moment, Haggard was nicked in the shoulder by a steel splinter. Otherwise okay, he got up and ran for his life with the other troopers who were zig-zagging toward the rear, stopping in holes to rest only momentarily before getting up to press on.[92]

It was then that Private Clarence Rohmann ran by and dropped into a shallow foxhole. He had been shot through the arm and into the abdomen, and was trying to hold both wounds. Rohmann saw Haggard. "I'm shot," cried Rohmann. "I need help." Haggard went to him. There were no medics and Haggard told him so. He couldn't see any blood – like the rest of them he had too many layers of clothing on – but he knew Rohmann was in bad shape. "Get up out of the hole and I'll help you," Haggard told him. "I can't do it," said Rohmann. "You have to," yelled Haggard. But it was no use. Rohmann was getting weaker and weaker. Pretty soon it was all over, he closed his eyes. Haggard got up, he had to leave him there.

Lieutenant Fann and Private Richard Murray were the last two men to withdraw. "Lieutenant Fann had the nerve, but nobody else did," commented Murray. In the midst of the confusion, Fann suggested, "Maybe we can get up a counterattack?" and sent Murray to round up as many men as he could while he did the same. It was a completely futile exercise – when they rejoined each other, neither had found a soul. Murray saw a damaged .30 caliber machine-gun abandoned in the snow and asked Lieutenant Fann if he could exchange its barrel for the one on a nearby jeep. "Go ahead if you want to," said Fann, but the lieutenant now realized the futility of his efforts and started to the rear himself.[93]

As Grice neared the woods, a shell exploded on the road. He threw himself down behind the frozen body of a German soldier for cover. "There were Germans lying everywhere and they just left them," explained Grice. "I guess they just left them till the ice melted." Grice looked into the corpse's face and remarked to him wryly, "I might be with you in a few minutes."[94]

When they reached Major Edwards' position, some troopers were handed ammunition, but rather than make a stand at the road junction, the men continued to withdraw back to the start line in the Bois des Valets. As Haggard approached the ammunition dump, he could see some of the panzers already had flanked the position to the north. A couple had been knocked out by bazookas, but seeing troopers were putting together Gammon grenades, he could tell the situation there was desperate, too. An officer from the regiment appeared and rallied some of the men, including Haggard, to make up some of the devices. They put in anything they could for shrapnel, but no one had any confidence in what was going to happen when a try with them was made. "I don't know how we're gonna win against tanks with these," Haggard said to himself. Then another order, retreat again, tanks were still coming down the road. They were leaving behind one medic and the wounded, and withdrawing. Haggard started across a field. It was supposed to be sown with antitank mines, but he hoped he wouldn't be stepping down hard enough to set any off.[95]

Having fought hard in their 'pillboxes' for nearly twenty-four hours straight, the surviving American tankers, seeing the rifle companies were withdrawing, abandoned their vehicles and took off for the rear themselves. Lieutenant Edgar Tommasino, the Battalion S-2, stayed behind at the ammunition dump with the twenty-five men and Lieutenant Rydesky's 81mm mortar platoon to cover the withdrawal. "Rydesky was a hell of a good mortarman," said Edwards. These men held until they had expended every round of ammunition at the dump, then made a run for it.[96]

It was about 1200 hours. With his men were still straggling in, Lieutenant Colonel Miller began reorganizing the battalion and salvaging what equipment he could. There were only about one hundred officers and men left, and more than ninety percent of these men were without ammunition. Those that did have ammunition had very little. The Germans, on the other hand, seemed to have "superior strength, equipment, and still had ammunition when theirs [the 2nd Battalion's] was gone." Fortunately, the German attack halted short of the battalion's new positions – perhaps because the fog hindered visibility, or perhaps because much of their supporting infantry had been killed by 2nd and 3rd Battalions.[97]

The medics, who had set up shop in a barn, prepared to evacuate a great many men via the ambulances that waited outside. Munafo and Private Tiberie C. Olivieri had taken their boots off; their feet blew up so much they couldn't get their boots back on and so they were both tagged for evacuation. Then, one medic found a bullet wound in Munafo's calf. Munafo was so cold he hadn't even felt it. "The next meat wagon," the medic ordered him, "you go." After nightfall, PFC Grice, who'd limped along for days and was suffering from the cold, was evacuated with trench foot. Staff Sergeant Seacott, who had frostbite and a shrapnel wound, was evacuated as well.[98]

Exhausted, Sarrell fell into a hole and just lay there for about a half hour. He soon ran into a couple of troopers who escorted him back to a tent – 2nd Battalion headquarters. They must have thought at first that he was a German in American uniform and grilled him a bit. They were eventually satisfied that he was American and returned him to F Company.[99]

PFC Sherlock was captured. Worse, when the Germans searched him, they found the Luger he'd captured on the fourth. A guard with a rifle was placed on Sherlock and a few other prisoners. The situation, however, was chaotic for both sides and this presented Sherlock with an opportunity. Rather than waiting to be executed, Sherlock decided to take a chance and broke away in a mad run. The guard fired, wounding him in the hand, but he nevertheless made good his escape.

Having fought until "all was quiet," that evening, two more E Company men straggled in. Both men reported that no man from their company had given up. Such sacrifice, however, was to no avail. Colonel Coutts had had no communication with the 2nd Battalion until their withdrawal into the Bois des Valets. Recognizing that the regiment "was then too weak to hold any strong enemy attack," General Miley moved the 507th Parachute Infantry Regiment, then in reserve, up behind the 513th. Miley then ordered the withdrawal of the 3rd Battalion from Flamierge.[100]

In Flamierge, the telephone line to the rear was cut in the first enemy attack leaving Major Anderson with no functioning signal equipment whatsoever. That morning, between fifteen and twenty German tanks hit Flamierge from the north, but 3rd Battalion, was well dug in and was able to hold. Severe casualties were inflicted upon enemy infantry as they advanced across the open country and bazooka fire pushed the panzers back to positions more than two hundred yards from the battalion's lines. When 2nd Battalion withdrew, however, the German effort at Flamierge intensified and casualties mounted. There were only two American aidmen to help the wounded, but "several German aidmen had been captured the day before" who gave good service to the wounded as well. Troopers who carried wounded buddies to the aid station returned to the line with more ammunition to continue the fight. Desperate for an opening, some Germans donned GI helmets and beckoned Anderson's men to come forward and into the open. The troopers, however, recognized the crude deception attempt and ruthlessly killed them.[101]

At 1400 hours, a radio on which repairmen had been working all morning was fixed and contact was established with Regiment. An artillery forward observer, who had the radio situated in a window, began to call corrections, "more by sound than by sight in the storm," Soon, three rounds of artillery hit the building and knocked in its walls. The radio operator and the battalion operations sergeant were wounded, and three civilians talking with Major Anderson were killed. Anderson was lightly wounded.[102]

At 1700 hours, three Germans were captured. Interrogation by the division's IPW teams the following day revealed that the attackers were from the *9th Panzer Reconnaissance Battalion* of the *9th Panzer Division*. After assembling in the woods north of Salle, they had attacked Flamierge during the morning. While Major Anderson tried to restore communications with Regiment, the *9th Panzer Reconnaissance Battalion* was then reorganizing in the same woods to make another attempt to wrest the town from 3rd Battalion's troopers.

Re-establishing communication with Regiment was critical. Realizing this, PFC Corley Wright, Major Anderson's personal radioman, volunteered to string a telephone line back to Regiment. No one believed it was possible including Wright himself, considering the fact that German tanks roamed the fields. Soon after he crawled into the field he was hit in the left arm but he kept going. He was hit twice more – through the chest and in the nose – and called Major Anderson on a check call to report that he would continue as long as he could. Anderson, however, ordered him to return. PFC Wright, in spite of his wounds, continued to help and later marched out with the battalion. The fighting remained heavy until nightfall at 1730 hours. At that time, the German armor withdrew save for two tanks that set up to fire down Flamierge's main street establishing a "killing ground." At 2100 hours these tanks stopped firing but the town continued to be shelled by mortars and artillery all night. Through it all, Major Anderson remained confident that Flamierge would be held.[103]

That night, Colonel Coutts ordered two three-man patrols from the Regimental S-2 to Flamierge with the withdrawal order. When the first of these patrols found the buildings on the edge of the town occupied by Germans, it withdrew, believing that Flamierge had been captured by the enemy and that Major Anderson's command was destroyed. On the way back they met the second patrol and returned together with the report. Colonel Coutts, fortunately, did not believe the patrols. Just as Coutts was preparing to send out another patrol, Lieutenant McGuire, 3rd Battalion's S-4, arrived with his own patrol from Flamierge.[104]

McGuire told Coutts that 3rd Battalion was still holding and that they had a radio repaired. He wanted regiment to "open their radio at 2100 for five minutes, and then again every thirty minutes." Major Anderson believed that the SCR-300 radios were drawing fire and did not want to use them any more than absolutely necessary. When Regiment failed to make contact at 2100, Colonel Coutts ordered one Corporal Gidley forward with an encoded message for Major Anderson and a radio. Gidley finally reached Anderson at 0100 hours on the morning of the ninth. Gidley asked if the battalion "had an M209 Code Converter" but Major Anderson informed Gidley that "all codes and code machines had been lost." Gidley therewith decided to cloak the withdrawal order within a casual conversation.[105]

"My favorite song has always been," began Gidley, articulating the message to withdraw, "When the Cowboy Herds His Doggies Back To The Old Corral!" "Stray doggies move faster," he continued, conveying Coutts' order for the men to split up into small groups. Gidley then passed the order for an officer to stay with and arrange the surrender of the wounded: "A wheel always stays with crippled doggies."

"That was the most uncomfortable time of my life," reported Major Anderson. "I was lying on a snow covered straw pile and was terribly cold. The messages took an hour to come thru [*sic*], and then I realized that our town would have to be given up. We wanted someone to come up to support us."[106]

Anderson passed the orders to withdraw immediately. Every man in the battalion was then defending the perimeter, so a third were ordered to remain in their positions until the main body of the battalion had moved out. Every house in the town was booby trapped with fragmentation or Gammon grenades and the stretcher cases were left behind with Lieutenant Charles A. Lewis who himself had been wounded in the head and foot and could not walk.[107]

It was a bitter retreat from Flamierge. "The men hated to leave. . . and said so," reported Anderson. Groups of eight to ten men, each led by an officer or NCO, were "sent out at odd times on compass courses varying from 147 to 155 degrees" – this heading led roughly to the junction of the Bastogne and Flamizoulle roads. The men were told to use the pass word "Phoenix City" which every paratrooper would easily recognize. All were burdened not only with their heavy loads of weapons and ammunition, but by knee-deep snow, frozen feet, and forty-eight hours without sleep or enough food. Enemy fire wounded four men, but all who started, "including the walking wounded, made the trip successfully." Stragglers continued to fall-back in small groups until daylight the next day.[108]

Major Anderson's party was the last to leave. It was almost dawn. The men had proceeded only 150 yards before the Germans began to shell Flamierge heavily. Carrying one of their number the final distance, Anderson's party at last reached friendly lines. Through the course of their assault on and defense of Flamierge, "3rd Battalion had lost more than half its strength." The wounded were evacuated but, after a hot meal, the rest of the battalion was sent back into the line.[109]

When 3rd Battalion evacuated Flamierge, inadvertently, several men were left behind. Bazookaman Private John Vafides of H Company and his assistant had manned an outpost along a long stone fence on the high ground bordering the western side of Flamierge. By late afternoon, they had completely exhausted their ammunition on the advancing German armor. Vafides left to scrounge more rockets and then returned. He continued to shift his position while, during the next hour, German tanks continued to shell him point blank with direct fire.

As evening and its colder temperatures approached, Vafides withdrew to a nearby barn to seek some warmth. He shared this shelter with a large, Belgian draught horse stabled inside. Soon, however, the Germans began to shell the barn, scoring several hits. The draught horse was killed and Vafides received multiple fragment wounds in the arm which began to bleed badly. He realized he needed immediate assistance so he walked into the center of the village looking for a medic. He found the town deserted – "not a single person there but [himself]."

Vafides wasn't sure what to do. It was about 1700 hours. Night was beginning to fall and he was losing a lot of blood. He walked back to the top of the hill several times, each time retracing his steps back to the center of town in a vain attempt to find other troopers. Finally, he decided to withdraw back along the same route on which H Company had advanced into town more than a day before. By now he realized only a miracle would see him safely back to friendly lines.

Just as he had made up his mind to leave, however, a medic emerged from the cellar of a nearby building and called Vafides inside. In the cellar, there were about twenty troopers from the 3rd Battalion, many of whom he recognized, all seriously wounded. The medic told Vafides that the battalion had pulled out and that trucks or tanks were supposed to return after dark to evacuate the wounded. Vafides decided that he would wait with the wounded.[110]

The promised trucks never came and the Germans reoccupied Flamierge at first light on the ninth. They ordered or carried out of the cellar all of the wounded troopers, including Vafides and the medic. The prisoners were lined up in the open, enduring freezing cold and snow for most of the morning while, one at a time, they were led to an adjacent building where they were operated on by a German surgeon. In the shell-torn building, the surgeon removed shrapnel and performed several amputations, all without anesthesia. Another German officer interrogated each of the men to glean from them any information he could.

While this took place, the Germans towed several of their disabled tanks to barns nearby where they were to be repaired. Vafides realized that they were being used as human shields for the withdrawal of the damaged German armor. Bitterly, he watched the armor that had been knocked out by 513th bazooka teams escape. After the tanks had been pulled back, the prisoners were put on trucks and driven away toward Germany and many months of captivity.[111]

F Company men found the bodies of 1st Lieutenant Robert Gilles and Staff Sergeant Pete Hellrigel sometime after sunup the next day. They had been executed by the Germans. Their hands had been bound with barbed wire and they had been shot through the head with captured German pistols they had been carrying. Their bodies were found with the pistols still in their mouths. All tolled, F Company, having lost seventeen more men on the eighth, now numbered only two officers and forty-nine enlisted men. With Captain Reynolds evacuated, Lieutenant Dean was now in command.

By the morning of 9 January, General Miley saw the Germans' capacity not only to resist but to aggressively challenge them with renewed perspective. "It didn't look like the enemy was withdrawing," commented Bud Miley in reference to the statement to the opposite made by Third Army's commander, General Patton, "and we were not able to fight tanks with our bare hands." In light of the division's losses, VIII Corps issued orders to General Miley instructing the 17th Airborne to go over to the defensive and to hold what it had. The battalion of the 507th that had been holding the position to the left of Colonel Miller's battalion and maintaining contact with the 87th Infantry Division on the evening of 7 January was replaced by the 139th Airborne Engineer Battalion. Then, the whole of the 507th Parachute

Infantry was moved into the line to the division's right and occupied Mande-St.-Etienne. On the division's far right was the 193rd Glider Infantry Regiment whose line extended all the way to Champs. The 193rd had taken over this sector from the 101st Airborne that was then preparing for an attack upon Noville, northeast of Bastogne.[112]

Coutts' regiment remained on the defensive until the late afternoon when it was ordered to the east to relieve elements of the 193rd Infantry just east of Monty. The sector was small and the battalions were disposed in depth in the order 2nd, 3rd and 1st, generally astride the Bastogne Highway south of Monty. No contact was made with the enemy though forward elements were subjected to intermittent artillery fire which caused light casualties. F Company evacuated five more men, PFC Jack Cook, PFC Morris W. Kelly, PFC Edward Logsdon, and Private Adolphus Hurbrough, Jr., all with frozen feet, and PFC Peter Blakney was evacuated with trench foot. Some men returned, however; Tec 5 Ray Rafalovich, who had gone to the hospital on 31 December, returned to duty, as did Private Lightcap, who that morning made his way back to the battalion and rejoined F Company. No one, including Lieutenant Dean, whom he found in charge, asked him where he'd been.[113]

On 10 January, Germans troops crossed the Rhine River to the south, in the zone of the Seventh U.S. Army. Although the crossing was only in battalion strength, Eisenhower was concerned enough by the new threat to order General Patton to stop Third Army's attack. Patton was irritated, "This is the second time I have been stopped in a successful attack due to the Germans having more nerve than we have." It was probably welcome news, however, to Miley who sent a memorandum to unit commanders of the 17th Airborne Division with orders to continue their defense in the division zone.

The 513th was placed in reserve for a few days rest and moved to the small town of Senonchamps, about two thousand yards southeast of Mande-St.-Etienne. From there, it could relax in relative safety, but could back up the positions of the 507th and 193rd Regiments if needed. By 1800 hours, F Company was established on the forward slope of a sparsely wooded hill facing northwest, approximately one thousand yards east of Mande-St.-Etienne, with E Company on its left and with D Company and Headquarters Company on the right. 3rd Battalion sat astride the Bastogne Highway south of 2nd Battalion and north of Senonchamps, and 1st Battalion was set up just to the east. There was no shelling in the 2nd Battalion zone, yet casualties due to the cold and wet weather continued. Three more F

Company men, PFC Jack Capell, PFC Jessie Guidry, and Private Paul Accomando, were evacuated with frozen feet or trench foot.[114]

While the 513th Infantry rested at Senonchamps, Miley's other regiments continued to defend the division front. In Flamierge, meanwhile, an estimated five hundred German soldiers were observed digging in during the afternoon. Fourteen panzers were also spotted in the area. Three tanks were flushed out of Flamierge by American fighter-bombers – the first Allied fighters seen since the division arrived – and destroyed on the Tronle road. Other American planes bombed and strafed enemy strongpoints in Renuamont, and worked over Flamizoulle where still more enemy troops had been observed. Meanwhile, the 17th Airborne's reconnaissance patrols continued to probe the enemy positions.[115]

The Germans, meanwhile, held their ground and continued to patrol themselves, but their grip on the area was loosening. By 11 January, German troops in the area were pulling out. The withdrawal of panzers and other tracked vehicles during the hours of darkness indicated that German formations were now concentrating at Gives, approximately three miles northeast of Flamierge on the road to Houffalize. When they pulled out, they left behind them scores of mine fields – eighty-four reported – throughout the Bastogne area. The German engineers' favorites were the motion-sensitive butterfly bombs – so sensitive that just blowing on them might set them off. The Germans continued to shell Mande-St.-Etienne and along the 17th Airborne's line, however; about half of the shells – at least in the zone of the 507th Parachute Infantry – were duds or solid, armor-piercing shot.[116]

On the eleventh, 513th Infantry was ordered north to positions just south of the large woods standing a mile east of Flamizoulle. The battalions again advanced in column, with 3rd Battalion leading, 2nd Battalion in center, and the 1st Battalion trailing. Patrols found the surrounding woods, which the enemy had so fiercely defended just a few days earlier, to be only lightly held. While there was little in the way of infantry resistance; the forward elements of the 513th were again subjected to intermittent shelling which caused a few more casualties.[117]

1st and 2nd Battalions dug in at the new position, but 3rd Battalion was ordered back into the line at 2000 hours, relieving the 1st Battalion of the 193rd Infantry. Major Anderson's battalion then maneuvered north and attacked the forest north of Mande-St.-Etienne in which D Company had been held up on 4 January. On their right, the 2nd Battalion of the 507th attacked into and occupied the woods between Flamizoulle and Champs overcoming light resistance.[118]

Intelligence gathered by patrols during the preceding several days indicated that on the night of 11-12 January, the German formations then facing the 17th Airborne Division – consisting mostly of the *3rd* and *15th Panzergrenadier Divisions* and the *77th Volksgrenadier Division* in the Givry-Rouette area – had completed the withdrawal of their main force. They left behind a delaying force, hundreds of mines, and snipers – supported by machine-guns, mortars, and artillery – to cover their departure. The enemy also gave up Flamizoulle and the woods to the east, but was still holding on to Flamierge in unknown strength. Givry and its neighboring woods were also held.[119]

Though the 17th was on the defensive, VIII Corps instructed Miley on the twelfth to maintain active patrolling so not to advertise 17th Airborne's posture to the enemy. As this patrolling continued, the 513th Infantry received instructions for an attack that would take place the next day. Coutts' men were to cross over to the west, behind the assaulting elements of the division who would be driving north in a renewed assault, and clear Flamierge. Miller's 2nd Battalion was to clear the surrounding woods and protect the division's left flank while Major Anderson's 3rd Battalion again attacked Flamierge. Regimental Intelligence warned of a small covering force, well equipped with mortars, automatic weapons, and artillery, and reported that before the Germans left, they had booby-trapped and mined the villages and woods.[120]

At 0830 hours the next morning, in the bitter cold and fog, the division pushed off once again for the Ourthe River line. Miley's instructions were to go straight forward as far as Houffalize – the same objective it had been assigned on 4 January. Using the Flamierge-Houffalize road, the division advanced with the 194th Infantry on the left, the 507th Infantry in the center, and the 193rd Infantry on the right. Where they had completed their withdrawal from the division sector, the enemy left in their wake an array of mines, booby traps and road blocks that would come to characterize their entire retreat. When the Germans overran an American ammunition dump at Bourcy, they had captured an estimated twenty thousand American land mines. These mines were starting to appear on the VIII Corps front, laid in the German pattern. Nevertheless, Miley's troopers reached the first phase line by 0930 and, after Gives was bombed at 1030 hours, made the second phase line, Givroulle-Gives, by the end of day in a two thousand yard advance.[121]

It was for their initial capture of the town on 7 January and their subsequent stand on the eighth, that Major Anderson's 3rd Battalion of the 513th was given the honor of retaking Flamierge. So, as the main body of the 17th Airborne Division began its move northward, Anderson's men, accompanied by the Regimental Headquarters, reoccupied the town at 1045 hours on the thirteenth. The effects of American shelling during their absence made it impossible for Anderson's men to determine the effects of the booby traps they'd left behind when they departed on the night of the eighth.[122]

Meanwhile, the 1st and 2nd Battalions moved into the forests at Trois Monts around 1700 hours harassed only by some light, sporadic shelling. F Company dug in along a cart path there. D Company set up just northwest of F Company, and E Company dug in about seven hundred yards away in the woods northeast of Tronle. The regiment remained in this location as Division Reserve while the rest of the 17th continued to attack northward. In the 513th's zone, only small bands of enemy troops – some with outposts employing dogs for warning – were encountered by patrols during the evening near the towns of Flamierge, Tronle, Givry, and Salle.[123]

That day, gains were made across the entire VIII Corps front. The 11th Armored Division continued its drive north toward the Houffalize bottleneck, while northeast of Bastogne, the 101st Airborne reoccupied Foy at 0915 after repulsing an attack by enemy tanks and infantry. The restoration of offensive movement by the American army, while it did not bring a resurgence in morale among American combat troops, increased manifold the suffering of the German army. With the first snow falls, men from both armies began stripping the dead for replacement articles, but, because they were so critically short of their own supplies by the latter stages of the battle, it was quite common to find German soldiers wearing American uniform parts. A wounded PW of the *9th Volksgrenadier Division* who was captured wearing American trousers stated under interrogation, "When I needed a new pair of trousers – due to a bowel movement – I asked my CO, Lieutenant Metzberg, for them. As there were no others available, he gave me this pair. I did not realize that there was anything wrong in that, and frankly, due to the condition I was in, I didn't care much either."[124]

The fall of Flamierge marked the end of the 17th Airborne Division's struggle for Dead Man's Ridge. The way to Houffalize now lay open and a new phase in the division's Winter campaign in Belgium had begun. Miley's division, however, had suffered a disproportionately high number of casualties, especially within Coutts' 513th Parachute Infantry. The regiment had lost sixty-three officers and 1,117 enlisted men since its move into the line around Monty on 3 January 1945; most of the casualties having been sustained in the two attacks of 4 and 7 January. These figures constituted a loss of fifty-four percent of the regiment's total strength, but more importantly, the 513th had lost more than seventy percent in its combat organizations. The remaining personnel of the regiment numbered an estimated eighty-one officers and 1,036 men. F Company could claim only Lieutenants Dean and Fann, and some thirty-two enlisted personnel.[125]

Captain John G. Westover, a historian assigned to VIII Corps who interviewed the officers of the 513th on 14-16 January 1945, remarked on what he saw as the defining characteristics of the engagement: "(1) The green troops showed exceptional courage in closing with the enemy. (2) The bald, open terrain over which they fought, covered with knee deep snow, was an extremely difficult area in which to operate. (3) The tactical plans of the attacks were "peculiar." (4) The casualties sustained by the unit were particularly high." According to Captain Westover, each of the officers interviewed was, in fact, "dazed by the losses of his unit."

Major Morris Anderson, who led the 3rd Battalion from the front during the entire battle, was, for his role in the eleven day Battle for Dead Man's Ridge, recommended for the Distinguished Service Cross. Lieutenant Colonel Miller, commanding 2nd Battalion, was complimented for the performance of his battalion on 4 January, but Miller himself was more proud of 2nd Battalion's stand on 8 January. In fact, Miller's command of the 2nd Battalion during its initial attack on 4 January had been erratic at best, yet he had seemingly been tempered by his experience and was able to command his battalion with renewed authority when its next test came four days later.

The officers of the 1st Battalion, Lieutenant Colonel Taylor and Major Kies, were still quite dumbfounded by the destruction of their battalion on 4 January. Indeed, Colonel Taylor had quickly broken under the stress of command, and, like Lieutenant Colonel Edward Kent, the commander of the 3rd Battalion, apparently had chosen to save himself at the expense of his command and his men.

"Colonel Coutts," wrote Westover, "seemed depressed about the operations, especially about his request to move on the final objectives on the 7th." Indeed, the decision to take the 513th Regiment into Flamierge on 7 January had been ill-advised, even reckless, and one which brings into question the competence of leaders from battalion to division. By 9 January, both Colonel Coutts, who had pushed the proposal to take Flamierge, and General Miley, who had allowed the 513th to continued their attack against his better judgment, realized they had made costly mistakes. Major Edwards, 2nd Battalion's Executive Officer, was severe in his criticism: "It was an uncoordinated effort," he explained, "the division was committed piecemeal." The 513th had gone into battle with the finest men the Airborne Effort could produce "and it was all wasted because they were mis-commanded."[126]

The battle also was an epic example of the misapplication of elite troops. Committing a parachute infantry formation, intended to be used as an invasion force of shock troops, to a prolonged battle of attrition required them to operate under conditions inconsistent with their intended mission and had led to their destruction. One could not expect such a light infantry unit, no matter how well trained or competently led, to take on heavy tank attacks directly without adequate antitank weapons and without proper air and artillery support.

Commenting on the outcome of the division's operations as a whole, General Miley stated: "For my money the prize son-of-a-bitch in this war is GENERAL REMMER of REMMER GROUP. He put more mines and booby traps over this area that I had ever thought possible and we lost a lot of men to them. There are shoe mines [*Schü-mine 42.*] under every tree. We haven't been able to move without an engineer sweep in front of us."

"He [Remmer] is a master in offensive-defensive delay and in organizing quick counter-attack," added General Whitelaw, the division Chief of Staff.

"Yes, he is that, too," acknowledged Miley, "in addition to being a son-of-a-bitch."[127]

While the Generals brooded, the men in the rifle companies continued to fight on with no relief and no end in sight. "Every morning you got up and knew you were on the offensive," explained PFC Sarrell. "Every night you think, 'tomorrow will be my last day.' You know you can't keep going, your luck can't run forever. With every narrow escape you think, 'Well, it's finally come. This is it.' You're scared but you're not, and the mornings get tougher and tougher."[128]

7

Nobody Goes Back

The Long March to the Our River
14 January - 10 February 1945

On 14 January 1945, the 17th Airborne Division reached the Ourthe River. Elements of the 507th Parachute Infantry met VII Corps' 24th Cavalry Reconnaissance Squadron in the village of La Roche at 1100 hours that day. The division then was ordered to "outpost the river line. . ." That same day, the 193rd Glider Infantry, attached in support of the 11th Armored Division, continued to fight its way north against stubborn enemy resistance.

As American combat forces tightened the noose around Houffalize, the town through which the *5th Panzer Army* still hoped to withdraw from the rapidly collapsing salient, they would find German resistance increase significantly. To stiffen the resolve of the Wehrmacht, small groups of *SS* men were being attached to regular troops. This also led many Americans to believe that larger *SS* formations were lurking nearby. With the Germans desperate to hold the roads through the town, the 193rd would have to remain with the 11th Armored until after the fall of Houffalize on 16 January.[1]

Meanwhile, the decimated 513th Parachute Infantry was detailed to begin salvage operations across the fields and woods over which the division had bled since 3 January. Regiment divided the old battlefield into four sections; one portion being assigned to each of the three battalions and one to Headquarters Company. In the 2nd Battalion's area, the collection points were the crossroads at Monty and the old Regimental Headquarters site in the Bois des Valets. Men searched the countryside for crew served weapons, small arms, ammunition, lost signal equipment, and other discarded material. Private Lightcap and his new foxhole buddy, Private Campbell Harris from Chattanooga, Tennessee – with whom Lightcap had buddied-up with in the Bois des Valets on the sixth – uncovered a Thompson submachine-gun in the snow. It was a bit rusty, but over the next three or four days, they cleaned it. After acquiring some magazines and ammunition from the quartermaster, they fired it a couple times to make sure it worked – and it worked just "dandy." Lightcap and Harris named her 'Betsy.'

The men also were also detailed to collect the dead. The bodies, both German and American, frozen in grotesque poses, the color of claret, were brought to the same collection points. Said PFC Sarrell, the men "were picking up casualties by the truck load."[2]

When night came, and salvage operations were ceased for the day, the men started looking for dry places to sleep. After a fruitless search, Private Ed Pierce laid down near the Monty intersection where a lot of other men already were bivouacked. Pierce took off his boots and put them under his head to use as a pillow, and then he hunkered down in his sleeping bag. He must have fallen very soundly asleep because when he woke up the next morning, his boots were gone. Somebody had stolen them. There was another trooper there that Pierce knew so he hollered at him, "Hey, has anybody seen my boots?"

"No," he answered.

"Well, my boots are gone. I need something," said Pierce angrily.

"Well, I'll go over here and see if I can get any boots for you," proposed Pierce's friend, motioning to the frozen bodies of several dead troopers stacked up near the intersection.

The trooper couldn't find any jump boots among the bodies, but he did find a pair of goulashes on one of the bodies and he gave these to Pierce. With four pairs of socks, the goulashes made fairly good shoepacs. Pierce wore them through the rest of the campaign and they probably saved him from getting frozen feet.[3]

Under heavy skies, the 17th Airborne Division, on 15 January, moved into positions in force along the Ourthe and established contact with Allied forces moving down from the north. Meanwhile, the 513th Regiment was ordered northeast to positions in reserve; 3rd Battalion to Gives, about two thousand yards further north, straddled the main highway. 1st and 2nd Battalions, and Regimental Headquarters, moved to positions in and around the village of Givry, a village of reasonable size east of the Houffalize road about four kilometers northeast of Flamierge.[4]

At 0905 hours the next morning, 16 January, Task Force Greene of the 11th Armored Division met elements of the 41st Infantry of the First Army's 2nd Armored Division at Houffalize. As far as the Allied High Command was concerned, this meeting signaled the end of the Battle of the Bulge. Though the campaign was 'officially' concluded, the Allies still had ten more miles to go to retake the line they had held a month earlier, before the battle began. It would take two more weeks to reach the Our River and the German border. For the men on the line, there would be no celebration, only more desperate days of fighting in the most appalling conditions.

With the divided American front now rejoined at Houffalize, the 17th Airborne was ordered to relieve the 11th Armored and 101st Airborne Divisions and take over the Houffalize-Bouvay line. At 1700 hours that day, the direction of the division's attack shifted to the east. Before them were the enemy, dug in, "with all the implements of war."[5]

The German troops facing the 17th included elements of the *9th* and *130th Panzer Divisions*, the *26th Infantry Division*, and a mixed formation of engineers – an estimated combined force of 6,500 men supported by thirty tanks. The enemy continued to be amply supported by mortars and artillery, and be protected by extensive minefields. The weather, which remained cold and gray, still favored the enemy because the overcast prevented air support, and the temperatures, often dipping to the twenty degree mark, made even the simplest tasks arduous.[6]

On 17 January, the 513th marched seven miles – through Gives, Bertogne, and Compogne – to new positions in division reserve. During the march, the morning fog and cold gave way to clearing skies and the temperature climbed to twenty-eight degrees Fahrenheit. In their new positions, in the woods about 2,600 yards north of Compogne, re-equipping was continued. Though resting, the regiment remained on alert, ready to move on two hours notice. Moreover, the Germans occasionally harassed them with light artillery, mortars, and occasional small arms fire.[7]

The men never had enough food and were always hungry so, whenever the supply trucks came up, everyone hustled over to get K-rations. PFC Dahlberg, however, who had a severe case of the GIs, wanted the toilet paper more than anything. In fact, almost every man had the GIs and Dahlberg was, himself, passing blood every time his stomach turned – he could hardly get out of his trousers let alone make it to a slit trench. Every few days, however, the cooks caught up with the battalion and served pancakes and coffee. After going two or three days at a time without warm food, Dahlberg thought they were the best meals he had ever had.

If he didn't have the GIs, it was still a struggle for a man to relieve himself. "If we could find a place to go, "explained Grice, "we did." Meanwhile, frontline infantrymen sometimes waited two or three days to relieve themselves. "We didn't eat much," said Grice, "and sometimes you just didn't worry about going to the bathroom."[8]

Dahlberg was always cold through and incredibly filthy. To keep from freezing to death, he worked on his foxholes through the nights. At last, with an increasing amount of blood in his stools, and shaking from a high fever, he went to the medics. "I have to go back," he begged them. The medics only gave him a couple of red pills and told him, "Nobody goes back." Dahlberg threw the pills in the snow. Sometimes he envied the men who had been wounded, even the men who'd been killed. At least they were out of this.

The weather on 18 January continued to be cold and cloudy, and rain and snow showers prevented air support for yet another day. The division line south of the Ourthe was held by the 507th Parachute Infantry on the left, and on the right glidermen of the 194th. The 4th French Parachute Battalion, meanwhile, patrolled north of the river line. Artillery and mortar fire harassed troopers all across the front while patrols exchanged fire with the enemy forward of the observation post line. Still in division reserve, the 513th Parachute Infantry moved east to Liheraine following behind the advancing 507th Parachute Infantry.[9]

In order to maintain the pace of advance, the 139th Airborne Engineers cleared mines, removed roadblocks, and improvised bridges. Through a combination of aggressive patrolling and a strong use of reconnaissance in force, the division advanced more than two miles on 20 January. In some places, the German withdrawal had been so rapid that they had not had the time to leave mines behind.[10]

The next day, the 17th Airborne, whose sector now stretched from Houffalize to Hardigney, Belgium, continued to advance on the towns of Hautbellain, Wattermal, and Espeler. The 507th jumping off on the division left supported by the 761st Tank Battalion (Colored), and the 194th jumping off on the right, attacked east to secure the Houffalize-Noville Road. The day's final objectives – the towns of Centturu, Bouitet, Steinbach, and Limerle – were captured by 1515 hours, and the front lines were advanced nearly four miles. Following the 507th, the 513th, still in reserve, moved to a new assembly area in the vicinity of Liheraine at 2000 hours.[11]

On 22 January, under clearing skies, the 513th moved into the line in the vicinity of Limerle. There, at 1100 hours, it attacked to the northeast, toward a wooded high ground. Opposition from scattered enemy infantry was overcome rapidly and the objective gained. Coutts then redeployed his battalions with the 1st on the left, the 3rd on the right, and Miller's 2nd Battalion in the center. Patrols soon contacted U.S. First Army units at Retigny, but 2nd Battalion patrols found enemy troops in the town of Wattermal and in the woods to its southeast. Before darkness fell on the Belgium-Luxembourg border, a twenty-four man combat patrol led by Lieutenant John Knight of the Divisional Reconnaissance Company entered Hautbellain and cleared the village after killing four Germans, capturing five, and routing another forty. Their hasty withdrawal notwithstanding, the enemy left the village heavily mined. The next day, after calling in the engineers, Hautbellain was occupied by the 193rd Glider Infantry who dug in east of the town.[12]

Despite a break in the weather, keeping Miley's advancing division supplied was becoming increasingly difficult. All the roads leading to Limerle were snow-drifted and impassable for vehicles, so supporting tank outfits quickly found themselves breaking trails and pulling in supplies. Later, engineers used a bulldozer to plow through the snow drifts, opening a line of communication. The Germans, however, found the roads even more unfit for travel. All day long, planes of the 9th and 19th Tactical Air Commands exacted a large toll on the thousands of German vehicles choking roads from the base of what remained of the Bulge to far beyond the Siegfried Line. Almost all traffic, airmen observed, was moving east. Fighter-bombers remained in contact until last light.[13]

The headlong German retreat came abruptly to a halt on the twenty-third. In front of the 513th Parachute Infantry, a German delaying force – elements of the *560th Volksgrenadier Division*, composed of hastily organized small units – was discovered in entrenched positions along commanding terrain on the outskirts of the town of Wattermal in a semi-circle defense. A patrol of the 4th Special Air Service Battalion (French) had located the enemy force digging in west of the village at 2000 hours the day before, but had not been able to determine its strength. Throughout the Bulge, scratch forces such as this were being left behind by the Germans to delay the American advance and buy time for the withdrawal of their best troops and armor.[14]

The 513th's attack on Wattermal got underway at dawn. The weather was cold
– about twenty-five degrees – and there were snow flurries. Supported by a platoon of light tanks from the 761st Tank Battalion, F Company's objective was a
woods southeast of the town. The survivors of the company had been combined
with the remnants of another 2nd Battalion company but all tolled, F Company's
fighting strength was a little less than that of a platoon. Lieutenant Sam Dean had
been evacuated with frozen feet on 16 January, so it was Lieutenant Isham Fann,
who had assumed command of the company who, that morning, led the men through
one stand of trees and out into an open field. Across this snowy expanse was another stand of tall, reforested pines, laden with snow. The troopers were sure the
Germans were waiting for them in there, and called up their armor, five Stuart
light tanks armed with 37mm guns. The tankers, with the hatches still open, pulled
up to the edge of the field and commenced shelling the woods. "When they started
firing, wood chips started flying," remembered Haggard. "It looked like a damn
sawmill [and] they [the tankers] thought it was funny as hell." After they had finished firing on the woods, the tank men reported to Major Edwards, "Sir, them
woods is cleared." Lieutenant Fann ordered the men forward and, making no contact with any enemy in the woods, F Company continued on towards the town.[15]

Around noon, however, the leading elements of 2nd Battalion came under
point-blank fire from an SP concealed in the woods about two hundred yards ahead
of their positions, and heavy small arms and sniper fire from around the town and
from the church steeple. "We were pinned down," recalled one F Company man,
when, on the order of Major Edwards, the tank platoon from the 761st again came
up in support. The tank platoon leader "got the radio and, from his position in the
commanders ring, radioed his men, 'All you Roses – all you Roses – this is Red
Rose. Load your pieces and shoot at you know what!' And Jesus, they did," recalled Major Edwards. The tanks leveled suppressing fire on the enemy's positions, and shot the church steeple to pieces, knocking it down. The combined force
then pressed forward. Like the tank crews who had earlier fought their knocked-
out tanks as pillboxes, these men had no lack of guts. "If they lost a tread," Edwards
recalled, "they'd unload and get their Thompson submachine-guns out and join
right in with the infantry. They just did a hell of a job. They were magnificent."
Enemy resistance, however, was too strong to overcome, and the troopers were
forced to withdraw. Through all, the tanks stuck with the infantry. "They rolled
down the street to get us, shooting like hell," remembered the men. "Get behind us

boys," the tank men yelled to the troopers, and, together, they backed out of the town.[16]

The twenty-fourth broke cloudy, gray, and cold – about twelve degrees. Visibility on the ground was poor, but Allied aircraft were flying in spite of it. Tec 5 Haggard, who had worked up a sweat while digging a foxhole during the night, woke up to discover he was frozen to the floor of his hole. As he pulled himself free of the ground's frosty grip, the throaty roar from a P-47's piston engine broke through the morning's stillness, followed by a great explosion. The fighter had dropped a bomb on the SP that had held up the attack the day before "and blew it to hell." At 1000 hours, Colonel Coutts received word from General Miley that a patrol of the division's reconnaissance company had entered Wattermal at 0700. Though the main body of the enemy force had pulled out, German artillery was still being directed on Wattermal. More importantly, although the town was clear of enemy troops, the enemy still held the wooded high ground to the south and southeast of the village which afforded observation for the German gunners. Enemy troops there were entrenched along the forward edges of the tree lines, and dispersed through the woods. Colonel Coutts' objective was to take this high ground and he gave the job to the 2nd Battalion. For the task, Ace Miller was given the support of Major Morris Anderson's 3rd Battalion of the 513th, the 761st Tank Battalion, Company B of the 811th Tank Battalion, C Battery of the 155th Anti-tank Battalion, and the entire 466th Parachute Field Artillery Battalion. At 1245, 2nd Battalion's attack jumped-off.

The leading elements advanced southeast, into a sunken cart path until they had drawn up adjacent to the objective, and then moved quickly east into a small copse of trees standing before the main woods. As the troopers advanced across the fields, Germans poured automatic and sniper fire down on them from positions further up the hillside. F Company moved through a small stand of pines and up along a firebreak to a position at the base of the steep hill. They then moved into the cover of a hillock at lower edge of the main woods. There, the company waited while Miller tried to organize a reconnaissance of the enemy positions forward. It was a dangerous task, a lieutenant from one of the other company's had already been killed, recalled Lightcap, when Miller sent him forward to "see what's up ahead."[17]

Lieutenant Fann sent Private Alvie Scott – a big, raw-boned boy with a country twang in his voice even though he was from New York State – out into the field to see if he could spot the enemy's positions. As soon as he left the protection of the trees, Scott was hit twice in the neck by German machine-gun fire and killed. Fann ordered Doc Sloan to go out and check to see if Scott was still alive.

"I don't believe I better do that," Sloan refused. "They're killing the medics."

While this exchange was taking place, Privates Lightcap and Campbell 'Whity' Harris had become pinned down behind the small hill, a hail of bullets was cracking loud and close over their heads. Suddenly, Lieutenant Colonel Miller appeared a short distance behind them and shouted to them to "Look up and see what's up there." Lightcap had seen the other two men killed and so told Harris to ignore the "dumb sonofabitch and just keep your head down." But after repeated demands by Miller to "look up ahead," Harris finally did. Harris was immediately struck in the head by machine-gun fire and killed. Lightcap was furious with Miller – men's lives were being thrown away needlessly and the attack was going nowhere – but he could do nothing.

By late afternoon, the German defense deteriorated into only a weak, rear guard action so, with steady pressure, 2nd Battalion succeeded in taking its objective. Despite the day's success, the men were very disturbed by Miller's performance under fire. "There was quite a bit of talk among the men about bumping-off Acey-Deucy" and, according to Sarrell, "some of these guys were dead serious." Miller, was a "bastard," said Lightcap, and a "lazy sonofabitch. He had a flunky who would dig his foxholes for him every night in the woods. The poor guy had diarrhea all the time – I can still hear that guy running for the woods [to relieve himself] now – but Miller had him digging the holes anyway. That's just the kind of a man [Miller] was." It was even rumored, recalled Sarrell, that Miller's flunky slept on the bottom of the foxhole and Miller slept on top of him to keep off the cold ground.[18]

Ed Pierce recalled once being given a message to deliver to Colonel Miller "and to him alone." As he approached Miller's CP – a two-story farmhouse made of stone – he was challenged by two of the Colonel's bodyguards. Pierce gave them the countersign and was allowed to enter. After delivering the message, Miller flatly told him, "Get out of here." Pierce left, but after going only a short distance he realized he'd omitted part of the message and turned around. Again, the two sentries challenged him, but now nervous, Pierce drew a blank. Just when he thought the guards would open fire, Miller burst out the door of his CP and into the middle of the road. There, surrounded by his bodyguards, Miller proceeded to drop his trousers and squat, all the while shouting orders at the men standing around him. As this was happening, the Germans began to shell the area. The men around Miller all went to the ground, but Miller just kept squatting and shouting out orders. In sight of this, Pierce didn't have the courage to deliver the rest of the message.[19]

Major Edwards described Miller as "a gutsy little bastard. He had that same type of guts that a lot of little men have." However, Edwards said, "he would do some horribly irrational acts." Once, in Belgium, when a radioman's sleeping bag became tangled in the handset's wire, Miller yanked at the sleeping bag so hard that the man hit the road. Miller then threw the offending article into a roadside culvert. "Those are the sort of things he'd do," recalled Edwards, "but then he'd turn around and give someone a decoration they shouldn't have received out of a Crackerjack box. He was irrational, not crazy, but *very* irrational."[20]

At 0830 on 25 January, the direction of the 513th's attack shifted to the south, toward the town of Hautbellain, just over a mile distant. Facing the regiment were the remnants of the *560th Volksgrenadier Division* – numbering about 250 men – and the *11th Panzergrenadier Regiment* – about ninety-five men. Offering only light small arms and artillery fire, and the usual sniping and *schü-mines*, the enemy were brushed aside by the 513th. By 1800 hours, the regiment had succeeded in capturing Hautbellain and the surrounding high ground. The *11th Panzergrenadier Regiment*, supported by three Panther medium tanks, inflicted a few casualties before withdrawing to Espeler. F Company's only casualties were Sergeant James E. Dornbos and PFC Rubin E. McLean, both of whom were evacuated with frozen feet.

On 26 January, the 513th Parachute Infantry attacked the village of Espeler. A German battle group – composed of the *560th VG Division* (estimated at 180-190 troops), the *9th Panzer Division*, and *9th SS Division Hohenstaufen*, a shattered formation then retreating through that area, held the town and the high ground surrounding it. A few tanks were in prepared positions supported by small groups of infantry with minimal artillery, and more infantry, supported by several heavy armored cars and a few half-tracks, occupied the woods to the south.[21]

With the same forces in support as on 24 January, the 513th pushed off at 0830 hours. It was another cold morning – sixteen degrees. Snow showers covered the advance and, therefore, the American attack came as an almost complete surprise to the enemy. The regiment's attack started just as the enemy was attempting to reinforce the Espeler garrison. Accurate supporting artillery provided by the 466th PFAB was very effective in engaging several approaching German columns and boxing the town. Those German soldiers who were able to escape, withdrew east to the vicinity of Thommen along with five enemy tanks which retreated to the east and northeast. After the 1st and 2nd Battalions took the high ground flanking the town to the northwest, the 3rd Battalion passed through the line of the 2nd Battalion and occupied the village against only light opposition. There, German troops "surrendered in large groups quite willingly."[22]

After Espeler was secured, the 513th Regiment was relieved by the 87th Infantry Division. At 2100 hours, the regiment withdrew to an assembly area near Limerle to prepare for a motor move the next day to the new divisional assembly area in the vicinity of Eschweiler, Luxembourg. There, the division came under the command of III Corps of Patton's Third Army, and moved into positions on high ground between the towns of Steinmaur and Marbourg where it overlooked the main Siegfried Line defenses on the east bank of the Our River. Like the other units in the III Corps, the 17th Airborne was ordered to "maintain an aggressive def[ense] in z[one] with the object of containing max[imum] number of enemy tr[oop]s." The sector that III Corps occupied was not suitable for offensive operations; Patton, therefore, ordered III Corps to increase its activity in its sector so as to pin down as many Germans there as possible and, thus, prevent them from being used to counter the attacks of Third Army's two other corps. The 17th Airborne Division's role in III Corps' mission was to clear the enemy from the west bank of the Our River, patrol across the river to probe the Siegfried Line defenses, and establish a limited bridgehead on the enemy side of the Our.[23]

It was here that Neal Haggard learned that the 17th Airborne Division had developed an unenviable reputation. Returning to F Company after spending a few days with the kitchens recovering from the GIs, Haggard came to a crossroads at which he and another trooper – Acey-Duecy's orderly – were hailed by a III Corps MP who was directing traffic. "What outfit you guys from?" he inquired.

"We're the 17th," Haggard replied.

"Oh, yeah?" the MP shot back, a sneer curling the sides of his mouth. "We heard all about you guys."

Haggard was at once curious and angry. "Yeah," he replied, "What'd ya hear?"

The MP charged right in. "Well, we all heard about you killin' prisoners up on the line there." Haggard frowned, the MP finished. "You've been nicknamed 'The Baggy Pocket Butchers'. "

"Well, listen you sonofabitch," Haggard replied, "don't stand back here at this intersection with a whistle directing traffic. Come along with me. I'm going back up to the front. We'll see how you do up on the front line."

The MP just stood blank faced and made no response. Satisfied that he'd made his point, Haggard kept walking. How that "rear echelon sonofabitch" could insult a fighting man by calling him a 'baggy pocket butcher' burned him up. He stewed on this until he reached the truck that would take him back to the company area, then he just decided to forget about it.

While the 513th's 1st and 3rd Battalions moved to a new assembly area in Noertrangle, Luxembourg to act as a division reserve, 2nd Battalion moved by truck to a rest area at Virton, France. There, Miller's men received both a twenty-four hour break, and a partial issue of winter shoes and gloves. PFC Dahlberg, Private Cogan, and PFC Brewer took the opportunity to head to the showers. There, Dahlberg stripped off his filthy, worn-out uniform – he didn't even recognize his own body. "I looked like a ninety-nine pound weakling," he remembered. The showers washed away much of the dirt, but couldn't get rid of the persistent smell of burnt powder that seemed to stick in his nostrils. It was wonderful nevertheless. That evening, as the men walked through the streets, they noticed a light peeking through the curtain of an otherwise blacked-out building. Curious, Dahlberg knocked on the door and the men were invited inside by the home's owners. There was a bowl of apples on the table and a tray of waffles. Brewer thought he'd died and gone to heaven for, while most of the men carried a picture of their wife or sweetheart in their wallets, Brewer carried a picture of waffles. "Here's what I really love!" he would tell his buddies whenever he produced the photograph.[24]

On the night of the 31 January, the 513th, after several days in reserve, moved into the line in the vicinity of Hosingen, relieving the 193rd Glider Infantry Regiment. "At Hosingen," explained Major Edwards, "it was about two thousand meters down to the Our River and another three or four thousand meters up the mountain on the other side – and the Krauts commanded the whole fucking area." With the rifle companies down to only a handful of men apiece, "we knew we weren't going to go anyplace against the Siegfried Line." Nevertheless, vigorous patrolling was begun. Though their morale was at an all-time low – PW reports indicated a high incidence of desertion in their ranks – the Germans were intent on defending the river until such time that they could be withdrawn behind the Siegfried Line.[25]

Lieutenant Fann set up the company CP in the cellar of an old school house in the town. Private Lightcap, who had been made a runner, made five or six trips a day from the CP down to the company positions a collection of foxholes situated above the river. Fann stayed in the school house, Lightcap did the running. The Germans were still pushing small patrols over to the west side of the Our so, during his trips, Lightcap kept on his toes, especially at night.[26]

Once the company set up in Hosingen, the food provided to the men improved. According to Private Ed Pierce, they "were able to get pretty good cooked meals – fried chicken, pork chops, and so forth – and there was plenty of it because the mess section was drawing rations for more men than were present." The men stuck out on the line, however, had to eat K rations, and if a soldier ate the frozen hash that was in some meals he would be in big trouble. "The grease in it went right through a man [and] caused the GIs," said Pierce. "Some of the guys didn't make it out of their sleeping bags and they messed themselves pretty bad."

On the night of 31 January, a patrol of the 2nd Battalion crossed on the now-frozen Our River to its east side in order to probe the enemy defenses and capture prisoners. The patrol located several enemy bunkers but, as they closed in, were fired upon by machine-guns and forced to retire. Despite its lack of success, this was, nevertheless, the first "penetration" into Germany proper by the 513th.[27]

At daylight the next day, the weather turned warmer with light snow changing to rain during the early morning hours. During the day, strong outposts were pushed to within fifteen hundred yards of the Our, and observations posts, which overlooked the river itself, were situated within eight hundred yards of the river bank. Patrolling continued actively, and German troops were discovered to be occupying Roderhausen and Eisenbach, towns to the regiment's northern and southern flanks respectively.[28]

Another patrol found some German troops holed up in a nearby railroad tunnel. As Private Ed Pierce recalled, several efforts were made to oust them to no avail. Watching the fracas from the top window of a two-story wooden frame house, Pierce saw a 'Long Tom' – a 155mm gun – towed up to the tunnel entrance by a half-track, followed by a number of supporting vehicles. It took a whole company of men to set the gun up, and when they were finished, it was aimed straight into the mouth of the tunnel. From where he was in the house – looking right over the barrel of the gun – Pierce thought, "Boy! I can get a ring side seat here. This will be great!"

The blast of the first round lifted Pierce a foot off the floor and shook the house so hard that he thought it would be knocked down. The gun crew quickly fired another round into the tunnel and then packed up and left. Apparently, that was the end of German resistance in the tunnel.[29]

With the exception of occasional German patrols and sporadic shelling, the sector was relatively quiet. The men of the 513th spent most of their time improving their defensive positions and patrolling. However, warmer temperatures and thinning ice lately had restricted foot patrols from crossing over the river.

2nd Battalion, nevertheless, was ordered to make another attempt at pushing a patrol across the Our and F Company drew the job. Just after midnight on the fourth, the patrol made its way down to the river where what PFC Goldfarb described as "canoes made of canvas" – four pontoon boats, each about twenty feet long, were waiting. The river wasn't very wide, only about two hundred feet, but the current was strong. Concrete pillboxes, set on steep heights across the river, dominated the whole area. As artillery was placed on these German positions, one at a time, the F Company men slid the boats into the swiftly running waters and scrambled in.

As quietly as they could, the men paddled toward the dark shore ahead. Before too long, with its occupants up and ready to spring out when the bow grounded, one boat reached the east bank. The second boat was about half way across, and the third boast was just starting to make progress. In the last boat, PFC Grice, who had rejoined the company from the hospital, had just started paddling when machine-guns started firing from the pillboxes.

Geysers leapt from the water all around the boats and bullets cut into their canvas sides. Grice jumped into the icy water and thrashed his way back to the river's west bank. The rest of the patrol withdrew as well, some in the boats, others wading through the water. Miraculously, although the boats were shot full of holes, no one had been hit.[30]

During the day, the weather changed to rain, further swelling the Our and reducing visibility. Patrols again attempted to cross the Our, but were frustrated at every attempt. The men of the 513th were forced to be content with calling down time-on-target artillery barrages on German troops that were spotted in nearby towns. The Germans also continued to harass the 513th with steady artillery fire.[31]

Because patrols were unsuccessful in crossing the river, Colonel Miller ordered forward observation posts established near the waterline. Miller instructed

PFC Dahlberg to take a sound-powered telephone down to the river and report any sign indicating the enemy was mounting a counterattack. Accompanied by Cogan and Brewer, Dahlberg went down the steep bank to a position a couple hundred yards from the river and there they started to dig in. The enemy soon spotted their position, however, and began mortaring them. The first round landed about twenty-five yards from their foxhole. The next only half that distance. "We better get out of here!" Dahlberg told his buddies. The three leapt from the hole and started running up the bank. The next shell landed right in the hole. Several more direct hits followed. Obviously, it wasn't safe along the river.

While on duty in another observation post, PFC Pierce noted that at around 1600 hours every day, a German soldier would emerge from his pillbox, walk towards the river to a gully, turn around, drop his pants, and relieve himself. Pierce mentioned the regularity of the enemy soldier's activity in passing to a friend in B Company who was a sniper.

"Well," his buddy told him, "stick around and we'll get that guy."

The next day, the sniper – equipped with a Springfield rifle upon which was mounted a telescopic sight – joined Pierce in his OP. Right on schedule, the German emerged from his bunker, walked to the gully, turned around, and dropped his pants. Just as the man squatted down, the sniper killed him. An exciting prospect at first, for Pierce the killing of the German was an anticlimax.

That night, Dahlberg, Cogan, and Brewer slept in the CP. They had decided that Brewer would pull the first guard, so the other two went to bed while Brewer stood vigil from the door. An enemy mortar shell came in suddenly and exploded in the doorway. Dahlberg and Cogan found Brewer lying prone with half of his head apparently torn away, but still alive. Evacuated, Brewer died of his wounds on 12 February 1945.

Early on the morning of the fifth, a patrol of the 2nd Battalion succeeded in crossing the river but were discovered when they tried to close on an enemy outpost. A hand-to-hand fight ensued in which an enemy NCO and three others were killed. The patrol suffered four men injured, all of whom returned with the patrol.[32]

As the days passed, the Germans became increasingly sensitive to the Americans' patrols. Edgy German gunners loosed bursts at the slightest sound in the darkness and fired flares that lit up the river like daylight. The weather, too, made patrolling more arduous. The temperature was rising and the swollen river was filled with small icebergs. A 1st Battalion patrol attempting to cross the river in boats was capsized by the heavy ice flows and the swift current and one trooper drowned.[33]

On 6 February, since patrols had not been able to force a breach in the Siegfried Line defenses, the Air Corps was called in to bomb them. PFC Pierce heard about the time of planned bombardment and, not wanting to miss another good show, climbed out of the third-story dormer window of a house overlooking the Our River and, holding on to chimney for balance, he perched himself on the peak of the roof.

At about 1445 hours, several P-47 Thunderbolts and P-51 Mustangs came roaring in over the town. Their target was a pair of German pillboxes situated across the river from Pierce's position. One by one the fighters swept down from the overcast and dropped napalm canisters on the German positions. Sheets of yellow flame and clouds of black smoke erupted around the pillboxes in a marvelous spectacle. Private Lightcap watched the planes from a spot near the battalion CP. From his vantage point, he couldn't see the bombs drop, but, after each plane passed, he did see the rising flames and smoke from the explosions. Not long after the fighter-bomber attacks ended, however, the same German guns the planes had been trying to knock out were throwing shells back over at the 2nd Battalion.

Earlier that afternoon, PFC Harry Goldfarb was called to the company CP. "There were only ten of us there," said Goldfarb, "and Lieutenant Fann gets a notice from headquarters: 'Send somebody back to Chalons-sur-Marne because the duffel bags came in this evening. Somebody's got to take care of the duffel bags'." Lieutenant Fann sent Goldfarb, a move that the soldier – weakened by the GIs – considered a great favor; the routine of patrols, river crossings, and constant shelling was dragging on, taking the lives of more men every day. When Goldfarb arrived in Chalons, he went through the duffel bags of the men who had been killed looking for clean underwear. "They couldn't use [it] anymore," reasoned Goldfarb. "I don't think they would have minded."

On the evening of 6 February, recalled Major Edwards, Colonel Miller, "got mad at the goddamned mess hall crew." Apparently, Miller had concluded that they had not pulled their share of the combat load. "You people have been doing nothing," he shouted at them. "You're gonna patrol tonight." According to one of F Company's machine-gunners, Private Richard Murray, the men of the mess section always said they wanted to go on a patrol. Now, like it or not, it had been arranged.

Miller gathered all the other rear echelon people he could find, even F Company's former supply sergeant, now a private, Willis Adams. Some of the mess crew asked Private Murray if he would go along, too, and he agreed. The patrol, eleven men all together, was led by 1st Lieutenant John W. Leary, 2nd Battalion's mess officer. Leary's objective was to establish a small "bridgehead across a long narrow strip of land edged by the Our River."[34]

The patrol waded across the river without a hitch. The river was shallow at the crossing point and there were several sand bar islands, however; the water was ice-cold. On the enemy shore, the men came upon a big pill-box. It was unoccupied, so Lieutenant Leary ordered the men forward toward another concrete-and-iron bunker. Surrounding it, the troopers groped in the snow and dark for communications wires leading from the bunker, hoping to cut them and isolate the Germans inside. From the noise the Germans inside were making, it sounded like a they were having a party and had no idea the paratroopers were outside. Wires were found and cut, then the troopers blew open the bunker with grenades and a bazooka round, killing at least three of the Germans inside. A second compartment was blasted with the bazooka. "We tried to pull it open," recalled Murray, but the Germans "were on the inside pulling it closed." Leary ordered the men to ignore the trapped Germans and instead make the area as secure as possible in order to establish the bridgehead.[35]

At that moment, one of the lookouts shouted, "Here comes the whole German army." A group of about twenty Germans, who were approaching rapidly, spotted the paratroopers and opened fire. Leary's men leveled a devastating fire of their own, however, and beat the Germans back. Shortly thereafter, the Germans counterattacked again in twice the strength. The patrol was holding its own "and a company was about to enter boats to reinforce them," when suddenly, Colonel Miller ordered the patrol to withdraw. Leary's men bolted down the steep bank into the river with the Germans giving chase. Though they were under fire, all of the men returned, wading back to the western shore, all except for Lieutenant Leary.[36]

Many in the patrol had been hit, and Dahlberg, Cogan, and a couple other troopers were sent to carry one of the wounded up the steep hill from the river. The man had been shot in the stomach and was damn mad about it, swearing "like a sailor." 1st Lieutenant John W. Leary's body was left on the enemy side of the river. Listed as missing in action, Leary was posthumously awarded the Silver Star. Sadly, nothing was gained by his sacrifice.[37]

On the night of 9 February, the 513th received orders to withdraw and for its positions to be turned over to elements of the 6th Armored Division. Relief of the 513th was soon begun by the 184th Engineer Combat Battalion and was completed by 0730 hours the next morning. The 513th then proceeded by motor convoy to an entraining point at Arlon, Belgium for the rail move to Chalons-sur-Marne, France – about thirty miles southeast of Rheims. There, its survivors would begin a period of rest and reorganization. Word of the withdrawal brought profound relief to the men of F Company. Their long ordeal was over, for a while at least.

Before departing, Private Pierce descended the river bank to take one last, long look out across the swollen Our. On the far shore, overlooked by the pillboxes on the heights, the body of the German soldier felled by B Company's sniper still lay in the mud along the river where he had fallen. Pierce's joy was tempered by grief; so many had been killed. He turned his back and walked away.

8

Reorganizing for Varsity

Bivouac Area, Chalons-sur-Marne, France
11 February - 23 March 1945

Upon arriving at the Chalons station, the men were moved the last eight miles to the camp area by truck. At about 1130 hours the next day, Sunday, 11 February 1945, the survivors of Colonel Coutts' regiment closed in their new cantonment near Chalons-sur-Marne, France where they were to reorganize and prepare for the soon to take place Airborne crossing of the Rhine – Operation VARSITY.[1]

There were scarcely enough men left in the regiment to organize a full-strength rifle company. F Company numbered just over a dozen men, 2nd Lieutenant Isham Fann, Sergeant Ben Faulk, Tec 5 Neal Haggard, PFC Ed Costello, PFC Ed Dahlberg, PFC Willie Grice, PFC Russell Hataway, PFC Morris Kelly, PFC Joe Kitson, Private Walter Balben, Private John Cogan, Private Sam Lightcap, Private Richard Murray, and Private James B. Williford. These men, and the rest of the men of the 513th, bore little resemblance to the cocky men who had left England less than two months before. All of them were suffering the effects of exposure, malnutrition, and fatigue.[2]

"Beards, mud, every kind of crud you could think of," said Lightcap. Some men got their first bath in almost eight weeks, "and nobody wanted to get out of the water either." Haggard hadn't put his grimy fingers in his mouth since Christmas, and, during his shower, all of his fingernails came off. He also discovered a small shrapnel wound in his shoulder. After seeing his friends maimed and killed, he figured it wasn't worth a Purple Heart so, he never reported the wound to the medics. Later, when he needed the extra five points to get him home, he would wish that he had.

On 13 February, F Company received its first new replacements, all officers. 1st Lieutenant Harold O. Diefenderfer took over 1st Lieutenant Sam Dean's job as company Executive Officer. 2nd Lieutenant Spencer G. Stanley, Jr. took Lieutenant Puckett's place as the new Third Platoon assistant. 2nd Lieutenant Francis C. Selzer was assigned as assistant to the recently promoted 1st Lieutenant Fann who took over Second Platoon. 2nd Lieutenant John A. Royston also joined, but would eventually be transferred to Headquarters, 2nd Battalion on 14 March. Arriving with the other officers was Captain Reynolds who had gone AWOL from the hospital in England in order to rejoin the company. Reynolds was elated to see his men and, according to Private Altmiller – who had been evacuated with the flu shortly before the regiment was relieved – told all of them, "You're entitled to a Purple Heart if you want it."[3]

Reynolds sent Lieutenant Fann, who had the flu, to the hospital, and put PFCs Sarrell and Dahlberg on KP. Still passing blood, Dahlberg at first could hardly even swing an ax to chop firewood. However, after a week or two of "good Army chow," he began to feel better. Returning to duty from the hospital, Sarrell discovered KP could be almost as dangerous as combat. When one of the other KPs was ordered to boil water, he inadvertently picked up a five gallon jerry can of gasoline and began pouring that into a pot. The resulting fire burned the mess hall down.[4]

It wasn't until 5 March, that F Company's regular mess crew was assigned. Among them was Tec 4 Henry Contreras, just eighteen years old and fresh from Ft. Benning. Contreras hailed from Mt. Rose, Colorado – "peach and apple country." They went to work right away. Up before dawn, the men prepared their small, four-burner gas stoves and started making the pancake batter. Breakfasts included sausage, bacon, toast, coffee, milk, and grapefruit juice. Dinners were mostly roast beef. While the mess crew made the practice jump, and trained with the company once in a while, they spent most of their days preparing meals for the rest if the men. In the evenings, while some of the cooks prepared for the next morning's meal, the rest ran around with the other men.[5]

After spending some five weeks in a general hospital at Metz, First Sergeant Donovan, arrived at Chalons on 14 February. He was astounded by the evidence of the casualties. "All but two tents on the company street were deserted," he remembered. He was further upset when he discovered all of F Company's morning reports had been destroyed when a shell had hit Captain Reynolds' jeep trailer. Donovan spent the next two weeks down at Division Headquarters, which had set up shop in old French army barracks in the village, resurrecting them. Returning with Donovan were Altmiller, Bassett, Sorenson, Harry Cook, Jack Cook, DePiero, Lloyd Elliott, Ramsey and Bob Greenstrand.[6]

After being evacuated on 6 January with frozen feet, PFC Bob Greenstrand was moved first to a hospital, then to Le Harve by train for evacuation to England – everyone on board had gotten a shot of penicillin – in the rump – every few hours regardless of the injury. Greenstrand felt a little embarrassed, though, when he compared his injuries to those of the some of the other men on the train. In Le Harve, German PWs loaded the wounded onto a hospital ship for the short trip across the Channel. After arriving in England, he was moved by another train to yet another hospital. There, Greenstrand was reunited with Sergeant Ray McClain from his own Second Platoon who had been shot in the thumb at Mande-St.-Etienne on 4 January. It was a short-lived reunion, however; Greenstrand was soon moved to a ward for men with frostbite injuries.[7]

"At the hospital," Greenstrand recalled, "men with frozen feet, trench foot, or frost bite were kept in a room with most of the windows open and the entire area that was frost bitten was never covered with sheets or blankets. Believe me, it got quite chilly in there. Guess they wanted to have the feet thaw out gradually because all we were supposed to do was rub them with mineral oil to get the circulation going. Mine came along quite well with the exception of the big toe on my right foot, and my left heel."[8]

A couple of weeks passed, and Greenstrand was enjoying the rest, and, therefore, was in no hurry to leave. One day, however, the doctor told him, "If that toe isn't better in a couple of days we'll have to take it off." Rather than being alarmed by the news, Greenstrand thought it was a good deal, just the thing to keep him out of combat. When the doctor had moved on to another patient, the nurse asked him quietly, "Greenstrand, are you sure you want to lose that toe? You could be a club foot, you know? The balance of your body is in you big toe." Now he was alarmed. Combat was one thing, walking funny the rest of his life was another. "Get that doctor back!" Greenstrand blurted out.

The nurse called the doctor over. "Doc," asked Greenstrand, "What can I do to save it?"

"No more than you've been doing," replied the doctor.

"I haven't been doing anything," Greenstrand answered. After the doctor gave him a good chewing out, he told Greenstrand to massage the toe with mineral oil. "Hell, I rubbed that thing till the skin came off," he recalled. A couple of days of this treatment, and the doctor proclaimed, "I think you did it, that toe is starting to look better."[9]

Greenstrand was discharged from the hospital in March, but, much to his disappointment, he wasn't going home. "I was going back to the 17th Airborne and more combat," he said. When Greenstrand hit the first replacement depot, he, and every other man from the 17th, was hustled right through. He wasn't happy about going back to combat, but he was comforted in the thought that he would soon be in the company of his old friends again.[10]

A day or so after settling into his new home at Chalons, he heard someone outside the tent ask, "Does anybody in here know how Bob Greenstrand was killed?" Greenstrand got up and went outside to see who was asking and found Max Gronewold, a boyhood friend from Grenada, Minnesota. After the eighth grade they kind of lost touch with each other – Gronewold quit school to help on the farm and Greenstrand moved to Blue Earth. When they enlisted – because they lived in separate counties – neither knew that the other had joined the 17th Airborne. When an article about Greenstrand appeared in a local paper, Gronewold's father wrote his son to tell him that Greenstrand was in F Company, 513th Parachute Infantry. Max told his buddy that when his regiment was on the line in the Bulge, a group from the 513th passed through their lines. When Max found out that it was F Company, he asked if anyone knew Bob Greenstrand and was told that Greenstrand had been killed. "Well, I wasn't dead and it had been some time since [we] had done any partying, so we each got passes and went to Nancy, France," remembered Greenstrand. "We really made up for lost partying."[11]

Along with the old timers returning to duty on 14 February, forty-three enlisted replacements joined the company. Among the new men were Privates Robert E. Guiles, Kenneth O. Olson, Anthony J. Rybka, and Donald K. Shay.

Private Olson, from Clear Lake, Wisconsin, had put in for a transfer out of the Army Air Forces because he wanted to see some action. He was assigned to the Third Platoon.[12]

PFC Don Shay was assigned to Third Platoon as well, third squad. Shay had entered service in June 1943 and, after basic training at Camp McQuade, California, he was assigned to a Coast Artillery battery near Port Townsend, Washington.

The unit was broken up a few months later and, in the spring of 1944, Shay was sent to Camp Barkley, Texas to be retrained on 155mm guns. The weather was too hot in Abilene and there were too many rattlesnakes, so Shay decided to apply for parachute training at Fort Benning. There, Shay met LeRoy Siegfried from Pennsylvania who landed in F Company as well. After training, Shay, Siegfried, and many other replacements departed by ship for Scotland on Christmas Eve, 1944. After six days at sea, the men were moved by troop train to Southampton where they boarded LSTs to cross the English Channel. The voyage was miserable; Shay and Siegfried were in the bottom of the boat with about six inches of water, a lot of sick soldiers, and plugged toilets. "Not a very good beginning," remarked Shay.

The next day, 15 February, 1st Lieutenant James J. Joyce, Jr. joined F Company as the new First Platoon leader. 2nd Lieutenant Richard B. Cross, his assistant platoon leader, was assigned to the company the same day, but was replaced on 12 March by 2nd Lieutenant William K. Wieland. Wieland "was a thin man with sort of a baby face with pimples on it," one trooper recalled. However, the men of the First Platoon soon dubbed him 'Wild Bill' because he had a tendency to go a little wild. "Boy did he get mad when the men called him Wild Bill," said the men. That evening, after the new men had made camp as comfortable as they could, they joined the old timers in enjoying a battalion party.[13]

On 16 February, after an inspection by Colonel Miller earlier that day, a further thirty-nine replacements joined F Company. These included Private William C. Bergmann, Private John E. Cobb, and Private Maurice C. Cuthbertson.

Private Cuthbertson, from Lisbon, New Hampshire, was twenty-seven, and married with a son and two little girls. He had had a deferment, but volunteered anyway.

Private Cobb was a young, good looking kid from Bridgeton, New Jersey. He had been in no rush to enlist, but he had made the mistake of telling a high school teacher whose husband was the head of the local draft board to go to hell. "She used to come down every day and ask me how old I was," Cobb recalled. "I turned eighteen on a Monday morning. I went and registered at eleven o'clock and when I got home that night my questionnaire was there. I got out of school June the sixth and I was in the Army June the seventh."[14]

At the induction center, Cobb first chose the Marine Corps, but he was refused. "Well, I want to be in the Navy," said Cobb. "No no no," said the sergeant, shaking his head. "You'll make a good infantryman." That was that. At Fort Dix, the call was raised for paratroopers. Cobb said to himself, I want to get the hell out of this infantry. I don't want to walk. "I never walked again," Cobb remarked with a laugh recalling that day. "I ran!"

After jump school, Cobb and the other replacements were sent by sea to Glasgow, Scotland, by train to London, and then by sea again across the English Channel to France. After a night's rest, they were trucked up close enough to the front to hear the sound of the guns. It was the Battle of the Bulge, they were told, but this information didn't seem to mean much to the men. Early the next morning, 16 February 1945, they arrived in Chalons-sur-Marne. The camp looked almost deserted. Cobb asked one of the NCOs, "Where in the hell is everybody at?"

"There's seven guys here," said the sergeant – only seven men left of the whole original company. The others, the sergeant added, "They're killed or in the hospital."

Private Kenny Halter, another F Company replacement who was also from Bridgeton looked at Cobb, his face a portrait of regrets. "What the shit did we get ourselves into?"

"Well," Cobb asked the sergeant, "what are we supposed to do?"

"Just go anywhere you want," the NCO said in an even tone, "in a little while they'll be coming back." Cobb, who sensed that the sergeant understood their anxiety, went and got something to eat at the single mess hall.

From Sedalia, Missouri, Private Bill Bergmann was inducted into the Army on 6 June 1944 at Ft. Leavenworth, Kansas. Impressed by the sharp appearance of troopers performing an exhibition jump at Camp Blanding, and drawn by the promise of jump pay, Bergmann and several other men volunteered for parachute training. After graduating The Parachute School on 24 November 1944 – what Bergmann described as a "glorious moment" – and a short leave, he and his buddies were shipped to Europe as replacements for the 17th Airborne Division at Chalons. On his way to his billet, they encountered "several questionable characters walking around the campsite who needed haircuts, shaves and clean uniforms." The next morning, he discovered that the "shaggy characters" they'd seen the night before were, in fact, F Company's survivors.[15]

By 17 February, F Company's strength had grown to 144 officers and men and more men arrived almost every day. For the first week or so, however, there was no attempt at any serious training. Instead the men played a lot of football. Cobb, being in the First Platoon, didn't know too many men from the other platoons except for Halter, but he met Johnnie Rutherford playing football, and then soon met Joe Kitson and Russell Hataway, who used to come up to First Platoon's area at night and sing. Kitson said he was from New York, but Cobb believed he was actually from Connecticut. Hataway was from Dry Prong, Louisiana, but the no one had said anything about Rebels since the company left the States.

When new replacements came in, Captain Reynolds lined them all up in front of the men who'd gone through the Bulge and said, "If you want to know anything about goddamned combat, you ask them. They went though it. They deserve the Congressional Medal of Honor." In the beginning, however, the new men only asked what Private Lightcap considered "stupid questions, like, "How many Germans did you shoot?" or "Did you use bayonets on 'em?" "Bayonets your ass!" replied some of the old timers. For their part, the veterans tried to impart what they considered critical advice, "Dig your holes fast and deep. Keep your head down. Cover your ass."

The veteran men in the company were dubious of the new officers, their Fort Benning tactics, and all the parade ground drilling they were now being put through, and they viewed the replacements dimly. "These are punks," thought Laufer. "They don't even know what it's all about yet." Bob Greenstrand admitted, though, that their inexperience gave them one advantage over the old F Company men: the new men followed orders immediately – during attacks especially. In combat it was often vital that men carried out orders like reflex reactions. The old timers, however, now often paused a split second to consider a command before moving. In later fighting, Greenstrand witnessed a couple of men get killed because they hesitated. "That didn't necessarily make the replacements better soldiers," said Greenstrand, "but it often made them safer soldiers." Many of the old timers stuck with the guys they knew and let the replacements fend for themselves, but some veterans soon began to forge new friendships. For example, PFC Laufer befriended PFC Ferdinand Aguirres from Raleigh, North Carolina. He and some of the other old timers nicknamed him "Pancho."[16]

Private Laufer had returned to duty on 25 February. When doctors in England offered to recommend he be assigned to a non-combat unit, Laufer declined. He wanted to go home – back to the 17th and back to F Company – and he was glad that his best buddy, Willie Grice, was there when he arrived. However, Laufer was not as pleased with the campsite. Cold and miserable, "Chalons-sur-Marne," as far as Private Laufer was concerned, "was just like the rest of France – a shit hole."

Whether or not conditions actually were so dire, the village of Chalons, surrounded by small farms, was typical of rural France, and the camp, three or four miles south of the village, was just a tent city. Just off post was a small farmhouse. A manure pile, usually swarming with flies, resided comfortably in the yard. When it rained, and it did frequently, the manure ran down into the street in brown currents. Disgusting as it was to Laufer, he couldn't escape it. All the local farms were identical. On the bright side, this farmer allowed the men to swim in his pond. Better yet, the farmer had a couple of attractive daughters. Nothing ever developed with them, however. When Captain Reynolds found out about them, they were put off limits at the farmer's insistence.[17]

Reynolds, in fact, had his hands full taking care of his men, and it was staggering how fast some of them could get into trouble. When Reynolds sent him and another trooper into town to get haircuts, Cobb recalled, they both landed in jail.

On the way into Chalons, they were picked up by MPs. "Where's your Eisenhower jackets?" the policemen asked.

"I just got over here, overseas," said Cobb. "All I've got is my combat jacket."

"Well," replied the MP, "you're not allowed to come to town in a field jacket."

"But I got to get a haircut," Cobb insisted, showing the MP his pass.

"Okay," said the MP, looking Cobb up and down. "You're from F Company too?" the MP asked the other trooper.

"Yeah."

"Well, let me see your pass," ordered the MP, sticking out an open hand at Cobb's companion. The MP looked over the passes, comparing the signatures. "Well, one of you's passes ain't no good," he said, "Which one of you's is it?"

"Mine's all right," Cobb blurted out. The other trooper insisted that his was all right, too.

"Well," the MP said flatly, "you're both going to jail."

After spending the night in a cell, Cobb appeared before the provost marshal.

"What are you doing here?" asked the official.

Cobb saluted him and gave his story. "I came to town to get a hair cut. The MP picked me up, he said I didn't have an OD dress jacket. All I've got is my combat jacket."

"That'll cost you fifteen dollars," announced the officer. Cobb's brief but sincere protestations had, apparently, fallen on deaf ears. Dejectedly, he returned to camp to face Captain Reynolds.

"What did you get thrown in jail for?" asked the Captain.

"I went to get a haircut, and I had a pass, and the other guy had a pass. . ."

"Well, he forged the damn pass," Reynolds disclosed with a huff. "How'd you make out?"

"I got fined fifteen dollars."

"That sonofabitch!" growled the Captain. "Fined you fifteen dollars – for what?"

"Cause I didn't take my hat off after I saluted him."

"Don't worry about it," assured the Captain.

On 6 March, F Company made its first and only practice jump from the new C-46 transport plane, the type which would carry them across the Rhine. The drop was made over a local orchard area, and went off without a hitch. "Within a period of six days, [5-10 March 1945] fifty-six planes of the 313th Group's squadrons jumped 3,246 paratroopers in 125 lifts and carried eighty-seven observers and thirty-nine parabundles." Officially known as the Curtiss C-46 Commando, the C-46 airframe originally had been created for the civilian market. Powered by two 2,000 horsepower Pratt & Whitney R-2800-51 Double Wasp radial piston engines, the C-46 could achieve a maximum airspeed of 269 miles per hour and maintain a fast cruising speed of 183 miles per hour. The first C-46s were delivered to the military on 12 July 1942, but Operation VARSITY would see their first use in a major airborne operation.[18]

Unlike the workhorse C-47 Skytrain with its single port-side jump door, the C-46 had jump doors on both sides of its massive fuselage. Because of the twin doors, twice as many men – about thirty-six – could jump in the same amount of time from the C-46 as could be jumped from the C-47. Designed to accommodate up to fifty-four passengers, it was widely held that the husky C-46 would give the 513th's sky troopers an important tactical advantage in VARSITY: more men would land closer together and, therefore, assemble faster. Having been trained exclusively in the C-47, it was difficult for the men jumping from the "wrong" side of the plane – the starboard side door – to adjust. It felt all wrong, unnatural, men had to concentrate. Men who were assigned to the regiment after 10 March practiced the new "wrong door" exiting technique by jumping out of a stationary C-46 into the back of a deuce-and-a-half.

Several faults accompanied the C-46's advantages. Pilots, like 1st Lieutenant Robert Kerr, thought the "big rascals" were "easy to fly" at altitude, yet admitted the Commando was not as stable as the C-47. Consequently, it was not easy to fly close to the ground. This problem could make formation flying difficult, especially at jump altitudes of less than eight hundred feet. Even more dangerous was the two thousand pound hydraulic booster system for the control surfaces which utilized an hydraulic fluid with a lower flash point than aviation fuel. If a plane's system sprang an hydraulic leak – and was hit with a tracer – "Friend, you've got one hell of a fire!" commented Kerr. Beyond this was the fact that none of the C-46s of the 313th Troop Carrier Group, the group scheduled to fly the planes in the upcoming Rhine mission, had been refitted with self-sealing fuel tanks. Troopers had minor dislikes, too – they hated the number of internal stowage racks because it allowed for a greater number of door and leg bundles – but these complications not withstanding, the men's first impression of the C-46 was that it was remarkable. However, they still didn't know about the planes other faults.[19]

After the practice jumps were completed on 10 March, Combat Infantryman's Badges were presented to the men of the 513th; Captain Reynolds distributed the CIBs to F Company's old timers. During the regimental review on 13 March, the Silver Star and Bronze Star medals were presented to General Miley. The sight made some of the men choke. To these men, Miley had performed no acts of valor deserving such recognition, while those that had, like PFC Bill Gibbs who had been killed in action of 4 January, had received no such honors.

On 15 March, the men embarked on an intense schedule with the regimental field tactical problem. Besides their practical aspects – developing unit cohesion and technical expertise – sports and training kept the men busy. "The busier you are," commented Private Laufer, rationalizing the Army way, "the more tired you are and the faster you go to sleep so you don't think very much." Training also served to keep the men from dwelling on what might happen when they got to Germany.

1st Lieutenant Sam Calhoun returned to duty on 18 March. It had been quite an odyssey. Wounded on 4 January, Calhoun was evacuated to the 101st Airborne Division's field hospital in Bastogne where medics redressed his wound, administered a gas gangrene shot, gave him sulfanilamide tablets, began a series of fourteen penicillin shots, and tagged him with a record of his shots and treatment. The medics told Calhoun that, if he lost his tag, they would start the series of shots all over again. Calhoun, therefore, was careful not to loose it. In the morning, Calhoun was moved via ambulance to another hospital located forty miles to the rear. Upon arrival, he was put-up in the basement ward and there, in the dark, he waited with several other men and tried to get a little sleep.

Some time later, Calhoun was awakened by an argument between some doctors and a trooper in the basement's stairway. The doctors were yelling for someone to sedate the man. When the shouting finally subsided, a doctor descended to the dark basement and in a soft voice he asked for Lieutenant Calhoun. Calhoun answered and the doctor came to where he was laying. The doctor explained that the commotion had been caused by a trooper who had learned that a German officer was being held in one of the rooms. Hoping to kill the German, the trooper was going around in the dark, indiscriminately stabbing patients. Medics had just put the man out with an injection. The doctor explained to Calhoun that an officer was needed to protect the German prisoner until he reached the next hospital along the line. Calhoun agreed, so they upgraded the lieutenant's status from walking wounded to a litter case, giving him a high priority for evacuation and Calhoun and the German officer, a real litter case, were put on the next ambulance.

The next hospital was a converted schoolhouse in which the classrooms were used as wards, the litters being placed on saw horses. Each ward had five rows of litters, six to a row. Methodically, doctors were working their way from litter to litter, row to row. There, Calhoun turned the German officer over to the medics.

The soldier immediately next to Calhoun in the ward was badly wounded and had been stripped naked. He was unconscious, waiting to be operated on, and there was a lot of giggling by the nurses when they passed him because the soldier had an erection. Every time a nurse passed it, she would reach out and flick the unconscious man's penis with her fingers. A doctor came over and placed a wet towel over the man. "If I'm going to get any work out of you women," he fumed, "I have to do this." Lying there waiting to be put under for his own operation, Calhoun wondered, if he too would have an erection when anesthetized. A nurse came to Calhoun carrying a syringe filled with sodium pentothal. As she stuck him in the vein with the needle she asked him, "Where are you from?"

"California," stated Calhoun.

"Where in California?"

Lieutenant Calhoun was being rolled down the hall by a medic. "Fresno," said the lieutenant.

"What did you say?" the medic asked.

"Fresno," said Calhoun again.

"Why did you say Fresno?" asked the medic curiously.

"The nurse asked me."

"There's no nurse here," replied the medic. It was about 0630 hours and the nurse had asked Lieutenant Calhoun the question more than four hours earlier.

When Calhoun was rolled into his ward, he met several officers from the 2nd Battalion including Lieutenants Gerner, Stositch, Hebert, and Sims. His reunion was cut short, however.

Lieutenant Calhoun was transported by ambulance to Paris to another hospital. In his ward there, Calhoun encountered Corporal John Eibert, F Company's clerk. Eibert had been wounded in the legs by German machine-gun fire on 4 January. Doctors had operated, but Eibert's leg continued to swell even after they'd removed a bullet. An x-ray revealed a second bullet in the same wound which had penetrated more deeply than the first and which was subsequently removed.

From the hospital in Paris, Calhoun was placed in a "fancy" U.S. Army hospital rail car, "with fancy bunk beds and thick mattresses," and started for Le Harve. Near Étampes, the train stopped to take on more wounded. During the stop, a doctor boarded Calhoun's car and, standing near Calhoun's bunk, asked a nurse if there was anyone in the car who might be moved to make room for a more seriously wounded soldier in one of the boxcars whom the doctor believed might die before the train reached Le Harve if he did not receive better accommodations. Calhoun volunteered to give up his place for the other young man. At first the doctor rejected Calhoun's offer citing the fact that the lieutenant was himself a litter case. Calhoun explained that he had been declared such only because he had been needed to protect a German Officer several days before. After giving Calhoun a quick examination, the doctor approved his offer and the two men traded places.

The hospital train arrived at the Le Harve docks where the USS *Saint Olaf* was moored and Calhoun was taken aboard. The next evening, the *Saint Olaf* docked at Southampton where hundreds of ambulances were waiting. Each ambulance was loaded with four patients and then set out, one by one, for one of the scores of American Army hospitals dotting southern England. Calhoun ended up in a hospital in Devon near the English seaside resort of Torbay.

According to official Army policy, if a wounded man could be returned to active service within thirty days, he would only travel as far as the first-line field hospitals for treatment. If the patient required sixty days to heal, he would be sent to first-line general hospitals on the continent. Ninety day patients were sent to hospitals in Britain. The most severely wounded were "ZI'd" – sent to hospitals in the Zone of the Interior (the United States).

The next day, surgeons performed the final operation on Calhoun's shoulder. The doctor was a fellow Californian, from San Francisco, and very friendly. After the operation, the doctor told the nurse that he would check on the wound in three days. This provided Calhoun with an opportunity – he put on his uniform and embarked for Torbay. Torbay was known as the 'Florida of England' because it boasted good beaches, comfortable hotels, and friendly pubs. Calhoun spent two days indulging in all the village could offer and, on the third day, he returned to the hospital. "I must have been pretty drunk," recalled Calhoun, "because the story in the ward was [that] they had men pulling on [my] legs and shoulders to get my boots off. Then they said someone [finally] decided to unlace them!" The next morning, the doctor, making his rounds of the ward, asked the nurse how Calhoun was fairing. "How would I know?" she replied. "He hasn't been here for two days!" The doctor just laughed. "It will be three days before I check him again," he said. Thus informed, Calhoun put his uniform back on and returned to Torbay. He "had met a beautiful English girl. . . whose father worked for an American airline." They were vacationing at the Imperial Hotel. Calhoun spent his nights dancing with the girl, and drinking with her father, and returned to the hospital every third day for his checkup.

After several weeks of this sort of routine, Calhoun's doctor certified him fit for limited duty. Calhoun pleaded to be approved for general duty, however; his outfit was going to make a combat jump, he told the doctor, and that he had to be with them when they did. The doctor finally consented and Calhoun went to the replacement depot at Lichfield, near Birmingham.

Berthed with five other officers, Calhoun sailed for Le Harve on HMS *Langibby Castle*. One of the other officers was a Catholic priest, Father Roncalli who had with him several Sundays' issue of sacramental wine which he generously shared with Calhoun and the other officers. When the men arrived at the replacement center at Le Harve, its commanding officer asked Father Roncalli to celebrate Mass on the next Sunday. But Calhoun and his fellow officers had drunk all the priest's wine on the voyage. Father Roncalli asked about post for any sacramental wine for the Mass, but there was none to be had. "Not to worry," said Father

Roncalli. "We'll go into town and see what we can come up with." Calhoun and Father Roncalli discovered that the only alcoholic beverage available in the town was calvados, a brandy distilled from apple cider. The strong liquor made sweat "pour down" Calhoun's face, but the little Father "would just rub his little round belly and smile while drinking it." It wasn't sacramental wine, the priest said, but he decided it would do.

Calhoun's next stop was the replacement depot at Étampes, France. He was looking forward to his arrival because men returning to the front lines through there usually received a three day pass to Paris. But when the train arrived at the Étampes station, down the platform came a jeep with MPs inside and a loudspeaker that blared, "Lieutenant Calhoun, report to the RTO (rail transport officer)."

Calhoun approached the jeep and was instructed, "Get your baggage and climb in." Calhoun was then driven to a dining hall and told to eat. "As soon as you get done," the MP said, "get back in the jeep. You're going back out on a troop train in about one hour."

"What about my pass to Paris?" Calhoun asked.

All the MP said was, "Sorry."

After Calhoun finished up his meal, the MPs informed him that some three hundred paratroopers had been given passes to Paris and more than half had gone AWOL. Those who had returned were being kept in the guard house to prevent them from going AWOL themselves. Since Lieutenant Calhoun was the only available parachute officer at the center, he was made responsible for shepherding all those in the guard house to the replacement center in Givet, Belgium. When Calhoun returned to the train, MPs marched the 'prisoners' onto the rail platform and into eight 'forty & eight' boxcars behind the train commander's personal coach. The cars forward of this coach were filled with 'legs' – regular infantrymen. "In big shipments," said Calhoun, "paratroopers were separated from non-parachutists to hold down fights and other problems." Calhoun was given a footlocker containing orders and the troopers' records. "The next morning, as we pulled into Paris South Station, all of my AWOL paratroopers came out of the station, through the yard, and loaded into the cars." Now he had three hundred to watch over.

That afternoon, the train pulled into the Metz station. From his car, Calhoun observed fifteen or twenty Frenchmen carrying boxes off of a rail car, one of many pieces of rolling stock which sat on a siding across from his own. The thieves escaped with the boxes through a hole in the fence. Calhoun's car was stopped just across from the open rail car the Frenchmen had been looting. From his vantage point, Calhoun saw it was loaded with cases of American beer, Carling's Black Label to be precise. Many of the men had not seen the American product for months.

Calhoun "notified the troop train commander, a major from the Transportation Corps, [about] what the Frenchmen had been stealing." The train commander told Calhoun, "Put a couple of cases on your car and let the men get what they can. We'll be pulling out in a few minutes." Calhoun first ordered some men to get a case of beer up to the major's car and then the men appropriated two or three cases for each of the other fifteen cars. Just as the last case of brew was being loaded into the cars, an MP jeep raced down the tracks, its siren wailing. The MPs "tried to delay the train for a search, but the train commander" informed them that his schedule required that the train depart immediately. The major then turned and quickly gave the signal to the engineer to go and the train started to move. As the last cars rolled past the frustrated MPs, the men on board pelted them with a storm of empty beer cans.

Lieutenant Calhoun figured the MPs had probably sold the contents of the rail car to French black marketers, and when Calhoun's men began appropriating some of the beer for themselves, the French thieves must have called their MP accomplices. Otherwise, he reasoned, the MPs would never have known.

When Lieutenant Calhoun's train arrived at Givet on 18 March, each airborne division retrieved their men and their records. Calhoun reached Chalons-sur-Marne at 1500 hours. No sooner had he arrived, then he was told to draw his equipment and was issued a bottle of whiskey, because the regiment was moving out at 2000 hours. Calhoun's regular liquor ration was four bottles, but the other officers had already drunk the rest. Reynolds, glad to see his favorite lieutenant, remarked to Calhoun, "You got back two days too late." Calhoun was curious and asked why. "If you'd come back two days earlier," Reynolds continued, "you'd have seen all [Lieutenant Manning's platoon] get decorated for a bayonet charge they hadn't been on." Manning had been awarded the Distinguished Service Cross. Calhoun had received no credit at all for his platoon's action on 4 January, and was damn steamed about it.

Captain Reynolds gave Lieutenant Calhoun Third Platoon with Lieutenant Greg Stanley as his assistant. Lieutenant Fann, Calhoun's old assistant, had received command of the Second Platoon. Fann survived the Bulge unscathed, but many of the men still held a grudge against him for missing the attack on 4 January by sleeping in a barn after a night out on patrol. Nevertheless, Reynolds wanted to leave Fann with the Second Platoon which he had always been with. Lieutenant Calhoun gathered the men of the Third Platoon and introduced himself: "The commander knows me and knows I'm a good leader. From now on, wherever F Company goes, *we* will be in the lead." Then he gave the men his bottle of whiskey.[20]

After dinner, the men "put all their gas masks in a pile in the company street" near the spot one of the men had erected an effigy of Colonel Miller. He had placed a helmet, a .45 holster, and a pair of boots in the street and everybody had saluted it. Then, after a short hop to the Chalons station, F Company's eight officers and 130 enlisted men loaded onto boxcars and, with the rest of the regiment, moved to their marshaling area at Achiet Airdrome, France – code named 'B-54'. "We knew where we were going," Private James Cox remembered. "I was young. . . it was a gung-ho deal."[21]

The regiment arrived the next day and, that evening, "security guards were posted at all entrances to Airstrip B-54 offering the first suggestion that a combat mission was close at hand." By the next morning, 21 March, the field was officially sealed off. The airfield was surrounded by barbed wire fences which were heavily guarded. Haggard was dismayed at being kept under guard like someone expected him and his comrades to run away from combat – worse yet, he was being guarded by more "rear echelon bastards" who would never see combat themselves. According to Private Bill Bergmann, for security against enemy spies, the men were ordered to remove their shoulder patches. "It didn't work, though, he remembered, "for a week we heard Axis Sally inviting us into Germany to be *killed*." The men of the 17th Airborne Division did not know it, but they were about to participate in the last major combat jump of the war.[22]

By February 1945, the Americans and British had once more seized the initiative and had driven all the way to the Rhine. But here they halted, faced with the most formidable river obstacle in Western Europe. Although the Allies were determined to cross the Rhine and enter Germany, the problem was how to cross it, and where.[23]

From its source in Switzerland as far as Cologne, the Rhine is narrow but girded by steep hills and rocky outcrops. For the Allies, therefore, it was necessary to choose crossing sites that would afford them the opportunity to exploit a bridgehead unhindered by difficult terrain. British Field Marshal Sir Bernard Law Montgomery, commander of the 21st Army Group, wanted to make the crossing north of Cologne where the land is flat on both sides of the river and, therefore, suitable for fast, mechanized forces. Simultaneously, American airborne planners had proposed Operation CHOKER, devised to support a crossing the Rhine in the Seventh U.S. Army's sector. However, after careful study of aerial photographs and intelligence reports, and much debate over various strategic considerations, Allied leaders eventually decided to adopt Field Marshal Montgomery's plan to cross the Rhine – Operation VARSITY-PLUNDER.[24]

The city of Wesel, which back in September had been under consideration along with Arnhem as the main target for Operation MARKET-GARDEN, would be the central focal point for the assault. In addition to the advantage offered by the level terrain around Wesel, the city itself was a prize. Wesel was the center of a major communications network and served as a principle artery for the shipment of coal and steel from the factories of the Ruhr to the rest of Germany. Coal barges traveled north on the Rhine to Wesel where the Lippe Lateral Canal, branching eastward just south of Wesel at Lipperdorf, ran to the Dortmund-Ems Canal that itself coursed northward 165 miles to Emden on the North Sea. Germany was in desperate need of Ruhr industrial products. Its second-largest source of such materials, Upper Silesia, was being overrun by the advancing Russian "steamroller." Moreover, Wesel, although small, as the hub of several water, road, and rail networks, would provide the Allies with a number of axes to advance across the northern side of the Ruhr industrial area while simultaneously driving deeper into the German interior. Wesel, therefore, was of premium strategic importance, lending credence to both Montgomery's desire to make his crossing there and to Hitler's wish to hold the west bank of the Rhine opposite Wesel at all costs.[25]

On 5 February, while the 17th Airborne Division was still deployed along the Our River, the first 'official word' of the upcoming Rhine airborne operation reached General Miley who was ordered to send his G-2 and G-3 staffs to conference with General Cutler at First Allied Airborne Army Headquarters. There, these officers found planning for the mammoth operation already at full swing. Meanwhile, several opportunities to 'bounce' the Rhine presented themselves to the Allies in the weeks that followed.[26]

On 10 March, after a grueling and costly month-long advance through the Reichswald, the British Guards Armored Division captured the Rhine town of Xanten. Unfortunately, the Guardsmen were unable to seize the nearby bridge across the Rhine at Wesel, which the Germans had destroyed that morning, and with it any British aspirations of an armored dash across the Rhine. This, perhaps, did not come as too great a disappointment to Field Marshal Montgomery. Undoubtedly, the British would have embraced any opportunity to "bounce the Rhine" had one presented itself to them. However, it was equally clear by this time that Montgomery would stop at nothing to see that his big set-piece crossing of the Rhine went ahead uninterrupted, even if it meant throwing roadblocks in way of his Americans allies.

Just to the south, the Ninth U.S. Army, under the control of 21st Army Group, had already closed on the Rhine during the evening of 1 March where they quickly attempted to seize bridges across the river at Neuss and Oberkassel. Neuss fell that day, but a patrol that crossed the Rhine discovered that the eastern span of the rail bridge there had been blown. Further south, the Oberkassel bridge was destroyed just as American tanks lumbered onto it. On the morning of 4 March, an additional attempt by the 379th Infantry and CCB of the 2nd Armored Division to capture the *Adolf Hitler* Bridge at Krefeld-Uerdingen was held up by the *2nd Fallschirmjäger Division* long enough for the Germans to blow that bridge. Regardless, the Krefeld crossing site, with a "first class highway" running along the east bank, and with the elevated west bank commanding the entire area, was deemed by General William H. Simpson, the commander of the Ninth Army, to be ideal – bridge or no bridge. By leaping the Rhine there, Simpson could turn north, clear the east bank of the Rhine, and drive on the Ruhr rail center Hamm. Simpson was sure a surprise crossing would meet with little opposition because the bulk of the German army was at that time still fighting on the west side of the Rhine. Additionally, Hamm's capture would deny the enemy a vital outlet for Ruhr industrial supplies and place Ninth Army in an excellent position to drive into the heart of Germany. What Simpson soon learned, however, was that any surprise crossing was to be an honor reserved by Montgomery for the British alone.[27]

Simpson's staff tried to gain permission to jump the Rhine at Krefeld, and even asked that an impromptu parachute assault be made on the eastbank to secure the crossing site, but Montgomery ordered Ninth Army to halt claiming he didn't want to get embroiled in urban fighting in the Ruhr. "Well, you get across," said Montgomery, "but then what can you do?" In reality, Montgomery was simply ignoring Simpson. Even before the attack had begun, on 21 January, Montgomery had announced that the Rhine crossing was to be the exclusive affair of the British

Second Army. And though under pressure Montgomery finally conceded a role for the Ninth Army in his upcoming set-piece crossing, he had no intention of being upstaged by the Americans before PLUNDER had gotten under way. "Had I been under General Bradley," fumed the usually mild Simpson, "I would have just sent a division over there, just like that, but being under Montgomery [I could not]. Right from the start he made it very plain that if he had a plan to do anything, he didn't want anybody to do anything to interfere with that plan." Perhaps the last great opportunity to shorten the war and save countless lives had been sacrificed to save British prestige.[28]

Typical Montgomery set piece, VARSITY-PLUNDER would be undertaken on a grand scale rivaling the Normandy invasion in size and complexity. The operation was composed of an amphibious crossing of the Rhine, to take place on the night of 23 March, and a coordinated airborne assault taking place the next morning at 1000 hours. PLUNDER, the amphibious component of the operation, called for elements of Montgomery's 21st Army Group to cross the river at three points opposite twenty miles of generally level ground east of the Rhine. XXX Corps was to cross opposite Rees, XII Corps opposite Xanten, and 1st Commando Brigade opposite Wesel. The Ninth U.S. Army would cross south of Wesel. PLUNDER would be covered by a "colossal smoke screen," stretching some sixty-six miles from Nijmagen, in Holland, to Dusseldorf. Behind this veil rolled LCMs, LCVPs, and trucks hauling innumerable tons of supply and men to the Rhine. What's more, the attack would be supported by the largest Allied artillery preparation of the war – 65,261 rounds eventually would be fired from eleven hundred guns parked "hub to hub" – beginning on the afternoon of the twenty-third and continuing on through the night.[29]

VARSITY, the airborne component of the operation, envisioning the largest single day airborne assault ever attempted, was designed to assist the amphibious troops in securing their bridgeheads around Wesel and bring to bear the maximum weight of troops in the bridgehead area as quickly as possible. VARSITY's main objective was the enemy gun area in the Diersfordter Wald, forested high ground between Wesel in south and the British bridgehead at Rees in the north. To this end, the sky men would be dropped "slap on top" of the enemy. The second objective was the capture of the bridges over the Issel River, northeast of Wesel, to prevent German reinforcements from interfering with the crossing until enough force had been mustered on the eastern bank of the Rhine to begin a breakout onto the Northern German Plain. Lastly, VARSITY's airborne men were to prevent enemy troops in Wesel from being used against the bridgehead.[30]

The strategic goals of Operation MARKET-GARDEN, the botched British invasion of Holland in September 1944, were almost identical to those of VAR-SITY-PLUNDER – namely, the seizing of a bridgehead over the lower Rhine from which the Allies could swing east across the Northern German Plain, encircle the Ruhr, and force a speedy end to the war. Vital for MARKET-GARDEN's success had been three consecutive days of adequate flying weather in which to drop all the airborne men, and a rapid link-up of the advancing ground forces and British Airborne sixty-four miles distant at Arnhem. Neither of these conditions were met and MARKET-GARDEN foundered. However, the hard lessons taught the Allies in MARKET-GARDEN served as a guide to the planners of VARSITY-PLUN-DER.

In a memorandum to General Eisenhower dated 22 December 1944, General Louis Brereton, Commander of the First Allied Airborne Army, advocated changes in airborne doctrine in light of the recent failure of airborne and ground forces to achieve the vital link-up during Operation MARKET-GARDEN.[31]

"[The enemy] has the ability to reinforce any threatened area quickly. Therefore, it is vital that the Airborne thrust be joined with the ground thrust in a minimum of time to avoid undue losses. The armament of airborne troops does not permit sustained operations against a prolonged attack by heavy weapons and armored forces."[32]

Operation VARSITY-PLUNDER left little to chance in this regard. VARSITY's airborne forces would be landed only after a bridgehead had been successfully established by 21st Army Group. Additionally, airborne forces could be supported by Allied artillery firing from the west bank of the Rhine.

Though it ultimately failed, MARKET, the airborne portion of the Holland operation, had successfully demonstrated that daylight operations were possible and, therefore, VARSITY, like MARKET, would take place in daylight. Also, contributing to MARKET-GARDEN's downfall was its air plan which spread the British 1st Airborne Division's lifts – as well as those of the American 82nd and 101st Airborne Divisions – over several days and, therefore, prevented a rapid build up of forces in the Arnhem bridgehead area. British and Polish Airborne forces were committed piecemeal to the battle and, although they fought gallantly, were ultimately destroyed. In light of the Arnhem failure, the framer of VARSITY's air plan, Air Vice-Marshal Scarlett-Streatfield, stated, "In future operations against an organized enemy, it may be found necessary to complete the entire lift within a matter of hours, landing every essential unit or load before the enemy can assess the situation, and not relying on airborne reinforcement or resupply." According to historian Martin Middlebrook, this was Scarlett-Streatfield's blueprint for the Rhine operation. In VARSITY, all American and British parachute and gliderborne forces, more than 21,700 men, were to be landed within about two hours. Their mission was not to establish an airhead in the enemy's rear but to, in the words of General 'Shan' Hackett, who had commanded the ill-fated 4th Parachute Brigade at Arnhem, effect a "dramatic extension in depth of a bridgehead already established." In fact, PLUNDER's forces, elements of the 1st Commando Brigade and the 15th Scottish Division of the 2nd Army, were to begin crossing the Rhine the evening before the jump to established a bridgehead and capture Wesel.[33]

VARSITY was to involve two Allied airborne divisions of the American XVIII Airborne Corps under the command of Lieutenant General Matthew B. Ridgeway, the American 17th Airborne Division and the British 6th Airborne Division. More than 3,100 planes and gliders, flying from sixteen airfields in the Paris area and eleven fields in East Anglia, would be flying the airborne men into battle.[34]

The 6th Airborne Division was commanded by Major General E. L. Bols who was handed the division on 8 December 1944 by its former commander, Major General Richard "Windy" Gale (for VARSITY, Gale would act as both executive under Ridgeway at XVIII Corps Headquarters, and replace Major General F. A. M. 'Boy' Browning as GOC, 1 Airborne Corps). After the British 1st Airborne Division was destroyed at Arnhem during MARKET-GARDEN, Browning was reassigned to Lord Mountbatten's Staff in the Far East.[35]

The 6th Airborne Division, a veteran outfit that had fought in Normandy, had, like the American 17th, been rushed to Belgium during the Battle of the Bulge. Arriving on Boxing day, 1944, the division spent more than a month in combat, eventually capturing the villages of Bures and Wavreille, and following the retreating enemy all the way to the banks of the Maas River near Venlo, Germany. Near the end of February, the division was moved to England's Salisbury Plain to begin exercises in preparations for what it hoped would be its last jump. 6th Airborne's mission was to disrupt the enemy defenses overlooking the crossing points and to capture the three bridges over the Issel River. To achieve its mission, 3rd Para Brigade would be landed atop the enemy defenses in the Diersfordter Wald, 5th Para Brigade would land and defend the division area from the north, and lastly, 6th Airlanding Brigade would arrive, "in their gliders, by battalions, to capture the crossings over the Issel and the village of Hamminkeln."[36]

At the same time, the 17th Airborne would begin landing on drop zones and landing zones south of the 6th Airborne sector. The mission given to the 17th Airborne Division was:

> "To drop during Daylight on D-Day; seize, clear and secure the Division Area with priority to the high ground East of DIERSFORDT in the general area (181449 - 183443 - 191441), and the bridges over the Issel River from (253439) to (235458) (both inclusive); protect the right (South) flank of the Corps; establish contact with the 1st Commando Brigade, the 12th British Corps and the 6th British Airborne Division. Objectives will be held at all costs."[37]

To accomplish their mission, the division planned to drop the 507th Combat Team – consisting of the 507th Parachute Infantry Regiment and the 464th Parachute Field Artillery Battalion – at 1000 hours onto DZ W, an area on the south side of the Diersfordter Wald near Fluren. There, the regiment would be in position to clear the southern portion of the forest and the high ground east of Diersfordt, and protect the right flank of the XVIII Airborne Corps area. The 513th Combat Team – composed of the 513th Parachute Infantry Regiment and the 466th Parachute Field Artillery Battalion – would drop next, at 1010 hours, onto DZ X. It was to clear the high ground east of Diersfordt and defend along the Issel Canal. The 194th Combat Team – composed of the 194th Glider Infantry Regiment and the 681st Glider Field Artillery Battalion – would land at 1030 hours in assault gliders on Landing Zone (LZ) S. It would secure bridges along the Issel Canal and protect the right flank of the XVIII Airborne Corps' area. Special Troops and Division Headquarters would land last on LZ N. The four DZs and the six LZs in the XVIII Airborne Corps zone were sited on fields or meadows, some two hundred to three hundred yards in length, and the entire area was only some five miles wide and six miles long. Although reconnaissance photographs revealed no 'Rommel Asparagus,' had been placed in the DZs and LZs, they were "criss-crossed with drainage ditches and wire fences."[38]

Colonel Coutts' orders to the 513th, stated in Field Order No. 16, were put forth simply: The regiment was to land at H-Hour on Drop Zone 'X', to occupy the area of their objective, and to hold it at all costs. Upon landing, Lieutenant Colonel Miller's 2nd Battalion troopers were to move to their objective in the heart of the Diersfordter Wald, clear it, and hold at all costs while contacting adjacent units, establishing protected roadblocks, and preparing counter attack plans to prevent enemy penetrations of the regimental zone from the west, southwest, and north-west. 2nd Battalion was to maintain patrols in its area of responsibility and recon-noiter the village of Schuttwick to determine if it was occupied by enemy troops and, if so, determine their strength and manner disposed.[39]

3rd Battalion's objective was to seize and hold the Issel Canal east of the proposed drop zones where Colonel Kent's men would tie in with British Airborne to the north. The battalion was to prepare for counterattacks from the east, north-east, and southeast and reconnoiter the village of Unter-Bauerschaft to determine if it was occupied by the Germans, determining their strength and manner dis-posed there. Both the 2nd and 3rd Battalions had a demolitions section attached.

1st Battalion would initially be 'combat team reserve,' ready to defend against counterattacks from the northwest, north, and northeast while reconnoitering to the north to determine whether British 6th Airborne troops were occupying their correct zone. If no contact was made, 1st Battalion was to push on to Hamminkeln, about five miles north of Wesel, to determine if the town was occupied by German infantry or armored units.[40]

The 466th Parachute Field Artillery Battalion would begin landing at H+8 minutes. It was to support the advance of the 513th Parachute Infantry Regiment's 2nd, 3rd, and 1st Battalions, in that order of priority, while being prepared to en-gage any enemy armored units attacking from the north or south. The 139th Air-borne Engineer Battalion, also attached to the regiment, was to begin landing on Drop Zone 'N' at H+1 hour and was to seize and clear the enemy from its area of responsibility. Battery C, 155th Airborne Antitank Battalion was to provide anti-tank protection for the regiment with special consideration given to enemy pen-etrations from the north and northeast.[41]

Upon landing, the glider pilots of the 440th, 441st, 442nd, and the 314th Troop Carrier Groups, carrying the division's 194th Glider Infantry Regiment to landing zones south of the 513th's, would be attached to the 513th and were to dig in in their assigned areas east of Diersfordt, in the 139th Engineer Battalion's zone, and defend themselves there. Also, all organizations down to platoon level were to maintain a reserve to defeat counterattacks, and battalions and attached units were to dispatch two messengers each to the regimental command post as soon as possible after landing. Radio silence would be maintained until H-Hour.[42]

Planning progressed rapidly as did the build up of supplies. Non-table of organization equipment – such as British leg bags, 57mm recoilless rifles (known to the men as the 'Shoulder 57'), yellow fluorescent handkerchiefs, BAR containers, hand grenades, and M1919A6 .30 caliber machine-guns – was obtained and distributed. Two K rations and one D ration would be issued to each man before the drop, and battalions were ordered to carry with them three-days supply of fresh batteries for the signal equipment.

270 tons of supplies of all categories would be dropped on D-Day by B-24 bombers flying from the United Kingdom, and a further 540 tons would be dropped on D+1. For the operation, 633 tons of ammunition were stockpiled for the division. 2,005 vehicles were required to transport the division's overland tail – carrying radios, crew served weapons, and other critical supplies as well as a further two hundred tons of ammunition – the 246 miles to the Rhine.[43]

On 19 March, the 313th Troop Carrier Group, that had "won the honor" of flying the 513th Parachute Infantry to their drop zones in seventy-two of the new C-46 transport planes, met at 52nd Troop Carrier Headquarters. "There, General Clark and his staff gave the detailed plans of the mission, code-named "Operation VARSITY" to the Commanding Officers and Intelligence and Operations Officers from each Group of the Wing. The 313th Troop Carrier Group was assigned to carry the men of the 513th over the Rhine. Field Order No. 5, along with photos and all necessary intelligence information were furnished by Colonel Disque of the Wing A-2 Section." The 313th assembled maps, photos, and intelligence information. The course was plotted with overlays of the route which were attached to the field order. That evening, "Squadron S-2s posted maps and overlays of the route and DZ in the S-2 Office in order to let the crews study them and thoroughly familiarize themselves with the possible problems concerned with the mission." Resulting from the meeting at 52nd Troop Carrier Wing Headquarters was Practice Mission TOKEN. Six C-46s from the 313th participated. Veteran pilots and aircrews, assigned to lead the formations of each of the 313th's four squadrons (the 49th, 29th, 48th, and 47th), flew a rehearsal mission simulating as close as possible VARSITY's planned route.[44]

The next day, however, concerns about VARSITY's limited objectives were voiced. As Major Robert R. Corey, the Assistant G-2 of the 17th Airborne recalled, "the division was told that there was some possibility that the operation would be pushed farther inland some ten miles to land on an alternate DZ. This would be in the vicinity of Erle, Germany. The feeling was prevalent that the ground forces would cross the river easily and that the operation might be to more advantage farther inland. In the marshaling areas maps and photographs to cover the alternate areas were received but they were never used. The problem of coordinating the entire operation," said Corey, "made the change impossible." So, although they were aware that VARSITY would probably provide little if any assistance to the amphibious forces, British Airborne planners forged ahead undeterred.

The 313th Troop Carrier Group's briefing of the squadron commanders took place in the Group Intelligence Office on the morning of 22 March "to begin work on the intelligence phase of the operation." Major George A. Smith, commander of the 49th TCS and Squadron S-3 Captain Jack L. Cardwell made an intensive study of the operation, scheduled for 24 March. Drop Zone X, the 513th's intended target, was a "rough quadrangle, some 2,500 yards long from east to west and about 1,000 yards wide, consisting mostly of small, flat fields." The DZ was about one and a quarter miles east of the Diersfordter Wald and about two and a half miles northwest of Wesel – to reach it, the C-46s would pass directly over the forested gun area. The double-track railroad that ran north from Wesel marked the western edge of the DZ and provided a highly visible landmark for Troop Carrier.[45]

Companies D, E, F, G, and I, Headquarters Company 2nd Battalion, and most of Headquarters Company 3rd Battalion would be carried in the 313th Troop Carrier Group's first serial of thirty-six planes. The rest of the regiment would arrive with the second serial on the heels of the first, while the artillery, engineer, and antitank elements attached to the regiment would be carried in the C-47s of another troop carrier group.[46]

On 22 March, Captain Reynolds called his officers and NCOs together to brief them on the F Company's mission in the coming operation. During the briefing, Reynolds informed them that F Company would have a special "point team" under Lieutenant Calhoun. Reynolds further stated that he needed a radioman to accompany the team. When Haggard informed the Captain that he was out of radiomen, Reynolds reiterated sternly, "I said I want a radioman." Haggard at first volunteered, but when that didn't suit Reynolds, Haggard spat out the name "Bob Greenstrand."

PFC Greenstrand was assigned by "that goddamned Haggard," as he put it, as radio-telephone operator for 1st Lieutenant Diefenderfer, who with five troopers, was to make a reconnaissance of the Diersfordter Castle in advance of Lieutenant Calhoun's platoon which had been given the task of leading the company through the Wald and securing the castle. Although it was believed to be unoccupied, Calhoun believed that such a structure was more than likely being used by the enemy as "some kind of a headquarters" and thus would be strongly defended. Since Greenstrand was the RTO, he went to the daily briefings at which huge sand tables, showing every feature of the countryside the 513th would jump into, were displayed. Said Greenstrand, "it must have taken thousands of aerial photographs and hours upon hours to construct and shape them. Everyday the sand tables were updated as new intelligence information was gathered. The high tension wires, farms, barns, houses, fences, creeks, location of enemy troops and big guns, everything you can imagine showed in their exact location on the ground," the works. It made the men feel like they were right there.[47]

On the evening of the twenty-second, F Company men were treated to a "Coca-Cola feast." Besides this, "there was very little other activity while we were [at Achiet], waiting for that steak that we all knew we were going to get," recalled Greenstrand. The men spent their time in the marshaling area studying the updated sand tables, sharpening knives, checking weapons and equipment, and trying to relax. Grice had finagled a 'Grease Gun' from one of the other men and talked Lieutenant Wieland into carrying it for him on the jump; Grice was already burdened with his machine-gun and a carbine, but wanted to take no chances. "Now don't lose my Grease Gun," Grice implored him.[48]

Just before moving to Achiet, Cobb was given "the great honor" of carrying First Platoon's M9A1 Bazooka, but he didn't get much time to practice. Cobb complained to Lieutenants Joyce and Wieland, "Let me go out and shoot this bazooka. I ain't shot this damn thing since Basic Training." Their reply was to laugh and say, "You'll learn how to do it." What his platoon leaders were telling him was that he was going to receive on the job training, only.

Another marshaling area activity was to get a 'Mohawk'-style haircut. German propaganda claimed that American paratroopers were a bunch of murderers who had had to kill their mothers and fathers before being allowed to join the paratroops and who could be identified by their Indian-style haircuts. Laufer decided to get a Mohawk – if the Germans were expecting murderers, Sid Laufer, for one, was going to look the part. Some men, including Grice, shaved their heads completely.[49]

The men were told that if they were captured by the Germans, they would probably be killed. An idea like that would make even the bravest trooper wonder why he'd ever volunteered for the parachute business to begin with. In turn, the men were given pointed instructions on their handling of German prisoners. "We had direct orders," explained Cobb. "We weren't allowed to shoot anybody that surrendered." After what had taken place during the Bulge, in which 17th Airborne troopers – and GIs from almost every fighting unit – had shot German soldiers right up front and in the open as they tried to surrender, something had to be done. Every fighting man knew already that if the Germans saw their own men being shot after they'd given up, the rest would never give up, but fight to the end. "They just preached and preached to us," said Cobb, " 'Don't shoot nobody. Don't shoot nobody'." Many officers, however, tempered the orders by telling their men, "If you do, make sure you don't do it out in the open." Regardless of orders, Laufer was going to think twice before he took any prisoners.[50]

At 0900 hours on 23 March, the 313th Troop Carrier Group's pilots, co-pilots, and navigators were briefed again on the mission by Lieutenant Colonel William A. Filer, commander of the 313th, and his staff. In attendance were Colonel Coutts, and Captain Gates Ivy, Jr., and the officers of the 513th. Each of the four squadrons of the 313th would "put up eighteen C-46s in two nine-ship formations." The 49th Troop Carrier Squadron, piloting the first flight of eighteen C-46s, would take the lead. F Company was assigned to planes with chalk numbers 11 through 15. Piloting the lead ship on which Lieutenant Colonel Miller would be carried, was Major George A. Smith; Lieutenant Colonel William A. Filer was his co-pilot.[51]

During the briefings, aircrews and paratroopers were warned that the most conspicuous danger posed to the mission was the thick concentrations of flak around the DZs. Reports still arriving on the afternoon of the twenty-third indicated that more anti-aircraft batteries were being placed to reinforce those already marked on the defense overlays. It was hoped, however, that any hazard presented by the flak would be minimized by the extensive system of navigational aids established along the flight path and the expectation that the C-46s would be over the DZ for only about ten minutes.[52]

Missing from all the preparations, however, was one crucial component that to Major Irwin Edwards could have provided some benefit; an appraisal of the operations in the Ardennes. First Sergeant Donovan broached the subject on several occasions to Captain Reynolds, and Reynolds assured Donovan that he had brought it up at battalion HQ, "but nothing came of it," said Donovan. It is more than likely that the question fell on deaf ears. In fact, as Major Edwards put it, "after the 17th Airborne Division returned to Chalons-sur-Marne, there was no meeting within the 2nd Battalion or the 513th to evaluate their combat experience. Everybody was happy the war was just about over and they were going to get to make this big combat jump. Everybody was hooped-up about it. There was no intelligent discussion."[53]

Under clear spring skies, Allied fighters and bombers had for a week hit targets all over the Ruhr in support of the impending ground assault. The heavies of the Eighth Air Force – diverted from their normal role as strategic bombers – pounded the cities of the Ruhr round the clock, while medium bombers and fighters struck transportation and communications targets and flak emplacements. "Daily sorties averaged 4,000, mounted to 8,000, and then, on March 24, reached an enormous total of 12,000 – 1,000 more than on D-Day."[54]

During the day of the twenty-third, the British Second Tactical Air Force hit enemy airfields and flak concentrations all along the Rhine and planes from Bomber Command demolished Wesel. At 2100 hours that evening, Field Marshall Montgomery's 21st Army group began its long-awaited crossing of the Northern Rhine. During his customary eve-of-battle address, Montgomery promised his troops, "we will crack into the plains of northern Germany, chasing the enemy from pillar to post." The amphibious assault was spearheaded by Highlanders of the British 51st Division who crossed north of the main objective, Wesel. An hour after the initial assault, 46 RM Commando crossed the Rhine two miles south of Wesel followed by three more divisions, the 15th Scottish, and the American 30th and 79th Infantry Divisions, at 0200 hours on the twenty-fourth. Though initially meeting heavy German resistance near Rees, British troops soon had ferries, delivering fresh men and equipment into the battle, operating across the Rhine. By daybreak, the commandos controlled the ruins of Wesel and the Americans were moving with great force.[55]

9

Like Bolts from Heaven

The Rhine Spearhead: Operation VARSITY
24 March 1945

A shrill voice jarred Greenstrand from uneasy sleep. It was dark, still very early, when the company was roused and ordered to fall out. "When F Company men went to breakfast that morning. . . the cooks plopped a big steak and a chunk of apple pie" in their mess kits. A meal like this meant only one thing – word spread quickly that the jump was on. "Frankly," recalled Greenstrand, "the steak didn't taste as good as you might imagine when we realized this was it."[1]

After breakfast, the men returned to the barracks to pack their duffel bags and give their weapons and gear the final once over. No one seemed to say much, especially those men with combat experience.

Over their brown wool shirts and trousers, the men wore the green M-43 combat suits. The parachute riggers had sewn deep cargo pockets on the trouser legs to hold rations and other essentials and then affixed tie-down-tapes to keep them secure. Trench knives were tied to one leg, above the jump boot, and the outfit was topped off with the ubiquitous steel helmet. British Gammon grenades were issued, as were K rations for three days and two D rations (emergency chocolate bars). Laufer stuffed four boxes of K rations, four fragmentation grenades, a poncho, a shelter half, an entrenching tool, and the parapack in his cargo pockets and mussette bag. Like many others, Laufer was much less concerned about food than he was about ammunition for his M1; he had two bandoleers and a cartridge belt full – 172 rounds. He considered that any more would be too burdensome. Laufer then discarded his shaving equipment and the gas mask he'd been holding on to – things he wouldn't need.[2]

Just before 0530 hours, word came down to F Company to fall out. After a brief formation they boarded trucks and were driven out to their planes to begin preparations for loading the aircraft. F Company drew their chutes from the hangers, the same T-7s with the quick-release harnesses they had used on their most recent practice jump. With some help, Laufer strapped on his chute – so tightly that he was forced to walk stoop-shouldered. Around him, everyone else was nervously tightening straps and sorting out equipment when, by accident, PFC Olson deployed his reserve chute, spilling it all over the hardstand. Sergeant Tom Harvey saw what had happened and, instead of bawling him out for his carelessness, told Olson, "Here, you take mine," and removed his own reserve and secured it to Olson's harness.[3]

Most of the heavy equipment, carried in bundles slung under the planes' fuselages, had been loaded already, however; the men had to jump with the bazookas and machine-guns in leg bags. Because one of the men who'd been assigned a bazooka was afraid to jump with it, Private Richard Murray was asked to do it. Murray agreed to take the bazooka but added a provision, "I'll jump it, but I'm not gonna use it." His terms accepted, Murray gave his machine-gun to someone else in exchange for a light M1A1 Carbine and the two-piece M9A1 Bazooka. To himself, Private Murray swore to ditch the cumbersome bazooka as soon as he got on the ground.[4]

Laufer had that hollow, nervous feeling in his gut a runner gets just before the start of a race. This isn't really happening, he thought. This just can't be real. Laufer took a last look around at his friends – Jack Cook, Grice who was adjusting the British leg bag containing his .30 caliber machine-gun, and Kondy – and wondered if he'd see them after this day was over. Outwardly they were all hyped-up – as ready as they'd ever be. Inside their stomachs were churning, that was true. Most of the men said a few words to the Big Trooper in the sky.[5]

F Company loaded on to five planes of the 49th Squadron's second flight – chalk numbers 11, 12, 13, 14, and 15. The planes were "parked on individual PSP [pierced steel planking] hardstands along the sides of the taxiways around the airfield." As the men boarded the planes, "a trooper on the bottom of the ladder. . . checked off the name and serial number of each man from the loading list." Lieutenants Joyce and Wieland were assigned to Number 11 with most of the First

Platoon. Private Cobb, with the bazooka, would be the first out the door. First Sergeant Donovan loaded with company headquarters and parts of Second and Third Platoons into Number 12. One of the lieutenants also loaded to act as jumpmaster. Lieutenant Fann was on 13 and Lieutenant Calhoun, and most of the Third Platoon loaded onto plane Number 14. Captain Reynolds, along with the remaining men, loaded into plane Number 15. Grice was the next to last to board – and with a couple of men helping – climbed awkwardly up Number 15's ladder, dragging the heavy bag containing his machine-gun. Just before getting on board himself, Captain Reynolds issued his final pre-battle instructions to F Company's officers: "Our first objective on the ground is to get together, and then give 'em Hell." By 0745 hours, the whole battalion had enplaned and was awaiting the order to take off.[6]

The last briefing for the aircrews of the 49th Troop Carrier Squadron (TCS) took place early that morning. The airmen were issued first aid kits, purses, and rice paper overlays of the fight route. Planes of the 49th TCS were loaded with "525 paratroopers and 102 bundles in parapacks, and door bundles, totaling 35,410 pounds of ammunition and equipment" for the 2nd Battalion of the 513th and elements of the 3rd Battalion. Two war correspondents also tagged along, each excited about the dangerous plane ride and anxious about getting the story first. One of them, the famed photographer Robert Capa, would go on Colonel Coutts' Number 46 ship.

When all had loaded aboard his Number 11 ship, 1st Lieutenant Robert Kerr walked back through the plane, sizing up the troopers. They all looked ready to go, like a football team going to the big game. "I don't understand you guys being so eager," he remarked to one of the F Company lieutenants on board.

"We just want to get in there and jump," said the lieutenant confidently.

"Let me know if you make it," Kerr said, and then he walked to the cockpit. They were something, he thought.

Now was the pay-off. Colonel Filer, Major Smith, and the war correspondent Robert Wilson were driven to their C-46 by staff car. Before boarding, they posed for photographs. Wilson felt privileged to be assigned to the lead plane – there were reporters with the other squadrons – but Wilson could write that he was the first reporter over the Rhine in the Commandos. "He intended to summarize his notes for early publication, during the return flight to Achiet." Also aboard were Lieutenant Colonel Miller and the 2nd Battalion staff. At 0800 hours, Major Smith's

C-46, leading the group, turned onto the runway. Smith throttled-up and the first of the twenty-one planes carrying the 2nd Battalion clawed its way into the sky.[7]

Inside the planes, the men were all terribly nervous because of the lack of information. PFC Laufer still didn't know exactly where he and his friends were headed. Although distracted by the deafening roar of the engines and the vibration they created, he tried to remember the sand table – the positions of the houses, the railroad, the river. The briefing officer had pointed out the numerous new German gun positions – the flak concentrations were going to be heavy over the drop zones. "This house should be taken immediately," he remembered one of the officers pointing out during the briefing. "The Germans know we're coming," he said to himself. Laufer kicked the idea around in his head.

Private Cobb sat calmly. Unlike Laufer, he "really didn't give a shit" where he was going. "What the hell?" he figured, "I'll go wherever they send me. What else can I do? Tell them I ain't goin'." The pilot opened-up the engines and the plane began to taxi.

The planes of the first flight took off in order, keeping to the right edge of the runway to counter the effect of the twenty to twenty-five mile-per-hour prevailing crosswinds. Captain Robert Blickensderfer, leading the second flight in Number 10 took off next, followed in order by the first of F Company's planes – Lieutenant Kerr's Number 11 and 1st Lieutenant Eugene Rothi's Number 12 ships.[8]

As he made a left turn onto the runway and throttled-up his Number 13 ship to takeoff speed, 1st Lieutenant Gilbert Whiteside was thinking about a conversation he and 1st Lieutenant Macel 'Mac' Mael, the pilot of the Number 14 ship, had had on both evenings prior to the mission. Mac had approached Lieutenant Whiteside about the turn out of the drop zone, concerned that Whiteside's ship might collide with his own during the maneuver. Whiteside figured Mac was a little nervous about the mission so on takeoff, he decided to use the left-center of the runway and leave Mael, who was to follow, as much room open on the right side of the runway as he could. This turned out, as Whiteside admitted, to be an error in judgment.

As the runway raced faster and faster past the open doors, Private James Cox, of the Second Platoon, noticed the plane was veering from side to side. The C-46, with its large fin and rudder was susceptible to crosswinds, and in the crosswinds lashing the field, Lieutenant Whiteside had his hands full.[9]

Using the brakes to make corrections – under sixty miles-per-hour, the C-46 could not be steered with the rudder – Lieutenant Whiteside tried to keep the ship on the hardstand but the wind was too strong and the ship's left landing gear drifted off the runway.

Whiteside had to make a decision fast. Trees stood at the end of the runway. If he tried to clear them – and blew an engine – he'd run right into them and kill everyone on board. He decided the best thing to do was to abort the takeoff and flop the plane. Whiteside first jettisoned the parapack bundles from their sponsons on the ship's belly, sending them tumbling. Fearing an explosion, men on the ground started to scatter. One man ran a half mile into the trees before he stopped. Sitting near the door watching the runway speed past, PFC Dahlberg was a little puzzled by the loud whining of the engines. "We should be off the ground by now," he mouthed silently. Just at that moment, the C-46 skidded off the runway, plowing into a motorcycle, seven jeeps, a fire truck, and a six-by-six truck. The left landing gear fell into a 40mm anti-aircraft gun position. As it was wrenched off, it whipped the right wing of the plane around, the wing tip striking a decontamination vehicle – its wooden box splintering like match sticks as the C-46 ground to rest. Someone yelled, "Fire!!!" The shaken troopers inside panicked and rushed to get to the doors. Fortunately, it was a false alarm and the heavily burdened men regained their composure.[10]

The men sat in the plane for a short time until a doctor came and asked if anyone was hurt. Two officers, Fann and Selzer, and thirty-two troopers were on Lieutenant Whiteside's C-46 and four of them, Fann and PFCs Edward Costello, Donald Hardy, and Boyd Ramsey, were injured in the wreck. Three two-and-a-half-ton trucks backed up to the plane and those who were able to continue climbed in while an Air Corps officer apologized to the men, telling them that they would get them underway as soon as possible so they could jump with their company. The paratroopers were driven to Captain Bobby Scott's C-46 – "Spare No. 1" – which was waiting on its hardstand. Each squadron maintained two "spare" aircraft and crews. "Engine trouble and a flat tire kept two [other] C-46s from taking off." Another with engine trouble returned. All these men were transferred to three more spare ships, the last departing B-54 at 0930 hours.[11]

Trucks loaded with paratroopers and the retrieved parapack bundles from Whiteside's plane arrived at Captain Bobby Scott's C-46. The parapacks were loaded on board with the troopers – there wasn't time to re-mount them on the belly so they were just stacked on the floor to be pushed out later. Scott's crew were surprised by their rapid change of fortune, but quickly resigned themselves

Two F Company men – chutes on and ready to go. (Robert Capa/Magnum Photos, Inc.)

Men of F Company's First Platoon assemble moments before takeoff. (Robert Capa/Magnum Photos, Inc.)

I Company, 513th troopers unload from a GMC cargo truck and march to their C-46, Chalk No. 34. (Robert Capa/ Magnum Photos, Inc.)

I Company troopers begin boarding their C-46. (Robert Capa/Magnum Photos, Inc.)

Heavily burdened with more than 150 pounds of equipment, troopers often required assistance in climbing into the planes. (Robert Capa/Magnum Photos, Inc.)

Reserve parachutes, like the one held by this trooper, were deemed useless at jump altitudes by many. Troopers on PFC Greenstrand's No. 14 ship unfastened theirs and left them behind when they jumped. (Robert Capa/Magnum Photos, Inc.)

Famed combat photographer Robert Capa exchanges a final word with Lieutenant Colonel Ward S. Ryan, the 513th's Executive Officer, before the mission. (Robert Capa/Magnum Photos, Inc.)

Chief of Staff of First Allied Airborne Army, Brigadier General Floyd L. Parks confers with Major General Miley prior to takeoff. (Signal Corps photo)

1st Lieutenant Gilbert Whiteside (back to the camera) stands amid the destruction wrought when, during takeoff, his C-46, Chalk No.13, skidded off the runway and into a motorcycle, seven jeeps, a fire truck, a six-by-six truck, and a decontamination vehicle. Four F Company men on board were injured in the crash. (Courtesy, 17th Airborne Division Association)

49th Troop Carrier Squadron C-46s taking off at Airstrip B-54 (Achiet) on the morning of VARSITY. F Company's No. 11, 12, 13, and 14 ships can be seen last in line on the taxiway. (Courtesy, Mrs. Rex Shama)

Officers of the 313th Troop Carrier Group – November 1944: Paulsel, Linsay, 1st Lieutenant Gilbert Whiteside, and Collins. (Courtesy, Mrs. Rex Shama)

The C-46 had jump doors on both sides of its massive fuselage. Twice as many men – about thirty-six – could jump in the same amount of time from the C-46 as could be jumped from the older C-47, a decidedly advantageous feature for the airborne men. Colonel Coutts is seated to the left. (Robert Capa/Magnum Photos, Inc.)

Cockpit view of Chalk No.46. (Robert Capa/Magnum Photos, Inc.)

En route to Germany, Colonel James W. Coutts, the 513th's CO, distributes sandwiches to the men on his No.46 ship. (Robert Capa/Magnum Photos, Inc.)

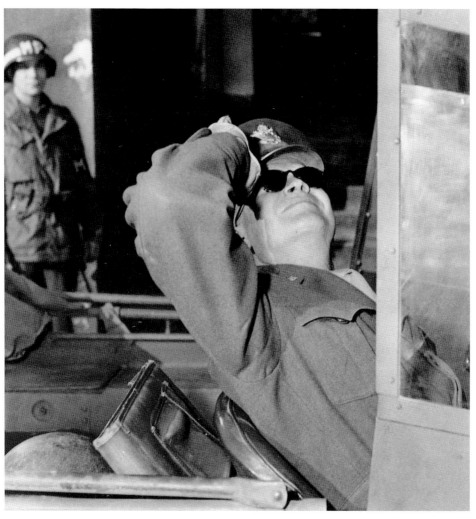

In the Ninth U.S. Army Sector, General Eisenhower pauses to watch the aerial procession, which stretched two hours and eighteen minutes in length, pass overhead. (Signal Corps photo)

When the green light was flashed, Colonel Coutts, left, was the first man aboard No. 46 to jump. (Robert Capa/ Magnum Photos, Inc.)

The 513th was dropped into fields west of Hamminkeln, almost three miles north of their intended drop zone. (Robert Capa/Magnum Photos, Inc.)

After landing in a cow pasture, a 513th bazookaman crawls toward safety. The thick ground haze, visible at top, which had obscured landmarks from the air, was a boon to the troops on the ground. (Robert Capa/Magnum Photos, Inc.)

Taking shelter in a slit trench, two Regimental Headquarters men from Colonel Coutts' plane keep a wary eye open for German troops. (Robert Capa/Magnum Photos, Inc.)

Small streams, open sewers, and irrigation ditches provided some of the only cover for assaulting troops landing in the fields north of Wesel. (Robert Capa/Magnum Photos, Inc.)

Paratroopers escort two of the nearly three thousand German prisoners captured by the 17th Airborne Division on D-Day. 1,252 prisoners alone were taken by the Lieutenant Colonel Miller's 2nd Battalion. (Robert Capa/Magnum Photos, Inc.)

Under sporadic fire, 17th Airborne troops evacuate a wounded comrade to the rear. (Robert Capa/Magnum Photos, Inc.)

Shortly after landing, 513th troops reorganize in a farmyard aid station. (Robert Capa/Magnum Photos, Inc.)

Paratroopers look skyward to the approach of British gliders which began landing at about 1030 hours. (Robert Capa/Magnum Photos, Inc.).

Glidermen of the 194th Regimental Combat Team hug the ground against enemy fire around a CG-4A Waco glider. (Robert Capa/Magnum Photos, Inc.)

Medical personnel make good use of local transportation to move wounded and supplies. In the background is the high tension wire, a landmark used by 513th troopers to orient themselves after the drop. (Robert Capa/Magnum Photos, Inc.)

Some of the many German prisoners captured by 17th Airborne troops on D-Day. (Signal Corps Photo)

British Second Army engineers constructing the 1,206-foot-long Lambeth Class 15 Bailey bridge over the Rhine about a kilometer north of Rees on the afternoon of D-Day. The first of five bridges built in the Second Army's sector, Lambeth was opened to traffic at 0830 hours on 26 March. (Robert Capa/Magnum Photos, Inc.)

German civilians, displaced from their homes by the fighting, flee past a damaged British Airspeed Horsa glider. (Robert Capa/Magnum Photos, Inc.)

PFCs Grice (front) and Laufer (top), Sergeant Rutherford (far right) and several other troopers from F Company's First Platoon ride the lead Churchill tank of the Scots Guards into Dorsten, Germany, 28 March 1945. (Courtesy, Willis Grice)

En route to Münster, Germany, infantrymen of the 513th pass through the smoldering remains of Appelhulsen, which fell to the regiment on 30 March 1945. (Courtesy, 17th Airborne Division Association)

On their way into Münster on 2 April 1945, men of the 513th pick up extra bandoleers of ammunition. (Signal Corps photo)

German prisoners are hustled past a Guards Churchill tank and to the rear by 513th troopers on the outskirts of Münster, 2 April 1945. (Signal Corps photo)

Supported by tanks of the Coldstream Guards, First and Third platoons of C Company of the 513th Parachute Infantry move into the ruins of Mecklenbeck on the outskirts of Münster, 2 April 1945. (Signal Corps photo)

After the fall of Münster, PFC Ed Sarrell, PFC Joe Gutt, PFC George Shaughnessy, PFC John Cogan, PFC Robert Guiles, Private Frank Apfel, and PFC Manuel Juarez on occupation duty in Gelsenkirchen, Germany. (Courtesy, Edward Sarrell)

"We were still on the line – we look it." Bob Greenstrand and Russell Hataway during occupation duty in Oberhausen, Germany. (Author's collection via Bob Greenstrand)

Private Herbert Potts, PFC Edmund Gonzalez, PFC Greenstrand and PFC Edward Logsdon rest on a park bench at Oberhausen. (Author's collection via Bob Greenstrand)

ABOVE: Dinslacken, Germany – April 1945. F Company men opened their mess line to German children and their mothers. (Author's collection via Neal Haggard)

ABOVE RIGHT: F Company men break for chow amid the ruins of Dinslacken, Germany, April 1945. (Courtesy, Neal Haggard)

RIGHT: Tech Sergeant Arther A. 'Snuffy' Bowers and Staff Sergeant James W. Galloway on patrol in Oberhausen, Germany, April 1945. (Author's collection via Bob Greenstrand)

PFC Donald K. Shay and Private James D. Chieloha enjoy victory near the Rhein-Hern Canal, April 1945. (Courtesy, Donald Shay)

Private John Cobb and Sergeant Russell Hataway at Oberhausen. (Author's collection via Sam Calhoun)

Private John Cobb and PFC Sidney Laufer in Oberhausen. (Author's collection via Sam Calhoun)

Oberhausen, Germany. Top: Staff Sergeant Howard R. McLain, Staff Sergeant William C. Kuntz, Sr., 1st Lieutenant Ivan Stositch, and unidentified; kneeling: unidentified, PFC Willis B. Grice, and Sergeant Johnnie A. Rutherford. (Courtesy, Bob Greenstrand)

A smiling Lieutenant Calhoun in the company of a young German woman. The Army's position on fraternization was clear-cut. However, the men were decidedly in disagreement. (Author's collection via Sam Calhoun)

Captain Marshall M. Reynolds in Germany after V-E Day. (Courtesy, Margaret Ellis)

Tantonville, France – July 1945. Sergeant Neal Haggard, First Sergeant Royal Donovan, and PFC Edward Schneck. (Author's collection via Neal Haggard)

Tech Sergeant Arthur Bowers and 1st Lieutenant Sam Calhoun pause during the trip in boxcars to Tantonville, France, in July 1945. (Author's collection via Sam Calhoun)

Captain Marshall McCormick Reynolds of Berryville, Virginia. A VMI graduate and veteran of Guadalcanal, Reynolds "was an animal," said the men, "a bulldog," and they loved him. (Author's collection via Bob Greenstrand)

1st Lieutenant Sam Calhoun spent V-E Day in Paris – it was "a crazy night of celebrating." (Author's collection via Sam Calhoun)

"Bob, Pat, Simone & Paul [Imre]. Chelmsford, Essex, ENGLAND. Sept. 1945." After being wounded on 5 January, Imre never again saw combat and went home with the 101st Airborne Division. (Courtesy, Paul Imre)

After V-E Day, Phil Cavaleri and Snuffy Bowers met while on furlough in Nice, France, Summer 1945. (Author's collection via Phil Cavaleri)

One of fifty-one F Company men killed in action between 3 January and 4 April 1945, Private Jean Paul Morin's grave in Hamm, Luxembourg stands as a poignant reminder of the cost of war. (Author's collection via Sam Calhoun)

to flying the mission. "It was the way it had to be," remembered Frank Joda, then a Tech Sergeant and the crew chief on Scott's ship. The plane's whole crew hurried through their pre-flight preparations because they knew it was going to be difficult if not impossible to catch up to the rest of the formation. Hustling to make up lost time himself, Captain Scott "barreled down the runway – gave it some flaps," and yanked the plane skyward, barely clearing the trees, remembered Joda. Once airborne, Scott "poured it on," while Joda watched out for signs of engine detonation.[12]

Despite the accident, Numbers 14 and 15 got off without a hitch. Private Laufer, with Grice and Captain Reynolds in 15, was much more than nervous. "There's a difference between being nervous and scared shitless," Laufer explained, and "I was scared shitless." He, like almost every man there, was worried about the battle he would soon face, and, chiefly, if he would survive it. As his C-46 climbed to altitude and joined the other planes, a pair of P-38 Lightnings rippled past the formation. It was going to be a long flight – 550 miles. Laufer settled back into his seat.

"Any Michigan guys?" Lieutenant Rothi yelled back over the engine noise to the F Company men seated in his Number 12 ship. No one answered. No Michigan men on board or, perhaps, no one felt like saying anything. Not much was said by any of the men in the troop transports as the sky train flew across the fields and villages of France and Belgium.

First Sergeant Donovan, who had curled up on the floor against a bulkhead on Number 12, had slept for most of the flight, but something roused him and when the stocky Irishmen cracked his eyes he suddenly felt a "hell of a lot better." What cheered him was the sight of Allied planes of all description, transports, bombers, and fighters that seemed to fill the sky.

Those who looked upwards from the villages and fields along the flight path were awe struck at the sight of hundreds of planes flying in close formation. "From the ground it must have been an awesome sight; staring up at the gigantic aerial procession far longer than the eye could see," remarked a pilot from the 436th Troop Carrier Group. The 17th Airborne Division's air column alone took two hours and eighteen minutes to pass one point and consisted of 226 C-47s and 72 C-46s carrying parachute troops, and 906 gliders towed by 610 C-47s. The British lift consisted of 420 gliders, forty-two C-54s and 752 C-47s. If anything could symbolize the amazing industrial strength and power of the Allies, this was surely it.[13]

Taking another nervous look around the cabin of the plane, Private Laufer saw the troopers crouching near the jump doors, among them the Captain, to watch the earth go by as the plane advanced with the formation. Most of the other men just sat still in their seats, their eyes closed tightly, as if they didn't want to see anything. Many, like PFC Cuthbertson who sat smoking a cigar, were consuming their smokes like mad. Laufer, who didn't smoke, had shoved a whole pack of Juicy Fruit into his mouth. He chewed it furiously until all the flavor was gone. He too had been heartened by the site of the armada of planes, but not enough to shake his fear.[14]

1st Lieutenant David Harvey, navigator on Captain Blickensderfer's Number 10 plane leading the second flight, had tuned in to Radio Berlin. Axis Sally – known as 'The Bitch' – was on, and she made an astounding announcement: Germany was aware that the 17th Airborne Division was marshaled at Troop Carrier airfields all over France. "Men of the 17th Airborne Division," she declared, "we know you're coming. We are waiting and ready for you on the Rhine. You won't need your parachute," she continued, "the flak will be so thick you can walk down."[15]

As early as mid-February, the Germans believed that an airborne assault in the Wesel area was not only possible, but probable, and had taken steps to defend against it. The "Special Order" of one of the defending German units, *Artillery Regiment Elbe*, dated 17 February 1945, stated, "Since we <u>can count</u> on an Airborne operation in this area all units have to take measure to engage in battle within the shortest time possible against any Airborne forces. 80% of officers and men must be committed against the Airborne units, the remainder to be used in guarding horses and equipment." By that date, *Elbe* had already prepared positions in the Diersfordter Wald.[16]

Some accountability for this must be shouldered by the Airborne planners themselves. While unit security was "generally good," news of Operation VARSITY had been leaked at the highest levels. Men of the 17th Airborne Division had been "given information while visiting higher headquarters as drivers or messengers" and general hints had even been given over American radio broadcasts. Also, the Germans must have realized the advantages the Wesel crossing site offered the Allies as much as Montgomery. When 21st Army Group's mammoth preparations for VARSITY-PLUNDER commenced opposite Wesel, there must have been little doubt left that a river crossing operation was imminent.[17]

The weather was spectacularly good. Visibility was unlimited in the skies over France and Belgium when the separate British and American air columns converged southeast of Brussels, over the city of Wavre (code-named MARFAK). From there, in two parallel airlanes, the Allied planes jabbed their way east toward the skies over the Third Reich. So far, no enemy fighters had been encountered and, overall, the operation was proceeding smoothly. The first in a series of mishaps, however, was about to occur.[18]

The two serials of C-46s were scheduled to reach the waypoint at Wavre at 0934 and 0938 hours. There, these planes would slip across the leading American glider element which would be entering the right airlane at 0936 hours – and into the left airlane which, at the time, would be temporarily unoccupied by British planes. Employing their great speed, the C-46s would pass the glider formations and take up their assigned position ahead of them in the right airlane just before the approach to the Initial Point (IP). As Major Smith's C-46s approached the glider formations at Wavre, he altered his course to the left considerably and, outpacing the gliders, brought the formation into its position in the right lane. In the conduct of the complex maneuver, however, Major Smith got off course and never regained the correct heading; a circumstance that would make finding the correct drop zone nearly impossible. Following behind Major Smith, the second serial climbed to two thousand feet and, without ever altering its course at all, flew over the glider formation in an effort to stay behind the planes of the first serial.[19]

Meanwhile, Spare Number 1 was still playing catch-up. After Captain Scott got on course, Tech Sergeant Joda took his station in the back of the plane near the jump doors and "waited for the fireworks." "We're gonna take a shortcut," Scott told the troopers. "We'll catch up to the group." Joda scanned the faces of the men for a reaction; he could tell not one of them believed they'd ever catch up to the formation. None of them looked altogether calm or happy either. Yet in spite of everything they appeared, to Joda at least, eager to get into the fight.[20]

On Number 11, PFC Sarrell sat next to First Sergeant Donovan, clutching the .30 caliber machine-gun that was resting in his leg bag. The red warning light came on and the order was given to stand up and hook up. The men quickly got to their feet and braced themselves. Joe Gutt, who was just behind him in the stick, and some of the other fellows helped Sarrell to his feet. Then, together with First Sergeant Donovan, he positioned in the door a "large equipment bundle which was to go out first."[21]

A few moments later, at 09:45 hours, the transports crossed the IP on their way to the Rhine. Soon they were met by anti-aircraft and small arms fire from the enemy on the far shore. Sarrell watched the Rhine pass underneath him. The intensity of the fire increased in volume as they neared the eastern bank. It was "incredibly heavy and incredibly accurate," observed Lieutenant Kerr piloting Number 11 – himself a veteran of many previous troop carrier missions in Normandy and Holland. At first, the ground appeared to be covered with thin clouds. Then, through the battle smoke and low-clinging ground haze, Kerr could distinguish the German anti-aircraft guns below. The 88s were "lined up like a motor pool." "What's that black smoke out there?" asked one of the troopers. His friend leaned over to him, "I think they're shooting at us." Lieutenant Rothi in Number 12 could see that the flak was concentrated in the Diersfordter Wald – "something that had not been anticipated." The flak was, in fact, the most destructive the veteran troop carrier pilots of the 313th had ever faced.[22]

Maneuvering to avoid the time-burst artillery, 20mm flak and small arms fire, Lieutenant Kerr suddenly banked left and the bundle Sarrell and Donovan had been holding fell inward and lay on the floor. Sarrell, with his .30 caliber machinegun in a leg bag strapped on, a carbine, ammunition, and all the rest of his gear, found it an effort just to move around let alone attempt to wrestle the bundle back to the door. Finally, Donovan and Sarrell managed to push the heavy bundle into the doorway and, together, they stood on it so the wind wouldn't take it out. Then they prayed.[23]

Among those who had come to witness the stream of planes and gliders headed over the Rhine were British Prime Minister Winston Churchill and the Supreme Commander, General Eisenhower. For those on the ground, the sight of the grand aerial precession inspired wild cheers. In the planes, however, it was a different story.

"A lot of black ones out there," Lieutenant Rothi remarked to his co-pilot, 2nd Lieutenant Harry Wilshire. "The flak, said Rothi in 1997, wasn't as bad as that he'd experienced in Holland "but it was bad enough."[24]

Men were awe-struck and terrified at once. Excitedly, the officer on Tec 4 Contreras' plane shouted, "Look out the window!" "Wow," thought Haggard. "This is gonna be something." Private Murray, standing near the door, watched the river pass below. Then he spotted British tanks already moving on the eastern shore. If the British are across, he wondered, what the hell were they doing?[25]

The command "Stand up and hook up!" had been given by Captain Reynolds well before the Rhine came into view below (the men were given the verbal warning fifteen minutes prior to the jump. The red light three minutes prior). When the flak started up, they were ready to get out. "As soon as we get across, let's go!" PFC Grice pressed Captain Reynolds. Grice was the number two man in Reynolds' stick and would jump right behind him. There were fourteen men in line behind Grice, and they all wanted to jump just as bad.[26]

"Yeah," said Reynolds, "I hear the flak hitting the bottom of the plane now."

Private Laufer could see the bursts in the air. Each puff of black smoke was followed by a dull, flat wham and a thunk-thunk-thunk as shrapnel rattled against the wings and fuselage of his C-46 and made the plane shutter. Laufer knew they were close to the drop zone.

"They're gonna shoot this plane down," shouted Grice.

Reynolds told Grice firmly, "We can't go until we get the green light."[27]

Lieutenant William Pully was navigator on C-46 Number 2. Pully's plane, carrying the regiment's pathfinders, followed Ace Miller's lead ship. Like all of the 313th's planes, Pully's C-46 was to guide on the Diersfordter Castle, situated in a 'V' shaped clearing – visible from the air – in the Diersfordter Wald, then cross the double-track railroad that marked the western most boundary of Drop Zone X. Here, the lead plane would break radio silence and the regiment would jump. As his plane flew along, Pully peered through the haze, watching for the checkpoints below. Due to battle smoke and ground haze, however, visibility was down to only a half mile. Also, many landmarks had been destroyed in the "softening-up" bombings prior to the drop.[28]

Although there was much jostling in the formations as pilots wrestled the unfamiliar planes, the C-46 formation stayed together. "The 313th came over the muddy Rhine at one thousand feet and there began to descend to six hundred feet," the designated jump altitude. While over the Rhine, Major Smith, piloting the lead ship, made a correction to bring the formation back on the right heading. By that time, however, the formation was far to the left of course and too far north to locate the colored marker panels, placed on the west bank of the Rhine, which designated the 313th's crossing point. Captain Blickensderfer, leading the second flight, merely followed Smith. The rest of the C-46s followed Blick, their pilots – like Lieutenant Kerr in Number 11 – flying with their "heads out of the cockpit" to keep the formation tight. All of the pilots were busy and trusted in 1st Lieutenant William Sussner, Smith's navigator in Number 1, to get them to the DZ.[29]

Approaching the drop zone, Lieutenant Calhoun, jumpmaster on his ship, stood near the door looking down. He could see German soldiers below firing up at the planes. Lieutenant Stanley, having had the opportunity to make a practice jump from the C-46, was to lead the men out the right jump door. Diefenderfer would lead the men out the port door. Lieutenant Calhoun would remain on board until all the men had exited, and then he would hook up and follow. Calhoun knew that, since it would take considerable time to hook up and jump, he would probably land about one hundred yards from the rest of the platoon.

At 1013 hours, the 313th's first nine C-46s came roaring in over the drop zone. Suddenly, Major Smith realized he was coming in too fast and, without warning, he throttled back his engines sharply. Smith's sudden decrease in speed took the rest of the pilots, each flying hard on the tail of the plane ahead, by surprise and the formation started to stack up. Lieutenant Kerr practically cut his engines. Planes in the second flight that couldn't slow down were forced to climb to avoid flying right into the planes ahead.

Colonel Miller, in the Number 1 aircraft with the Major Smith, could not make out the double-track railroad – the landmark that was to signal the battalion's jump – through the ground haze, swirling smoke, and dust raised by the artillery barrage. In fact, 2nd Battalion was two to three miles north of their assigned drop zone. Furthermore, as the planes dropped their speed to one hundred knots for the pass over the DZ, they became easy targets for the flak gunners.[30]

The murderous flak was bouncing Number 14 around like a yo-yo. It was Greenstrand's understanding that they were going to jump at four hundred feet, but the plane looked like it was climbing to eight hundred. Most of the men were unfastening their reserve chutes – at four hundred feet, a reserve would probably be useless. Greenstrand unhooked his and tossed it back in his seat. With a roar, a shell exploded near the plane. The crew chief, Tech Sergeant Graff, standing in the back of the plane near the door, was caught in the gut by a piece of shrapnel and spun around. Graff then went forward and collapsed.[31]

Over the DZ, the planes of the first flight were below the planes of the second and taking most of the flak. The plane in which Colonel Miller flew was hit repeatedly. Directly in front of him, Captain Blickensderfer could see the Number 1 C-46, "burning from wingtip to wingtip." Planes seemed to burst into flames all across the sky. Miller's lead plane began to go in. Moments later, Number 2, heavily damaged by small arms fire, heeled over toward earth (the paratroopers and Lieutenant Pully managed to jump clear of the C-46, but the pilot, the co-pilot, and the crew chief were killed in the crash. Number 2's radio operator also managed to jump but he landed in a tree and was shot by the Germans). Number 11 had nearly stalled when Lieutenant Kerr, with the sound of the flak in his ears, dropped his flaps and blasted the throttle. Then, at 1014 hours, the green light was flashed and 2nd Battalion jumped.[32]

"Out you go!" cried Number 15's jumpmaster. "I'll never forget the look on Captain Reynolds [*sic*] face as he looked back toward the *stick*. . .," wrote Bill Bergmann, who was the number three man in the stick behind the CO. With the left engine burning, "engulfed in flames," Reynolds turned to Grice, his face was white and streaked with beads of sweat. It was the only time Reynolds had ever displayed fear. "Okay," said the Captain, his voice shallow. "Let's go!" Then Reynolds went out with Grice right behind. Then Bergmann jumped right behind him. Gripped by a terrible fear, and with the rest of the men behind him pushing like hell, Private Laufer too went out the door. Troopers and camouflage parachutes filled the air around them.

The men were pressing so hard they'd pushed Cobb right on past the door, but as soon as the light came on in 11, Lieutenant Joyce kicked Cobb in the butt and out the door he went. Once Cobb had recovered from the opening shock, he saw another trooper right next to him, screaming and hollering. It was Bill Bergmann.[33]

"After my chute opened (violently, it seemed)," wrote Bergmann, "there was an explosion nearby and I felt myself being propelled thru [*sic*] space. I couldn't even open my eyes as the pressure was so great." Small arms fire or a 20mm flak burst had ignited one of the white phosphorus grenades Bergmann had been carrying on his harness showering him with flaming phosphorus pellets. "Suddenly I realized I was on fire. . . the reserve chute was ignited. The smoke from burning nylon and the heat led me to believe 'Bill, you're not going to make it.' Having been raised by Christian parents I immediately said a prayer to the Lord, may His will be done."

"It seemed like a long time before I *klanked* [*sic*] to the ground. I was on the edge of a small brook [or irrigation ditch] and just had to roll over the embankment to put out the fire. The British *quick-release* button that was supposed to allow the chute straps to come off with one tap was encrusted with melted nylon and so I had to reach down and get my trench knife strapped to my right leg and cut the harness loose. About that time [I heard] the sound of another trooper hitting the earth and it turned out to be John Cobb. . ."[34]

Cobb, who'd lost his helmet in the jump and "felt a bit naked without it," helped Bergmann out of the water. Then, they decided to cross the road nearby and Cobb started 'slauntering' (slouching and sauntering) over it. Suddenly, bullets began cutting the branches out of the trees above them – a German machine-gun had the road zeroed-in. "Cobb stopped slauntering and ran at top speed." Bergmann followed next, crossing the road in "record time."[35]

With all the flak hitting the plane, the men on First Sergeant Donovan's C-46 knew they were close to the DZ. The intense groundfire was too much for the jumpmaster – one of the replacement lieutenants – to endure. He "chickened-out," said Donovan, and went to the front of the plane leaving the job to the first sergeant. PFC Sarrell and Donovan, still standing on the door bundle, watched helplessly as black smoke started to pour out of Number 11's left engine. Then, a flak shell burst close and the ship bucked. Sergeant Harvey, who was standing in the right door, was knocked back onto the floor, killed by shrapnel. Donovan lifted Harvey's body and pushed it out of the plane – there was nothing else he could do. Then the buzzer sounded and the green light came on. Donovan and Sarrell "got off the bundle, gave it a little push, Donovan followed and [Sarrell] was right behind. With the engine on fire everyone was pushing to get out," remembered Sarrell. PFC Ken Olson went out with the static line under his arm and was whipped around when the chute deployed. He landed in a field in about five inches of water.[36]

Lieutenant Kerr was doing his best to keep his ship level, pushing forward on the yoke as the troopers ran to the back of the plane. He figured he was at about five hundred feet and at a normal speed. When the last man cleared the ship, Kerr pushed the throttle forward as far as it would go and headed for the ground, picking up speed for the turn home.

Lieutenant Mael's Number 14 ship was doing 110 mph at seven hundred feet when he hit the drop zone. Just before they got the green light, a string of bullets ripped a line up through the floor of the troop compartment. Then something "the size of a truck" hit the left wing – a direct hit – and rolled the C-46 over on its right side. The left motor was burning and flames were streaming from it and past the door. "Oh Jesus, how are those guys gonna get out of there?" thought Greenstrand. Lieutenant Calhoun ordered all the men out the starboard door. Leading the men out, Lieutenant Diefenderfer was hit several times on the way down. Greenstrand went out right behind him, his chute oscillating wildly. He was glad the canopy was spilling air because he'd be on the ground quickly, but he also knew he was in for a hard landing. Greenstrand's chute took one last big swing and then he hit the ground at the same time as the canopy. "Ouch, what a landing!" he recalled. Greenstrand looked up for his ship; he was sure he'd seen it going down.[37]

Lieutenant Calhoun was the last man out. Having only been released from the hospital six days before, Calhoun missed the practice jumps and was given only a brief explanation of the new quick-release parachute. "Upon leaving the aircraft," he was told, "pull the safety fork and give the quick-release a half turn. When you're ten feet off the ground, press the quick-release and you'll hit the ground running!" Remembering these instructions, he pulled the safety fork and gave the quick-release a half turn. It was then he saw an empty parachute harness float past – its former occupant lay four hundred feet below, dead where he fell. Concluding that the dead man had either released the harness by accident, or that the quick-release device had been hit by shrapnel after the man removed the safety fork, Calhoun quickly replaced his own safety fork and rode the chute all the way to the ground.

As successive serials reached the drop zones, green lights were flashed and jumpmasters yelled "GO!!!!!" Thousands of canopies were filling the sky over Wesel. The concussion of exploding flak caused some troopers to oscillate crazily in their chutes as shrapnel ripped through the sky. Under the intense fire, the descent to earth seemed to take an eternity. In a desperate effort to escape the German gunners, some troopers, floating defenselessly, climbed their suspension lines, hitting the ground "with their heads in the silk." Many C-46s were damaged and some crashed, many before the paratroopers on board were able to jump clear. Floating down in his chute, Sergeant Hataway watched a C-46 plunge toward earth and strike a high wire, exploding.[38] Some 513th troopers, wounded by flak or groundfire while still in the planes, chose to jump rather than risk another moment in the "flaming coffins."[39]

Lieutenant Rothi dropped his paratroops and put Number 12 into a slow right turn away from the drop zone. His plane came under small arms fire as it passed over the Issel and was hit. Tech Sergeant Elder Loney, the crew chief, was pulling in the static lines when a single round "entered the plane just behind the pilot's seat and underneath the fuselage at an angle which severed the hydraulic lines in the compartment containing the put-put engine." "Is anybody hit?" Rothi called back. But no one had been injured. Rothi had a time getting the wheels to drop but eventually landed safely.[40]

After Number 14's crew chief, Tech Sergeant Marvin Graff, informed its pilot, Lieutenant Mael, that all the troopers had jumped clear, Mael pulled maximum power and began a climb-turn to the right. As he did, three flak rounds detonated in close proximity to the ship and a fourth entered behind the bulkhead separating the pilots' and the navigator's compartments and exploded inside the plane. The explosion blew a large hole in the right side of the fuselage, but, amazingly, no one was injured, nothing vital was hit, and the plane continued to fly unimpaired. Lieutenant Mael throttled back to 2150 rpm for the trip home while Tech Sergeant Graff and Staff Sergeant Angel Garcia, the radio operator, watched for fire in the rear of the plane.[41]

As his formation was approaching the drop zones, Captain Ed Yarborough, commander of a squadron of the 314th Troop Carrier Group, saw the C-46s of the 313th returning from the east side of the Rhine. VARSITY was Yarborough's fifth troop carrier mission, having flown four such prior missions in Sicily, at Salerno, at Normandy, and in Holland in his C-47 *Turf and Sport Special*. As his plane approached the Rhine, Yarborough first observed the thick smoke and haze blanketing the ground. Then he saw the C-46s. "They weren't flying in any kind of formation, the ships were just spread out in disarray. The formation was really chopped up and many were in trouble."[42]

On the ground, troopers collapsed their chutes with relative ease in the light winds, however; a lot of the troopers had trouble unfastening the leg straps of the quick-release harness making them relatively easy targets for German troops around the drop zones. Several men, including D Company's commander, Lieutenant Edgar C. Tommisino, were killed before they could get out of their parachute harnesses.[46] Several men had landed amid the high tension wires or in trees where their chutes became entangled and they swung in plain view of the enemy. Chutes hung, some empty, some "sagging under the weight of their lifeless burdens," all over the drop zone.[43]

Lieutenant Joyce came down atop a raised road and immediately came under the fire of a German machine-gun firing straight down it. Still in his harness, Joyce dived for the ditch and, in the process, rolled himself up in his canopy. More embarrassed than scared, Joyce untangled himself and set out to find his men.

Private Cobb saw Joyce run by and called to him, but Joyce, apparently not hearing, kept right on moving. Then another lieutenant appeared and yelled to Cobb, "You got a bazooka?"

"Yeah," Cobb responded.

"Get her out," the lieutenant ordered, and then led Cobb to a ditch where they prepared to take on a tank that was sitting in a field ahead of them. At first, an enlisted man with the lieutenant tried to help Cobb load the bazooka, but he didn't know how to wrap the wires extending from the rocket's motor onto the electrical leads. The lieutenant impatiently ordered the man, "Get out of here," and immediately took his place loading the weapon. Cobb fired twice, hitting the tank in the tracks with both shots. The tracks were broken, but after the second shot, the tank's turret began to swing around toward them. Cobb quickly suggested to the officer, "We better move down the street a little bit." The lieutenant agreed and together the men took off. However, a few stout-hearted troopers waited around and finished off the tank crew when they decided to abandon their vehicle.

Upon hitting the ground, Lieutenant Calhoun quickly pulled off the safety fork and started pounding on the quick-release mechanism. Nothing happened, however; he hadn't remembered to give the quick-release the half turn necessary to disengage the harness. As Calhoun struggled, a German PzKpfw Mk IV tank began backing out of a farm building not more than twenty-five yards away.

With his heart racing, Calhoun rolled into a nearby ditch, still frantically beating the quick-release as he did in an attempt to free himself before he was spotted by the German tank. He finally decided to cut himself loose. With his dull M3 trench knife, he sawed through the webbing, accidentally cutting the straps off his mussette bag in the process. He quickly stuffed whatever contents from the bag he could into the pockets of his jump suit.

Then, Lieutenant Calhoun cautiously rose up a little from the ditch and peeked at the tank. Its driver was trying to steer the tank away from the building without snagging a track and breaking it. The tank commander had his head sticking out from the hatch, apparently concerned only with directing his driver. Calhoun raised his M1A1 Carbine and squeezed off a shot at him. The tank commander grabbed his neck and turned around, and looked right into Calhoun's eyes. "Holy shit!" Calhoun exclaimed, as the tank began to swing its 75mm gun around, toward his hole. Calhoun sunk as deep into the ground as he could, hoping the tank could not depress its gun enough to fire into the hole. With a crack, the tank fired. The round plowed deep into the soft earth before it exploded. All Calhoun got was the concussion and a pile of dirt on top of him. Calhoun lay there a few moments, and then heard the tank moving off. He then got up and made it around the other side of the barn. There he found a medic, a BAR gunner, two riflemen, and a British paratrooper with a Sten gun. "Okay," thought Calhoun, "I've survived the jump!" and together with these men, he started off across a field in the direction Calhoun thought F Company should be.

Private Murray came down in a small field surrounded by low, bushy hedgerows. As soon as he hit the ground, a German on the other side of the hedgerow took a shot at him. Murray rolled into a ditch. "Are you hurt?" came a shout from another trooper on the far end of the field. "No," Murray replied. "Shake a bush," the other man shouted. Murray understood. He rattled some shrubbery and the German on the other side of the hedge took another shot. The trooper on the other side of the field again yelled to Murray, "Shake a bush again." Murray heard one shot from an M1. "Okay," yelled the trooper, "Go ahead." Private Murray inspected the bazooka he'd jumped with. It was a wreck – the pistol grip had been ripped right off.[44]

Coming in, PFC Sarrell watched the tracers and flak but didn't watch his landing. Therefore, he landed in what was probably the only tree in the drop zone. Suspended just above the ground, Sarrell had a difficult time getting out of his harness. Although he made a good target, amazingly, he wasn't shot. When he finally got out of his chute, he flopped down into the ditch next to the tree and waited until he'd caught his breath.[45]

The opening shock of Grice's chute was so severe that it ripped the leg bag in which he carried his machine-gun off his parachute harness. The machine-gun fell into oblivion. A flak burst close by sent shrapnel whining through the air, slightly wounding his hand. Then Grice, like Sarrell, came crashing down into a seemingly lone tree sticking up in the middle of a field. When he stopped, he was hanging several feet in the air, praying he wouldn't be hit, and struggling to get down fast. The night before, Grice had told the green men that they were in for a rough time. So far, it looked like he was right. Worried he was going to he shot if he didn't move fast, Grice dug into the top of his mussette bag and found his switchblade. He quickly cut the risers and dropped into the ditch below. The knife fell into the knee-deep water in the ditch when he landed, but he did not take the time to look for it. Instead, with his heart pounding heavily, he threw his mussette bag over his head, and pulled his M1A1 Carbine from its belt scabbard and loaded it.

A couple of other troopers were close by and Grice told them, "Let's go get that house," and motioned to a two story farmhouse less than fifty yards distant. The house was surrounded by level, cleared land, and there was an orchard to its left. The three men started firing and moved slowly forward until they were close enough make a rush. Still firing, they burst in the front door.[46]

Inside they discovered fifty Germans, all crowded together, waiting to surrender. They were mostly Luftwaffe personnel – and these were old men – but there were a few SS men bunched in among them. Grice relieved one of the Luftwaffe men of his Luger and its holster and told the rest to put down their weapons. The Germans responded sheepishly and the three troopers marched the prisoners out into the farm yard. Presently, the prisoners sat down, took out their mess kits, and started cooking their breakfast. The spread was too much for Grice to resist – eggs, bacon, ham, biscuits, jelly – so he sat down and joined in. "Do ya think it's poison?" one of the other troopers asked him. "Heck, no!" said Grice, his mouth full. After eating, Grice returned inside and broke the Germans' weapons, Mauser rifles, against a door jam. Grice and one of the other troopers then searched the house, finding in the pantry a one and a half foot slab of dry-cured bacon. Grice cut a big piece off for himself and tucked it into his mussette bag. "What are you gonna do with that?" his friend asked. "If I get a chance, I'm gonna cook it."[47]

The wind was gusting a bit when PFC Greenstrand landed on the soft, sandy ground, blowing the gun smoke that hung thickly in the air. Greenstrand almost couldn't believe the peculiar sight that greeted him. There, in front of him, was a one-armed British officer, carrying a pistol in his good hand, and "barking orders like mad." Greenstrand, however, had a more important concern and quickly turned his attentions to getting out of his parachute harness. Greenstrand turned the quick release, but it didn't open. Then he started pounding on it, but he still couldn't get it to work. Finally, he decided to cut the parachute off at the risers. Greenstrand readied his carbine, and then threw his mussette bag over his head and shouldered his Handy-Talky. Just as he began heading for a nearby ditch, another trooper being dragged by his chute blew past him. Greenstrand ran after the man and helped him collapse his chute until they came under machine-gun fire. Greenstrand then decided he better get in the ditch he'd been headed for.[48]

When he jumped in, Greenstrand discovered waist-deep water and several water-soaked paratroopers. One of these men was a sergeant who took charge and led the small group in an attack upon a nearby barn from which the enemy was firing. After a short exchange of small arms fire, the Germans inside surrendered. With the fighting growing steadily more intense, none of the paratroopers were happy about taking prisoners because they would have to hold them until they ran across some glider pilots whose responsibility it was to guard them.[49]

Greenstrand's group grew when a lieutenant arrived a few minutes later and took over for the sergeant. He directed them in clearing out the rest of the farm buildings in the immediate area and then led them toward the assembly area, prisoners in tow.[50]

As they walked, one of the other men said to Greenstrand. "You've got crap hanging all off you from that back pack. Why don't you take that goddamned parachute harness off?"

"It's jammed." explained Greenstrand.

"Pull the damn pin, stupid!"

Greenstrand looked down and pulled the pin and just touched the quick release. The harness fell right off. Greenstrand's crotch was raw from being wet, wearing the harness, and running all around the fields and, even worse, he now felt stupid. An aidman gave him some Vaseline. Although it didn't help his pride much, it did ease the rawness in his crotch.[51]

Just moments after leaving his plane, Private Laufer was on the ground feeling utterly alone and naked. "Oh my God, what am I doing here?" Laufer appealed to Heaven. Unfastening his harness, he anxiously looked around for a familiar face and soon saw a staff sergeant from the Second Platoon, and then Lieutenant Wieland, his platoon leader, appeared.

"Well, should we go on a patrol?" asked Wieland.

"You're the boss," voiced Laufer in approval of the idea. The sergeant agreed, too, and struck out immediately toward a nearby farmhouse with Laufer and Wieland following. Wieland peeled off to scout up ahead toward the assembly area while the sergeant kicked in the door and walked inside. Within, a young girl and her parents were cringing in fear. The sergeant took hold of the girl and ordered the father and mother upstairs. The sergeant then turned to Laufer. "I bet you don't think I'll fuck her," he said. Laufer didn't know what to say, and the sergeant raped the girl while Laufer just stood there, stunned. When he was finished, the sergeant told Laufer that it was his turn, but Laufer refused. The sergeant merely left and headed for the assembly area. Laufer followed.

When First Sergeant Donovan landed, he came immediately under fire. Still, he couldn't resist the temptation to cut out a big piece of his canopy for a scarf before seeking shelter. His silk in hand, he moved out toward a farmhouse situated among some trees. There, he found a wounded 2nd lieutenant who had been shot in the heel and said he could not walk. Although enemy machine-gun fire was intensifying, after the lieutenant pleaded for a while, Donovan agreed to take him to an aid station and picked him up. After carrying the lieutenant for nearly a half mile under fire, Donovan found the aid station. When the medics removed the lieutenant's boot, they discovered the wound, although bloody, amounted only to a nick. Donovan "wanted to kill that damn lieutenant."[52]

As PFC Cuthbertson cut himself out of his parachute, he saw Private John Brown emerge from the woods, his face and chest covered with blood. Cuthbertson thought that Brown had been hit but soon discovered that when Brown's chute opened, the risers had pushed his helmet forward sharply and "gave him a hell of a nose bleed." Don Shay landed in a pasture among several frantic dairy cows and one equally frantic bull. "He was not my biggest worry. . . finding cover was," said Shay. He found a ditch and jumped in. The ditch turned out to be an open sewer but, with all the 20mm flak and machine-gun fire going on around him, he didn't mind. Shay soon joined some other troopers and set out to join-up with the rest of F Company.[53]

Captain Bobby Scott's Spare Number 1, carrying the men from Number 13's takeoff accident, crossed the Rhine at 1025 hours. The men had been told that their plane would catch up with the formation; they wanted to jump with the rest of F Company, but this, of course, had never been more than a remote possibility. Up and ready to jump, PFC Dahlberg searched the sky, but no other C-46s were in sight. Because they were late – Spare Number 1 had met a glider formation approaching the landing zones at the same altitude – Captain Scott was forced a half mile right of course before reaching the river. With battle smoke and haze obscuring landmarks, and unable to pick up a Eureka Beacon signal from the DZ, Scott was uncertain of his exact position.[54]

By the time Scott ascertained his true position, he had already passed the DZ. As the plane passed over the Issel Canal it started to draw small arms fire, but this did no visible damage. Yet, Spare Number 1's ordeal had only begun. Tech Sergeant Joda peered out the door to the battle below. He could see the "gun flashes down in the woods." Gun smoke and the smell of cordite whipped through the open jump doors. Now he knew what it was like to be a duck on the first day of hunting season. With the ship now some distance east of the DZ, Scott immediately made a 180 degree turn and headed back toward the drop zone.

The troopers lurched back and forth as the pilot altered his speed. Flying sometimes fast and sometimes slow, Captain Scott was doing his best to dodge the 88s. The flak was so thick that it sounded like hail bouncing off the wings. On the ground, Private Greenstrand, stared up at the lone, lumbering transport. "The flak around that plane was unbelievable," he remembered.

Just as the plane reached the DZ, it ran into another glider formation. Scott was forced to make a large 360 degree turn and again the plane took small arms fire as it passed over the Issel Canal. At the completion of the turn, the C-46 was about a half mile east of the canal and Captain Scott daringly headed for the northern edge of the drop zone, still determined to get his troops out on target.[55]

As Scott brought the plane on a heading to pass over the drop zone, Tech Sergeant Joda and Sergeant Erb began tossing out the 270-pound parapack bundles. As the C-46, now heading west, passed over the Issel Canal for the fourth time, it caught two flak bursts. . . one about a foot behind the right door and the other underneath the right side." Blood splattered the inside of the plane and the right engine almost immediately caught fire.[56]

Inside the plane, panic broke out. Tech Sergeant Joda had been hit by flak fragments that shattered his right arm, severing nerves and arteries, and pierced his body in twenty-five places including his penis. Sergeant Erb was hit in the ear. At the end of the sticks, PFC Jack Cook accidentally spilled his parachute. Private James Cox, just eighteen, fell into the floor and couldn't get up, crushed by a terrible, weighty fear. Dahlberg started praying for all he was worth.[57]

Upon reaching the DZ, Captain Scott again had to maneuver – veering right this time – to miss gliders. By the time he recovered and the DZ was recognized, he had passed over the double-track railroad marking the DZ's western edge. Scott would not give the green light because if the men jumped then, they would land in the Diersfordter Wald. Instead, he continued to fly west to make a turn and come back for another pass over the DZ. As he started this turn, Captain Scott remembered, "the left rudder fell to the floor useless and when I tried to bring the wing up with the ailerons I discovered they would not operate [either] so I cranked it up with the rudder trim tab. With only elevators and rudder trim tab control it was impossible to make another pass at the DZ so I could only hold the heading I had."[58]

One of the aircrew told the paratroopers: "We're gonna crash land in a field." A kind of deliberateness now overtook the men – they wanted to jump. Scott began looking for a suitable field on the west side of the Rhine. One field "looked like it was growing telephone poles" – Rommel Asparagus, remembered Dahlberg. The next field looked good, however, and as soon as Scott reached it, he flashed the green light. The men clamored out as fast as they could go over parapack bundles piled in the floor. Three troopers – Sergeant Erb, Private James Cox who still lay in the floor, and PFC Jack Cook – stayed with the plane.[59]

The C-46 was only at three hundred feet when PFC Dahlberg jumped. The opening shock was so violent it ripped his mussette bag – with six 60mm mortar shells – from his harness. The chute had barely opened before he hit the ground. Dahlberg saw a lot of men running towards him and, unaware that he had landed on the friendly-held side of the Rhine, figured they were Germans and that he was done for. Much to his pleasure, Dahlberg realized he had landed among the guns of a British artillery battery and that the men were Englishmen. The gunners helped him from his harness, gave him a cup of tea and some chocolate, and generally made him feel at home.

When the troopers had cleared the plane, the radio operator, Staff Sergeant Vincent Russo, went to Joda's aid, applying a tourniquet to Joda's upper right arm "to stop the blood from spurting out." Joda could hear the engine misfiring; it had been "sputtering" since they crossed the Rhine. Russo yelled to the captain, "We're losing a lot of gasoline from the right engine or tanks." Joda knew his ship was going in.

A C-47 pulled along side Scott's ship and its pilot motioned for him to cut the burning engine, but Scott had already decided to make a crash landing and didn't want to sacrifice it – the engine was only running in "spurts" but it still had some power. Scott spotted a large "field straight ahead, dropped half flaps, and started in." He maintained 110 mph on his approach, cutting the power as soon as the plane cleared the trees at the edge of the field. 2nd Lieutenant Fred Davis, the co-pilot, "cut the switches and the fuel tank selector switches." Meanwhile, Joda, Erb, Cook, and Private Cox who had recovered and retaken his seat, braced themselves.

Scott finessed the plane in. With a terrible noise, dirt flew as the propellers bent into the soft earth killing the engines. The plane slid almost silently to a smooth stop about two miles southeast of airstrip B-100 at about 1050 hours – a perfect belly flop. The bottom of the plane had been flattened and there were a few holes in flaps and ailerons left by the fence posts the ship had run over. The flak shell that had struck near the right jump door had continued out through the left door and there was a bullet hole in the right wing center fuel tank.

The casualties, Joda and Sergeant Erb, were evacuated to the hospital immediately. Before departing, Joda was given Last Rites by a captured German priest. He did not die, however, but he never regained the use of his right arm. Privates Cox and Cook took off to rejoin F Company. Captain Scott and the rest of the crew began their journey home.[60]

After recovering from their individual landing ordeals, the 513th's troopers set out to silence the German defenses. Moving quickly, E Company's commander, Captain Harry J. Kenyon, destroyed a German machine-gun nest that was inflicting heavy casualties on his men, but was killed trying to subdue a second. Sergeant John F. Queenen crossed two hundred yards of open ground to convince a group of German riflemen firing on his men to surrender. Other men were being fired on from a building above which a Red Cross flag was being flown. When the troopers returned fire, the Germans displayed a white flag and the paratroopers closed in to take possession of the building. When the troopers were close to the building, the white flag was withdrawn and the Germans opened fire again, wounding several men. A few rounds from a bazooka eventually convinced these Germans to surrender. Company aidmen, exposed to the same crippling fire, constantly exposed themselves to recover the equipment bundles containing plasma and other vital medical supplies. One medic crawled from casualty to casualty, heedless of the enemy fire, until a sniper shot him through the head, the round punching straight through the red cross painted on his helmet.[61]

The Germans were throwing everything from small arms to 88s at 2nd Battalion, and from all sides, but the ground haze and smoke that blanketed the area and obscured landmarks for the American airmen turned out to be a boon to the paratroopers on the ground. Together with the flat terrain, and tall hedgerows which limited visibility to three hundred yards, the smoke kept the Germans from directing observed artillery fire upon Miller's men.[62]

PFC Pat Phillips had recovered his .30 caliber machine-gun from his leg bag and joined Podkulski, Spivy, and Sergeant La Riccia. Together, they started moving south, but were stopped by the sight of a large – and suspicious – haystack in front of a farmhouse. Phillips soon spotted the barrel of a German MG-42 machine-gun sticking out of it. The four troopers worked their way to the back of the farmhouse and then broke through the door. Inside was the German farm family who, Phillips could see, had just taken their photographs of Hitler off the walls and stacked them in a corner. They were prattling away in German and obviously terrified by the presence of the paratroopers. Podkulski motioned for them to get down on the floor as the rest of the men looked around for the entrance to the basement. They found the trap door and braced themselves. Then one of them threw it open revealing six German soldiers playing cards, apparently oblivious to the pandemonium outside. Without hesitation, the F Company men shot them down. Phillips went down in the basement and discovered a tunnel leading out to the haystack where the machine-gun was positioned.[63]

At another farmhouse, a German-speaking trooper in Haggard's group managed to talk the German defenders into surrendering. The German-speaking trooper then directed the prisoners to the rear and told them to "Go double-quick." The Wehrmacht machine-gunners went off at a run, but a tall, smartly dressed SS officer who was with them walked to the rear at a deliberately slow pace. Upset by this obvious defiance, one of the men fired at the man's heels with his Grease Gun. The SS officer, startled by the shots, jumped at first, but then stopped and looked back over his shoulder, fixing his gaze on the young troopers. The SS man smirked at them contemptuously and then turned and started walking off as slowly as before. The trooper who had fired raised his Grease Gun, ready this time to kill the officer, but Haggard told him to let the man go. Haggard admired the SS officer's guts, even though he thought it was only a fool's courage.[64]

As Lieutenant Calhoun and his little band moved to join F Company, he ran into a group of about ten enemy soldiers. With the small band of men he'd picked up at the barn following his lead, Calhoun jumped into a nearby hole and started firing. The Germans, having no cover, flopped down in the field. The Germans' officer quickly produced a white handkerchief and waved his surrender. Calhoun's band disarmed the Germans and, kicking the officer in his rear end, he sent them running for the rear. Calhoun fretted over the decision, however; MPs and glider pilots were supposed to take charge of the prisoners, but since there were abandoned weapons all over the fields, any German soldier who so desired could, amid the reigning confusion, rearm himself before the MPs got to him.

Most of the crew and troopers on Lieutenant Colonel Miller's Number 1 C-46 had become casualties. Miller's radio operators and runners had all been killed. Also lost were the operations sergeant, several wiremen, and Miller's S-3, Captain Jack D. Lawler, who was shot on the ground while trying to free himself from his parachute harness. All told, only four or five men from the Number 1 ship had survived the drop unscathed. Of more immediate consequence to Miller, however, was the loss of the two SCR-300 radios being carried on his plane. He would need them if he was to direct the organization of the battalion.

Almost immediately upon landing, Miller realized that his battalion had jumped on the wrong area – the double-track railroad was nearby, but the terrain features were not as they were supposed to be. The high tension line, visible above the tall hedgerows, was some distance to the east. The big question in Miller's mind was, "how far north or south he had dropped from the proposed DZ." The Colonel consulted his map and within five minutes had oriented himself. 2nd Battalion was to have landed on the western edge of Drop Zone X, but instead had been dropped about two thousand yards west of Hamminkeln in a British drop zone – more than two miles northwest of DZ X. Presently, Miller was joined by Lieutenant Horton, Lieutenant Walter Rydesky, and 1st Lieutenant Joyce from F Company, who had all landed nearby. Accompanied by these officers, Miller struck out for the high tension line to begin gathering his scattered command.[65]

The one thing Miller had going for him was that 2nd Battalion's troopers had not been widely separated in the drop. In fact, the entire regiment had landed together in a space no bigger than two square kilometers. Briefed to guide on a north-south power line which intersected Drop Zone X, troopers who landed east moved west towards it while those to the west moved east. Small bands of men drifted together, reducing enemy strong points as they went. Lieutenant Colonel Miller arrived at the power line where it crossed a field less than a thousand yards west of Hamminkeln. There, an SCR-300 was presented to the Colonel and within about thirty minutes he had gathered two to three hundred men on his spot. There were men from every company of the regiment and the Colonel organized them into an ad-hoc battalion. Under constant fire, but with at least a portion of his men assembled, Miller's force then set out for DZ X, Miller at the head of the column. Private Cobb saw Miller there, waving his .45 and yelling at the prone troopers, "Let's go! Get up off the ground and let's go!" The men got up, observed Cobb, and he led them. The troopers advanced in a skirmishing formation, guiding on the power line. Along the way, Miller picked up a 57mm recoilless rifle team.[66]

Suddenly, a German machine-gun, firing from the second story window of a farmhouse ahead, drove the men of Miller's force to the ground. On the right, closest to the farmhouse, was a haystack which a few troopers hid behind, out of view of the German gunner. The rest of the men were spread out across the new-plowed fields, pinned by fire. Every time a man moved, the gun in the window fired. Colonel Miller, watching impatiently from a patch of woods on the left that effectively covered him from the effects of the fire, yelled to the men behind the haystack, "Get that damn machine-gun." When no one dared to move forward, Miller, chafing at the delay in his advance, yelled again, "I said get up and get that damn machine-gun!" Again no one responded to the command. Now infuriated, Miller howled, "I wish I had the old 2nd Battalion, I'd show you how to get that machine-gun."

Incensed by Miller's remark, one of the troopers laying on the ground hollered back, "If you hadn't got the old 2nd Battalion all killed in the Battle of the Bulge, you'd have the old 2nd Battalion to take that machine-gun nest."

Miller jumped upright. "Who said that?" he demanded, almost coming apart with anger. "Who said that?" No one answered, but the men finally, and cautiously, moved forward, surrounding the farmhouse and inducing the German machine-gunners to give up. It was clear, however, that 2nd Battalion men were no longer willing to rush headlong into unnecessary risks simply to carry out one of Miller's gung-ho orders.[67]

At 1030 hours, the first gliders – British Horsas with their sirens wailing, and double-towed CG-4A Wacos – began to approach their landing zones. The troopers watched as glider after glider cut loose and dropped for earth. It was a harrowing experience. Not a single paratrooper would have traded places with the glidermen, "not if they gave me the whole airplane *and* the glider," remarked Laufer. If a tow plane got hit, the pilot released his glider right then and there, no matter where it was. Some of the gliders hit the trees, some snagged power lines, and others landed in the Rhine or the Issel Canal. Private Sarrell saw a big Horsa smash right through a farmhouse and drag a long stretch of wire and fence posts with it. Greenstrand saw one British Horsa's undercarriage strike the top of a barn. "The glider just kind of stopped and those Brits came out of there like popcorn." PFC Olson watched one glider smash into the embankment running along the Issel Canal and then saw the Germans rake it with machine-gun fire. In trying to escape, the glidermen were mowed down under the wing. Cobb looked up and saw a glider hit by an 88; the glider came apart and the 57mm cannon, the jeep towing it, and the driver went careening to earth. One glider pilot's body lay on the field, its arms and legs burned off.[68]

Major Edwards, who had come down about one hundred yards from one of the Issel Canal bridges east of Hamminkeln, also had stopped to watch the gliders land. During the sand table briefings at Achiet, Edwards had asked what organization was responsible for securing the nearby canal bridge, a steel span of some seventy-five yards – because it lay on the northern boundary of the 2nd Battalion's objective. "That will be taken care of by the British landing team," the briefing officer had told him.[69]

Edwards "heard this whistling noise that the CG-4A made when it was coming in. That sonofabitch [the British glider pilot] lined himself up – and he hit the entrance to the bridge and sheared both wings. The fuselage then rattled right on across the bridge coming to rest on the far [eastern] side with all the British personnel inside happy and well. In less than two minutes they had their machine-guns out and ready to go."[70]

Major Edwards was very favorably impressed with the skill, courage, and attitude of the British airborne troops. On the jump, the first man that Major Edwards had met and talked to was "a one-armed British brigadier general – a man tougher than hell." Edwards accompanied him to his headquarters and had a cup of tea. "Don't be in any hurry," was how Edwards understood their approach to war.[71]

By 1100 hours, Miller's force had advanced about a thousand yards south, but was held up by direct artillery fire and a German Mark IV tank. The tank, supported by other guns, succeeded in pinning down the left flank of Miller's advance. Just then, however, more British gliders began landing among the troopers. From a gigantic Hamilcar glider, a small Tetrarch light tank emerged and immediately engaged the Mark IV with its machine-gun, but a single hit from the Mark IV's 75mm high-velocity gun was enough to set the little tank ablaze. The 57mm recoilless rifle team fired two rounds, scoring a hit that broke one of the Mark IV's tracks. The panzer crew abandoning the vehicle were swiftly cut down by the troopers' rifle fire.[72]

Private Anthony Rybka was one of the Shoulder 57 gunners in F Company. "The damn thing was heavy," some sixty-five pounds, he explained, but, that aside, it was a terrific weapon. It had real stopping power and a range more than three times that of the M1 bazooka. The Shoulder 57 teams were made up of a gunner, sometimes an assistant, and two ammunition bearers each carrying six rounds. Schneck and Podkulski carried ammunition for Rybka. More accurate, with greater armor penetration and greater range than the underpowered bazooka, the 57mm recoilless rifle was a welcome addition to the Airborne men's arsenal. These guns were so important, in fact, that when Rybka was given it after the drop, Lieutenant Wieland told him, "You'll die first before you leave that weapon behind."[73]

With the tank knocked out, 2nd Battalion passed forward and Colonel Miller and company reached DZ X by 1145 hours.[74]

When he arrived, Colonel Miller was greatly relieved to discover the 466th Parachute Field Artillery Battalion had been dropped on the correct spot and was holding the ground. The artillery had a hard go of it, explained Edwards. They came in, "all ready to man their guns and [instead landed] on the hottest spot in the DZ." By the time Miller arrived, however, the artillerymen had achieved some semblance of order.

Mixed groups of 17th Airborne Division troopers – large and small – continued to join Miller's command. Most of the paratroopers quickly realized that they had jumped on the wrong field and, guiding on the high tension line, moved swiftly to the correct assembly area. Soon more than one thousand men, including the aid stations which had accompanied him, had assembled.[75]

When PFC Bergmann and Private Cobb rejoined the battalion, then assembling on DZ X, the first F Company men they saw were PFC Grice, Staff Sergeant Ben Faulk, their squad leader, and Sergeant Hataway, his assistant. Faulk took one look at Bergmann's charred uniform and multitude of burns and a stunned expression grew on his face. "What the hell happened to you, Bergmann?" he asked. A machine-gunner, Bergmann had jumped with two belts of .30 caliber ammunition draped around him. When the white phosphorus grenade he had been carrying on the jump went off, the heat from the explosion had caused nearly every round to cook off, yet none had pierced his body. The belts of empty cartridges were still wrapped around him. Bergmann's face, hands, and arms had all been badly burned by the searing phosphorus pellets, and though he wanted to stay, Faulk ordered him to go immediately to the aid station. Eventually evacuated to a Paris hospital, Bergmann spent the next two months convalescing.[76]

2nd Lieutenant Wieland, Staff Sergeant Kuntz, and PFC Laufer arrived soon after Bergmann departed. Wieland saw Grice and asked him, "Where's your machine-gun?"

"It's somewhere between here and the Rhine River," said Grice and explained what had happened.

Wieland apparently understood. "Here's your Grease Gun," he then said, putting it into Grice's hand, which had been bandaged by a medic. "I'm gonna put you at the head of the assault squad." Formed by combining two of the First Platoon's squads, the 'assault squad' had been had been organized at the marshaling area to carry out all of F Company's patrolling duties, flank patrols, and rear guards. To maximize their firepower at close-quarters, each of the men in the squad was issued a .45 caliber M3 submachine-gun.[77]

Meanwhile, the other battalions in the same area were beginning to assemble as well. Jumping right behind the men of the 2nd Battalion and onto the same DZ, troopers of the 1st and 3rd Battalions shared an equally rough time landing and assembling, and high tension wires, houses, trees, and the heavy German fire proved just as deadly.

By "hollering himself hoarse" for more than an hour, Major Morris Anderson, the 3rd Battalion Executive, collected a mixed force of about three hundred men and organized them into two companies of 150 men each. After orienting himself, he advanced toward Drop Zone X, guiding on the high tension line. However, Anderson's group met fierce resistance from German soldiers holed-up in nearly every house along the way.

By collecting four and five men at a time, Colonel Edward F. Kent, the 3rd Battalion CO who had resumed command of the battalion after the Battle of the Bulge, assembled about 150 troopers himself. Kent, however, unlike Major Anderson, was unsure of his position. 3rd Battalion's objective was to secure the eastern side of the regimental zone along the Issel Canal. Apparently concluding that the canal lay to the northeast, Kent set out in that direction, gathering men along the way. After covering only a short distance, Kent saw a spire and realized that it was the steeple of the church in Hamminkeln. Kent was surely able at this point to fix his position, but rather than turning southeast, toward his objective, he instead decided to continue on toward Hamminkeln anyway. On the outskirts of the town, Kent learned from British paratroopers that the 6th Airborne Division had entered Hamminkeln amid stiff German resistance and were heavily engaged; the pitched rattling sounds of German machine-guns were reverberating in the town. Kent decided then to fix his position at a crossroads, and turned his troops southeast.

Despite his detour to Hamminkeln, Lieutenant Colonel Kent reached DZ X at 1330 hours, about seventy-five minutes ahead of Major Anderson.[78]

Upon landing, Major Harry F. Kies, 1st Battalion's Commander, was immediately aware that he had been dropped in the wrong spot, but mistakenly believed that the main body of the 1st Battalion had been dropped on target. Therefore, accompanied by 1st Lieutenant Peter White, 1st Battalion's S-3, Kies set out to find DZ X where he believed his men were waiting. When Kies found no 1st Battalion troopers on the DZ, he decided to continue searching toward Heidi, a village about a half mile to the south. There, Major Kies and Lieutenant White were taken prisoner. Their captors relieved them of their small arms and knives, but, amazingly, failed to discover the grenades both officers were carrying. Kies and White were held prisoner for three hours during which time they acted as intermediaries between their German captors and elements of the 194th Glider Infantry Regiment who then were fighting in the area. Eventually, Kies and White talked their captors into surrendering and started back to DZ X to join their unit.[79]

Meanwhile, at "a farmhouse from which they could see the church spire at Hamminkeln," Lieutenant Richard Cosner, the Commander of Headquarters Company, 1st Battalion, and several officers from the battalion's rifle companies, began gathering their men. No one, including Cosner, knew exactly where they had landed, but when gliders started landing among the men, they concluded they had been dropped too far north. Cosner was just west of the high tension line – which was visible to nearly everyone on the ground – and only a few hundred yards south of Lieutenant Colonel Miller's 2nd Battalion rallying point. Cosner observed men from the other battalions moving south and deduced they were heading for the proper DZ, so Cosner got his men up and headed them south as well, guiding on the power line. Sporadic shelling and sniper fire caused several casualties during the advance, but Lieutenant Cosner's group soon arrived at the designated assembly area.

As the men assembled at DZ X, they were directed by their officers to clean up the last resistance in the area. PFC Cuthbertson saw Miller on the DZ, exhorting his men to attack. "He was there, waving his .45 in the air and yelling, 'Go get 'em boys. Go get 'em!' " Miller wanted the men to cross over the railroad embankment on the west side of the DZ, but machine-gun fire raked the top and the men were wary of exposing themselves. PFCs Cuthbertson and Sarrell sat tight and ignored the command. Suddenly, some ammunition boxes were hit by tracers from the German machine-gun and started exploding. "Miller got behind a house pretty quick," Cuthbertson remembered.[80]

This notwithstanding, with steady pressure, 513th troopers overcame most of the enemy's prepared positions and occupied farm buildings in the area, and, by mid-afternoon, organized enemy resistance around the assembly area ceased. A large number of German prisoners had been taken by the regiment. These Germans, lined up in long rows, appeared to be mainly young kids and old men, "the scraping of the barrel," according to Laufer. However, he took no chances. "You had to watch the young kids" said Laufer, "cause they were vicious little bastards."[81]

Once relative calm had been established, Colonel Miller reorganized the 2nd Battalion. Though a few men had shot every round they had by 1100 hours, there was no general shortage of ammunition – little had been expended during the advance toward the assembly area. The battalion's signal equipment and ordnance situation, however, was more critical. F Company had lost three of its nine M1919A6 .30 caliber machine-guns in the jump and D and E Companies were in similar situations. Headquarters Company, 2nd Battalion still had its four machine-guns but had only five of its radios in operation. The rifle companies still had most of their Handy-Talkies so they could stay in touch with Battalion, but these often were unreliable and their batteries rarely lasted longer than nineteen hours. On the bright side, 2nd Battalion had captured a number German trucks and cars, as well as bicycles, motorcycles, and various horse-drawn vehicles, so at least there was no problem moving what equipment they had.[82]

At about 1300 hours, came the resupply mission. Directed by 2nd Battalion's S-4, Lieutenant Raymond Stem, C-46s, C-47s, and B-24 Liberator bombers dropped 270 tons of supplies in parapack bundles from an altitude of between 250 to 300 feet. The drops were accurate – one bundle fell so close to Colonel Miller that it knocked him over. The bundles were full of rations and every type of ammunition as well as other non-lethal cargoes. When he arrived an hour later, First Sergeant Donovan kicked one open and in it he found bales of *Stars and Stripes* – printed that morning. The low flying B-24s, however, were subjected to anti-aircraft fire near as deadly as that which had been directed at the troop transports. In all, twenty B-24s were lost resupplying the 17th Airborne Division that day. This was a high price, especially when considering there was no great need for either food or ammunition, and that "more than adequate" supplies of all categories would be dropped the next day and would arrive with the overland tail.[83]

Meanwhile, troopers continued to drift into the assembly area. At about 1400 hours, First Sergeant Donovan, who was driving a captured German half-track, arrived with a group of about fifty F Company men. "What are you doing?" Haggard hollered to him. "I'm going out fraternizing," answered Donovan, grinning. "How do you know how to shift it?" Haggard yelled to him with a laugh. "I just put it in gear and see if we go," the First Sergeant replied. Donovan spotted Captain Reynolds – he could recognize the "tough little bastard" even from a distance – and reported. Donovan said to Reynolds: "I was told you were dead." Reynolds shot back that he had heard the same thing about Donovan. Needless to say, both men were glad the reports were false.[84]

On his way to the assembly area, Private Greenstrand had ended up with a bunch of troopers, numbering thirty to thirty-five men, led by Lieutenant Colonel Ward Ryan, the 513th's Executive Officer. Though the group never grew to more than fifty men, it was nevertheless a formidable fighting force. And Ryan, who had radio contact with Colonel Coutts, had taken about a dozen prisoners and quite a few civilians, too, many of whom had been laying in open ditches or hiding in cellars all morning until rounded up. After several hours of fighting, "Ryan's Raiders," as they came to be known, arrived at the assembly area with the civilians and prisoners in tow. Major Edwards, who'd recently rejoined battalion headquarters, noticed that two of the German soldiers were "drunker than hell." Both were getting hard to handle, but one, who kept talking to the other prisoners and civilians, had made them frightened and agitated. Edwards started toward him, intending to knock him unconscious by striking him over the head with his Grease Gun. Suddenly, Colonel Ryan grabbed an MP's Thompson submachine-gun, and walked over and pulled the man out of the group. Ryan then marched him fifteen yards away, recalled Edwards, "and shot this poor drunk sonofabitch and cut him in two – at about ten feet." The killing of this man made the rest of the Wehrmacht prisoners shut up, but the civilians became very frightened. There was a little girl among the civilians with a badly injured arm, and the men reported this to Doc Warner, the head surgeon of the 513th. Warner attended to the girl's arm and gave her mother a note to take her to the American aid station. This act of kindness seemed to ease the civilians' fears.[85]

When Colonel Coutts arrived on the drop zone, he ordered Lieutenant Colonel Miller out to accomplish 2nd Battalion's mission: to seize and hold the ground around a one thousand yard stretch of the Rees-Wesel Highway running through the Diersfordter Wald about 1,200 yards north of the village Diersfordt and to the west of the regimental zone. By about 1630 hours, enough men and supplies had been gathered for the battalion to begin its attack and so Miller moved the men out with E Company on the left and D Company on the right in a skirmishing formation. F Company was in reserve.[86]

Entering the eastern edge of the Wald, the men stormed a four-gun battery of single-trail 105mm field guns. The gun crews – 250 Germans including a full colonel – surrendered to the Miller's men without having put up much of a fight. Taking off his helmet to bare his shaved head, Grice taunted the prisoners and lunged at them like a wild man. The performance had desired effect. "They were scared to death," Grice recalled.[87]

The attack continued into the woods toward the Rees-Wesel Highway, encountering very little opposition along the way until the battalion reached its objective. There, at 1915 hours, Lieutenant Colonel Miller ordered his men to dig in along the road.[88]

Patrols were sent out and the men took turns on guard duty, everybody comforted by the steady pounding of the British guns firing on the west bank of the Rhine. Meanwhile, officers came and went from briefings at the battalion CP throughout the night. Since he was a radioman, Greenstrand was ordered to go out with a wire team to string a land line from F Company's position back to Battalion. It was getting dark, so he and his partner hustled, laying it right on the ground, and then quickly beat it back to the company. The assignment was, however, mercifully uneventful.

The night passed cold, and many of the men, like Laufer, tossed and turned in the freezing night air. Laufer's Mohawk haircut, though fearsome, didn't keep his head warm. He pulled his 'cunt cap' (a brown wool knit cap) down over his ears and shivered. Private Shay was cold, too, so he sought shelter in a shed. He found a blanket inside, but when he picked it up he discovered it was covering the bodies of two dead German soldiers. Shay had never been so close to the enemy and at first was startled. Though very cold, he left the blanket over the bodies.[89]

That afternoon, on the west bank of the Rhine, PFC Dahlberg had watched the men of a quartermaster unit playing baseball, carrying on as if completely removed from the war. On the east bank of the Rhine, men were dying. How abstract a scene it was, he thought. After dark, Dahlberg and the other troopers from Spare Number 1 were taken across the Rhine in a Navy LCVP. British engineers were already hard at work building a pontoon bridge across the river. Meanwhile, German planes occasionally appeared overhead, attempting to harry the engineers' work. After all the flak that had been fired that day, thought Dahlberg, the flak now being fired over the Rhine was Allied.

By the end of D-Day, the other battalions of the 513th, as well as the other regiments of the 17th Airborne Division, had taken all of their assigned objectives, too. Lieutenant Colonel Kent, having reorganized the 3rd Battalion of the 513th during the afternoon, had, by nightfall, established an all-round defense at the far eastern edge of the regimental zone with the 139th Airborne Engineers to the left rear, 1st Battalion of the 513th to the west, and the 466th Parachute Field Artillery Battalion between the 1st Battalion and themselves. 3rd Battalion remained in defensive positions through the evening, preparing to move across the Issel Canal in the morning. Some enemy movement was detected during the night, but the men felt certain that it was the noise of enemy soldiers trying to escape "the pocket" rather than attempting to slip patrols in through their lines.[90]

Major Kies and Lieutenant White finally rejoined the 1st Battalion of the 513th at 1630 hours. By that time, 1st Battalion, which was being held in regimental reserve, had prepared defensive positions in an orchard on the northern portion of DZ X. 1st Battalion's jeeps had arrived with the gliders and, since that time, the company supply sergeants had attempted to pick up the scattered parapack bundles containing heavy equipment and extra ammunition. However, because they remained under enemy fire until after dark, it was impossible to recover many of the bundles the first day.

The 507th Parachute Infantry Regiment, with the 464th Parachute Field Artillery Battalion attached, had been ordered to seize the southern portion of the Diersfordter Wald. The 507th's 2nd and 3rd Battalions landed on target, but 1st Battalion was dropped on the wrong DZ. Nevertheless, all of the regiment's objectives were secured by the end of the day. The 194th Glider Infantry Regiment, with the 681st Glider Field Artillery Battalion attached, began landing at 1030 hours. By noon, the combat team was seventy-five percent assembled, and by the end of the day had secured all of its objectives. Moreover, thirty eight of the fifty-one artillery pieces delivered with the division were in action by 1800 hours.[91]

What's more, British Airborne, too, had faired well in what was described as "an accurate and generally excellent drop," while to the south, the Ninth U.S. Army, successfully crossing the Rhine south of Wesel without the benefit of an airborne assault, had advanced their bridgehead even deeper than that of the British Second Army, and with fewer casualties.

The combined total D-Day casualties suffered by the American 30th and 79th Infantry Divisions of the Ninth Army were forty-one men killed, 450 wounded, and 163 missing in action. By comparison, the casualties suffered by the 17th Airborne Division during the assault, on the drop zones, and in the initial fighting were excessively high. Among the American airborne troops, there were 282 men missing in action, 834 wounded, and 393 men killed, almost twenty times that of either the 30th or 79th Infantry Divisions. British losses were at least as heavy. In addition, IX Troop Carrier Command suffered and additional forty-one killed, 153 wounded, and 165 missing.[92]

Of the 637 men of Lieutenant Colonel A. C. Miller's 2nd Battalion taking part in the operation, fifty-eight were either lightly wounded or injured, three were seriously wounded, and thirty-one were killed in action on the first day. Of these, at least thirty-one F Company men had been killed, wounded, or injured – over twenty-two percent. Not as bad as 4 January, but bad enough. Two of the battalion's jump casualties were fractured femurs – and were believed to have been initiated by parachute failures. At least one man fell to his death when his main and reserve parachutes caught fire and burned, and several company commanders and staff officers had been killed.[93]

Several explanations were offered for the high casualty rates among the airborne men. Officers of the 513th concluded that mechanical problems with the T-7 parachute were partially to blame, and believed, also, that their men had needed more training with the quick-release system prior to the operation. After removing their shoulder straps upon landing, many men found it impossible to unfasten their leg straps and had to instead cut their way loose. Lieutenant Rollie Cantley, the commander of H Company of the 513th, cut three men free himself. Delays in removing their parachute harnesses left many men exposed to murderous crossfire in open fields. Captain Arthur Young, a medical officer in the 3rd Battalion of the 513th, estimated that, among the men of his organization, over one hundred casualties, precipitated by mechanical failures in the T-7 system or by the men's inexperience in using it, were sustained on the drop alone – nineteen percent of the

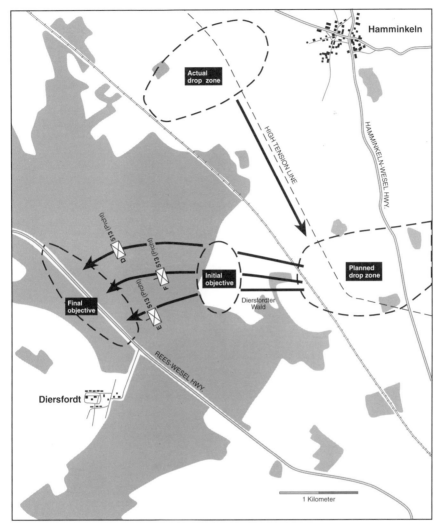

Initial landings and movement to objectives by the 2nd Battalion, 513th Parachute Infantry Regiment during Operation Varsity – Wesel, Germany, 24 March 1945. (Rick Brownlee/R&B Graphic Designs)

original 640 man force. Almost every parachute organization of the 17th Airborne Division suffered similarly.[94]

During Operation MARKET, 17-25 September 1944, only twenty-nine C-47s total had been lost by IX Troop Carrier Command while carrying American paratroopers to Holland. Comparatively, American aircraft losses during VARSITY were high, especially among the C-46 Commandos of the 313th Troop Carrier

Group which saw twenty-two of their C-46 aircraft shot down in only minutes over the drop zones. Of the six Commandos that carried F Company across the Rhine, one, Number 13, crashed on takeoff. Its replacement, Spare No. 1, crash landed. Number 11 received a "small hole," Number 12 had its hydraulic cables shot out and received a "small hole," Number 14 received a "large hole" from flak hits but returned, and Number 15 was only slightly damaged. Overall, aircraft losses can be attributed to the heavy concentrations of German flak batteries in the Wesel area and to the expertise of their gun crews, many of whom had been engaging Allied bombers for three years or longer. To these gunners, the slow, low-flying troop transports had presented easy targets.[95]

Glider and tow plane losses were comparable or only slightly heavier than that of earlier Airborne operations. Because the landing zones had not first been secured by paratroopers, many gliders, though landing directly on their objectives, were immediately taken under point blank fire by enemy artillery and machine-guns. Frequently, artillerymen, engineers, and glider pilots had to fight alongside the glider infantrymen to secure their LZs before carrying out their own missions. Ultimately, only 148 of the 902 CG-4A Waco assault gliders participating in the operation could be salvaged. "Those that were not shot up or wrecked on landing were vandalized by civilians for their clocks, compasses, and other parts." Twelve of the C-47 tug planes were lost, too.[96]

Despite having succeeded in securing all of its D-Day objectives, ultimately there remains the question of Operation VARSITY's relative contribution to the overall operation. It was the personal opinion of Major Robert Corey, Assistant G-2 of the 17th Airborne Division, "that the critical need of the operation had been overcome before the troops became airborne. The British landing of twelve hours prior had been so successful that there was no doubt of the success of the Rhine crossing before the Div[ision] started. At the last moment [I] figured that there might be a change[,] for the British were very successful in their crossing and had almost closed on the DZ area," however, the mission went ahead as planned. "Without doubt," continued Corey, "the operation did speed the British operations. Probably at the last moment, when the crossing of the Rhine was assured, [and before the planes had become airborne] the operation was mounted with this idea in mind. The airborne operation was not canceled as it was felt that the added speed was worth the cost." However, for all the sacrifices of the sky men, the Ninth U.S.

Army, without the aid of an Airborne assault, had, by the end of D-Day, expanded their bridgehead deeper in their zone than VARSITY had in the British Second Army zone to the north. Thus, when compared to the light casualties sustained by Ninth Army troops, the heavy casualties suffered by the Airborne troops are all the more grave. Moreover, Operation VARSITY may be seen as simply a lavish attempt by British Airborne planners to redeem themselves for their failure to secure a bridgehead over the Rhine at Arnhem the previous September. Though successful within its limited scope, the contribution to PLUNDER rendered by VARSITY, in the end, had not been worth the cost.[97]

10

Spearheading East

Breakout to the Herman Goering Barracks
25 March - 4 April 1945

On the morning after the drop, Division intelligence located the German front lines – which took the "form of a series of small unit positions, partially dug in, only lightly supported by artillery, and manned by assorted units comprising remnants of the *84th* and *180th Divisions* plus new units from *B.G. Karst*" – running roughly along the Paris Line from Brunen to Drevenack. Those elements of the German *84th* and *180th Divisions* still fighting in the Wesel bridgehead were dissolving rapidly. Even with the entry of the new *Kampfgruppe Karst* – composed of several well-organized combat teams – into action at Brunen and to the southeast, and the threat of German reserves entering the line, the enemy apparently was only capable of launching weak, local counterattacks before falling back on new defensive lines. Though the infantry regiments were still cleaning out isolated pockets of resistance in the airhead area, the 17th Airborne Division used most of the twenty-fifth to secure their zone and reorganize before striking east.[1]

Dawn found Miller's 2nd Battalion dug in along the Rees-Wesel road, a short distance from the Diersfordt Castle, and about five miles north of Wesel. Most of the troopers had sat up through the night listening to the guns, watching anti-aircraft fire light up the sky, and shivering in the cold night air. At 0515 hours, orders were passed down to Colonel Miller instructing the 2nd Battalion to attack west, through the woods, and clear out the area between their present position and the Rhine River. Miller put F Company on the point, with E Company, Headquarters Company, and D Company following in that order.

With its assault squad leading, Lieutenant Wieland's platoon was spread out across a two hundred yard front. Second and Third Platoons lined up on either flank. Reynolds instructed his men to shoot anything that moved, and F Company started through the woods, expecting all hell to break loose. "The forest was riddled with bullets," commented Contreras, "some of those trees looked like they been attacked by woodpeckers." The whole area was littered with the dead of both sides, but the scouts, well out in front, were only occasionally slowed by sniper fire. No other contact was made "except for a big buck deer that made [Cuthbertson] jump some when [it] took off."[2]

In the forested area, F Company discovered a number of dead paratroopers, men who had landed in trees and, as they hung defenseless twenty feet from the ground, were shot dead by the Germans. While some men stood gaping at the grim spectacle, suddenly, shots echoed through the trees from up ahead, the thumping staccato of a Grease Gun. Lieutenant Wieland turned to his men and asked, "Who's doing all that firing?" "That's Grice," one of the men laughingly answered. There were bunkers all through the woods, evidence that the Germans had at least at one time intended to defend the Diersfordter Wald fiercely. Whenever he came upon one, Grice burst into it recklessly, firing up a storm, but found them empty. Just when he figured the enemy in the area had all disappeared, Grice came to a group of about ten Germans standing quietly outside their bunker, their hands raised dazedly. Grice searched them and then pointed them to the rear.[3]

Greenstrand, with Third Platoon's Handy-Talky, stuck close to Lieutenant Stanley. He still remembered Mande-St.-Etienne, and the gloom of these woods made him nervous. Sergeant Haggard's voice crackled over the radio. "What do you got out there?" inquired Haggard from company headquarters – well to the rear. Greenstrand reported that they had not made contact. As the company edged deeper into the woods, Haggard's calls became more frequent. Tired of the constant hails, and afraid the radio noise was giving away his position, Greenstrand declared hoarsely, "Nothing! If I see anything, I'll call you. Don't call me!" Greenstrand was immensely relieved when the advance finally broke into thinner woods and then out onto open countryside.

After two hours, the objective was occupied and the battalion prepared to defend it. While F Company dug in on the right flank and prepared emplacements, additional ammunition, weapons, and signal equipment were brought up on captured or commandeered vehicles. Meanwhile, E Company set up on the left and D

Company was made the reserve and placed in the line behind F Company. The battalion's heavy weapons and the machine-guns were then set up to defend along the line and further plans were made to repulse counterattacks from the northwest, southwest and west. Contact was soon made with the 3rd Parachute Regiment of the British 6th Airborne Division to the north and, to the south, with the 507th Parachute Infantry. The troopers also "liberated" a group of B-24 and C-47 crews who had "barricaded themselves inside a farmhouse." By 0800 hours, fifty enemy prisoners had been taken and 2nd Battalion's mission was accomplished: troops crossing the Rhine could "proceed eastward without danger of receiving fire from this area."[4]

At 1715 hours, 2nd Battalion was placed in regimental reserve for the division's attack east toward Brunen and returned to the assembly area on the drop zone. As another day ended, Lieutenant Calhoun watched Service Company men and the "jockstraps" (men from the division's baseball team) picking up the bodies of the dead and stacking them – six feet high – on jeep trailers. Private Lightcap was with the graves registration personnel that day. Among the dead, Lightcap found the body of Sergeant Tom Harvey, who had been killed while still on board Number 12 on D-Day. According to Ken Olson, Harvey's body had come down in a tree after it was thrown from the plane. Lightcap removed Harvey's personal effects, including a photo of his wife and child, then buried his body.

Ever occupied by thoughts of food – he even admitted he'd rather carry food than ammunition – PFC Grice asked his buddies, "Y'all want some chicken?"

"Where you gonna get that," they asked skeptically.

Grice pointed to a small farm a few hundred yards to the south. "That yard's full of them down yonder," Grice said and then announced that he was going to ask for a few chickens. Everyone agreed it was a good idea, so Grice picked up his Grease Gun and walked down to talk to the farmer.

As Grice approached, the farmer, who appeared to be about sixty-five, came out to meet him. Grice pointed to three chickens and informed the farmer that he wanted them. The farmer, however, had no intentions of giving anything to an American. "No chickens. No chickens," he repeated, his body language alone sufficient to make himself understood. At about that moment, a young woman stuck her head out one of the windows of the house to see what all the commotion was about. Grice took one look at the girl and let out a big "Whoo-whee!" implying that, if the farmer refused to part with the chickens, then he might have to take the girl as conciliation.

The farmer immediately gave up the three chickens and then led the husky paratrooper into his house where he pressed shortening, flour, and a frying pan into his hands. Grice, who couldn't believe his good fortune, thanked the farmer and walked off back to his platoon-mates.

Everyone was elated over Grice's coup, especially Grice. After he cleaned the birds, singing off the feathers he hadn't been able to pull off, he began frying them. His buddies asked, "Where did you learn to cook chicken?"

"I've lived on a farm for years," Grice said proudly.[5]

Seven F Company men separated from the company since the jump, including Staff Sergeant Dornbos, Sergeant Sorenson, and PFC Olson, returned that day as well. Olson and two other troopers had spent the night huddled in a slit trench under the wing of a smashed up glider. All night they listened as German patrols walked around, searching for the enemy in the dull moonlight. Olson knew they were Krauts because the rattling sound their gas mask containers made gave them away. Toward morning, and with better light, they could see patrols coming, so Olson's little band dug in while one man kept a look out. Then, when they felt it was safe, they made their way back to the company.[6]

While Miller's 2nd Battalion was working its way back toward the Rhine, the 1st and 3rd Battalions of the 513th crossed over the Issel Canal at about 1430 hours to take up positions along the Autobahn. Relieving elements of the 194th Glider Infantry Regiment, Major Kies' 1st Battalion moved into new positions along a three thousand yard section of the highway around the village of Bruner Bruch. Meanwhile, using a captured foot bridge or simply by wading the three or four feet deep water in the canal, Lieutenant Colonel Kent's 3rd Battalion pushed across the Issel and two hundred yards further east to dig in on 1st Battalion's left. That evening, the two battalions consolidated their positions and mopped up the remaining German resistance in their zones, capturing numerous enemy vehicles and sixty-three prisoners. Beyond the Autobahn, patrols later found several houses to be strongly held by the enemy.[7]

At the close of 25 March, the 17th Airborne Division was in a firm position along the Issel Canal with the 513th Combat Team on the left, contacting the 6th British Airborne Division; and the 194th Combat Team on the center contacting both flank elements; while the 507th Regimental Combat Team, on the south or right flank, contacted the British 1st Commando Brigade – attached to the division in reserve – which was firmly established in Wesel. Bridges had been secured intact across the Issel River, armored attachments had joined their respective combat teams, and the teams had re-grouped and relocated. Morale was reported to be high throughout the 17th Airborne Division and casualties had been light.[8]

On 26 March, the 17th Airborne Division renewed its attack, jumping off from the line of departure 'London'. The 30th U.S. Infantry Division was advancing along the south side of the Lippe Canal on the division right, contacting elements of 1st Commando Brigade, and the 6th British Airborne Division was on the division's left.[9]

The 17th Airborne faced a mixed bag of enemy formations ranging in quality from German parachute troops to line infantry to anti-aircraft units, even 'stomach battalions'. The enemy, however, had no strong reserves available with which he might intervene on his front and General Miley's G-2 believed the enemy was withdrawing to more defensible positions along the line Bocholt-Dorsten. A few large enemy vehicle concentrations were observed, but these were apparently moving east, away from the battle area.[10]

The 513th's attack, which was conceived to expand the bridgehead while preventing the Germans from containing it, was begun at 0900 hours. The attack of the 1st Battalion, which was ordered to capture the town of Stratman which lay astride the 'New York' phase line, was almost immediately held up by heavy German small arms fire which caused several casualties including the B Company commander. C Company, in reserve on the west side of the canal, was soon committed and, after battling its way across the canal, reached the Autobahn by 0945 hours. Major Kies reorganized his battalion and, at 1300 hours, the attack was resumed and this time made good progress, reaching the Brunen-Wesel Highway. There, the battalion was again stopped by German troops "in strong entrenched positions with panzerfausts, light and heavy machine-guns and small arms." Four artillery concentrations broke the enemy's defenses and the battalion then pushed on into Stratman, taking some 250 prisoners.

Lieutenant Colonel Kent's 3rd Battalion, on the regimental left, was ordered to seize the tall hill west of Brunen along the 'New York' phase line. Short rounds from Corps artillery's ten minute preparatory barrage caused four casualties among Kent's men, but nevertheless, the attack jumped off on time. G and I Companies, supported by the fires of three British SPs and a platoon of Shermans from the 771st Tank Battalion, ran into stiff opposition right from the start. However, this was swiftly overcome and, after taking more than two hundred prisoners, the battalion then moved ahead quickly across a 1,500 yard front. A twenty-five minute artillery preparation was placed on the battalion's objective as it approached and, after it was finished, the assault companies advanced up the hill with walking fire and under the direct fire support of the British SPs and Shermans. With the shelling keeping the enemies' heads down, the battalion stormed the hill killing several Germans and capturing sixty more prisoners at a cost of twenty casualties to the 3rd Battalion. Kent then pushed into the outskirts of Brunen were he contacted elements of British Airborne on his left and Kies' 1st Battalion on his right.

At 0945, while the 1st and 3rd Battalion were attacking east, the 2nd Battalion of the 513th moved out, following behind the leading elements of the regiment. Just after noon, 2nd Battalion began encountering some light enemy opposition, and then, at 0215 hours, word reached Lieutenant Colonel Miller from regiment that the Germans were mounting a counterattack from the vicinity of Brunen. Strong security was posted in the 2nd Battalion area, but the enemy's counterattack, which proved only to be in company strength, was soon interrupted by the arrival of British Mosquito fighter-bombers.[11]

Air support during and after VARSITY was coordinated by British air-liaison teams – known as 'Tentacle' teams – which had been attached to the 17th Airborne two weeks prior to the operation. The RAF provided excellent support to the men on the ground. Rocket-firing Tempest fighter-bombers struck targets ahead of the advancing troops, in some cases within ten minutes of a mission being requested.[12]

Though the threat of a counterattack seemed to be diminishing, F Company men remained on edge. The only incident occurred in the afternoon, when Grice spotted a bicycle rider approaching his position and opened fire with a .30 caliber machine-gun. Bullets ripped up the earth around the bicycle, spilling the rider into the road. When he approached to investigate, the rider, who had been hit in the foot, turned out to be a young woman dressed in men's clothing. Grice applied a dressing to the wound, and then picked her up and carried her to the medics.[13]

By day's end, the 17th Airborne Division, including the 513th, had advanced three thousand yards and taken all of its objectives. In their advance east, troopers of the 513th Parachute Infantry had destroyed five 88mm and two 20mm enemy guns, and captured 497 prisoners. At 2100 hours, 2nd Battalion, which, by that afternoon, had assembled about two miles west of Brunen, was relieved from reserve by the 1st Canadian Parachute Battalion, 3rd Parachute Brigade. The balance of the 513th was relieved by the British 6th Airborne early on the morning of the twenty-seventh. The 1st Battalion then reverted to division reserve and the 2nd Battalion was ordered to move into the line.[14]

On 27 March, the 513th moved to the vicinity of Peddenberg, east of Wesel, where it was attached to the 6th Guards Armored Brigade to act as infantry support. The Guards were assigned to the XIX U.S. Corps, that had assumed responsibility for that sector of the line from the XVIII Airborne Corps.[15]

At about 1100 hours, the 3rd Battalion marched to an assembly area near Peddenberg and joined up with a fifty tank task force of the Coldstream Guards. The battalion mounted the tanks and, against only light and sporadic shelling, proceeded along the Wesel-Münster Highway, halting about five miles west of Dorsten. 1st Battalion too moved to new positions west of Peddenberg, but remained there in division reserve.[16]

At 1125 hours, on the heels of the 3rd Battalion, Lieutenant Colonel Miller's battalion marched south to Peddenberg where they too were to join a British tank unit. As they neared the town, F Company's lead men came upon a lone house on the edge of the village. To enter Peddenberg, the company had to cross the open, flat field that lay in front of it. The men were leery, the house might still contain an enemy machine-gun. Deciding a detour would take too much time, Reynolds ordered a cautious advance. Some troopers entered the house, turning up a civilian man and woman, and one German soldier who was cooking his lunch and seemed only too happy to give himself up. As the company continued on into town, they walked past a Standard Oil gas station and, in its drive, was a 1937 Chevrolet pickup truck, painted camouflage. Haggard went over to take a look but was disappointed when he couldn't find any keys.

Soon the company was walking into the town center where tanks of the 3rd Battalion, Scots Guards, commanded by Lieutenant Colonel Claude I. H. Dunbar, were dispersed. Colonel Dunbar's tank battalion was composed of fourteen British Churchill tanks, seven American tank destroyers, and several little Bren Gun Carriers. F Company men were told that the Guards had been in the line for more than one hundred days, and the vehicles showed every hour of it. The tanks were banged up, rusty, and dirty from weeks and months of hard fighting. "Hell," commented Donovan, "they were just worn out." The twenty-eight ton A22 Churchill Infantry Tanks boasted six inches of armor in front, but with a plodding road speed of only 15 miles-per-hour and their inadequate 75mm main guns, they were out-classed by every German tank they met. Nevertheless, the paratroopers were impressed. "Any German that doesn't put up a white flag when he sees this must be crazy," thought PFC Dahlberg as he looked at the long column.[17]

The British battalion was divided into three squadrons and a rifle company from the 2nd Battalion was attached to each. Lieutenant Calhoun packed Third Platoon on board the first three tanks in the column; the rest of F Company climbed onto the next seven. Private Cobb got on Calhoun's tank carrying his bazooka. "We're heading into Germany!" one of the men shouted. At 1645 hours, the column moved out, through the positions of the 507th, bound for Dorsten.[18]

After advancing for only thirty minutes along the Wesel-Münster Highway, Colonel Dunbar's column came under fire from enemy self-propelled guns, but soon the enemy was forced to withdraw. Nightfall, however, then caused the column to halt and while the tankers waited for the moon to rise. The troopers dismounted and dug shelters, but no enemy fire was received during the halt.

The 17th Airborne Division's attacks on the twenty-seventh made large gains and the division captured more than five hundred prisoners. 1st Battalion of the 507th Parachute Infantry advanced some 1,500 yards east before 0900, and then continued to the 'Detroit Line' where it made contact with the 30th U.S. Infantry Division on the south side of the Lippe Canal. On the division left, the 194th Glider Infantry Regiment advanced approximately two thousand yards.

By the twenty-eighth, the 17th Airborne Division, in cooperation with the 6th Guards Armored Brigade, had driven a 33,000 yard salient into the German lines, placing them well ahead of the Ninth U.S. Army formations to the south that were up against more determined resistance. All indications were that the 17th Airborne had pierced the enemy's main line of resistance, the weight of the attack completely demoralizing the enemy. The attacks of the division's 194th and 507th Combat Teams on 28 March captured Wulfen and closed on the 'Miami Line' at 2200 hours. Throughout the day, only token resistance was encountered.[19]

At 0055 hours that morning, F Company troopers mounted the British tanks and Colonel Dunbar's task force resumed its advance northeast toward Holsterhausen and Dorsten. Dunbar's advance, however, was again delayed east of Peddenberg by fire from German SPs. The enemy strongpoint was eliminated and the task force again pushed forward, toward Schermbeck. Though some of the tankers had been killed or wounded in the action, no troopers were injured.[20]

The enemy tried various passive methods to slow the spearheads down. Sometimes holes were dug in the middle of the highway, recalled Private Lightcap. "If you weren't privy to it, you'd just drop right in." Just underneath a viaduct, he recalled, was a favorite place for this sort of trap. The Germans also placed heavy abatis in the roads, forcing the tanks to maneuver through muddy fields to get around them. Once, when his tank turned into a plowed field to bypass one of these obstacles, PFC Olson was thrown off into the mud. Sarrell alertly stuck out a hand and pulled Olson back on before he was left behind. The column was pressing on quickly and would stop for no one.[21]

Snipers firing at the column from roadside farmhouses posed a more immediate threat, and were dealt with ruthlessly. Troopers systematically doused any house harboring a sniper with gasoline and burned it to the ground. Quite a few houses were burned down on the road to Dorsten.[22]

At Schermbeck, still about seven kilometers from Dorsten, an enemy roadblock and a self-propelled gun firing timed charges forced Colonel Dunbar to bypass the town. Tanks followed the leader across the sodden ground, once again jostling the riding troopers. Private Shay was perched on the fender as his tank churned through the field. Mud, carried up on the tracks, began to "ball-up" under the fender, rolling it up. Suddenly, Shay was thrown off and in the darkness, with his cries drowned out by the din of the engines struggling to get the tanks through the mud, no one noticed. Shay reached out and grabbed the tank's hand-hold and "held on for dear life," all the while hollering at the top of his lungs for help and thinking he was a "goner." Finally, his cries were heard over the engine's roar, and a fellow trooper got the attention of the tank commander who stopped the tank long enough for Shay to climb back on. This incident not withstanding, and although two tanks became bogged in the soft fields and were left behind, Dunbar's column outflanked the enemy positions to the south and, cutting across country, emerged on the road east of Schermbeck.[23]

The two British tanks and their riders, left behind at Schermbeck that morning by Colonel Dunbar when they became mired in the mud, were attacked by German infantry as they tried to catch up with the rest of the column. Some German soldiers bypassed by the column earlier that morning apparently had lain in wait on the highway for just such an opportunity. The leading tank was struck and damaged by a panzerfaust antitank weapon, a short-range recoilless antitank grenade launcher tipped with a hollow-charge warhead capable of penetrating up to ten inches of armor plate. "Being hit with a panzerfaust," suggested Staff Sergeant Charles J. Bailey, who joined F Company as a replacement on 25 March, "was like being hit by an 88." The tank's driver was killed and three troopers riding on the engine deck were wounded. The paratroopers drove off the ambushers with small arms fire, and then little group continued toward Dorsten to rejoin the command.[24]

A more serious problem facing the task force was the inadequate communications arrangement between the tankers and the paratroopers. Typically, the tank column commander issued orders to individual tanks over the tanks' radio net, however; these transmissions caused interference in the radios of the 2nd Battalion. In addition, the tanks' engines caused static in the battalion radio net and the noise of the motors often drowned out communications – verbal or via radio – altogether. The length of the column also prevented close communication and the speed of the advance kept communications between 2nd Battalion and Colonel Coutts' headquarters "spotty." Furthermore, there was no way for the paratroopers on the tanks to communicate – except in the most rudimentary ways – with the tank crews. The consequence was that the paratroopers often ran unprepared into a fight. Therefore, Sergeant Haggard advised the men on his tank to watch the tankers and if they buttoned up, it was the one sure way of knowing they were getting ready to see some shooting.[25]

As the column neared Dorsten, Lieutenant Calhoun's platoon, riding the leading Churchills, was afforded no such warning when the head of the column, which had reached the village of Holsterhausen, was taken under fire by German machine-guns. The fire forced the troopers to scramble off the Churchills and run for the safety of the ditches. The column halted momentarily, but moved forward suddenly, leaving Lieutenant Calhoun's men to hoof it behind them, through the enemy fire, the last mile.

The column rumbled into the outskirts of Dorsten, a town of moderate size but possessing an important network of rail lines, at 0710 hours. The Germans still occupied the town, although not too strongly, and were firing down from the buildings at the column. Those paratroopers still riding dismounted and, on either side of the street, cautiously advanced into the town supported by the tankers whose tactics were to fire at anything moving or visible. Cobb, up front with his bazooka, was surprised by a German tank which "stuck his head right around a building" at him. "He [the tank's commander] seen me," recalled Cobb, "and he took off." The Germans were ready to run and Cobb couldn't blame them. Resistance quickly crumbled as the men began cleaning out the houses. Germans threw down their steel helmets and put on *kaput* hats. Last to leave, a squad of German infantry, each armed with a bazooka, were chased from the town leaving behind a great number of dead and wounded. This took about an hour and when the area was fairly secure, Dunbar's task force received orders to remain in Dorsten throughout the day and evening, and await further orders to move.[26]

Captain Reynolds, who had picked the *Hervest-Dorsten Bahnhof* (train station) in the center of the town for F Company's CP, ordered Sergeant Haggard to set up his radio in the basement. Haggard remembered this well because the body of a young German girl, apparently killed during the fighting for the town, lay in the yard outside. Meanwhile, Lieutenant Calhoun had been ordered to dig in his platoon along the forward edge of a nearby railroad embankment which was about twenty feet tall, and on which were at least four rail lines. The other platoons began digging in on nearby embankments, too. As the men worked on their holes, they were harassed by light enemy small arms fire and sporadic shelling.[27]

While his men were busy digging in, Calhoun set up his CP in a house nearby. When everything there was in order, Calhoun started back toward the railroad embankment to check on his platoon's disposition. The artillery that had been sporadic up until now, suddenly intensified. Calhoun sprang into one of a line of boxcars standing on a siding for cover. With the shelling's pitch increasing, Calhoun started leapfrogging from one car to another, back toward his CP. It seemed that each time he reached the safety of another car, a shell would splinter the one he'd last occupied. Finally, he reached a shelter, and it was then he spotted the little U.S. Army 'grasshopper' flying above.[28]

It was fortunate that Reynolds ordered the men to dig in because the Ninth Army was unaware that the 513th Parachute Infantry had captured Dorsten and, apparently, was shelling the town while one of their spotter planes was flying overhead, correcting fires. The men had no sooner finished their holes when the first shells struck.

"We didn't dare get out of our holes," said Sarrell, but after several minutes of the pounding he turned to the man with him, PFC Joe Gutt, and said, "We got to get out of this thing." Sarrell and Gutt slid down the back side of the embankment and joined several other men taking cover under the tanks. PFC Dahlberg was already there, and the shrapnel from the exploding shells was clanking like hail against the tanks' armor. More men presently joined them, including an F Company sergeant who kicked one private in the butt to make room for himself. When the sergeant crawled under one of the Churchills, he became wedged and later had to be dug out. Some men went into the basements for protection, but not Sergeant Haggard. When the shelling started, he sprang out of the train station and ran for a nearby bomb shelter. It wasn't very spacious, but the concrete walls were thick and it offered good protection. The Germans, Haggard thought, must have had the shelter's location zeroed-in because "they were pounding the hell out of it." Finally, word reached Ninth Army that the men being shelled were British and American, but not before several 2nd Battalion men were injured and one man was killed.[29]

Though Ninth Army's artillery was now silent, the men were still under sporadic German artillery fire. Nevertheless, Reynolds decided it was time to get a look at the company's positions for himself. Reynolds found Calhoun on the railroad embankment and had just begun talking with him when some shells struck close by. Reynolds took a piece of shrapnel in his ear and tumbled down the embankment. Though the wound made his neck stiff and sore, he refused to be evacuated.

Haggard, who had returned to the station and was now peering out of one of its tiny basement windows, watched as Reynolds returned. "What happened to you, Captain?" asked Haggard, noticing the bleeding gash.

"Well," said Reynolds in an undisturbed tone as he pressed a red-stained handkerchief against his injured ear, "those sonsabitches took a shot at me. I think the sonsabitches are trying to kill me." Reynolds then turned and went about his business. Haggard stood there for a minute, a little surprised the Captain could remain so composed while bleeding so profusely. Reynolds then climbed into a makeshift bed where he remained until it was time for him to get the battalion attack order for the next day.

Soon after settling himself, Reynolds remembered that he still needed to send a message to one of the platoons. Since he didn't have radio contact, he ordered Haggard to send a runner with the message. Haggard picked a man for the task and gave him the message, but since the shelling was still going on, Haggard told him, "Wait a couple of seconds until this barrage stops, then scoot." But the barrage continued and Reynolds got up momentarily and asked Haggard, "Did you send that guy yet."

I'm getting ready to send him now," Haggard answered. "He's gonna wait till this barrage is over."

"You send him right now," said Reynolds. "I don't give a damn if a barrage is going on or not. You get that man out of here."

The man turned around and gave Haggard a wide-eyed look. Haggard just told him, "You gotta go." The man went, and soon came back okay. If Reynolds didn't have any fear, he didn't expect anyone else should either, Haggard thought when he considered why the Captain insisted on sending the runner.

After the shelling had ceased, Lieutenant Calhoun set out to get the feel of the area. Occasionally, a German civilian waved at him as he walked alone through the houses. After about a mile, he was met by Tech Sergeant Norman Arrow, the Battalion Sergeant Major, who was leading a patrol from 2nd Battalion. Arrow informed Calhoun that at a slag pile ahead, he had discovered several hundred foreign laborers living in caves they had carved into the mounds of spent coal. Arrow asked Calhoun if he would accompany him back to the area to investigate further and Calhoun agreed. Somehow, these people had acquired weapons, but they surrendered them at Calhoun's request. The arms were stacked in a pile and set on fire by Arrow's men. Calhoun then departed to finish scouting the area and later returned to his CP to get some rest.[30]

While Calhoun was getting the lay of the land to the north and east, Lieutenant Wieland approached PFC Grice and told him that he'd found him a machine-gun. He explained further that Germans were attempting to cross a field southwest of First Platoon's position; therefore he instructed Grice to set his gun up on the railroad embankment on the south side of the town. From atop the embankment, Grice could clearly see Germans soldiers across the Lippe River, in groups of two and three, darting south across the fields about six hundred yards away. Grice went to his deadly work right away. "I'd wait till they got to the middle of the field," Grice explained. When they did, Grice opened up with the machine-gun. Since every fifth round was a tracer, he knew where the bullets were hitting and he raked the Germans to make sure they were dead. Every so often a German ambulance drove out from a barn on the edge of the field to pick up the wounded. Grice figured they were using the barn for an aid station and, therefore, didn't fire on it or the ambulance. Germans, meanwhile, continued to run headlong out onto the fields, where Grice caught them in the deadly hail storm of bullets. Though Grice passed at firing on the ambulances, eventually some of the mortarmen came up, set up their mortars, and began firing on the ambulances themselves. They missed the trucks, but hit several German soldiers.

Wieland located a German who was perched in a house's window using a pair of binoculars and pointed him out to Grice who took a look as well.

"You think you can hit that guy?" asked Wieland, peering through his own binoculars.

"I know I can," said Grice confidently. Grice then aimed carefully and fired. The two men watched as the tracers streamed into the window, knocking the man back into the room.

Grice stayed at his gun until dark. Almost three dozen Germans had tried to cross that field and Grice had hit at least twenty of them. Grice remarked, "I had a field day that day." Grice had no qualms about his actions; his philosophy of battle was simple: "After they killed several of my buddies I got mad. I decided from now on it's just kill or be killed – I ain't gonna take no pity on them."[31]

As night fell, Lieutenant Wieland decided it would be dangerous to stay in such an exposed spot overnight and told Grice to withdraw to a new, more covered position. That night, the Germans lobbed several grenades into his previous position. "See there," Grice told Wieland after viewing the explosions, "we'd have been dead."[32]

On the afternoon of the twenty-eighth, 2nd Battalion received orders to capture a bridge over the Lippe River at Haltern. The plan called for one platoon from E Company, under the company commander, Lieutenant David L. Blunt, accompanied by its troop of tanks, to advance along the north bank of the Lippe River east of Dorsten to the bridge. Simultaneously, Lieutenant Frank Hebert, the 2nd Battalion S-2, would lead a sixteen man combat patrol across the river and, advancing between the river and the canal, on to the bridge.

Lieutenant Hebert's patrol reached the bridge in advance of Blunt's force only to have it blown up in their faces. Hebert returned with this information and forty-four German prisoners.[33]

Plans were then made by Lieutenant Colonel Dunbar and Lieutenant Colonel Miller for the next day's movement. The principal concentration of enemy resistance was located on the high ground on the south side of the Dorsten-Haltern Highway about five miles southeast of Haltern. There, on an island that lay between the Lippe River and the Lippe Canal, German 88s were emplaced and, from there, they maintained a commanding presence over the road, effectively preventing any attacks towards Münster via the main Wesel-Münster Highway. If the 513th

Parachute Infantry was to advance, these guns would have to be dealt with and the job of disposing of them fell to Acey's boys.[34]

In the late afternoon, Lieutenant Calhoun was told to report to Captain Reynolds. Calhoun got up from where he was resting and made his way along a brick-paved street toward the company CP. As he was walking, four P-47 fighters thundered eastward, and Calhoun stopped to watch them pass. He then noticed the flight turn. Perhaps, Calhoun thought, they had spotted the armored column parked on the shoulder below them and wanted to investigate. Calhoun was smack in the middle of the street when one of the fighters made a recognition passover, firing a burst from its .50 caliber machine-guns across the road in front of him scattering shattered bricks for yards. Calhoun went down immediately and when he arose saw the British tankers, whose tea break had been disturbed, spreading out their gold, aerial recognition panels on the tops of their Churchills. When fighter returned, it again raced overhead, but this time wagging its wings.

Lieutenant Calhoun found Captain Reynolds in bed. Without getting up, Reynolds apprised Calhoun of the attack planned for the morning, describing how the attack would proceed. Supported by the tanks and 2nd Battalion's 81mm mortars, D and F Companies would cross over the river and onto the island. From there, they would sweep east, capturing the enemy guns that were holding up their advance. Meanwhile, E Company would advance along the north bank of the river to cover the battalion's left flank. After explaining this, Reynolds then told Calhoun that one platoon had been assigned to lead the battalion onto the island and then cover the right flank of the battalion's advance.

"And who do you think is going to lead the movement?" Reynolds asked Calhoun.

"Not me!" moaned Calhoun in surprised frustration.

Reynolds confirmed Calhoun's suspicions. "Colonel Miller specifically said: 'Lieutenant Calhoun's platoon will be leading the movement'." Lieutenant Calhoun, after leading the battalion onto the island, would somehow cross over the Lippe Canal on the island's south side, and then advance parallel to the main body of the battalion. From the north side of the canal, Major Edwards would assist Calhoun in coordinating the movement of his platoon.[35]

At 1300 hours on the twenty-eighth, while the 2nd Battalion was halted at Dorsten, the 3rd Battalion of the 513th, riding with the tanks of the Coldstream

Guards, passed through the town and, by using another road, pressed east in hopes of reaching Lippramsdorf, a few miles to the northeast, or even Haltern by nightfall. When the task force passed through to the far side of Lippramsdorf, they encountered a mixed enemy column and opened fire. The Germans, in turn, retaliated, directing artillery upon the British tanks. Lieutenant Colonel Kent dispatched G Company to clear the neighboring houses on the right side of the road and H Company to clear those on the left. Most of the Germans they encountered "seemed more anxious to surrender than to fight."

Then, in the gathering darkness, H Company pursued the retreating Germans on foot toward Haltern. On the outskirts of Haltern the column ran into two enemy strong points and panzerfaust fire, but no tanks were hit and G Company, riding the leading tanks, moved into the town. Veiled by the night's darkness, G Company and the tanks proceeded into the center of Haltern and to the cathedral where they halted. Alarm bells were ringing in the town, but the enemy took no action to stop them. H Company then passed on through the town to its far side in order to seize the Lippe River bridges there. One bridge was captured intact, but the enemy then blew the others and withdrew. The 1st Battalion of the 513th was then moved to Haltern to assist in securing and outposting the town.[36]

The twenty-eighth had been another successful day for the men of the 17th Airborne Division and the 6th Guards Armored Brigade. Nearly two hundred more prisoners had been taken – 127 by the 513th Parachute Infantry alone – bringing the total number of captured enemy troops for the whole operation to over four thousand for the five day period 24 to 28 March 1945.

Back at home, newspapers were reporting on the close comradeship that was developing between the men of the 6th Guards Armored Brigade and those of the 513th Parachute Infantry Regiment. "A British armored brigade which has been moving without sleep for days and nights highly praised their new buddies from the 17th Airborne Division," proclaimed the Danville (Virginia) Commercial-News. "'You could not meet finer fighters,' a British colonel said. 'We admire them enormously. They are brave men and delightful companions. They have been a tonic to us.'"[37]

For their part, and for many reasons, F Company men admired the British tankers. The British officers, like one young lieutenant who wore a pair of matching Colt .45 automatic pistols with pearl grips, were flamboyant characters. Guards officers wore chukka boots instead of the regulation ammunition boots, long sweaters under their battledress jackets, and eschewed their wool battledress trousers for corduroy pants. They then topped off their outfits with colorful scarves. F Company troopers were perplexed, however, by the tankers' ritual stops for tea. At 1000 and 1500 every day, the British stopped to 'brew up' a pot of the strong stuff. "We got so goddamned mad at them bastards [making tea]," recalled Donovan. "At night they were always rattling around." Tec 4 Contreras, riding at the back of the tank column with F Company's mess crew, discovered that even when contact was made with the enemy at the front of the column – an event which often caused those tanks at the rear to stop and wait – the crews on the waiting tanks would employ the time to brew up more tea. The British, however, were always ready to share their tea and crumpets with the paratroopers. The crumpets, according to PFC Laufer, were nothing more than a round biscuit that was "so goddamned hard if you'd let it soak for a week you'd never get it soft." But the sharing made for a good relationship between the soldiers of the two nations. Laufer always reciprocated the British soldiers' courtesy by offering them American cigarettes, a gift the British truly appreciated.[38]

At Dorsten the next morning, 29 March, the main force of Lieutenant Colonel Miller's 2nd Battalion's moved out at 1025 hours toward the island. D Company was leading, followed by the First and Second Platoons of F Company, and then by elements of 2nd Battalion's Headquarters Company. It was planned that their attack would be supported by Lieutenant Rydesky's 81mm mortar platoon as well as E Company and the tanks of the Scots Guards. The British tankers maneuvered to a point overlooking the river and there, on the highway between Haltern and Dulmen, they prepared to provide supporting fire. Rydesky's mortars went with the tanks to assist them in covering the battalion's crossing the Lippe River and their advance east. E Company was ordered to advance east along the north bank of the Lippe River in order to clear the area between it and the highway of any resistance and to assist in covering the crossing of the battalion. Contact between the elements of the battalion and the tanks was maintained exclusively by radio. Once the mortars and tanks were in place, they began firing a short preparation.[39]

Leading 2nd Battalion's movement onto the island was Lieutenant Calhoun's platoon. Calhoun walked with the Staff Sergeant Gresher's point squad, and gave

Lieutenant Stanley the task of bringing up the rest of the platoon. Proceeding east to the outskirts of Dorsten, Calhoun took the road south to a bridge that crossed the Lippe River. Once he was across, Calhoun planned to cross the canal and, advancing parallel to the main force, cover its right flank. When he reached the designated crossing point, however, Calhoun discovered the steel bridge had been blown, its center had collapsed into the middle of the river, forming a 'V'. Calhoun stood looking at the twisted remains when, abruptly, some of Gresher's men began firing their weapons toward the woods on the opposite bank. One of the men had observed a group of German soldiers moving up on the other side of the river. No one was sure if they'd hit any of the enemy, but the firing had dispersed them.

Lieutenant Calhoun was determined to cross the bridge and ordered Lieutenant Stanley, "Take two squads and form a line to cover the squad that's going to cross the bridge." Sure now that German soldiers were on the other side of the river, Calhoun didn't want to take any chances. Calhoun, accompanied by his runner, PFC Lloyd 'Flat Top' Elliot, and his radioman, Private Bob Greenstrand, was set to go when Staff Sergeant Gresher told Calhoun that he would not lead his men across. Although incensed by this attitude, Calhoun didn't have time to argue with Gresher. So, he shouted "Follow me" to Gresher's squad and, without even looking back to see if they were following, he started across the buckled span. Calhoun, Greenstrand, and Elliot hurdled the water at the bottom of the trestle and carefully made their way over the foot-wide beams on the other side. Calhoun prayed all the way across and, when he reached the river's south bank, he turned and saw his prayers had been answered – Gresher's squad had followed him. Calhoun spread out the squad and motioned to Stanley to bring the rest of the platoon across.[40]

Calhoun had orders to "extend his platoon to the Lippe Canal about 200 yards south of the river," and sweep east until he found a bridge over the canal he could cross. The men spread out in a skirmish line, about fifty feet from each other across the width of the island. The land was pastoral and sparsely dotted with small trees that would not provide much cover. Once the platoon was in formation, Calhoun moved east as quickly as possible, planning to check in succession each of the three bridges over the canal he'd marked on his map the day before. As Calhoun's men advanced warily across the open ground, the Germans who had so recently withdrawn reappeared and started "clipping" at them. No one was hit, however, and Third Platoon even took a few of the sniping Germans prisoner. They were well equipped, the men found, but very young.[41]

Calhoun stopped to examine the first bridge, but decided it was in too poor a condition to cross safely. As Calhoun pressed into a stand of woods, moving toward the second bridge, the platoon "ran into a German prisoner of war camp." The camp, about four hundred yards square, was surrounded by a barbed wire fence about twenty feet high. A guard tower stood in each of the corners. Calhoun walked to the open gate where he was met by a tall French chaplain. "The Germans," the chaplain told Calhoun in English, "have moved all the American prisoners out to the east yesterday." Those prisoners that still remained were in very shabby condition from their captivity although the chaplain, in comparison, was relatively well attired. Calhoun, accompanied by a few of his men, investigated the wooden barracks the prisoners were billeted in. The prisoners had no bunks. They slept on the floor, lice ridden straw their only comfort. Overall, the barracks were in as decrepit a state as the prisoners themselves. Calhoun returned to the French chaplain. "You're in charge," he told him. "There is a battalion of American paratroopers about two hundred yards behind me, and they'll shoot at anything that's moving through these woods. So, keep your soldiers under control and in camp until Colonel Miller arrives. He will contact people to repatriate [your men]."

Lieutenant Calhoun then pulled his men together and moved out for the second bridge. Unfortunately, this bridge also was too badly damaged to be used and so the lieutenant moved on toward the last. Upon reaching the third bridge, he found that it too had been blown. At that moment, one of the men spotted a German soldier on the opposite side of the canal and the platoon started firing. The German, however, managed to avoid being hit and escaped over the levee to warn his friends. "They knew we were coming," Greenstrand recalled, "and that was bad."

Calhoun directed the platoon into a stand of trees next to the river to wait while he tested the waters one hundred yards further east to see if his men could wade the canal. He found, however, the canal was too deep to ford. As Calhoun returned to where his men sat, the Germans began shelling the area, the shell bursts creeping closer and closer to the platoon's position in the woods. "Man, if they don't stop, tree bursts are gonna get all of us," Ed Sarrell told his assistant gunner, PFC Manuel Juarez. By the time Calhoun had reached his men, he had decided they could try and swim the canal. He remarked to Greenstrand, "We're gonna have to cross this thing." Then, without further explanation, Calhoun slid down the bank and jumped in. When he hit the water, however, he just disappeared. "Calhoun couldn't swim a lick," remembered Greenstrand. "The lieutenant jumped into the water and didn't come up for a long time. The current started taking him away and his ass damn near drowned." Calhoun actually was an accomplished swimmer, having grown up swimming in the numerous irrigation canals of his native Fresno, California, but weighted down by nearly sixty pounds of equipment and ammunition he didn't stand a chance. After Greenstrand and Elliot dragged him out – no easy task because the bank was fairly steep – Lieutenant Stanley suggested that by crawling on hands and knees over the girders, the platoon might be able to cross the bridge. With the artillery increasing, Lieutenant Calhoun decided that was a better idea.[42]

Stanley told PFCs Sarrell and Juarez to stay in the stand of trees on the north side of the canal to cover them with their machine-gun. The other troopers in the platoon dropped machine-gun ammunition with Sarrell and the men started across. As PFC Bob Guiles, the lead scout passed, Juarez asked him, "Are we supposed to cross?" Guiles shrugged. "I don't know," he answered, and ran to catch up with Calhoun.

Lieutenant Calhoun took the right side of the bridge and Stanley took the left and, moving delicately from girder to girder, made it across. Calhoun and Stanley jumped off the bridge and moved to the edge of the embankment. Calhoun then turned his attention back to the bridge. PFC Guiles, who apparently was less worried about falling in the river than about being shot, was just sprinting the last few yards to the bank, and the rest of the platoon had started across with Apfel and Shaughnessy leading, and the others right behind.[43]

When Calhoun turned back to the front, he was staggered by the sight of a company of Germans approaching from over the dike ahead. When their commander, a smartly dressed captain, came forward with his arms in the air and told Calhoun that he wanted to surrender his men, Calhoun breathed as sigh of relief. Lieutenant Calhoun instructed the officer to bring his men forward and have them throw their weapons, helmets, and all other equipment into the canal. Then, while Calhoun brought his platoon across on the left side of the bridge, he sent the Germans across on the right side. Staff Sergeant Robin E. McClain counted them as they crossed, ninety-eight in all. The prisoners were turned over to Major Edwards, who arrived and was waiting for them on the north bank of the canal. Calhoun spread his men out in a short skirmish line and began to push east, sticking close to the canal while following the movement of the main body of the battalion which he now observed coming up on the island to his left.

As Third Platoon advanced atop the levee, a concrete bunker came into view about one hundred yards to their front. Though a white flag flew above it, no one took any chances. Just as the platoon started to close, the Germans inside opened up on them with small arms and machine-guns, pinning down the platoon for a short time. Calhoun decided to withdraw below the canal's flood bank, a dike some eighteen feet high and thirty feet across at the base. Once there, the platoon could bypass the bunker safely, keeping the dike between the enemy position and themselves. The men slid back on their guts and, after a few minutes, they bypassed the bunker and pushed on as before.

Meanwhile, PFCs Sarrell and Juarez had waited about thirty minutes, but Calhoun had given them no orders to follow nor sent anyone back for them. The two troopers decided to move east, along the north side of the canal, until they ran into the main body of the company. Sarrell picked up the gun and Juarez the four or five boxes of ammunition that had been left with them and they started off. In about a half hour, they met the company assembled at another demolished bridge. Captain Reynolds spotted them coming and walked straight up to Sarrell. He could see the Captain was furious about something. Before Sarrell could even open his mouth Reynolds directed: "Take these guys' guns away and put them under arrest." Reynolds walked off immediately. Sarrell just stood there with is mouth agape. Reynolds had arrested them for desertion.[44]

Lieutenant Calhoun's platoon walked along the road running below the canal's high bank. The Germans apparently knew the platoon was down there on the narrow path, but didn't appear up to coming over the dike themselves. Instead, they threw a few mortar rounds and stick grenades over the dike. The men took cover every time this happened, but the shells and grenades only splashed harmlessly in the canal and no one was injured. In any case, according to Greenstrand, none of the troopers wanted to go over the dike to get at the Germans either.

Coming to a point where the canal bent southward, Guiles, the point man, surprised a German soldier who was relieving himself. The German had his back to the approaching paratroopers and was acting as if he hadn't thought there were any Americans within "fourteen thousand miles of him," remembered Greenstrand. "*Auf geben und ich will nicht schiezen* [Give up and I won't shoot]," yelled Greenstrand in his best German. The troopers started laughing as the startled German turned, and in alarm started up over the bank, trying to pull his pants up while slipping down with every step. The troopers were laughing so hard they let him get away. "Guaranteed he hadn't even taken time to wipe," recalled Greenstrand. But it was the third time an enemy soldier had been allowed to escape carrying a warning of Third Platoon's approach and Greenstrand was a little disgusted with it.[45]

. A few men went up the dike to see where the German went. From the top, they could see there was a farm house on the other side of the dike and several men were sent to clear it out. They soon returned with a few prisoners and the platoon started off again, this time double-timing it along the path below the dike with the prisoners in tow.

Calhoun's final objective, still a mile distant, was a bridge which spanned the canal south of the German gun positions 2nd Battalion was attempting to seize. D Company, meanwhile, on the north side of the canal and advancing against heavy sniper fire, had just come up on line, contacting Third Platoon. Calhoun was pressing on quickly when the sound of metal striking metal and alarmed shouts from the D Company men on the other side of the canal alerted him to danger. Calhoun instantly wheeled to look behind him and saw a German soldier rising from a spider hole which had been concealed by a plot of tall grass. The German pointed his MP-40 machine-pistol directly at Calhoun. Suddenly, a rifle butt came crashing down over the German's head, the impact making a sharp crack as the heavy walnut stock splintered against the gray steel helmet. Thirty-eight year old PFC Robert 'Pop' Rieger – a cook sent with Lieutenant Calhoun to act as an interpreter because he spoke fluent German – had broken his M1 over the head of the German soldier knocking him cold.[46]

Troopers pulled the stunned German, apparently only sixteen or so, out of his hiding place. D Company troopers shouted over at Lieutenant Calhoun, demanding that he be sent across the canal so they could shoot him. The D Company men said the German had shot one of their men just moments earlier. "You'll have to wait till all my men are pulled back across the canal tonight," replied Calhoun. "Then you can have him." Calhoun's decision was prompted by his concern about any possible reprisals. "There were many incidents," recalled Calhoun in 1996, "where some paratrooper shot a German prisoner in cold blood where other German soldiers witnessed it. And whenever [the Germans] captured a parachutist, they would execute [him] in the same manner. I was not going to subject my men to this fate."

As Calhoun's platoon closed on their final objective, they began to receive very heavy small arms and machine-gun fire from dug-in infantry on the wooded the high ground surrounding the bridge site. Fortunately, the fire was inaccurate. Calhoun had orders to clear this area before coming back across the canal and so pressed his attack. The platoon advanced in bounds and, by this manner, soon closed with the enemy. As the troopers neared, some of the German soldiers threw down their weapons and put on their kaput hats. More and more presently followed suit until the firing slackened and then finally ceased. Lieutenant Calhoun's men rounded up nearly one hundred more old men and boys. The prisoners told the troopers that the SS had loaded their rifles and machine-guns and ordered them to fire on the Americans until their ammunition was exhausted – only then could they surrender.

While Calhoun and Rieger were conducting an interrogation of the prisoners, two Germans riding bicycles were spotted trying to escape about a quarter mile further east. A fusillade of rifle fire erupted as everyone tried to shoot them off their mounts, but when the first rounds popped past them, the riders dumped their bicycles and hit the ditch "goddamned fast," remembered Greenstrand. Out of targets, the men dug in and waited until evening, when Lieutenant Calhoun withdrew his men and their bag of prisoners across the Lippe River to rejoin the armored column. PFC Olson and another trooper, accompanied by the now-unarmed PFC Sarrell, escorted the prisoners to an open field and watched them until the MPs came to take them to the rear. One of the prisoners was a doctor and spoke English. "You know," he remarked to Olson arrogantly, "For me, the war is over. For you, it's just beginning." Olson didn't like his attitude, even though he realized the man was right.[47]

While Calhoun's men had been advancing along the canal, D and F Companies had pushed east across the island against heavy artillery fire and, as they neared the final objective, concentrated small arms fire. Enemy resistance was eliminated around 1330 hours and fifty-six German prisoners were taken. The battalion then secured the objective and continued to mop-up the area until 1700 hours. Troopers discovered large quantities of enemy small arms and equipment, but the 88s that were supposed to be covering the road had apparently escaped.[48]

The capture of the island opened the Wesel-Münster Highway for the passage of the Guards Armored and Airborne units. D and F Companies returned to the north side of the Lippe River during the evening and joined the Churchill tanks which were standing on the highway at the spot from which they had fired in support of that day's attack. The troopers then mounted up and the column pushed on until late that night when Colonel Dunbar called a halt at a group of buildings in the vicinity of Dulmen, which had been captured by the 3rd Battalion earlier that day. There, a group of women came out of their homes, apparently to greet them, but when they saw they were not German tanks but British, the women scattered.

For their part, the tanks plowed into the farmyards, tearing ruts in the ground and knocking over stone fence posts before halting. The troopers jumped off and began digging in for the evening. Sarrell rested in a large barn for a while, but left for fear that German stragglers might be hiding out in the loft. He was still unarmed – still under arrest. Later that night, however, whatever trouble Sarrell and Juarez were in was evidently resolved because the officers returned their weapons to them, albeit without explanation.[49]

At his nightly meeting, Lieutenant Colonel Dunbar noted that Lieutenant Calhoun's men had jumped off before entering Dorsten and then had to run to keep up with the tanks. Not wanting a repeat of that episode if they ran into trouble the next day, he concluded, "In the future, no matter how hot the fire gets around our tanks, the infantry will stay on top of the tank until I give you an order to dismount."[50]

After capturing the towns of Haltern and Dulmen, two regiments of the 17th Airborne Division were assigned the task of holding open the main highway, which ran between the two towns, so that elements of the XIX and XIII U.S. Corps could pass through and attack east. The 513th Parachute Infantry Regiment, meanwhile, was ordered to continue its attack toward Münster. In hopes of outflanking the retreating Germans, Lieutenant Colonel Miller's 2nd Battalion, resting near Dulmen, received orders to continue their advance northeast, towards Potthoff. Accordingly, at 1025 hours on 30 March, the column moved out with F Company again in the lead.[51]

It was an easy start. In fact, operations had gone incredibly well since D-Day, yet F Company's faces bore little outward expression of ease or confidence. The men were constantly "shook up and fearful," said Dahlberg. After all, there was still the very real prospect that violent death was waiting for them at every new bend in the road. "You just took things as they came and tried to relax when you could," Dahlberg explained.[52]

About a mile or so from the road, a British plane was strafing Germans positions. Every time the plane made a pass, the Germans fired "like hell at it," remembered Greenstrand. The strafing continued for a while until, on its fourth pass, the plane was hit and its engine started sputtering. The pilot turned west and passed over the tank column, gaining altitude, and then bailed out. He landed a few hundred yards from the road and some F Company men were sent across the fields in a Bren Gun Carrier to pick him up before the Germans did. "He was one happy guy when he seen us rolling up," recalled Greenstrand.

The tank column soon passed through Dulmen, where the 3rd Battalion was resting, and pressed on. Ahead was Potthoff.[53]

Not long afterward, two more planes flew over the tank column, German Me 109s, heading west. Within fifteen minutes, the 109s flew overhead again, only they were traveling east this time and fast, pursued by three American P-38 Lightnings. From their engine deck seats on the Churchills, the troopers gazed up at the unfolding show in awed expectation. As the P-38s began to overtake the slower German planes, the enemy pilots began climbing and then separated, each pilot making a run for it alone. Two P-38s went after one of the Me 109s while the third Lightning chased the other. In just seconds, the first Messerschmitt was aflame and spinning towards earth, and the pair of P-38s wheeled to help their buddy who was closing on the last plane. Far in the distance, the troopers watched as the second 109 was sent spiraling in. The men's cheers drowned out the engines of the Churchills.[54]

For the attack on Potthoff, F Company, supported by the tanks, was to deploy up the road leading to the town. E Company, meanwhile, was to hold down the right flank of the battalion while D Company acted as battalion reserve. At a road junction, the Bren Gun Carriers, moving about a quarter mile ahead of the lead Churchill, led the column onto a dirt secondary road which meandered into a wood. The commander of the lead tank turned to Lieutenant Calhoun and asked, "When we come to the end of the trees, about a quarter of a mile to our front, the German front lines will be about a quarter of a mile further out. Do you want to get off now?"

"You heard your CO say no one gets off until he says we can," replied Calhoun over the noise of the engine. "We're waiting his orders."

About five hundred yards beyond the road junction, as promised, Lieutenant Calhoun's tanks cleared the tree line and were met by heavy enemy machine-gun and rifle fire coming from a group of buildings and a line of foxholes about a hundred yards ahead. Everyone started firing, shooting for any head that appeared from a foxhole while the tankers fired their 6 pounders at the German machine-gun positions. In the midst of the confusion, the little Bren Gun Carriers ran up and down the area, firing their weapons at the Germans, too. Calhoun's tank continued forward along the road and drove fifty yards straight through the line of German foxholes. The second tank stopped among the German positions and the third tank, with the rest of Calhoun's platoon, pulled up about fifty yards short of the enemy line. The order came to dismount and the troopers scrambled off and charged right into the German positions.

With the sounds of rifle fire and Schmeissers coming from up ahead, F Company's First and Second Platoons dismounted in the woods and were spread out in skirmish lines about two hundred yards on the right side of the road. The men moved forward and, working their way through a wood to the right, flanked the enemy positions. The Germans then quickly gave up and the paratroopers pulled them from their foxholes.

Shortly after the prisoners were rounded up, enemy SP fire started coming in and F Company could advance no further. E Company, which was supposed to have advanced on the right, was held up at the road junction. Lieutenant Blunt, the company commander, and the British tank commanders with E Company, decided to try to flank the enemy SPs by going around through the fields to the left. Four tanks attempted the maneuver but three were destroyed and the last was forced to return to the road. Lieutenant Blunt was forced, therefore, to deploy E Company in the fields and woods and send out patrols. Later that evening, E Company returned to the road junction.[55]

F Company was out in front alone, and still about two miles southwest of the objective – Potthoff. Because of the SP fire being directed against them, which was shortly joined by enemy small arms, Reynolds chose to stay on foot. Several hundred yards of flat farmland lay ahead so, to move F Company across the open ground, Captain Reynolds led half the company up the shallow ditches on the right side of the road and instructed Lieutenant Calhoun to take the rest of the company up the ditches on the left. Calhoun again sent PFC Guiles ahead to act as lead scout while a second trooper acted as connecting file. Guiles worked his way forward cautiously – on either side of him were spring plowed fields, but little cover. While the troopers advanced up the ditches, the tanks, at some distance, followed on the tree-lined road.

As the company advanced, they began to receive some light small arms fire from a bunker about five hundred yards ahead and on the right. The tanks were called up and battered it terribly. The firing quickly ceased and the one of the defenders emerged, waving a white flag. The First Platoon, that had taken up a position to the right of the road, took a half dozen prisoners from the bunker. Always pragmatic, PFC Laufer sympathized with the Germans' decision: It was "better to be alive and walking than dead and in the ground." Presently, the SP fire that had been harassing the tanks stopped, too, and since there was now only sporadic Schmeisser and rifle fire being directed against them, Reynolds put the men back on the tanks.

It was then that PFC Olson came jogging back. During the firing, he had worked his way around under a stone wall to a farmhouse. There, the German farmer gave him water and some cold milk.

By about 1400 hours, Dunbar's tanks had advanced forward to within six hundred yards of the village, about a quarter mile west of the Koesfeld-Nottuln Tilbeck crossroads. The column was pressing down the hedgerow flanked country road when a German self-propelled gun, camouflaged with brush, fired from a wooded hill several hundred yards ahead. The SP then withdrew to cover in the woods. "The Germans always waited to see if Allied tanks would be involved before committing to an action," explained Sid Laufer. "If the Allies were employing tanks, the Germans concentrated their efforts first against them before turning their attention to any accompanying infantry." The SP again rolled forward and fired on Lieutenant Calhoun's tank. The shell missed, instead splintering a tree beside the road. Within seconds, more self-propelled gun, tank, machine-gun, sniper, and small arms fire erupted from enemy positions on the hill immediately forward of Reynolds' men. The column stopped abruptly and the paratroopers jumped for cover in the ditches.

On the left side of the road, Haggard was clinging to the earth near Captain Reynolds. Shells were coming in so close that their concussion was rattling his helmet off his head. About two hundred yards ahead, between F Company and the SPs on the hill, a German tank rolled out from behind a farmhouse, situated on a ridge where the road bent left, and fired.

Captain Reynolds planned to send one of his platoons to take out that tank and went to a British major and asked him for a couple of the Churchills to support his men. The British major, however, flatly refused. "I'm not pulling my tanks out in front of that gun," he said.

The response made Reynolds mad. "Okay," he said sharply, "I'll get it with my own men."

"Well," the British officer offered, "I'll give you smoke mortar support" (the Churchills had smoke mortars on the sides of the turrets).

"I don't need it!" Reynolds shot back angrily.

"Calhoun," called Captain Reynolds, "Get over here!"

Calhoun – wondering why Reynolds never called for Lieutenant Joyce or Lieutenant Fann to get over to him – raised up from his position in the roadside ditch to see what Reynolds wanted. A German machine-gun fired to his left front – and he felt something go through his field jacket and rip across his back. The feeling was the same one he'd had when he was hit in the shoulder during the attack on the woods north of Mande-St.-Etienne in January.

Calhoun hit the ground and called excitedly to the man in the ditch behind him, "Take a look at my back!"

The man crawled forward and pulled up the lieutenant's jacket and shirts. "The hole goes through your jacket, shirt, and undershirt, but there's only a little white line across your skin," the trooper told him.

"Calhoun, get over here!" called Captain Reynolds again.

"A machine-gun has me zeroed in," Calhoun called back. "I have to move forward a little, then I'll come across." Calhoun moved down the ditch about ten feet then made a made dash across the road, hitting the ground next to Captain Reynolds. The odor of human feces hung heavily around him.

"Did you shit your pants, Calhoun?" asked Reynolds.

"Hell no!" Calhoun declared sharply, but as he rolled over he saw that the front of his jacket was covered with "the remains of some German soldier's bowels." Someone, perhaps a German soldier, had apparently chosen that spot to relieve himself sometime earlier and Calhoun had landed in it. He took off his field jacket and threw it away.

Reynolds instructed Calhoun to go back down the road, and find a shoulder 57mm team and bring them forward to knock out the German tank. Calhoun found the recoilless rifle team back down the tree lined road, over a low hill and around a bend where the British tanks were standing among some buildings, their crews brewing tea of all things. Calhoun brought the men forward to a position in the field on the north side of the road. The crew knelt down, loaded the weapon and fired one round. The German tank immediately answered, the shell killing or wounding all of the team, and then withdrew behind the building.[56]

Captain Reynolds then ordered Lieutenant Calhoun's platoon to make an attempt to flank the positions and attack the enemy from the rear. Calhoun ordered Staff Sergeant Gresher to take his squad up the left side of the road to clean out the farmhouse on the right side of the bend that the tank was using for cover. "Our objective was to capture a barn [farmhouse] that was occupied by German soldiers," remembered rifleman Don Shay. Gresher's squad inched forward along the ditch in single file, keeping as low as possible. A bullet cracked past PFC Shay's head, the trooper in line behind him had accidentally discharged his M1. The round pierced the helmet of a soldier about three men ahead of Shay, the bullet passing between the man's skull and the inside of the helmet, and exiting out its front right side. The shaken trooper turned around to the soldier, "You dirty sonofabitch," he said furiously, "you ruined my helmet." He was too stunned by what had happened to realize that the bullet had taken the top of his ear off. The wounded man was evacuated. Sergeant Gresher was furious.

Gresher then moved his men ahead a little farther until he was hit in the chest by shrapnel and went down. Gresher was rushed back to where the Churchills were gathered and laid in the yard. His eyes were open, but he was shaking all over, like he was freezing to death, one trooper observed. Still, he was making eye contact with people as he lay there. Sergeant Haggard could see he was going into shock – his eyes were glazing over. The wounds didn't look too bad, Haggard thought, and he was surprised when Gresher, the friend he used to talk with about Chicago, suddenly died.

At the same time, Sergeant Sorenson ordered First Platoon, on the right, to "Get up and get that goddamned gun!" "We were running across a field to take a woods 120 yards ahead," recalled Grice. PFC Jack Cook appeared all by himself in the ditch well forward of the advancing platoon waving and shouting "Come on, come on, come on," to the rest of the men. All of a sudden, Cook was hit by small arms fire and went down. Somebody yelled, "Cook's been hit."

"My mind just lapsed," recalled Grice. He remembered joshing Cook back in basic: "You're not old enough to be in the service. You don't even shave." Cook had just grinned in reply. Even Reynolds knew Cook was too young to be in the Army and had tried to get him discharged, but Cook wouldn't have any of it.[57]

A tank was sent forward to cover the men who had run to Cook's aid, and soon, one of the medics was carrying him back in his arms. He was evacuated but died on 6 April. For his gallant action that day, Cook was posthumously awarded the Silver Star and promoted to sergeant. About a week after he had been hit, a message was received by Captain Reynolds regarding a discharge for Cook; the Army had discovered that he was only sixteen.

For two more hours, F Company battled against a determined enemy. Finally, artillery was in position to assist. The men all let out great "war whoops," and at 1730 hours, under a terrific artillery barrage, F Company stormed the enemy positions in a frontal assault. The hill was gained, but the enemy SPs, except for one that had been destroyed in the shelling, managed to escape.[58]

Two dozen defenders, however, came out of their holes to surrender. "The Germans came running down the road with their hands up," remembered Grice, "and I hauled off and hit them in the back when they passed, rolling them down the hill." Meanwhile, Private Contreras and another cook, who were waiting on one of the tanks at the rear of the column, were driven up to where the prisoners were waiting. There, the two cooks were ordered to escort the prisoners to the rear. Contreras could see they were just kids. "I felt sorry for them," said Contreras. "A lot of them were crying." It is likely the prisoners believed they were going to be shot by the American paratroopers. And, indeed, they were lucky Grice had settled on just knocking them down. He wanted to shoot them, badly, but his friends had stopped him. F Company's had lost two men killed and another eight wounded in this fight. The Army, apparently, considered this number of casualties to be light.[59]

With F Company having broken through the German lines, the column began to advance rapidly against only sporadic fire, pursuing a retreating enemy. The advance never stopped, not even for prisoners – they were simply ushered to the rear – sometimes with their rifles still slung over their backs. The armor-infantry column rolled forward until it was within three miles of Nottuln where, at 1900 hours, the battalion set up a perimeter defense and dug in for the night.

Meanwhile, Lieutenant Calhoun's platoon, making a reconnaissance of the area ahead of the column, ran into in a group of retreating German armor. The British were reluctant to tangle with them in the dark, but Calhoun dismounted his men, and with the Churchills following, pursued them into the village of Girieve on foot. Once they reached the village, Calhoun was informed by radio that he was cut off from the rest of the battalion and, therefore, was instructed to form a perimeter around the village for the night.

Third Platoon set up in a farm house set back in a big wooded area. There was a barn and numerous other buildings located nearby. The large, two-story home was well furnished, but the residents were long gone. In the dining room, the men found a fine silver service. One trooper got the idea to set the table and they all ate their K rations on it. It had grown very late by then, but no one slept much – they all knew they were surrounded so, except for those enjoying the dining accommodations, they kept super alert. Guards were posted to make sure the Germans didn't come through their perimeter without warning. Lieutenant Calhoun and his platoon sergeant, Staff Sergeant McLean, checked the surrounding buildings and discovered three women, the farmer's wife, mother-in-law, and daughter. Calhoun left McLean with the daughter and grandmother, and instructed the mother to give him a tour of the house. The lieutenant unearthed a treasure when the woman led him upstairs to a cold storage room housing a variety of fresh and preserved meats. Calhoun casually mentioned his discovery when he rejoined McLean. Later that night, several men from the platoon stripped the place clean.[60]

Early the next morning, 31 March, 2nd Battalion set its sights on the town Roxel, west of Münster. To reach Roxel, their column first had to pass through Nottuln. At about 0100 hours, the Battalion S-2, 2nd Lieutenant Frank Hebert, equipped with a radio, led a patrol composed of F Company's assault squad, armed heavily with Grease Guns, bazookas and shoulder 57s, toward Nottuln. "The squad was pulled out and brought their stuff to the HQ," remembered PFC Maurice Cuthbertson, who, with PFC Delbert Cox, was assigned as a point man. The men stripped themselves of most of their equipment; the patrol's extra gear would be brought forward with the battalion when it moved up. Cuthbertson could hear the rest of F Company's men "loading their weapons in their holes around the perimeter" as he departed the HQ. He didn't think that was a good sign, but, of course, it didn't matter how he felt about it. He had his orders and went.

The patrol – twelve to fourteen men – moved out slow and cautious with their eyes and ears open. Cox and Cuthbertson pushed out across a field, feeling their way along until their eyes got used to the blackness. It was very dark. "We made sure we were in contact with someone, and we always had an officer in the middle directing things." Single houses loomed out of the darkness on the outskirts of town, and soon the scattered dwellings gave way to concentrations of buildings and a factory in Nottuln's center. "It was pretty eerie," Cuthbertson recalled of entering the village. "An ammunition dump [had blown up nearby] . . . and that lit up everything." White flags were waving from the buildings, illuminated crazily by the burning munitions fires. When Cuthbertson reached a large abatis blocking the middle of the street, he heard the sound of a man coming towards him from the opposite direction. The rest of the patrol crept up to the barricade and when the man came close, a trooper stuck a gun in the stranger's gut. When the man was recognized as just a terrified civilian, they let him go. Then, while a few men kept guard, Lieutenant Hebert and the others scouted the rest of the town. At about 0330 hours, Hebert radioed battalion that he had observed the German defenders – ten tanks and about two hundred infantry – pulling out of the village. Within half an hour of placing this radio call, the patrol had secured the center of town without much resistance.[61]

At 0545, the rest of the battalion, except for Lieutenant Calhoun's platoon, rode up on the tanks. The men then cleared and secured the rest of Nottuln, in the process taking several more prisoners. The battalion then was reorganized and strong defensive positions were established outside the town. While F Company waited, one of the men spotted a vehicle approaching on the road that intersected their own. They didn't know what it was, but fired on it anyway, running it into the ditch. F Company men approached the small truck and pulled out the driver. The man – a civilian bread truck driver – was rattled but otherwise unharmed and the men turned him loose right away.[62]

It turned out that Lieutenant Calhoun's men spent the night cut-off in Girieve. During the evening, Lieutenant Colonel Dunbar, Major Edwards, and Captain Reynolds crammed into a small armored car and, via radio, informed the British officer with Calhoun that they were going to lead a convoy of ammunition and fuel for Calhoun's tanks through German lines and into Girieve. Around 0200 hours, the British tank officer with Third Platoon asked Calhoun to accompany him to the road junction to help direct the convoy in. Calhoun agreed and the two started out. German soldiers were still trying to escape through the area, so Calhoun kept his guard as he approached the crossroads.

Nearing the road junction, Calhoun spotted "something that looked like black-out lights on an army vehicle" off to the right. Cautiously, Calhoun crept closer, whispering, "Follow me," to the British officer. In the darkness, Lieutenant Calhoun advanced one hundred yards further down the road toward the lights. Suddenly, he ran right into a dozen German soldiers and both Calhoun and the party of Germans hit the ground immediately.

Calhoun thought fast. "*Handy hoch! Nicht schiezen!*" he commanded. Pretty soon one of the Germans, an officer, produced a white handkerchief on the end of a stick and, still lying prone on the road, waved it above himself and his men.

Lieutenant Calhoun yelled to the British officer, "Keep me covered," and began to search the Germans and relieve them of their weapons. Then Calhoun called for the officer to "come on in." There was no response, and Calhoun realized he was all alone. Calhoun put on a confident face, and bluffed the Germans into thinking there was indeed someone covering him. Then he got the Germans on their feet and double-timed them back to the road junction. "He [Sam Calhoun] was one brave bastard," commented Greenstrand. Calhoun later learned that when he had seen lights on the road, the British officer had seen similar lights in the other direction and walked the other way, thinking Calhoun was following him.

The tank officer wasn't at the crossroads when he arrived with his prisoners, so Calhoun pointed the Germans toward Girieve, where his platoon was located, and marched them on. About half way to his own perimeter, Calhoun was halted by the British officer, who now was with Captain Reynolds. Calhoun, relieved to be once again among friends, marched his prisoners to the shed where about fifty more Germans, who had been captured during the night while trying to escape to the east, were already being kept. Calhoun opened the door and ordered his bag in with the rest.

Major Edwards visited the barn where the German PWs were imprisoned. Most of them, exhausted, were sleeping. They were down to *Volkssturm* – sixteen year old boys and sixty year old men, observed Edwards. "It was just shooting fish in a barrel." The German prisoners in there moaned all night, and "if I was in there I would have moaned too," commented Greenstrand. According to him, Major Edwards "went in their and took his pants down, and took a shit right in there amongst them." Calhoun put it in more mild terms: Edwards "had relieved himself in the building where the prisoners were being held."[63]

While Lieutenant Calhoun was busy capturing Germans, the British tankers were busy refueling and rearming their Churchills. Now, with full daylight to accompany him, Lieutenant Calhoun led his platoon to join up with the main body then waiting on orders in Nottuln. On the road between Girieve and Nottuln, Lieutenant Calhoun's tanks were subjected to some light, harassing fires. Unexpectedly, a German tracer, deflecting off the tanks armor, hit a pool of gasoline spilled during the recent refueling, igniting it. Suddenly, Calhoun "had one hell of a problem."

Tank fires were not an uncommon occurrence. The Churchill's covered exhaust pipes ran just behind the Churchill's turret. The covers alone were so hot a trooper could get burned just by touching them. "Some men burned the hell out of their boots," recalled Haggard. If the cover got ripped off, which sometimes happened, the red hot pipes became exposed. The British tied five gallon jerry cans up to exposed exhaust pipes to heat water for tea. The cans stayed so hot the men slept next to them at night. The exposed pipes were hot enough to ignite spilled fuel, too. When a fire started, the tank crew would usually pull out a little squirt-gun contraption and put it out. Then, away they'd go.

When the gasoline fire erupted, Lieutenant Calhoun yelled down inside the turret and got the attention of the tank commander. "Try to put it out if you can," he replied. "We can't stop now." Calhoun and the other troopers on the tank fought the blaze and finally smothered it. When their Churchills arrived in Nottuln a little while later, the Third Platoon troopers dismounted. Lieutenant Fann, who had returned to the company the night before, was seated in a rocking chair on the front porch of a nearby house, and waved to his former platoon leader. As Calhoun started across the road toward Fann, he began walking on the side of his boot. Although he did not realize it initially, he had been badly burned while battling the fire. He looked down and could see that his boot was burned and was smoldering, and that the leather was beginning to shrink.

Calhoun asked PFC Guiles to help him get the boot off. Guiles obeyed, cut the boot and pulled it from the lieutenant's foot, taking burnt skin with it. The pain became excruciating. One of the medics wrapped Calhoun's foot and immediately called for an ambulance.

Since there was nothing he could do himself to aid the lieutenant, PFC Greenstrand went looking for food. Once on German soil, the GIs' attitude toward civilian property was that it was there for the taking. PFC Greenstrand and his buddy picked a modest farmhouse and boldly walked in. Inside, a German woman greeted them nervously. The two soldiers paid little attention to her as soon as they heard her chickens' noisy clucking from the back of the house. Greenstrand went out to the coup, liberated several eggs, and returned to look for a frying pan. When he found it, he handed it to the woman and ordered her fry them up. While the woman cooked, Greenstrand continued to search the dwelling, turning up a loaf of black bread which he had the woman slice and serve the eggs on.

When a couple more troopers came in, they just couldn't believe it. "Where'd you get the eggs?" they asked eagerly. Greenstrand's explanation prompted a more thorough search of the house. They struck gold – a whole basket of eggs – and the German woman was pressed into cooking these as well. "After she had fried one egg," recalled Greenstrand, "she would try to sneak out. About that time another trooper would come in, and the men would grab her again and make her fry a couple more." Soon, F Company men had eaten every one of the white treasures. As he left, Greenstrand took two chickens to roast that night.

Meanwhile, some of the other men had discovered a bar – a bar that still had some liquor remaining – and they proceeded to try and empty the bottles as quickly as they could. When, several minutes into the drinking, a cuckoo clock erupted marking the half hour, one of the men raised his M1 and shot it off the wall. The firing apparently alarmed the crew of a British tank because they stuck their Churchill's main gun right through the bar's front window. The British, however, had not been invited to this private F Company-only affair and the troopers ordered them to, "Get the hell out!"

The British tankers were just as relentless in their pursuit of spoils and they expropriated anything useful – down to the last chicken. Staff Sergeant Charles E. Bailey, from Memphis, Tennessee, was a replacement who had just joined Third Platoon at Nottuln. "The British tank man always had ham and other goodies in his pack," he remembered. After a few days with the British, Bailey came to see that "it was incumbent for any soldier to lift goodies from houses for himself if he could. . . to liberate them you might say. That was our job [after all] – *Liberation!*" When the column left Nottuln, remembered Dahlberg, it looked like a "rolling delicatessen."[64]

K rations were distributed shortly after sun up, but before the men could eat them, orders came down for the whole battalion to get on the move again, this time to Appelhulsen a few miles to the southeast. Colonel Miller's battalion arrived at Appelhulsen at 0945, but was forced to wait on the outskirts because Major Kies' 1st Battalion was still fighting in the town against an unorganized yet determined defense made by the *193rd Volksgrenadiers* and the *3rd Parachute Training Battalion* (on the 513th Parachute Infantry's front, the Germans were fighting a delaying action between Appelhulsen and the village of Albachten, just to the east in Münster's suburbs). A message was received from higher British headquarters at 1230 hours with orders to be ready at a moments notice, but it was not until after the 1st Battalion had secured Appelhulsen at 1330 hours that Miller's battalion could proceed.[65]

An hour later, the column moved out again, its destination Boesensell (east of Appelhulsen). The 2nd Battalion column turned off the main highway and fought "cross-country" toward the town. The Germans harassed the advance, lobbing in a few 88s, mortar shells, and the usual rifle fire, but to no avail. At around 2000 hours, the column entered Boesensell and a brief pause in the attack was allowed. This break was cut short by orders, received at 2030, to push forward again to Roxel, another suburb west of Münster. Troopers had just enough time to scrounge a little and make a reconnaissance of the road ahead. While hunting for souvenirs, PFC Grice discovered a barracks filled with slave laborers. Perhaps 150 of these "thin men," as Grice described them, lay in bunkbeds in the barracks, emaciated and weakened by months of privation. Grice and the other men did what they could, giving them cigarettes and some of their rations, and then re-boarded the Churchills.[66]

Meanwhile, a patrol was sent forward to reconnoiter a path to Roxel and Münster. The patrol was formed of intelligence personnel, radio operators, and the assault squad from F Company under 2nd Battalion's Lieutenants Frank Hebert and Don Mort. Near a country crossroads, Private Rybka and his 57mm team were ordered to wait in a roadside ditch while the rest of the patrol scouted up ahead. The three men hunkered down to wait, but soon heard the sounds of German voices approaching. Suddenly, Rybka felt a sneeze coming on. He put his face down into the mud and choked off the noise. The Germans passed, never seeing the three paratroopers crouching just a few feet away. The patrol never returned to pick them up, and since the other two men were egging him to get out of there, Rybka and his team made their way back to the company.[67]

Up ahead with the patrol, Lieutenant Hebert radioed back to Miller at 2015 hours telling him that there were barricades of felled trees and branches and road blocks in the highway ahead. Just as he finished up his report, intense small arms fire broke out around him. Grenades and panzerfausts shells exploded among Hebert's men and small arms fire popped from every direction. Fortunately for Hebert, it was only a probing attack, and the Germans were driven off after suffering three or four killed, and some fifteen more captured. The only American killed was Private Kenneth M. Eide, one of the original F Company men from the Alabama Area days. Though Eide had been transferred to Battalion Headquarters on 1 September 1944, F Company men considered his loss their own.

Knowing the Germans had prepared effective roadblocks ahead, and assured that the enemy were prepared to defend them, Lieutenants Hebert and Mort thought it wiser to find an alternate route for the advance to Roxel and so informed battalion. Around midnight, however, the Brigadier commanding the 6th Guards Armored ordered Lieutenant Colonel Dunbar to cancel the contemplated move altogether and the patrol was called in at 0130 hours 1 April.[68]

The halt came as a relief to the men; they were all dead tired. Guards were posted and everyone dug in for the night. Sometime in the middle of the evening, PFC Greenstrand was roused by an irate Captain Reynolds and another officer. "Why aren't you on guard duty?" demanded Reynolds. Greenstrand replied that he knew he had been scheduled to pull a shift on guard, but that the man he was to relieve never woke him. That trooper was sleeping nearby; Reynolds woke him up and started questioning him. The other trooper told the captain that when he woke Greenstrand, Greenstrand said, "I'll be right there." Greenstrand must have just rolled back over and gone to sleep never remembering ever being wakened. Reynolds asked the other trooper what he'd done after waking Greenstrand up. The soldier replied that he had gone to bed. That saved Greenstrand's skin. Reynolds chewed out the other trooper for not waiting to be "properly relieved." It was a major screw up, and Greenstrand knew it. This wasn't England or Tennessee, they were on the front lines now.[69]

With his foot wrapped, Lieutenant Calhoun was on his way back across the Rhine and to a hospital. Along the road, the ambulance in which Calhoun rode passed a British tank shepherding a herd of more than a thousand German PWs to the rear. A couple miles further on, the British driver stepped down on the brakes, bringing the ambulance to an abrupt halt. "There's about a battalion of armed German soldiers on the road ahead!" he exclaimed excitedly.

"How far?" asked Calhoun.

"About one hundred yards," the driver answered.

"If they haven't started shooting at us by now, something's wrong," Calhoun said, considering the situation. "Drive up and bring the officers around to me and I'll find out what they want." Cautiously, the driver complied.

When Calhoun questioned them about their intentions, they answered in good English that their men were out of ammunition, had not eaten in two days, and were tired of war. In short, they wanted to surrender. Calhoun ordered the Germans to line up on the northern side of the road and there to discard all the weapons and equipment they carried. Calhoun informed the officers of the approaching British tank his ambulance had passed a few miles back. Once in their hands, he assured the prisoners, the surrendered men would be taken to a holding area where they would be fed and otherwise attended to. Calhoun then asked the driver to wait until the tank arrived, and when it did, then they continued.

When Calhoun reached the hospital, he was placed on a metal cot. Orderlies wrapped a large belt around his chest and another about his legs, tying him fast to the cot. Then two men sat on Calhoun's legs and chest. Calhoun then was given a five inch piece of broom handle and told by the doctors attending him, "Bite on it. You can scream, yell, and cry but there's no way to operate on a burn with pain-killing anesthetics." The doctors planned to remove burned tissue, but also had to know when they were tearing off live skin. The only way to do so was by the volume of Calhoun's screaming. In twenty minutes all of the burnt skin was removed and the doctors sprayed the wound with "some medicine that killed the pain." Calhoun was evacuated by plane shortly thereafter to the 108th General Hospital in Paris.

With the exception of the 507th Combat Team, which remained at Haltern to hold open the main Wesel-Münster Highway for XIX Corps, the 17th Airborne Division was, on 1 April, assigned to XIII U.S. Corps. Due to the change in the command structure, the 6th Guards Armored Brigade, to which the 513th Combat Team had been attached since the twenty-seventh, was now placed under the command of the 17th Airborne Division. The overall mission, however, remained unchanged. The sky men and the Guards still had their eyes set on Münster – an attack that would resume that day. The 513th Parachute Infantry, whose front lines ran from Albachten three-thousand meters north to Roxel, were to continue their advance northeast, guiding on the Dulmen-Münster Highway (Route 51). Miller's 2nd Battalion, on the regiment's left, was moving towards Münster's western suburbs. 1st Battalion, on the right, was advancing along the track of the main road toward the city's southwest limits.[70]

Regiment had decided that 2nd Battalion, supported by the tanks, would attack the city from the west, and Miller's battalion had two objectives: first, to capture the main road junction west of the Aa River; second, to capture the high ground west of Münster near Gievenbecker. From the dominating high ground,

Miller could launch his final attack on the city. After Miller's infantry had crossed the Aa River, the Scots Guards would bridge the river and follow the paratroopers, first into Gievenbecker and then into Münster proper.

On 1 April, near to 1600 hours, 2nd Battalion mounted up and pushed forward, through Albachten, and north towards Roxel. Along the way, one of the tank turrets stripped its gears and swung around wildly, pinching PFC Richard Murray's leg between the swinging barrel and an ammunition crate. The impact shattered his femur. Gripping his carbine, Murray rolled onto the tank's treads and nearly fell into the road. The spinning track grabbed his broken limb and threw it behind him. He held on for dear life because he knew the column wouldn't stop for him if he fell off. At that moment, a jeep with a pair of medics pulled along side.

"What's wrong?" one shouted.

"My leg's broke," Murray yelled. By that time, the other men on he tank had gotten the commander's attention. The Churchill pulled out of line and Murray was put hurriedly on a stretcher on the hood of the jeep. Since there were bypassed German soldiers all over the place, the medics asked, "Can you still shoot?" Murray told them he could and then the medics told him to hold on, they "were gonna go like hell."

Doctors put Murray in a cast up to his hip and he was ZIed. In the United States he was told a steel rod would eventually have to be put in the break, but in the meantime, he could return to Boothbay, Maine. When he arrived at home, it was haying time, and he worked in the fields, cutting wheat with a hand scythe. When he returned to the hospital, the doctors discovered the leg, though now slightly shorter, had healed.[71]

The armor-infantry column advanced north along the highway about eight hundred yards without opposition until it approached Hs. Forkenbeck. There, after the lead tanks emerged from a small wood that flanked the road, the column came under small arms, artillery, and SPs fires of medium intensity. Colonel Miller deployed D Company into the woods on the left side of the road and E Company on the right, both arrayed in skirmish line formations. Together, they swiftly cleared the opposition. Meanwhile, F Company was kept in battalion reserve.[72]

After Hs. Forkenbeck had been secured, Colonel Miller wheeled the 2nd Battalion right, and brought them up along a line of railroad tracks in preparation for an advance to the northeast and Gievenbecker. The rail line was established as the line of departure, and two phase lines were drawn between it and the objective three thousand yards ahead. At 2130 hours, in a claustrophobic darkness, D and E Companies crossed the tracks. F Company, in reserve, followed behind D Company while the mortar platoon from Headquarters Company fired in support of the assault companies.

Two thousand meters beyond the line of departure, the main north-south road that connected Roxel to the smaller village of Mecklenbeck, almost four kilometers southeast, was designated Phase Line 1. The Roxel-Mecklenbeck road, a main, hard-surfaced highway some four meters wide, would be an easily recognizable line on which the battalion's assault companies could reform before closing on the Aa River line.

With its initial objective to reach this road, D Company, spread across a five hundred yard front on the battalion's right, struck out onto the hilly, hedgerow-encircled fields. Control was difficult to maintain as the troopers pushed ahead in the almost pitch black. Soon, however, D Company men were entering the woods which lay ahead. Beyond these trees was Phase Line 1.

Attacking on the battalion's left, E Company, too, advanced, out onto the rolling, stream-crossed fields. The company reached the main northwest-southeast road at Hohenfeld without overmuch difficulty and from there, a twenty-four man combat patrol was sent north to quiet an enemy artillery battery harassing the company's advance. The patrol quickly captured the four-gun 88mm battery along with two hundred prisoners. Hundreds more Germans soldiers came out of the woods behind the battery's position to give themselves up, but the men did not wait to accept their surrender; they were simply ushered to the rear. As they marched in tattered columns through the battalion's line, F Company men could plainly see these Germans had no fight left in them and simply waved them on.[73]

D and E Companies' leading elements reached Phase Line 2 – the Aa River, which ran roughly northwest to southeast about a kilometer southwest of Gievenbecker – around midnight. There, they discovered that the road bridge over the river had been blown. The Aa was not wide, but was chest deep, and the men had no alternative but to wade into the bracing water. At 0130 hours, 2 April, D Company, maintaining contact with E Company on their left, and while slowed only by "scattered" small arms fire, waded across the Aa's slippery bed and, after pausing briefly to reorganize on the far bank, continued their attack up the pitched river bank. There, they captured a gasoline truck driven by a German woman. D Company then quickly overran the enemy defenses on the wooded hill ahead where they captured some sixty prisoners. Although enemy infantry kept up a constant harassing fire on D Company with machine-guns and machine pistols, the men dug in and then reconnoitered the high ground on their right.[74]

D Company had little chance to rest, however; they received orders to push on to the final objective, the high ground around Gievenbecker that dominated Münster. With their prisoners in tow, they continued on. Resistance had, in the two hour interval between reaching the Aa and crossing it, slackened somewhat, and German soldiers in their path now offered only limited resistance to the advance. Upon reaching the objective – a knoll overlooking the Herman Goering Barracks complex's southeast side – D Company men engaged a small covering force of enemy infantry and four 81mm mortars that had been left to defend the hill. In a sharp engagement, all of the enemy were killed or captured and D Company then pressed forward again. Advancing a thousand yards further to the northeast, D Company occupied the high ground due east of the barracks area and there dug in. It was then 0300 hours.[75]

E Company crossed the Aa River at about 0130 hours as well, and advanced northeast among hedgerows and fields until they were caught in the crossfire of four machine-guns. The automatic fire, and several grenades, wounded twelve men in E Company's leading platoon. The remaining platoons, in spite of a communications problems imposed by the darkness, were able to quickly organize and destroy the guns. The company then moved to the southeast corner of the Herman Goering Barracks "where they entered the garrison one platoon at a time" in bounds so that the advancing platoon would always be supported by a base of fire from the other two. Though unsupported by the British tanks, E Company quickly overran the German defenses.

Clearing the buildings was tough work, but one trooper devised a devastating tactic. "The Krauts would sandbag the four corners of rooms in the buildings of Münster," recalled Major Edwards. "If a grenade was thrown in there, the Germans would jump behind the sandbags. A man picked up by the 2nd Battalion who'd been separated from his own unit figured out that if he took a pineapple grenade and, without pulling the pin, threw it in through the window or the ventilator. . . [he could] then [just] walk in. As the Germans raised up from behind the sandbag walls, he'd shoot 'em all. 'American ingenuity'." Edwards was sorry he lost track of the man after the fight. "I sure as shit would have decorated him for having the brains to figure that out."[76]

E Company captured 212 prisoners and four 88mm guns, and the barracks' west wing was cleared of the enemy. A strong defensive position was then established. At 0430 hours, Colonel Miller radioed Regiment that the "Herman Goering Barracks, on outskirts of Münster, [is] fairly secure [and] in our hands."[77]

While D and E Companies were wading the Aa, F Company had remained with the tanks to assist them in their crossing. It was determined, however, that the river was too deep for the tanks to ford and that the point at which the assault companies had crossed was not suitable for bridging. Therefore, another crossing site had to be found. Captain Reynolds moved to the north and there, at a point three kilometers north of the intended spot, F Company and the tanks forded the river at 0830 hours on the morning of the second.[78]

Instructed by Colonel Miller to proceed to Gievenbecker, where the rest of the battalion was assembling, Reynolds began heading south on a secondary road which ran along the east side of the river. Trees lined the right side of the narrow road the tanks traveled on. The sounds of battle reverberated clearly above the roar of the plodding Churchills' engines, but F Company's morning had been, so far, fairly calm. PFC Laufer, riding behind the turret of the lead tank with PFC Grice, his platoon sergeant Tech Sergeant Harry Cook, Tec 5 Bob Anderson, and Doc Sloan the medic, was suddenly shaken alert by the sight of a ball of fire racing straight towards his tank. With a hissing crack, a high velocity shell passed, high overhead. No one had time to move before the next round struck. The second shot was a direct hit and the Churchill exploded violently, a huge hole torn in the front. Sergeant Cook, Anderson, and Sloan were thrown from the tank. The concussion made blood run from their noses and ears, covering their faces, Anderson had a long cut across his face. Grice and Laufer were also thrown off the tank, but with the exception of ringing ears, the two hadn't received a scratch. None of the Churchill's crew escaped. The men then saw the problem: From a low, one story wooden structure sitting a few hundred yards to the left, a captured American tank destroyer was firing at the column.[79]

Another British tank then erupted with a violent crash, its turret was thrown completely off and into the ditch as the chassis rolled to a stop some forty feet further on. Cobb, on the next tank in line didn't wait around for orders to dismount and jumped off. The whole company soon leapt from the tanks and went running for the deep ditches flanking both sides of the road or into the trees.[80]

Wieland and Joyce quickly got the First Platoon men started through the trees on the right in hopes of getting around on the tank. Then, remembered Grice, "man, it just started coming in on us." German artillery fell thickly in the woods causing a lot of tree bursts. Because of the intense shelling, First Platoon abandoned their initial attack and tried to go around a different way, advancing up another road. There, they met a tremendous amount of small arms fire – the pop of rifles and the crackling of Schmeissers. While the Churchills were moving across the fields on the left to fire on the enemy strongpoint, Private Cobb drifted off to the right into the edge of a small copse of trees, where he lay prone. There, he spied a telephone wire strung low across the ground. Cobb, who had only his bazooka, looked over to one of the men who was nearest him and told him, "Come on. I don't have a gun, come on."[81]

Cobb and his partner followed the wire deeper into the trees. Suddenly, three German kids armed with a machine-gun came into view in front of them. Cobb screamed as loud as he could and pointed the bazooka at them. Without hesitation, they threw their hands up. The two troopers rushed in quickly and disarmed the boys. There, in their hole, the three Germans had a telephone set. Apparently, they were spotting for the German gunners.

Cobb told the trooper with him, "Grab that machine-gun. I'll shoot that sonofabitch. I ain't got no gun."

"No," refused the other trooper, "the Americans will kill us." When fired, the MG-42 made a distinctive sound that could well have drawn friendly fire from other paratroopers, and although Cobb didn't really know his partner, he knew he was one of the older men in the company and figured he knew best. About three minutes later, one of Dunbar's M10 tank destroyer approached, and Cobb, much relieved to have support, identified himself and turned over the three Germans to the British crew.

The prisoners were brought roughly to where the First Platoon was assembled. PFC Laufer looked them over. He then kicked the biggest one in the crotch. The other two he belted in the mouth, knocking them both down. One was bleeding. Laufer then took off his cunt cap and showed the boys his Mohawk – he was, he admitted, "one miserable looking sonofabitch." His face was covered with four or five days' growth and streaked with sweat. The boys' facial expressions altered and they started shaking uncontrollably, believing they would be shot right then and there. "I'm a Jew!" he bellowed in delight. Laufer was still angry over Jack Cook being hit and wanted to shoot the kids, but decided to walk away instead. About that time Grice appeared, bleeding, and madder than hell.

Shortly after the fight started, Grice, moving through the woods on the right, had been wounded by a tree burst and blacked out. When, some time later, he came to, he was all alone, the firing had died down. Grice had a bad wound in the back of his neck, where the shrapnel had bumped his spine. He figured his friends had left him for dead. It was a sinking feeling. Grice grabbed his helmet up and put it on, grabbed his Grease Gun, and went looking for his platoon. When he arrived, and saw the three German prisoners, Grice raised his Grease Gun to shoot them, but another trooper pushed the muzzle away, saying "Don't kill them." "Look at the hole in my neck," snapped Grice. Grice soon cooled down and another trooper escorted the boys away. Meantime, most of the enemy had been routed by the tanks and several prisoners were taken, including twenty-six officers.[82]

Laufer's Churchill, still burning fiercely, sat in the road. Nearby, the six troopers wounded in the engagement were put on a Bren Gun Carrier and started to the rear to where an ambulance was waiting. As the carrier retraced the column's route back up the road, they were fired on by enemy machine-gunners who'd gotten around behind the company. Grice, and a couple of the other wounded men who had been hanging on the outside of the tiny British vehicle, had to jump off and crawl, two hundred yards along the roadside ditch, until they were clear of the enemy fire. Then they climbed back on and headed for the ambulance. F Company and the remaining tanks, meanwhile, continued forward and joined the main body of the 2nd Battalion which had assembled on the high ground east of the Herman Goering Barracks. There, Reynolds informed Colonel Miller about the presence of the enemy pocket of resistance they had passed.[83]

The fall of Münster was officially recorded at 1610 hours, 2 April 1945. By midday, the whole of the city had been more or less surrounded by elements of the XIX U.S. Corps: the 5th U.S. Armored Division had circled the city to the north; the 194th Glider Infantry Regiment was rapidly closing on positions to the northwest; the 513th and the 6 Guards Armored Brigade had closed in positions to the west and south of the city; and the 507th Combat Team, returned to the 17th Airborne Division at 1000 hours that day, had completed Münster's encirclement to the east. Throughout the day, scores of the disheveled German defenders came in to surrender. The 17th Airborne Division captured some 1,500 German prisoners, of more than five hundred were credited to the 513th. The fighting, however, was far from over.[84]

On the morning of 3 April, Colonel Miller assembled the 2nd Battalion on the high ground west of Münster. It was from here that he had planned to launch his final attack on the city, an attack which F Company was picked to lead. Though Münster had fallen 'officially' the day before, no one had related this to the Germans. There were still many waiting amid the shattered remains of the city prepared to fight, and fight hard.

George Dorsey, a staff writer for the *Stars and Stripes*, was with the men of the 17th Airborne Division when they entered the city. He reported: "A few scattered intact houses in the outskirts – that's all that remains of Münster." Once a center of German culture, Münster had been bombed ninety-nine times, the last raid coming the day before, 1 April – in a "big softening-up air raid," in preparation for the ground assault. The city's Gothic cathedral, having withstood the previous ninety-eight raids, was numbered among the casualties of the final air attack.

With the tanks, Reynolds' men started into the town at 0730 hours. As the company passed a roadside barn, Private Dahlberg heard the voices of German soldiers from inside and he and another trooper went to investigate. The two climbed up a pile of straw and poked their heads into the loft – expecting full well to come face to face with the muzzle of a German Mauser. What Dahlberg found instead was a pair of young boys, both in brand new uniforms with brand new rifles who couldn't wait to surrender. Dahlberg got them down out of the loft and pushed them towards the rear.

"We could see clearly the town of Münster down below," recalled Contreras, who watched the battle from atop the high ground. "The town was just rubble, some of the buildings were on fire. The cooks took turns firing one of 2nd Battalion's .50 caliber machine-guns in support of the attack. "We fired at anything that moved." The troopers advanced into the outskirts of the city along both sides of the main thoroughfare – house by house – covering each other and the Churchills which drove with one track on the sidewalk and one track in the street, knocking down every telephone pole in their path.[85]

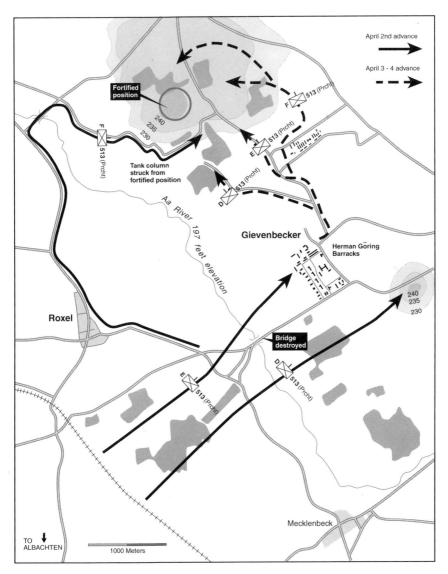

Fighting in the western suburbs of Münster, Germany, by 2nd Battalion of the 513th Parachute Infantry, 2-4 April 1945. (Rick Brownlee/R&B Graphic Designs)

Not much resistance was initially encountered and civilians cooperated willingly with the men when questioned. Yet, resistance began to stiffen as the company moved further into the city, and the sound of firing was growing to the rear, in the northwestern part of the city.[86]

As the troopers moved into the city proper, they entered a business area of large buildings. A lot of small arms fire came from German troops holed up in a factory building ahead and slowed the attack's progress considerably. Edging forward around the corner of a building, one of the men ran face to face into a German soldier. Both soldiers just stood there for a second, gaping at each other in surprise. Then, the F Company man recovered and killed the German.

Suddenly, another German soldier popped out of a window above the street. Sergeant Haggard had spotted him, but too late to stop him. The German pressed his pistol against the top of PFC Beaumont Hunter's helmet and fired one round. As Hunter collapsed onto the street, the German withdrew back into the darkness behind the window. Two troopers tossed in grenades while another man ran to get Cobb and the bazooka. Cobb jogged up quickly and fired a rocket into the house. Then they went in after him. When the troopers reappeared, they were dragging with them a middle-aged SS officer. The man was bleeding from a deep cut in the top of his bald head and from stomach wounds. The F Company men took him to the medics. Rudolph, the aidman, could see that with his stomach wound the SS man probably wouldn't make it but he wanted to make sure. Rudolf twisted the top off his canteen poured the whole contents in the German's mouth, filling him full of water. "He gave him a drink," said Cobb and that surely finished him.[87]

German infantry were waiting in the ruins of the botanical gardens and zoo complex and it was F Company's job to clean the snipers out. Rounding one of the zoo's big buildings, troopers spotted more Germans fleeing into a basement. One of the riflemen crept forward to throw a grenade, but was shot in the neck and seriously wounded. Two grenades tossed into the basement by PFCs Olson and Gutt finished resistance there. Another clutch of German soldiers was spotted dashing around the side of a building and into another basement. Third Platoon's bazooka team put a round through the basement's window, and more than half a dozen Germans crawled out to surrender. A subsequent search of the basement uncovered about a dozen more Germans killed and wounded. Before long, the volume of sniper fire had increased so the British tanks were called forward to blast out pockets of resistance. "If there was suspicion of the enemy being in a certain building," explained Greenstrand, "they would simply blow the hell out of it."

Escaped zoo animals, released by the repeated bombings of the past several days, darted in and out of the rubble. First Sergeant Donovan was nearly trampled by a giraffe when it bolted out from around a corner, down the street, and out of view. Other men chased parakeets, parrots, or monkeys to keep as pets.[88]

In spite of the slow going, F Company was inflicting a great number of casualties on the defenders and sending scores of prisoners – they eventually numbered over two hundred – to the rear. The Germans typically put up a great deal of resistance until the Americans closed on them. When things began to look desperate, the enemy would surrender. "Most of them were far older than you might expect," said Greenstrand. "[They] simply didn't have the will to hang on and fight."[89]

All morning, as the company moved into Münster, troopers had listened to the rumble of a 'mini-war' growing louder to their rear. While the balance of E Company had continued its advance into the city, one platoon from E Company had been detached to clear the same pocket of resistance that had engaged F Company northwest of the barracks the day before. What the E Company platoon soon discovered was that they were facing a well armed, well entrenched, and extremely determined force, and they needed help fast. Colonel Miller was apprised of the situation and in turn, he called Captain Reynolds.

Reynolds was ordered to pull out of the line and return to the Herman Goering Barracks. Reynolds quickly informed his tank squadron commander that another company was coming up to take over for them, and that F Company was leaving to relieve the E Company platoon.[90]

Captain Reynolds reassembled the company in the lately captured barracks area and told the men to drop all of their equipment – mussette bags, entrenching tools – everything but their weapons and ammunition. He then explained the situation to the men, and told them that the rest of the battalion would soon be attacking as well.[91]

Reynolds initially believed that the main concentration of enemy resistance was located at a second barracks complex, located about 1,200 yards north of the main Herman Goering Barracks, and therefore, proceeded to maneuver the company northward along the highway. There were more than two dozen large buildings at the site, and Reynolds ordered the men to clear them out. The muffled thuds of detonating grenades and the slow rattle of M3s erupted all around. With a couple men covering, Greenstrand tossed a grenade in through a window. After the blast, the men stormed into the room and pulled out some dazed German soldiers. Greenstrand and another man had to carry one of the wounded Germans out on a door, and then commenced interrogating the man right there. When they discovered he didn't want to talk, they "dropped the sonofabitch on the ground." "It was a bad thing to do," remembered Greenstrand. "He was wounded bad, but that's the way war was." Since there weren't a lot of enemy troops defending this part of the barracks complex, Reynolds realized that the enemy concentration must be located in another area. It was just as Reynolds was about to return to his start line that, from a hill to the northwest, F Company received a large volume of fire from the well entrenched enemy force the E Company platoon was battling.[92]

Captain Reynolds hustled the company down the road to a farm yard on the southeast side of the barracks complex and then northwest to a farm area which was located behind a hospital the battalion had passed that morning. Here, F Company was approximately one thousand yards due east of the German positions and there was a dense wood standing between the farm and the area where the battle was taking place. Reynolds set up his CP in the farmhouse and then issued orders for the company to attack through the woods with the farm yard as the line of departure.

The company moved out cautiously – it was almost impossible to see through the dense growth of trees. As they neared the battle area, F Company was pinned down by tree burst artillery, a couple of men were hit. Cuthbertson was stung by shrapnel on the sleeve where he wore his watch, but it didn't penetrate. However, Private Russell E. Dolan, a seventeen year old from Washington State who had been on point, was killed instantly. The fire was so hot that Reynolds ordered the men to fall back around the farm. When the company withdrew, the artillery ceased. Reynolds tried to push through the woods one more time but again the attack failed. Then, one of the men told Reynolds, "Every time we get into the woods, I hear a bell ringing." Something was up and Reynolds knew it. On the next attack, the captain left a man in the house. The men pushed into the woods but were again forced to retire under a stiff barrage of 88s. Reassembling at the farmhouse, the man Reynolds had left behind reported that he had bagged a German in the farmhouse's cupola. The German spotter had been warning the enemy gunners that F Company was coming by ringing a bell.[93]

F Company once more attacked through the woods but was nevertheless stopped by heavy fires from 88s, Schmeissers, and MG-42s. Reynolds could see it would be impossible to advance from the southeast so he called on Corps artillery to lay down a barrage and withdrew his men, leaving behind a covering force to keep the Germans occupied while the rest of the company pulled back. The men were all short of ammunition, so Reynolds led them back to the Herman Goering Barracks to rejoin the rest of the battalion. There, at 1500 hours, Colonel Miller "took charge of the situation and at 1530, reorganizing his command, committed the battalion with E Company leading, D on the left, and F on the right" with the mission of sealing off the pocket from the rear. The battalion started its advance northwest along the main road, hoping to quickly surround the German pocket of resistance.[94]

Lying astride the highway, E Company, got pinned down right away by heavy fire from 88s and a captured Sherman tank firing white phosphorous – the first time it had been used against the battalion. E Company called for artillery and mortar support. Mortarmen fired as fast as they could drop the rounds, but it was difficult to gauge the effect due to the dense woods and growing darkness. The enemy fire did ease, however, and E Company continued to advance on a 250 yard front, their left on a river that ran parallel to the road. Clearing snipers from houses as they went, they reached a house within three hundred yards of the enemy position where they reorganized.[95]

At that moment, F Company, circling to the north, neared the chain of trees that shrouded the enemy bunker complex. Grasshoppers – artillery forward observation planes – were flying above the German positions directing fire, and the Germans were trying to shoot them down with machine-guns. Staff Sergeant Bailey was instructed by one of the officers: "Sergeant, run across that field and take those two men with you." This was supposed to draw the enemy's fire and give the rest of the company the opportunity to close in on the enemy positions. The field, on F Company's left, was about one hundred yards wide with trees bordering it on the far end. Just in front of the trees was an abandoned ammunition storage bunker and the Germans were only about a hundred yards forward of that. Bailey had transferred from the Air Corps because he wanted to see some action. Well, he figured, he was about to.

"You follow me. Let's go!!" he told two men, and started out across the field, the two troopers following. Bailey didn't know their names. He was so new he didn't really know anybody. He did know that was the way for leaders to give orders in combat: simply "Follow me." "Everybody understands that," explained Bailey. The leader had to lead from the front. "There was no time to be scared. That was something you realized, [that you'd been scared], when it was all over."

When Bailey's group took off, the Germans started firing. Bullets splattered into the mud all around them, but all three made it to the earth-covered ammunition bunker in one piece. Meanwhile, the rest of the company started pushing into the German positions. They didn't get anywhere, however.

The Germans started firing white phosphorous rounds, several slamming into the face of the storage bunker Bailey and his two men were using for cover. Bailey could smell the wood of the bunker burning after the explosions. Machine-gun and occasionally rifle fire raked the area. This was no place to be, Bailey thought, "the ruse didn't pay off." At this point, Bailey didn't care about anything but keeping himself, and the two fellows with him, alive. They started crawling away, slowly, and finally rejoined the company.[96]

Though they had been unable to enter the German bunker complex, F Company men had successfully moved around on the right and surrounded the place. The battalion was, therefore, going to have to blast the Germans out with artillery. As the shelling commenced, the men were told to prepare to stay there all night. Since F Company didn't have their entrenching tools, the troopers took cover as best they could. It was late and the men were hungry. All most of them had was D bars, but K rations were finally brought forward.

As it got dark, the word was passed that all efforts were to be directed toward the complete annihilation of the Germans in the pocket – not a single one was to be allowed out alive. All through the night, the enemy made attempts to break out but were fiercely driven back into the killing ground by the troopers. The battalion's mortars pounded the enemy unceasingly. "I can't imagine where they came up with that amount of ammunition," commented Greenstrand. Squads were rotated off the line and the men did get a chance to rest, but it was a long night and no one got any sleep.[97]

Around midnight, Captain Reynolds picked six men to go on a patrol around to the west side of the German bunker complex. The men got going through the woods and then started heading south toward a road that was the objective of the patrol. When PFC Sarrell heard the sounds of Germans marching and talking, the patrol ran for the ditches which, of course, were filled with water. What looked like one hundred Germans walked past, talking, Sarrell recalled. The patrol lay there for what seemed hours watching them go by. They were unarmed, it appeared to Sarrell, but the patrol took no chances and stayed tight. After things quieted down, the six troopers got up and began back-tracking out of there with Sarrell on the point. He was "walking down the road and, from around the curve, here comes this German soldier on a bike." The German stopped dead and looked right at Sarrell. Then Sarrell told him: "Get your butt out of here." The German took off back up the road. As Sarrell explained, "It was tough to shoot a guy like that."[98]

Meanwhile, from his position in the house along the highway, Lieutenant Blunt had recognized a bunker, only forty yards away, as the center of resistance and ordered his E Company men to attack. Blunt's men had assailed the bunker but were driven back. D Company had also attacked from the west but were also repulsed with three of Musick's men having been captured. Both companies called for additional white phosphorous grenades for the next attack, but both company commanders, Lieutenants Blunt and Musick, wanted to wait for daylight to take another crack at the German position.[99]

Under the cover of darkness, small German patrols again strained to break free of the pocket, engaging 2nd Battalion troopers with grenades and panzerfausts. A platoon from D Company, led by First Sergeant Jobie K. Boggs, intercepted a six-man German patrol, well armed with grenades and panzerfausts, sent out to destroy a shoulder 57mm that they had mistakenly identified as a tank. A serious firefight began when Boggs and his men surprised the heavily armed patrol. Boggs "killed two of the enemy with his carbine, then grappled with and killed a third with his trench knife." When shrapnel from a grenade broke Boggs' leg the remaining three Germans were able to escape.[100]

Just after midnight, Lieutenant Selzer went out to check on one of F Company's outposts. With all the Germans trying to break out of the pocket, the men were a little edgy. It was pitch black, and the lieutenant strayed into E Company's area and was challenged by a sentry. Lieutenant Selzer had "the very bad habit of mumbling the password whenever he was challenged." Most of the F Company men recognized him, and he had been warned about his bad habit many times. The E Company sentry took no chances, however, and shot first, wounding Selzer in the chest.

Selzer was laying on the ground heaving when PFC Dahlberg got to him. "Pound sand in the wound," Selzer repeated over and over again. "He was delirious," said Dahlberg who was helpless to stop the bleeding. PFC Greenstrand and another man were sent to bring Selzer back to the farm house. Cobb was there when the medic arrived. Rudolph removed the lieutenant's jacket and shirts. Selzer had a sucking chest wound and Rudolph knew he wasn't going to make it. Greenstrand returned to his post. A little while later, Lieutenant Selzer died. The men were dismayed by the senselessness of Selzer's death, but "everybody had a trigger finger," Dahlberg explained.[101]

Sometime in May 1945, F Company men received a letter from Mrs. Mable E. Selzer, Lieutenant Selzer's mother. She wrote:

> I have mailed some requested packages of foods to our son, 2nd Lieutenant Francis C. Selzer, O-1059276,- Co. F. 513th Prcht. Inf. Reg't, A.P.O. 452. I would like very much for you to give this food to Co. F. if you are allowed to do so. Our son, Francis, died of wounds in Germany and cannot use the foods. If Co. F. does not exist now, give it to some of the 513th P.I.R. If the 513 is no more give these foods as you see best. There is a watch in the mail for Lieutenant Francis C. Selzer. I want that back.
>
> Can you let me know what you do with the foods?

As F Company continued to hold its positions on the right of the battalion, some of the officers, were becoming irritable – they had a great deal of responsibility for young men. The tension had had no effect on Staff Sergeant Bill Kuntz, however. Early in the morning, he pulled up in front of the company CP on a commandeered German motorcycle and invited Cobb to jump on. "Your gonna get us both killed," Cobb told him. Kuntz turned out to be very drunk and didn't care that much about it. With Cobb, stone sober and holding on tight, he took off on a wild joy ride through the streets of Münster.

Early on the morning of the fourth, Major Edwards took charge of D and E Companies and led them in three successive assaults on the enemy positions. Colonel Miller, who witnessed the attack, reported the assault as follows:

On the night of 3-4 April 1945 the Second Battalion, 513th Parachute Infantry launched an attack against a strongly fortified position in the vicinity of Müsnter, Germany.

The enemy, numbering about 175 fanatical Nazis commanded by a major, occupied concrete emplacements 10 to 20 feet thick, 10 to 12 feet high and interconnected by underground passages. In addition to massed fires of eight 88 mm guns, numerous 20 mm flak guns, machine-guns, panzerfausts and small arms, the enemy had at its disposal five tanks, including two Churchills, one of them in good condition and the other immobilized but still able to fire. The battalion attacked with a full combat load of ammunition and, besides artillery support, had at its disposal 16 shoulder type 57 mm AT guns.

With Major IRWIN A. EDWARDS, battalion Executive Officer, leading Companies "D" and "E", the battalion came under 88 fire about 400 yards from the nearest gun. Without regard for his own safety, I saw Major EDWARDS guide the two companies across an open field that afforded the best approach under the circumstances and close with the enemy. He led and inspired the battalion in hand to hand combat until its ammunition load was exhausted and it was forced to fall back. The battalion was re-supplied and I saw Major EDWARDS lead it in a second assault at about 2300 but heavy firepower and the nature of the concrete bunkers prevented capturing the objective after troops of our battalion had penetrated the emplacements and passageways. When our troops were forced to withdraw after again exhausting their ammunition supply Major EDWARDS volunteered to stay in the advanced position, observing the enemy and coordinating the third assault. By this time we were separated and he told me his decision by radio. He then continued in constant contact with me, assisting greatly in coordinating the attack while beating off all efforts of the enemy to dislodge him in close fighting. As soon as the battalion was resupplied he guided it forward at 0100 and led the third assault which resulted in complete routing of the enemy force and capture of a large amount of material.

The fighting was the hardest I witnessed in the entire operation. The courage and calm leadership of Major EDWARDS in remaining within the enemy fortifications against all odds to coordinate our attack was a deciding factor in our favor.

At 0100 hours, Lieutenant Blunt was called from the bunker by PFC Robert J. Fox, one of the men taken in the first assault. Fox had apparently convinced the German garrison that, in the face of 2nd Battalion's relentless pressure, their resistance was futile and that they should surrender. At dawn, black silhouettes began walking through the woods towards F Company's lines. Staff Sergeant Bailey didn't know whether to fire or not – they were so close, but the Germans were coming out to surrender. The German officer commanding the position had been terribly wounded during the fight and, this, too, may have had some bearing, it was thought, on the garrison's decision to surrender. Regardless of the reason, the decision spared the lives of eighty-seven German soldiers. 2nd Battalion's medics came up and began treating the German wounded. "Some of them looked like the concussion from the artillery had blown their clothes and skin right off of them," remembered Staff Sergeant Bailey.[102]

F Company got up and walked into the pocket to mop it up. "We cautiously started through the area," remembered Greenstrand, "[and] discovered bodies all over the place. There were huge bunkers built and covered with earth with many dead Germans inside. They had held off an entire battalion for many hours and," Greenstrand added, "must be given credit as fearless soldiers." [103]

An ambulance and a jeep had come forward with the medics. Both had gotten stuck in the mud, but the drivers, who had left them unattended, had left the engines running. Olson and several others freed the jeep and, even though it had one flat tire, piled on. They were about to take off when an officer came by and told them to get out. The company was moving back to the barracks and Olson had to walk like everyone else.[104]

2nd Battalion returned to the Herman Goering Barracks to pick up their equipment, change clothes, and get a rest. The rest of the regiment already were billeted there and, by this time, had already started looking for souvenirs. The barracks was a trophy hunter's paradise and the men plucked up anything they could lay their hands on, from Nazi ashtrays to Nazi flags to Nazi P-38s (the thought that a lot of their treasures would be sold for booze money as soon as they hit New York never crossed their minds). The cooks had set up a mess line in a farmhouse and, at 0730 hours, F Company was served their first hot meal since D-Day. "Everyone enjoyed it," remarked Contreras. In the afternoon, the men received their second hot chow and began preparations for a move that would take place the following day.[105]

The next morning, the 17th Airborne Division moved by motor convoy to the vicinity of Duisburg, in the Ruhr, to began occupation duty. Thirty-two days later the war in Europe ended.

Epilogue

The fall of Münster meant that, for the 17th Airborne Division and, thus, for F Company, the war was all but over. All that remained was the 'mopping up' and occupation duties – and lording it over the conquered Germans – as everybody waited for the German high command to realize what had become plainly evident to the men in the field on both sides: Germany was defeated.

It took another month for the generals to acknowledge this fact and surrender to the Allies. Supreme Commander Dwight D. Eisenhower's announcement of the end of the war in Europe was terse, but to the point. "The mission of this Allied force was fulfilled at 0241 local time, May 7, 1945."

So, it was over. The war had taken F Company from Alabama to Germany via England, France, Belgium, and France again. More than 380 men had served in its ranks, and of these, F Company had suffered at least fifty-one killed and more than 135 wounded or injured in action. Seven men received decorations for valor, one of which was a posthumous award. Most important, however, F Company had defeated Hitler's Germany.

In the broad scheme of things, however, F Company was, in many ways, not much different than all the units which had fought in Europe, taking part in what Eisenhower called, "The Great Crusade" – from the tankers of the 761st Tank Battalion to the aircrews of the 313th Troop Carrier Group. The men of F Company were, as the British would say, "in at the death," had fought in one of the

European Campaign's most desperate battles, and had participated in the largest Airborne operation of the war, however; there would be no singular treatment for it as a unit or its men as individuals. One by one, the men were sent home or assigned to other units for occupation duty. As it was formed – little by little and with a complete absence of ceremony – so too F Company was disbanded.

Appendices

Appendix I: Unit Roster

Name, Last rank held before 4 April 1945, and Combat wounds.

*Accomando, Paul J., Private (LIA 1/10/45)
*Adams, Wayland, Private
Adams, Willis J. R., Staff Sergeant
Adler, James E., Private (LIA 1/4/45)
Adragna, Jack, Private (KIA 1/16/45)
Aguirres, Ferdinand, PFC
Alger, Acey E., Tech Sergeant
Alt, Victor R. G., PFC (LWA 3/30/45)
Altmiller, Frederick W., PFC (NBC 2/5/45)
*Anderson, Robert J., Tec 5 (NBC 1/8/45, LWA 4/2/45)
*Anderson, Walter E., Private
*Andrews, Donald L., Private (LIA 2/1/45)
Andrews, Floyd, PFC
Apfel, Frank, Private
Arango, Angle, Private (LWA 1/30/45)
Armus, Louis, Private (MIA 3/24/45)
*Arrowood, James W., PFC (LIA 1/6/45)
Asher, Forrest E., Sergeant
*Auer, Dale J., PFC (NBC 1/16/45)

*Bacon, Donald A., Private (Drummed out of the Airborne).
Bailey, Charles E., Staff Sergeant
*Balben, Walter H., Tec 5
*Barber, Asa F., PFC
*Barbera, Edward, Private
*Barth, Albert W., PFC (LWA 1/7/45)
Barton, Paul E., Tec 5
*Bassett, James F., Tech Sergeant (LWA 1/4/45)
Benson, Maynard R., Private (LIA 1/16/45)
*Berg, Warren C., Private (NBC 1/4/45)
Bergmann, William C., PFC (LWA 3/24/45)
Black, Donald E. (SWA 1/4/45, DOW 1/14/45)
*Blakney, Peter J., PFC (NBC 1/9/45)
Bohn, Jack F., Private (SWA 1/3/45)
*Borchers, Alfred E., Private
*Bowers, Arthur A., Tech Sergeant (LIA 1/4/45)
*Brewer, Wilmer T., PFC (SWA 2/4/45, DOW 2/12/45)
Bricmont, Arthur E., PFC (LWA 1/3/45)

*Brooks, William F., Private
*Brown, Donald, Private (Dropped from rolls 8/6/44)
Brown, James A., PFC (KIA 1/4/45)
Brown, John V. Jr., PFC
Bubenchick, Milo, Private
Burroughs, Herbert L., Private
Burke, Eugene L., Private (LIA 1/16/45)
*Butcher, Clifford W., Sergeant

*Calhoun, Samuel, 1st Lieutenant (LWA 1/4/45, LIA 3/31/45)
*Cappell, Jack N., Private
Cantwell, Henry J., Staff Sergeant (LWA 4/2/45)
Carter, Donald W., Private (KIA 3/24/45)
Cater, William G., Corporal (KIA 3/24/45)
*Caton, Dwight E., PFC (SWA 1/3/45)
*Cavaleri, Philip, PFC (LIA 1/7/45)
*Chappell, Frank, 1st Lieutenant
Chutas, Charles, PFC (SWA 4/3/45)
Chieloha, James D., Private
*Clark, Arthur A., First Sergeant
Cobb, John E., Private
Coburn, Robert E.
*Cogan, John W., PFC.
Collins, Horace P., Private
Common, Adair W., 1st Lieutenant
Connolly, Thomas E., Private (LWA 1/4/45)
Contreras, Henry, Tec 4
*Cook, Harry E., Tech Sergeant (LWA 1/6/45, LWA 4/2/45)
*Cook, Jack, PFC. (LIA 1/9/45, SWA 3/30/45, DOW 4/6/45)
Cornale, Joseph M., Private
*Costello, Edward F., PFC (LWA 3/24/45)
Cox, Delbert J., PFC
Cox, James G., Private
Coyle, John W. Private
Craddock, Charles E., (KIA 1/4/45)
Craddock, Howard A., Private (KIA 3/24/45)
Cross, Richard B., 2nd Lieutenant
Crowley, Thomas B. Private (KIA 1/16/45)
Cuthbertson, Maurice C., PFC

Dabbs, Robert J., PFC
*Dahlberg, Edward R., PFC

*Dauer, Harry E., PFC (LIA 1/6/45)
Davenport, Herbert C., Sergeant (KIA 3/30/45)
*Davis, Ralph N., Private
Day, Walter A., Private (LWA 1/4/45)
*Dean, Samuel C., 1st Lieutenant (LIA 1/16/45)
*DeHaven, Wayne H., Tec 5 (LWA 1/7/45)
*DePiero, Jeno A., Sergeant
DeSanto, Frank D., Private (KIA 1/16/45)
Dick, Robert E., PFC
Diefenderfer, Harold O., 1st Lieutenant (LWA 3/24/45)
Dolan, Russell E., Private (KIA 4/3/45)
Donovan, Royal W., First Sergeant (NBC 1/7/45)
Dornbos, James E., Staff Sergeant (LIA 1/25/45, 4/3/45)
Dougherty, John A., Tec 5 (LWA 3/30/45)
Drago, Paoli O., Private
Dreith, John C., Private
Driggers, Alver S., Private (LWA 1/4/45)
Driscoll, Elmer C., Tec 4 (NBC 1/31/45)
*Duncan, Norman E., Private (LWA 1/4/45)
*Duprey, Lawrence J., PFC (SWA 1/3/45)
Durant, Donald H., Private

*Edwards, Schley E., Private
*Eibert, John M., Corporal (LWA 1/4/45)
*Eide, Kenneth M., Private (KIA 3/31/45)
*Eide, Raymond O., Sergeant (LWA 1/4/45)
Elliot, Lloyd K., PFC (LIA 1/8/45, LIA 4/3/45)
Engel, Rubin, Private
English, Billy J., Private (LWA 1/4/45)
*Erb, Donald S., Sergeant (SWA 1/3/45, LWA 3/24/45)
*Evans, Paul M., Private (LWA 1/16/45)

Fann, Isham, 1st Lieutenant (LWA 3/24/45)
*Faulk, Benson, Staff Sergeant
Fellman, Edwin J., Private
*Fine, John "Tex" C., Private
Fischer, Lawrence V., Tec 4
*Fisher, Robert G., Private
Flynn, John J., PFC
Forbes, Chester H., Private
Ford, William L., Tec 5
Fortunato, Carmine J., Private

Franklin, Robert P., PFC
*Fredenburg, Wesley E., Sergeant (LIA 1/16/45)
*Fuller, Charles, Private
*Funinez, Michael, Private

Gallardo, Tommy S., Private
Galloway, James W., Corporal
Garcia, Perfecto, Jr., Private (LIA 1/4/45)
Garrett, Robert T., Private
Gatter, Charles R., Private
Gauthreaux, Llewellyn V., PFC
Geddie, Earl M., Private
*George, Joseph E., Private
Gerner, Louis J., 1st Lieutenant
*Giard, Francis J., PFC (LIA 1/8/45)
*Gibbs, William L., Private (KIA 1/4/45)
*Gilles, Robert E., 1st Lieutenant (KIA 1/8/45)
Girvin, Robert C., PFC (LWA 3/30/45)
Glanowski, Bernard E., Private (LIA 1/7/45)
Glasgow, Nolan G., Private
Glavas, John N., Private (NBC 4/1/45)
Goble, Frank J., PFC
*Goddard, Howard W., PFC (KIA 3/24/45)
Goetsch, Roland W., Private
*Gohn, George H., Jr., Sergeant (KIA 1/4/45)
Goins, Doyle E., PFC
Goldfarb, Harry, PFC
Gonzalez, Edmundo, Private
*Graupensperger, George H., PFC (LWA 1/4/45)
Grealis, John T., PFC (LWA 3/30/45)
Green, Daniel, Private (LWA 1/6/45)
*Greene, Dolph, Private
*Greenstrand, Elwyn "Bob" H., PFC (MIA 1/16/45)
Gresher, James J., Staff Sergeant (KIA 3/30/45)
*Grice, Willis B., PFC (NBC 1/8/45, LWA 4/2/45)
*Griffin, Boyd W., Private
*Grubb, Joseph R., PFC (KIA 1/4/45)
*Guidry, Jessie J., PFC
Guiles, Robert E., PFC
Gutt, Joseph B. PFC

*Haggard, Neal, Sergeant
*Hall, John I., PFC (LWA 1/4/45)
*Halley, Leroy D., PFC (LWA 1/4/45)
Halter, Kenneth D., Private
Hamby, Dolph R., Jr., Private
Hammilton, Russell R., Private
Hamorski, Joseph, Private
Haney, Ernest C., Private (LIA 3/24/45)
Harbrough, Adolphus D., Jr., Private (LIA 1/9/45)
*Harding, Clifford T., PFC (LIA 1/4/45, LWA 4/3/45)
Hardy, Donald F., PFC (LWA 3/24/45)
Harris, Campbell L., (KIA 1/24/45)
*Harris, Marvin C., Corporal
Harrison, William T., First Sergeant
*Hart, Walter (NMI), Private
*Harvey, Thomas D., Sergeant (KIA 3/24/45)
*Hataway, Russell A., Sergeant
Heaton, Howard J., Private (SWA 1/5/45)
Heckman, William A., PFC (NBC 4/4/45)
Hellrigel, Peter J. Staff Sergeant (KIA 1/8/45)
Henderson, Mabron E., Private (LWA 1/7/45)
Helton, James A., Private
*Henriett, Floyd C., Private
Hernandez, Eulalio G., Private
Herrin, John M., PFC (LWA 3/24/45)
*Hester, Charles A., Private (KIA 1/4/45)
*Hester, Okel T., Private
Hewitt, Hollis C., Private
Hickman, William L., Private
*Hill, Henry C., Tec 5
*Hinkley, Harold E., Staff Sergeant (LIA 1/6/45)
Hinman, Thomas W., Private
*Hriesik, Jacob, Private (MIA 1/5/45)
*Holine, Russell E., Tec 5
Hoover, Arthur C., Private
*Howell, Robert G., PFC
*Hultman, Robert C., PFC (LIA 1/20/45)
Hunter, Beaumont R., PFC (KIA 4/3/45)
Hurst, Delmar W., Private (LWA 1/16/45)
Hutto, Herbert F., Staff Sergeant

*Imre, Paul (NMI), PFC (LIA 1/4/45, LWA 1/5/45)
Imber, John P., Corporal (LIA 1/16/45)
Imhof, Raymond P., Private
*Ivy, Gates, Jr., Captain

*Jacob, James J., PFC (SWA 1/8/45, MIA 1/16/45)
Jacobs, Raymond J., PFC (LWA 1/4/45)
Jakes, William E., Captain
Jordan, Dennis, PFC (LWA 1/6/45)
*Jordan, John J., Private
Johnson, James R. (KIA 1/4/45)
Johnson, Otto T., PFC (LWA 1/4/45)
Jones, Arthur E., Private
Jones, Paul R., Private
Joyce, John J., 1st Lieutenant
Juarez, Manuel, PFC

*Kaczmarek, Henry, Private (LIA 1/5/45)
*Keeling, Jr., Edward A., Corporal (LWA 1/7/45)
Keese, Andrew J., PFC (LWA 3/24/45)
*Keller, Jr., Frank, PFC
*Keller, Patrick M., Private (KIA 1/4/45)
Kelly, Morris W., PFC (LIA 1/9/45, NBC 4/4/45)
*Kerber, Francois A., Private
*Kinkus, Jr., Frank J., PFC (KIA 1/4/45)
*Kirkup, Robert I., Private
*Kitson, Joseph R., Sergeant (LWA 3/24/45)
*Knigge, Clarence F., Jr., Staff Sergeant (LWA 1/7/45)
*Kondiditsiotes, Evangelos J., PFC (LWA 1/4/45)
Krohs, Henry H., Tec 4
*Kuntz, William C., Sr., Staff Sergeant (LWA 1/4/45)

LaChance, George C., Private
*Lage, Virgil P., Private
Landers, Raymond H., Tec 4 (LWA 3/24/45)
La Riccia, John D., Sergeant (SWA 1/8/45)
*Laufer, Sidney, PFC (SWA 1/3/45)
Lawrence, George S., Private (LIA 1/16/45)
Lawson, Clarence E., Private (LWA 1/4/45)
LeDuc, Clifford F., Private (LIA 3/31/45)
Lightcap, Raymond L., PFC
Lincoln, Lawrence E. (KIA 1/5/45)

*Logan, James M. Private (KIA 1/7/45)
Logsdon, Edward T., PFC (LIA 1/9/45)
Lown, Leonard B., Sergeant
Lubbuck, John L., (KIA 1/16/45)

MacKenzie, Roderick, A., Jr., PFC (LWA 1/4/45)
Madere, Francis X., Jr., Private (NBC 1/16/45)
*Mahoney, John J., Private
Mallon, Robert C., PFC (LIA 1/4/45, LWA 3/28/45)
Mandis, Josph E., Private
Marchand, John E., Private
Masterjohn, Donald D., Corporal
Masterson, John W., Tec 5 (LIA 3/26/45)
Maxwell, William W. Private (DOW 1/7/45)
McCall, John T., Corporal
*McClain, Howard R., Sergeant (LWA 1/4/45)
McLean, Rubin E., Staff Sergeant (LIA 1/5/45)
McDevitt, Francis V. Staff Sergeant (KIA 1/4/45)
McGoldrick, Fred, Captain
McMahon, David P., Staff Sergeant (LWA 3/24/45)
Merzoian, Arthur, Private
Michalik, Stanley J., Tec 5
Mihalsky, Leonard J., Private (LWA 1/4/45)
Miller, Herbert C., PFC
Miller, Robert B., Tec 4
Miller, William L., Tec 5 (KIA 3/24/45)
Ming, Joel Y., Private (KIA 3/24/45)
Mixon, Philip M., Tec 4
Molchan, Michael A., Tec 5
*Moon, Robert B., Tec 5 (LWA 3/24/45)
Moore, Adolph J., PFC
*Morin, Jean Paul, Private (KIA 1/4/45)
*Munafo, Frank, Private (LWA 1/8/45)
*Murray, Richard H., PFC (LWA 4/2/45)
Myers, Manuel W., PFC (NBC 3/24/45)

Nekrassoff, Boris S., PFC (SWA 1/8/45)
Newhouse, Donald O., Private (NBC 1/6/45)
*Nix, Raymond A., Staff Sergeant
*Nobles, Henry D., Private

*O'Donnell, Lawrence P., 2nd Lieutenant
*Olivieri, Tiberie C., Private
Olson, Kenneth O., PFC

Parkinson, Thomas H., PFC (KIA 3/24/45)
*Paton, William B., Private
*Paul, John O., Tech Sergeant (SWA 1/4/45)
Pellegrino, Harold L., Private
*Penwith, James J., Private
Peri, Narcisco H., PFC (LWA 4/3/45)
Peterson, Earl K., Private (KIA 1/4/45)
Phillips, Patrick E., PFC (LWA 1/4/45, LWA 3/24/45)
Pieper, Wilhelm F., Staff Sergeant
Pierce, Edward, Private
*Pilger, Jr., Joseph J., Private
*Pippin, Jack P., Sergeant (LWA 1/4/45)
*Platt, Chester O., Corporal
Platzek, Max W., Private
*Plumb, Sanford M., Private (LIA 1/4/45)
*Podkulski, William C., PFC
Popik, Charles W., Private
*Porter, James J., Private
Porterfield, Ralph E., Private
Potts, Herbert L., Private
Pruzkowski, John, Private
Puckett, Charles D., 2nd Lieutenant (LWA 1/7/45)

*Quinn, Eugene D., PFC

*Rafalovich, Ray R., Tec 5 (NBC 12/31/44, 1/28/45)
Rambo, Paul A., Staff Sergeant
Ramsey, Boyd E., PFC (NBC 1/4/45, LWA 3/24/45)
Renner, Harold A., Private (SWA 3/24/45)
*Revels, Maurice, Private
Reynolds, Marshall M., Captain (LWA 1/8/45)
Rieger, Joseph J., PFC
*Rituh, Julien N. E., Private
Roberts, Homer, Private (LIA 1/28/45)
*Roberts, Paul E., Private
*Robinson, Thomas E., Private
Rock, Stanley, Private (LIA 1/16/45)
*Roebke, Rex A., PFC (LIA 1/5/45)

*Rogers, Eugene F., Private (LWA 1/4/45)
*Rohmann, Clarence E., PFC (KIA 1/8/45)
Row, James W., Private
Rowland, William W., Private (NBC 2/24/45, LWA 3/24/45)
Royston, John A., 2nd Lieutenant
*Royston, John A., Private
Rudolph, Robert G., Tec 5
Ruthenberg, William, PFC (LWA 4/2/45)
*Rutherford, Johnnie A., Sergeant (NBC 1/6/45)
Rybka, Anthony J., PFC

Sandhoefner, Bernard D., PFC (LWA 3/30/45)
Sarrell, Edward R. PFC
Scarbrough, Lawrence E., Private
Schmidt, Ervin D. Private (KIA 1/8/45)
*Schneck, Edward PFC (LWA 1/4/45)
Schultz, Glenn R., Private
Scott, Alvie L. PFC (KIA 1/24/45)
Seacott, August C., Staff Sergeant (LWA 1/8/45)
Self, Clarence T., PFC
Selzer, Francis C., 2nd Lieutenant (KIA 4/3/45)
Siegfried, LeRoy M., PFC
Sigal, David A., Private
Simpson, Charles W., Private (LWA, 1/4/45)
Sims, Leonard P., 2nd Lieutenant
*Sitavich, Albin S., Private (LWA 1/4/45)
Shaughnessy, George L., PFC (LWA 1/4/45)
Shay, Donald K., PFC
Sheffield, Clifford M. Private (KIA 1/5/45)
Sherlock, Vincent J., Jr., Private (LWA 1/8/45)
Schock, W. George, PFC
Sharkey, Neil J., 2nd Lieutenant
Sloan, Erna L., Tec 4
*Slocomb, Raymond W., Private (KIA 1/4/45)
Smart, Walter H., PFC
*Smith, Milton C., Tech Sergeant (KIA 1/3/45)
Smosna, Max, Corporal
*Sorenson, Edward D., Sergeant
Soucy, Roger O. Private (LWA 1/4/45)
*Sperling, Larry J., Sergeant (KIA 1/7/45)
*Spivey, Louis B., Private (LIA 1/8/45)
Stanley, Spencer G., Jr., 2nd Lieutenant (LWA 3/30/45)

*Stositch, Ivan, 1st Lieutenant (LWA 1/4/45)
*Studinarz, Stanley J., PFC (LWA 1/4/45)
*Susal, Edward J., PFC
Swazuk, John, Private

Tresize, Harry E., Private (LWA 1/8/45)
Templeton, Lawrence J., Jr., Tec 4
Tomasch, Jack, PFC (KIA 1/4/45)
Tom, Chin T., Private (KIA 3/24/45)
*Thomson, William I., (KIA 1/4/45)

Underwood, Thomas A., Private
Unsworth, Thomas J., PFC
Utt, Dean H., Staff Sergeant (LIA 1/5/45)

Vasteno, James A., Private
*Vaughn, Percy M., Private
Veach, Earl E., PFC
Vendt, Albert W., Private
*Vondrasek, George, Tec 4

*Walker, Louis P., Tec 4
Ward, William E., Sergeant (LIA 1/5/45)
Waters, John S., Private (DOW 1/4/45)
Watkins, Harrison G., Tec 5 (LWA 3/24/45)
*Weghorn, Wayne W., PFC
Westbrook, Henry W., Jr., PFC
*Wheat, Wallace V., Private
White, Richard W., Private (LWA 1/4/45)
Wieland, William K., 2nd Lieutenant
Williford, James B., PFC
Wisner, Arthur D., PFC (KIA 1/4/45)

*Original to F Company (compiled from November-December 1943 payroll records).

Appendix II: Morning Reports, 1 August 1944 - 4 April 1945.

MORNING REPORT 1 August 1944
Assigned & Joined: 1
Private Boris S. Nekrassoff.
Misc. Losses: 3
PFC Lawrence J. DuPrey (duty to seven day furlough), Private Wilmer T. Brewer (duty to AWOL), and Private James W. Row (duty to confined to the division stockade awaiting trial).
Aggregate Losses: 3
Present for Duty: 135; 8 officers and 127 enlisted men (T/O & E Strength was 176).

MORNING REPORT 2 August 1944
Record of Events: Tec 5 George Vondrasek, promoted to Tec 4.
Misc. Losses: 1
Private Raymond P. Imhof (duty to transferred to to 11th Detachment Special Troops, 2nd Army).
Aggregate Losses: 1
Present for Duty: 134; 8 officers and 126 enlisted men.

MORNING REPORT 3 August 1944
Record of Events: Corporal Albert W. Vendt, reduced to Private
Misc. Losses: 2
Staff Sergeant John O. Paul and PFC George H. Graupensperger (duty to detailed to Camp McCoy, Wisconsin to return a prisoner (5 days)).
Aggregate Losses: 2
Present for Duty: 132; 8 officers and 124 enlisted men.

MORNING REPORT 4 August 1944
Record of Events: Corporal Walter H. Balben, AWOL, to arrest in quarters.
Returned to Duty: 2
PFC Evangelos J. Kondiditsiotes (six day furlough, to RTD). Private Wilmer T. Brewer (AWOL to RTD).
Misc. Losses: 1
PFC Asa F. Barber (duty to transferred to The Parachute School).
Aggregate Increase: 1
Present for Duty: 133; 8 officers and 125 enlisted men.

MORNING REPORT 5 August 1944
Misc. Losses: 1

PFC Evangelos J. Kondiditsiotes (duty to hospital (NLD)).
Aggregate Losses: 1
Present for Duty: 132; 8 officers and 124 enlisted men.

MORNING REPORT 6 August 1944
Record of Events: Private Donald (NMI) Brown (AWOL to dropped from F Company's rolls).
Misc. Losses: 1
Private Louis B. Spivey (duty to three day emergency furlough).
Aggregate Losses: 1
Present for Duty: 131; 8 officers and 123 enlisted men.

MORNING REPORT 7 August 1944
Record of Events: Private Albert W. Vendt, promoted to PFC.

MORNING REPORT 8 August 1944
Record of Events: Tec 5 Harrison G. Watkins, promoted to Tec 4. Private Thomas J. Unsworth, promoted to Tec 5. Private Joseph H. Pilger, confined in the division stockade, to transferred to The Parachute School. Private Maurice Revels (atchd), AWOL to arrest in quarters awaiting trial.
Returned to Duty: 2
Staff Sergeant John O. Paul & PFC George H. Graupensperger (detailed to Camp McCoy, Wisconsin to return a prisoner, Private Maurice Revels (atchd), on 3 August), returned to duty).
Misc: Losses: 2
Corporal John T. McCall (duty to confined to the division stockade). Private Boris S. Nekrassoff (duty to the hospital (NLD)).
Present for Duty: No Change

MORNING REPORT 9 August 1944
Returned to Duty: 4
Corporal Walter H. Balben, placed under arrest in quarters on 3 August, returned to duty; Corporal John T. McCall, confined to the division stockade the day before to returned to duty; Private Boris S. Nekrassoff and PFC Evangelos J. Kondiditsiotes, hospital (NLD), to returned to duty; and Private Louis B. Spivey, emergency furlough to returned to duty.
Aggregate Increase: 4
Present for Duty: 135; 8 officers and 127 enlisted men.

MORNING REPORT 10 August 1944
Returned to Duty: 4
Private Maurice Revels (formerly under arrest in quarters). Private Warren C.

Berg, Private Jack (NMI) Cook, and Private Jean Paul Morin, confined in the division stockade, returned to duty.

Misc. Losses: 11

Staff Sergeant Willis J. Adams, Tec 4 Chin T. Tom, Tec 4 Philip M. Mixon, Tec 4 Harrison G. Watkins, Corporal Edward A. Keeling, Tec 5 Elmer C. Driscoll, Tec 5 Erna L. Sloan, Tec 5 Thomas J. Unsworth, Private Earl K. Peterson, Private William I. Thomson, and Private Maurice (NMI) Revels were relieved from attachment to F Company. Private James W. Row, confined in the division stockade, was transferred to the 11th Detachment, Special Troops, 2nd Army. Private Lewis P. Walker, formerly in the division stockade, was transferred to 1457th Special Coverage Unit (SCU).

Aggregate Losses: 7

Present for Duty: 128; 8 officers and 120 enlisted men.

MORNING REPORT 15 August 1944

Misc. Losses: 1

Private Dolph (NMI) Greene went to the hospital (LD).

Aggregate Losses: 1

Present for Duty: 127; 8 officers and 119 enlisted men.

MORNING REPORT 16 August 1944

Assigned & Joined: 1

Private Chester H. Forbes joined from A Company, 513th.

Aggregate Increase: 1

Present for Duty: 128; 8 officers and 120 enlisted men.

MORNING REPORT 19 August 1944

Record of Events: Private Dolph (NMI) Greene, formerly in hospital, transferred to Boston POE.

MORNING REPORT 30 August 1944

Returned to Duty: 1

1st Lieutenant Robert J. Gilles returned to F Company from temporary duty.

Assigned & Joined: 3

F Company's three medics, Tec 5 Erna L. Sloan, Private Earl K. Peterson, and Private William I. Thomson were attached to F Company on 30 August for "rations, quarters, duty, and administration" from the Medical Detachment, 513th Parachute Infantry.

Aggregate Increase: 4

Present for Duty: 132; 9 officers and 123 enlisted men.

MORNING REPORT 1 September 1944
Misc. Losses: 5
  PFC Eugene D. Quinn, and Private Kenneth M. Eide, Private Milo Bubenchick, Private Herbert L. Burroughs, and Private Joseph Hamorski, transferred out of F Company to HQ 2nd Battalion.
Aggregate Losses: 5
Present for Duty: 127; 9 officers and 118 enlisted men.

MORNING REPORT 4 September 1944
Assigned & Joined: 20
  Staff Sergeant August C. Seacott, Sergeant Dean H. Utt, Corporal William E. Ward, PFC Otto T. Johnson, and Private Jack Tomasch, Private Richard W. White, Private William W. Maxwell, Private Clifford M. Sheffield, Private Roger O. Sousy, Private Charles W. Simpson, Private James B. Williford, Private James E. Dornbos, Private Harry E. Tresize, Private Patrick E. Phillips, Private Robert C. Mallon, Private Morris W. Kelly, Private Edward R. Sarrell, Private Vincent J. Sherlock, Jr., Private John D. La Riccia, and Private Alvie L. Scott joined F Company from the 54th Replacement Battalion.
Misc. Losses: 1
  2nd Lieutenant Lawrence P. O'Donnell went to the hospital (LD).
Aggregate Increase: 19
Present for Duty: 146; 8 officers and 138 enlisted men.

MORNING REPORT 5 September 1944
Misc. Losses: 1
  PFC Joseph R. Kitson went on special duty to HQ Co., 513th (PX Detail).
Aggregate Losses: 1
Present for Duty: 145; 8 officers and 137 enlisted men.

MORNING REPORT 6 September 1944
Record of Events: Corporal Walter H. Balben was reduced to Private
Assigned & Joined: 10
  Corporal Jack Adragna, Private Walter A. Day, Private Francis R. Henry, Private Raymond J. Jacob, Private Edward T. Logsdon, Private Rubin E. McLean, Private Donald O. Newhouse, Private Ervin D. Schmidt, Private David A. Sigal, and Private John S. Waters joined F Company from the 54th Replacement Battalion.
Aggregate Increase: 10
Present for Duty: 155; 8 officers and 147 enlisted men.

MORNING REPORT 11 September 1944
Assigned & Joined: 4
  Private Donald E. Black, Private George S. Lawrence, Private Clifford F. LeDuc,

Private Roderick MacKenzie, and Private John Swazuk joined F Company from the 4th Replacement Depot.
Aggregate Increase: 4
Present for Duty: 159; 8 officers and 151 enlisted men.

MORNING REPORT 13 September 1944
Record of Events: Seven officers and 119 enlisted men.were awarded the European-African-Middle Eastern Theater Ribbon.

MORNING REPORT 14 September 1944
Record of Events: 1st Lieutenant Samuel C. Dean assumed command (Captain William E. Jakes, from Service Company, was assigned as the new CO but did not join as he was sick and in the hospital). Corporal Edward A. Keeling was attached to F Company from Service Company but did not join as he was sick and in the hospital.
Assigned & Joined: 1
Staff Sergeant Willis J. Adams was attached from Service Company.
Misc. Losses: 2
Captain Fred McGoldrick was relieved and transferred to the Service Company. Private John G. Dreith, duty to AWOL.
Aggregate Losses: 1
Present for Duty: 158; 7 officers and 151 enlisted men.

MORNING REPORT 15 September 1944
Record of Events: The thirty-five enlisted men assigned to F Company after 1 September were awarded the European-African-Middle Eastern Theater Ribbon.
Misc. Losses: 1
Private John S. Waters, who joined F Company 6 September, went AWOL.
Aggregate Losses: 1
Present for Duty: 157; 7 officers and 150 enlisted men.

MORNING REPORT 16 September 1944
Record of Events: A dedication and review ceremony was held and 513th was officially designated an Expert Infantry Regiment. Three officers and 104 enlisted men from F Company qualified for the Expert Infantry Badge, most of F Company's 160 men. F Company was awarded a streamer for their guideon.
Misc. Losses: 1
Tec 5 Erna L. Sloan went to the hospital (LD).
Aggregate Losses: 1
Present for Duty: 156; 7 officers and 149 enlisted men.

MORNING REPORT 17 September 1944
Returned to Duty: 1
Private John G. Dreith, formerly AWOL, returned to duty.
Misc. Losses: 1
PFC Clarence E. Rohmann went to the hospital.
Present for Duty: No Change

MORNING REPORT 18 September 1944
Assigned & Joined: 1
2nd Lieutenant Charles D. Puckett joined F Company from E/513th.
Aggregate Increase: 1
Present for Duty: 157; 8 officers and 149 enlisted men.

MORNING REPORT 19 September 1944
Record of Events: Private James W. Arrowood, Private Jack Cook, Private James J. Gresher, Private John I. Hall, Private Harry Goldfarb, Private Clifford T. Harding, Private Robert C. Hultman, Private William C. Podkulski, Private Alvie L. Scott, and Private Edward J. Susol were promoted to PFC.
Misc. Losses: 1
Tec 5 Russell E. Holine and Private Eugene L. Burke went to the hospital.
Aggregate Losses: 1
Present for Duty: 156; 8 officers and 148 enlisted men.

MORNING REPORT 20 September 1944
Assigned & Joined: 1
PFC Joseph B. Gutt joined F Company from A/513th.
Misc. Losses: 1
Private John G. Dreith was confined in the regimental stockade to await trial.
Present for Duty: No Change

MORNING REPORT 21 September 1944
Misc. Losses: 2
PFC Jacob Hriesik and Private Wilmer T. Brewer went to Sniper School at Tidworth.
Aggregate Losses: 2
Present for Duty: 154; 8 officers and 146 enlisted men.

MORNING REPORT 26 September 1944
Returned to Duty: 1
Corporal Edward A. Keeling returned to duty from the hospital.
Misc. Losses: 1
Private Virgil F. Lage went to the hospital (LD).
Present for Duty: No Change

MORNING REPORT 27 September 1944
Record of Events: Corporal Francis V. McDevitt, Corporal Johnnie A. Rutherford, and Corporal Harold E. Hinkley were promoted to Sergeant. Sergeant Benson Faulk was reduced to Private Private John S. Waters, AWOL since 15 September and taken into the custody of military authorities in London 1930 hours on 23 September, was confined in the regimental stockade.

MORNING REPORT 1 October 1944
Misc. Losses: 2
  PFC Paul Imre and Private Richard W. White went to the hospital (LD).
Aggregate Losses: 2
Present for Duty: 152; 8 officers and 144 enlisted men.

MORNING REPORT 5 October 1944
Record of Events: Captain William E. Jakes, in hospital on LD, was relieved from Command of F Company and transferred to the Service Company.
Assigned & Joined: 1
  Captain Marshall M. Reynolds joined F Company from the 16th replacement depot and assumed command.
Aggregate Increase: 1
Present for Duty: 153; 9 officers and 144 enlisted men.

MORNING REPORT 10 October 1944
Record of Events: 2nd Lieutenant Lawrence P. O'Donnell, in hospital (LD), was relieved and transferred as a patient to another hospital.

MORNING REPORT 13 October 1944
Returned to Duty: 1
  PFC Jacob Hriesik and Private Wilmer T. Brewer returned to duty from Sniper School.
Misc. Losses: 1
  Private Sanford M. Plumb went to Sniper School at Tidworth.
Present for Duty: No Change

MORNING REPORT 15 October 1944
Record of Events: Private John G. Dreith escaped from the stockade and went AWOL again.
Misc. Losses: 1
  Private William W. Maxwell went to the hospital (LD).
Aggregate Losses: 1
Present for Duty: 152; 9 officers and 143 enlisted men.

MORNING REPORT 16 October 1944
Returned to Duty: 1
Private John S. Waters, confined in the stockade since 27 September, returned to duty.
Aggregate Increase: 1
Present for Duty: 153; 9 officers and 144 enlisted men.

MORNING REPORT 17 October 1944
Record of Events: Staff Sergeant Henry Kaczmarek and Corporal John T. McCall were reduced to Private
Returned to Duty: 1
Private Clarence E. Rohmann, formerly in hospital, returned to duty.
Misc. Losses: 1
Private John S. Waters went to the hospital (LD).
Present for Duty: No Change

MORNING REPORT 19 October 1944
Record of Events: Entrucked to engage the 507th Parachute Infantry in a three-day tactical problem, arrived at bivouac area at 1630 hours.
Assigned & Joined: 1
Private George L. Shaughnessy joined from B Company.
Misc. Losses: 4
PFC John J. Flynn, PFC Albert Vendt, and Private John T. McCall were transferred to the Service Company. Private Charles W. Simpson went to the hospital (LD).
Aggregate Losses: 3
Present for Duty: 150; 9 officers and 141 enlisted men.

MORNING REPORT 21 October 1944
Returned to Duty: 1
Private Eugene L. Burke, in hospital since 19 September, returned to duty.
Aggregate Increase: 1
Present for Duty: 151; 9 officers and 142 enlisted men.

MORNING REPORT 23 October 1944
Returned to Duty: 1
Private Richard W. White, in hospital since 1 October, returned to duty.
Aggregate Increase: 1
Present for Duty: 152; 9 officers and 143 enlisted men.

MORNING REPORT 26 October 1944
Misc. Losses: 1

2nd Lieutenant Lawrence P. O'Donnell was relieved from assignment and transferred to Service Company.

Aggregate Losses: 1

Present for Duty: 151; 8 officers and 143 enlisted men.

MORNING REPORT 27 October 1944

Returned to Duty: 1

Private John S. Waters, in hospital since 17 October, returned to duty.

Aggregate Increase: 1

Present for Duty: 152; 8 officers and 144 enlisted men.

MORNING REPORT 29 October 1944

Returned to Duty: 1

Private Sanford M. Plumb, on temporary duty at Sniper School, returned to duty.

Misc. Losses: 1

Private Edward Barbera was transferred to the Service Company.

Present for Duty: No Change

MORNING REPORT 31 October 1944

Non-Battle Casualties: 1

PFC Lawrence J. Duprey, went to the hospital as a non-battle casualty.

Aggregate Losses: 1

Present for Duty: 151; 8 officers and 143 enlisted men.

MORNING REPORT 4 November 1944

Returned to Duty: 1

Tec 5 Erna L. Sloan, in hospital since 16 September, returned to duty.

Non-Battle Casualties: 1

PFC Clifford W. Butcher went to the hospital as a non-battle casualty.

Present for Duty: No Change

MORNING REPORT 5 November 1944

Record of Events: Staff Sergeant Willis J. Adams and Corporal Edward A. Keeling were transferred to F Company from Service Company.

Assigned & Joined: 1

PFC Marvin C. Harris was attached to Service Company for quarters, rations, duty, and administrative purposes.

Misc. Losses: 1

2nd Lieutenant Neil J. Sharkey left on detached service to the 1st AAA.

Present for Duty: 151; 7 officers and 144 enlisted men.

MORNING REPORT 6 November 1944
Record of Events: Staff Sergeant John O. Paul and Staff Sergeant Milton C. Smith were promoted to Tech Sergeant; Sergeant James F. Bassett and Sergeant Dean H. Utt were promoted to Staff Sergeant; and Corporal Peter J. Hellrigel, Corporal William E. Ward, and Corporal Howard R. McClain were promoted to Sergeant
Non-Battle Casualties: 1
Private Jeno A. DePiero went to the hospital as a non-battle casualty.
Misc. Losses: 1
2nd Lieutenant Samuel Calhoun went on temporary duty in connection with Airborne activities.
Aggregate Losses: 2
Present for Duty: 149; 6 officers and 143 enlisted men.

MORNING REPORT 8 November 1944
Record of Events: Tec 5 Erna L. Sloan was promoted to Tec 4. Tec 5 Russell E. Holine, in hospital since 19 September, was transferred to Co. Detachment of Patients, 4124 Hospital.
Misc. Losses: 2
Private Maynard R. Benson and Private Leonard J. Mihalsky were placed under arrest in quarters.
Aggregate Losses: 2
Present for Duty: 147; 6 officers and 141 enlisted men.

MORNING REPORT 9 November 1944
Assigned & Joined: 1
2nd Lieutenant Louis J. Gerner joined from the 12th Replacement Depot.
Aggregate Increase: 1
Present for Duty: 148; 7 officers and 141 enlisted men.

MORNING REPORT 14 November 1944
Assigned & Joined: 3
Private Jack F. Bohn, Private Howard J. Heaton, and Private John L. Lubbuck joined F Company from GFRS.
Non-Battle Casualties: 1
Private Vincent J. Sherlock went to the hospital as a non-battle casualty.
Aggregate Increase: 2
Present for Duty: 150; 7 officers and 143 enlisted men.

MORNING REPORT 15 November 1944
Record of Events: F Company and the 513th left Barton Stacey at 0745, 15 November for Chilbolten Airfield to participate in a Division review at 1400 hours.
Returned to Duty: 1

2nd Lieutenant Samuel Calhoun, on temporary duty since 6 November, returned to duty.
Aggregate Increase: 1
Present for Duty: 151; 8 officers and 143 enlisted men.

MORNING REPORT 16 November 1944
Returned to Duty: 2
Private Maynard R. Benson and Private Leonard J. Mihalsky, placed under arrest in quarters 8 November, returned to duty.
Misc. Losses: 2
PFC James J. Jacob and PFC Boris S. Nekrassoff went on detached service to 17th A/B glider pilot school.
Present for Duty: No Change.

MORNING REPORT 19 November 1944
Record of Events: PFC Marvin C. Harris was promoted to Corporal

MORNING REPORT 20 November 1944
Assigned & Joined: 18
Corporal John P. Imber, PFC Arthur E. Bricmont, Jr., PFC Raymond L. Lightcap, Private Homer Roberts, Private James E. Adler, Private Boyd E. Ramsey, Private Lawrence E. Lincoln, Private Frank D. DeSanto, Private Thomas R. Crowley, Private Clarence E. Lawson, Private James R. Johnson, Private Delmar W. Hurst, Private Mabron E. Henderson, Private Campbell L. Harris, Private Daniel Green, Private Bernard E. Glanowski, Private Perfecto Garcia, Jr., and Private Thomas Connolly joined F Company from the 12th Replacement Depot.
Aggregate Increase: 18
Present for Duty: 169; 8 officers and 161 enlisted men.

MORNING REPORT 21 November 1944
Record of Events: Sergeant Arthur A. Bowers was promoted to Tech Sergeant; Sergeant Harry E. Cook, Sergeant Peter J. Hellrigel, and Sergeant Clarence F. Knigge were promoted to Staff Sergeant; Corporal Larry J. Sperling, Corporal Thomas D. Harvey, PFC Wesley E. Fredenburg, Private John D. La Riccia and Private James E. Dornbos were promoted to Sergeant; PFC Ray R. Rafalovich was promoted to Tec 5; and Corporal Jack Adragna and Corporal James M. Logan were reduced to Private
Misc. Losses: 1
Private William L. Hickman was promoted to Sergeant and transferred to HQ Co., 513th.
Aggregate Losses: 1
Present for Duty: 168; 8 officers and 160 enlisted men.

MORNING REPORT 22 November 1944
Assigned & Joined: 1
  Private Adolphus D. Harbrough, Jr. joined from HQ 2/513th.
Misc. Losses: 1
  Private John Swazuk was transferred to HQ 2/513th.
Present for Duty: No Change.

MORNING REPORT 27 November 1944
Returned to Duty: 1
  PFC Lawrence J. Duprey, in the hospital since 31 October, returned to duty.
Non-Battle Casualty: 1
  Sergeant Thomas D. Harvey went to the hospital as a non-battle casualty.
Present for Duty: No Change.

MORNING REPORT 28 November 1944
Non-Battle Casualties: 2
  PFC Edward F. Costello and Private Clifford F. Leduc went to the hospital as non-battle casualties.
Aggregate Losses: 2
Present for Duty: 166; 8 officers and 158 enlisted men.

MORNING REPORT 29 November 1944
Misc. Losses: 1
  1st Lieutenant Louis J. Gerner was transferred to E Company, 513th.
Aggregate Losses: 1
Present for Duty: 165; 7 officers and 158 enlisted men.

MORNING REPORT 30 November 1944
Returned to Duty: 3
  Private William W. Maxwell (15 Oct.), Private Charles W. Simpson (19 Oct.), and Private Vincent J. Sherlock (14 Nov.), returned to duty from the hospital.
Aggregate Increase: 3
Present for Duty: 168; 7 officers and 161 enlisted men.

MORNING REPORT 1 December 1944
Misc. Losses: 1
  PFC William C. Podkulski was placed under arrest in quarters.
Aggregate Losses: 1
Present for Duty: 167; 7 officers and 160 enlisted men.

MORNING REPORT 2 December 1944
Non-Battle Casualty: 1

Private Walter H. Balben went to the hospital as a non-battle casualty.
Aggregate Losses: 1
Present for Duty: 166; 7 officers and 159 enlisted men.

MORNING REPORT 3 December 1944
Assigned & Joined : 1
2nd Lieutenant Isham Fann was transferred to F Company from E/513th.
Aggregate Increase: 1
Present for Duty: 167; 8 officers and 159 enlisted men.

MORNING REPORT 4 December 1944
Record of Events: Private Jeno A. DePiero, in hospital since 6 November, was transferred to 4109 U.S. Army Hospital.
Non-Battle Casualty: 1
Private Francis R. Henry went to the hospital as a non-battle casualty.
Aggregate Losses: 1
Present for Duty: 166; 8 officers and 158 enlisted men.

MORNING REPORT 6 December 1944
Record of Events: Private Dennis Jordan, Private Morris W. Kelly, Private Arthur D. Wisner, Private Robert C. Mallon, Private Stanley J. Studinarz, Private Patrick E. Phillips, Private Jack Tomasch, Private Edward R. Sarrell, Private Donald E. Black, Private Roderick A. MacKenzie, Private Joseph R. Grubb, Private John L. Lubbuck, Private James A. Brown, Private Jack N. Capell, Private Francis J. Altmiller, Private Francis J. Giard, Private Wilmer T. Brewer, Private Albert W. Barth, Private Rubin E. McLean, Private Raymond J. Jacob, Private George L. Shaughnessy, and Private Edward T. Logsdon were promoted to PFC. PFC William C. Podkulski was reduced to Private

MORNING REPORT 7 December 1944
Record of Events: PFC Clifford W. Butcher, Private Clifford F. Leduc and Private Walter H. Balben, in hospital, were moved to another hospital for further observation and treatment.

MORNING REPORT 8 December 1944
Returned to Duty: 1
PFC Paul Imre returned to duty.
Non-Battle Casualties: 1
PFC Howard W. Goddard went to the hospital as a non-battle casualty.
Present for Duty: No Change.

MORNING REPORT 11 December 1944
Record of Events: Left Barton-Stacey Camp A at 1040 hours and moved sixty miles by truck to a marshalling area, arriving at 1345 hours.

MORNING REPORT 13 December 1944
Record of Events: F Company practiced loading planes for a jump.

MORNING REPORT 15 December 1944
Record of Events: F Company left the marshalling area at 1445 and returned to Barton-Stacey Camp A at 1730 hours.

MORNING REPORT 19 December 1944
Record of Events: F Company is alerted for departure.
Returned to Duty: 1
  Private William C. Podkulski, under arrest in quarters, returned to duty.
Aggregate Increase: 1
Present for Duty: 167; 8 officers and 159 enlisted men.

MORNING REPORT 20 December 1944
Returned to Duty: 2
  PFC James J. Jacob and PFC Boris Nekrassoff, on temporary duty to the Glider Pilot School, return to duty.
Aggregate Increase: 2
Present for Duty: 169; 8 officers and 161 enlisted men.

MORNING REPORT 21 December 1944
Record of Events: Left Barton-Stacey Camp "A" at 0900 enroute by truck to unknown air field. Arrives air port 1015. Departure delayed.

MORNING REPORT 22 December 1944
Record of Events: Departure delayed. Usual marshalling area duties.

MORNING REPORT 23 December 1944
Record of Events: Departure delayed. Usual marshalling area duties.

MORNING REPORT 24 December 1944
Record of Events: Left Chilbolten airfield at 1005 enroute by plane to Couvron airfield. Arrived at 1300. Left Couvron airfield at 1330 enroute by truck to Camp de Mourmelon le Grande and arrived at 1435. Morale high.

MORNING REPORT 25 December 1944
Record of Events: Left Camp Mourmelon, 1900 hr, destination secret. Mode of travel, truck convoy.

MORNING REPORT 26 December 1944
Record of Events: F Company stationed one half mile northwest of Stenay guarding approached to the town.

MORNING REPORT 27 December 1944
Record of Events: Twelve French enlisted men are attached to F Company. Enemy aircraft sighted at 2230 hours.

MORNING REPORT 28 December 1944
Record of Events: Outpost positions and roadblocks were improved, and roads were prepared for mines. Morale high. 2nd Lieutenant Leonard P. Sims sent to Division for action (approximation of date).
Returned to Duty: 1
   PFC Howard W. Goddard returns from the hospital to duty.
Aggregate Increase: 1
Present for Duty: 170; 8 officers and 162 enlisted men.

MORNING REPORT 29 December 1944
Record of Events: Second Platoon improved the roadblock.
Returned to Duty: 1
   PFC Clifford W. Butcher returned to duty.
Aggregate Increase: 1
Present for Duty: 171; 8 officers and 163 enlisted men.

MORNING REPORT 30 December 1944
Record of Events: Six cooks were attached to F Company from HQ 2/513th.

MORNING REPORT 31 December 1944
Record of Events: F Company departed Stenay at 1030 hours by truck for Aincreville, 15 miles distant. Arrived at 1100. Went into bivouac area. The French enlisted personnel were releaved from attachment.
Non-Battle Casualties: 1
   Tec 5 Ray R. Rafalovich went to the hospital as a non-battle casualty.
Aggregate Losses: 1
Present for Duty: 170; 8 officers and 162 enlisted men.

MORNING REPORT 1 January 1945
Record of Events: Company enjoyed New Years day, turkey dinner. Morale high.

MORNING REPORT 2 January 1945
Record of Events: Left Aincreville at 1230, enroute by truck 1 mile N.W. of Bercheux. Arrived at 2200 & went into bivouac area. Private John G. Dreith, AWOL, was transferred to Casualty Pool of the 70th Replacement Depot (AAF).

MORNING REPORT 3 January 1945

Record of Events: F Company moved to Monty by truck, travelling ten miles; arrived at 0830. Shelled by enemy artillery in village. Private Francis R. Henry, sick in hospital, was transferred to the Parachute Replacement Regiment at The Parachute School.

Lightly Wounded In Action: 1

PFC Arthur E. Bricmont, Jr. LWA (Rifle wound).

Seriously Wounded In Action: 5

Sergeant Donald S. Erb (shell fragments), PFC Lawrence J. Duprey (shell fragments), Private Jack Bohn (shell fragments), Private Dwight E. Caton (shrapnel wound), and Private Sidney Laufer (gunshot wound). All evacuated to the 109th Evac. Hosp.

Killed In Action: 1

Tech Sergeant Milton C. Smith KIA (Sniper).

Misc. Losses: 1

PFC Howard W. Goddard goes to hospital (LD).

Aggregate Losses: 8

Present for Duty: 162; 8 officers and 154 enlisted men.

MORNING REPORT 4 January 1945

Returned to Duty: 1

PFC Edward F. Costello returned to duty (LD).

Lightly Wounded In Action: 34

1 Lieutenant Ivan Stositch, 2 Lieutenant Samuel Calhoun, Tech Sergeant John O. Paul (Machine-gun fire), Sergeant Raymond O. Eide, Sergeant Howard R. McClain, Corporal John M. Eibert, Tec 4 George Vondrasek, PFC George H. Graupensperger, PFC John I. Hall, PFC Leroy D. Halley, PFC Raymond J. Jacobs, PFC Otto T. Johnson, PFC Evangelos J. Kondiditsiotes, PFC Roderick A. MacKenzie, PFC Patrick E. Phillips, PFC Jack P. Pippin, PFC Edward Schneck, PFC George L. Shaughnessy, PFC Stanley J. Studinarz (Artillery), Private Thomas E. Connolly, Private Walter A. Day, Private Alver S. Driggers, Private Norman S. Duncan, Private Billy J. English, Private Chester H. Forbes, Private William C. Kuntz, Sr., Private Clarence E. Lawson, Private Leonard J. Mihalsky, Private Eugene F. Rogers, Private Charles W. Simpson (and Frostbite), Private Albin S. Sitavich, Private Roger O. Soucy, and Private Richard W. White.

Seriously Wounded In Action: 1

PFC Donald E. Black (Shrapnel).

Killed In Action: 16

Staff Sergeant Francis V. McDevitt, PFC James A. Brown, PFC Charles E. Craddock, PFC George H. Gohn, PFC Joseph R. Grubb, PFC Charles A. Hester, PFC Patrick M. Keller, PFC Frank J. Kinkus, Jr., PFC Jack Tomasch, PFC Arthur D. Wisner, Private William L. Gibbs, Private James R. Johnson, Private John Paul

Morin, Private Earl K. Peterson, Private Raymond W. Slocomb, and Private William I. Thomson.

Died Of Wounds: 1

Private John S. Waters.

Lightly Injured In Action (Frozen Feet): 8

Tech Sergeant Arthur A. Bowers, Staff Sergeant James F. Bassett, PFC Clifford T. Harding, PFC Paul Imre (also LWA 1/5/45), Private James E. Adler, Private Perfecto Garcia, Jr., Private Robert C. Mallon, and Private Sanford M. Plumb.

Non-Battle Casualties (Trench Foot): 2

Private Warren C. Berg, and Private Boyd E. Ramsey.

Aggregate Losses: 61

Present for Duty: 101; 6 officers and 95 enlisted men.

MORNING REPORT 5 January 1945

Seriously Wounded In Action: 1

Private Howard J. Heaton.

Killed In Action: 3

Private Lawrence E. Lincoln, Private Joseph Malinowski, and Private Clifford M. Sheffield.

Lightly Injured In Action (Frozen Feet): 5

Staff Sergeant Dean H. Utt, Sergeant William E. Ward, PFC Rubin E. McLean (Frostbite), PFC Rex A. Roebke, Private Henry Kaczmarek (Frozen feet, Battle casualty).

Missing in Action: 1

PFC Jacob Hriesik (PW).

Aggregate Losses: 10

Present for Duty: 91; 6 officers and 85 enlisted men.

MORNING REPORT 6 January 1945

Lightly Wounded In Action: 3

Staff Sergeant Harry E. Cook, PFC Dennis Jordan, and Private Daniel Green.

Lightly Injured In Action (Frozen Feet): 3

Sergeant Harold E. Hinkley (Battle Casualty), PFC James W. Arrowood (Battle casualty), and PFC Harry E. Dauer.

Non-Battle Casualties (Trench Foot): 2

Sergeant Johnnie A. Rutherford and Private Donald O. Newhouse.

Aggregate Losses: 8

Present for Duty: 83; 6 officers and 77 enlisted men.

MORNING REPORT 7 January 1945

Record of Events: Private James B. Williford, MIA Battle Casualty/then RTD.

Lightly Wounded In Action: 6

2nd Lieutenant Charles D. Puckett, Staff Sergeant Clarence F. Knigge, Jr., Corporal Edward A. Keeling, Tec 5 Wayne H. DeHaven, PFC Albert W. Barth, and Private Mabron E. Henderson. All listed LWA (Shrapnel wound).

Killed In Action: 1

Private James M. Logan (Rifle fire).

Died Of Wounds: 2

Sergeant Larry J. Sperling (Shrapnel wound) and Private William W. Maxwell (31375766, Battle casualty).

Lightly Injured In Action (Frozen Feet): 2

PFC Philip Cavaleri and Private Bernard E. Glanowski.

Non-Battle Casualties: 1

First Sergeant Royal W. Donovan evacuated as non-battle casualty.

Aggregate Losses: 12

Present for Duty: 71; 5 officers and 66 enlisted men.

MORNING REPORT 8 January 1945

Record of Events: Private Vigil P. Lage, absent in hospital, is transferred to another hospital.

Lightly Wounded In Action: 6

Captain Marshall M. Reynolds, Staff Sergeant August C. Seacott (Shrapnel wound), Sergeant John D. La Riccia, Private Vincent J. Sherlock, Private Harry E. Tresize, and Private Frank Munafo.

Seriously Wounded In Action: 2

PFC James J. Jacob, and PFC Boris S. Nekrassoff (Shrapnel wound).

Killed In Action: 4

1st Lieutenant Robert J. Gilles, Staff Sergeant Peter J. Hellrigel, PFC Clarence E. Rohmann (88 Shrapnel), and Private Ervin D. Schmidt (88 Shrapnel).

Lightly Injured In Action (Frozen Feet): 4

Sergeant Edward D. Sorenson, PFC Lloyd K. Elliott, PFC Francis J. Giard (Battle Casualty), and Private Louis B. Spivey.

Non-Battle Casualties (Trench Foot): 2

Tec 5 Robert J. Anderson, and PFC Willis B. Grice (Trench foot).

Aggregate Losses: 18

Present for Duty: 53; 3 officers and 50 enlisted men.

MORNING REPORT 9 January 1945

Returned to Duty: 1

Tec 5 Ray R. Rafalovich returned to duty (LD).

Lightly Injured In Action (Frozen Feet): 4

PFC Edward T. Logsdon, PFC Jack Cook, PFC Morris W. Kelly, and Private Adolphus D. Harbrough, Jr. were evacuated with frozen feet.

Non-Battle Casualties (Trench Foot): 1

PFC Peter J. Blakney.

Aggregate Losses: 4
Present for Duty: 49; 3 officers and 46 enlisted men.

MORNING REPORT 10 January 1945
Lightly Injured In Action (Frozen Feet): 3
PFC Jack N. Capell, PFC Jessie J. Guidry, and Private Paul J. Accomando (trench foot).
Aggregate Losses: 3
Present for Duty: 46; 3 officers and 43 enlisted men.

MORNING REPORT 13 January 1945
Record of Events: Private Perfecto Garcia, Jr., LWA 4 January (and in hospital), Attached unassigned to assigned and joined company.

MORNING REPORT 14 January 1945
Record of Events: PFC Donald E. Black, SWA 4 January, to DOW (Shrapnel).

MORNING REPORT 16 January 1945
Record of Events: Private John W. Cogan was evacuated as a non-battle casualty, but returned to duty on the same date. PFC James J. Jacob, listed as SWA 8 January, was listed as MIA.
Lightly Wounded In Action: 2
PFC Paul M. Evans (Burn), and Private Delmar W. Hurst.
Killed In Action: 4
PFC John L. Lubbock, Private Jack Adragna, Private Thomas B. Crowley, and Private Frank D. DeSanto.
Lightly Injured In Action (Frozen Feet): 6
1 Lieutenant Samuel C. Dean, Sergeant Wesley E. Fredenburg, Corporal John P. Imber, Private Maynard R. Benson, Private Eugene L. Burke, and Private George S. Lawrence, Jr. (Frozen feet).
Missing in Action: 3
PFC Elwyn H. Greenstrand, Private Thomas B. Crowley, and Private Stanley Rock.
Non-Battle Casualties (Trench Foot): 2
PFC Dale J. Auer and Private Francis X. Madere, Jr.
Aggregate Losses: 17
Present for Duty: 29; 2 officers and 27 enlisted men.

MORNING REPORT 17 January 1945
Record of Events: Private Chester H. Forbes (in hospital) from attached unassigned to assigned.

MORNING REPORT 18 January 1945
Record of Events: Sergeant Thomas D. Harvey (in hospital) from attached unassigned to assigned & joined company.

MORNING REPORT 19 January 1945
Record of Events:
Returned to Duty: 1
  Private Harry E. Tresize, LWA 8 January, returned to duty.
Aggregate Increase: 1
Present for Duty: 30; 2 officers and 28 enlisted men.

MORNING REPORT 20 January 1945
Returned to Duty: 1
  PFC Jack P. Pippin, LWA 4 January, rejoined company.
Lightly Injured In Action (Frozen Feet): 1
  PFC Robert C. Hultman was evacuated (Frostbite).
Present for Duty: No Change.

MORNING REPORT 22 January 1945
Record of Events: Moved approximately eight miles northeast of old position into new tactical position.
Returned to Duty: 2
  PFC Morris W. Kelly (LIA 9 January) and PFC George L. Shaunessy (LWA 4 January) rejoined company.
Aggregate Increase: 2
Present for Duty: 32; 2 officers and 30 enlisted men.

MORNING REPORT 23 January 1945
Assigned & Joined: 4
  Corporal James H. Helton, Tec 5 Stanley J. Michalik, Private John N. Glavas, and Private John Pruzkowski were assigned to and joined F Company from HQ Company, 17th Airborne Division.
Lightly Injured In Action: 1
  PFC Edward R. Sarrell (Battle casualty).
Aggregate Increase: 3
Present for Duty: 35; 2 officers and 33 enlisted men.

MORNING REPORT 24 January 1945
Returned to Duty: 2
  Private Walter H. Balben (who went to the hospital 2 December 1944 NBC) and Private Delmar W. Hurst (LWA 16 January) rejoined company.
Killed in Action: 2

Private Campbell L. Harris, and PFC Alvie L. Scott.
Present for Duty: No Change.

MORNING REPORT 25 January 1945
Record of Events: CP Location in Field of Battle.
Lightly Injured In Action: 2
Sergeant James E. Dornbos, and PFC Rubin E. McLean.
Misc. Losses: 1
2nd Lieutenant Leonard P. Sims was relieved and transferred to A Company, 513th.
Aggregate Losses: 3
Present for Duty: 32; 1 officer and 31 enlisted men.

MORNING REPORT 27 January 1945
Returned to Duty: 1
Sergeant Donald S. Erb, wounded 3 January, returned to duty.
Aggregate Increase: 1
Present for Duty: 33; 1 officer and 32 enlisted men

MORNING REPORT 28 January 1945
Record of Events: 2nd Lieutenant Samuel Calhoun and 2nd Lieutenant Isham Fann promoted to 1 Lieutenant (as per SO#24 Hq 3rd Army 25 January).
Lightly Injured In Action (Frozen Feet): 2
PFC James J. Gresher and Private Homer Roberts.
Non-Battle Casualties (Trench Foot): 1
Tec 5 Ray R. Rafalovich.
Aggregate Losses: 3
Present for Duty: 30; 1 officer and 29 enlisted men

MORNING REPORT 29 January 1945
Assigned & Joined: 1
Private Harold L. Pellegrino was assigned and joined company.
Aggregate Increase: 1
Present for Duty: 31; 1 officer and 30 enlisted men

MORNING REPORT 30 January 1945
Record of Events: On 30 January, the 17th Airborne relieved the 26th and 80th Infantry Divisions and moved into the line. F Company's CP was moved to Wiltz. PFC Edward T. Logsdon (in Hospital) from attached unassigned to assigned and joined company.

MORNING REPORT 31 January 1945
Record of Events: Moved CP from Wiltz to HosinGeneral

MORNING REPORT 1 February 1945
Record of Events: Staff Sergeant Willis J. Adams was reduced to Private, PFC James J. Gresher was promoted to Staff Sergeant, and Private Benson Faulk was promoted to Sergeant
Lightly Injured In Action (Frozen Feet): 1
 Private Donald L. Andrews.
Aggregate Losses: 1
Present for Duty: 30; 1 officer and 29 enlisted men

MORNING REPORT 2 February 1945
Returned to Duty/Assigned & Joined: 1
 Private Joel Y. Ming was assigned and joined F Company.
Aggregate Increase: 1
Present for Duty: 31; 1 officer and 30 enlisted men

MORNING REPORT 3 February 1945
Record of Events: 2 Lieutenant Charles D. Puckett promoted to 1st Lieutenant

MORNING REPORT 4 February 1945
Returned to Duty: 1
 PFC Willis B. Grice.
Seriously Wounded in Action: 1
 PFC Wilmer T. Brewer (Mortar Fire).
Present for Duty: No Change.

MORNING REPORT 5 February 1945
Non-Battle Casualties: 1
 PFC Fredrick W. Altmiller was evacuated with the flu.
Aggregate Losses: 1
Present for Duty: 30; 1 officer and 29 enlisted men

MORNING REPORT 8 February 1945
Record of Events: Rear echelon departed from St.-Mard, Belgium at 0930 hours. Arrived at Chalons, France at 1600 hours.

MORNING REPORT 10 February 1945
Record of Events: Moved from Hosingen to base camp located one mile south of Chalons-sur-Marne, France. Private John G. Dreith, AWOL to Apprehended by Military Authorities, Brussels, Belgium 2020 hr.

MORNING REPORT 11 February 1945
Record of Events: Private Richard W. White (LWA) was transferred to Ft. Benning.

MORNING REPORT 12 February 1945
Record of Events: PFC Wilmer T. Brewer, DOW.

MORNING REPORT 13 February 1945
Returned to Duty/Assigned & Joined: 5
Captain Marshal M. Reynolds returned to duty. 1st Lieutenant Harold O. Diefenderfer, 2nd Lieutenant John A. Royston, 2nd Lieutenant Francis C. Selzer, and 2nd Lieutenant Spencer G. Stanley, Jr. were assigned and joined F Company.
Non-Battle Casualties:
1 Lieutenant Isham Fann went to the hospital with the flu.
Aggregate Increase: 4
Present for Duty: 34; 5 officers and 29 enlisted men.

MORNING REPORT 14 February 1945
Returned to Duty: 10
First Sergeant Royal W. Donovan, Staff Sergeant James F. Bassett, Staff Sergeant Harry E. Cook, Sergeant Edward E. Sorenson, PFC Fredrick W. Altmiller, PFC Jack Cook, PFC Lloyd K. Elliott, PFC Elwyn H. Greenstrand, PFC Clifford T. Harding (approximation), Private Jeno A. DePiero, and Private Boyd E. Ramsey.
Assigned & Joined: 43
Tech Sergeant Acey E. Alger, Staff Sergeant Paul A. Rambo, Tec 4 Lawrence V. Fischer, Tec 4 Raymond H. Landers, Corporal James W. Galloway, Corporal William G. Cater, Corporal Herbert C. Davenport, Jr., Corporal Max Smosna, PFC Ferdinand Aguirres, PFC Edmundo Gonzalez, PFC Donald F. Hardy, PFC Andrew J. Keese, PFC Ralph E. Porterfield, PFC Henry W. Westbrook, Jr., Private Victor R. C. Alt, Private Richard A. Anderson, Private Floyd Andrews, Private Frank Apfel, Private Angel Arange, Private Louis Armus, Private William T. Fulton, Jr., Private Charles R. Gatter, Private Llewellyn V. Gauthreaux, Private John T. Grealis, Private Earl M. Geddie, Private Robert E. Guiles, Private Ernest C. Haney, Private Eulalio C. Hernandez, Private John L. Horrin, Private Manuel W. Myers, Private Kenneth O. Olson, Private Joseph J. Rieger, Private William Ruthenberg, Private Anthony J. Rybka, Private Bernard D. Sandhoefner, Private Lawrence Scarbrough, Private George W. Schock, Private Glenn R. Schultz, Private Clarence T. Self, Private Donald K. Shay, Private LeRoy M. Siegfried, Private Charles E. Sigle, Private Walter H. Smart, Private James A. Vasteno, and Private Earl E. Veach.
Aggregate Increase: 56
Present for Duty: 90; 5 officers and 85 enlisted men.

MORNING REPORT 15 February 1945

Record of Events: F Company made camp comfortable and enjoyed battalion party.

Assigned & Joined: 2

1st Lieutenant John J. Joyce, Jr. and 2nd Lieutenant Richard B. Cross.

Aggregate Increase: 2

Present for Duty: 92; 7 officers and 85 enlisted men.

MORNING REPORT 16 February 1945

Record of Events: F Company was inspected by Colonel Miller; continued to work on camp.

Returned to Duty: 1

Tec 5 Ray R. Rafalovich.

Assigned & Joined: 37

First Sergeant William T. Harrison, Staff Sergeant Henry J. Cantwell, Staff Sergeant Herbert F. Hutto, Tec 4 Robert B. Miller, Tec 5 John A. Dougherty, Tec 5 William L. Ford, Tec 5 William L. Miller, PFC Robert J. Dabbs, PFC Beaumont R. Hunter, PFC Manuel Juarez, PFC Herbert C. Miller, Private William C. Bergmann, Private John V. Brown, Jr., Private Donald W. Carter, Private Charles Chutas, Private James D. Chieloha, Private John E. Cobb, Private Joseph M. Cornale, Private Delbert J. Cox, Private Howard A. Craddock, Private Maurice C. Cuthbertson, Private Robert B. Dick, Private Russell B. Dolan, Private Carmine J. Fortunato, Private Robert T. Garrett, Private Robert C. Girvin, Private Nolan G. Glasgow, PFC Frank J. Goble, Private Doyle E. Goins, Private Dolph F. Hamby, Jr., Private Kenneth D. Halter, Private William A. Heckman, Private Thomas W. Hinman, Private Authur E. Jones, Private Leonard B. Lown, Private Joseph E. Mandis, and Private Adolf J. Moore.

Non-Battle Casualties: 1

Private William A. Heckman to hospital (listed on 15 February).

Aggregate Increase: 38

Present for Duty: 130; 7 officers and 123 enlisted men.

MORNING REPORT 17 February 1945

Record of Events: Inspected by Colonel Coutts; continued to "beautify area."

Assigned & Joined: 3

Private James G. Cox, Private George C. LaChance, and Private Narcisco H. Peri.

Aggregate Increase: 3

Present for Duty: 133; 7 officers and 126 enlisted men.

MORNING REPORT 18 February 1945

Returned to Duty: 1

PFC Robert C. Mallon.

Assigned & Joined: 4

Corporal Donald D. Masterjohn, Private Paul R. Jones, Private William L. Hickman, and Private Herbert L. Potts joined from HQ 2/513th.

Aggregate Increase: 5

Present for Duty: 138; 7 officers and 131 enlisted men.

MORNING REPORT 20 February 1945

Assigned & Joined: 1

Sergeant David P. McMahon joined from HQ/513th.

Aggregate Increase: 1

Present for Duty: 139; 7 officers and 132 enlisted men.

MORNING REPORT 22 February 1945

Record of Events: Combat Infantryman's Badges were awarded to the men of the regiment. Captain Reynolds received these and passed them out to all the returning F Company men. Sergeant Benson Faulk and PFC Rubin E. McLean were promoted to S/Sgt; PFC Joseph R. Kitson was promoted to Sergeant Staff Sergeant August C. Seacott and Staff Sergeant Dean H. Utt (in hospital) were reduced to Private

Assigned & Joined: 1

Private William W. Rowland assigned & joined company.

Aggregate Increase: 1

Present for Duty: 140; 7 officers and 133 enlisted men.

MORNING REPORT 24 February 1945

Assigned & Joined: 3

Tec 5 John W. Masterson joined from Service Co. PFC Robert P. Franklin and PFC Robert G. Rudolph were attached from Medical Det.

Non-Battle Casualties: 1

Private William W. Rowland went to hospital.

Misc. Losses: 2

First Sergeant William T. Harrison was transferred to H/513th; Private Willis Adams transferred to HQ 2/513th.

Present for Duty: No Change.

MORNING REPORT 25 February 1945

Returned to Duty: 2

PFC Edward Schneck and Private Sidney Laufer.

Aggregate Increase: 2

Present for Duty: 142; 7 officers and 135 enlisted men.

MORNING REPORT 27 February 1945
Returned to Duty: 1
  1 Lieutenant Isham Fann returned from hospital.
Aggregate Increase: 1
Present for Duty: 143; 8 officers and 135 enlisted men.

MORNING REPORT 1 March 1945
Record of Events: Corporal James H. Helton reduced to Private
Misc. Losses: 1
  PFC Harry Goldfard was transferred to HQ 2/513th.
Aggregate Losses: 1
Present for Duty: 142; 8 officers and 134 enlisted men.

MORNING REPORT 2 March 1945
Non-Battle Casualties: 1
  Corporal Donald D. Masterjohn went to the hospital.
Aggregate Losses: 1
Present for Duty: 141; 8 officers and 133 enlisted men.

MORNING REPORT 3 March 1945
Returned to Duty/Assigned & Joined: 5
  Staff Sergeant James J. Gresher, Sergeant James E. Dornbos, Private Warren C.
Berg, and Private William A. Heckman returned to duty. Private Harold A. Renner
joined from HQ/513th.
Aggregate Increase: 5
Present for Duty: 146; 8 officers and 138enlisted men.

MORNING REPORT 5 March 1945
Assigned & Joined: 6
  Sergeant Wilhelm T. Pieper, Tec 4 Henry H. Krohs, Tec 5 Elmer L. Driscoll, Tec
5 Michael A. Molchan, Tec 5 Harrison G. Watkins, and Private Chin T. Tom joined
from HQ 2/513th.
Misc. Losses: 2
  Private James H. Helton went AWOL at 0630, and Private Harry E. Tresize to
hospital.
Aggregate Increase: 4
Present for Duty: 150; 8 officers and 142 enlisted men.

MORNING REPORT 6 March 1945
Returned to Duty: 3
  Tec 5 Robert J. Anderson, PFC Patrick E. Phillips, and Private Clifford F. LeDuc
returned to duty.

Aggregate Increase: 3
Present for Duty: 153; 8 officers and 145 enlisted men.

MORNING REPORT 8 March 1945
Misc. Losses: 1
Private Herbert L. Potts went AWOL 0600 Hrs.
Aggregate Losses: 1
Present for Duty: 152; 8 officers and 144 enlisted men.

MORNING REPORT 9 March 1945
Returned to Duty: 1
Private Homer Roberts returned to duty.
Misc. Losses: 14
Tec 4 Lawrence J. Templeton, Tec 5 William L. Ford, PFC Frank J. Goble, PFC Herbert C. Miller, PFC Edward J. Susol, Private Richard A. Anderson, Private Joseph M. Cornale, Private Nolan G. Glasgow, Private Eulalio C. Hernandez, Private Thomas W. Hinman, Private George LeChance, Private John Pruskowski, Private Lawrence F. Scarbrough, and Private James A. Vasteno transferred to HQ 2/513th:
Aggregate Losses: 13
Present for Duty: 139; 8 officers and 131 enlisted men.

MORNING REPORT 11 March 1945
Misc. Losses: 4
PFC Donald F. Hardy, PFC Robert C. Mallon, Private John N. Glavas, and Private Chester H. Forbes went AWOL, 0630 hours.
Aggregate Losses: 4
Present for Duty: 135; 8 officers and 127 enlisted men.

MORNING REPORT 12 March 1945
Record of Events: Private William C. Kuntz, Sr. and Sergeant David McMahon were promoted to S/Sgt; Corporal Herbert C. Davenport and Tec 5 Neal Haggard were promoted to Sgt; and Private Walter H. Balben was promoted to Tec 5. Private Herbert L. Potts, AWOL, was arrested by military authorities in Paris.
Assigned & Joined: 1
2nd Lieutenant William H. Wieland joined from HQ 2/513th.
Misc. Losses: 3
2nd Lieutenant Richard B. Cross was transferred to HQ 2/513th, and Staff Sergeant James F. Bassett and Private Kenneth D. Halter went to the hospital.
Aggregate Losses: 2
Present for Duty: 133; 8 officers and 125 enlisted men.

MORNING REPORT 13 March 1945
Returned to Duty: 2
   PFC Donald F. Hardy and Private James H. Helton, formerly AWOL, returned to duty.
Misc. Losses: 1
   Private Clarence T. Self was transferred to the division MP Platoon.
Aggregate Increase: 1
Present for Duty: 134; 8 officers and 126 enlisted men.

MORNING REPORT 14 March 1945
Record of Events: Sergeant Wilhelm F. Pieper promoted to Staff Sergeant; PFC Russell A. Hataway promoted to Sergeant; and Tec 5 Elmer G. Driscoll promoted to Tec 4.
Misc. Losses: 2
   2nd Lieutenant John A. Royston transferred to HQ 2/513th, and PFC Jack P. Pippin went to hospital.
Aggregate Losses: 2
Present for Duty: 132; 7 officers and 125 enlisted men.

MORNING REPORT 15 March 1945
Record of Events: PFC Robert G. Rudolph was promoted to Tec 5; and PFC Robert C. Mallon from AWOL to arrested in quarters.
Returned to Duty: 1
   PFC Robert C. Hultman returned to duty.
Aggregate Increase: 1
Present for Duty: 133; 7 officers and 126 enlisted men.

MORNING REPORT 16 March 1945
Record of Events: The following EM were appointed PFC: Private Victor R. C. Alt, Private Floyd Andrews, Private John V. Brown, Private Charles Chutas, Private John W. Cogan, Private Delbert J. Cox, Private Morris G. Cuthbertson, Private Robert B. Dick, Private William T. Fulton, Private Llewellyn V. Gauthreaux, Private Robert C. Girvin, Private Doyle E. Goins, Private John T. Grealis, Private Robert E. Guiles, Private William A. Heckman, Private John M. Herrin, Private Sidney Laufer, Private Manuel W. Myers, Private Adolph J. Moore, Private Kenneth O. Olson, Private Narcisco H. Peri, Private Boyd E. Ramsey, Private Joseph J. Rieger, Private William Ruthenberg, Private Anthony J. Rybka, Private Bernard D. Sandhoefner, Private George W. Schock, Private Glenn R. Schultz, Private Donald K. Shay, Private LeRoy M. Siegfried, Private Walter H. Smart, Private Earl M. Veach, and Private James B. Williford.

MORNING REPORT 17 March 1945
Misc. Losses: 1
Private Raymond L. Lightcap was transferred to the Service Company.
Aggregate Losses: 1
Present for Duty: 132; 7 officers and 125 enlisted men.

MORNING REPORT 18 March 1945
Record of Events: Company alerted for departure.
Returned to Duty: 6
1 Lieutenant Samuel Calhoun and Tec 5 Robert J. Anderson returned to duty.
PFC Robert C. Mallon (from AinQ to duty). PFC Morris W. Kelly, Private Chester
H. Forbes, and Private John N. Glavas from AWOL to duty at 1700 hours.
Aggregate Increase: 6
Present for Duty: 138; 8 officers and 130 enlisted men.

MORNING REPORT 19 March 1945
Record of Events: Staff Sergeant James F. Bassett (in hospital), and Staff Sergeant Harry E. Cook were promoted to Tech Sergeant; PFC Clifford W. Butcher, PFC Jack P. Pippin, and Private Leonard B. Lown promoted to Sergeant; and Sergeant James E. Dornbos was promoted to Staff Sergeant
Returned to Duty: 1
Private William W. Roland returned to duty.
Misc. Losses: 2
Private Warren C. Berg went to the hospital, and Private William L. Hickman discovered AWOL.
Aggregate Losses: 1
Present for Duty: 137; 8 officers and 129 enlisted men.

MORNING REPORT 20 March 1945
Record of Events: F Company entrucked for Chalons at 1530 hr. and arrived at 1600 hr. Entrained at 1630 hr., destination unknown.
Assigned & Joined: 1
PFC Thomas J. Unsworth joined from HQ 2/513th.
Aggregate Increase: 1
Present for Duty: 138; 8 officers and 130 enlisted men.

MORNING REPORT 21 March 1945
Record of Events: Detreained at 0500 hr. Arrived at marshalling area at 0630 hr.

MORNING REPORT 22 March 1945
Record of Events: Company briefed on coming operation. Company enjoyed a "Coca-Cola feast."

MORNING REPORT 23 March 1945
Record of Events: "Loaded planes in morning. Morale good – chow not so good."

MORNING REPORT 24 March 1945
Record of Events: Left marshalling area at 0530 hr. for airfield. Took off for airborne operation at 0800 hr. Landed via parachute at 1017 hr.
Lightly Wounded in Action: 13
   1st Lieutenant Harold O. Diefenderfer (Sniper fire), Staff Sergeant David P. McMahon, Sergeant Donald S. Erb, Sergeant Joseph R. Kitson, Tec 5 Harrison G. Watkins (MG fire), Tec 4 Raymond H. Landers (Rifle fire), PFC William C. Bergmann (Flak), PFC Harry E. Dauer, PFC John M. Herrin (Parachute jump), PFC Andrew J. Keese (Rifle fire), PFC Patrick E. Phillips (Shrapnel, possibly on 29 March), Private Robert B. Moon (MG fire), Private William W. Rowland (Shrapnel).
LWA in plane crash of C-46 Number 13: 4
   1st Lieutenant Isham Fann, PFC Edward F. Costello, PFC Donald F. Hardy, and PFC Boyd M. Ramsey.
Seriously Wounded in Action: 1
   Private Harold A. Renner (MG fire).
Killed in Action: 9
   Sergeant Thomas D. Harvey, Corporal William G. Cater, Tec 5 William L. Miller, PFC Donald W. Carter, PFC Howard A. Craddock, PFC Howard W. Goddard, PFC Thomas H. Parkinson, Private Joel Y. Ming, and Private Chin T. Tom.
Lightly Injured in Action: 1
   Private Ernest C. Haney (Jump).
Missing in Action: 1
   Private Louis Armus.
Non-Battle Casualties: 2
   PFC Manuel W. Myers (Exhaustion), and Tec 5 Walter H. Balben was absent sick (LD).
Aggregate Losses: 31
Present for Duty: 107; 6 officers and 101 enlisted men.

MORNING REPORT 25 March 1945
Record of Events: Private Jeno A. DePiero was promoted to Sergeant

MORNING REPORT 26 March 1945
Lightly Injured in Action: 1
   Tec 5 John W. Masterson.
Aggregate Losses: 1
Present for Duty: 106; 6 officers and 100 enlisted men.

MORNING REPORT 28 March 1945
Lightly Wounded in Action: 1
  PFC Robert C. Mallon (Shrapnel).
Aggregate Losses: 1
Present for Duty: 105; 6 officers and 99 enlisted men.

MORNING REPORT 30 March 1945
Record of Events: F Company moved from bivouac area in Dulmen toward Münster. Held up by enemy pockets five miles from Dulmen. Set up defensive positions near Nottuln for the night. 75 prisoners taken.
Returned to Duty: 4
  1st Lieutenant Isham Fann, PFC Edward F. Costello, PFC Donald F. Hardy, and PFC Boyd M. Ramsey.
Lightly Wounded In Action: 7
  2nd Lieutenant Spencer G. Stanley (Enemy action), Tec 5 John A. Dougherty, PFC Victor R. C. Alt, PFC Jack Cook (Small arms fire), PFC Robert C. Girvin, PFC John T. Grealis, and Private Angel Arango.
Killed In Action: 2
  Staff Sergeant James A. Gresher, Sergeant Herbert C. Davenport, Jr.
Lightly Injured In Action: 1
  PFC Bernard D. Sandhoefner (Enemy action).
Aggregate Losses: 6
Present for Duty: 99; 6 officers and 93 enlisted men.

MORNING REPORT 31 March 1945
Record of Events:
Assigned & Joined: 16
  Staff Sergeant Charles E. Bailey, Sergeant Forrest E. Asher, Tec 5 Paul E. Barton, PFC Wayne W. Weghorn, Private Paoli O. Drago , Private Donald H. Durant, Private Rubin Engel, Private Edwin J. Fellman, Private Tommy S. Gallardo, Private Roland W. Goetsch, Private Russell R. Hamilton, Private Hollis C. Hewitt, Private Arthur C. Hoover, Private John E. Marchand, Private Arthur Merzoian, Private Thomas A. Underwood.
Lightly Injured In Action: 2
  1st Lieutenant Samuel Calhoun (Burn), and Private Clifford F. LeDuc (Enemy action).
Non-Battle Casualties (Trench Foot): 1
  Tec 4 Elmer C. Driscoll.
Aggregate Increase: 13
Present for Duty: 112; 5 officers and 107 enlisted men.

MORNING REPORT 1 April 1945
Returned to Duty: 2
Private Donald L. Andrews (LIA 1 February) and Private Sanford M. Plumb (LIA 4 January).
Lightly Wounded In Action: 1
PFC Richard H. Murray (Tank).
Non-Battle Casualties: 1
Private John N. Glavas.
Present for Duty: No Change.

MORNING REPORT 2 April 1945
Lightly Wounded In Action: 5
Tech Sergeant Harry E. Cook, Staff Sergeant Henry J. Cantwell, Tec 5 Robert J. Anderson, PFC Willis B. Grice, and PFC William Ruthenberg (Enemy Action).
Misc. Losses: 1
Tec 4 Erna L. Sloan was returned to the Regimental Medical Detachment.
Aggregate Losses: 6
Present for Duty: 106; 5 officers and 101 enlisted men.

MORNING REPORT: 3 April 1945
Record of Events: Company moved from Herman Goering Division barracks to clean out a sector of Münster. Moved from sector in Münster to attack positions one mile NW of Münster.
Lightly Wounded In Action: 2
PFC Clifford T. Harding, and PFC Narcisco H. Peri (Enemy action).
Seriously Wounded In Action: 1
PFC Charles Chutas (Enemy action).
Killed In Action: 2
PFC Beaumont R. Hunter (Sniper), and Private Russell E. Dolan.
Died Of Wounds: 1
2nd Lieutenant Francis C. Selzer, carried on morning report as LWA (Small arms fire).
Lightly Injured In Action: 2
Staff Sergeant James E. Dornbos, and PFC Lloyd K. Elliott (Enemy action).
Aggregate Losses: 8
Present for Duty: 98; 4 officers and 94 enlisted men.

MORNING REPORT 4 April 1945
Record of Events: Company moved from positions one mile NW of Münster to Bivouac in the Herman Goering Barracks. Company enjoyed a good hot meal.
Non-Battle Casualties: 2
PFC William A. Heckman and PFC Morris W. Kelly.

Aggregate Losses: 2
Present for Duty: 96; 4 officers and 92 enlisted men.

According to War Department records, the 513th Parachute Infantry Regiment suffered some 453 men Killed in Action/Died of Wounds during World War II. Fourteen companies made up the regiment. Evenly distributed, this would have totaled some thirty-two men killed per company, however, fifty-one were suffered by F Company alone (11.25 percent of the total casualties). F Company, therefore, suffered 59 percent more men killed than average.

Appendix III: T/O & Es.

T/O & E 7-37T, INFANTRY RIFLE COMPANY, PARACHUTE.

Company headquarters consisted of twenty-nine officers and men: the Company Commander (Captain), the Executive (1st Lieutenant), the First Sergeant (First Sergeant), Mess Sergeant (Staff Sergeant), a Supply Sergeant (Staff Sergeant), a Communication Sergeant (Sergeant), a Company Clerk (Corporal), Armorer-artificer (Tec 5), Bugler (Private), two Cooks (Tec 4), a Cook (Tec 5), two Cook's Helpers (Privates), two Messengers (Privates), a Radio-Telephone Operator (Private), and twelve Basic Privates (Privates).

Each of the three Rifle Platoons, each of forty-nine officers and men, consisted of a Platoon Commander (1st Lieutenant), an Assistant Platoon Commander (2nd Lieutenant), a Platoon Sergeant (Tech Sergeant), a Platoon Guide (Staff Sergeant), two Messengers (Privates), and a Radio-Telephone Operator. Each of the three rifle squads within the platoons consisted of a Squad Leader (Staff Sergeant), an Assistant Squad Leader (Sergeant), a Machine-gunner, .30 caliber M1919A6 (Private), an Assistant Machine-gunner (Private), an Ammunition Bearer (Private), and seven Riflemen (Privates). The Mortar Squad consisted of the Squad Leader (Sergeant), a Mortar Gunner, 60mm M2 (Private), an Assistant Mortar Gunner (Private), and three Ammunition Bearers (Privates).

The company was allotted: nine M1919A6 .30 Caliber Browning Machine-guns with M3 tripod mounts (one per rifle squad); six M3A1 .45 Caliber Submachine-guns; twenty-two M7 Grenade Launchers; four M9A1 2.36-in Rocket Launchers; three M2 60mm Mortars with M3 Mounts; four M9 Hand Pyrotechnic Projectors; nine M1918A2 .30 Caliber Browning Automatic Rifles (one per rifle squad); 144 M1 (Garand) .30 Caliber U.S. Rifles; three M1C .30 Caliber U.S. Rifles (one per platoon); and thirty-two M1A1 .30 Caliber Carbines.

T/O & E 7-36, HQ AND HQ CO, INFANTRY BATTALION, PARACHUTE.

The 513th Parachute Infantry Regiment consisted of the Regimental Headquarters and Headquarters Company, the Service Company, and three Parachute Infantry Battalions. Each of the three infantry battalions consisted of three Parachute Infantry Rifle Companies (as described above), and a Battalion Headquarters and Headquarters Company. The Battalion Headquarters and Headquarters Companies were organized along the following lines:

Battalion Headquarters consisted of five officers: Battalion Commander (Lieutenant Colonel), Executive (Major), Operations and Training, S-3 (Captain), Intelligence, S-2 (1st Lieutenant), Supply, S-4 (1st. Lieutenant), and Adjutant and S-1 (Warrant Officer).

Headquarters Company consisted of the Company Headquarters, a Headquarters Platoon, a Light Machine-gun Platoon (with eight .30 caliber M1919A6 light machine-guns), and an 81mm Mortar Platoon (with four M1 81mm mortars).

Appendix IV: Awards.

Medals of Valor awarded to F Company men before 7 May 1945.

The Silver Star Medal

Private First Class Jack Cook for gallantly in action near Potthoff, Germany, on 30 March 1945 (Posthumous).

First Lieutenant Samuel C. Dean for gallantly in action in Belgium.

Private William C. Kuntz, Sr. for gallantly in action in Belgium and Luxembourg.

Captain Marshall M. Reynolds for gallantly in action in Belgium.

The Bronze Star Medal for Valor

Private First Class Joseph R. Kitson for heroic and meritorious service in Belgium and Luxembourg.

Private Vincent J. Sherlock for heroic and meritorious service in Belgium and Luxembourg.

Sergeant Wilhelm Pieper.

Distinguished Unit Citation for Operation VARSITY.

CITATION

SECOND BATTALION, 513th PARACHUTE INFANTRY REGIMENT for extraordinary heroism, achievement and gallantry in action against the enemy in the vicinity of WESEL, GERMANY on 24 March 1945. Encountering heavy anti-aircraft resistance, this battalion landed amid strong enemy positions. In spite of the stiff resistance encountered on the ground, the battalion assemble and organized to reduce 6 - 88mm guns and capture 1252 prisoners during the day's action. Although suffering sever [*sic*] casualties both in the air and on the ground, the courageous and heroic action demonstrated by members of this unit assisted materially in gaining the successful exploitation of the airborne invasion of Germany. In spite of having lost an estimated 27% of their transport planes to hostile anti-aircraft fire, the efforts of this [2nd] Battalion, 513th Parachute Infantry Regiment made the overall success of the mission possible.[83] *(Awarded December 28, 1945)*

Appendix V: Sergeant Neal Haggard's Letter Home.

On 7 April, while in a house F Company occupied along the Rhein-Herne Canal in the Ruhr, Sergeant Haggard found time to sum up his experiences in Operation VARSITY in a letter to his folks – typed, incidentally, on a captured typewriter:

Sergeant N. Haggard (37604488)
Co.F. 513 Parcht. Inf.

April 7, 1945
Germany

Dear Mom & All,

I dropped you a few lines the other day and as I am not too busy now, I will write again. I am writing this letter to you from a beautiful German home that we have taken over, with running water, lights, bath-tub, radio and all. It is almost heaven to us. There is a big still next door. We ran the civilians out. They were truly pro-Nazis. The German soldiers are just two or three hundred yards from us. We are shooting mortar shells at them now as I am writing you. They snipe at us with machine-guns all day. I promised to tell you about the Rhine jump – so here goes.

Mom, I'll always remember that day. Before we left France, we were briefed on it and knew it would be a coordinated attack between us, the British Airborne and the British Commandos. When we climbed into our chutes that morning and into the planes, we were all tense; some of us knew what battle was like. Others didn't, I think we were all pretty cool. I can't say just what I felt like, because I can't explain. We were in the air about two hours when all of a sudden we saw the Rhine go past us below. It would be in a few minutes now. The haze was in the shy below us, smoke to cover us. Then the order came to STAND UP. Any second now. All of a sudden hell broke. Flak was coming up. GO-! We were tumbling out of the door. My mind became hazy. I hardly remember leaving the door. The minute I got my opening shock, I started fighting to get out of part of my chute on the way down. Noise! Noise, everywhere. A flak shell burst very near me. I looked back. A plane was going down in flames – MY PLANE. Thousands of planes and gliders roaring above me; some coming in, some on fire. Shells and machine-guns were firing and land-ing below me. After a time that seemed like a year, I was on the ground. My rifle almost knocked me out. I finally got out of my chute and started running for the field which was being shelled by 88's and mortars. I saw a shell land in the middle of five boys. It got all of them, only one of them moved a little.

We started to wipe out or capture the artillery gun positions and pillboxes. In a few minutes we had lots of prisoners. Other guns were still trying to shoot down gliders coming in by the thousands. They got some of them. I saw a British glider come in, and crash. Still the men came out. Every gun they had blazing at a gun to their left. In all this turmoil civilians were waving white flags. Farm animals were all over. After a few hours when things had quieted down, the boys were driving captured vehicles, horses, bicycles and even pulling mortar ammunition in baby carriages. We captured more men than was in our regiment inside of a few hours. We really gave the Germans hell. We jumped right in the middle of the higher [corps] headquarters. We met the forces that crossed the Rhine by boat two days later. It was an experience and sight I'll never forget. Neither will the other boys that were there. I guess there isn't much else to say about it now. Try and get all the clippings on it you can.

Don't worry I am safe and O.K.

By by,

Neal

Notes

Prologue Notes

1. James A. Huston, *Out of the Blue: U.S. Army Airborne Operations in World War II*, (West Lafayette, Indiana: Purdue Research Foundation, 1972), viii.

2. Major General James M. Gavin, *Airborne Warfare*, (Washington: Infantry Journal Press, 1947), vii.

3. Huston, *Out of the Blue*, 47, and Gordon Rottman, *US Army Airborne, 1940-90*, (London: Osprey Publishing, 1990), 4-5.

4. Huston, *Out of the Blue*, 47-9, Gavin, *Airborne Warfare*, vii-viii, Bruce Quarrie, *German Airborne Troops, 1939-1945*, (London: Osprey Publishing, 1983), 4-5, and Rottman, *US Army Airborne, 1940-90*, 5.

5. Quarrie, *German Airborne Troops, 1939-1945*, 4

6. Ibid., 4-7.

7. Huston, *Out of the Blue*, 48.

8. Rottman, *US Army Airborne, 1940-90*, 5.

9. Ibid.

10. Gavin, *Airborne Warfare*, viii.

11. Rottman, *US Army Airborne, 1940-90*, 5.

12. Ibid., 5-6.

13. Ibid., 7.

14. Huston, *Out of the Blue*, 49.

15. Ibid., 54.

16. Ibid.

17. Ibid., 47-54.

Chapter 1 Notes

1. Frank Munafo, Interview with Author, Hasbrouck Heights, NJ, 26 May 1997.

2. Kurt Gable, *The Making of A Paratrooper: Airborne Training and Combat in World War II*, (Lawrence: University of Kansas Press, 1990), 46-7, 79.

3. Marvin Harris, Interview with Author, 12 February 1998.

4. Walter A. Rydesky, Interview with Author, 27 February 1997.

5. Munafo, Interview, 26 May 1997.

6. Willis Grice, Interview with Author, 10 February 1998.

7. Sidney Laufer, Interview with Author, Boca Raton, FL, 5 March 1997.

8. Ibid.

9. Ibid.

10. Ibid.; According to Paul Fussell, 'Chickenshit,' could be easily recognized because it never had "anything to do with winning a war;" petty, demeaning, or cruel treatment. (Paul Fussell, *Wartime: Understanding and Behavior in the Second World War*, (New York: Oxford University Press, 1989), 80).

11. Laufer, Interview, 5 March 1997.

12. Palmer, Wiley, and Keast, *The Procurement and Training of Ground Combat Troops*, (Washington, DC: Office of the Chief of Military History, Department of the Army), 6.

13. Paul Imre, Interview with Author, Columbia, MD, 28 September 1996.

14. Munafo, Interview, 26 May 1997; and Interview with Author, 16 January 1997.

15. Neal Haggard, Interview with Author, Troy, IL, 30 March 1997.

16. Ibid.

17. John O. Paul, Interview with Author, 13 May 1997.

18. Laufer, Interview, 5 March 1997. John O. Paul remembers that when women looked Lieutenant Stositch's way, the gentile, soft spoke, and bashful Stositch would turn beet-red.

19. Colonel I. A. Edwards, Interview with Author, Phoenix, AZ, 6 March 1997.

20. Headquarters, Army Ground Forces, Camp Mackall, N.C., *File: 321-GHVDT, Subject: Activation of the 513th Parachute Infantry Regiment*, 2 May 43; and *History of the 513th Parachute Infantry*, 317-INF(513)-0.1 (23963), 11 Jan 43 - 6 Sept 45, courtesy the 17th Airborne Division Association.

21. Haggard, Interview, 30 March 1997; and Philip Cavaleri, Interview with Author, Orlando, FL, 22 September 1996.

22. Cavaleri, Interview, 22 September 1996.

23. Munafo, Interview, 26 May 1997.

24. Bob Greenstrand, *My World War II Service Years*, 1998, 2.

25. Samuel Calhoun, Interview with Author, Orlando, FL, 22 September 1996.

26. Donald Newhouse, Interview with Author, 20 January 1998.

27. Laufer, Interview, 5 March 1997.

28. Munafo, Interview, 26 May 1997; and Richard Murray, Interview with Author, 3 January 1998.

29. Haggard, Interview , 30 March 1997; and Grice, Interview, 10 and 13 February 1998.

30. Laufer, Interview, 5 March 1997.

31. The Platoon Guide was the second-highest ranking non-commissioned officer in a rifle platoon. In combat, he was responsible, among other things, for bringing up the platoon's rear in an advance, and in defense, redistributing ammunition among the squads and guiding the platoon to secondary positions during a withdrawal.

32. Calhoun, Interview with Author, 22 September 1996; Harris, Interview, 12 February 1998; and Greenstrand, *World War II Service*, 2.

33. Munafo, Interview, 26 May 1997.

34. *Parachute School U.S.A.*, 4-5; and War Department, *FM 31-30: Tactics and Technique of Airborne Troops*, (Washington, United States Government Printing Office, 1945), 62-5.

35. Laufer, Interview, 5 March 1997; Maurice Cuthbertson, Interview with Author, 15 January 1998; *Parachute School U.S.A.*, 4, 6-19; and Imre, Interview, 28 September 1996.

36. Haggard, Interview, 30 March 1997; and John La Riccia, Interview with Author, 31 December 1997.

37. La Riccia, Interview, 31 December 1997; and Laufer, Interview, 5 March 1997.

38. War Department, FM *31-30*, 62-5, 89; Laufer, Interview, 5 March 1997; and Imre, Interview, 28 September 1996.

39. Greenstrand, *World War II Service*, 4; and Harris, Interview, 12 February 1998.

40. Munafo, Interview, 16 January 1997. Munafo states, "Sergeant Paul wouldn't do push-ups!"

41. War Department, *FM 31-30*, 88-9, 111, 113.

42. Ibid., 111-2.

43. Ibid.

44. Ibid., 113-4.

45. Gable, *The Making of a Paratrooper*, 81-4.

46. War Department, *FM 31-30*, 114-5.
47. Ibid., 115.
48. Grice, Interview, 10 February 1997.
49. Laufer, Interview, 5 March 1997.
50. Ibid.; and Munafo, Interview, 26 May 1997.
51. Munafo, Interview, 26 May 1997.
52. Cavaleri, Interview, 22 September 1996.
53. Greenstrand, *World War II Service*, 5.
54. Ibid.
55. Willis Grice, Interview with Author, 18 February 1998.
56. Imre, Interview, 28 September 1996.
57. Laufer, Interview, 5 March 1997.
58. Samuel Calhoun, Interview with Author, Fresno, CA, 23 February 1997; and Imre, Interview, 28 September 1996.
59. Murray, Interview, 3 January 1998.
60. Laufer, Interview, 5 March 1997.

Chapter 2 Notes
1. Lee Kennett, *GI: The American Soldier in World War II*, (New York: Charles Scribner's Sons, 1987), 77-8, 209.
2. Munafo, Interview, 26 May 1997.
3. Ibid.
4. Ibid.
5. Ibid.
6. Calhoun, Interview, 23 February 1997; and Laufer, Interview, 5 March 1997.
7. *Parachute School, USA*.
8. Prima Cord is fabric-covered TNT 'rope' used to lash charges together and, when set off with a blasting cap or other igniter, simultaneously detonate a chain of explosive charges.
9. Newhouse, Interview, 20 January 1998.
10. Cuthbertson, Interview, 15 January 1998.
11. Calhoun, Interview, 23 February 1997.
12. Munafo, Interview, 26 May 1997.
13. Laufer, Interview, 5 March 1997.
14. Munafo, Interview, 26 May 1997.
15. Ibid.
16. Ibid.; and Anthony Rybka, Interview with Author, 7 February 1998.
17. Munafo, Interview, 26 May 1997.
18. Royal Donovan, Interview with Author, 9 October 1997.
19. Munafo, Interview, 26 May 1997.
20. Donovan, Interview, 9 October 1997.
21. Laufer, Interview, 5 March 1997.
22. Stephen E. Ambrose, *Band of Brothers: E Company, 506th Regiment, 101st Airborne From Normandy to Hitler's Eagle's Nest*, (New York: Simon & Schuster, 1992), 33.
23. Calhoun, Interview, 23 February 1997.
24. King Harris, "Adventures of Ace Miller." *Alta Vista Magazine*. (Sunday, 27 January 1991): 6-9, 16.
25. Ibid., 7.
26. Ibid., 7, 16.
27. Ibid., 6, 8; Royal Donovan, Interview with Author, 17 October 1997; and John O. Paul, Interview with Author, Orlando, FL, 22 September 1996.
28. Edwards, Interview, 16 March 1997.
29. Haggard, Interview, 30 March 1998.
30. Ibid.
31. Harris, Interview, 12 February 1998.
32. Greenstrand, *World War II Service*, 6.
33. Donovan, Interview, 9 October 1997. Lieutenant Purcell was later killed in the Battle of the Bulge.

34. Greenstrand, *World War II Service*, 7,8; and Calhoun, Interview, 23 February 1997.

35. Frank Paskowski, Interview with Author, Centreville, MD, 4 June 1999.

36. Carlo D'este, *Patton, A Genius for War*, (New York: Harperperennial, 1996), 392-397.

37. Munafo, Interview, 26 May 1997.

38. Harris, Interview, 12 February 1998; and Forrest Asher, Interview with Author, 24 March 1998.

39. Harris, Interview, 12 February 1998; and Grice, Interview with Author, Nashville, TN, 6 June 1997.

40. Haggard, Interview, 30 March 1998.

41. Ibid.

42. Ibid.; and Laufer, Interview, 5 March 1997.

43. Grice, Interview, 13 February 1998.

44. Ibid.

45. Harris, Interview, 12 February 1998.

46. "Night Bivouac To Highlight 2-Day Problem," The Talon, 1:1 (26 May 1944) as reprinted in *Thunder From Heaven* 39 (June 1992): 46. On 5 June 1944, Colonel Coutts was appointed commander of the 17th Airborne Division Parachute School two classes for three thousand officers and enlisted men were held.

47. Munafo, Interview, 26 May 1997.

48. Greenstrand, *World War II Service*, 9-10.

49. Ibid., 10; and Newhouse, Interview, 20 January 1998. When Greenstrand and company arrived in England, they all were sent to the stockade for punishment.

50. "Paratroop Play Is Due Tonight," *The Huntsville Times*, (29 June 29 1944); and "Paratroop Show is Big Success," *The Huntsville Times*, (30 June 1944), as reprinted in "Headlines from 50+ Years Ago," *Thunder From Heaven*, 43 (March/April 1996): 66.

Chapter 3 Notes

1. Cavaleri, Interview, 22 September 1996.

2. U.S. Naval Institute, "The Wakefield," *Thunder From Heaven*, 44 (Winter 97): 75-6.

3. Ibid.

4. Haggard, Interview, 30 March 1997.

5. "The USS Wakefield," *Thunder From Heaven*, 39 (June 1992): 8.

6. Munafo, Interview, 27 May 1997.

7. Charles Puckett, Letter to Author, 27 April 1997.

8. Munafo, Interview, 27 May 1997.

9. Ibid.; and John La Riccia, Interview with Author, 31 December 1997.

10. Charles Simpson, Interview with Author, 5 February 1998.

11. Newhouse, Interview, 20 January 1998.

12. Roderick MacKenzie, Interview with Author, 5 February 1998.

13. Donovan, Interview, 9 October 1997.

14. Ibid.; Haggard, Interview, 30 March 1997; Newhouse, Interview 20 January 1998; and Paul, Interview, 13 May 1997. Within a week of acquiring their stoves, F Company men, through careless stoking, burned down at least two of their tents.

15. Newhouse, Interview, 20 January 1998.

16. Norman Longmate, *The GI's: The American in Britain, 1942-1945*, (New York: Charles Scribner's Sons, 1975), 225.

17. La Riccia, Interview, 31 December 1997.

18. Neal Haggard was promoted to Technician 5th Grade before leaving the States.

19. Haggard, Interview, 30 March 1997; and La Riccia, Interview, 31 December 1997.

20. Newhouse, Interview, 20 January 1998.

21. Ibid.

22. Edward Dahlberg, Interview with Author, 4 August 1998.

23. Newhouse, Interview, 20 January 1998.

24. Laufer, Interview, 5 March 1997.

25. Lee Kennett, *GI: The American Soldier in World War II*, (New York: Charles Scribner's Sons, 1987), 32-3; John Sloan Brown, *Draftee Division: The 88th Infantry Division in World War II*, (Lexington: The University Press of Kentucky: 1986), 43; and Newhouse, Interview 20 January 1998.

26. Donovan, Interview, 14 October 1997; La Riccia, Interview, 31 December 1997; Greenstrand, *World War II Service*, 11; and Newhouse, Interview 20 January 1998.

27. Donovan, Interview, 14 October 1997.

28. Ibid.; Newhouse, Interview, 20 January 1998; and Greenstrand, *World War II Service*, 11.

29. Edward Sarrell, Interview with Author, 16 January 1998.

30. Laufer, Interview, 5 March 1997.

31. August Seacott, Interview with Author, 26 December 1997.

32. Greenstrand, *World War II Service*, 11.

33. Newhouse, Interview, 20 January 1998.

34. Ibid.; Calhoun, Interview, 23 February 1997; and Greenstrand, *World War II Service*, 11.

35. Ibid.

36. Calhoun, Interview, 30 September 1997; and Sarrell, Interview, 16 January 1998.

37. Charles Puckett, Letter to Author, 28 April 1997.

38. Imre, Interview, 28 September 1996; and Cavaleri, Interview, 22 September 1996.

39. Puckett, Letter, 28 April 1997.

40. Grice, Interview, 18 February 1998; and Puckett, Letter, 28 April 1997.

41. Munafo, Interview, 27 May 1997.

42. Sarrell, Interview, 16 January 1998.

43. Newhouse, Interview, 20 January 1998.

44. Munafo, Interview, 27 May 1997.

45. Kennett, GI, 76-7.

46. Ibid., 77-8, 209.

47. Sarrell, Interview, 16 January 1998; Newhouse, Interview, 20 January 1998; and Donovan, Interview, 9 October 1997.

48. Newhouse, Interview, 20 January 1998.

49. Munafo, Interview, 27 May 1997.

50. Laufer, Interview, 5 March 1997. Gin & Lemon was, apparently, the drink of choice!

51. Thomas Connolly, Interview with Author, 12 January 1999.

52. Laufer, Interview, 5 March 1997.

53. O'Neill, *A Democracy at War*, page 264.

54. Longmate, *The GI's*, 208-16)

55. Kennett, G*I*, 123, 208.

56. Munafo, Interview, 27 May 1997; George Finnelli, Interview with Author, Chestertown, MD, 28 November 1997; and Sarrell, Interview, 16-17 January 1998.

57. Newhouse, Interview, 20 January 1998.

58. Greenstrand, *World War II Service*, 12; and Laufer, Interview, 5 March 1997. Scott Belliveau suggested the comparison to Reynolds and a freight train; 'Cannonball' reference from the VMI Yearbook, *The Bomb*, 1940.

59. Marshal M. Reynolds, Letter to General Charles Kilbourne, 10 June 1945, VMI Archives.

60. Wayne DeHaven, Interview with Author, 15 July, 1997.

61. Munafo, Interview, 27 May 1997; Laufer, Interview, 5 March 1997; and Greenstrand, Interview, 16 March 1997.

62. Connolly, Interview, 12 January 1999.

63. Edwards, Interview, 16 March 1997; Munafo, Interview, 27 May 1997; and Newhouse, Interview, 20 January 1998.

64. Dahlberg, Interview, 4 August 1998; and John Vafides, "A POW Story," *Thunder from Heaven*, (Fall 1994), 68.

65. Donald R. Pay, *Thunder From Heaven: The Story of the 17th Airborne Division, 1943-1945*, (Boots, 1947), 17.

66. Raymond Lightcap, Interview with Author, Hazel Green, WI, 6 July 1997.

67. Ibid.

68. Ibid.

69. Grice, Interview, 18 February 1998.

70. Pay, *Thunder From Heaven*, 17-8.

71. La Riccia, Interview, 31 December 1997.

Chapter 4 Notes

1. William K. Goolrick and Ogden Tanner, *The Battle of the Bulge*, (Alexandria, VA: Time-Life Books, 1979), Chapter 2; and Eric Sjogren, *Fodor's The Netherlands, Belgium, Luxembourg*, (New York: Fodor's Travel Publications, 1993), 269.

2. Goolrick, *The Battle of the Bulge*, Chapter 2.

3. Ibid.

4. Ibid.

5. Ibid.

6. Ibid.; and Dwight D. Eisenhower, *Crusade in Europe*, (Garden City: Doubleday & Company, Inc., 1948), 348-9.

7. Clay Blair, *Ridgeway's Paratroopers: The American Airborne in World War II*, Garden City, New York: The Dial Press, 1985), 360-5; Eisenhower, *Crusade in Europe*, 368-9.

8. Russell Weigley, *Eisenhower's Lieutenants: The Campaigns of France and Germany, 1944-1945*, (Bloomington: Indiana University Press: 1981), 570; Clay Blair, *Ridgeway's Paratroopers*, 360-5; James M. Gavin, *On to Berlin*, (New York: The Viking Press, 1978), 204-21. It was not until 1415 hours on 18 December that word reached General Ridgeway that his Corps was to be deployed. By 2030 hours, Ridgeway and his XVIII Airborne Corps staff were enroute to Rheims in fifty-five planes of the IX Troop Carrier Command. Ridgeway resumed command of his Corps on 19 December at Werbomont.

9. Clay Blair, *Ridgeway's Paratroopers*, 360-5.

10. Goolrick, *The Battle of the Bulge*, Chapter 2.

11. Ibid.

12. Eisenhower, *Crusade in Europe*, 350;

13. Shama, *Pulse & Repulse*, 295; and Clay Blair, *Ridgeway's Paratroopers*, 361-5.

14. Haggard, Interview, 30 March 1998; and Seacott, Interview, 26 December 1997.

15. Newhouse, Interview, 22 January 1998.

16. 513th Parachute Infantry Regiment, *Summary of Operations*, 2 February 1945; and Sarrell, Interview, 16 January 1998.

17. Simpson, Interview, 5 February 1998.

18. Irving, War, 348-9.

19. Ibid., 351-2.

20. Shama, *Pulse & Repulse*, 294-5.

21. 513th Parachute Infantry Regiment, *Summary of Operations*, 2 February 1945.

22. 513th Parachute Infantry Regiment, *S-1 Memorandum, First Serial*, 20 December 1944.

23. 513th Parachute Infantry Regiment, *Air Movement Table*, 19 December 1944; and *S-1 Memorandum*, Headquarters 513th Parachute Infantry Regiment, 21 December 1944. As a footnote, Colonel Coutts forbade officers from wearing leather flight jackets as outer garments. Gammon grenades were composed of a fuse and a sock-like bag which was usually filled with plastic explosives.

24. Sarrell, Interview, 16 January 1998.

25. Newhouse, Interview, 22 January 1998.

26. 513th Parachute Infantry Regiment, *S-1 Memorandum, First Serial*, 20 December 1944.

27. Shama, *Pulse & Repulse*, 295.

28. The radios (610s, 300s, and 536s) were all short-range devices. The 536 was the 'Handy-Talky,' the 300 series was a backpack radio called the 'Walky-Talky,' and the 610 was a vehicle-portable model. Airguards were soldiers who spotted incoming enemy aircraft.

29. 513th Parachute Infantry Regiment, *Summary of Operations*, 2 February 1945; and Shama, *Pulse & Repulse*, 295. Thirty-five from the 439th, seventeen from the 440th, thirty-five from the 441st, and twenty-five from the 442nd.

30. Donovan, Interview, 14 October 1997; and Edwards, Interview, 16 March 1997. Before taking off, Major Edwards "personally counted every sonofabitch on the airplanes with the 2nd Battalion. And when we flew into France, I counted them off the planes. I froze 'em in the planes till I came by and there were 736 men." Note the discrepancy.

31. William Johnson, Sr., "Christmas Eve 1944," *Thunder From Heaven*, 42 (Spring 1995): 47; 513th Parachute Infantry Regiment, *Summary of Operations*, 2 February 1945; Shama, *Pulse & Repulse*, 295; and Donovan, Interview, 14 October 1997.

32. Newhouse, Interview, 22 January 1998.

33. Major General William M. Miley, *17th Airborne in the Bulge*, 19 January 1945.
34. Ibid.
35. Ibid.
36. 513th Combat Team, *Field Order No. 7*, 251800 December 1944.
37. Shama, *Pulse & Repulse*, 301.
38. Newhouse, Interview, 22 January 1998.
39. Shama, *Pulse & Repulse*, 301; and 513th Parachute Infantry Regiment, *Summary of Operations*, 2 February 1945
40. Letter courtesy of Mrs. Dwight Caton.
41. Shama, *Pulse & Repulse*, 301; and Greenstrand, *World War II Service*, 12.
42. Shama, *Pulse & Repulse*, 301; 513th Parachute Infantry Regiment, *Summary of Operations*, 2 February 1945; and Greenstrand, *World War II Service*, 13.
43. Lightcap, Interview, 6 July 1998.
44. Greenstrand, *World War II Service*, 13.
45. Seacott, Interview 26 December 1997; Connolly, Interview, 12 January 1998; and James Arrowood, Letter to Author, 28 February 1999.
46. Connolly, Interview, 12 January 1998.
47. Puckett, Letter, 28 April 1997; Headquarters, VIII Corps, *Defense of Raodblocks*, 27 December 1944; and Laufer, Interview, 5 March 1997.
48. Newhouse, Interview, 22 January 1998; and Greenstrand, *World War II Service*, 13.
49. Newhouse, Interview, 22 January 1998.
50. Seacott, Interview 26 December 1997.
51. Newhouse, Interview, 22 January 1998, and Arrowood, Letter, 28 February 1999. Sergeant Dean Utt did return to duty before F Company went into action.
52. Puckett, Letter, 28 April 1997.
53. Greenstrand, *World War II Service*, 13; and Field Message from Lieutenant E. C. Tommasino, 2nd Battalion's S-2 to Colonel Coutts, 26 December 1944.
54. Greenstrand, *World War II Service*, 13.
55. Irving, *War*, 362,70.
56. Headquarters, 17th Airborne Division, *G-2 Summary No. 2*, 17 December 1944.
57. Commanding General, 17th Airborne Division, *Annex No. 1 to Letter of Instruction, "Reconnaissance and Security,"* 27 December 1944.
58. Puckett, Letter, 28 April 1997; and Greenstrand, *World War II Service*, 13.
59. Newhouse, Interview, 22 January 1998; Grice, Interview, 18 February 1998; and Haggard, Interview, 30 March 1998.
60. VIII Corps, *G-2 Periodic Report No. 209*, 12 January 1945.
61. Calhoun, Interview, 23 February 1997; Paul, Interview, 2 May 1997; and G-2, 17th Airborne Division, *Mutual Recognition Between French and American Forces*, 27 December 1944. Due to a mutual lack of recognition, however, several incidents had occurred between American and French patrols.
62. 513th Combat Team, *Field Order No. 8*, 29 December 1944.
63. Ibid.; and Captain Gates Ivy, Jr., *Message No. 5*, 29 December 1944.
64. Clay Blair, *Ridgeway's Paratroopers*, 360-5
65. Newhouse, Interview, 22 January 1998; and Cavaleri, Interview, 22 September 1996.
66. Major General William M. Miley, *Letter to Division*, 1 January 1945.
67. 17th Airborne Division, *G-2 Summary No. 6*, 1 January 1945.
68. Miley, *Airborne in the Bulge*; and VIII Corps, *Interview of officers, 11th Armored Division, 30 Dec.-15 Jan. 1945.*
69. 513th Parachute Infantry Regiment, *Summary of Operations*, 2 February 1945; and Combat Interview by Captain John G. Westover, "513th Parachute Infantry Regiment, 17th Airborne Division, 2-13 January 1945," 14-16 January 1945, 1-2.
70. Calhoun, Interview, 23 February 1997.
71. Seacott, Interview, 26 December 1997.
72. Lightcap, Interview, 6 July 1998.
73. Simpson, Interview, 5 February 1998.
74. Newhouse, Interview, 22 January 1998.

75. Edward Costello, Letter to Author, 18 February 1998.

76. Sarrell, Interview, 16 January 1998; Puckett, Letter, 28 April 1997; Paul, Interview, 2 May 1997; Dahlberg, Interview, 4 August 1997; Donovan; Interview, 14 October 1997; and Calhoun, Interview, 23 February 1997.

77. Irving, War, 370.

78. Greenstrand, *World War II Service*, 13; and Seacott, Interview, 26 December 1997.

79. Paul, Interview, 2 May 1997; and Seacott, Interview, 26 December 1997.

80. Dahlberg, Interview, 4 August 1997; and Lightcap, Interview, 6 July 1998.

81. Seacott, Interview, 26 December 1997; Calhoun, Interview, 23 February 1997; Puckett, Interview, 2 May 1997, Munafo, Interview, 26 February 1997.

82. 513th Parachute Infantry Regiment, *Summary of Operations*, 2 February 1945; and *513th Regimental History*.

83. Puckett, Interview, 2 May 1997.

84. Dahlberg, Interview, 4 August 1997.

85. Munafo, Interview, 26 February 1997.

86. Calhoun, Interview, 23 February 1997; Cavaleri, Interview, 22 September 1996; and Seacott, Interview, 26 December 1997.

87. Newhouse, Interview, 22 January 1998.

88. Lightcap, Interview, 6 July 1998.

89. Dahlberg, Interview, 4 August 1997; and Combat Interview by Captain John G. Westover, "513th Parachute Infantry Regiment, 17th Airborne Division, 2-13 January 1945," 14-16 January 1945, 2.

90. Donovan, Interview, 14 October 1997.

91. Dahlberg, Interview, 4 August 1997; Combat Interview by Captain John G. Westover, "513th Parachute Infantry Regiment, 17th Airborne Division, 2-13 January 1945," 14-16 January 1945, 2; and Newhouse, Interview, 22 January 1998.

92. Combat Interview by Captain John G. Westover, "513th Parachute Infantry Regiment, 17th Airborne Division, 2-13 January 1945," 14-16 January 1945, 2.

93. VIII Corps, *Interview of 41st Tank Battalion, CCB, 11th Armored Division, 20 Dec.-15 Jan. 45*, 1-3.

94. Ibid., 3-5.

95. Ibid., 5-7, 10.

96. Ibid., 7-8.

97. Ibid.

98. Ibid., 8-10.

99. Edwards, Interview, 16 March 1997.

100. Laufer, Interview, 5 March 1997; Newhouse, Interview, 22 January 1998; and Munafo, Interview, 26 February 1997. '10-in-1s' were field rations packed in a case so as to provide one days ration for ten men or ten days rations for one man. They were generally preferred over the K-ration.

101. Calhoun, Interview, 23 February 1997; Cavaleri, Interview, 22 September 1996; and Combat Interview by Captain John G. Westover, "513th Parachute Infantry Regiment, 17th Airborne Division, 2-13 January 1945," 14-16 January 1945, 2-3.

102. Newhouse, Interview, 22 January 1998.

103. Irving, War, 371. The 41st Tank Battalion had lost 112 men (25 were killed), and twelve Shermans in taking the town – the losses of the division were so great, in fact, that it prompted General Patton to write, "The 11th Armored division is very green and took unnecessary losses to no effect."

104. Combat Interview by Captain John G. Westover, "513th Parachute Infantry Regiment, 17th Airborne Division, 2-13 January 1945," 14-16 January 1945, 3; and Newhouse, Interview, 22 January 1998.

105. Imre, Interview, 28 September 1996.

106. Dahlberg, Interview, 4 August 1997; and Sarrell, Interview, 16 January 1998.

107. Laufer, Interview, 5 March 1997

108. Edward Pierce, Interview with Author, Phoenix, AZ, 16 March 1997.

109. La Riccia, Interview, 31 December 1997.

110. Cavaleri, Interview, 22 September 1996.

111. Dahlberg, Interview, 4 August 1997; Puckett, Interview, 2 May 2 1997; and Combat Inter-

view by Captain John G. Westover, "513th Parachute Infantry Regiment, 17th Airborne Division, 2-13 January 1945," 14-16 January 1945, 3. According to Colonel Miller, as 2nd Battalion entered Mande-St.- Etienne, the Germans threw nine heavy tanks into the fight in an effort to penetrate WHITE's lines, but he ordered the bazooka teams sent out to face them. Miller claimed that four of the enemy tanks were knocked-out in a very short time by troopers in individual attacks. His account, however, cannot be supported.

112. Combat Interview by Captain John G. Westover, "513th Parachute Infantry Regiment, 17th Airborne Division, 2-13 January 1945," 14-16 January 1945, 2.

113. 513th Parachute Infantry Regiment, *Summary of Operations*, 2 February 1945.

114. Combat Interview by Captain John G. Westover, "513th Parachute Infantry Regiment, 17th Airborne Division, 2-13 January 1945," 14-16 January 1945, 3.

115. Ibid., 2.

116. Paul, Interview, 2 May 1997.

117. Ibid., and Dahlberg, Interview, 4 August 1997.

118. Combat Interview by Captain John G. Westover, "513th Parachute Infantry Regiment, 17th Airborne Division, 2-13 January 1945," 14-16 January 1945, 3.

119. Ibid., 3-4.

120. Ibid., 2-4.

121. Major General William M. Miley, *17th Airborne in the Bulge*, 19 January 1945.

122. 513th Parachute Infantry Regiment, *Summary of Operations*, 2 February 1945; 17th Airborne Division, *Field Order No. 1*, 3 January 1945; Combat Interview by Captain John G. Westover, "513th Parachute Infantry Regiment, 17th Airborne Division, 2-13 January 1945," 14-16 January 1945, 4; and 513th Combat Team, *Annex to Field Order No. 9*, 3 January 1945.

123. Combat Interview by Captain John G. Westover, "513th Parachute Infantry Regiment, 17th Airborne Division, 2-13 January 1945," 14-16 January 1945, 4-5; and Edwards, Interview, 16 March 1997. Edwards, who was checking the 2nd Battalion's disposition at the time, missed the officers' meeting.

124. Combat Interview by Captain John G. Westover, "513th Parachute Infantry Regiment, 17th Airborne Division, 2-13 January 1945," 14-16 January 1945, 5.

125. The Nebelwerfer was a six-barreled rocket launcher sometimes called a 'screaming meemie' by GIs.

126. Greenstrand, *World War II Service*, 14.

127. Calhoun, Interview, 23 February 1997; and Cavaleri, Interview, 22 September 1996.

128. Newhouse, Interview, 22 January 1998; and Greenstrand, "WWII Service," 15.

129. Greenstrand, *World War II Service*, 15. Greenstrand went back to the spring house to get more machine-gun ammunition. That was the last time he saw his friend Dolph Green. Green got transferred out of F Company to headquarters special troops; Green was apparently an actor in civilian life.

130. Cavaleri, Interview, 22 September 1996.

131. Pay, *Thunder From Heaven*, 19-20.

132. Calhoun, Interview, 23 February 1997; Edwards, Interview, 16 March 1997; and Newhouse, Interview, 22 January 1998.

133. Paul, Interview, 2 May 1997; and Puckett, Interview, 2 May 1997.

134. Combat Interview by Captain John G. Westover, "513th Parachute Infantry Regiment, 17th Airborne Division, 2-13 January 1945," 14-16 January 1945, 4.

135. Dahlberg, Interview, 4 August 1997.

136. Munafo, Interview, 26 February, 1997.

137. Newhouse, Interview, 20 January 1998.

138. Combat Interview by Captain John G. Westover, "513th Parachute Infantry Regiment, 17th Airborne Division, 2-13 January 1945," 14-16 January 1945, 4.

139. Sarrell, Interview, 17 January, 1997; and Pay, *Thunder From Heaven*, 20.

Chapter 5 Notes

1. Combat Interview by Captain John G. Westover, "513th Parachute Infantry Regiment, 17th Airborne Division, 2-13 January 1945," 14-16 January 1945, 5.

2. Royal Donovan, Interview with Author, 14 October 1997.

3. Ed Dahlberg, Interview with Author, 8 April 1997.

4. Lieutenant Colonel Ward S. Ryan, "Summary of Operations, 513th Parachute Infantry Regiment," 2 February 1945.

5. Don Newhouse, Interview with Author, Ft. Indiantown Gap, PA, 22 January 1998.

6. Ibid.

7. Major Samuel Calhoun, "Critique and Correction of Two War Stories Mentioning the Bayonet Charge Made At Mande St. Etienne;" and Bob Greenstrand, "My WWII Service Years," 1998, 15.

8. Don Newhouse, Interview with Author, Ft. Indiantown Gap, PA, 22 January 1998; Charles Simpson, Interview with Author, 5 February 1998; and Combat Interview by Captain John G. Westover, "513th Parachute Infantry Regiment, 17th Airborne Division, 2-13 January 1945," 14-16 January 1945, 6.

9. Major Samuel Calhoun, "Critique"; Bob Greenstrand, "WWII Service," 16; and Don Newhouse, Interview with Author, 16 January 1998.

10. Bob Greenstrand, "WWII Service," 16.

11. Don Newhouse, Interview with Author, Ft. Indiantown Gap, PA, 22 January 1998.

12. Don Newhouse, Interview with Author, Ft. Indiantown Gap, PA, 23 January 1998.

13. Bob Greenstrand, "WWII Service" 16.

14. Don Newhouse, Interview with Author, Ft. Indiantown Gap, PA, 22 January 1998.

15. Royal Donovan, Interview with Author, 14 October 1997.

16. Edwards, Interview.6 March 1997.

17. Neil Haggard, Interview with Author, 18 December 1997.

18. Bob Greenstrand, "WWII Service" 16-7.

19. Bob Greenstrand, "WWII Service" 17.

20. Ibid.

21. Ibid.

22. Major Samuel Calhoun, "Critique"; Bob Greenstrand, "WWII Service" 17.

23. Bob Greenstrand, "WWII Service" 17.

24. Ibid.

25. Combat Interview by Captain John G. Westover, "513th Parachute Infantry Regiment, 17th Airborne Division, 2-13 January 1945," 14-16 January 1945, 5.

26. Walter A. Rydesky, Interview with Author, 27 February 1997.

27. Combat Interview by Captain John G. Westover, "513th Parachute Infantry Regiment, 17th Airborne Division, 2-13 January 1945," 14-16 January 1945, 6; Major Samuel Calhoun, Interview with Author, Fresno, CA, 23 February 1997; and Bart Hagerman, *War Stories: The Men of The Airborne*, (Paducah: Turner Publishing Company, 1993), 150.

28. Edwards, Interview.6 March 1997.

29. Bob Greenstrand, "WWII Service," 19.

30. Rod MacKenzie, Interview with Author, 5 February 1998.

31. Don Newhouse, Interview with Author, Ft. Indiantown Gap, PA, 23 January 1998.

32. Bob Greenstrand, "WWII Service," 19.

33. Don Newhouse, Interview with Author, Ft. Indiantown Gap, PA, 23 January 1998.

34. Neil Haggard, Interview with Author, 18 December 1997. According to Haggard, Private Hataway always "carried a chip" on his shoulder toward the Germans because Hataway's brother had been killed in Europe earlier in the war.

35. Charles Puckett, Interview with Author, 12 May 1997. Lieutenant Puckett says that when he counted the prisoners, there were fourteen.

36. Hagerman, War Stor*i*es, 150-1.

37. Ibid., 151.

38. Combat Interview by Captain John G. Westover, "513th Parachute Infantry Regiment, 17th Airborne Division, 2-13 January 1945," 14-16 January 1945, 6.

39. Paul Imre, Interview with Author, Orlando, FL, 22 September 1996.

40. Russell Hataway, Interview with Author, 19 April 1997; and Don Newhouse, Interview with Author, Ft. Indiantown Gap, PA, 22 January 1998.

41. Neil Haggard, Interview with Author, 18 December 1997.

42. Paul Imre, Interview with Author, 22 September 1996.

43. Combat Interview by Captain John G. Westover, "513th Parachute Infantry Regiment, 17th Airborne Division, 2-13 January 1945," 14-16 January 1945, 5.

45. Ibid., 7.

46. Ibid.

47. Ibid., 8; and Edwards, Interview, 6 March 1997. Edwards also had a personal dislike for the man: "Kies, a Canadian born in Three Rivers, Canada, was a worthless sonofabitch," said Edwards. "He was a cock-hound; he tried to fuck all of his junior officer's wives and girlfriends – that sort of a guy."

48. Ibid.; and Edward Sarrell, Interview with Author, 17 January 1998.

49. Frank Munafo, Interview with Author, Hasbrouk Heights, NJ, 26 May 1997; and John O. Paul, Interview with Author, 2 May 1997.

50. John O. Paul, Interview with Author, 2 May 1997; Charles Puckett, Interview with Author, 12 May 1997; and John La Riccia, Interview with Author, 31 December 1997.

51. John La Riccia, Interview with Author, 31 December 1997.

52. Patrick Phillips, Interview with Author, 13 October 1997.

53. John La Riccia, Interview with Author, 31 December 1997.

54. Frank Munafo, Interview with Author, 9 May 1997.

55. Ibid.

56. Frank Munafo, Interview with Author, Hasbrouk Heights, NJ, 26 May 1997; and John La Riccia, Interview with Author, 31 December 1997. Sorenson kept his shaving kit to maintain the red goatee he wore throughout the war.

57. John O. Paul, Interview with Author, 2 May 1997.

58. Richard Murray, Interview with Author, 3 January 1998.

59. John La Riccia, Interview with Author, 31 December 1997.

60. John O. Paul, Interview with Author, 2 May 1997.

61. Ibid.

62. Frank Munafo, Interview with Author, 16 January 1997; 9 May 1997; and Hasbrouk Heights, NJ, 26 May 1997.

63. Frank Munafo, Interview with Author, Hasbrouk Heights, NJ, 26 May 1997.

64. Charles Puckett, Interview with Author, 12 May 1997; and John O. Paul, Interview with Author, 13 May 1997. While Paul was in the hospital, he received a letter from his platoon guide, Staff Sergeant James F. Bassett. Bassett apparently felt guilty for not trying to save Paul himself: "I don't want you to think I was yellow," Bassett wrote, "but Lieutenant Puckett gave an order." John Paul believes that Lieutenant Puckett ordered the rest of the platoon: "Don't go any further forward. Everyone up their is dead," and that it was that order that prompted Munafo to act. Puckett denies ever giving such an order, and Munafo himself remembered no such order being given.

"If something was going to screw up, it was going to be Frank," commented John O. Paul in 1997. In Basic, Munafo, "he got into so much trouble – but it wasn't intentional." Lieutenant Stositch visited Munafo in the hospital after the battle. "I've got to be honest with you," Stosh told Munafo. "You're a fuckup, but when the chips are down – you're there!"

Later, Private Munafo received a letter from Sergeant Paul's Mother:

To: Private Frank Munafo
Co. "F", 2nd Bn., 513th Prcht. Inf.
A.P.O. 452
c/o Post Master, New York, New York

Mrs. Ailleen Paul
326 Main Street
Pineville, Louisiana

Dear Frank,

I know you are wondering who I am and why I am writing. I'm the mother of Technical Sergeant John O. Paul who was wounded in Belgium January 4th. I received a letter from Johnny today. He said if it were not for you he would not be alive today. We wish to thank you from the bottom of our hearts for saving Johnny's life. I wish there was something we could do for you to show our thanks. I suppose you know Johnny is still in the hospital in England. He writes that he is doing very well and can not use either right hand or arm. He writes with his left hand. We would like very much to here from you. We will remember you in our prayers. May God bless you and bring you home safely to your loved ones.

Sincerely,

Mrs. Aileen Paul

"I never wrote her a letter," lamented Frank Munafo in 1997.

Letter courtesy John O. Paul.

65. Charles Puckett, Letter to Author, 19 July 1997.
66. Charles Puckett, Interview with Author, 12 May 1997.
67. Ibid.
68. Ibid.
69. Ibid.
70. Ibid.
71. Ibid.; and Royal Donovan, Interview with Author, 14 October 1997.
72. John O. Paul, Interview with Author, 2 May 1997; and Charles Puckett, Interview with Author 12 May 1997.
73. Edward Sarrell, Interview with Author, 17 January 1998.
74. Ibid.
75. Ibid. Sarrell believed that his group was the first to enter the woods. Royal Donovan, however, who watched the attack, confirmed that Lieutenant Calhoun's group was indeed the first.
76. Frank Munafo, Interview with Author, Hasbrouk Heights, NJ, 26 May 1997.
77. August Seacott, Interview with Author, 26 December 1997.
78. John La Riccia, Interview with Author, 2 January 1998.
79. Richard Murray, Interview with Author, 3 January 1998.
80. John O. Paul, Interview with Author, 2 May 1997; and 13 May 1997.
81. Major Samuel Calhoun, Interview with Author, Fresno, CA, 23 February 1997; and Orlando, FL, 22 September 1997.
82. Paul Imre, Interview with Author, Orlando, FL, 22 September 197; and George Finnelli, 3/506, Interview with Author, Chestertown, MD, 28 November 1997.
83. Combat Interview by Captain John G. Westover, "513th Parachute Infantry Regiment, 17th Airborne Division, 2-13 January 1945," 14-16 January 1945, 6.
84. Royal Donovan, Interview with Author, 14 October 1997. In the end, however, it is likely that Calhoun's story is the accurate account; a hanging would have been a lot of trouble to arrange when just shooting them was the obvious solution.
85. Combat Interview by Captain John G. Westover, "513th Parachute Infantry Regiment, 17th Airborne Division, 2-13 January 1945," 14-16 January 1945, 7.
86. Ibid.
87. Clarence Knigge, Interview with Author, 19 April 1997.
88. Edward Sarrell, Interview with Author, 17 January 1998.
89. Bob Greenstrand, "WWII Service," 20.
90. Don Newhouse, Interview with Author, 20 January 1998.
91. Clarence Knigge, Interview with Author, 19 April 1997; and in Orlando, FL, 22 September 1997.
92. Ibid.
93. Bob Greenstrand, "WWII Service," 19.
94. Don Newhouse, Interview with Author, Fort Indiantown Gap, PA, 23 January 1998.
95. Charles Puckett, Interview with to Author, 12 May 1997.
96. Ibid.; and Charles Puckett, Letter to Author, 19 July 1997.
97. Bob Greenstrand, "WWII Service," 19-20; and Don Newhouse, Interview with Author, Fort Indiantown Gap, PA, 23 January 1998.

98. Frank Altmiller, Interview with Author, 6 February 1998.

99. Don Newhouse, Interview with Author, Fort Indiantown Gap, PA, 23 January 1998.

100. Bob Greenstrand, "WWII Service," 20.

101. Don Newhouse, Interview with Author, Fort Indiantown Gap, PA, 23 January 1998.

102. Philip Cavaleri, Interview with Author, Orlando, FL, 22 September 1997; and Willis Grice, Interview with Author, 18 & 27 February 1998.

103. Philip Cavaleri, Interview with Author, Orlando, FL, 22 September 1997.

104. Ibid.

105. Thomas Connolly, Interview with Author, 12 January 1998.

106. Philip Cavaleri, Interview with Author, Orlando, FL, 22 September 1997.

107. Ibid.

108. Thomas Connolly, Interview with Author, 12 January 1998. In hospital in England, Connolly nearly lost one of his feet to a French surgeon, but he refused to let him take it and eventually recovered. It had been a close call, however; men's legs were being amputated right in the ward.

109. Combat Interview by Captain John G. Westover, "513th Parachute Infantry Regiment, 17th Airborne Division, 2-13 January 1945," 14-16 January 1945, 7. When interviewed, Colonel Miller stated that F Company had met resistance in the two stands of trees to the north of the forest, knocking out two German tanks with Germination grenades in the wood on the east while also taking fire from the wood on the left. Although this western copse of trees was in the 1st Battalion's sector, Miller stated that F Company cleared it anyway. Miller went on to say that F Company continued to push due north to the woods south at Gammon (at 49.3-62.3), advancing well to the left of 2nd Battalion's area. Most F Company men stated they ever advanced further than the big woods, and none it seems, save the small group that patrolled to Flamizoulle, advanced any further on 4 January.

110. Charles Puckett, Letter to Author, 19 July 1997.

111. Ibid.

112. Combat Interview by Captain John G. Westover, "513th Parachute Infantry Regiment, 17th Airborne Division, 2-13 January 1945," 14-16 January 1945, 6.

113. Major General William Miley, "17th Airborne in the Bulge," 19 January 1945.

114. Combat Interview by Captain John G. Westover, "513th Parachute Infantry Regiment, 17th Airborne Division, 2-13 January 1945," 14-16 January 1945, 8.

115. Combat Interview by VIII Corps, "513th Parachute Infantry Regiment, 2-13 January 1945," 14-16 January 1945, 8. Coutts ordered a company from the 139th Airborne Engineers to take over for Headquarters company which reverted to regimental reserve.

116. Ibid.

117. Lieutenant Colonel Ward S. Ryan, "Summary of Operations, 513th Parachute Infantry Regiment," 2 February 1945; and Combat Interview, "22nd Tank Battalion, 29 December-16 January 1945," 30 January 1945.

118. Combat Interview, "Off-the-Record Remarks, 11th Armored Division," No date, 2.

119. Edwards, Interview.6 March 1997.

120. Combat Interview by Captain John G. Westover, "513th Parachute Infantry Regiment, 17th Airborne Division, 2-13 January 1945," 14-16 January 1945, 9.

121. MacKenzie, Interview, 5 February 1999.

122. Don Newhouse, Interview with Author, Fort Indiantown Gap, PA, 23 January 1998.

123. Paul Imre, Interview with Author, Orlando, FL, 22 September 1996.

124. Haggard, Interview, 27 August 1999.

125. Don Newhouse, Interview with Author, Fort Indiantown Gap, PA, 23 January 1998.

126. Charles Puckett, Interview with Author, 23 May 1997; and Bob Greenstrand, "WWII Service," 20.

127. Royal Donovan, Interview with Author, 14 October 1997; and Edward Sarrell, Interview with Author, 17 January 1998.

128. Richard Murray, Interview with Author, 3 January 1998.

129. Don Newhouse, Interview with Author, 20 January 1998.

130. Bob Greenstrand, "WWII Service," 20; and Philip Cavaleri, Interview with Author, Orlando, FL, 22 September 1996.

131. John La Riccia, Interview with Author, 2 January 1998.

132. Ed Dahlberg, Interview with Author, 4 August 1998.

133. Royal Donovan, Interview with Author, 14 October 1998.

134. Combat Interview by Captain John G. Westover, "513th Parachute Infantry Regiment, 17th Airborne Division, 2-13 January 1945," 14-16 January 1945, 9.

Chapter 6 Notes

1. Edwards, Interview, 16 March 1997; and 513th Parachute Infantry Regiment, *S-3 Periodic Report No. 8*, 051000 January 1945.

2. 513th Parachute Infantry Regiment, *S-3 Periodic Report No. 8*, 051000 January 1945.

3. 513th Parachute Infantry Regiment, *Summary of Operations*, 2 February 1945.

4. Major General William M. Miley, *17th Airborne in the Bulge*, 19 January 1945.

5. Murray, Interview, 3 January 1998.

6. Donovan, Interview, 17 October 1997.

7. Puckett, Interview, 29 September 1997.

8. Combat Interview by Captain John G. Westover, "513th Parachute Infantry Regiment, 17th Airborne Division, 2-13 January 1945," 14-16 January 1945, 10.

9. Puckett, Interview, 29 September 1997.

10. Combat Interview by Captain John G. Westover, "513th Parachute Infantry Regiment, 17th Airborne Division, 2-13 January 1945," 14-16 January 1945, 10; and Edwards, Interview, 16 January 1997.

11. Lightcap, Interview, 6 July 1997.

12. Seacott, Interview, 26 December 1997.

13. 17th Airborne Division, *Intelligence Directive*, 5 January 1945; and Combat Interview by Captain John G. Westover, "513th Parachute Infantry Regiment, 17th Airborne Division, 2-13 January 1945," 14-16 January 1945, 10.

14. Combat Interview by Captain John G. Westover, "513th Parachute Infantry Regiment, 17th Airborne Division, 2-13 January 1945," 14-16 January 1945, 10.

15. Cavaleri, Interview, 22 September 1996.

16. Newhouse, Interview, 20 January 1998.

17. Philip S. Edwards, "This I Remember," *Thunder From Heaven*, 42:3 (Spring 95): 27-8.

18. Irving, *War*, 372-3. Uneasy over the slow progress of his army, General Patton noted in his diary, "We can still loose this war. However, the Germans are colder and hungrier than we are, but they fight better. I can never get over the stupidity of our green troops. We simply have to keep attacking," he continued, "or he will."

19. Ibid.; and Edwards, Interview, 16 March 1997.

20. Combat Interview by Captain John G. Westover, "513th Parachute Infantry Regiment, 17th Airborne Division, 2-13 January 1945," 14-16 January 1945, 10; Major General William M. Miley, *17th Airborne in the Bulge*, 19 January 1945; and Field Message from General Miley to Lieutenant Colonel Kent, 070830 January 1945.

21. Combat Interview by Captain John G. Westover, "513th Parachute Infantry Regiment, 17th Airborne Division, 2-13 January 1945," 14-16 January 1945, 10.

22. Ibid.

23. Combat Interview by Captain John G. Westover, "513th Parachute Infantry Regiment, 17th Airborne Division, 2-13 January 1945," 14-16 January 1945, 10; 513th Parachute Infantry Regiment, *Field Order No. 10*, 6 January 1945; 17th Airborne Division, *Field Order No. 2*, 6 January 1945.

24. 513th Parachute Infantry Regiment, *Summary of Operations*, 2 February 1945; and Sarrell, Interview, 17 January 1945.

25. Munafo, Interview, 26 May 1997.

26. Newhouse, Interview, 23 January 1998.

27. Newhouse, Interview, 20 January 1998.

28. Greenstrand, "WWII Service," 21.

29. Ibid.

30. Donovan, Interview, 17 October 1997; and *Field Message from Surgeon Commanding to Colonel Coutts*, Attn: Surgeon, 070910: "Notify your surgeons that NP [Neuropsychiatric] or NP diagnosis are not, repeat, not to be used on EMT's. Use the term 'Combat Fatigue' or 'Combat Exhaustion' for all NP cases."

31. 513th Parachute Infantry Regiment, *Summary of Operations*, 2 February 1945; Major General William M. Miley, *17th Airborne in the Bulge*, 19 January 1945.

32. 17th Airborne Division, *G-2 Periodic Report No. 9*, 7 January 1945.

33. Combat Interview by Captain John G. Westover, "513th Parachute Infantry Regiment, 17th Airborne Division, 2-13 January 1945," 14-16 January 1945, 11.

34. Ibid.

35. Ibid.; Combat Interview, "22nd Tank Battalion, 29 December-16 January 1945," 30 January 1945; Major General William M. Miley, *17th Airborne in the Bulge*, 19 January 1945; and General Miley to Lieutenant Colonel Kent, *Field Message*, 070830, January 1945.

36. Combat Interview by Captain John G. Westover, "513th Parachute Infantry Regiment, 17th Airborne Division, 2-13 January 1945," 14-16 January 1945, 11-2.

37. Ibid., 12.

38. Ibid., 12-3; and Combat Interview, "22nd Tank Battalion, 29 December-16 January 1945," 30 January 1945.

39. Combat Interview by Captain John G. Westover, "513th Parachute Infantry Regiment, 17th Airborne Division, 2-13 January 1945," 14-16 January 1945, 12-3.

40. Ibid., 13; and Major General William M. Miley, *17th Airborne in the Bulge*, 19 January 1945.

41. Combat Interview by Captain John G. Westover, "513th Parachute Infantry Regiment, 17th Airborne Division, 2-13 January 1945," 14-16 January 1945, 13.

42. Ibid., 13-4; and 513th Parachute Infantry Regiment, *Narrative of Action*, 2 February 1945.

43. Combat Interview by Captain John G. Westover, "513th Parachute Infantry Regiment, 17th Airborne Division, 2-13 January 1945," 14-16 January 1945, 14.

44. Ibid.

45. Ibid., 14-5. Lieutenant Puckett recalls that F Company, not E, was in the lead.

46. Combat Interview by Captain John G. Westover, "513th Parachute Infantry Regiment, 17th Airborne Division, 2-13 January 1945," 14-16 January 1945, 15.

47. Sarrell, Interview, 17 January 1998.

48. Ibid. Puckett recalls only two shots being fired at the sniper.

49. Combat Interview by Captain John G. Westover, "513th Parachute Infantry Regiment, 17th Airborne Division, 2-13 January 1945," 14-16 January 1945, 15; and Combat Interview, "22nd Tank Battalion, 29 December-16 January 1945," 30 January 1945.

50. DeHaven, Interview, 15 July 1997; Grice, Interview, 15 June 1998; and Lightcap, Interview, 6 July 1998.

51. Combat Interview by Captain John G. Westover, "513th Parachute Infantry Regiment, 17th Airborne Division, 2-13 January 1945," 14-16 January 1945, 15.

52. Puckett, Interview, 29 September 1997.

53. Combat Interview by Captain John G. Westover, "513th Parachute Infantry Regiment, 17th Airborne Division, 2-13 January 1945," 14-16 January 1945, 15.

54. Major General William M. Miley, *17th Airborne in the Bulge*, 19 January 1945.

55. Ibid.; and Combat Interview by Captain John G. Westover, "513th Parachute Infantry Regiment, 17th Airborne Division, 2-13 January 1945," 14-16 January 1945, 15.

56. Ibid.

57. Combat Interview by Captain John G. Westover, "513th Parachute Infantry Regiment, 17th Airborne Division, 2-13 January 1945," 14-16 January 1945, 16.

58. Sarrell, Interview, 17 January 1998.

59. Combat Interview by Captain John G. Westover, "513th Parachute Infantry Regiment, 17th Airborne Division, 2-13 January 1945," 14-16 January 1945, 16-18; Dahlberg, Interview 13 October 1997. Reports suggest F Company's strength was eighteen men.

60. Grice, Interview, 18 February 1998.

61. Harris, Interview, 12 February, 1998.

62. Cavaleri, Interview, 22 September 1996.

63. Donovan, Interview, 20 October 1997.

64. Cavaleri, Interview, 22 September 1996.

65. Ibid.

66. Combat Interview by Captain John G. Westover, "513th Parachute Infantry Regiment, 17th Airborne Division, 2-13 January 1945," 14-16 January 1945, 16-7.

67. Ibid., 17.

68. Ibid.

69. Combat Interview by Captain John G. Westover, "513th Parachute Infantry Regiment, 17th Airborne Division, 2-13 January 1945," 14-16 January 1945, 17; and 17th Airborne Division, *G-2 Periodic Report No. 10*, 8 January 1945.

70. Combat Interview by Captain John G. Westover, "513th Parachute Infantry Regiment, 17th Airborne Division, 2-13 January 1945," 14-16 January 1945, 17. Colonel Coutts stated after the battle that the telephone lines to the rear had not been established. Major Anderson believed at the time that his request had been refused because he was unable to verify the targets. Wherever the truth lay, failing to support Anderson's request for artillery would prove a grave error on the part of Coutts.

71. Lightcap, Interview, 6 July 1997.

72. Combat Interview by Captain John G. Westover, "513th Parachute Infantry Regiment, 17th Airborne Division, 2-13 January 1945," 14-16 January 1945, 18; and Sarrell, Interview, 17 January 1998.

73. Combat Interview by Captain John G. Westover, "513th Parachute Infantry Regiment, 17th Airborne Division, 2-13 January 1945," 14-16 January 1945, 17-9.

74. Sarrell, Interview, 17 January 1998.

75. Ibid.

76. Altmiller, Interview, 6 February 1998; and Donovan, Interview, 17 October 1997.

77. Lightcap, Interview, 6 July 1997.

78. Ibid.

79. Grice, Interview, 18 February 1998.

80. and Donovan, Interview, 20 October 1997; Combat Interview by Captain John G. Westover, "513th Parachute Infantry Regiment, 17th Airborne Division, 2-13 January 1945," 14-16 January 1945, 19; and Seacott, Interview, 26 December 1997.

81. Altmiller, Interview, 6 February 1998

82. Munafo, Interview, 26 May 1997.

83. Combat Interview by Captain John G. Westover, "513th Parachute Infantry Regiment, 17th Airborne Division, 2-13 January 1945," 14-16 January 1945, 19-20.

84. Ibid., 20.

85. Ibid.; and 513th Parachute Infantry Regiment, *Summary of Operations*, 2 February 1945; Combat Interview, "22nd Tank Battalion, 29 December-16 January 1945," 30 January 1945; and Edwards, Interview, 16 March 1997.

86. Grice, Interview, 18 February 1998.

87. Grice, Interview, 22 September 1996; Altmiller, Interview, 6 February 1998. Colonel Miller stated that it was when the artillery FO's radio was destroyed by fire that he knew he couldn't hold. That, however, does not jibe with Altmiller's testimony.

88. Seacott, Interview, 26 December 1997.

89. Sarrell, Interview, 17 January 1998.

90. Grice, Interview, 22 September 1996.

91. Dahlberg, Interviews, 22 September 1996 and 30 September 1997.

92. Haggard, Interview, 22 December 1997.

93. Murray, Interview, 3 January 1998.

94. Grice, Interview, 18 February 1998.

95. Haggard, Interview, 30 March 1997.

96. Edwards, Interview, 16 March 1997; Dahlberg, Interview, 22 September 1996; Combat Interview by Captain John G. Westover, "513th Parachute Infantry Regiment, 17th Airborne Division, 2-13 January 1945," 14-16 January 1945, 20.

97. Combat Interview by Captain John G. Westover, "513th Parachute Infantry Regiment, 17th Airborne Division, 2-13 January 1945," 14-16 January 1945, 20. Newhouse said he never encountered a German tank that was out of fuel or out of ammunition during the battle.

98. Grice, Interview, 24 February 1998.

99. Sarrell, Interview, 17 January 1998.

100. Combat Interview by Captain John G. Westover, "513th Parachute Infantry Regiment, 17th Airborne Division, 2-13 January 1945," 14-16 January 1945, 20-2.

101. Ibid., 21.

102. Ibid., 21-2.

103. Ibid.

104. Ibid., 22.

105. Ibid., 22-3.

106. Ibid., 23.

107. Ibid.

108. Ibid., 23-4

109. Ibid., 24.

110. John Vafides, "A POW Story," *Thunder From Heaven*, (Fall 1994): 68-9.

111. Ibid.

112. Major General William M. Miley, *17th Airborne in the Bulge*, 19 January 1945.

113. 513th Parachute Infantry Regiment, *Summary of Operations*, 2 February 1945.

114. Irving, *War*, 377; and Combat Interview by Captain John G. Westover, "513th Parachute Infantry Regiment, 17th Airborne Division, 2-13 January 1945," 14-16 January 1945, 24.

115. 17th Airborne Division, *G-2 Periodic Report No. 12*, 10 January 1945.

116. 17th Airborne Division, *G-2 Periodic Report No. 13*, 11 January 1945; VIII Corps, *G-2 Periodic Report No. 209*, 12 January 1945.

117. 513th Parachute Infantry Regiment, *Summary of Operations*, 2 February 1945.

118. 513th Combat Team, *G-3 Periodic Report No. 15*, 11 January 1945; and 17th Airborne Division, *G-3 Periodic Report No. 9*, 12 January 1945.

119. 17th Airborne Division, *G-2 Periodic Report No. 14*, 12 January 1945.

120. Ibid. American tactics in general were improving, however. Most troops were now by-passing towns occupied by the enemy. Enemy artillery was zeroed-in on these strongpoints and the Germans, according to one captured enemy officer, were disappointed when American soldiers "did not come in." 513th Parachute Infantry Regiment, *Summary of Operations*, 2 February 1945; and VIII Corps, *G-2 Periodic Report No. 209*, 12 January 1945.

121. Major General William M. Miley, *17th Airborne in the Bulge*, 19 January 1945; 17th Airborne Division, *G-3 Periodic Report No. 11*, 14 January 1945; 17th Airborne Division, *G-3 Periodic Report No. 10*, 13 January 1945; 17th Airborne Division, *G-2 Periodic Report No. 16*, 14 January 1945; and 513th Parachute Infantry Regiment, *Summary of Operations*, 2 February 1945.

122. Combat Interview by Captain John G. Westover, "513th Parachute Infantry Regiment, 17th Airborne Division, 2-13 January 1945," 14-16 January 1945, 24.

123. Ibid.; 513th Combat Team, *G-3 Periodic Report No. 16*, 14 January 1945; and 513th Parachute Infantry Regiment, *Summary of Operations*, 2 February 1945.

124. VIII Corps, *G-2 Periodic Report No. 210*, 13 January 1945.

125. Combat Interview by Captain John G. Westover, "513th Parachute Infantry Regiment, 17th Airborne Division, 2-13 January 1945," 14-16 January 1945, 1.

126. Ibid.; and Edwards, Interview, 16 March 1997.

127. Major General William M. Miley, *17th Airborne in the Bulge*, 19 January 1945.

128. Sarrell, Interview, 16 January 1998.

Chapter 7 Notes

1. 17th Airborne Division, *G-2 Periodic Report No. 16*, 14 January 1945; Major General William M. Miley, *17th Airborne in the Bulge*, 19 January 1945; and Pallud, *Battle of the Bulge: Then and Now*, 448.

2. Sarrell, Interview, 16 January 1998.

3. Pierce, Interview with Author, Phoenix, AZ, 16 March 1997.

4. 17th Airborne Division, *G-3 Periodic Report No. 12*, 15 January 1945; and Major General William M. Miley, *17th Airborne in the Bulge*, 19 January 1945.

5. Pay, *Thunder From Heaven*, 23; and 17th Airborne Division, *G-3 Periodic Report No. 13*, 16 January 1945; Major General William M. Miley, *17th Airborne in the Bulge*, 19 January 1945.

6. 17th Airborne Division, *G-2 Estimate No. 1*, 161200 January 1945.

7. 513th Parachute Infantry Regiment, *Summary of Operations*, 2 February 1945; 17th Airborne Division, *G-2 Periodic Report No. 18*, 17 January 1945; and 17th Airborne Division, *Field Order No. 5*, 17 January 1945.

8. Grice, Interview, 24 February 1998.

9. 17th Airborne Division, *G-2 Periodic Report No. 18*, 17 January 1945; 17th Airborne Division, *G-3 Periodic Report No. 15*, 18 January 1945; 17th Airborne Division, *G-2 Periodic Report No. 19*, 18 January 1945; 513th Parachute Infantry Regiment, *Summary of Operations*, 2 February 1945.

10. Pay, *Thunder From Heaven*, 23; and 17th Airborne Division.

11. 17th Airborne Division, *G-2 Periodic Report No. 18*, 17 January 1945; and 17th Airborne Division, *Field Order No. 6*, 20 January 1945.

12. 513th Parachute Infantry Regiment, *Summary of Operations*, 2 February 1945; 17th Airborne Division, *Field Order No. 8*, 21 January 1945; and 513th Combat Team, *G-2 Periodic Report No. 24*, 23 January 1945; and 17th Airborne Division, *G-2 Periodic Report No. 23*, 22 January 1945.

13. VIII Corps, *G-2 Periodic Report No. 219*, 22 January 1945.

14. Ibid.

15. Pierce, Interview, 16 March 1997; and Haggard, Interview, 22 December 1997.

16. Greenstrand, Interview, 16 March 1997; Edwards, Interview, 16 March 1997; and Donovan, Interview, 20 October 1997.

17. Lightcap, Interview, 6 July, 1997.

18. Ibid.; Sarrell, Interview, 19 January 1997; and 513th Parachute Infantry Regiment, *Summary of Operations*, 2 February 1945.

19. Pierce, Interview, 16 March 1997.

20. Edwards, Interview, 16 March 1997.

21. 513th Combat Team, *Field Order No. 12*, 26 January 1945; 513th Parachute Infantry Regiment, *Summary of Operations*, 2 February 1945; 17th Airborne Division, *G-2 Periodic Report No. 27*, 26 January 1945; and 17th Airborne Division, *Consolidated IPW Report*, 26 January 1945.

22. 513th Parachute Infantry Regiment, *Summary of Operations*, 2 February 1945.

23. Ibid.; Headquarters, 17th Airborne Division, *Summary of Operations*, 14 February 1945; and 17th Airborne Division, *Narrative of Action*.

24. 513th Parachute Infantry Regiment, *Summary of Operations*, 2 February 1945; and Dahlberg, Interview, 13 October 1997.

25. Edwards, Interview, 16 March 1997; and 513th Parachute Infantry Regiment, *Summary of Operations*, 2 February 1945.

26. Lightcap, Interview, 6 July 1997.

27. Headquarters, 17th Airborne Division, *Summary of Operations*, 14 February 1945.

28. 513th Parachute Infantry Regiment, *Summary of Operations*, 2 February 1945; and 513th Parachute Infantry Regiment, *Summary of Operations*, 14 February 1945.

29. Pierce, Interview, 16 March 1997.

30. Grice, Interviews, 22 September 1996 and 10 February 1998.

31. 513th Parachute Infantry Regiment, *Summary of Operations*, 14 February 1945.

32. Ibid.

33. Ibid.

34. Ibid.; Dahlberg, Interview, 30 September 1997; and Murray, Interview, 3 January 1998.

35. 513th Parachute Infantry Regiment, *Summary of Operations*, 14 February 1945; and Murray, Interview, 3 January 1998.

36. Ibid.; and Haggard, Interview, 30 March 1998.

37. *History of the 513th Parachute Infantry* (317-Inf(513)-0.1, 45), NARA; and Dahlberg, Interview, 30 September 1997.

Chapter 8 Notes

1. 513th Parachute Infantry Regiment, *Summary of Operations*, 14 February 1945.

2. Ibid.; and Pierce, Interview 16 March 1997.

3. Donovan, Interview, 20 October 1997; and Altmiller, Interview, 6 February 1998.

4. Sarrell, Interview, 17 January 1998.

5. Henry Contreras, Interview with Author, 14 January 1998.

6. Donovan, Interviews, 17 and 20 October 1997.

7. Greenstrand, "World War II Service," 21-2.

8. Ibid., 22.

9. Ibid., 22-3. Apparently, no Purple Hearts were awarded to men with frozen feet.

10. Ibid., 22.

11. Ibid., 22-3.

12. Ken Olson, Interview with Author, 11 January 1998; and James Cox, Interview with Author, 11 January 1998.

13. John Cobb, Interview with Author, Bridgeton, NJ, 22 November 1998.

14. Ibid.

15. Bill Bergmann, Letter to the Author, 24 February 1999.

16. Altmiller, Interview, 6 February 1998.

17. Sarrell, Interview, 17 January 1998.

18. Rex Shama, *History of the 49th Troop Carrier Squadron*; Bergmann, Letter, 24 February 1999, and David Mondey, *The Concise Guide to American Aircraft of World War II*, (New York: Smithmark Publishers, 1996), 71-2.

19. Gil Whiteside, Interview with Author, New Castle, DE, 1997; Robert Kerr, Interview with the Author, 1997; and Major J.F. O'Sullivan, *Interview of the Officers, 1st Battalion, 513th Parachute Infantry Regiment*, 9 April 1945.

20. Robert Guiles, Interview with Author, Mt. Pocano, PA 17 September 1998.

21. Cox, Interview, 11 January 1998; and Cuthbertson, Interview, 15 January 1998.

22. Rex Shama, *History of the 49th Troop Carrier Squadron*, and Bergmann, Letter, 24 February 1999.

23. Franklin M. Davis, Jr., and the Editors of Time-Life Books, *Across the Rhine*, (Chicago: Time-Life Books, 1980), 47; and RAF Film Production Unit, *Operation VARSITY*.

24. RAF Film Production Unit, *Operation VARSITY*.

25. Ibid.; and Davis, *Across the Rhine*, 47, 83.

26. Captain John G. Westover, *Interview of Major Robert R. Corey, Assistant G-2 of the 17th Airborne Division*, 31 March 1945.

27. B. H. Lidell Hart, *History of the Second World War*, (New York: G. P. Putnam's Sons, 1971), 678; Russell F Weigley, *Eisenhower's Lieutenants: The Campaigns of France and Germany, 1944-1945* (Bloomington: Indiana University Press, 1977) 612-16; and Alexander McKee, *The Race for the Rhine Bridges: 1940, 1944, 1945*, (New York: Stein and Day, Publishers, 1971), 298-302.

28. Ibid., and David Iving, *The War Between The Generals: Inside The Allied High Command*, (New York: Congdon & Lattes, Inc., 1981) 389.

29. RAF Film Production Unit, *Operation VARSITY*; and "Wehrmacht Begins to Break Apart Under Punishment of Allied Arms," *Newsweek*, 25:14 (2 April 1945): 25.

30. RAF Film Production Unit, *Operation VARSITY*; Ferguson, *The PARAS*, 29; Hynes, *Reporting World War II*, 652; Franklin, *Across the Rhine*, 96.

31. Martin Wolfe, *Green Light: A Troop Carrier Squadron's War From Normandy to the Rhine*, (Washington, D.C.: Center for Air Force History, 1993), 274,8.

32. 17th Airborne Division, *Narrative of Action*.

33. Martin Middlebrook, *Arnhem 1944: The Airborne Battle, 17-26 September*, (Boulder, CO: Westview Press, 1944), 443; Ferguson, *The PARAS*, 29, and Samuel Hynes, et. al.; and *Reporting World War II: Part II, American Journalism, 1944-1946*, (New York: The Library of America, 1995), 652.

34. Army Pictorial Service, *The First Allied Airborne Army in Operation Varsity, 24 March 1945*.

35. Ferguson, *The PARAS*, 28-9.

36. Ibid.; and RAF Film Production Unit, O*peration VARSITY*.

37. 17th Airborne Division, *Historical Report of Operation Varsity*, 1945, 1.

38. Ibid., 1-9.

39. 513th Parachute Infantry Regiment, *Field Order No. 16*, with *Annex Nos. 1 and 2 (Intelligence)*, March 17, 1945

40. Ibid.

41. Ibid.

42. Ibid.

43. 17th Airborne Division, *Historical Report of Operation Varsity*, 1945, 23.

44. Wolfe, *Green Light*, 380; Rex Shama, *History of the 49th Troop Carrier Squadron*; and 49th Troop Carrier Squadron, 313th Troop Carrier Group, *Narrative of Operation VARSITY*.

45. 49th Troop Carrier Squadron, 313th Troop Carrier Group, *Narrative of Operation VARSITY*; and Rex Shama, *History of the 49th Troop Carrier Squadron*.

46. The first serial of 36 planes would carry D Company in planes 1-5, E Company in planes 6-10, F Company in planes 11 through 15.HHC 2/513th in planes 16-21, G Company in planes 22-26, most of HHC 3/513th in planes 27-31, and I Company in planes 32-36. The second serial of 36 planes

would carry H Company H and the remainder of HHC 3/513th in planes 1-6, Regimental Headquarters and the Service Company in planes 7-15, A Company in planes 16-20, B Company in planes 21-25, C Company in planes 26-30, and HHC 1/513th in planes 31-36.

47. Greenstrand, "World War II Service," 22-3; Harold Diefenderfer, Interview with Author, 1997. Haggard was promoted so Sergeant on 12 March 1945 and was made company communications sergeant.

48. Grice, Interview, 18 February 1998.

49. Ibid.; and Cobb, Interview, 22 November 1998.

50. Cobb, Interview, 22 November 1998.

51. Rex Shama, *History of the 49th Troop Carrier Squadron*

52. 49th Troop Carrier Squadron, 313th Troop Carrier Group, *Narrative of Operation VARSITY*.

53. Donovan, Interview, 20 October 1997.

54. "Wehrmacht Begins to Break," 25.

55. RAF Film Production Unit, *Operation VARSITY*.

Chapter 9 Notes

1. Greenstrand, "WWII Service," 24.

2. Ibid., 23-4.

3. Olson, Interview, 11 January 1998.

4. Murray, Interview, 3 January 1998.

5. Greenstrand, "WWII Service," 25.

6. Ibid.; Shama, *Pulse & Repulse*, 335; Contreras, Interview, 14 January 1998; and 2nd Battalion, 513th Parachute Infantry Regiment, *Journal*, 232400-242400 March, 1945.

7. Shama, *Pulse & Repulse*, 335; and Major J.F. O'Sullivan, *Interview of the Officers, 2nd Battalion, 513th Parachute Infantry Regiment*, 8 April 1945.

8. Shama, *Pulse & Repulse*, 335-6.

9. Ibid.; Cox, Interview, 11 January 1998; and Gilbert Whiteside, Interview with Author, New Castle, DE, 27 July 1997.

10. Whiteside, Interview, 27 July 1997; and Shama, *Pulse & Repulse*, 336.

11. Cox, Interview, 11 January 1998; Shama, *Pulse & Repulse*, 336-7; and Shama; *History of the 49th Troop Carrier Squadron*, 172.

12. Frank Joda, Interview with the Author, 21 July 1997; and Frank Joda, *Operation VARSITY*, April 1990.

13. *17th Airborne Division Historical Report of Operation Varsity*, 1945, 1; and Private Robert M. Gilmore, Editor in Chief, "Airborne Invasion of the Rhine,"*513th Parachute Infantry History*, (Vittle, France: A Talon Publication, July 25, 1945).

14. Cuthbertson, Interview 15 January 1998.

15. Shama, *History of the 49th*, 104; Laufer, Interview, 5 March 1997; and Hagerman, *War Stories*, 217.

16. XVIII Corps, *G-2 Periodic Report No. 3, Annex No. 2*; *17th Airborne Division Historical Report of Operation Varsity*, 1945, 9.

17. *17th Airborne Division Historical Report of Operation Varsity*, 1945, 9.

18. Army Pictorial Services Film, *The First Allied Airborne Army in Operation Varsity*, 1945.

19. Warren, Dr. John, "Airborne Operations in World War II," USAF Historical Studies, Research Studies Institute, Maxwell AFB, AL., Sept 56., page Apdix C-4, from Shama, *History of the 49th*, 172.

20. Cox, Interview, 11 January 1998; and Joda, *Operation Varsity*, April 1990.

21. Altmiller, Interview, 6 February 1998.

22. The initial point (IP) was code named 'Yalta.' It was the last check point reached before the run to the drop zones. Robert Kerr, Interview with Author, 21 July 1997; Eugene Rothi, Interview with Author, 21 July 1997; and Army Pictorial Services Film, *The First Allied Airborne Army in Operation Varsity*, 1945.

23. Ed Sarrell, Letters to Author, 2 January 1998 and 17 January 1998.

24. Rothi, Interview, 21 July 1997.

25. Contreras, Interview, 14 January 1998.

26. Shama, *History of the 49th*, 172.

27. Grice, Interview, 13 February 1998.

28. Shama, *History of the 49th*, 172; and William Pully, Letter to Author, 1996.

29. Kerr, Interview, 21 July 1997; Shama, *History of the 49th*, 172; and Pully, Letter, 1996.

30. Shama, *History of the 49th*, 172; Pully, Letter, 1996; 2nd Battalion, 513th Parachute Infantry Regiment, *Enclosure No. 3*, 29 April 1945; and 2nd Battalion, 513th Parachute Infantry Regiment, *Narrative of Action*, 24 March 1945.

31. Greenstrand's information is not substantiated by contemporary accounts.

32. Donovan, Interview, 17 October 1997; and Pully, Letter, 1996.

33. Cobb, Interview, 22 November 1998.

34. Bergmann, Letter, 24 February 1999.

35. Ibid.

36. Donovan, Interviews, 17, 20 October 1997; Sarrell, Letter, 2 January 1998; and Olson, Interview 11 January 1998.

37. Greenstrand, Interview, 16 March 1997; and Pat Phillips, Interview with Author, 13 October 1997.

38. Hataway, Interview, 19 April 1997.

39. 2nd Battalion, 513th Parachute Infantry Regiment, Journal, 232400-242400 March 1945; Martin Wolfe, *Green Light: A Troop Carrier Squadrons War From Normandy to the Rhine*, (Washington, D.C.: Center for Air Force History, 1993), 380; and Gilmore, "Airborne Invasion of the Rhine."

40. Rothi, Interview, 21 July 1997, and Lieutenant Eugene Rothi, *After Action Interview by 313th Troop Carrier Group*, 24 March 1945.

41. Lieutenant Macel Mael, *After Action Interview by 313th Troop Carrier Group*, 24 March 1945.

42. Colonel Edward Yarborough, USAAF (Ret.), Interview by author, October 5, 1996, notes, Dover Air Force Base Museum, Delaware. Major General James Gavin jumped from Yarborough's plane in Sicily. Yarborough cites the C-46's hydraulic system as the biggest culprit in their losses over the drop zones.

43. Gilmore, "Airborne Invasion of the Rhine;" 2nd Battalion, 513th Parachute Infantry Regiment, N*arrative of Action*, 24 March 1945; and Major J.F. O'Sullivan, *Interview of the Officers, 2nd Battalion, 513th Parachute Infantry Regiment*, 8 April 1945, 3.

44. Murray, Interview, 3 January 1998.

45. Sarrell, Letter, 2 January 1998.

46. Grice, Interviews, 13, 18 February 1998.

47. Ibid.

48. Greenstrand, "WWII Service, 26-7.

49. Ibid., 26.

50. Ibid.

51. Ibid.

52. Donovan, Interviews, 17, 20 October 1997.

53. Cuthbertson, Interview, 15 January 1998.

54. Captain Robert Scott, *After Action Interview by 313th Troop Carrier Group*, 24 March 1945.

55. Ibid.

56. Ibid.; Joda, *Operation Varsity*, April 1990; and Cox, Interview, 11 January 1998.

57. Joda, *Operation Varsity*, April 1990; and Cox, Interview, 11 January 1998.

58. Captain Robert Scott, *After Action Interview by 313th Troop Carrier Group*, 24 March 1945.

59. Cox, Interview, 11 January 1998; and Dahlberg, Interview, 29 July 1997.

60. Joda, *Operation Varsity*, April 1990; and Captain Robert Scott, *After Action Interview by 313th Troop Carrier Group*, 24 March 1945.

61. Major J.F. O'Sullivan, *Interview of the Officers, 2nd Battalion, 513th Parachute Infantry Regiment*, 8 April 1945; and 2nd Battalion, 513th Parachute Infantry Regiment, *Narrative of Action*, 24 March 1945.

62. Major J.F. O'Sullivan, *Interview of the Officers, 2nd Battalion, 513th Parachute Infantry Regiment*, 8 April 1945.

63. Phillips, Interview, 13 October 1997.

64. Haggard, Interview, 30 March 1998.

65. Major J.F. O'Sullivan, *Interview of the Officers, 2nd Battalion, 513th Parachute Infantry Regiment*, 8 April 1945.

66. Shama, *History of the 49th*, 173; and Cobb, Interview, 22 November 1997.

67. Haggard, Interview, 30 March 1998.

68. Sarrell, Letter, 2 January 1998; Greenstrand, "WWII Service," 27; and Olson, Interview, 11 January 1998.

69. Edwards, Interview, 16 March 1997.

70. Ibid.

71. Ibid.

72. Major J.F. O'Sullivan, *Interview of the Officers, 2nd Battalion, 513th Parachute Infantry Regiment*, 8 April 1945, 3.

73. Rybka, Interview, 7 February 1998.

74. Major J.F. O'Sullivan, *Interview of the Officers, 2nd Battalion, 513th Parachute Infantry Regiment*, 8 April 1945, 3.

75. Edwards, Interview, 16 March 1997; and

76. Major J.F. O'Sullivan, *Interview of the Officers, 2nd Battalion, 513th Parachute Infantry Regiment*, 8 April 1945, 3-4.

77. Cuthbertson, Interview, 15 January 1998; and Grice, Interviews, 13, 18 February 1998.

78. Major J.F. O'Sullivan, *Interview of the Officers, 2nd Battalion, 513th Parachute Infantry Regiment*, 8 April 1945, 3.

79. Major J.F. O'Sullivan, *Interview of the Officers, 1st Battalion, 513th Parachute Infantry Regiment*, 9 April 1945.

80. Laufer, Interview, 5 March 1997; Grice, Interviews, 13, 18 February 1998; and Cuthbertson, Interview, 15 January 1998.

81. 2nd Battalion, 513th Parachute Infantry Regiment, N*arrative of Action*, 24 March 1945.

82. Major J.F. O'Sullivan, *Interview of the Officers, 2nd Battalion, 513th Parachute Infantry Regiment*, 8 April 1945, 3-6; D Company lost five M1919A6 LMGs and F Company lost three; HHC 2/513 had only four of their twelve SCR 300 radio sets delivered in the drop. Two more were later delivered by jeep. 16-18 of the 24 SCR 536s were in use.

83. Donovan, Interview, 28 October 1997; and *17th Airborne Division Historical Report of Operation Varsity*, 1945, 23.

84. Donovan, Interview, 17 October 1997

85. Greenstrand, "WWII Service," 28; and Edwards, Interview, 16 March 1997.

86. 513th Parachute Infantry Regiment, *S-3 Journal*, 24 March 1945 1000 Hrs to 0001 Hrs, March 25, 1945; and 2nd Battalion, 513th Parachute Infantry Regiment, *Narrative of Action*, 24 March 1945.

87. Grice, Interview 18 February 1998.

88. Major J.F. O'Sullivan, *Interview of the Officers, 2nd Battalion, 513th Parachute Infantry Regiment*, 8 April 1945, 4; 2nd Battalion, 513th Parachute Infantry Regiment, Journal, 232400-242400 March 1945; and 17th Airborne Division, *Summary of Combat Operations*, 24 March - 31 March 1945.

89. 2nd Battalion, 513th Parachute Infantry Regiment, *Narrative of Action*, 24 March 1945; and Greenstrand, "WWII Service," 28-9.

90. Major J.F. O'Sullivan, *Interview of the Officers, 2nd Battalion, 513th Parachute Infantry Regiment*, 8 April 1945, 3-4; and Major J.F. O'Sullivan, *Interview of the Officers, 3rd Battalion, 513th Parachute Infantry Regiment*, 7 April 1945, 3.I Company had six of nine LMGs, G and H Companies both had only three of nine. HHC 3/513 had only two of eight LMGs.

91. 17th Airborne Division, *Summary of Combat Operations*, 24 March - 31 March 1945.

92. "Operation Varsity," *Thunder from Heaven*, V 39 (3 June 1992), 26.

93. Major J.F. O'Sullivan, *Interview of the Officers, 2nd Battalion, 513th Parachute Infantry Regiment*, 8 April 1945, 3-4; and 2nd Battalion, 513th Parachute Infantry Regiment, *Battle Casualty Report*, 11 June 1945. 2nd Battalion would sustain thirty-six percent casualties by 5 April.

94. Major J.F. O'Sullivan, *Interview of the Officers, 3rd Battalion, 513th Parachute Infantry Regiment*, 7 April 1945.

95. "Operation Varsity," *Thunder from Heaven*, V 39 (3 June 1992), 26; Shama, *History of the 49th TCS*, 105-6; and Shama, *Pulse and Repulse*, 336-7.

96. "Operation Varsity," *Thunder from Heaven*, V 39 (3 June 1992), 26.

97. Captain John G. Westover, *Interview of Major Robert R. Corey, Assistant G-2, 17th Airborne Division*, 31 March 1945, 3-4; and Weigley, *Lieutenants*, 649.

Chapter 10 Notes

1. 17th Airborne Division, *Summary of Combat Operations, 24 March-30 April 1945*; and 17th Airborne Division, *G-2 Periodic Report No. 2*, 26 March 1945.

2. Cuthbertson, Interview, 15 January 1998; and Contreras, Interview, 14 January 1998.

3. Sarrell, Letter, 2 January 1998; and Grice, Interview, 18 February 1998.

4. 2nd Battalion, 513th Parachute Infantry Regiment, Na*rrative of Action*; and Greenstrand, "WWII Service," 29.

5. Grice, Interviews, 13,18 February 1998.

6. Olson, Interview, 11 January 1998.

7. 513th Parachute Infantry Regiment, *After Action Report, 24-31 March 1945*, 4 April 1945.

8. 17th Airborne Division, *Summary of Combat Operations, 24 March-30 April 1945*.

9. Ibid.

10. XVIII Corps (Airborne), *G-2 Periodic Report No. 3*, 26 March 1945.

11. Ibid.; and Donovan, Interview, 20 October 1997.

12. *17th Airborne Division Historical Report of Operation Varsity*, 1945, 35.

13. Grice, Interviews, 18 February 1998.

14. 513th Parachute Infantry Regiment, *After Action Report, 24-31 March 1945*, 4 April 1945; and 17th Airborne Division, *Summary of Combat Operations, 24 March-30 April 1945*.

15. 17th Airborne Division, *Summary of Combat Operations, 24 March-30 April 1945*.

16. 513th Parachute Infantry Regiment, *After Action Report, 24-31 March 1945*, 4 April 1945.

17. Ibid.; Donovan, Interview, 20 October 1997; and Christopher F., Foss, Ed, *World War II Tanks and Fighting Vehicles*, (New York: Arco Publishing, Inc., 1981), 80-5.

18. 2nd Battalion, 513th Parachute Infantry Regiment, *Narrative of Action*; and 17th Airborne Division, *Summary of Combat Operations, 24 March-30 April 1945*.

19. 17th Airborne Division, *Summary of Combat Operations, 24 March-30 April 1945*.

20. 513th Parachute Infantry Regiment, *After Action Report, 24-31 March 1945*, 4 April 1945.

21. Olson, Interview, 11 January 1998.

22. Greenstrand, Interview, 17 March 1997; and Greenstrand, "WWII Service," 30.

23. Major J.F. O'Sullivan, *Interview of the Officers, 2nd Battalion, 513th Parachute Infantry Regiment*, 8 April 1945; and Greenstrand, Interview, 17 March 1997.

24. Charles Bailey, Interview with Author, 24 December 1997.

25. Major J.F. O'Sullivan, *Interview of the Officers, 3rd Battalion, 513th Parachute Infantry Regiment*, 7 April 1945.

26. Major J.F. O'Sullivan, *Interview of the Officers, 2nd Battalion, 513th Parachute Infantry Regiment*, 8 April 1945.

27. Ibid.; and Sarrell, Interview 18 January 1998.

28. Calhoun, Interview, 22 December 1998.

29. Ibid.; Sarrell, Interview 18 January 1998; Dahlberg, Interviews, 29 July 1997 and 13 October 1997; and Cuthbertson; Interview, 15 January 1998.

30. Calhoun, Interview, 23 February 1998.

31. Grice, Interviews, 13,18 February 1998.

32. Ibid.; and Cobb, 22 November 1998.

33. 2nd Battalion, 513th Parachute Infantry Regiment, Narrativ*e of Action*.

34. Major J.F. O'Sullivan, *Interview of the Officers, 2nd Battalion, 513th Parachute Infantry Regiment*, 8 April 1945.

35. Edwards, Interview, 16 March 1997.

36. Major J.F. O'Sullivan, *Interview of the Officers, 2nd Battalion, 513th Parachute Infantry Regiment*, 8 April 1945.

37. Danville Commercial-News (2 April 1945), as reprinted in "Headlines From 50+ Years Ago," *Thunder From Heaven*, 43:2 (March/April 1996): 68.

38. Olson, Interview, 11 January 1998; Donovan, Interview, 20 October 1997; and Contreras, Interview, 14 January 1998.

39. Olson, Interview, 11 January 1998.

40. Calhoun, Interview, 23 February 1998.

41. Olson, Interview, 11 January 1998.

42. Sarrell, Interview, 16 January 1998; Olson, Interview, 11 January 1998; and Interview, 11 January 1998.

43. Sarrell, Interview, 16 January 1998.

44. Ibid.

45. Greenstrand, "WWII Service," 31.

46. Olson, Interview, 11 January 1998.

47. Ibid.; and 2nd Battalion, 513th Parachute Infantry Regiment, *Narrative of Action.*

48. 2nd Battalion, 513th Parachute Infantry Regiment, *Narrative of Action*; and Major J.F. O'Sullivan, *Interview of the Officers, 2nd Battalion, 513th Parachute Infantry Regiment*, 8 April 1945.

49. 2nd Battalion, 513th Parachute Infantry Regiment, *Narrative of Action*; and Sarrell, Interview, 16 January 1998.

50. 2nd Battalion, 513th Parachute Infantry Regiment, *Narrative of Action.*

51. 17th Airborne Division, *Summary of Combat Operations, 24 March-30 April 1945*; and 513th Parachute Infantry Regiment, *After Action Report, 24-31 March 1945*, 4 April 1945.

52. Dahlberg, Interviews, 29 July 1997 and 13 October 1997.

53. Greenstrand, "WWII Service," 30.

54. Ibid., 34.

55. 2nd Battalion, 513th Parachute Infantry Regiment, Narr*ative of Action*; and Major J.F. O'Sullivan, *Interview of the Officers, 2nd Battalion, 513th Parachute Infantry Regiment*, 8 April 1945.

56. Colonel Dunbar ordered his tanks into the farm yards and behind the buildings in order to prevent them being seen by the enemy SPs. Meanwhile, the infantry had to go it alone.

57. Grice, Interviews, 18 February 1998; and Cox, Interview, 11 January 1998.

58. 513th Parachute Infantry Regiment, *After Action Report, 24-31 March 1945*, 4 April 1945.

59. Grice, Interviews, 18 February 1998; and Contreras, Interview, 14 January 1998.

60. Greenstrand, "WWII Service," 33; and Calhoun, Interview, 23 February 1998.

61. Cuthbertson, Interview, 15 January 1998.

62. Haggard, Interview, 30 March 1997.

63. Edwards, 16 March 1997; and Calhoun, Interview, 23 February 1998.

64. Bailey, Interview, 24 December 1997; Greenstrand, "WWII Service," 32-3; Lightcap, Interview 6 July 1998; and Dahlberg, Interviews, 29 July 1997 and 13 October 1997.

65. 513th Parachute Infantry Regiment, *After Action Report, 24-31 March 1945*; Major J.F. O'Sullivan, *Interview of the Officers, 2nd Battalion, 513th Parachute Infantry Regiment*, 8 April 1945; and Cuthbertson, Interview, 15 January 1998.

66. Major J.F. O'Sullivan, *Interview of the Officers, 2nd Battalion, 513th Parachute Infantry Regiment*, 8 April 1945; and Grice, Interview 19 February 1998.

67. Rybka, Interview 7 February 1998.

68. Major J.F. O'Sullivan, *Interview of the Officers, 2nd Battalion, 513th Parachute Infantry Regiment*, 8 April 1945.

69. Greenstrand, "WWII Service," 33.

70. 17th Airborne Division, *Summary of Combat Operations, 24 March-30 April 1945.*

71. Murray, Interview, 3 January 1998.

72. Major J.F. O'Sullivan, *Interview of the Officers, 2nd Battalion, 513th Parachute Infantry Regiment*, 8 April 1945.

73. Ibid.; and Dahlberg, Interview, 13 October 1997.

74. Major J.F. O'Sullivan, *Interview of the Officers, 2nd Battalion, 513th Parachute Infantry Regiment*, 8 April 1945; 2nd Battalion, 513th Parachute Infantry Regiment, *Narrative of Action*; and 513th Parachute Infantry Regiment, *After Action Report, 24-31 March 1945*, 4 April 1945.

75. Major J.F. O'Sullivan, *Interview of the Officers, 2nd Battalion, 513th Parachute Infantry Regiment*, 8 April 1945.

76. Edwards, Interview, 16 March 1997.

77. Major J.F. O'Sullivan, *Interview of the Officers, 2nd Battalion, 513th Parachute Infantry Regiment*, 8 April 1945, 9-10; and 2nd Battalion, 513th Parachute Infantry Regiment, *Narrative of Action*, 6-7.

78. Ibid.

79. Grice, Interview, 13 February 1998.

80. Sarrell, Interview, 18 January 1998.

81. Laufer, Interview, 5 March 1997; Cox, 11 January 1998; and Grice, Interview, 13 February 1998.

82. Laufer, Interview, 5 March 1997; and Grice, Interview, 13 February 1998.

83. Grice, Interview, 13 February 1998.

84. 17th Airborne Division, *Summary of Combat Operations, 24 March-30 April 1945*; and 513th Parachute Infantry Regiment, *After Action Report, 24-31 March 1945*, 4 April 1945.

85. Dahlberg, Interview, 13 October 1997; Contreras, Interview, 14 January 1998; and Major J.F. O'Sullivan, *Interview of the Officers, 2nd Battalion, 513th Parachute Infantry Regiment*, 8 April 1945, 9-10.

86. Greenstrand, "WWII Service," 35.

87. Haggard, Interview, 30 March 1998; and Cobb, Interview, 22 November 1998.

88. Greenstrand, "WWII Service," 35; and Donovan 14 October 1997.

89. Greenstrand, "WWII Service," 35.

90. Major J.F. O'Sullivan, *Interview of the Officers, 2nd Battalion, 513th Parachute Infantry Regiment*, 8 April 1945; 2nd Battalion, 513th Parachute Infantry Regiment, *Narrative of Action*, 7.

91. Greenstrand, "WWII Service," 35.

92. Ibid.; and Greenstrand, Interview, 17 March 1997.

93. Ibid.; Cox, Interview, 11 January 1998; and Cuthbertson, Interview, 15 January 1998.

94. Major J.F. O'Sullivan, *Interview of the Officers, 2nd Battalion, 513th Parachute Infantry Regiment*, 8 April 1945, 9-10.

95. Ibid.; and Greenstrand, "WWII Service," 36.

96. Bailey, Interviews, 24, 26 December 1997.

97. Greenstrand, "WWII Service," 36.

98. Sarrell, Interviews, 18-19 January 1998.

99. Major J.F. O'Sullivan, *Interview of the Officers, 2nd Battalion, 513th Parachute Infantry Regiment*, 8 April 1945.

100. 2nd Battalion, 513th Parachute Infantry Regiment, *Narrative of Action*.

101. Bailey, Interviews, 24, 26 December 1997; Greenstrand, "WWII Service," 36; and Dahlberg, Interviews, 29 July 1997 and 13 October 1997.

102. Major J.F. O'Sullivan, *Interview of the Officers, 2nd Battalion, 513th Parachute Infantry Regiment*, 8 April 1945; Bailey, Interviews, 24, 26 December 1997; and 513th Parachute Infantry Regiment, *After Action Report*, 3 May 1945.

103. 513th Parachute Infantry Regiment, *After Action Report*, 3 May 1945; Major J.F. O'Sullivan, *Interview of the Officers, 2nd Battalion, 513th Parachute Infantry Regiment*, 8 April 1945; and Greenstrand, "WWII Service," 37.

104. Olson, Interview, 11 January 1998.

105. 513th Parachute Infantry Regiment, *After Action Report*, 3 May 1945; Greenstrand, "WWII Service," 37; Cox, Interview, 11 January 1998; and Contreras, Interview, 14 January, 1998.

Published Sources

Adams, Michael C. C. *The Best War Ever: America and World War II*. Baltimore: The Johns Hopkins University Press, 1994.

Allen, Peter. *One More River: The Rhine Crossings of 1945*. New York: Charles Scribner's Sons, 1980.

Ambrose, Stephen E. *Band of Brothers: E Company, 506th Regiment, 101st Airborne From Normandy to Hitler's Eagle's Nest*. New York: Simon & Schuster, 1992.

— . *Citizen Soldiers: The U.S. Army from the Normandy Beaches to the Bulge to the Surrender of Germany, June 7, 1944 to May 7, 1945*. New York: Simon & Schuster, 1998.

— . *D-Day, June 6, 1944: The Climactic Battle of World War II*. New York: Simon & Schuster, 1994.

Astor, Gerald. *A Blood-Dimmed Tide: The Battle of the Bulge By the Men Who Fought It*. New York: Dell Publishing, 1994.

Bradley, Omar N., General. *A Soldiers Story*. New York: Popular Library, 1964.

Breuer, William B. *Geronimo: American Paratroopers in World War II*. New York: St. Martin's Press, 1989.

— . *Storming Hitler's Rhine: The Allied Assault: February-March 1945*. New York: St. Martin's Press, 1989.

Brown, John Sloan. *Draftee Division: The 88th Infantry Division in World War II*. Lexington: The University Press of Kentucky, 1986.

Cortesi, Lawrence. *Last Bridge to Victory*. New York: Kensignton Publishing Corporation (Zebra Books), 1984.

D'este, Carlo. *Patton, A Genius for War*. New York: Harperperennial, 1996.

Devlin, Gerard M. *Paratrooper: The Saga of the U.S. Army and Marine Parachute and Glider Combat Troops During World War II*. New York: St. Martin's Press, 1979.

Doubler, Michael D. *Closing with the Enemy: How GIs Fought the War in Europe, 1944-1945*. Lawrence: University Press of Kansas, 1994.

Dower, John W. *War Without Mercy: Race & Power in the Pacific War*. New York: Pantheon Books, 1993.

Egger, Bruce E., and Lee MacMillan Otts. *G Company's War: Two Personal Accounts of the Campaigns in Europe, 1944-1945*. Tuscaloosa: The University Press of Alabama, 1992.

Eisenhower, Dwight D. *Crusade in Europe*. Garden City: Doubleday & Company, Inc., 1948.

Eisenhower, John S. D. *The Bitter Woods*. New York: Da Capo Press, 1969.

Eubank, Keith. *The Origins of World War II*. Arlington Heights, Il: Harlan Davidson, Inc., 1990.

Ferguson, Gregor. *The PARAS: British Airborne Forces 1940-1984*. London: Osprey Publishing, 1984.

Forty, George. *U S Army Handbook, 1939-1945*. Phoenix Mill, England: Alan Sutton Publishing Limited, 1979.

Foss, Christopher F., Ed. *World War II Tanks and Fighting Vehicles*. New York: Arco Publishing, Inc., 1981.

Fussell, Paul. *Wartime: Understanding and Behavior in the Second World War*. New York: Oxford University Press, 1989.

Gable, Kurt. *The Making of A Paratrooper: Airborne Training and Combat in World War II*. Lawrence: University Press of Kansas, 1990.

Gavin, Major General James M. *Airborne Warfare*. Washington: Infantry Journal Press, 1947.

Goolrick, William K, and Ogden Tanner. *The Battle of the Bulge*. Alexandria: Time-Life Books, Inc., 1979.

Harris, King. "Adventures of Ace Miller." *Alta Vista Magazine*. (Sunday, January 27, 1991), 6-9, 16.

Hoyt, Edwin P. *Airborne: The History of American Parachute Forces*. New York: Stein and Day, 1979.

— . *The GI's War: The Story of American Soldiers in Europe in World War II*. New York: McGraw-Hill Book Company, 1988.

Huston, James A. *Out of the Blue: U.S. Army Airborne Operations in World War II*. West Lafayette, Indiana: Purdue Research Foundation, 1972.

Hynes, Samuel, et. al. *Reporting World War II: Part II, American Journalism, 1944-1946*. New York: The Library of America, 1995.

— . *The Soldiers' Tale: Bearing Witness to Modern War*. New York: The Penguin Press, 1997.

Iving, David. *The War Between The Generals: Inside The Allied High Command*. New York: Congdon & Lattes, Inc., 1981.

Kennett, Lee. *GI: The American Soldier in World War II*. New York: Charles Scribner's Sons, 1987.

Laughlin, Cameron P., and John P. Langellier. *U.S. Army Uniforms: Europe 1944-1945*. London, Arms and Armor Press, 1986.

Lidell Hart, B. H., *History of the Second World War*. New York: G. P. Putnam's Sons, 1971.

Longmate, Norman. *The GI's: The American in Britain, 1942-1945*. New York: Charles Scribner's Sons, 1975.

MacDonald, Charles B. *The Mighty Endeavor: The American War In Europe*. New York: Da Capo Press, 1992.

Martin Middlebrook. *Arnhem 1944: The Airborne Battle, 17-26 September*. Boulder, CO: Westview Press, 1944.

McKee, Alexander. *The Race for the Rhine Bridges: 1940, 1944, 1945*. New York: Stein and Day, Publishers, 1971.

Mondey, David. *The Concise Guide to American Aircraft of World War II*. New York: Smithmark Publishers, 1996.

O'Neill, William L. *A Democracy At War: America's Fight At Home & Abroad In World War II*. New York: The Free Press, 1993.

Palmer, Wiley, and Keast. *The Procurement and Training of Ground Combat Troops*. Washington, DC: Office of the Chief of Military History, Department of the Army.

Parachute School U.S.A. Atlanta: Albert Love Enterprises, 250-252 Peachtree Street. No date.

Pay, Donald R. *Thunder From Heaven: The Story of the 17th Airborne Division, 1943-1945*. Boots, 1947.

Pyle, Ernie. *Brave Men*. New York: Henry Holt and Company, 1943.

Quarrie, Bruce. *German Airborne Troops, 1939-1945*. London: Osprey Publishing, 1983.

Raff, Colonel Edson D. *We Jumped to Fight*. New York: Eagle Books, 1944.

Rottman, Gordon. *US Army Airborne, 1940-90*. London: Osprey Publishing, 1990.

Shama, H. Rex. *Pulse and Repulse: Troop Carrier and Airborne Teams in Europe During World War II*. Austin, Eakin Press, 1995.

— . *History of the 49th Troop Carrier Squadron, 313th Troop Carrier Group, 1942-1945*. 1990.

Standifer, Leon C. *Not In Vain: A Rifleman Remembers World War II*. Baton Rouge: Louisiana State University Press, 1992.

Stanton, Shelby L. *World War II Order of Battle*. New York: Galahad Books, 1984.

Stokesbury, James L. *A Short History of World War II*. New York: William Morrow and Company, Inc., 1980.

Thompson, Leroy. *U.S. Special Forces of World War II*. London, Arms and Armor Press, 1986.

Toland, John. *Battle: The Story of the Bulge*. New York: Random House, 1959.

Trezzvant, W. *Come Out Fighting: The Epic Tale of the 761st Tank Battalion, 1942-1945*. Salzburge Druckerei und Verlag, 1945.

Webster, David Kenyon. *Parachute Infantry: An American Paratrooper's Memoir of D-Day and the Fall of the Third Reich*. Baton Rouge: Louisiana State University Press, 1994.

Weigley, Russell F. *The American Way of War: A History of United States Strategy and Policy*. Bloomington: Indiana University Press, 1977.

— . *Eisenhower's Lieutenants: The Campaings of France and Germany, 1944-1945*. Bloomington: Indiana University Press, 1981.

War Department: *FM 31-30: Tactics and Technique of Air-borne Troops*. Washington: United States Government Printing Office, 1942.

v . *The Officers Guide*. 9th ed. Harrisburg: The Military Service Publishing Company, 1942.

Wilson, George. *If You Survive*. New York: Ivy Books, 1987.

Wolfe, Martin. *Green Light: A Troop Carrier Squadron's War From Normandy to the Rhine*. Washington, D.C.: Center for Air Force History, 1993.

Index